Reader's Digest

North American Wildlife

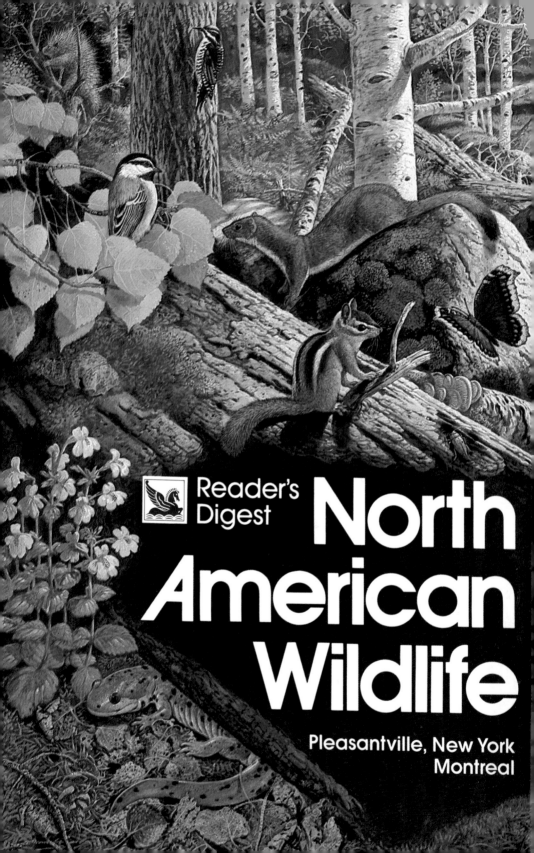

Reader's Digest

North American Wildlife

Pleasantville, New York
Montreal

North American Wildlife

Editor: Susan J. Wernert

Art Editor: Richard J. Berenson

Associate Editors: James Dwyer
                     Sally French

Designers: Ken Chaya
             Larissa Lawrynenko

Editorial Assistant: Annette Koshut

Contributing Editor: Katharine R. O'Hare

Picture Editor: Robert J. Woodward

With special assistance from
Associate Editor: James Cassidy
Designers: Virginia Wells Blaker
             Karen Mastropietro
Research Editors: Mary Vanaman O'Gorman
                    Georgea Atkinson Pace

The acknowledgments and credits that
appear on the facing page and page 576 are
hereby made a part of this copyright page.

Copyright © 1982
The Reader's Digest Association, Inc.
Copyright © 1982
The Reader's Digest Association (Canada) Ltd.
Copyright © 1982
Reader's Digest Association Far East Ltd.
Philippine Copyright 1982
Reader's Digest Association Far East Ltd.

The Library of Congress has cataloged this work as follows:

Reader's Digest North American wildlife / [editor,
    Susan J. Wernert].—Pleasantville, N.Y.:
    Reader's Digest Association, c1982.

    559 p.: ill. (some col.); 24 cm.

    Includes index.
    ISBN 0-7621-0020-6

    1. Zoology—North America.   2. Animals—Identification.
3. Botany—North America.   4. Plants—Identification.
I. Wernert, Susan J.   II. Reader's Digest Association.
III. Title: North American wildlife.

QL151.R395   574.97—dc19   81-50919
                                         AACR 2 MARC

Printed in the United States of America
Nineteenth Printing, March 1998

Contributing Artists

Biruta Akerbergs
Dorothea Barlowe
George Buctel
Eva Cellini
John D. Dawson
Howard S. Friedman
John Hamberger
William H. Howe
Robert Jones
Mary Kellner
Gwen Leighton
Elizabeth McClelland
Michael B. Merlin
Robert Mullen
Lorelle Raboni
Chuck Ripper
Allianora Rosse
Alan D. Singer
Ray Skibinski
Karen Lidbeck Stewart
Wayne Trimm
Guy Tudor
Nina Williams
John Cameron Yrizarry

Contributors

Michael Harwood

Thomas W. Burke
George S. Fichter
Sally Diana Kaicher
Paul Lehman
Peter R. Limburg
David Simon
John Cameron Yrizarry
Mary A. Yrizarry

Copy Editor:
Patricia M. Godfrey

Contents

Wildlife Communities
10–41

About This Book

NORTH AMERICAN WILDLIFE is a book intended to be used. Use it to explore nature—to discover what alligators eat, where Wood Ducks build their nests, why mushrooms are so often found near certain kinds of trees. Use it to identify species—to give a name to the cheerful little songster perched in the treetops or the delicate wildflower that appeared so unexpectedly and confirmed the approach of spring. Most of all, use it to marvel—at the amazing richness of our flora and fauna, at their intricate ways, at the breathtaking beauty inherent in all forms of life.

Unique in its coverage, this book spans the continent from ocean to ocean and includes more than two thousand plants and animals of all types—everything from delicate ferns to mighty whales. It does not show or describe all species (no book—not even a dozen books—could do that), but instead highlights species that are common, conspicuous, or important in some other way.

Innovative Features

With its thousands of color portraits and fact-filled text, NORTH AMERICAN WILDLIFE is a book to be enjoyed indoors as well as out. Its value extends far beyond its usefulness as an identification guide—but when you use it for that purpose, you'll find it has a variety of timesaving innovations.

Each page has a **name tab** printed at the edge, its color and position varying according to section. (See the lineup at right.) Visible even when the book is closed, these tabs make it easy to find the section you're looking for; sometimes even the precise pages within that section are pinpointed by the tab. The invertebrate section, for example, has one tab for the mollusks, one for the insects, and one for such miscellaneous creatures as jellyfish and crabs.

Each section also has a color-coded **introduction**, which explains how the section is organized and gives general identification tips. (As the Contents page indicates, several sections have their introductions split into two parts.) For the two biggest sections (wildflowers and birds), the introductions contain special **identification charts**—speedy alternatives to the flipping-through-the-pages method of identifying species.

In a book for identification purposes, all the facts needed to identify a species should be close together and easy to find. So in NORTH AMERICAN WILDLIFE, the information important for identification (size, markings, and the like) has been taken out of the text and placed in separate **identification capsules**. Generally each species shown has its own identification capsule. (The fish and invertebrate sections are organized in slightly different ways.) By using the capsules, you can quickly find out, for example, that a particular lizard pictured in the book is far too big to be the one you spotted sunbathing among the rocks—and look for another one that is about the right size.

The identification capsules are intended to be used together with the color portraits, for certain features mentioned in the capsules have been highlighted with **checkmarks** on the art. These "Idento-checks" point out traits to be observed in identifying a species. They do not necessarily point out *the* single feature most important in identification.

In every section of this book there are some species—Raccoons, Cardinals, Luna Moths, Bloodroot—that can be recognized quickly and easily by their appearance alone. Where you find these particular plants and animals doesn't much matter (for identification purposes, at least). For others, where you find them is often an important clue as to what they might or might not be. The **range maps** in

MAMMALS

BIRDS

REPTILES AND AMPHIBIANS

FISH

INVERTEBRATES

TREES AND SHRUBS

WILDFLOWERS

NONFLOWERING PLANTS

MUSHROOMS

7

female

male

Scarlet Tanager
Piranga olivacea

Length: 6–7 in.
What to look for: *male scarlet, with black wings and tail (in fall, red replaced by yellowish green); female yellowish green, with darker wings and tail.* **Habitat:** *thick deciduous woodlands, suburbs, parks.*

The Scarlet Tanager's song is not hard to pick out: listen to a robin sing for a while, then listen for the same song with a burr in it. The species also has a distinctive, hoarse call—*chick-kurr* in the East, sometimes *chip-chiree* elsewhere. Scarlet Tanagers devour many destructive caterpillars and wood-boring beetles, most often but not exclusively in oaks. Young males may be principally orange or splotched with red and yellow.

BIRDS

Western Tanager
Piranga ludoviciana

Length: 6–7 in.
What to look for: *male bright yellow, with red head and black on upper back, wings, and tail (no red on nonbreeder); female greenish above, yellowish below (only female tanager with wingbars).* **Habitat:** *open mixed and coniferous woodlands; other forests (migration).*

The song of the Western Tanager is much the same as that of the Scarlet Tanager—a series of short phrases separated by pauses. Its call is two- or three-syllabled—*pit-ic, pit-it-ic.* On migration, flocks of Western Tanagers pass through valleys, plains, and foothills. They nest mostly in the mountains, in firs and pines, often at high elevations. Like other tanagers, they lay three to five eggs. The female alone incubates, but both parents share the care and feeding of the nestlings.

female

male

Summer Tanager
Piranga rubra

Length: 6–7½ in.
What to look for: *yellowish bill; male red; female yellowish green above, yellow below.* **Habitat:** *woodlands; in uplands, drier forests*

Sugar Maple
Acer saccharum

Size: 60–80 ft. tall; leaves 3–6 in. wide.
What to look for: *leaves 5-lobed, bright green above, paler below; 2 joined seeds with nearly parallel wings (autumn); bark gray, with furrows, flakes, or both.* **Habitat:** *moist, rich soils in uplands and valleys,*

Maples *Acer*

With lobed leaves growing in pairs, most maples are easy to distinguish from other trees. (A few maples, such as the Boxelder, have compound leaves.) Maples also have distinctive fruits called samaras—winged, paired seeds that spin to the earth like tiny helicopters. Some species bear the samaras in spring, others in fall. All produce large quantities of sweet sap in late winter and early spring, but only the Sugar Maple's sap contains enough sugar to warrant commercial tapping and boiling for sugar. Transplanted maple species abound in North America. Pollution-resistant Norway

flowers

Norway Maple
Acer platanoides

Size: 60–80 ft. tall; leaves 4–6 in. wide.
What to look for: *leaves with 5–7 lobes, dark green above, bright green below; crushed stem exudes milky sap; 2 joined seeds with wings spread wide (autumn).* **Habitat:** *streets, lawns.*

Red Maple
(Swamp Maple)
Acer rubrum

Size: 50–70 ft. tall; leaves 2–6 in. wide.
What to look for: *leaves with 3–5 lobes, coarsely toothed, light green above, gray-green below; flowers red, preceding leaves; 2 joined seeds, often red, with wings in narrow V (spring).* **Habitat:** *swamps; bottomlands and uplands in moist soils.*

this book will help out here. Much easier to use than a lengthy written-out description of range, these maps show the general part of the continent where a species is likely to occur. Any animal, of course, will move about, and plants travel as seeds or spores, so the ranges shown should be considered approximations only.

Below the range maps are specially designed **habitat symbols**. The symbols, interpreted below, are a sort of shorthand—something that tells you, say, whether a bird is a desert or a forest species. The habitat part of the identification capsule explains in detail where the plant or animal lives. If most species in a section occur in the same habitat (for example, mollusks generally live in or near the ocean), the symbols have been omitted but the habitat part of the capsule retained.

Because habitat is so useful in identifying species, and because a true understanding of nature requires looking not just at individual species but also at the ways they interact, a special section called **Wildlife Communities** is included in this book. Beginning on the next page, it offers lists of species and places as well as photographs and descriptive text—a unique combination certain to enhance your enjoyment and appreciation of our wildlife heritage.

Habitat symbols
are another quick device
you can use to narrow
down the possibilities.
Birds without a
tree symbol, for example,
are unlikely to be seen
in a forest.

 deserts, sagebrush, other arid lands

 grasslands, meadows, brushy areas, tundra

 forests, woodlands

 roadsides (used for wildflowers only)

 urban and suburban areas, farms

 ponds, lakes, rivers, streams, freshwater marshes

 rocky and sandy shores, salt marshes, ocean

 brackish water (certain sections only)

---

*Many species have **more than one** illustration. Where appropriate, trees have insets of flowers or silhouettes; birds may be shown in different plumages.*

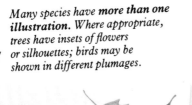

Autumn leaves. Leaves are green because they have chlorophyll, the substance that enables them to manufacture food. Other pigments—red, orange, yellow—are also present but are masked by the green. As the days shorten in fall, chlorophyll synthesis ceases, the green color disappears, and other pigments begin to dominate. The leaves of certain species typically turn a uniform color (yellow on aspens and birches, scarlet on the Red Maple); others are more variable.

*Special features, printed in blue, highlight items of unusual interest and provide tips on identification. You'll find additional tips in the overall **introduction** to each section.*

le)

all;
ng.
r:
with 3-7
coarse-toothed
low-green;
h
(autumn).
atercourses;

flowers

Striped Maple
(Moosewood)
Acer pensylvanicum
Size: 20-30 ft. tall; leaves 5-6 in. long.
What to look for: leaves 3-lobed, finely toothed, pale below; young bark smooth, bright green with white stripes; flowers bright yellow, on long drooping stalk.
Habitat: wooded valleys and slopes in moist soils.

Titles often provide **alternative names.** *You may know the species by yet another name.*

9

Wildlife Communities

Why plants and animals live where they do, and how their lives are intertwined, make fascinating stories in themselves. But this section also serves a practical function: from it you'll get a head start on recognizing species in the wild.

Grass traps energy from the sun and makes it into food; grasshopper eats grass; wren eats grasshopper; hawk eats wren; and so on through the cycle. The most dramatic interactions among plants and animals concern food; that is, the transfer of energy through the food chain or, to express it more simply, eating and being eaten.

But relationships among members of a wildlife community are much more intricate than this—not only because food chains are infinitely varied (and are themselves interwoven into webs) but because the relationships extend far beyond food. Plants "use" animals for pollination and for dispersing their seeds. Animals rely on plants for shelter and for support; a moth cocoon needs something from which to hang. Animals have their interactions too; witness the owls, snakes, and other creatures that live in prairie dog burrows.

Beyond this, there are relationships between living things and the physical aspects of their environment—among them, temperature, light, moisture, and minerals. That the flora and fauna of North America are so diverse (more than 600 breeding bird species, more than 50 species of oaks) is a reflection of the diversity of living conditions. For no habitat, be it desert, tundra, or even hot spring, can be considered truly hostile to life; chances are that some species have adaptations that allow them to survive there.

In many cases the entries in NORTH AMERICAN WILDLIFE explore relationships such as these, treating species in the context of their surroundings. No discussion of pitcher plants would be complete without a mention of their insect-eating habits and the environment that has "forced" them to behave in this unplantlike way; nor would any discussion of Barn Owls be complete without a mention of barns. But the species-by-species organization of this book does not altogether lend itself to extensive overviews; hence this section.

Who eats whom is only one of the intricate relationships between plants and animals. This illustration encompasses some of the interactions in Everglades National Park.

Slash Pine
Saw-palmetto
Spanish Moss
Butterfly Orchid

LAND PLANTS

PLANT-EATING ANIMALS

White-tailed Deer
Cardinal
Eastern Box Turtle
Tiger Swallowtail

PREDATORS AND SCAVENGERS

Bobcat
Turkey Vulture
Red-bellied Woodpecker
Indigo Snake

NUTRIENTS

DECAY

Red Mangrove
Narrowleaf Cattail
Pickerelweed
Sea Lettuce

WATER PLANTS

Manatee
Loggerhead
Pinfish
Angel Wing

PLANT-EATING ANIMALS

PREDATORS AND SCAVENGERS

Anhinga
American Alligator
Cottonmouth
Blue Crab

How to Use This Section

This section has a practical function: getting you acquainted with the flora and fauna of a particular area in advance. If you're planning a trip to the West Coast, for example, you'll want to look up at least three communities: Pacific Coast Forest, Pacific Sandy Shore, and Rocky Pacific Coast. Each community has its own page, where you'll find a scene-setting photograph, descriptive text, and two lists: one with places and the other with species.

Directly following the descriptive text for most communities is a list of places in the United States and Canada where the community occurs. National parks, national wildlife refuges, and state and provincial parks are among the areas included. If a park falls in more than one state or province, it is listed under the one where the greatest portion is found.

The list, of course, is only a sampling; there are many other places where the flora, the fauna, and their interrelationships are essentially the same. And a park listed as an example of one particular type of community should not be assumed to have nothing else there. Most large areas have more than one type, and several parks are included in more than one list. A few pages have no place lists. Those communities tend to be very common—Lake and Pond, for example.

The other list names some of the characteristic plants and animals. Emphasis is on the larger forms of life; that is, mammals, birds, trees, and wildflowers. The names are followed by page references, making it easy to look up the pictures of the species (or close relatives) and get a head start on identifying them in the wild.

Wildlife is not divided into such neat packages as these lists imply, and an observant eye will notice that a number of species occur on more than one list. Some, such as many shorebirds and other migrating species, are part of different communities at different times of year. Others range over much of the continent or live in a variety of habitats; the Black Bear, for example, is listed for six different ones.

An Invitation to Explore

Below is the Table of Contents for this section. Though North American wildlife can be divided into groups in an infinite number of ways, the 30 communities depicted in the pages that follow have been carefully chosen to represent most of the major types. As the titles suggest, some communities are defined by specific plant inhabitants (Cypress Swamp, for example); others, more by locale (Great Plains Grassland).

We hope that you'll explore each and every community—if not by actually going there, then by discovering them through this book. For though the visible beauty of North American wildlife may be found in an individual species (the Painted Bunting's spectacular plumage, the Redwood's majestic height), it is only by viewing the full panorama, by looking at the entire picture, that one can fully appreciate the splendid diversity of this land.

Contents of This Section

In a British Columbia forest young hemlocks and a hefty Douglas-fir share a patch of sunlight with a ground cover of ferns.

Pacific Coast Forest

A strip of coniferous forest lies along the western edge of the continent from Alaska to northern California. Nowhere wider than a hundred miles, the narrow band boasts some of the world's tallest trees—and not as isolated giants but in great assemblages of 250-foot spruces, hemlocks, and firs.

*The coastal region is damp and fog-shrouded throughout. On Washington's Olympic Peninsula, unusually heavy rainfall has produced North America's only temperate zone rain forest. Mosses drip in festoons from the trees; ferns, mosses, lichens, and other moisture-loving plants blanket the earth. Where a break occurs in the towering evergreens, an undergrowth of deciduous shrubs supplies browse for Elk and deer. Other large mammals (especially the Black Bear and Mountain Lion) are elusive, though their tracks may be visible along national park trails. Nor are birds conspicuous, except for noisy jays and small flocks of nuthatches and chickadees. Sounding to some like a chickadee is the Chickaree (or Doug-*las' Squirrel), *a relative of the Red Squirrel that lives only in the Pacific Coast forest.*

Farther south, along the coast of northern California, is the redwood forest, where ground cover is sparse and animal life more readily seen. The trees here grow even taller than the spruces and firs to the north; many Redwoods top 300 feet, and several have been measured at more than 360. Though only scattered groves of these majestic trees have escaped the lumberman's saw, the sight of the huge rust-red trunks, soaring unbroken by branches above the sun-dappled earth, cannot fail to impress.

Places to see this habitat include:
British Columbia Garibaldi, MacMillan, and
  Manning provincial parks
California Redwood National Park; Six Rivers
  National Forest; Muir Woods
  National Monument; Big Basin, Humboldt,
  and Jedediah Smith Redwoods state parks
Oregon Cape Lookout, Cape Sebastian, and
  Saddle Mountain state parks
Washington Olympic National Park; Beacon Rock,
  Deception Pass, Larrabee, and Moran state parks

On the eastern slopes of the Cascades, tall Ponderosa Pines grow well apart, with other, younger conifers closing the scene at the rear.

Sierra-Cascade Forest

Parklike forests, aromatic with the scent of sun-warmed cedar and pine, climb the western foothills and lower slopes of California's rugged Sierra Nevada. John Muir, who explored these forests beginning in 1869, wrote of their "inviting Openness"; fires, often lightning-sparked, spaced the trees and kept the earth free of dead wood and other debris. Today, because fires have been controlled, the forests are becoming increasingly dense.

The middle-elevation Sierras—from 4,500 to 7,000 feet—are notable for the world's biggest trees. Almost as tall as the Redwoods, the Giant Sequoias are much more massive, with heavy trunks and thick angular limbs. They grow in scattered groves, in company with Ponderosa Pines, in a narrow belt about 250 miles long. The Cascade Range of Washington and Oregon lacks the giant trees, but the ponderosa forests offer the same sunlit vistas. A ground cover of wildflowers and shrubs supplies seeds and berries for many birds and small mammals. Lively squirrels are plentiful, deer and bear are frequently seen, and even the elusive Mountain Lion occasionally wanders through these open forests.

Places to see this habitat include:

California Kings Canyon, Lassen Volcanic, Sequoia, and Yosemite national parks; Inyo, Lassen, Shasta-Trinity, Sierra, and Stanislaus national forests; Calaveras Big Trees State Park
Oregon Crater Lake National Park; Deschutes and Fremont national forests
Washington Snoqualmie and Wenatchee national forests.

Animal life includes:
Deer Mouse *p. 51*
Golden-mantled Ground
  Squirrel *other ground*
  squirrels p. 55
Marten *p. 60*
Black Bear *p. 64*
Mule Deer *p. 67*
Pygmy Owl *p. 115*
White-throated Swift *p. 116*
Acorn Woodpecker *p. 118*
Olive-sided Flycatcher *p. 123*
Steller's Jay *p. 124*
Clark's Nutcracker *p. 125*
Mountain Chickadee *p. 127*
Yellow-rumped Warbler *p. 141*
Western Tanager *p. 147*
Fox Sparrow *p. 156*

Plant life includes:
Lodgepole Pine *p. 290*
Ponderosa Pine *p. 290*
White Fir *p. 294*
California Red Fir *p. 294*
Giant Sequoia *p. 295*
California Black Oak *p. 305*
Quaking Aspen *p. 310*
Manzanitas *p. 325 and p. 377*
Ceanothuses *p. 328*
Snow Plant *p. 379*
Lupines *p. 391*
Giant Red Paintbrush *p. 431*
Leopard Lily *p. 485*

Animal life includes:
Porcupine *p. 44*
Red Squirrel *p. 54*
Snowshoe Hare *p. 57*
Black Bear *p. 64*
Mountain Sheep *p. 66*
Mule Deer *p. 67*
Wapiti (Elk) *p. 68*
Golden Eagle *p. 108*
Bald Eagle *p. 108*
Blue Grouse *other grouse p. 110*
Pygmy Owl *p. 115*
Gray Jay *p. 124*
Clark's Nutcracker *p. 125*
Common Raven *p. 125*
Mountain Chickadee *p. 127*
Varied Thrush *p. 134*
Mountain Bluebird *p. 135*
Western Tanager *p. 147*
Evening Grosbeak *p. 148*
Red Crossbill *p. 150*
White-crowned Sparrow *p. 155*
Fox Sparrow *p. 156*

Plant life includes:
Lodgepole Pine *p. 290*
Ponderosa Pine *p. 290*
Engelmann Spruce *p. 293*
Subalpine Fir *other firs p. 294*
Douglas-fir *p. 295*
Quaking Aspen *p. 310*
Blue Columbine *p. 345*
Larkspurs *p. 346*
Pipsissewa *p. 378*
Bunchberry *p. 397*
Explorer's Gentian *p. 408*
Glacier Lily *p. 487*

Aspens like showers of molten gold light up a mountainside near the Continental Divide in Colorado.

Rocky Mountain Forest

Along the great curve of the Rockies, several types of forests cover the rugged terrain. On the lower slopes of the central and southern Rockies, and the surrounding plateaus, pines are the dominant trees. They grow tall in open stands, interrupted here and there by grassy meadowlands grazed by herds of deer —and in Yellowstone, by Bison as well.

Slopes higher up or farther to the north are cloaked with spruces and firs. But this subalpine forest is not exclusively evergreen. Where moisture seeps through or where fire has opened clearings, the wide, somber sweep of conifers is broken by airier patches of aspen, also found lower on the mountain. At

the tree line, twisted pines cling to life with tenacious roots. Precipitous crags may tower above, home to soaring eagles and surefooted wild sheep and goats.

Places to see this habitat include:
Alberta Banff, Jasper, and Waterton Lakes
   national parks; Bow Valley Provincial Park
Colorado Rocky Mountain National Park;
   White River National Forest
Idaho Boise, Challis, Payette, and Sawtooth
   national forests
Montana Glacier National Park; Flathead and
   Lewis and Clark national forests
Wyoming Grand Teton and Yellowstone national
   parks; Shoshone National Forest

Pinyon–Juniper Woodland

In parts of the Great Basin, pygmy cone-bearing trees, adapted to the paucity of water, grow in a narrow strip between the Sierra Nevada and the Rocky Mountains. (A similar habitat occupies the tops and sides of some mesas and plateaus.) In these warm, dry areas, trees grow singly or in scattered clumps on rocky or gravelly soil, which is sparsely covered with low-growing vegetation. Although the diversity of plant life is limited, the species that do thrive here supply food, particularly in winter, for a number of mammals and birds. As the cold sets in, deer descend from the higher coniferous forests to browse; Coyotes and Mountain Lions follow their prey. There are bird migrants, too—among others, Clark's Nutcrackers, which feed on pinyon nuts, and Robins, which feast on the junipers' berrylike cones. Permanent residents include several species seldom found elsewhere. One is the Pinyon Jay, a gray-blue bird with a short tail and no crest; another is the white-footed Pinyon Mouse, a close relative of the Deer Mouse.

Places to see this habitat include:

Arizona Grand Canyon National Park; Canyon de Chelly and Navajo national monuments
Colorado Mesa Verde National Park; Colorado and Dinosaur national monuments
Nevada Humboldt and Toiyabe national forests; Cathedral Gorge and Valley of Fire state parks
New Mexico Cibola National Forest; Bandelier National Monument; San Andres National Wildlife Area
Utah Arches, Bryce Canyon, Canyonlands, Capitol Reef, and Zion national parks

Animal life includes:
Porcupine *p. 44*
Cliff Chipmunk
  other chipmunks p. 55
Black-tailed Jackrabbit *p. 57*
Coyote *p. 63*
Mountain Lion *p. 65*
Mule Deer *p. 67*
Red-tailed Hawk *p. 107*
Black-chinned Hummingbird
  p. 117
Scrub Jay *p. 124*
Clark's Nutcracker *p. 125*
Mountain Chickadee *p. 127*
Plain Titmouse
  other titmice p. 128
Bushtit *p. 128*
Canyon Wren
  other wrens pp. 130–131
Loggerhead Shrike *p. 132*
Sage Thrasher *p. 133*
American Robin *p. 134*
Mountain Bluebird *p. 135*

Plant life includes:
Pinyon *p. 289*
Utah Juniper *p. 296*
Utah Serviceberry
  other serviceberries p. 313
Buckbrush *p. 328*
Common Sagebrush *p. 331*
Rabbitbrush *p. 331*
Plains Prickly Pear *p. 355*
Claret Cup Cactus *p. 356*
Desert Plume *p. 375*
Porcupine Grass *p. 474*
Sego Lily *p. 486*

On a rocky Colorado plateau, a compactly growing pine and a spiky-leaved yucca defy the drought. A juniper has succumbed.

15

*As far as the eye can see, dense forest mixes
with watery muskeg near Mount McKinley, Alaska.*

Northern Coniferous Forest

*Also called the boreal forest (from Boreas, the north wind), a
great expanse of evergreens stretches across Canada. North of the
trees lies the tundra. To the south the forest reaches the shores of
Lake Superior, with extensions into the Adirondack and Appalachian mountains.*

*This enormous area is glacial land, scoured down to bedrock by
advancing ice sheets and now sprinkled with thousands of lakes
and bogs. Though the soil is often shallow, trees grow densely;
where sunlight penetrates, the forest floor is a carpet of delicate
wildflowers. Many species of birds nest in these northern conifers,
including grosbeaks, crossbills, and a number of warblers more
familiar as migrants in areas to the south. The large mammals are
not usually visible, but their presence adds a special excitement for
those who visit the area by trail or canoe.*

Places to see this habitat include:
Alberta Banff, Jasper, and Prince Albert national parks
Maine Acadia National Park; Baxter State Park
Michigan Isle Royale National Park
Minnesota Superior National Forest
New Hampshire White Mountain National Forest
New York Adirondack Park Preserve
Ontario Lake Superior and Quetico provincial parks
Quebec Gaspé Provincial Park

Animal life includes:
Beaver *p. 45*
Red Squirrel *p. 54*
Snowshoe Hare *p. 57*
Mink *p. 61*
Gray Wolf *p. 63*
Black Bear *p. 64*
Lynx *p. 65*
Moose *p. 68*
Caribou *p. 69*
Spruce Grouse
  other grouse p. 110
Three-toed woodpeckers *p. 119*
Gray Jay *p. 124*
Boreal Chickadee *p. 127*
Red-breasted Nuthatch *p. 129*
Ruby-crowned Kinglet *p. 136*
Tennessee, Magnolia,
  Black-throated Green, and
  other warblers *pp. 138–143*
Red Crossbill *p. 150*
Pine Grosbeak *p. 150*
Dark-eyed Junco *p. 153*
White-throated Sparrow *p. 155*

Plant life includes:
Tamarack *p. 292*
Black Spruce *p. 292*
White Spruce *p. 293*
Balsam Fir *p. 294*
Goldthread *p. 344*
One-sided Pyrola *p. 378*
Starflower *p. 382*
Bunchberry *p. 397*
Wild Sarsaparilla *p. 404*
Twinflower *p. 445*
Canada Mayflower *p. 495*

16

Sphagnum Bog

Often occupying a glacial depression, a sphagnum bog—named for its characteristic mosses—conserves the cold of winter and acts as an insulated microclimate. Here such tundra shrubs as Labrador Tea and Leatherleaf can survive far south of their normal range; rare orchids and insect-eating plants may also occur. Because of the acid water and lack of oxygen, fish and many other forms of aquatic life are generally absent; birds and mammals are mostly transient visitors from the surrounding forest.

Bogs display with great clarity the gradual development of an area from open water to forested land. First, a floating fringe of mosses and sedges encircles the pool of water; then shrubby growth appears, supported by the floating mass of vegetation that penetrates farther toward the center. Eventually, a bog undergoing these changes dries out, its mosses become peat, and the spruces and larches surrounding the bog invade the area.

Places to see this habitat include:

Maine Acadia National Park
Michigan Isle Royale National Park; Hiawatha National Forest; Tahquamenon Falls State Park
Minnesota Voyageurs National Park
New Jersey Wharton State Forest
Ohio Brown's Lake Bog (Wayne County)
Ontario Quetico Provincial Park
Quebec Gatineau Park; Laurentides Provincial Park
West Virginia Cranberry Glades (Monongahela National Forest); Canaan Valley State Park
Wisconsin Chequamegon National Forest

Animal life includes:
Southern Bog Lemming *p. 49*
Moose *p. 68*
Yellow-bellied Flycatcher *p. 122*
Olive-sided Flycatcher *p. 123*
Gray Jay *p. 124*
Winter Wren *p. 130*
Hermit Thrush *p. 134*
Cedar Waxwing *p. 136*
Golden-crowned Kinglet *p. 136*
Northern Waterthrush *p. 139*
Palm Warbler *p. 141*

Plant life includes:
Black Spruce *p. 292*
Tamarack *p. 292*
Northern White-cedar *p. 296*
Labrador Tea *p. 324*
Swamp Laurel
   other laurels p. 325
Bog Rosemary *p. 325*
Leatherleaf *p. 325*
Northern Pitcher Plant *p. 368*
Roundleaf Sundew *p. 369*
American Cranberry *p. 377*
Butterwort *p. 440*
Porcupine Sedge *p. 472*
Cottongrass *p. 472*
Yellow Lady's Slipper *p. 500*
Dragon's Mouth *p. 501*
Rose Pogonia *p. 501*
Orange Fringed Orchid *p. 503*
Nodding Ladies' Tresses *p. 505*
Grass Pink *p. 505*

A mat of low-growing laurel and an outer ring of larch circle the eye of this deep, cold Michigan bog.

Eastern Mixed Forest

This mixed forest, a transitional habitat where spruces and other northern conifers mingle with broad-leaved maples and beeches, occupies land once covered by ice. Now the terrain is varied, dissected by mountains, valleys, and ravines; there are rocky outcrops and huge boulders, left as the glaciers retreated.

Before the land was extensively settled, the mixed forest extended from the midwestern prairies east to Nova Scotia. Today, though it survives spottily elsewhere, it is best seen in the Green Mountains of Vermont, in the Catskills of New York, and along the ridges of the Allegheny Mountains. Trees are tall, towering over several layers of shrubs, both evergreen and deciduous. Because of the variety of food and nesting sites available, birds from hawks and owls to warblers and finches are numerous. The soil—a rich, dark humus—nourishes an outstanding succession of wildflowers, beginning with the delicate blossoms of early spring.

Places to see this habitat include:
New Brunswick Fundy National Park
New Hampshire White Mountain National Forest
New York Allegheny State Park; Catskill Park Preserve
Ontario Lake Superior Provincial Park
Pennsylvania Allegheny National Forest
Vermont Green Mountain National Forest
Virginia Shenandoah National Park
West Virginia Monongahela National Forest

Animal life includes:
Gray Squirrel *p. 54*
Eastern Chipmunk *p. 55*
Raccoon *p. 58*
Foxes *p. 62*
Bobcat *p. 65*
White-tailed Deer *p. 67*
Red-tailed Hawk *p. 107*
Ruffed Grouse *p. 110*
Pileated Woodpecker *p. 118*
Great Crested Flycatcher *p. 121*
Blue Jay *p. 124*
Black-capped Chickadee *p. 127*
Tufted Titmouse *p. 128*
Hermit Thrush *p. 134*
Veery *p. 135*
Red-eyed Vireo *p. 137*
Black-throated Blue and
   other warblers *pp. 138-143*
Scarlet Tanager *p. 147*

Plant life includes:
Eastern White Pine *p. 288*
Eastern Hemlock *p. 293*
American Beech *p. 303*
American Basswood *p. 308*
Red Maple *p. 318*
Sugar Maple *p. 318*
Witch-hazel *p. 323*
Round-lobed Hepatica *p. 344*
Mayapple *p. 350*
Bloodroot *p. 351*
Dutchman's Breeches *p. 352*
Spring Beauty *p. 360*
Pipsissewa *p. 378*
Partridgeberry *p. 443*
Jack-in-the-pulpit *p. 479*
Trilliums *p. 488*

The maples' blaze of color, set off by dark spruces and pines and the white trunks of an occasional birch, glorifies a mixed forest in the Green Mountains.

White Oaks and Shagbark Hickories mingle their varied greens in this western Illinois forest.

Oak-Hickory Forest

Oaks of many species dominate two major forested areas. (They also form an extensive woodland in California.) One extends from the Ozarks of Missouri and Arkansas south to Texas and up the Mississippi to Illinois. The other runs along the lower slopes of the Appalachians as far north as New York and New England. In times past the eastern oaks shared supremacy with the mighty Chestnut. With the Chestnut almost completely killed by blight, the oaks are now most often associated with hickories, interspersed with other broad-leaved trees and pines.

The oak-hickory forest is dry and the soil often somewhat sandy. The trees are widely spaced, with a low undergrowth of shrubs and vines. In the East the oaks are usually tall and widely branching; west of the Mississippi they tend to be scrubby, forming stands that cover the slopes of river valleys and push into the prairies. Among the birds partial to oaks for nesting are vireos and tanagers. Raccoons, squirrels, deer, and wild Turkeys all feast on nature's bounty—the acorns and hickory nuts produced by mature trees.

Places to see this habitat include:
Alabama Talladega National Forest
Arkansas Ouachita and Ozark national forests
Illinois Starved Rock State Park
Kentucky Daniel Boone National Forest
Mississippi Holly Springs National Forest; Hugh White State Park
Missouri Mark Twain National Forest
New York Bear Mountain State Park
North Carolina Blue Ridge Parkway
Oklahoma Osage Hills State Park
Texas Davis Mountains, Garner, and Possum Kingdom state parks
Virginia Shenandoah National Park; George Washington and Jefferson national forests

Animal life includes:
Opossum *p. 44*
Gray Squirrel *p. 54*
Eastern Chipmunk *p. 55*
Eastern Cottontail *p. 57*
Raccoon *p. 58*
Gray Fox *p. 62*
White-tailed Deer *p. 67*
Broad-winged Hawk *p. 106*
Ruffed Grouse *p. 110*
Wild Turkey *p. 111*
Whip-poor-will *p. 116*
Red-bellied Woodpecker *p. 118*
Northern Flicker *p. 119*
Blue Jay *p. 124*
Red-eyed Vireo *p. 137*
Scarlet Tanager *p. 147*
Summer Tanager *p. 147*
Rose-breasted Grosbeak *p. 149*

Plant life includes:
Pitch Pine *p. 291*
Tuliptree *p. 298*
Sweetgum *p. 300*
Shagbark Hickory *p. 302*
Mockernut Hickory *p. 302*
Northern Red, Blackjack, White, Bur, and other oaks *pp. 304-306*
Eastern Redbud *p. 314*
Flowering Dogwood *p. 317*
Spicebush *p. 323*
American Hazel *p. 324*
Rhododendrons *p. 325*
Mountain Laurel *p. 325*
Birdfoot Violet *p. 370*
Goat's Rue *p. 389*
Climbing Bittersweet *p. 398*
Wild Geranium *p. 401*
Big Merrybells *p. 487*
Solomon's Zigzag *p. 495*
Catbrier *p. 499*
Moccasin Flower *p. 500*

Southern Appalachian Forest

A summer sea of green covers the gently rolling ridges of the southern Appalachians. This magnificent forest is especially impressive in the Great Smoky Mountains, where the most extensive stands of virgin timber in the East cloak the middle elevations. In the rich soil of sheltered valleys (called coves), many species of trees and shrubs reach maximum size. On exposed ridges and plateaus, treeless "balds" are famous for the springtime display of rhododendron and azalea.

The variety of plant species in the Smokies is astounding: more than 130 trees and 1,600 wildflowers have been recorded. Tropical species like the Filmy Fern as well as Arctic representatives occur in the area. Because these mountains were never glaciated, many plants are isolated relics of an ancient botanical community that once stretched across North America to Asia.

The Appalachian region is well known for the salamanders that shelter beneath decaying logs and leaves. Birds are easier to spot, especially when the forest comes alive in spring. Some of the species are merely passing through; others remain to nest and fill the towering woods with song.

Places to see this habitat include:
Georgia Chattahoochee National Forest
North Carolina Pisgah and Nantahala national forests; Blue Ridge Parkway
Tennessee Great Smoky Mountains National Park; Cherokee National Forest; Cove and Harrison Bay state parks
Virginia Shenandoah National Park; George Washington and Jefferson national forests
West Virginia Monongahela National Forest; Blackwater Falls, Kanawha, and Watoga state parks

Animal life includes:
Red Squirrel *p. 54*
Gray Squirrel *p. 54*
Eastern Chipmunk *p. 55*
Foxes *p. 62*
Black Bear *p. 64*
White-tailed Deer *p. 67*
Turkey *p. 111*
Pileated Woodpecker *p. 118*
Carolina Chickadee
    other chickadees p. 127
Brown Thrasher *p. 133*
Wood Thrush *p. 134*
Solitary Vireo *p. 137*
Hooded, Black-throated Blue, and other warblers *pp. 138-143*
Scarlet Tanager *p. 147*
Northern Cardinal *p. 148*

Plant life includes:
Tuliptree *p. 298*
Bitternut and other hickories *p. 302*
American Beech *p. 303*
Chestnut, White, and other oaks *pp. 304-306*
American Basswood *p. 308*
Black Cherry *p. 312*
Downy Serviceberry *p. 313*
Eastern Redbud *p. 314*
Black Tupelo *p. 316*
Yellow Buckeye
    other buckeyes p. 317
Red Maple *p. 318*
White Ash *p. 321*
Rhododendrons *p. 325*
Mountain Laurel *p. 325*

Wave upon wave of forest beckons beyond a flowery roadside in Shenandoah National Park.

Birch, aspen, and spruce invade a Michigan clearing.

Abandoned Field

A field slowly reverting to the wild after logging or cultivation is more than a piece of untended property. It is also an example of an early stage of plant succession—the transition from low-growing species to shrubs and finally to trees. Corresponding changes in animal life are also taking place.

When soil is laid bare, the first plants to sprout are such annual herbs and grasses as ragweed and Lamb's Quarters—plants with wind-dispersed seeds and the ability to thrive in sunny places with widely varying temperatures. Subsequent years see the rapid establishment of milkweed, thistles, and other perennials, which, because they need not grow anew each year, have a head start each spring over the annual plants. This stage is the oft-photographed "old-field stage," the landscape sparkling with butterflies, ringing with meadowlark and bobolink song, basking in the warmth of the summer sun. Shrubs and vines spread from woodland and hedgerow, creating dense tangles favored by catbirds and quail. Woodchucks burrow in the openings; skunks, foxes, and other predators move in.

Trees take root some 15 or 20 years after the bare-earth stage. Which ones are first depends largely on geography. Around the upper Great Lakes, and at corresponding latitudes in the East, aspen and birch grow before conifers and longer-living hardwoods. Black Cherry, its seed distributed by fruit-eating birds, is a successful pioneer tree throughout much of the eastern United States. Southward it is commonly joined by persimmon, Sassafras, and various nut-bearing trees planted by enterprising squirrels; in the Deep South, wind-seeded pines are likely to be the first successful trees. Left undisturbed, an abandoned field will usually become just what it was before the land was cleared—a piece of forest characteristic of the surrounding countryside.

Animal life includes:
Woodchuck *p. 56*
Eastern Cottontail *p. 57*
White-tailed Deer *p. 67*
Killdeer *p. 97*
Bobwhite *p. 110*
Mourning Dove *p. 112*
Horned Lark *p. 123*
Northern Mockingbird *p. 132*
Eastern Bluebird *p. 135*
Common Yellowthroat and
other warblers *pp. 138-143*
Bobolink *p. 144*
Meadowlarks *p. 144*
American Goldfinch *p. 151*
Rufous-sided Towhee *p. 151*
Sparrows *pp. 152-157*

Plant life includes:
Shortleaf Pine *p. 290*
Loblolly Pine *p. 290*
Eastern Redcedar *p. 296*
Common Juniper *p. 296*
Sassafras *p. 299*
Paper Birch *p. 307*
Quaking Aspen *p. 310*
Common Persimmon *p. 311*
Black Cherry *p. 312*
Staghorn Sumac *p. 320*
Brambles *p. 327*
Pokeweed *p. 353*
Lamb's Quarters *p. 359*
Virginia Creeper *p. 401*
Queen Anne's Lace *p. 406*
Milkweeds *pp. 412-413*
Common Mullein *p. 436*
Asters *p. 451*
Common Ragweed *p. 453*
Black-eyed Susan *p. 455*
Oxeye Daisy *p. 460*
Common Yarrow *p. 461*
Thistles *p. 463*
Broomsedge *p. 476*

Animal life includes:
Southeastern Pocket Gopher
  other pocket gophers p. 53
Raccoon *p. 58*
Gray Fox *p. 62*
Bobcat *p. 65*
White-tailed Deer *p. 67*
Pileated Woodpecker *p. 118*
Red-bellied Woodpecker *p. 118*
Great Crested Flycatcher *p. 121*
American Crow *p. 125*
Tufted Titmouse *p. 128*
Brown-headed Nuthatch
  other nuthatches p. 129
Carolina Wren *p. 130*
Northern Parula *p. 138*
Yellow-breasted Chat *p. 140*
Yellow-throated Warbler *p. 142*
Pine Warbler *p. 143*
Northern Cardinal *p. 148*

Plant life includes:
Shortleaf Pine *p. 290*
Loblolly Pine *p. 290*
Slash Pine *p. 291*
Longleaf Pine *p. 291*
Blackjack, Post, and
  other oaks *pp. 304–306*
Loblolly-bay *p. 308*
Hawthorns *p. 313*
Waxmyrtle *p. 323*
Saw-palmetto *p. 331*
Wiregrass *other
  three-awns p. 474*
Bluestems *p. 476*
Yellow Stargrass *p. 490*

A mature Slash Pine stands out against a background of young trees. The setting: Florida's Gulf Coast.

Southern Pine Forest

A forest of widely spaced pines spreads over much of the coastal plain from eastern Texas to North Carolina. Four species of pine dominate the area, sometimes growing in pure stands, sometimes associating with one another or with oaks or other broad-leaved trees. Were it not for frequent fires, large stretches would be oak-hickory, not pine.

This is young land, geologically speaking; much of the region has only a thin layer of sandy, rather sterile soil atop compacted clay, or hardpan. Sandy spots may be dotted with mounds excavated by tortoises and pocket gophers; spadefoot toads burrow into the sand to escape heat and drought. Drainage is often poor. Water collects in boggy spots called pocosins (an Indian word), home to insect-eating plants and evergreen shrubs.

On land that is slightly elevated, especially in Florida, the deeper, richer soil supports the growth of magnolias and other broad-leaved trees in characteristic communities known as hammocks.

Places to see this habitat include:
Alabama Conecuh National Forest; Geneva State
  Forest; Chewacla and Chickasaw state parks
Florida Apalachicola National Forest;
  Austin Carey Memorial Forest; Hillsborough
  River and O'Leno state parks
Georgia Oconee National Forest; Piedmont
  National Wildlife Refuge; Hard Labor Creek;
  Franklin D. Roosevelt and Little Ocmulgee
  state parks
Mississippi Bienville and De Soto national
  forests; Clarkco and Shelby state parks
South Carolina Francis Marion National Forest;
  Aiken, Lee, and Little Pee Dee state parks

Cypress Swamp

What classifies a wetland as a swamp instead of a bog or a marsh is the presence of trees—in many swamps of the southeastern United States, Baldcypress trees. Plant growth is luxuriant in any swamp, but in cypress swamps it is overwhelming. The towering trees, often standing in water, are draped with vines and covered with Spanish Moss, ferns, orchids, and other epiphytes ("air plants"). Atop the still water, duckweed or water lettuce may grow in a vivid green slick.

In the southernmost swamps like Big Cypress and Okefenokee, alligators bask on the banks or lie half-submerged in their holes; turtles sun themselves on logs. The many snakes range from harmless species to the sluggish but venomous Cottonmouth. (Both alligators and snakes can often be observed without trepidation from along a boardwalk.) Mammals are always present, though usually unseen, but bird life can be spectacular: one of the great sights of a cypress swamp is the homeward flight of storks or ibis to nighttime roosts in the giant trees.

Places to see this habitat include:

Florida Big Cypress National Preserve; Corkscrew Swamp Sanctuary; Wakula Springs State Park

Georgia Okefenokee National Wildlife Refuge

North Carolina Croatan National Forest; Great Dismal Swamp, National Wildlife Refuge

South Carolina Francis Marion National Forest; Santee State Park

Tennessee Reelfoot State Park

Virginia Great Dismal Swamp National Wildlife Refuge

Animal life includes:
Raccoon *p. 58*
Black Bear *p. 64*
Bobcat *p. 65*
Anhinga *p. 83*
Great Blue Heron *p. 84*
Snowy Egret *p. 85*
Great Egret *p. 85*
Wood Stork *p. 86*
White Ibis *other ibises p. 86*
Sandhill Crane *p. 87*
Wood Duck *p. 90*
Vultures *p. 106*
Red-shouldered Hawk *p. 107*
Barred Owl *p. 114*
Pileated Woodpecker *p. 118*
Red-bellied Woodpecker *p. 118*
Northern Parula *p. 138*
Prothonotary Warbler *p. 138*
Yellow-throated Warbler *p. 142*

Plant life includes:
Baldcypress *p. 295*
Sweetbay *p. 299*
Sweetgum *p. 300*
Black Willow *p. 309*
Black and other tupelos *p. 316*
Possumhaw *p. 316*
Red Maple *p. 318*
White Waterlily *p. 340*
Yellow Pondlily *p. 340*
Greater Bladderwort *p. 440*
Wapato *p. 468*
Spanish Moss *p. 478*
Pickerelweed *p. 480*
Swamp Lily *p. 491*
Yellow Flag *p. 497*
Epidendrums *p. 506*

Cypresses with protruding knees (at left) line the swampy shores of a Florida river.

The dark green of live oaks contrasts with the tawny grasses in the hill country back of Monterey, California.

California Oak Woodland

To a botanist, California is the land of oaks, a region where oaks of more than a dozen species (and innumerable hybrids as well) grow in nearly every wild setting but the driest deserts and the highest slopes. Especially prominent in the foothills, clusters of oaks alternate with rolling grasslands and pockets of chaparral. The oaks occupy the moister areas, often canyons and north-facing slopes, but even there they must cope with long summer droughts. Some species—among others, the live oaks—are evergreen, with small leathery leaves that minimize water loss; hairy leaves on other species help retain water.

An oak woodland has obvious attractions for acorn-eating animals. Mule Deer feed on the fallen nuts; squirrels bury them, helping renew the woodland by "planting" far more acorns than they will ever retrieve. Above the ground, Acorn Woodpeckers drill their holes in oaks and in other trees—not in pursuit of insects but to create storage space for their acorn food. Once studded with nuts, the trees will serve as larders not just for the woodpeckers but also for marauding squirrels and jays.

Places to see this habitat include:

California Kings Canyon and Sequoia national parks; Angeles and Los Padres national forests; Pinnacles National Monument; Cuyamaca Rancho, Henry W. Coe, Malibu Creek, Mount Diablo, Mount Tamalpais, Samuel P. Taylor, and Topanga state parks; Griffith Park (Los Angeles); Oak Grove Park (Pasadena)

Animal life includes:
Western Gray Squirrel
    other gray squirrels p. 54
California Ground Squirrel
    other ground squirrels p. 55
Coyote *p. 63*
Mule Deer *p. 67*
Red-tailed Hawk *p. 107*
Swainson's Hawk *p. 107*
California Quail *p. 111*
Western Screech-owl
    other screech-owls p. 115
Acorn Woodpecker *p. 118*
Scrub Jay *p. 124*
Bushtit *p. 128*
White-breasted Nuthatch
    p. 129
Western Bluebird
    other bluebirds p. 135
Northern Oriole *p. 146*
Black-headed Grosbeak *p. 149*
Lark Sparrow *p. 153*

Plant life includes:
California-laurel *p. 299*
Tanoak *p. 303*
Coast Live, California Black, Valley, and other oaks
    pp. 304–306
Pacific Madrone *p. 311*
California Buckeye
    other buckeyes p. 317
Yellow Lupine *p. 391*
Fiddleneck *p. 423*
Yerba Buena *p. 424*
Annual Bluegrass
    other bluegrasses p. 473
Ithuriel's Spear *p. 482*
Mariposa lilies *p. 486*
Goldenstars *p. 490*

Rolling hills, protruding rocks, and bristly bushes metamorphosing from green to brown— this California landscape is typical of chaparral in early summer.

Chaparral Country

Named for the Spanish for "scrub oak," the chaparral is a unique plant community, most prominent on hot, dry California slopes. Chaparral is a mixture of various evergreen shrubs, some of them bushy versions of trees found in nearby woodlands. With roots that tap deep sources of water, the shrubs can survive on parched soil. Though winter rains bring on a season of bloom, the waxy leaves turn dry as tinder during the long, hot summer. Fire sweeps periodically through the chaparral. When it rains again, seedlings germinate and new shoots sprout, reclaiming the land.

Chaparral forms dense thickets nearly impenetrable to man or large animals. (Chaparral and chaps—chaps being the protective leggings donned by cowboys riding through the brush—are closely allied.) But thanks to an abundance of berries, acorns, and seeds, the scrubby landscape is a haven for small animal life. Woodrats, chipmunks, and rabbits scurry about; skinks and other lizards are much in evidence on sunny slopes. Ground-foraging quail and towhees dart through low passageways in the thickets; hard-to-see wrentits, seldom found elsewhere, flit from twig to twig.

Places to see this habitat include:
California Sequoia National Park; Angeles, Cleveland, Los Padres, Mendocino, and Shasta-Trinity national forests; Pinnacles National Monument; Santa Monica Mountains National Recreation Area; Cuyamaca Rancho, Fremont Peak, and Mount Diablo state parks; Griffith Park (Los Angeles)

Animal life includes:
Dusky-footed Woodrat
  other woodrats p. 52
Brush Rabbit
  other cottontails p. 57
Gray Fox *p. 62*
Coyote *p. 63*
Bobcat *p. 65*
Mule Deer *p. 67*
California Quail *p. 111*
Anna's Hummingbird *p. 117*
Scrub Jay *p. 124*
Wrentit *p. 128*
Bushtit *p. 128*
Bewick's Wren *p. 131*
California Thrasher *p. 133*
Rufous-sided and
  other towhees *p. 151*
White-crowned Sparrow *p. 155*
Fox Sparrow *p. 156*
Song Sparrow *p. 156*

Plant life includes:
Coast Live Oak and
  other oaks *pp. 304–306*
Hollyleaf Cherry
  other cherries p. 312
Birchleaf Cercocarpus *p. 313*
Our Lord's Candle
  other yuccas p. 322
Manzanitas *p. 325*
Toyon *p. 327*
Chamise *p. 327*
Buckbrush and
  other ceanothuses *p. 328*
Deerweed *other trefoils p. 390*
Chia *p. 430*
Nuttall's Bedstraw
  other bedstraws p. 444
Ithuriel's Spear *p. 482*

Sagebrush Desert

Our largest, highest, and coldest desert covers Nevada, Utah, and areas of neighboring states. This bleak upland, known as the Great Basin, seems an infinite expanse of nothing but fragrant gray-green sagebrush, the plants separated by virtually bare ground. But the landscape is more varied than it at first appears—broken by many conifer-cloaked parallel ridges, traversed by tree-lined streams, dotted with playas, the salt-encrusted, water-collecting depressions that may contain marshes or lagoons.

To animal life, the clumps of sagebrush furnish welcome shelter as well as a valuable, fat-rich food. Certain species are so closely associated with this environment that their names cement the relationship: the pale little Sagebrush Vole, the spiny Sagebrush Lizard, the black-bellied Sage Grouse, the sweet-singing Sage Thrasher, and the secretive Sage Sparrow, a tail-flicking relative of the Black-throated Sparrow.

Places to see this habitat include:
California Modoc National Forest
Colorado Dinosaur National Monument
Nevada Humboldt and Toiyabe national forests; Ruby Lake and Sheldon national wildlife refuges; Desert National Wildlife Refuge
Oregon Malheur National Wildlife Refuge; Hart Mountain National Antelope Refuge
Utah Dixie National Forest; Snow Canyon State Park

Animal life includes:
Sagebrush Vole
  other voles p. 49
Great Basin Pocket Mouse
  other pocket mice p. 50
Ord's Kangaroo Rat *p. 51*
Black-tailed Jackrabbit *p. 57*
Pygmy Rabbit
  other cottontails p. 57
Badger *p. 58*
Kit and Gray foxes *p. 62*
Coyote *p. 63*
Pronghorn *p. 66*
Mule Deer *p. 67*
Swainson's Hawk *p. 107*
Golden Eagle *p. 108*
Prairie Falcon *p. 109*
Sage Grouse *other grouse p. 110*
Burrowing Owl *p. 115*
Western Kingbird *p. 120*
Horned Lark *p. 123*
Sage Thrasher *p. 133*
Savannah Sparrow *p. 152*
Vesper Sparrow *p. 152*
Black-throated Sparrow *p. 153*
Brewer's Sparrow *p. 154*

Plant life includes:
Four-wing Saltbush *p. 324*
Sagebrushes *p. 331*
Rabbitbrush *p. 331*
Opuntia cacti *p. 355*
Wild buckwheats *p. 363*
Locoweeds *p. 388*

Spring brings new growth to sagebrush and cactus. The mountains at the horizon—a spur of the southern Rockies—belie the elevation of this long flat expanse: 7,500 feet.

After winter rains in southern Arizona, a living yellow-green carpet blends with the hues of less ephemeral plants—stately Saguaros, bushy cholla, and whiplike ocotillo.

Cactus Desert

North America has four distinct deserts. The northernmost is the Great Basin desert, sagebrush-dominated and colder than the others. The Mojave, in Nevada and California, is small but famous: Death Valley is there, and so are the dagger-leaved Joshua-trees. The Chihuahuan, best known for its century plants (agaves), occurs in Texas and New Mexico but is for the most part a Mexican desert. Much of the Sonoran desert, too, is in Mexico, though portions extend into Arizona and California.

Nowhere in the world are plants of the desert as dramatic and diversified as in the Sonoran. Not only do cacti reach their peak here, with more than a hundred species; there are also succulent shrubs and, after the winter and summer rains, brilliant wildflower displays. Like trees in a forest, the giant cacti nurture life. Flickers and other woodpeckers excavate nest holes in the trunks; Elf Owls, North America's tiniest owls, eventually make them their own. Doves pollinate the blossoms and feast on the fruits and seeds; hawks nest in the crooks of the angular arms.

Places to see this habitat include:

Arizona Chirichua and Organ Pipe Cactus national monuments, Saguaro National Park; Arizona-Sonora Desert Museum (Tucson); Boyce Thompson Southwestern Arboretum (Superior); Desert Botanical Garden (Phoenix) *California* Death Valley and Joshua Tree national parks; Cuyamaca Rancho and Anza-Borrego Desert state parks; Living Desert Reserve

A Bison grazes the dry mixed-grass prairie at Wind Cave National Park, South Dakota. The solitary tree is a Bur Oak, an intruder from farther east.

Great Plains Grassland

When nature is allowed to take its course, the amount of rainfall largely determines which grasses grow where in the central part of the continent. In areas with greater moisture, Big Bluestem and other tallgrass species surpassing 4 feet in height form deep-rooted sod. In drier areas the shallow-rooted shortgrasses—Blue Grama and others that rarely top 16 inches—grow in scattered bunches. There are also midgrasses, including Little Bluestem, of intermediate height.

Because the Rocky Mountains block rain from reaching the Midwest, the area just to the east of the mountains is shortgrass country, the "home-on-the-range" land of Pronghorn and Bison. To the east of the shortgrass, the midgrasses mingle with other species in a mixed-prairie community covering most of the Dakotas, Nebraska, Oklahoma, and parts of Texas. Still farther east is the tallgrass prairie and then the forest, the boundaries of each zone shifting during years of drought or heavy rain. The 20 national grasslands in the United States include examples of all types.

Places to see this habitat include:
Alberta Waterton Lakes National Park; Cypress Hills Provincial Park
Colorado Comanche and Pawnee national grasslands
Kansas Cimarron National Grassland
Manitoba Riding Mountain National Park
Montana Benton Lake, Black Coulee, Bowdoin, Hewitt Lake, and Medicine Lake national wildlife refuges; National Bison Range
Nebraska Nebraska National Forest; Crescent Lake, Fort Niobrara, and Valentine national wildlife refuges
North Dakota Long Lake and Lostwood national wildlife refuges
Oklahoma Wichita Mountains Wildlife Refuge
Oregon Hart Mountain National Antelope Refuge; Lawrence Memorial Grasslands Preserve
Saskatchewan Prince Albert National Park; Cypress Hills Provincial Park
South Dakota Badlands and Wind Cave national parks; Lacreek National Wildlife Refuge; Custer State Park
Texas Caddo and Lyndon B. Johnson national grasslands
Wyoming Hutton Lake National Wildlife Refuge

Animal life includes:
Northern Grasshopper Mouse *p. 50*
Hispid Pocket Mouse *p. 50*
Plains Harvest Mouse *p. 51*
Plains Pocket Gopher *p. 53*
Ground squirrels *p. 55*
Black-tailed Prairie Dog *p. 55*
Jackrabbits *p. 57*
Badger *p. 58*
Coyote *p. 63*
Pronghorn *p. 66*
Bison *p. 69*
Long-billed Curlew *p. 95*
Killdeer *p. 97*
Marsh Hawk *p. 109*
Prairie Falcon *p. 109*
American Kestrel *p. 109*
Sharp-tailed Grouse *p. 110*
Short-eared Owl *p. 115*
Burrowing Owl *p. 115*
Horned Lark *p. 123*
Western Meadowlark *p. 144*
Brewer's Blackbird *p. 145*
Lark Bunting *p. 151*
Lark and other sparrows *pp. 152-156*
Chestnut-collared Longspur *p. 157*

Plant life includes:
Pale Larkspur *p. 346*
Prairie Buttercup *p. 347*
Plains Prickly Pear *p. 355*
Poppy Mallow *p. 366*
Scarlet Globe Mallow *p. 367*
Wild Pumpkin *p. 373*
Fragrant Leadplant *p. 388*
Prairie and other evening primroses *p. 396*
Indian paintbrushes *p. 431*
Pink Plains and other beardtongues *p. 433*
Gumweeds *p. 448*
Pale Purple Coneflower *p. 455*
Golden Tickseed *p. 457*
Skeleton Plant *p. 465*
Prairie Dandelion *p. 466*
Blue Grama, Sandburs, and other grasses *pp. 473-477*
Mariposa lilies *p. 486*
Wild Onion *p. 489*

Tallgrass Prairie

Rolling hills, waving grasses, occasional dark green patches of trees—but the serenity metamorphoses into a bustle of activity in spring. Prairie chickens boom on their mating grounds. Sandhill Cranes stage their elaborate courtship dance in and around the wetlands. Bobolinks sing on the wing. And all this activity takes place amid the developing grasses and flowers that will transform the prairies into a medley of scarlet, purple, and gold.

    The tallgrass prairie originally stretched eastward across Canada's prairie provinces and south along the border of Minnesota and the Dakotas through Iowa, eastern Nebraska, and Kansas, with another section on the western Gulf Coast. Although most of the region, with its deep, moist, humus-rich soil, has been converted to cropland or built up into towns and cities, a few remnants of the prairie grandeur that was have been preserved here and there.

Places to see this habitat include:

Illinois Goose Lake Prairie State Park
Iowa Pilot Knob State Park; Crossman and Mark Sand prairies;
    Freda Haffner Preserve; Caylor, Hayden,
    and Kaslow state prairie preserves
Kansas Flint Hills National Wildlife Refuge; Konza Prairie
Manitoba Living Prairie Museum (Winnipeg)
Minnesota Pipestone National Monument; Audubon, Blazing Star, Bluestem,
    Chippewa, Ottertail, and Zimmerman prairies; Compass Prairie Preserve
North Dakota Arrowwood and Tewaukon national wildlife refuges
Ohio Irwin Prairie Nature Preserve
Ontario Ojibway Prairie Provincial Nature Reserve
South Dakota Waubay National Wildlife Refuge; Samuel H. Ordway
    Memorial Prairie
Texas Attwater Prairie Chicken National Wildlife Refuge

Animal life includes:
Prairie Vole
  other voles p. 49
Meadow Jumping Mouse *p. 50*
Deer Mouse *p. 51*
Hispid Cotton Rat *p. 52*
Plains Pocket Gopher *p. 53*
Upland Sandpiper *p. 101*
Marsh Hawk *p. 109*
American Kestrel *p. 109*
Short-eared Owl *p. 115*
Bobolink *p. 144*
Meadowlarks *p. 144*
Grasshopper, Vesper, and
  other sparrows *pp. 152-156*
Lapland Longspur *p. 157*

Plant life includes:
Prairie and other violets
  pp. 370-371
Shooting Star *p. 380*
Queen of the Prairie *p. 385*
Tall Cinquefoil *p. 386*
Prairie False Indigo *p. 392*
Purple Prairie Clover *p. 393*
Rattlesnake Master *p. 407*
Bluebells *p. 409*
Prairie Rose Pink *p. 410*
Scarlet Paintbrush *p. 431*
Blazing Stars *p. 448*
Tall Goldenrod *p. 449*
Rosinweeds *p. 454*
Prairie Coneflower *p. 455*
Tickseed *p. 457*
Yellow Indian Grass,
  Big Bluestem, and other
  grasses *pp. 473-477*
Prairie Iris *p. 496*
Prairie Fringed Orchid *p. 503*

*The Flint Hills of Kansas, interlaced with streams,
form the largest area of tallgrass prairie left in the United States.*

Animal life includes:
Meadow Vole *p. 49*
Deer Mouse *p. 51*
Pocket gophers *p. 53*
Golden-mantled Ground Squirrel
    other ground squirrels p. 55
Marmots *p. 56*
Pika *p. 56*
Mountain Sheep *p. 66*
Mountain Goat *p. 66*
Wapiti (Elk) *p. 68*
Golden Eagle *p. 108*
White-tailed Ptarmigan *p. 110*
Horned Lark *p. 123*
Mountain Bluebird *p. 135*
Water Pipit *p. 153*
White-crowned Sparrow *p. 155*

Plant life includes:
American Globeflower *p. 343*
Blue and other columbines *p. 345*
Western Anemone *p. 348*
Moss Campion *other catchflies p. 358*
Bitterroot *p. 361*
White Heather *p. 377*
Mountain Heather *p. 377*
Mountain Douglasia *p. 380*
Mountain Primrose *p. 380*
Roseroot and
    other stonecrops *p. 383*
Gordon's Ivesia *p. 385*
Explorer's Gentian *p. 408*
Mountain Phlox *p. 418*
Rattlebox *p. 432*
Elephant Heads *p. 437*
Alpine Gold *p. 458*
Alp Lily *p. 482*
Quamash *p. 494*
Alkali Grass *p. 495*

Fiery red paintbrush
brightens a stony meadow
in the Canadian Rockies.

Alpine Meadow and Tundra

High on the western mountains (and, to a far lesser extent, in the Appalachians of the East), exquisite natural gardens stage a colorful show during their brief season of bloom. Some blossoms are alpine versions of buttercups and other lowland plants; others, such as douglasias, are strictly mountain species —in nature, at least (cultivated rock gardens are their second home). Mountain flowers tend to be hardy perennials, the ones in exposed places growing low and in the form of cushions or mats, which retain heat and moisture. In winter the plants are protected by snow cover, while animal life tends to disappear. Marmots hibernate in burrows for eight months a year; Meadow Voles scuttle about under the snow. Flocks of rosy finches, pink-winged birds found only in western mountains and the Far North, descend several thousand feet when winter sets in, only to fly up again in mild weather for a day's outing.

Places to see this habitat include:
Alaska Denali (Mount McKinley) National Park
    and Preserve; Denali State Park
Alberta Banff, Jasper, and Waterton Lakes
    national parks
British Columbia Manning Provincial Park
California Sequoia and Yosemite national parks
Colorado Rocky Mountain National Park;
    White River National Forest
Montana Glacier National Park; Absaroka-Beartooth
    Bob Marshall, Cabinet Mountains, and
    Mission Mountains wilderness areas
Utah High Uintas Wilderness Area
Washington Mount Rainier, North Cascades,
    and Olympic national parks
Wyoming Grand Teton National Park

Near Mount McKinley, Alaska, sedges extend into a summertime reflecting pool. Rolling hills alternate with watery lowlands throughout the tundra.

Arctic Tundra

A soggy treeless plain extends from the northern coast of the continent south to the evergreen forest. Because the Arctic tundra has a permanently frozen layer (called the permafrost) beneath the surface, water cannot seep down into the ground—hence the wetness of the terrain, despite low precipitation.

Slight changes in elevation offer variety in the landscape. There are rocky ridges blanketed by lichens and moss; rounded hillocks supporting stunted shrubs; gravelly streambeds lined with scraggly birch. Specialists of the wetlands, sedges form sweeping prairies. Crowberry, Bearberry, and other dwarf evergreens creep along the ground, their names hinting at their linkage with animal life.

Though geographically remote, the Arctic tundra shares at least one feature with temperate lands: its birds. Most of the geese that winter in lower latitudes nest there, for goslings can feed round the clock during the long summer days; numerous shorebirds also breed on the tundra. The significance of these lands as a nesting ground cannot be denied—nor should the subtle beauty be underrated.

Places to see this habitat include:
Alaska Denali (Mount McKinley) National Park and Preserve; Arctic National Wildlife Refuge
Manitoba Cape Churchill Wildlife Management Area
Northwest Territories Auyuittuq and Nahanni national parks
Ontario Polar Bear Provincial Park
Yukon Territory Kluane National Park; Peel River Game Preserve

Animal life includes:
Brown Lemming
   other lemmings p. 49
Arctic Ground Squirrel
   other ground squirrels p. 55
Arctic Hare *other hares p. 57*
Arctic Fox *other foxes p. 62*
Gray Wolf *p. 63*
Polar Bear *p. 64*
Caribou *p. 69*
Tundra Swan *p. 88*
Snow Goose *p. 89*
Canada Goose *p. 89*
American Golden-plover *p. 96*
Ruddy Turnstone *p. 97*
Red Knot *p. 98*
Sandpipers *pp. 98–101*
Rock Ptarmigan
   other ptarmigan p. 110
Snowy Owl *p. 114*
Horned Lark *p. 123*
Lapland Longspur *p. 157*
Snow Bunting *p. 157*

Plant life includes:
Dwarf Birch *other birches p. 307*
Dwarf Willow *other willows p. 309*
Dwarf Bilberry *other blueberries and cranberries p. 326*
Bearberry *p. 377*
White Heather *p. 377*
Mountain heathers *p. 377*
Purple Saxifrage
   other saxifrages p. 384
Marsh Cinquefoil *p. 386*
Rushes *p. 471*
Cottongrass *p. 472*
Sedges *p. 472*

Glimmering like a jewel in its alpine setting, Maligne Lake, in Jasper National Park, Alberta, is fed by glacial waters from nearby peaks.

Lake and Pond

An amazing number of lakes and ponds are scattered over North America. Some regions, like the canoe country of Minnesota and Ontario, are networks of both large and small bodies of water. These lakes, like the Finger Lakes in New York, are the product of glaciers, which gouged out depressions and formed the prairie ponds and potholes. Movements of the earth's crust created Lake Tahoe in the Sierra Nevada, Lake Okeechobee in Florida, and Reelfoot Lake in Tennessee. Other lakes, usually circular and very deep, occupy the craters of extinct volcanoes; Oregon's Crater Lake is in the caldera, or collapsed crater, of an ancient peak.

The depth of a lake determines its plant and animal life. Deep lakes, with a layer of cold water at the bottom, often do not contain enough microscopic food or vegetation to nurture many forms of life, and ducks and other water birds shun their crystal-clear waters. Shallow lakes and ponds, on the other hand, are rich in algae and small animals.

Freshwater Marsh

Marshes are treeless wetlands. Freshwater ones develop in ponds and lake shallows and at the edges of quiet streams—places where a slow current (or none at all) permits cattails, sedges, and water-loving grasses to push out from shore. Marshes often represent a transition stage between water and dry land. Waterlilies take root on the deepwater side; other aquatic plants float at the surface. Muskrats, ducks, and coots feed on rootstocks, seeds, and leaves; herons and egrets, on the amphibians and fish.

All of these animals—and human beings too—benefit from the hundreds of marshes in North America. Found all across the continent but especially prominent in the Upper Midwest, many of the marsh areas in the United States are protected as part of the national wildlife refuge system. Established primarily to increase waterfowl populations, the refuges are breeding grounds for hundreds of thousands of ducks and stopovers for millions more. Beyond that, the refuges are increasingly appreciated for the nongame species—hawks, owls, shorebirds, songbirds—that visit to feed or nest in these protected surroundings.

Places to see this habitat include:
British Columbia Creston Valley Wildlife Management Area
California Lower Klamath and Tule Lake national wildlife refuges
Delaware Bombay Hook National Wildlife Refuge
Idaho Camas National Wildlife Refuge
Maine Moosehorn National Wildlife Refuge
Manitoba Delta Marsh; Oak Hammock Marsh Wildlife Management Area
Massachusetts Great Meadows National Wildlife Refuge
Michigan Seney National Wildlife Refuge
Minnesota Agassiz National Wildlife Refuge
Montana Red Rock Lakes National Wildlife Refuge
Nevada Ruby Lake National Wildlife Refuge
New Jersey Great Swamp National Wildlife Refuge
New York Montezuma National Wildlife Refuge
North Dakota Upper Souris National Wildlife Refuge
Ontario Point Pelee National Park
Oregon Malheur National Wildlife Refuge
Utah Bear River Migratory Bird Refuge

Animal life includes:
Muskrat *p. 45*
Raccoon *p. 58*
Herons *p. 84*
Egrets *p. 85*
American Bittern *p. 85*
Glossy Ibis *p. 86*
Sandhill Crane *p. 87*
Virginia and other rails *p. 88*
Common Gallinule *p. 89*
Canada Goose *p. 89*
Green-winged Teal
    and other ducks *pp. 90–93*
Common Snipe *p. 100*
Franklin's Gull *p. 103*
Black and other terns *pp. 104–105*
Marsh Hawk *p. 109*
Marsh Wren *p. 130*
Red-winged Blackbird *p. 144*
Yellow-headed Blackbird *p. 144*
Sharp-tailed Sparrow *p. 152*

Plant life includes:
Yellow Pondlily *p. 340*
Marsh Marigold *p. 341*
Marsh Mallow *p. 367*
Swamp Candles *p. 381*
Water Pennywort *p. 407*
Buckbean *p. 409*
Yellow and other
    monkey flowers *p. 432*
Water Speedwell *p. 436*
Arrowheads *p. 468*
Rushes *p. 471*
Bulrushes *p. 471*
Sedges *p. 472*
Reedgrass *p. 473*
Indian Rice *p. 475*
Cattails *p. 477*
Calamus *p. 479*
Southern Blue Flag *p. 497*

This Shoveler is but one of more than 20 species of ducks—and more than 200 kinds of birds overall—sighted at the Ruby Lake refuge in Nevada.

33

Animal life includes:
Water Shrew *other shrews p. 48*
Raccoon *p. 58*
Mink *p. 61*
River Otter *p. 61*
Spotted Sandpiper *p. 100*
Belted Kingfisher *p. 113*
American Dipper *p. 129*
Louisiana Waterthrush
  other waterthrushes p. 139

Plant life includes:
Eastern and other hemlocks
  p. 293
Mountain Alder
  other alders p. 307
Pussy Willow *p. 309*
Elkslip *p. 341*
Watercress *p. 376*
Forget-me-not *p. 422*
Scarlet and other
  monkey flowers p. 432
Stream Orchid *p. 507*

*A mountain stream in
northern Georgia,
flecked with autumn
leaves, threads its way
through its stony bed.*

Swift Stream

Many a mighty river begins as a fast mountain stream. Chuckling and murmuring in its rocky bed, the stream gives little evidence of its power, but when a steep slope or a sudden spring freshet adds force, even a little brook can move quantities of silt, sand, and gravel. In most swift streams, shallow riffles alternate with deeper pools; where the gradient drops sharply, waterfalls and white-water rapids take shape.

Because of the current, swift streams have few aquatic plants other than algae and moss. Nevertheless, animal life is abundant, nourished partially by leaf fall from streamside plants and resisting the force of the current with flattened or streamlined bodies, suckers, and other adaptations. Myriads of insects live beneath stones and gravel or cling to rough surfaces, using friction pads or clawlike grapples; others attach themselves with silken strands. Several species of salamanders, including the Dusky and the Two-lined, also spend most of their lives underwater, feeding on insect larvae and laying their eggs under stones. Aquatic insects are food for fish as well. On both sides of the continent salmon ascend even small streams to spawn in the riffles; trout lurk in quiet backwaters and pools. Fishermen and canoeists have always appreciated these rivers, but a growing public awareness of their beauty and vitality led to the creation of the U.S. Wild and Scenic Rivers System in 1968. Today portions of more than two dozen rivers and streams, including the Allagash in Maine, Ohio's Little Miami, the Chattooga in the Southeast, and Montana's Flathead, are preserved in this system.

Slow-moving River

When a rushing river reaches a flat expanse, such as the southeastern coastal plain, it undergoes a change. The waters spread out and slow down, depositing their load of silt and creating a soft, muddy bottom. In many cases the river becomes a series of meanders and oxbows, the horseshoe-shaped bends that turn into isolated lakes if the river changes course. Away from the main channel, bayous and sloughs—quiet waters that conjure up a host of images but resist precise definition—take shape.

The land drained by a slow-moving river resembles a huge sponge, with an almost infinite capacity for absorbing water. Yet when swelled by rains or melted snow, the river will overflow its banks, inundating the bottomland forest and turning the region into a vast wooded swamp. The boundaries of the slow-moving river, its channel less defined than that of a headwater stream, are fixed neither in space nor in time.

In the sluggish part of a river the water is warmer, richer in nutrients, and more conducive to plant growth than it is upstream. The luxuriant growth of waterlilies and other vegetation shelters a number of amphibians (including both big salamanders and very small frogs), reptiles (mud turtles and snappers, among others), and such large fishes as sturgeon and gar. Hunting in the muddy shallows for crustaceans and small fish, birds are as disrespectful of boundaries as the river itself; slow rivers share many species of birds, and other animals as well, with swamps, marshes, and other standing waters.

Animal life includes:
Muskrat *p. 45*
Raccoon *p. 58*
Anhinga *p. 83*
Great Blue Heron *p. 84*
Green Heron *p. 84*
Wood Stork *p. 86*
Gallinules *p. 89*
Wood Duck *p. 90*
Spotted Sandpiper *p. 100*

Plant life includes:
Baldcypress *p. 295*
Sycamore *p. 299*
Willow Oak *p. 305*
Black and other willows *p. 309*
Black and other tupelos *p. 316*
Yellow Pondlily *p. 340*
Yellow Lotus *p. 341*
Arrowheads *p. 468*
Pondweed *p. 469*
Water Hyacinth *p. 480*

Tall cottonwoods shade the marshy edges and quiet waters of this slough on the floodplain of the Sacramento River.

35

Tidal Marsh

Land meets sea in the marshes fringing Cape Cod Bay. Crab holes exposed by an outgoing tide can only hint at the abundance of animal life.

All too easily viewed as vacant land, salt marshes—blanketed with vegetation, abounding in shellfish, nurturing the young of many commercial and sport fish—are the most productive of all natural habitats. Vivid green in summer, tawny gold in fall, with shifting patterns of water, shadow, and sun, they offer wild beauty throughout the year.

A walk at low tide, when fewer channels have to be forded, quickly dispels any impression of uniformity. As in other low-lying areas, a slight difference in elevation means a dramatic difference in plant life. Salt-tolerant spartina grasses dominate the lower region, one kind growing tall and coarse along tidal creeks, another, shorter and finer, in drier places. The tall, dark Blackgrass grows in areas not ordinarily swept by the tides; the jointed, fleshy-stemmed Glasswort, at the edge of depressions, called pannes or pans, that retain water when the tide goes out.

Places to see this habitat include:
California Elkhorn Slough Estuary Sanctuary
Florida Chassahowitzka and St. Marks national wildlife refuges;
   Gulf Islands National Seashore; Waccasassa Bay State Preserve
Louisiana Sabine National Wildlife Refuge
Maryland Assateague Island National Seashore
Massachusetts Parker River National Wildlife Refuge; Cape Cod
   National Seashore; Wellfleet Bay Audubon Sanctuary
New Jersey Edwin B. Forsythe National Wildlife Refuge (Brigantine Division)
North Carolina Cape Hatteras and Cape Lookout national seashores
Oregon South Slough Estuarine Sanctuary
South Carolina Cape Romain National Wildlife Refuge
Texas Aransas National Wildlife Refuge
Virginia Chincoteague National Wildlife Refuge

Animal life includes:
Muskrat *p. 45*
Herons *p. 84*
Egrets *p. 85*
Sora and other rails *p. 88*
Black Duck *p. 91*
Willet *p. 95*
Laughing Gull *p. 103*
Forster's Tern *p. 104*
Common Tern *p. 104*
Black Skimmer *p. 104*
Marsh Hawk *p. 109*
Marsh Wren *p. 130*
Savannah, Sharp-tailed, and
   Seaside sparrows *p. 152*
Diamondback Terrapin *p. 162*

Plant life includes:
Groundsel-tree *p. 331*
Sea Lavender *p. 364*
Swamp Rose Mallow *p. 366*
Sea Milkwort *p. 382*
Silverweed *p. 386*
Large Marsh Pink *p. 410*
Seaside Gerardia *other gerardias
   p. 430*
Seaside Goldenrod *p. 449*
Blackgrass *other rushes p. 471*

Mangrove Swamp

Prominent along the southwestern coast of the Everglades and in the Florida Keys, mangrove swamps, the tropical counterparts of tidal marshes, are dramatic examples of succession, the replacement of one plant community by another as living conditions change. Scattered along the seaward edge are seedlings of the Red Mangrove. As they grow and develop into a thicket, their arching prop roots trap silt and detritus. One of the very few trees that can survive in saltwater, the Red Mangrove fares poorly in the oxygen-poor mud that develops beneath its "feet." Not so the Black-mangrove, with its erect roots, called pneumatophores, that poke through the mud and help the plant to breathe. Eventually Black-mangrove takes over—only to be replaced, in turn, by Button-mangrove, which often forms a transition zone between swamp and dry land.

Mangrove tangles, with their intermeshing roots and stems, are virtually impenetrable to man, but channels and other open-water areas furnish excellent opportunities for photography and birding. As a boat approaches, clouds of large, impressive birds waft up from the mangroves, circle for a while, and then settle down, near others of their own kind. On one mangrove island herons were observed to nest in the interior, cormorants on the outside, and ibises in between—a zonation paralleling that of the mangroves themselves. Divisions of plants and animals into ecological zones such as these occur not only in mangrove swamps but on rocky shores, in northern sphagnum bogs, and in nearly every other wildlife community on earth.

A Red Mangrove's prop roots arch over a limestone beach in the Florida Keys. If nature is allowed to take its course, this place may in time become dry land.

Animal life includes:
Raccoon *p. 58*
Manatee *p. 71*
Pelicans *p. 82*
Double-crested Cormorant *p. 83*
Anhinga *p. 83*
Great Blue Heron *p. 84*
Egrets *p. 85*
Wood Stork *p. 86*
White Ibis *other ibises p. 86*
Roseate Spoonbill *p. 86*
Bald Eagle *p. 108*
Osprey *p. 108*

Plant life includes:
Red Mangrove *p. 316*
White-mangrove *p. 316*
Black-mangrove *p. 321*

Between headlands of wave-resistant rock in Oregon, sand has accumulated, forming a broad beach.

Pacific Sandy Shore

Although many of the cliffs that line the western coast have a narrow ribbon of sand at their feet, extensive beaches are more the exception than the rule. Sand collects in the lee of headlands and in other protected locations, creating isolated "pocket beaches"; sand spits take shape on the borders of estuaries and bays. Dunes are uncommon except for several stretches in California and a magnificent Lawrence-of-Arabia landscape halfway down the Oregon coast. Most of the beaches are backed by rocky cliffs or steeply rising ground.

With an abundance of small animal life, sandy shores and their finer-particled counterparts, mud flats, serve as "roadside restaurants" for many a migrating shorebird. Although most species nest in the Arctic, their southward migration is in full swing well before autumn, creating delightful opportunities for summertime bird-watching; and even in the northern states, some species frequent the winter beach. Many shorebirds roost during high tide on sandbars or on the upper beach, then probe for burrowing animals when the tide goes out. Sanderlings patrol the water's edge, snatching up drifting bits of food; plovers gather morsels from beach wrack, higher on the shore.

Places to see this habitat include:
British Columbia Pacific Rim National Park
California Channel Islands and Redwood national parks; Humboldt Bay National Wildlife Refuge; Santa Monica Mountains National Recreation Area; Point Reyes National Seashore; Morro Bay State Park
Oregon Oregon Dunes National Recreation Area
Washington Olympic National Park; Fort Canby State Park

Animal life includes:
Brown Pelican *p. 82*
Marbled Godwit *p. 95*
Willet *p. 95*
Semipalmated, Snowy, and Black-bellied plovers *p. 96*
Dunlin *p. 98*
Sanderling *p. 98*
Western and Least sandpipers *p. 99*
Western and other gulls *pp. 102–103*
Pacific Razor, Pismo, and other clams *pp. 256–260*
Sand dollars *p. 285*

Plant life includes:
Rock Sandwort *p. 356*
Carpetweed *p. 362*
Ice Plant *p. 362*
Sea Milkwort *p. 382*
Silverweed *p. 386*
Beach Pea *p. 388*
Quail Plant *p. 423*
Western Vervain other vervains *p. 424*
Mat Sandbur *p. 476*

Waving beach grass and fruiting wild rose bind a Cape Cod sand dune, while the ocean gnaws at its base.

Eastern Sandy Shore

From Florida to Cape Cod the Atlantic coast is blessed with long stretches of beach. In sharp contrast with the mountainous Pacific shore, the eastern edge of the continent (and the Gulf coast as well) is for the most part a gently sloping lowland, often protected from the surf by barrier islands and shoals. In many places the landward side of the beach is backed by dunes, their sands shifting ever so slowly downwind until beach grasses and other salt-tolerant plants halt their advance.

As on the Pacific shore, countless small animals live beneath the surface, cooler, moister, and safer than they would be elsewhere. Tiny sand fleas ("beach hoppers") emerge at night or on cloudy days; pale-colored Ghost Crabs scurry to and from their burrows, maneuvering easily on land but entering the water frequently to moisten their gills. Lower down on the shore, diminutive mole crabs rise from below the surface as each wave recedes, straining plankton from the backwash with their feathery antennae and then burrowing back into the sand as the next wave rolls in.

Places to see this habitat include:
Delaware Cape Henlopen State Park
Florida Canaveral and Gulf Islands national seashores;
    Captiva and Sanibel islands
Georgia Cumberland Island National Seashore; Jekyll Island State Park
Maryland Assateague Island National Seashore
New York Fire Island National Seashore; Montauk Point State Park
North Carolina Cape Hatteras and Cape Lookout national seashores
South Carolina Cape Romain National Wildlife Refuge
Texas Padre Island National Seashore
Virginia Chincoteague National Wildlife Refuge

Animal life includes:
Pelicans *p. 82*
American Oystercatcher *p. 94*
Black-necked Stilt *p. 94*
Marbled Godwit *p. 95*
Willet *p. 95*
Semipalmated and other
    plovers *pp. 96–97*
Dowitchers *p. 98*
Sanderling *p. 98*
Dunlin *p. 98*
Sandpipers *p. 99*
Gulls *pp. 102–103*
Terns *pp. 104–105*
Loggerhead *p. 165*
Moon snails *p. 243*
Atlantic Jackknife, Florida
    Coquina, and other clams
    pp. 256–260
Shore crabs *p. 283*
Atlantic Horseshoe Crab *p. 284*

Plant life includes:
Beach Plum *other plums p. 312*
Bayberries *p. 323*
Roses *p. 327*
Dusty-miller
    other sagebrushes p. 331
Prickly Pear Cactus
    other opuntia cacti p. 355
Rock Sandwort *p. 356*
Beach Heather *p. 372*
Sea Milkwort *p. 382*
Silverweed *p. 386*
Beach Pea *p. 388*
Poison Ivy *p. 398*
Quail Plant *p. 423*
Cleavers *p. 444*
Seaside Goldenrod *p. 449*
Sea Oats *p. 473*
Adam's Needle *p. 499*

39

Rocky Pacific Coast

As the Pacific shoreline retreats before the onslaught of the sea, its rocky cliffs are sculpted into arches, caves, towers ("sea stacks"), and other wave-cut forms. Seabirds nest in these isolated fortresses, as well as on the cliffs themselves. Sea lions bask on rocks at the base; Sea Otters frolic in the kelp offshore; whales maneuver close to land, migrating along the coast or hunting for prey.

Areas swept by surf, its force intensified by the vastness of the ocean and the eastward-blowing winds, offer little sanctuary to either man or wildlife. Shores protected by headlands, islands, kelp beds, or offshore reefs are far better for curious naturalists to explore. As the tide retreats, mirrorlike pools remain as natural aquariums, populated with life-giving algae, an occasional small fish, and invertebrates of all types. Pistol shrimps noisily snap their claws; light-sensitive chitons cling to the underside of rocks; and octopuses in their lairs delight visitors to this evanescent world.

Places to see this habitat include:
British Columbia Pacific Rim National Park
California Channel Islands National Park; Cabrillo National Monument; Point Reyes National Seashore; Andrew Molera State Park; Asilomar State Beach; Point Lobos State Reserve
Oregon Cape Meares National Wildlife Refuge; Cape Blanco and Seal Rock state parks; Sea Lion Caves (near Florence)
Washington Olympic National Park; Fort Canby State Park

Luxuriant seaweeds drape the rocks on a Washington beach.
A brightly colored starfish is just touching the water at right.

*Below a canopy of conifers,
waves break against the
Maine coast, shaped
by glaciers and the sea.*

Northeastern Coast

Thousands of years ago this rugged land was weighed down by glaciers, then inundated when they melted and the sea level rose. Saltwater flooded the coast, hills became islands, valleys turned into bays, and the deeply indented, island-dotted northeastern shoreline—an excellent example of what geologists call a drowned coast—slowly came into being.

From Labrador to southern Maine the coast is predominantly rocky. Twice a day the tide ebbs and flows, generally on a more regular schedule than along the Pacific shore. In places where the water rises especially high (the world's highest tides, in the Bay of Fundy, can exceed 50 feet), vertical zones of life are particularly conspicuous. Vertical zonation, most noticeable among the plants, occurs on seacoasts around the world.

High on the shore, in the splash zone, are blue-green algae and certain lichens, plants that can survive saltwater spray and near-drought conditions. Just below, exposed to the air for a good part of the day, are yellow-brown rockweeds. Irish Moss and other red seaweeds thrive lower on the shore; below them are the leathery brown kelps, characteristic not only of the shore but also of the waters beyond.

Places to see this habitat include:
Maine Acadia National Park; Cobscook Bay
    and Quoddy Head state parks
New Brunswick Fundy National Park;
    Grand Manan Island
Newfoundland Terra Nova National Park
Nova Scotia Cape Breton Highlands National Park
Quebec Forillon National Park; Bonaventure Island
    Wildlife Sanctuary

41

Mammals

*Chipmunks and squirrels please us with their lively antics;
deer, with their gentle nature and soulful eyes.
Impressions of other mammals may be more fleeting,
more tantalizing, more evocative of the spirit of the wild.*

Although North America has some 400 species of mammals, most are by no means easy to find. True, Raccoons catch our attention when they prowl around our homes, and Bison are much too big to stay hidden in the grass. But the majority of mammals survive by being elusive. Many, for example, avoid the light of day (a behavior pattern that also keeps them cool). Opossums and Mink are primarily nocturnal; deer and rabbits are active mainly about dawn and dusk.

Regardless of the hours they keep, mammals in general are difficult to spot, for they blend into their background with ease. Their fur—a feature unique to mammals (another unique trait is that they nurse their young)—is usually some shade of brown; some, such as the Varying Hare, even change color with the seasons to achieve year-round camouflage. Stripes or other patterns often break up the image (fawns are a prime example). Many mammals, and other animals too, are pale on the underside, which offsets any shadow that might make them stand out from their surroundings. And few mammals are noisy enough to attract your attention with sound.

With their high sensitivity to odor and sound, mammals often sense an approaching human in ample time for them to hide or flee. Whether predator or prey (often both), a mammal depends on a keen awareness of its surroundings, and anyone hoping to observe mammals in the wild should be aware of that awareness. Specific dos and don'ts are provided at right.

Searching for Mammals

To increase your chances of spotting mammals, don't just *hope* they'll pass your way; turn detective. Look for clues to where they have been—and where they might return to. Cracks or ridges running along the surface indicate mole tunnels below. Dome-shaped heaps of grasses in water say Muskrat.

Be alert too for food-related signs. Squirrels build up heaps of "used" pine cones. Mouse-like Pikas prepare winter larders—piles of dried plant materials. Beavers and Porcupines leave tooth marks in trees.

Tracks reveal the presence of mammal life. Although the form they take varies with the speed of the animal and with the surface (tracks in the snow look different from those in mud), certain species make very distinctive tracks, and some of these patterns are shown in this book alongside the animal that makes them. Look for animal footprints in the soft, moist edges of brooks and ponds, in snow, and in seashore or desert sand—and remember that mammals are creatures of habit who, once familiar with a certain place, tend to return to it again and again. In this way visible trails are created, whether by voles tunneling through the grass or deer traveling established routes.

Identifying Mammals

Mammals are for the most part more difficult to identify than birds; few have the distinctiveness of a Robin or a Cardinal, and there are a large number of little rodents that look pretty much alike. You should have little problem identifying mammals that you've had the luxury of observing out in the open for a long period of time. But if one crosses your path only briefly, try to extract from the encounter a general impression of its shape and color, and also a rough estimate of the size of its ears and the length of its tail. With such information at hand, you'll have a much easier time giving the creature a name.

Specific information about the habits of mammals shown in this book is given in the individual entries for each species. In this section, as in the others, closely related animals are generally grouped together; the hoofed mammals, for example, are shown on pages 66 through 69. The species on the first two pages belong to several different groups.

The habitat symbols used in this section are: ⊞ *desert* 🌿 *grassland/meadow/brush* 🌲 *forest*

Tips on Observing Mammals

• Don't wear clothing that contrasts sharply with the landscape; in a wooded area, for instance, browns, greens, and grays are preferred. Patterned fabrics—camouflage cloth and the like—have the added advantage of breaking your image into smaller, less conspicuous parts. Choose clothing that doesn't rustle or swish when you walk, and avoid shiny fabrics, jewelry, and other items likely to reflect the sun.

• Keep your voice low, and move slowly and quietly. Take advantage of shrubs and other cover when approaching an animal or a possible viewing site. Literally keep a low profile (sometimes it's best to crawl on all fours), and stay away from open hilltops where you might be silhouetted against the sky. Don't make hand movements that will give you away.

• Don't smoke. To animals the smell of tobacco means danger. Some authorities recommend that smokers and nonsmokers alike looking for mammals give their clothes a natural aroma—say, by covering them with pine needles for a day or two.

• If you plan to spend some time at a promising site (a muddy riverbank with numerous animal footprints is one example), a folding stool or foam-rubber cushion will add to your comfort. Before you settle down, note which way the breeze is blowing and try to position yourself downwind.

• Merely encountering wild mammals can be a thrill in itself, especially if they are of the more furtive kind. But if you're very lucky, patient, or skilled, you may be able to watch the animals *doing* something—feeding, drinking, interacting with you or with others of their own kind. The illustrations on this page show some of the types of behavior you may be able to observe.

Threat Behavior

Though few can observe the gesture with the proper degree of scientific detachment, the Spotted Skunk's handstand is a threat, to be followed with a well-aimed spray should the intruder not retreat. Animals often threaten in a way that focuses attention on their weaponry. Moose lower their antlers; wolves and Coyotes bare their teeth. To observe threat gestures, you should listen as well as look. Opossums hiss; Porcupines gnash their teeth.

Play

Even more so than among humans, it is the young animals who play (though adult cats—wild *and* domestic —also toy with their prey). Often taking the form of wrestling or chasing, play is a repetitive, exuberant activity that helps the youngsters learn. Such social animals as prairie dogs seem to love to play.

Parental Care

The care mammals give their young is unique. Usually the females nurse their offspring, protect them, and keep them warm (sometimes the males help out too). Seals and sea lions breed in colonies that are out in the open, and they use the same sites year after year—conditions that make mother and young rather easy to observe. Be sure to use binoculars, however, and do your best not to disturb the colonies.

Fighting

Often preceded by threats, fighting occurs among the males of many species as they attempt to set up territories or take possession of a female. The purpose of fighting is not to kill but to drive the opponent away. Small mammals wrestle and bite; Mountain Sheep use their horns.

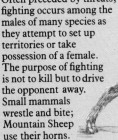

 urban/suburban ≊ freshwater ≋ saltwater ⧫ brackish water

Opossum
Didelphis virginiana

Length: *head and body, 13½–21 in.; tail, 9½–20 in.*
What to look for: *nose long, pointed, pinkish; white face; large leaflike ears; tail long, rounded, sparsely haired; pale gray in northern states, darker in southern states.* **Habitat:** *farmland, forests; usually near water.*

North America's only marsupial (pouched mammal) bears litters of up to 14 kits, each about the size of a honeybee. Immediately after birth the tiny creatures crawl into their mother's pouch, where they nurse for several months. After emerging from the pouch, they ride about on their mother's back for another few weeks. As their 50 teeth (more than those of any other North American land mammal) develop, the young switch from mother's milk to an extraordinarily diverse diet of insects, other small animals, birds' eggs, mushrooms, grain crops, fruit, and carrion. Though their food habits bring them close to man, opossums often go unnoticed because they are active mainly at night. They occasionally "play possum" when cornered, curling up into a trancelike state that may last several hours. It is believed that potential predators may leave such animals for dead and seek more active prey elsewhere.

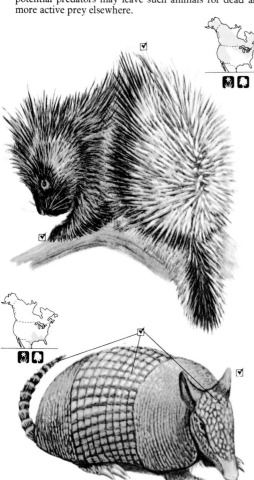

Porcupine
Erethizon dorsatum

Length: *head and body, 18–23 in.; tail, 6–11 in.*
What to look for: *chunky body; short legs; long, stiff quills; slow-moving gait.*
Habitat: *forests (commonly in trees); occasionally in brushy areas.*

Contrary to popular belief, the Porcupine does not shoot its quills. When threatened by the weasellike Fisher or some other predator, it turns its back to the enemy, raises its approximately 30,000 quills, and strikes out with its tail. The barbed quills, which are really modified hairs loosely attached to the skin, become embedded on contact. The Porcupine is a large nocturnal rodent. If seen during the day, it appears as a round, dark shape high in a tree. At night it clambers from tree to tree, often causing serious damage by feeding on buds, twigs, and bark. In areas where trappers have eliminated the Porcupine's predators, its population has increased dramatically—much to the dismay of foresters.

Nine-banded Armadillo
Dasypus novemcinctus

Length: *head and body, 15–17½ in.; tail, 13–15½ in.*
What to look for: *bony plates on body, tail, and top of head; large ears; long, squarish snout.*
Habitat: *brushy or rocky areas; forests (pines in East).*

The armadillo's lizardlike skin and bony-plated shell look like the perfect defense against predators. Although on rare occasions the animal may curl into a ball when attacked, it is more likely to protect itself by quickly digging a hole or fleeing into its burrow. The burrow is a multichambered tunnel where the females give birth, always to quadruplets that are always of the same sex. Close relatives of anteaters and sloths, armadillos are extending their range.

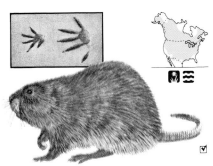

Muskrat
Ondatra zibethicus

Length: *head and body, 9–15 in.; tail, 7½–10½ in.*
What to look for: *color reddish brown, except for light gray belly; tail black, scaly, vertically flattened.*
Habitat: *marshes, ponds, lakes, slow streams with reeds and cattails.*

This aquatic mammal persists despite the widespread drainage of marshes, for it can survive in a variety of wetland habitats. Its versatile diet is also an asset; though it feeds mainly on aquatic plants, it also eats snails, clams, crayfish, and frogs and may travel hundreds of feet from water to harvest land plants. It reproduces rapidly: several litters a year, each with up to 11 young. Muskrats use aquatic lodges that are smaller than beaver lodges and made of grasses and sedges instead of sticks and mud.

Nutria
Myocastor coypus

Length: *head and body, 20–26 in.; tail, 12–17 in.*
What to look for: *grayish-brown rodent midway in size between a Muskrat and a Beaver; tail long, almost hairless, round (not flattened).*
Habitat: *freshwater marshes, ponds, lakes, swamps.*

Native to South America, Nutrias, or Coypus, were brought to this continent in the 1930's. Some individuals escaped from fur ranches, others were released to control vegetation in lakes, and the species became part of the wildlife of North America. Though their diet, habitat, and fertility are similar to the Muskrat's, Nutrias are larger and highly competitive. In certain areas they have displaced the Muskrat, usurping its lodges, burrows, and feeding areas. Man and alligators are their main enemies.

Beaver   *Castor canadensis*

Length: *head and body, 27–38 in.; tail, 9–12 in.*
What to look for: *front teeth prominent, orange; tail large, paddlelike, scaly.* **Habitat:** *lakes and streams, bordered with poplars, birches, or other food trees.*

Famed for their dam-building ability, North America's largest rodents begin by making an underwater foundation of mud and stone. Then they gnaw down trees, leaving characteristic cone-shaped stumps, and drag or float cuttings to the dam site, where they are incorporated into the foundation with more mud. As a pond forms behind the dam, the pair of Beavers build a stick-and-mud lodge with underwater entrances and an inside platform raised above the water. Here they remain much of the day, emerging at dusk to forage for succulent plants or to cut trees and shrubs. In late summer and fall the cuttings are stored in an underwater food pile, to be eaten in winter. The kits are born in spring and stay in the home pond until they are two years old.

Little Brown Bat
Myotis lucifugus

Size: *length, 3-4½ in.; wingspan, 8-10 in.*
What to look for: *low, zigzagging flight;
small size; dark, shiny fur.* **Habitat:** *flies near
wooded areas and water; roosts in caves,
hollow trees, buildings.*

Probably the most abundant bat in North America,
this mammal is common in and around cities. On
summer days thousands may hang upside down in an
attic or loft. These sleeping groups are composed
solely of females and young, for Little Brown Bats,
like many other species, separate by sex before the
young are born. Males also roost during the day but
usually as solitary individuals.

Silver-haired Bat
Lasionycteris noctivagans

Size: *length, 4-4½ in.; wingspan, 10-12½ in.*
What to look for: *flight relatively high,
straight, and slow; fur dark, with white tips
on back.* **Habitat:** *flies in forests; roosts
mainly in trees near water.*

Although most North American bats give birth to a
single young, this species produces twins. (The tree-
roosting Red Bat, *Lasiurus borealis*, occasionally has
quadruplets.) Bats give birth while hanging at their
roosts, then nurse their offspring for several weeks.
Young ones cling to their mothers' bellies until they
can fly independently.

Big Brown Bat
Eptesicus fuscus

Size: *length, 3½-5 in.;
wingspan, 10-13 in.*
What to look for: *strong, steady flight;
large size.* **Habitat:** *flies in forests; roosts in caves,
hollow trees, buildings (especially in summer).*

Occasionally seen flying during the day, Big Brown
Bats usually emerge at twilight to pursue prey over
meadows, suburban streets, and city traffic. They
detect beetles and other insects by emitting high-
pitched sounds that bounce off objects and come back
as echoes. The same technique, known as echolocation and used by other insect-eating bats, also helps
them avoid obstacles.

Brazilian Free-tailed Bat
Tadarida brasiliensis

Size: *length, 3½-4 in.; wingspan, 11-13 in.*
What to look for: *flight high, straight, fast;
long tail.* **Habitat:** *roosts in buildings and caves,
especially in Carlsbad Caverns, New Mexico.*

Bats are the only true flying mammals. They wing
through the air on thin membranes stretched between
their elongated "fingers." A smaller membrane usually connects the hind limbs and spans the tail, which
extends well beyond the membrane in free-tailed
bats. This bat summers in enormous numbers in
southwestern caves, and winters in Mexico.
Most bats in temperate regions
hibernate in winter.

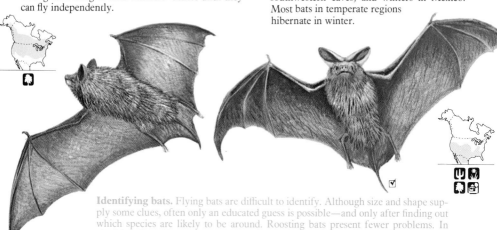

Identifying bats. Flying bats are difficult to identify. Although size and shape supply some clues, often only an educated guess is possible—and only after finding out
which species are likely to be around. Roosting bats present fewer problems. In
checking them, however, remember that bats should never be handled with bare
hands. All are believed to be able to transmit rabies.

Star-nosed Mole
Condylura cristata

Length: *head and body, 4½–5 in.; tail, 2½–3½ in.*
What to look for: *nose large, pinkish, with fleshy projections; long hairy tail.*
Habitat: *moist, low-lying soil.*

This burrowing mammal is equally at home in water and on land. Frequently its winding tunnels end in a pond or stream. An excellent swimmer, the Star-nosed Mole uses its broad front feet as paddles and its thick tail as a scull. It dives after much of its food—aquatic insects, crustaceans, snails, and even small fish. Excess food is converted into fat and stored in its tail, to be used as an energy source during times of scarcity. The 22 projections on its nose are sensitive feelers, which help it locate prey; the two round holes in the center are the nostrils. Moles characteristically have a highly developed sense of touch, but their eyesight is poor.

Broad-footed Mole
Scapanus latimanus

Length: *head and body, 5½–6½ in.; tail, 1½–2 in.*
What to look for: *front feet greater in width than in length; fur blackish brown to black; tail nearly hairless.*
Habitat: *soft soil in meadows and forests.*

Active night and day beneath the surface, the Broad-footed, or California, Mole seems to swim through the soil as it tunnels along, wedging its spindle-shaped body into the sod. Its powerful feet act as shovels; its fleshy nose packs the dirt. Earthworms and other prey are detected by their vibrations. Like other moles, the Broad-footed species has an extremely high metabolic rate, causing the animal to burn up so much food that it must eat its own weight in food every day. This mole resembles two other western species—the Townsend's Mole (*Scapanus townsendii*) and the Coast Mole (*Scapanus orarius*).

Eastern Mole
Scalopus aquaticus

Length: *head and body, 4½–6½ in.; tail, 1–1½ in.*
What to look for: *soft, velvety fur, gray in north, golden to darker brown elsewhere; hairless tail.*
Habitat: *moist, sandy soils in grassy areas.*

The Eastern Mole spends most of its life beneath the surface of the earth. After a rain it moves through shallow tunnels, searching for earthworms, insect larvae, and other prey. Its permanent passageway, which lies 10 inches or more beneath the surface, is also a retreat during drought or cold spells. Moles are not hibernators, and remain active throughout the winter. Notorious for their inability to tolerate others of their kind (chance encounters sometimes lead to death), they are solitary except during the breeding season. Eastern Moles mate in spring. Four weeks later the female, which is slightly smaller than the male, gives birth in an underground nest lined with dried plant material. Raised ridges in the soil (pushed up as the mole tunnels along) and molehills (mounds of excavated earth) are more likely to be seen than the animal itself. Though moles may wreak havoc on a lawn, they do accomplish some good by eating insects and aerating the soil.

Moles versus shrews. People occasionally confuse these two groups of mammals. Here's how to tell them apart:
• OVERALL SHAPE. Moles are larger and fatter. Shrews are mouse-size or smaller.
• SNOUT. Both groups have long snouts. The mole's is naked and pink; the shrew's is furred nearly to the tip.
• EYES. Eyes are small in both groups but minuscule in moles. Certain moles are blind, with skin covering their eyes.
• FEET. Unlike shrews, moles have huge front feet; the soles face outward.
• TAILS. Mole tails are stubby and can be either haired or hairless (this varies according to species). Most shrews have longer, thinner tails with stiff hairs.

Masked Shrew
Sorex cinereus

Length: *head and body, 1¾–2½ in.; tail, 1–2 in.*
What to look for: *grayish-brown color; tail longer than that of other shrews.*
Habitat: *moist soil in grasslands, brushy areas, and forests.*

This tiny bundle of fierce energy, also called the Common Shrew, is found in a greater variety of habitats than any other North American mammal. Throughout the northern part of the continent it seems equally at home in grassy fields, salt marshes, coniferous forests, and high mountain slopes. Active at any hour (though more so at night than during the day), it furiously searches for food and eats more than its weight each day in insects, mollusks, earthworms, and occasionally carrion. It is not much of a burrower and often hunts in tunnels dug by other mammals. Like other shrews, this species does not hibernate but is active throughout the year. Several litters of up to 10 young are produced each year from spring until fall. Few live for much more than a year.

Least Shrew
Cryptotis parva

Length: *head and body, 2–2½ in.; tail, ½–¾ in.*
What to look for: *cinnamon brown color; very short tail.* **Habitat:** *open fields, freshwater marshes, sparse brush.*

Also known as the Bee Shrew, this very small mammal occasionally nests in beehives and feeds on bees and their larvae. More frequently it nests in fallen leaves and utilizes the surface runways of voles as it searches, nose aquiver, for insects and other small prey. Its digestion, like that of other shrews, is remarkably rapid: the hard parts of insects pass through its alimentary tract in about 90 minutes. Shrews are the world's smallest mammals and form an important intermediate link in the food chain, serving as food for such animals as owls, hawks, and snakes. There are about 30 kinds of shrews in North America, but many of them are restricted to rather small areas.

Sorting out small mammals.
At first glance, many small mammals look similar because of their size. However, closer observation reveals important differences among the shrews, voles, lemmings, mice, and rats.
• SHAPE. Shrews have elongated bodies and pointed noses. Voles and lemmings are stocky and rounded, with little separation between head and body. The heads of mice and rats are better defined.
• EARS. The ears of mice and rats are prominent. Those of voles and lemmings are somewhat obscured by long, soft fur; those of shrews are almost imperceptible.
• EYES. Mice and rats have large eyes; voles and lemmings, small beady ones; and shrews even smaller ones.
• TAILS. In proportion to the rest of the animal, the tails of mice and rats are long; those of shrews, voles, and lemmings are usually shorter.

Short-tailed Shrew
Blarina brevicauda

Length: *head and body, 3–4 in.; tail, ¾–1 in.*
What to look for: *dark metallic gray color; relatively short tail.*
Habitat: *all land habitats except deserts.*

This abundant species is unique among North American mammals in having venomous saliva, which probably aids it in subduing mice and other mammals that equal or surpass it in size. More shrewlike is its habit of eating insects, including many pests: Short-tailed Shrews are believed to have killed 60 percent of the Larch Sawfly larvae in eastern Canada. This shrew has two breeding seasons, one in spring and one in fall. During these periods males pursue females, making clicking sounds during the chase; an unreceptive female rebuffs her suitor with loud squeaks and chattering. Litters of up to eight furless young are born three weeks after mating, and weaning occurs after another three weeks.

Southern Bog Lemming

Synaptomys cooperi

Length: *head and body, 3½–4½ in.; tail, ½–¾ in.*
What to look for: *back brownish gray, belly gray; tail short; ears nearly hidden.* **Habitat:** *bogs and wet meadows with thick vegetation.*

Volelike in habits and appearance, the Southern Bog Lemming is a social rodent that lives in colonies of from several to several dozen animals. It is also found in the company of other small mammals, including voles, shrews, and moles, and may utilize their runways and burrows. It feeds mainly on leaves and stems but also relishes berries, seeds, bark, and insects. Similar in appearance but slightly larger is the Northern Bog Lemming (*Synaptomys borealis*), an inhabitant of wet mountain areas across much of Canada. The Brown Lemming (*Lemmus sibiricus*) lives on the tundra farther north. Lemmings in Scandinavia are famous for their periodic population explosions, which often result in mass migrations.

Southern
Bog Lemming

Southern Red-backed Vole

Clethrionomys gapperi

Length: *head and body, 3½–4½ in.; tail, 1–2 in.*
What to look for: *back reddish brown, sides grayer, belly whitish; sometimes gray all over.*
Habitat: *forests, usually in moist areas.*

With a trotting gait this small creature moves rapidly along the forest floor. An agile climber, it scrambles over fallen tree trunks and even up living ones to feed or seek out nest sites; it has been known to kill trees of up to a foot in diameter by gnawing the bark. Though it has many predators (as do other small rodents), it reproduces so prolifically that it is often the most abundant mammal on the forest floor.

Meadow Vole

Meadow Vole

Microtus pennsylvanicus

Length: *head and body, 3½–5 in.; tail, 1½–2½ in.*
What to look for: *back and sides brown to dark brown; gray below.*
Habitat: *grasslands with dense vegetation; open forests, orchards, forest edges.*

Runways of closely cropped grasses reveal the comings and goings of the Meadow Vole, or Field Mouse, a stocky creature with some impressive statistics. Populations frequently number several hundred per acre and during one "mouse plague" reached an estimated 10,000 per acre. A female can produce a hundred young within just one year. These prolific rodents may be highly destructive to hay and other forage crops, but they are an important food supply for birds of prey and small carnivorous mammals.

Southern Red-backed Vole

Woodland Vole

Microtus pinetorum

Length: *head and body, 3–4 in.; tail, ½–1 in.*
What to look for: *soft fur, reddish brown on back, gray below; very short tail.*
Habitat: *forest floors covered with thick duff (decaying vegetation); orchards.*

The smallest North American vole, also called the Pine Vole, lives among pines only in the South; elsewhere it prefers broad-leaved forests, especially where the soil is loose. Though the Woodland Vole tunnels through leaf litter at the surface, it also burrows to depths of 12 inches. It has a rather short tail, short ears, soft fur, small eyes, and strong front feet—all adaptations to a subterranean way of life. The underground parts of plants are its usual diet; these include not only wild plants but—to the dismay of farmers—peanuts and potatoes as well.

Woodland Vole

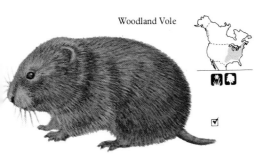

49

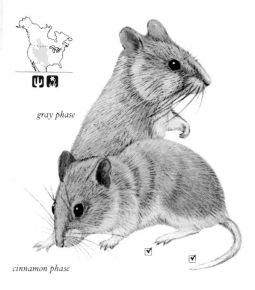

gray phase

cinnamon phase

Northern Grasshopper Mouse
Onychomys leucogaster

Length: *head and body, 4½-5½ in.; tail, 1-2½ in.*
What to look for: *plump body; short tail; gray or cinnamon above, white below; white feet and tip of tail.* **Habitat:** *prairies, deserts.*

A veritable tiger among mice, this nocturnal rodent feeds not only on grasshoppers but also on beetles, crickets, caterpillars, spiders, lizards, and small mammals. The larger prey is stalked, seized with a rush, and then killed with a bite on the neck. Because of its taste for scorpions, it is sometimes called the Scorpion Mouse, as is the Southern Grasshopper Mouse (*Onychomys torridus*), a smaller creature with a more southerly range. Grasshopper mice nest in burrows, often preempting those made by other small rodents. Occasionally they are spotted standing on their hind feet and pointing their noses into the air, uttering shrill sounds at the same time. This behavior is similar to the territorial call of prairie dogs and certain grassland ground squirrels.

Hispid Pocket Mouse
Chaetodipus hispidus

Length: *head and body, 4½-5 in.; tail, 3½-4½ in.*
What to look for: *relatively large size; tannish brown above, whitish below; coarse hair.*
Habitat: *grassy areas; along roads and fences.*

Pocket mice carry seeds to their burrows in expandable pouches on the outside of their cheeks. Once inside the burrows—usually dug with the entrance beneath a shrub—they force out the seeds by pressing against the pouches with their front feet. Pocket mice seldom, if ever, drink water, evidently depending on the "metabolic water" produced as they digest their food. All 20 or so species of pocket mice are found in dry regions west of the Mississippi. Similar in general appearance and habits (all are active only at night), they vary in size, color, and the texture of their fur. The Hispid Pocket Mouse (*hispid* means "bristly") is the largest of the pocket mice.

Meadow Jumping Mouse
Zapus hudsonius

Length: *head and body, 3-3½ in.; tail, 4½-6 in.*
What to look for: *yellowish brown above, white below; large hind feet; tail long, sparsely haired.*
Habitat: *meadows, clearings.*

Meadow
Jumping
Mouse

Western
Jumping
Mouse

Using its long tail for balance and its long hind legs to spring into the air, the Meadow Jumping Mouse can leap across distances of 5 feet or more. Primarily nocturnal, this diminutive creature evades owls, weasels, and other predators with a zigzagging series of jumps across meadow and field. Unlike most mice, it uses a burrow not for year-round refuge but only during its winter-long hibernation. A grassy nest in a tussock or beneath a log serves as its nursery and summer shelter. Meadow Jumping Mice mate soon after waking in spring; litters averaging about five blind, hairless young are born several weeks later. They breed again in late summer. A closely related species, the Western Jumping Mouse (*Zapus princeps*), bears but one litter a year.

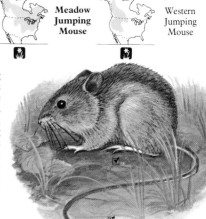

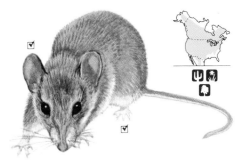

Plains Harvest Mouse
Reithrodontomys montanus

Length: *head and body, 2½–3 in.; tail, 2–2½ in.*
What to look for: *small size; pale grayish to tan above, lighter below; faint stripe on back.*
Habitat: *uplands with low-growing plants.*

This little mouse is a versatile reaper, bending stalks of grass downward to nibble at the fruiting tips or picking up seeds from the ground. It is also a weaver, shaping grass into a round nest. Located on the ground or slightly above it in a bush or thick grass, the nest may be abandoned in cold weather for a burrow. North America has five kinds of harvest mice, which together range over most of the lower 48 states. All look much like the common House Mouse. A good way of telling harvest mice from the House Mouse—but one that involves capturing the creature in question—is to look at the teeth. Only the harvest mice have a vertical groove on each upper incisor.

Deer Mouse
Peromyscus maniculatus

Length: *head and body, 3–4 in.; tail, 2–5 in.*
What to look for: *white feet and belly; tail dark above, white below; prominent ears.*
Habitat: *nearly every habitat except very wet places; will enter buildings.*

Only the liveliest imagination would see a resemblance between Deer Mice and deer, for the two have little in common except the dark-above, light-below pattern of their fur. Varying in color from region to region, the Deer Mouse is one of the most widely distributed mammals in North America. It is a social creature, with groups of up to a dozen or more huddling together in winter. Active throughout the year, Deer Mice depend on stored seeds for survival in winter. They are nocturnal and usually rest during the day in logs, burrows, trees, buildings, and even bird nests.

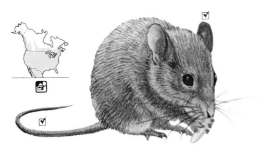

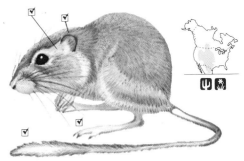

House Mouse
Mus musculus

Length: *head and body, 3–3½ in.; tail, 2½–4 in.*
What to look for: *dull color (grayish brown on back, gray below); long, scaly tail; prominent ears.*
Habitat: *around buildings.*

This uninvited house guest thrives not only on food intended for man but also on such prosaic items as soap and glue. For nest material it helps itself to anything soft, including pillow feathers and shredded newspapers. Like many pest species, the House Mouse is not native to North America. Originally from Asia, it first reached the New World as a 16th-century stowaway from Europe. Its reproductive capacity is enormous. Under certain conditions a female may produce eight litters a year, with up to a dozen young in a single litter. The mice are ready to breed when little more than a month old.

Ord's Kangaroo Rat
Dipodomys ordii

Length: *head and body, 4–4½ in.; tail, 5–6 in.*
What to look for: *large size; long hind legs; long, striped, tufted tail; small ears; light patch behind eye.* **Habitat:** *dry, sandy areas.*

Often seen hopping across a road at night, this long-legged leaper can make a sharp turn in midair and cover 2 feet in a single bound. This species is the most widespread of the kangaroo rats—rodents noteworthy not only for their jumping ability but also for their seed-carrying technique. Like pocket mice, they stuff seeds into external cheek pouches (the openings are on the outside of the cheeks) and carry the food into burrows, storing it there for later use. Burrows also serve as nurseries and provide daytime relief from the desert sun. Kangaroo rats obtain most of the water they need as a product of digestion.

51

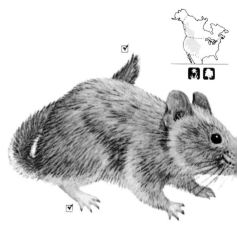

Hispid Cotton Rat
Sigmodon hispidus

Length: *head and body, 6–8 in.; tail, 3½–5½ in.*
What to look for: *fur long, coarse; dark brown mixed with buff, whitish below; inconspicuous ears.*
Habitat: *moist meadows, ditches.*

This abundant rodent is named for the coarse, or hispid, quality of its fur. Common in farmlands, it damages cotton, alfalfa, and other crops and is regarded as a serious agricultural pest. Like many other rats, it adjusts its diet according to availability; for example, cotton rats in ditches sometimes feed almost exclusively on crayfish and fiddler crabs. Because cotton rats tend to have small home ranges, numerous individuals may occur in close proximity. One count revealed 513 cotton rats in a single rat-ridden acre, although the usual number is only about a dozen.

Bushy-tailed Woodrat
Neotoma cinerea

Length: *head and body, 7–10 in.; tail, 5–7½ in.*
What to look for: *tail bushy (though less so than a squirrel's); pale reddish gray to black above, white below (including tail); white feet.*
Habitat: *rocky areas, coniferous forests.*

Occasionally a camper falls victim to a peculiar "theft": some small trinket is stolen and a stick or stone left in its place. The culprit is likely to be a woodrat, a soft-furred rodent also known as a trade rat or packrat. Woodrats do not really trade objects but may drop items they are carrying in order to pick up something else. Stolen items are incorporated into stick-and-bone nests, often constructed in rock crevices or shrubbery. The Bushy-tailed Woodrat has a relatively modest nest compared with that of the Dusky-footed Woodrat (*Neotoma fuscipes*). Built in trees or on the ground, the impressive stick tower of this California resident may measure some 6 feet tall.

Norway Rat
Rattus norvegicus

Length: *head and body, 7–10 in.; tail, 5½–8 in.*
What to look for: *coarse fur; dull gray-brown above, paler (but not white) below; tail long, scaly, nearly hairless, not bicolored.*
Habitat: *buildings, wharves, dumps; sometimes in fields.*

Originally from Asia, the world's most destructive mammal reached North America by ship about 1775. It has been an economic and a health problem since that time. The Norway Rat eats almost anything of proper size, plant or animal, dead or alive. It spreads disease and contaminates food. It has a high reproductive rate—an average of 5 litters a year, with 8 to 10 rats in a litter. The Black, or Roof, Rat (*Rattus rattus*), also native to Asia, usually stays close to seaports. Though its fur is darker and its tail somewhat longer, the distinction is unimportant in human terms: the Black Rat would probably cause as much destruction if the Norway Rat did not drive it away.

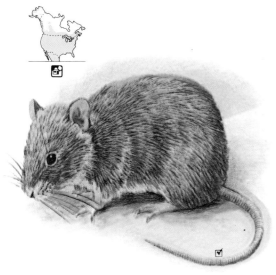

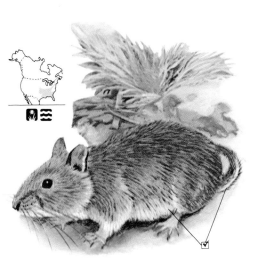

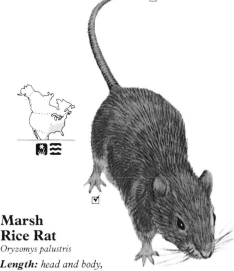

Florida Woodrat
Neotoma floridana

Length: *head and body, 8–9 in.; tail, 6–8 in.*
What to look for: *soft fur; grayish brown above, white below (including tail); tail furred, shorter than rest of animal.* **Habitat:** *usually in open places, including swamps and rocky areas.*

When threatened or otherwise excited, the Florida Woodrat chatters its teeth, vibrates its tail against the ground, and thumps its hind feet. (Certain rabbits and mice also drum on the ground.) This rodent is usually solitary, living alone in a bulky nest built in a rock crevice or under a shrub. Young woodrats, two to four per litter, are nursed in the nest until about four weeks old; the mother's elongated teat fits into a gap between the two top front teeth of the newborn, an adaptation that helps her to carry them about. Adult woodrats feed on fruit, seeds, and nuts, and do man no economic harm, although some people dislike them merely because of their name and appearance.

Marsh Rice Rat
Oryzomys palustris

Length: *head and body, 4½–5½ in.; tail, 4¼–7½ in.*
What to look for: *gray-brown above, grayish or dull yellow below; tail long, scaly; whitish feet.*
Habitat: *marshes; other wet or moist areas with grasses or sedges.*

As its name implies, the rice rat thrives on the tender shoots and ripened grain of rice and other plants. It also eats fish and snails. Though generally nocturnal, this slender rodent may feed at any hour and is active throughout the year. Rice rats are semiaquatic, often diving and swimming a considerable distance underwater when alarmed. They are vulnerable to predatory attacks in the water (from Water Moccasins and Mink), on the land (skunks and weasels), and from the sky (hawks and owls). The young are born in a nest of dry leaves, which is usually perched a foot or more above the high-water level in a tangle of rushes or other plants. Breeding may occur at any time of year in the southern part of its range.

Plains Pocket Gopher
Geomys bursarius

Length: *head and body, 5½–9 in.; tail, 2–4½ in.*
What to look for: *chunky body; tail short, nearly hairless; prominent yellow teeth.*
Habitat: *grasslands, pastures, prairies.*

Pocket gophers' pockets are outside cheek pouches, invisible unless crammed with roots, bulbs, or other food. These burrowing rodents live solitary lives (except during the brief spring mating season) and will battle any other gopher that invades their home. Fan-shaped mounds marking tunnel openings are common sights in gopher territory. Pocket gophers are easily distinguished from most other mammals, for their teeth are visible even when their mouths are closed. About 18 different species are recognized scientifically, although telling one from another is a task for a specialist. The Plains Pocket Gopher, for example, is the only species with two distinct grooves on the outside of each upper incisor.

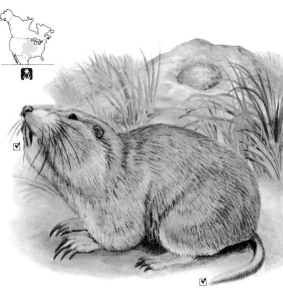

53

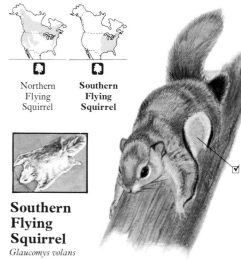

Northern
Flying
Squirrel

**Southern
Flying
Squirrel**

Red Squirrel
Tamiasciurus hudsonicus

Length: *head and body, 7½–8½ in.; tail, 4–6 in.*
What to look for: *rusty above, whitish below; smaller than Gray Squirrel; tail less bushy.*
Habitat: *northern and mountain forests.*

These noisy rodents, which announce an intruder with a harsh, strident call, are especially active just after sunrise and just before sunset. In midsummer they spend much of their time cutting cones from pines, spruces, and other trees and carrying them to caches near a log, under a tree, or in a burrow. The seeds in the cones will serve as food during the next winter. Red Squirrels are able to eat certain mushrooms that are deadly to man. Their diversified diet also includes buds, sap, and even bird eggs and nestlings. The squirrels are in turn an important food source for birds of prey.

Southern Flying Squirrel
Glaucomys volans

Length: *head and body, 5½–6 in.; tail, 3½–5 in.*
What to look for: *grayish brown on back, white below; folds of skin between front and back legs; large eyes.* **Habitat:** *broad-leaved and mixed forests.*

A flying squirrel cannot truly fly. It glides downward, using wide flaps of skin along its sides to help slow its descent. To become airborne, this mammal leaps and spreads its legs; to control the glide, it moves its legs and uses its tail as a rudder. Immediately after a flying squirrel lands (usually 20 to 30 feet from its starting point), it may scramble to the far side of the tree—just in case an owl is in pursuit. Like owls, flying squirrels are nocturnal. All other North American squirrels are active during the day.

nest, or dray

Western
Gray
Squirrel

Gray Squirrel
Sciurus carolinensis

Length: *head and body, 8–11 in.; tail, 8–10 in.*
What to look for: *usually gray on back and sides, whitish below (many northern ones are all black); large, bushy tail.*
Habitat: *broad-leaved forests, parks, suburbs.*

Gray Squirrels breed twice a year, an event accompanied by fights, chases, and other noisy activities. Late winter or spring litters are usually born in tree hollows; summer ones, sometimes in leafy nests out along the branches of a tree. Males play no role in raising the young, which average three per litter and nurse for several months. Both the Gray Squirrel and its western relative (*Sciurus griseus*) are active all year, relying on buried food (as well as stolen birdseed) for winter sustenance.

**Gray
Squirrel**

Squirrel language.
Gray squirrels are noisy. Although some vocalizations are probably idle chatter, others have a specific meaning:
• A rapid *kuk, kuk, kuk* means immediate danger.
• A drawn-out *ku-u-uk*, sounded at 2-second intervals, warns of less immediate danger.
• A slow *kuk, kuk, kuk* indicates the danger has passed. Gray squirrels convey a variety of messages with their tails:
• Rapid jerks are a threat gesture.
• Rapid waves (looser than jerks) are a sign of agitation.
• Holding the tail against the back may mean that danger has passed.

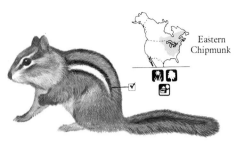

Eastern
Chipmunk

Least
Chipmunk

Least Chipmunk *Tamias minimus*

Length: *head and body, 3½–4½ in.; tail, 3–4½ in.*
What to look for: *small, slim body; stripes on head, sides, and back; back stripes extend to base of tail.* **Habitat:** *varied; includes tundra, forests, forest edges, sagebrush.*

The smallest chipmunks are among the most active, scurrying over the ground and occasionally into trees. Piles of fruit pulp and nut trimmings mark their feeding sites. Least Chipmunks hibernate underground in winter and mate in spring. About a month later the female gives birth to a litter with up to seven young, which remain with her for several months. The Least Chipmunk is one of more than a dozen species of western chipmunks. Usually smaller and grayer than the Eastern Chipmunk, they vary in color according to their location. Desert inhabitants tend to be paler than forest ones, and individuals living in sun-dappled forests tend to have well-defined stripes.

Black-tailed Prairie Dog

Cynomys ludovicianus

Length: *head and body, 10–14 in.; tail, 3–4 in.*
What to look for: *broad head; fat, yellowish-brown body; black-tipped tail.*
Habitat: *short- and mixed-grass prairies.*

Not a dog at all, this stocky rodent takes its name from its bark, an alarm signal that sends all in the vicinity scurrying into their burrows. A prairie dog burrow is an elaborate network of tunnels at the base of a plunge shaft, which sometimes extends more than a dozen feet below the surface. Black-tailed Prairie Dogs are noted for their colonies ("towns"), which formerly covered many square miles and contained millions of inhabitants. Towns are divided into territories, each used by a group commonly dominated by a single male. The members of a group share their burrows, groom one another, and communicate through a variety of gestures and sounds. White-tailed Prairie Dogs (*Cynomys leucurus*) are less social.

Eastern Chipmunk *Tamias striatus*

Length: *head and body, 5½–6½ in.; tail, 3–4½ in.*
What to look for: *stripes on head, sides, and back; back stripes extend only to rump.*
Habitat: *forests, brushy areas, gardens.*

Chipmunks are ground-dwelling squirrels. They spend most of their lives at or below the surface, although they will also climb trees. Their extensive burrows are up to 12 feet long and may include a storage chamber, sleeping room, dump, and latrine, along with several concealed entrances. The pantry holds up to half a bushel of nuts and other food, all carried there in the chipmunk's outsized cheek pouches. Eastern Chipmunks partially hibernate in winter (they wake frequently and feed). The females give birth in spring or midsummer, producing litters of two to eight young. Like other members of the squirrel family, chipmunks are naked, blind, and helpless at birth.

Thirteen-lined Ground Squirrel

Spermophilus tridecemlineatus

Length: *head and body, 4½–6½ in.; tail, 2–5 in.*
What to look for: *many stripes on sides and back (some broken into dots); small ears.*
Habitat: *brushy areas, overgrown fields, small stands of trees, open areas.*

This is the Federation Squirrel, so called because of its pattern of "stars and stripes." Ground squirrels are burrowing animals, using their underground labyrinths as nurseries, hibernation dens, and temporary refuges. Active during the day, they retreat to their burrows at night and when skies are overcast. The Golden-mantled Ground Squirrel (*Spermophilus lateralis*), often seen around campgrounds in western parks, is sometimes confused with a chipmunk. Larger than any chipmunk, it has a single stripe on each side of the body but none on the head.

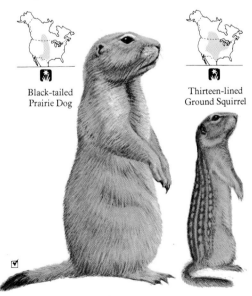

Black-tailed
Prairie Dog

Thirteen-lined
Ground Squirrel

Woodchuck (Groundhog)
Marmota monax

Length: *head and body, 14–20 in.; tail, 4½–6½ in.*
What to look for: *large head; chunky body; short legs; small bushy tail; no special markings.* **Habitat:** *open forests, forest edges, rocky areas, roadsides.*

Contrary to legend, the Woodchuck, or Groundhog, does not emerge from its burrow on February 2 to look for its shadow or anything else. Instead, this stocky rodent usually hibernates in its burrow (an extensive system of tunnels, chambers, and multiple entrances) until late winter. Soon after emerging, male Woodchucks battle one another, using their teeth as weapons, and then seek out the females. The young are born four weeks after mating. Although blind, hairless, and extremely small at birth, they are ready for sorties outside the burrow within a month. Adults are frequently seen sunbathing atop the entrance mound, sitting upright on guard for predators, or waddling along as they stuff themselves with clover, alfalfa, and other plants.

Yellow-bellied Marmot
Marmota flaviventris

Length: *head and body, 14–20 in.; tail, 5½–8½ in.*
What to look for: *bulky body; white markings on dark face; bushy tail.* **Habitat:** *rocky slopes, valleys.*

Unlike the Woodchuck, the Yellow-bellied Marmot is a social animal, living in colonies of several dozen individuals. Often one marmot seems to be doing sentry duty while others in the colony graze in the alpine meadows. At the approach of danger (an eagle, for example), the sentry whistles sharply, causing marmots within earshot to scamper toward their burrows. Burrow entrances are usually located beneath rocks, so this large rodent is also known as the Rockchuck. A second species—the larger, grayer Hoary Marmot (*Marmota caligata*)—lives at higher elevations and is found farther to the north. Both species hibernate for more than half the year. Rockchucks may also become torpid and remain underground in hot weather.

Pika
Ochotona princeps

Length: *head and body, 6½–8½ in.*
What to look for: *ratlike head and body; small, rounded ears; no visible tail.* **Habitat:** *rock-strewn slopes.*

The Pika, or Coney, harvests a variety of plants during the short mountain summer, stacks them in piles to cure in the sun, and eventually moves the "hay" to sheltered sites among the rocks. Between forays the little mammal dozes in the sunshine, nearly invisible as it sits hunched on a rock. Although the Pika looks like a rodent, it is technically a cousin of rabbits and hares. It remains active all winter, as do its relatives, but only the Pika stores hay for winter use. Much more vocal than rabbits and hares, the Pika communicates with others of its kind by sharp, nasal bleats and is occasionally called the Whistling, or Piping, Hare. It is something of a ventriloquist—a skill to keep in mind when trying to locate the animal by its calls.

Black-tailed Jackrabbit

Lepus californicus

Length: *head and body, 17–21 in.; tail, 4 in.*
What to look for: *ears very long, black-tipped; large hind feet; dark streak on tail.*
Habitat: *grasslands, deserts.*

Black-tailed Jackrabbit   White-tailed Jackrabbit

The Black-tailed Jackrabbit is superbly adapted to life in open places. Relying on its speed to flee Coyotes and other predators, it can leap across distances of up to 20 feet and cover the ground at 30 to 35 miles an hour. During the day it rests in slight depressions, called forms, beneath shrubs, beside rocks, or in long grass. Its long ears act as antennas and air conditioners, picking up sound and dissipating body heat. The White-tailed Jackrabbit (*Lepus townsendii*) is similar in appearance but turns white in winter. The Antelope Jackrabbit (*Lepus alleni*), found mainly in Mexico, has even larger ears. All jackrabbits are technically hares, not rabbits.

Snowshoe Hare

Lepus americanus

Length: *head and body, 15–18½ in.; tail, 2 in.*
What to look for: *large hind feet; dark brown color (white in winter).* **Habitat:** *northern and alpine forests, swamps, brushy areas.*

Twice a year this whiskered mammal, also called the Varying Hare, changes its coat. Beginning in September the brown summer coat is gradually replaced by white-tipped hairs, a process lasting up to three months; the reverse process begins in March. The name Snowshoe Hare reflects another seasonal change: in autumn the animal develops dense fur pads on its feet. (The pads supply insulation and enhance mobility in snow.) Diet also changes with the seasons. When green plants are no longer available, the hare feeds on twigs and buds, leaving a characteristic slanted cut on the severed end of the branch. Like other hares and rabbits, it rests in thick cover during the day. Camouflaged by its color, it may reveal its whereabouts only by its tracks.

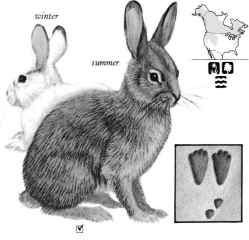

winter

summer

Eastern Cottontail

Sylvilagus floridanus

Length: *head and body, 13½–16 in.; tail, 2 in.*
What to look for: *short-eared, short-tailed rabbit; white tail conspicuous when running.*
Habitat: *brushy areas, forest edges, swamps.*

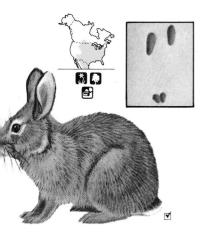

This rabbit flourishes almost everywhere east of the Rocky Mountains. (Other kinds of cottontails occur in the West.) Cats, foxes, hawks, and owls help to keep its numbers under some control; human hunters also take a heavy toll. But the rabbit's legendary fecundity means that the population is constantly being renewed. Each year a female cottontail produces several litters, each with up to seven young, and rabbits born in early spring may breed that very summer. Rabbits bear naked, blind young; hares (including the jackrabbits) are born furred and with their eyes open. Another difference is their gait: rabbits have shorter legs and are better suited for running.

Raccoon
Procyon lotor

Length: *head and body, 16–26 in.; tail, 8–12 in.*
What to look for: *dark eye mask; bushy, ringed tail.* **Habitat:** *bottomlands, forested edges of streams, lakes; rocky cliffs near water.*

Equally at home in suburban, rural, and forested areas, the wily Raccoon is unperturbed by the presence of man. Having learned to pry the lids from garbage cans, it makes regular nightly raids in certain locales, and will eat almost any type of food, including nuts, berries, grain, bird eggs, carrion, rodents, insects, and crayfish. According to a popular myth, Raccoons wash everything they eat. Though in captivity they often dunk their food, this behavior is not related to cleanliness; instead, it is believed to reflect their natural habit of finding food in water. Raccoons mate in late winter and give birth to litters averaging four young in spring. Mother and young may remain together during the first winter. Raccoons do not hibernate but may be inactive for long periods during cold weather.

Ringtail
(Cacomistle)
Bassariscus astutus

Length: *head and body, 14–16 in.; tail, 14–15½ in.*
What to look for: *light-colored body; tail very long, bushy, ringed, tipped with black.* **Habitat:** *rocky hills, cliffs, chaparral; usually near water.*

The 2-pound Ringtail, smaller and more lithe than the Raccoon, is most at home in wooded and rocky areas of the southwestern states. This nocturnal hunter usually pounces from ambush and kills its prey (mainly birds and small mammals) with a bite on the neck. It was formerly kept in mines to control the rodent population—hence the alternative name of Miner's Cat. Ringtails are agile climbers and use their tails for balance. During the day they sometimes sleep high in trees, invisible except for their long, dangling tails. In the southern part of their range they are known as Cacomistles, a name derived from Indian words for "half" and "mountain lion."

Badger
Taxidea taxus

Length: *head and body, 18–23 in.; tail, 4½–6 in.*
What to look for: *flattened body; short legs; shaggy fur; black facial pattern; white stripe on top of head.* **Habitat:** *dry, treeless areas.*

A tough and tenacious fighter, this heavy-bodied member of the weasel family has scent glands that emit a strong odor and long front claws capable of tearing flesh. The Badger is a remarkable burrower that can rapidly dig out of sight when danger threatens. Large holes dug as it pursues rodents are more likely to be seen than the animal itself, which is active mainly at night. Badgers are usually solitary except in late summer, during the breeding season. Though the word *badger* has come to mean *annoy*, this does not stem from the animal's scrappy disposition. Instead, it comes from badger-baiting, a former "sport" in which the European species was tormented by dogs.

Spotted Skunk
Spilogale putorius

Length: *head and body, 8–14 in.; tail, 5–9 in.*
What to look for: *variable black and white pattern, with white spots on head and many stripes or spots on body; white tip on bushy tail.*
Habitat: *open woods, brushy and rocky areas, prairies; usually near water.*

The Spotted Skunk's warning is a handstand: the animal puts its weight on its front feet, raises its hindquarters into the air, and aims the openings of its scent glands at the source of provocation. The spray is even sharper and more acrid than the Striped Skunk's. It eats the same type of food but depends more on mammals (especially mice and rats) than its larger relative. The diets of both change with the seasons. A study of Spotted Skunks in Iowa found mammals to be the most important winter food. The proportion of insects increased in spring and summer, and fruits were eaten mainly in the fall.

Striped Skunk
Mephitis mephitis

Length: *head and body, 15–19 in.; tail, 7–10 in.*
What to look for: *white facial stripe, neck patch, and V on back; mottled bushy tail.*
Habitat: *open forests, farmlands, brushy areas, prairies; usually near water.*

When provoked, the Striped Skunk arches its back, raises its tail, stamps its front feet, and shuffles backward. If the warning is not heeded, the animal ejects a fine spray of acrid, blinding fluid from its anal glands. As a result, few animals other than large owls prey on skunks. The Striped Skunk ambles about at dusk and after nightfall in search of animal and plant food. It is especially fond of grasshoppers, ground beetles, and even bees, excavating their nests and eating the larvae. It becomes fat in autumn and spends the winter in a den, emerging in warm weather to forage.

Wolverine
Gulo gulo

Length: *head and body, 28–34 in.; tail, 8–9½ in.*
What to look for: *dark fur; broad, yellowish bands on forehead and sides; bushy tail.* **Habitat:** *high mountains, Arctic tundra.*

This animal goes by a variety of names. As one, Skunk-bear, suggests, it looks like a cross between a skunk and a bear. (It is actually a member of the weasel family, as are the skunks.) The name Wolverine probably stems from its predatory nature. For an animal of its size, the Wolverine is exceptionally strong; under certain circumstances it can kill animals as large as a deer. It is a slow plodder but can cover long distances through the snow. Also called the Indian Devil, it raids traps and food caches and is a nuisance to trappers. It eats not only mammals but also fish, berries, and carcasses left by other predators. Not surprisingly, another of the Wolverine's names is Glutton.

Marten
Martes americana

Length: *head and body, 13½–20 in.; tail, 6½–9½ in.*
What to look for: *slender body; long, bushy tail; tail and underparts darker than back; buffy patch on throat and breast.*
Habitat: *coniferous forests, cedar swamps.*

Usually a nighttime hunter, this arboreal weasel is occasionally seen during the day as it leaps and runs along branches in pursuit of squirrels. It also feeds on other small mammals, birds, insects, and berries. Martens are solitary; the males are quarrelsome and associate with females only in summer, during the mating season. Young martens are not born until spring. Though this period of gestation may seem exceptionally long, the embryos do not develop throughout the entire time. Instead, they undergo a spurt of growth only during the month before birth. This phenomenon, called delayed implantation, occurs in other mammals, including the Nine-banded Armadillo, Black Bear, and Fisher (*Martes pennanti*), a large, all-dark relative of the Marten.

Marten

Fisher

Ermine
Mustela erminea

Length: *head and body, 5–9½ in.; tail, 2–4 in.*
What to look for: *long, slim body; tail black at tip; summer fur dark brown above, white below; winter fur white except for tail tip.*
Habitat: *forests, brushy areas; usually near water.*

This ferocious little carnivore, also called the Short-tailed Weasel, is quick and agile. With a slender, almost serpentine body, it can easily move through small burrows in nocturnal pursuit of rodents. It also climbs well and chases squirrels and chipmunks into trees, usually killing them with a bite in the neck. Often the Ermine does not immediately eat all that it kills but returns to the carcass for several meals. Twice a year, in spring and fall, the Ermine changes color dramatically. The white winter pelts are luxury furs, usually obtained from animals trapped in Europe, Asia, and Canada.

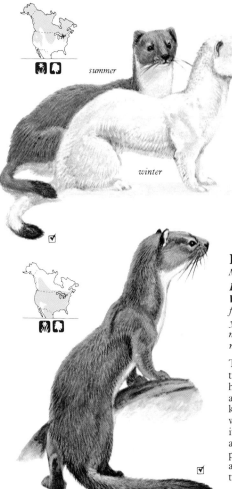

summer

winter

Long-tailed Weasel
Mustela frenata

Length: *head and body, 7½–15 in.; tail, 3½–7 in.*
What to look for: *long, slim body; tail black at tip; feet and legs brown; body brown above, pale below; yellowish white (except tip of tail) in winter in northern part of range.* **Habitat:** *open country, forests, many other areas; usually near water.*

Though larger and more powerful than the Ermine, the Long-tailed Weasel feeds primarily on the same type of prey. It also hunts birds, especially ground-nesters, and can cause considerable damage in a chicken coop. (It benefits man, however, by killing rats and mice in fields and barns.) Like the Ermine, this weasel changes color twice a year, except in the southern part of its range. Molting occurs during a period of about four weeks, and the gradual nature of the process explains the part-white, part-brown individuals that are sometimes encountered. Molts are triggered mainly by changes in day length, though temperature also plays a role.

Mink

Mustela vison

Length: *head and body, 11½–20 in.; tail, 5–9 in.*
What to look for: *long, slim body; fur dark red-brown, except for small pale area on chin and scattered white spots on underside.*
Habitat: *along rivers, streams, and lakes; occasionally in tidal marshes.*

Mink never live far from water. They are excellent swimmers and prey on both aquatic and terrestrial animals, including Muskrats, fishes, rabbits, and snakes. The males are larger than the females and have a more extensive hunting area. Mink are fierce and seemingly fearless fighters that scream, spit, hiss, and—like other members of the weasel family (including skunks)—emit a pungent odor when provoked. Adults are usually solitary except in the breeding season. Mating occurs in winter (both sexes are polygamous), and litters of 2 to 10 kits are born in spring. By early summer the young follow their mother on hunting forays; by autumn they are able to fend for themselves. Though some Mink are still being trapped, ranch-raised individuals supply most of the commercial market.

River Otter

Lutra canadensis

Length: *head and body, 20–35 in.; tail, 10–18½ in.*
What to look for: *weasellike shape; dark brown fur, often with golden gloss on head and shoulders; thick, furry tail, tapering toward tip.*
Habitat: *rivers, streams, lakes, and neighboring areas; occasionally in coastal waters.*

Otters truly seem to enjoy life. These sociable animals wrestle, play tag, slide down muddy or snowy riverbanks, and roll about in grasses and reeds. They express themselves vocally through chirps, whistles, growls, and screams. Although male and female stay together for part of the year, the female drives her mate away before giving birth to a litter of two or three young in early spring. Blind at birth but fully furred, the young grow slowly and do not venture out of the den—a hollow log or a beaver or muskrat burrow—until they are 10 to 12 weeks old. Then the mother begins teaching them to swim, dive, and hunt, aided by the father after the young are about six months old. Though otters are mainly fish eaters, they also feed on frogs, crayfish, and other small animals. Their streamlined bodies, webbed toes, and eyes and ears that can be closed underwater make them well adapted to an aquatic life.

otters sliding on snow

Red Fox
Vulpes vulpes

Length: *head and body, 20–30 in.; tail, 14–16 in.*
What to look for: *usually reddish on back and face, white on underparts; tail bushy, white-tipped; black legs and feet.*
Habitat: *farmlands; forests with open areas.*

Red Foxes are not always red. Though the fur of this species usually has a reddish cast, some individuals (known as silver foxes) are black, with silver guard hairs; others (cross foxes) are red or brown, with dark areas on the underparts extending up along the shoulders and back. Such color variation, caused by genetic differences, can occur even among pups in the same litter. Red Foxes are born in spring and weaned when one month old or more. Active throughout the year, they are best observed in early morning and late afternoon. These notorious chicken thieves are actually quite opportunistic in diet: although they prey mainly on small mammals and birds, they also eat insects, carrion, and fruits.

Kit Fox
Vulpes velox

Length: *head and body, 14–22 in.; tail, 9–11½ in.*
What to look for: *smaller than Red Fox; fur pale rusty-gray, with white belly; black-tipped tail; large ears.* **Habitat:** *flat, open, sandy areas; deserts; near pinyon pines.*

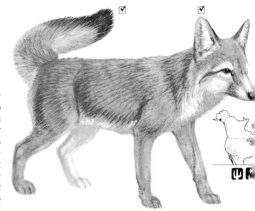

The smallest fox in North America has exceptionally large ears, which are believed to enhance its ability to detect rodents and other prey moving across the open land. Like the Red Fox, this species mates in winter and often uses burrows excavated by other mammals as maternity dens. Vixens (females) produce one litter a year, usually of four or five pups. Although Kit Foxes may move about near their dens during the day, these dainty animals are basically nighttime hunters. Poisoned bait intended for other predators has caused their numbers to decline.

Gray Fox
Urocyon cinereoargenteus

Length: *head and body, 22–30 in.; tail, 10–15 in.*
What to look for: *coat coarse, salt-and-pepper gray, with orange and white markings; tail bushy, black-tipped, with black stripe on top.*
Habitat: *open woodlands, chaparral, desert edges.*

Foxes belong to the dog family (Canidae), and canids are noticeably deficient in tree-climbing ability. But the Gray Fox is unusual: it climbs trees readily by clasping the trunk with its front legs and pushing itself up with its hind feet. Like other foxes, this grizzled animal uses ground burrows for escape holes and birthing sites. Gray Foxes den in hollow logs, tree trunks, and rock.

Coyote
Canis latrans

Length: *head and body, 32–40 in.; tail, 12–15 in.*
What to look for: *gray on back, with red on flanks; tawny legs, feet, and ears; tail held between legs when running.*
Habitat: *prairies, open forests, brush.*

The Coyote's nocturnal serenades – a chorus of howls, barks, and wails – epitomize the American West. But Coyotes have drastically extended their range and now commonly occur throughout the United States. They adapt well to the presence of man (even to the extent of raiding garbage cans) and have moved into areas extensively cleared for farming. Frequently condemned as livestock-killers, they are primarily predators on rodents, rabbits, and other small animals. Occasionally several adults cooperate in hunting large prey such as deer. Coyotes belong to the dog family. They resemble German shepherds and have been known to mate with domestic dogs.

Gray Wolf
Canis lupus

Length: *head and body, 40–52 in.; tail, 13–19 in.*
What to look for: *large doglike animal; fur usually gray but varies from silvery white to black.*
Habitat: *open forests, tundra.*

Maligned through the ages as a vicious predator, the wolf might better be admired for its complex social organization. The wolf pack, usually numbering four to seven individuals, is a society of parents, young, and close relatives that follows a rigid hierarchy. The leader, or alpha male, appears to control the pack's activities and is often the only male to breed; usually he is paired with the dominant female. Wolves have a wide repertoire of social behavior, communicating by posture, voice, and scent. They cooperate in feeding, protecting, and training the pups. They are mainly big-game hunters, preying on deer and other large mammals, but will also attack smaller mammals and birds. The Gray, or Timber, Wolf is native to both North America and Eurasia; the rapidly disappearing Red Wolf (*Canis rufus*) is strictly a resident of the southeastern states.

Grizzly Bear
Ursus arctos horribilis

Size: *head and body length, 6–7 ft.; shoulder height, 3–3½ ft.*
What to look for: *fur ranging from yellow to dark brown or black; tips of hairs usually whitish (grizzled); hump on shoulder; tail almost hidden in fur.* **Habitat:** *mountain forests, tundra.*

Lacking natural enemies, this giant does not always conceal itself when disturbed but rears up on its hind legs to get a better view of the situation. Like its even larger relative, the Kodiak Bear (*Ursus arctos middendorffi*), it can run as fast as a horse for short distances. Although sometimes capable of killing Moose and Caribou, it generally feeds on smaller animals (such as rodents and fish) and on plant material. It is dangerous to man only when surprised, cornered, wounded, or with cubs.

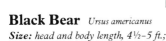

Black Bear *Ursus americanus*

Size: *head and body length, 4½–5 ft.; shoulder height, 2–3 ft.*
What to look for: *fur varying from cinnamon to black; brown snout; no shoulder hump; small white breast spot often present.* **Habitat:** *forests, swamps, mountains.*

Omnivorous in diet, Black Bears feed on animals ranging in size from insects to large mammals, as well as on plant material, carrion, and garbage. In autumn these bears gain weight and retreat into dens under fallen trees, in caves, or in other protected areas. There they sleep for several months, living off stored fat. Black Bears are not true hibernators: their body temperature does not drop drastically, and occasionally they wake up and wander away from their dens. Cubs are born about the end of January, while the sows (females) are still in their dens. Bears produce exceptionally small offspring relative to adult size: a Black Bear weighs about half a pound at birth, but a mature sow averages 300 pounds.

Polar Bear
Ursus maritimus

Size: *head and body length, 6½–8 ft.; shoulder height, 3–4 ft.*
What to look for: *yellowish-white fur.*
Habitat: *barren rocky shores, islands, ice floes.*

With powerful shoulders, webbed paws, streamlined bodies, and thick, oily fur, Polar Bears are strong swimmers. But they are not agile enough to catch swimming seals; they either stalk basking individuals or wait for a seal to surface at its breathing hole in the ice. More carnivorous than other bears, Polar Bears spend much of the year on and around ice floes. In late summer, however, they come ashore and forage for small animals, plants, and garbage. Pregnant females winter and give birth in dens excavated in the snow; other individuals may den for shorter periods of time. Churchill, Manitoba, is a prime area for seeing these massive creatures, which rival the great Alaskan bears in size.

Mountain Lion
Felis concolor

Length: *head and body, 42-60 in.; tail, 24-36 in.*
What to look for: *fur tawny to gray, spotted only in young; small head; long, dark-tipped tail.*
Habitat: *mountains, forests, swamps, deserts.*

Puma, Cougar, Panther, Painter, Catamount, Mountain Lion—all are names of the same secretive creature, believed to be the most widely distributed carnivore in the New World. Usually solitary and nocturnal, the Mountain Lion hunts deer and other mammals by stalking and rushing or by pouncing from trees and overhanging rocks. Like other large cats, it often kills by biting the neck of its prey. Neck bites of a gentler sort also occur during mating. Although breeding may occur at any time of year, most births take place in summer. The spotted kittens nurse for five or six weeks, grow unspotted coats at about six months, and remain with the mother for as long as two years. This is one of the few cat species in which the adult's fur has no spots or stripes.

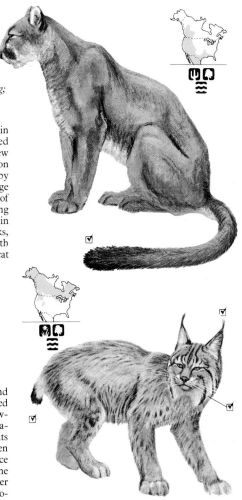

Lynx
Lynx lynx

Length: *head and body, 30-38 in.; tail, 4 in.*
What to look for: *tufted ears; short, black-tipped tail; fur varied in color but usually grayish tan; scattered spots (more in summer); furry ruff.* **Habitat:** *northern forests, swamps; occasionally on tundra.*

This shy, elusive animal is an agile climber, swims well, and travels with ease among fallen timbers and moss-covered boulders. In winter its broad, well-furred feet act as snowshoes, allowing swift movement in deep snow. Lynx populations undergo ups and downs that closely follow those of its chief prey animal, the Varying (or Snowshoe) Hare. When hares are abundant (about every 10 years), the cats produce larger litters and their population increases. Eventually the hare population crashes, and a decline occurs in the number of Lynx. A similar relationship exists between owl and rodent populations, but the cycle recurs at shorter intervals.

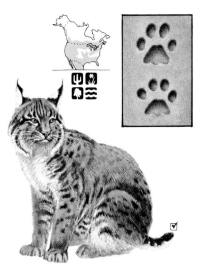

Bobcat
Lynx rufus

Length: *head and body, 26-36 in.; tail, 5 in.*
What to look for: *tail short, black on top only; fur varies from dark (forests) to light (open areas); spotted belly; spots more conspicuous than on Lynx.*
Habitat: *canyon country, chaparral, forests, swamps.*

The Bobcat is doing relatively well in the modern world. The commonest wild feline in North America, it occurs in a variety of habitats, adapts well to the presence of man, and is increasing in number in some areas—all in sharp contrast to the Lynx, a close relative with which it is often confused. Both Lynx and Bobcats are essentially solitary animals with individual hunting ranges that vary in size according to the availability of prey. (When prey is abundant, the cats stay within a smaller area.) Though rabbits and hares are the Bobcat's usual food, it will eat almost any mammal, reptile, or bird and has even been known to capture bats roosting in caves. Caves, hollow logs, and rocky ledges are used as denning sites by pregnant females. Kittens are usually born in spring, although females in the southern part of the range may have a second litter later in the year.

Mountain Sheep

Ovis canadensis

Size: *head and body length, 5-6 ft.;
shoulder height, 2½-3½ ft.*
What to look for: *ram's horns massive,
spiraling; ewe's horns much smaller, slightly
curved; fur brown or grayish brown; whitish rump.*
Habitat: *rugged, sparsely wooded mountain slopes.*

Also known as the Bighorn (its horns measure up to 4 feet), this heavy-bodied sheep has a remarkable capacity for climbing and jumping, thanks to the structure of its hooves. The halves of each hoof separate, so that the feet cling firmly to rocky terrain. The soles are soft and cushionlike, allowing the Bighorn to keep its balance as it moves across uneven or slippery ground. Mountain Sheep are gregarious animals. Groups of old rams roam together in summer, then separate to join bands of ewes and young in fall; they all move to lower valleys for the winter. Though in winter they may rely on willows and other woody plants, they are primarily grass-eating creatures.

Mountain Goat

Oreamnos americanus

Size: *head and body length, 5-5½ ft.; shoulder
height, 3-3½ ft.* **What to look for:** *fur white, long;
horns black, curving backward; bearded chin.*
Habitat: *steep slopes, cliffs, woods;
usually above timberline.*

This sure-footed animal grazes well above the timberline, preferring steep mountainsides and cliffs to sheltered valleys. It generally moves quite slowly. But when danger threatens, it rapidly scales cliff faces, reaching nooks and crannies that are inaccessible to predators. Avalanches are a chief cause of death, though Mountain Lions, wolves, foxes, and eagles sometimes take young goats, or kids. Born in April or May, the kids are able to stand up only a few minutes after birth and can follow their mother over difficult terrain within several days.

Pronghorn

Antilocapra americana

Size: *head and body length, 4-4½ ft.; shoulder
height, 3-3½ ft.* **What to look for:** *fur tan,
white on belly and rump; 2 white stripes on breast;
horns slightly curved, with single forward-projecting prong.*
Habitat: *prairies, sagebrush flats.*

North America's swiftest mammal, sometimes called an antelope, can reach speeds of more than 40 miles an hour, cover 20 feet in one leap, and outdistance nearly all predators. Adapted to the temperature extremes of the open plains, it maintains a constant body temperature by adjusting its loose, hollow-haired fur. When the hairs lie flat, cold air is kept out; when hairs are erect, air circulates near the skin and allows body heat to escape. In dangerous situations, and also during courtship, it signals to other Pronghorns by raising the white hairs on its rump. Pronghorns are the only animals that shed the outer part of their horns once a year.

White-tailed Deer
Odocoileus virginianus

Size: *head and body length, 4-6 ft.; tail length, 7-11 in.; shoulder height, 2¾-3½ ft.* **What to look for:** *tail white on underside, raised when alarmed; antlers (males) have main beam with several prongs; fur reddish (summer) or grayish brown (winter).* **Habitat:** *forests, swamps; adjacent brushy areas.*

The cutting of forests and clearing of land for farming have favored these graceful deer, now the most abundant hoofed mammals in North America. Early morning and dusk are the best times to see them; at other times of day they usually rest and digest their food. Except in winter, they are not gregarious and seldom appear in groups of more than three animals (a doe and two fawns). Females normally have no antlers. Males begin growing them several months after birth, shed them each winter, and develop them anew each spring and summer. The age of a deer cannot be told by the size of the antlers or the number of points (tines), for antler development is determined by nutrition, not age.

Mule Deer
Odocoileus hemionus

Size: *head and body length, 4½-6½ ft.; tail length, 4½-9 in.; shoulder height, 3-3½ ft.* **What to look for:** *tail black-tipped or all black on top ("Black-tailed Deer"); antlers (males) fork into 2 nearly equal branches; fur reddish brown (summer) or grayish (winter); large ears.* **Habitat:** *mountain forests, wooded hills and valleys, chaparral, brushy deserts.*

Unlike the White-tailed Deer, the Mule Deer (named for its large, mulelike ears) avoids areas of human activity. On summer evenings single individuals or groups of Mule Deer can be seen near forest edges in western parks; in winter large, loosely structured herds assemble on brushy slopes in the foothills where browse (the twigs and buds of woody plants) is available. The animals move to higher elevations in spring. Like other deer, this species ruts in autumn, when males contest for and associate briefly with the females. Spotted fawns, usually twins, are born in spring and weaned at about six weeks of age. Young females may stay with their mother for two years, but males leave in their first year.

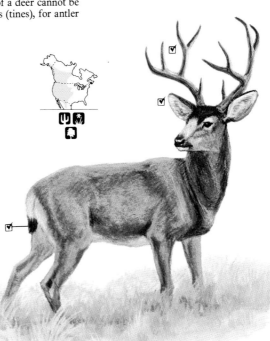

Wapiti (Elk)

Cervus elaphus

Size: *head and body length, 7½–9½ ft.; tail length, 4½–8 in.; shoulder height, 4–5 ft.*
What to look for: *large size; huge antlers (males); red-brown fur; pale rump; short tail.*
Habitat: *mountain meadows, forested areas, lakeshores; valleys, grassland edges (winter).*

Wapiti is an Indian word for "white," a reference to the light rump color of this gregarious deer. Though Wapiti are less common today than in the past (they formerly roamed even the eastern states), herds are widely distributed in mountain forests and adjacent valleys of the West. In summer Wapiti cows and calves graze together in groups; bulls form separate herds. In autumn the bulls' loud, resonant bugling announces the rut, or mating season, when they fight (sometimes to the death) for possession of a harem. Males and females forage together in winter, then separate for the birth of the young. The calves have spotted fur, unlike Moose and Caribou calves.

Moose

Alces alces

Size: *head and body length, 7½–10 ft.; tail length, 2½–3½ in.; shoulder height, 5–6½ ft.*
What to look for: *large size; antlers (males) massive, flattened, pronged; fleshy dewlap on throat; upper lip overhangs lower.* **Habitat:** *northern forests; often around freshwater.*

Moose are the largest members of the deer family; males in autumn may weigh more than a thousand pounds. Standing or swimming in lakes and ponds, they feed on many kinds of aquatic plants. Moose are not social animals; they are solitary or associate in small groups most of the year. In the fall the males become restless and aggressive, engaging in antler-to-antler combat and searching for a series of mates. Calves (often twins) are born in spring. Weak at birth, these gangling, unspotted creatures remain hidden and inactive for several days. Wolves and bears prey on the calves, as they also do on the aged and weak, but few predators can successfully challenge a healthy adult. Moose swim well and run easily through the snow, and they possess formidable weapons in their legs and hooves. Males shed their antlers in winter and begin to grow them again in spring.

Caribou
Rangifer tarandus

Size: *head and body length, 5½–7½ ft.;*
tail length, 4–5½ in.; shoulder height, 3½–4 ft.
What to look for: *stocky body; antlers*
branching into 3 slightly flattened tines, one
extending over brow; white neck, rump, and "socks."
Habitat: *northern forests, bogs; tundra.*

Unlike other deer, Caribou of both sexes usually have antlers, although the males' far surpass those of the females. The Caribou has another peculiarity: as it moves, a tendon in its foot rubs against a bone and produces an audible click. The sound becomes especially noticeable when the animals move in great numbers, as they do during the migration of the tundra-dwelling race (known as the Barren-ground Caribou). Sometimes considered a separate species, the tundra animals winter in the scattered spruce-fir forests south of their summer range. Although 100,000 animals may band together just before migration, the typical herd is much smaller and relatively homogeneous in age and sex. The Reindeer of the Old World are considered by many to belong to the same species as the American Caribou.

Bison
Bison bison

Size: *head and body length, 7–11½ ft.; tail length, 20–26 in.; shoulder height, 5–6 ft.*
What to look for: *large head; shoulder hump; horns on sides of head; long, shaggy fur*
on shoulders and front legs. **Habitat:** *prairies; open woodlands in north.*

Bison once grazed the continent from the mountain grasslands of the West as far east as Georgia. Hunted nearly to extinction by the end of the 19th century, these shaggy creatures were bred in zoos and on ranches and then released in parks and refuges. Today they can be seen in such areas as Yellowstone National Park (Wyoming), Wood Buffalo National Park (Alberta), and the National Bison Range (Montana). Often called Buffalo, they belong to the same family as sheep, goats, and cattle. All have horns with a bony core that are retained from year to year. Bison travel in bands commonly numbering 60 or more but occasionally form larger herds. Calves follow their mothers closely for two to three weeks after birth, then often band together in playful nursery groups. Weaned at about seven months, they feed on a variety of green plants for the rest of their lives. Bison have been known to produce calves at 30 years of age.

Northern Fur Seal
Callorhinus ursinus

Length: *4½-6½ ft.*
What to look for: *blackish above, reddish below; brown face; gray shoulders; small, pointed ears.*
Habitat: *cold seas; comes ashore only for breeding.*

The Northern Fur Seal, valued for its lustrous pelt, breeds on three groups of islands in and around the North Pacific. The largest herd is found on the Pribilof Islands, off the Alaskan coast. After a winter at sea the mature bulls (harem masters) arrive on the beaches in late spring. Then come the females, which give birth shortly after arrival and then mate; offspring from these matings will be born the following year. After suckling their young for about a week, the females leave for a week or so at sea. They hunt fish and squid, return to nurse their pups for a day, and maintain this schedule until the young are weaned. In autumn the bulls, weakened by constant fighting and lack of food (they do not eat during the breeding season), are the first to depart. In winter the seals may swim as far south as southern California—a journey of several thousand miles.

Harbor Seal   *Phoca vitulina*

Length: *4½-5½ ft.*
What to look for: *fur varying in color (dark gray with brown spots, dark brown with gray spots, all gray, or all brown); no visible ears.*
Habitat: *coastal waters, estuaries, harbors; occasionally in lakes.*

Few seals spend as much time ashore as this common species, which is believed to have the widest range of any seal. Harbor Seals wait out low tide on the beach and normally take to the water only as the tide comes in, sometimes following the tidal flow far into an estuary as they fish. Like elephant seals, they submerge by slipping beneath the surface; in contrast, fur seals and sea lions arch their backs, thrust forward, and dive. Harbor Seals can reach depths of 300 feet and stay underwater for nearly half an hour. They mate both in water and on land and on occasion have been known to give birth in the sea. Birth normally occurs on sandbars, ledges, offshore islands, or ice floes.

California Sea Lion
Zalophus californianus

Length: *6-8 ft.*
What to look for: *brown fur (blackish when wet); high forehead; small, pointed ears; animal barks frequently.*
Habitat: *rocky coasts, surf, open sea.*

Although the names "sea lion" and "seal" are often used interchangeably, the animals are not the same. There are two major differences: sea lions, and also fur seals, have visible, external ears; and they can turn their flippers forward when walking on land. The trained "seals" of circuses, zoos, and aquariums are usually California Sea Lions. In their natural habitat these graceful swimmers ride the surf, leap in and out of the water, and playfully cavort near shore. They spend much of the day basking on land and are believed to feed mainly at night on a typically seallike diet of mollusks and fish. The Northern, or Steller, Sea Lion (*Eumetopias jubatus*) is a larger creature with lighter-colored fur.

Sea Otter   *Enhydra lutris*

Length: *head and body, 29–39 in.; tail, 9½–12 in.*
What to look for: *fur glossy, blackish brown,*
with white-tipped hairs; head area lighter in color; webbed,
flipperlike feet. **Habitat:** *kelp beds along rocky shores.*

The Sea Otter is the smallest marine mammal. Almost wholly aquatic,
it comes ashore only in severe storms. In water it propels itself by
alternate strokes of the broad hind feet, spending much of the time
backstroking, with its head above the surface. The Sea Otter feeds in
relatively shallow water, searching the bottom for abalone and also
preying on squid, octopus, and sea urchins. It carries food to the surface, uses its belly as a table as it floats on its back, and cracks shells by
placing a flat rock on its chest and hitting them against the rock.

Manatee

Trichechus manatus

Length: *7½–12½ ft.*
What to look for: *bulky body; lips cleft*
in center, covered with bristles; no rear
flippers; tail flattened, rounded at tip.
Habitat: *shallow lagoons, estuaries,*
coastal rivers; usually in brackish water.

Although this odd-looking creature occasionally
noses onto a riverbank to graze, it never comes completely ashore. Water is its home, but like all other
mammals, it must have air to breathe. Manatees are
born underwater. Immediately after birth, the
mother brings the calf to the surface and is said to
dunk it repeatedly until it can submerge on its own.
To nurse, she holds the calf against her breast with
her flippers. Manatees are rare animals, with a total
estimated population of about 1,000. The best places
to look for them are weed beds and, in winter, the
warm outflow from power plants.

Northern Elephant Seal

Mirounga angustirostris

Length: *males to 20 ft.,*
females to 11 ft.
What to look for:
large size; skin
brown to grayish,
nearly hairless;
snout flabby,
overhanging on
old males; ears not visible.
Habitat: *sandy beaches,*
warm waters.

This seal takes its name from its great size
and overhanging snout. Bulls weigh several tons; when alarmed or defending their
harems, they bellow through and inflate
their snouts. Usually rather lethargic,
Northern Elephant Seals were easy victims for 19th-century hunters who sought
their blubber as a source of oil. Only one
small colony, on an island off the coast of
Baja California, remained by the 1890's.
Protected by Mexico since 1911, Northern
Elephant Seals have made a remarkable
recovery: they now number
more than 10,000 and have
extended their range up
the Pacific coast to
San Francisco.

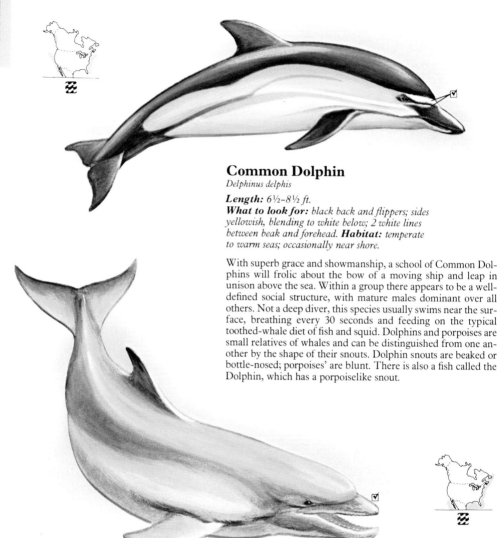

Common Dolphin
Delphinus delphis

Length: *6½–8½ ft.*
What to look for: *black back and flippers; sides yellowish, blending to white below; 2 white lines between beak and forehead.* **Habitat:** *temperate to warm seas; occasionally near shore.*

With superb grace and showmanship, a school of Common Dolphins will frolic about the bow of a moving ship and leap in unison above the sea. Within a group there appears to be a well-defined social structure, with mature males dominant over all others. Not a deep diver, this species usually swims near the surface, breathing every 30 seconds and feeding on the typical toothed-whale diet of fish and squid. Dolphins and porpoises are small relatives of whales and can be distinguished from one another by the shape of their snouts. Dolphin snouts are beaked or bottle-nosed; porpoises' are blunt. There is also a fish called the Dolphin, which has a porpoiselike snout.

Whales and their kin.
Dolphins and porpoises are essentially small versions of whales. All members of the group of mammals known as cetaceans, they have certain features in common:
• They are strictly aquatic, remaining in water even to breed.
• They are relatively large. Even the smallest species grows to lengths of 5 feet or more.
• The front limbs are paddlelike flippers. Hind limbs are not visible.
• The tails are flattened horizontally and notched in the center. Each half of the tail is called a fluke.
• Hair is absent except for a few bristles around the mouth.

Bottle-nosed Dolphin
Tursiops truncatus

Length: *9–12 ft.*
What to look for: *short projecting snout; grayish above, somewhat paler below.*
Habitat: *along Atlantic and Pacific coasts.*

The playfulness, friendliness, and intelligence of the Bottle-nosed Dolphin have won it fame as a star performer in marine aquariums and films. This especially vocal animal emits complicated whistles and chirps as it communicates with others of its kind. Like all toothed whales, it also sends out ultrasonic signals that help it navigate and locate prey. (This technique, also used by bats, is called echolocation or sonar.) Friendly toward man, it turns fierce when its young are menaced by sharks. One or more individuals have been observed repeatedly ramming an attacking fish at high speed until the molester was killed. This is the commonest dolphin along the Atlantic shore; a close relative, Gill's Bottle-nosed Dolphin (*Tursiops gillii*), lives in the Pacific.

Harbor Porpoise

Phocoena phocoena

Length: *4-6 ft.*
What to look for: *blunt nose; black back; pink sides; white belly; black line from mouth to flipper; triangular dorsal fin.* **Habitat:** *along Atlantic and Pacific coasts; harbors; occasionally in rivers.*

Traveling in pairs or larger groups, Harbor Porpoises cruise just below the surface and rise to breathe about four times a minute. Like whales, dolphins and porpoises take in and expel air through blowholes near the top of the head. (Dolphins, porpoises, and toothed whales have single blowholes; baleen whales have two.) Although the Harbor Porpoise is not as playful as some of its relatives, the male and female swim together, touch, and vocalize in an elaborate courtship. A single calf is born after a year's gestation.

Killer Whale

Orcinus orca

Length: *15-30 ft.*
What to look for: *large, high dorsal fin; black and white pattern.*
Habitat: *Pacific and Atlantic waters; often near shore.*

Weighing up to 20,000 pounds, Killer Whales, or Orcas, are formidable predators. They slice through the water at a top speed of 30 knots. They pursue their prey in packs of up to 50 individuals, swimming in close formation and often leaping and diving in unison. A pack will herd a school of tuna or salmon into a cove, where the fish are easier to catch. Killer Whales are the only whales to prey frequently on warm-blooded animals (mammals and birds). They will surround even a large whale and tear away chunks of flesh with knife-like teeth. In Antarctic waters they capture penguins and seals by crashing through ice floes and dislodging their victims. In spite of their fearsome reputation, they have never been known to attack man. The Killer Whale is one of the easiest whales to identify—not only by species, but even by sex. Males are longer than females and have larger, more triangular fins.

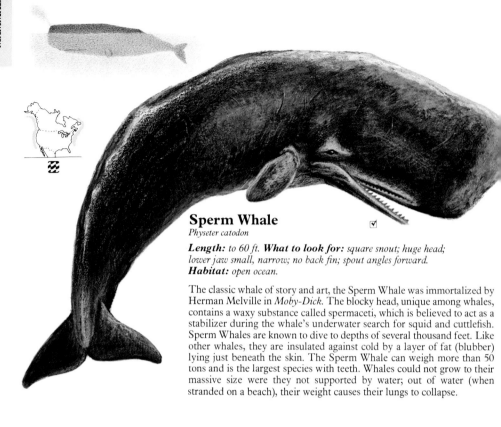

Sperm Whale
Physeter catodon

Length: *to 60 ft.* **What to look for:** *square snout; huge head; lower jaw small, narrow; no back fin; spout angles forward.*
Habitat: *open ocean.*

The classic whale of story and art, the Sperm Whale was immortalized by Herman Melville in *Moby-Dick*. The blocky head, unique among whales, contains a waxy substance called spermaceti, which is believed to act as a stabilizer during the whale's underwater search for squid and cuttlefish. Sperm Whales are known to dive to depths of several thousand feet. Like other whales, they are insulated against cold by a layer of fat (blubber) lying just beneath the skin. The Sperm Whale can weigh more than 50 tons and is the largest species with teeth. Whales could not grow to their massive size were they not supported by water; out of water (when stranded on a beach), their weight causes their lungs to collapse.

Fin Whale
Balaenoptera physalus

Length: *to 80 ft.* **What to look for:** *grayish above, white below; dorsal fin small, toward rear of body; fan-shaped spout extends to 20 ft.*
Habitat: *Atlantic Ocean south to Caribbean Sea;*
Pacific Ocean south to Baja California.

Finbacks belong to the group of whales known as rorquals and characterized by deep grooves in their throats. All rorquals, as well as the Gray and the Humpbacked Whale, lack teeth. Instead, they have strips of a hard, flexible substance called baleen (or whalebone) that hang from the upper jaw and act as a sieve. To feed, they gulp mouthfuls of water, close their jaws, and force water out through the baleen plates. The fringed edges of the baleen retain food organisms—usually tiny shrimplike animals called krill. In summer, whale food is most abundant in Arctic and Antarctic waters. Twice a year, therefore, baleen whales migrate between polar feeding grounds and breeding grounds nearer the Equator. The Blue Whale (*Balaenoptera musculus*), a baleen whale with a more mottled appearance than the
Fin Whale, is the largest animal that has ever lived on earth.

Identifying whales. Those lucky enough to spot a whale rarely see the entire animal. Whales come to the surface mainly to breathe, and for this only their blowholes need be exposed.
• Knowing which species are likely to be in the area helps to narrow down the possibilities. So does estimating the size of the whale. Keep in mind, however, that species overlap in size; a large Fin Whale and a small Blue Whale may be about the same size.
• Look at the color of the whale and the pattern of light and dark. Does the whale have a dorsal (back) fin? If so, note its shape. And if possible, note the shape of the head.
• Especially from a distance, the spout (shape, angle, and height) furnishes important clues.

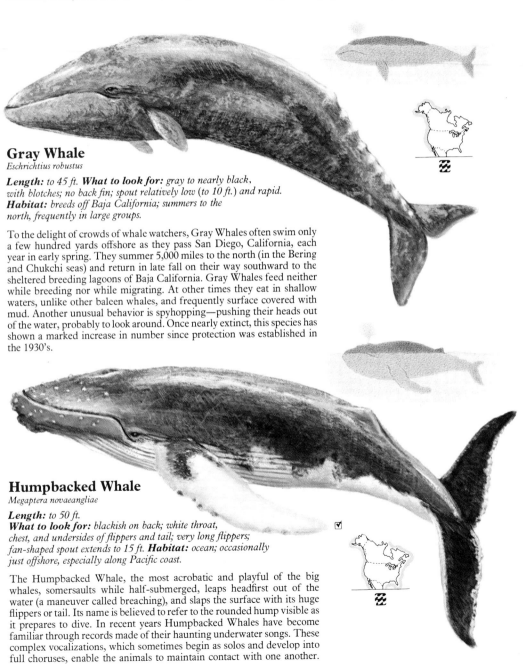

Gray Whale
Eschrichtius robustus

Length: *to 45 ft.* **What to look for:** *gray to nearly black, with blotches; no back fin; spout relatively low (to 10 ft.) and rapid.* **Habitat:** *breeds off Baja California; summers to the north, frequently in large groups.*

To the delight of crowds of whale watchers, Gray Whales often swim only a few hundred yards offshore as they pass San Diego, California, each year in early spring. They summer 5,000 miles to the north (in the Bering and Chukchi seas) and return in late fall on their way southward to the sheltered breeding lagoons of Baja California. Gray Whales feed neither while breeding nor while migrating. At other times they eat in shallow waters, unlike other baleen whales, and frequently surface covered with mud. Another unusual behavior is spyhopping—pushing their heads out of the water, probably to look around. Once nearly extinct, this species has shown a marked increase in number since protection was established in the 1930's.

Humpbacked Whale
Megaptera novaeangliae

Length: *to 50 ft.* **What to look for:** *blackish on back; white throat, chest, and undersides of flippers and tail; very long flippers; fan-shaped spout extends to 15 ft.* **Habitat:** *ocean; occasionally just offshore, especially along Pacific coast.*

The Humpbacked Whale, the most acrobatic and playful of the big whales, somersaults while half-submerged, leaps headfirst out of the water (a maneuver called breaching), and slaps the surface with its huge flippers or tail. Its name is believed to refer to the rounded hump visible as it prepares to dive. In recent years Humpbacked Whales have become familiar through records made of their haunting underwater songs. These complex vocalizations, which sometimes begin as solos and develop into full choruses, enable the animals to maintain contact with one another.

Birds

*For some it is joy enough simply to see a bird and
observe its actions. Others want to identify the bird,
to know its life-style, to understand its behavior.
We appreciate, and encourage, both points of view.*

More than any other type of wildlife, it is
birds that hold man in their spell. They
are active and attractive. They make beautiful
music. They please us with their willingness to
come to feeders, their preoccupation with
nests and nestlings, their miraculous, mysterious ability to fly.

Part of the fascination of birds lies in their
diversity and ubiquitousness. Upwards of 650
species are regular breeders or frequent visitors north of the Mexican border. Birds nest on
sandy beaches and rocky cliffs, in marshes and
deserts, along city streets and country roadsides. Although their numbers vary from place
to place (and from season to season), you can
watch them just about anywhere. Especially
rewarding are places where birds fly or perch
out in the open—near a feeder or woodland
pool, for example.

To maximize your opportunities to observe
birds, keep in mind their flighty nature. Walk
slowly and steadily, or not at all. (Birds are less
skittish if you stay in the car.) Keep quiet.
Don't wear bright clothing. And do get out
early in the day, especially if you're looking for
land birds in spring; they are noisiest and most
active from dawn to midmorning.

Getting Started
Beginning or intermediate birders need little
equipment. Most important is a pair of binoculars with central focusing and a seven- or eight-
fold magnification. Popular sizes for general
use are 7 x 35 and 8 x 40. (The first number refers to magnification; the second, indirectly to
light-gathering power.) Other aids you may
want to carry along are a pocket-sized field
guide and a notebook. Sooner or later, even
casual bird-watchers start to keep records that,
whether mere lists of species seen and
identified or more extensive notes, serve as a
jog to the memory, a running diary of birding
experiences.

Many birders enjoy going out by themselves, and there is much to be said for a solitary early-morning walk or a restful hour near
a pond or stream. But birding in a group that
includes at least one experienced observer will
speed up the learning process—and furnish
companionship and extra pairs of eyes as well.
Many parts of the country have bird clubs that
schedule meetings and outings where you can
meet helpful birders. Try calling the biology
department of a high school or college or the
nearest natural history museum to find out
about such clubs and events.

How to Use This Section
Only abundant, wide-ranging, or conspicuous
birds are pictured here, although mention is
made of many other species. To simplify recognition, swimming and wading birds have been
separated from land birds. Within these two
major divisions, species are arranged in cur-
rently accepted scientific groupings. (The
Starling, the House Sparrow, and several other
species have been taken out of sequence and
placed near species they resemble.) Once you
have become accustomed to this sequence, and
to the basic characteristics of each group, you
should have little trouble locating a particular
bird. In the meantime, use the two-page
spread that follows to pinpoint birds with distinctive traits.

Where appropriate, the maps have been
subdivided to show separate breeding, wintering, and migration ranges. A word of caution,

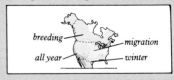

however: individual birds (and even large populations) may stray far from their usual range,
and changes in ranges are inevitable over time.
The maps in this book are a guide, not an abso-
lute; be delighted rather than dismayed should
you find a bird in the "wrong" place or at the
"wrong" time of year.

The habitat symbols used in this section are: U *desert*   ⚘ *grassland/meadow/brush*   ♣ *fore*

As the descriptions in this section indicate, many species have more than one distinctive plumage, and in many cases more than one form is illustrated in this book. (See, for example, the Orchard Orioles at right.) For other species with major sexual or seasonal differences, the individual shown in this book is a male and in breeding ("summer") plumage unless otherwise noted.

Orchard Oriole

Female

First-year (fall) male

Adult male

In many species the most strikingly colored bird is the adult, breeding male. Young birds often look like the female.

Tips on Identifying Birds

Posture and movement. The way a bird sits or moves often gives away its identity. Wrens cock their tails; woodpeckers and goldfinches have an undulating pattern of flight. Illustrations cannot always communicate this type of information, so check the species descriptions in this book for such behavioral clues.

Size and proportions. When you see a bird you don't recognize, compare its size as best you can with a Robin, crow, or other familiar species. Note also whether the unknown bird is streamlined or robust, and whether its bill or legs seem

unusually long. Closely related species in this book have been pictured in scale with one another, making differences in size or proportion readily apparent.

Songs and calls. Recognizing a bird by sound is often easier than by sight, especially with small birds flitting in foliage. First, of course, one has to learn the sounds—by listening to recordings (a method not recommended for beginners) or by hearing a song or call, spotting the bird that is making it, and then identifying the bird. This book can only hint at the rich

variety of vocalizations, best appreciated by spending a few early morning hours in spring near a woodland pool.

Color and markings. These are the attributes that most tellingly reveal a bird's identity, though you may not always be able to see a bird as closely or for as long a time as you may need. With experience, you will be able to take in more and more at a glance, and to immediately "go for" the characteristics that separate closely related species—the bill color on a tern, the presence or absence of wingbars on a vireo.

Bill shape and color can be important in identification.

Crown

Nape

Throat may have distinctive color or pattern.

Back is sometimes striped, barred, or streaked.

Speculum

Breast may be spotted, streaked, or unmarked.

Belly

Leg color may vary among closely related species.

Wing may have speculum, stripe, patch, or bars.

Tail may be spotted or banded. Note shape and length.

Mallard (male)

Bright crown   Dark crown stripe

Pointed bill   White eye ring

Unstreaked throat   Olive back

Streaked breast   Pink legs

Ovenbird

To improve your ability to identify birds, train your eye to observe a variety of features, as described for the duck at left. The illustration above shows what a trained observer will see on one type of warbler.

Birds with Distinctive Traits

To identify birds with a distinctive appearance or behavior, consult the lists that follow. The lists include only those species shown in this book, but the text accompanying an illustration may mention other species with similar traits. Because plumage may vary according to age, sex, season, and other factors, not all birds of a given species necessarily have the particular trait for which they are listed.

BIRDS

Blue
prominent color or markings

SMALL
Eastern Bluebird *p. 135*
Mountain Bluebird *p. 135*
Northern Parula *p. 138*
Black-throated Blue
  Warbler *p. 142*
Blue Grosbeak *p. 148*
Indigo Bunting *p. 149*

MEDIUM
Blue Jay *p. 124*
Scrub Jay *p. 124*

LARGE
Belted Kingfisher *p. 113*
Steller's Jay *p. 124*

Mostly Black
may show iridescence

SMALL
Chimney Swift *p. 116*
Lark Bunting *p. 151*

MEDIUM
*Leach's Storm-petrel *p. 80*
*Black Tern *p. 105*
Purple Martin *p. 127*
Phainopepla *p. 137*
Red-winged Blackbird *p. 144*
Brown-headed Cowbird *p. 145*
Brewer's Blackbird *p. 145*
European Starling *p. 145*

LARGE
*Common Gallinule *p. 89*
*American Coot *p. 89*
*Black Duck *p. 91*
*Black Oystercatcher *p. 94*
American Crow *p. 125*
Common Grackle *p. 145*

VERY LARGE
*Double-crested Cormorant *p. 83*
*Anhinga *p. 83*
*Glossy Ibis *p. 86*
Turkey Vulture *p. 106*
Common Raven *p. 125*

Rose, Red, or Orange
prominent color or markings

SMALL
Rufous Hummingbird *p. 117*
Vermilion Flycatcher *p. 123*
American Redstart *p. 139*
Blackburnian Warbler *p. 143*
Painted Bunting *p. 149*
Purple Finch *p. 150*
House Finch *p. 150*
Red Crossbill *p. 150*
Common Redpoll *p. 151*

MEDIUM
Red-bellied Woodpecker *p. 118*
Red-headed Woodpecker *p. 118*
Yellow-bellied Sapsucker *p. 119*
American Robin *p. 134*
Varied Thrush *p. 134*
Red-winged Blackbird *p. 144*
Scarlet Tanager *p. 147*
Western Tanager *p. 147*
Summer Tanager *p. 147*
Northern Cardinal *p. 148*
Rose-breasted Grosbeak *p. 149*
Black-headed Grosbeak *p. 149*
Pine Grosbeak *p. 150*

LARGE
Pileated Woodpecker *p. 118*

VERY LARGE
*Roseate Spoonbill *p. 86*

Bright Yellow *prominent color or markings*

SMALL
Verdin *p. 128*
Northern Parula *p. 138*
Prothonotary Warbler *p. 138*
MacGillivray's Warbler *p. 139*
American Redstart *p. 139*
Canada Warbler *p. 140*
Hooded Warbler *p. 140*
Common Yellowthroat *p. 140*
Magnolia Warbler *p. 141*
Yellow-rumped Warbler *p. 141*
Palm Warbler *p. 141*
Yellow Warbler *p. 141*

White
dominant color

SMALL
*Snowy Plover *p. 96*
Snow Bunting *p. 157*

MEDIUM
*Sanderling *p. 98*
*Least Tern *p. 104*

LARGE
*Snowy Egret *p. 85*
Cattle Egret *p. 85*
*Common Goldeneye *p. 93*
*Bufflehead *p. 93*
*Ring-billed Gull *p. 102*
*Bonaparte's Gull *p. 103*
*Forster's Tern *p. 104*
*Common Tern *p. 104*
*Caspian Tern *p. 105*
White-tailed Ptarmigan *p. 110*

VERY LARGE
*American White Pelican *p. 82*
*Northern Gannet *p. 83*
*Great Egret *p. 85*
*Wood Stork *p. 86*
*Whooping Crane *p. 87*
*Mute Swan *p. 88*
*Tundra Swan *p. 88*
*Snow Goose *p. 89*
*Herring Gull *p. 102*
Snowy Owl *p. 114*

Black-throated Green
  Warbler *p. 142*
Yellow-throated Warbler *p. 142*
Blackburnian Warbler *p. 143*
Pine Warbler *p. 143*
American Goldfinch *p. 151*

MEDIUM
Northern Flicker *p. 119*
Western Kingbird *p. 120*
Great Crested Flycatcher *p. 121*
Horned Lark *p. 123*
Yellow-breasted Chat *p. 140*
Western Meadowlark *p. 144*
Yellow-headed Blackbird *p. 144*
Scott's Oriole *p. 146*
Evening Grosbeak *p. 148*

*associated mainly with water

Crest or Tufts

SMALL
Tufted Titmouse   p. 128

MEDIUM
California Quail   p. 111
Scaled Quail   p. 111
Eastern Screech-owl   p. 115
Horned Lark   p. 123
Blue Jay   p. 124
Cedar Waxwing   p. 136
Phainopepla   p. 137
Northern Cardinal   p. 148

LARGE
*Horned Grebe   p. 81
*Wood Duck   p. 90
*Hooded Merganser   p. 93
*Tufted Puffin   p. 105
Ruffed Grouse   p. 110
Greater Roadrunner   p. 113
Belted Kingfisher   p. 113
Great Horned Owl   p. 114
Long-eared Owl   p. 115
Pileated Woodpecker   p. 118
Steller's Jay   p. 124

VERY LARGE
*Common Merganser   p. 93

Long Tail

SMALL
Barn Swallow   p. 126
Wrentit   p. 128
Blue-gray Gnatcatcher   p. 136

MEDIUM
American Kestrel   p. 109
Mockingbird   p. 132
Gray Catbird   p. 132
Brown Thrasher   p. 133
California Thrasher   p. 133
Sage Thrasher   p. 133

LARGE
*Northern Pintail   p. 90
*Forster's Tern   p. 104
*Common Tern   p. 104
Sharp-shinned Hawk   p. 106
Marsh Hawk   p. 109
Prairie Falcon   p. 109
Peregrine Falcon   p. 109
Sharp-tailed Grouse   p. 110
Mourning Dove   p. 112
Yellow-billed Cuckoo   p. 113
Greater Roadrunner   p. 113
Scissor-tailed Flycatcher   p. 120
Black-billed Magpie   p. 125
Common Grackle   p. 145

VERY LARGE
Ring-necked Pheasant   p. 111

Very Long Bill

SMALL
Ruby-throated Hummingbird   p. 117
Anna's Hummingbird   p. 117
Rufous Hummingbird   p. 117
Black-chinned Hummingbird   p. 117

MEDIUM
*Virginia Rail   p. 88
*Long-billed Dowitcher   p. 98
*Dunlin   p. 98
*Common Snipe   p. 100
American Woodcock   p. 100
California Thrasher   p. 133

Hovering Birds

SMALL
Ruby-throated
  Hummingbird   p. 117
Anna's Hummingbird   p. 117
Rufous Hummingbird   p. 117
Black-chinned
  Hummingbird   p. 117

MEDIUM
*Least Tern   p. 104
*Black Tern   p. 105
American Kestrel   p. 109
*Belted Kingfisher   p. 113

LARGE
*Forster's Tern   p. 104
*Common Tern   p. 104
Red-tailed Hawk   p. 107
*Osprey   p. 108

Soaring and Gliding Birds

SMALL
Chimney Swift   p. 116
White-throated Swift   p. 116
Tree Swallow   p. 126
Barn Swallow   p. 126

MEDIUM
Purple Martin   p. 127

LARGE
*Ring-billed Gull   p. 102
*Herring Gull   p. 102
Red-tailed Hawk   p. 107

LARGE
*Northern Shoveler   p. 91
*American Oystercatcher   p. 94
*American Avocet   p. 94
*Black-necked Stilt   p. 94
Long-billed Curlew   p. 95
*Marbled Godwit   p. 95
*Black Skimmer   p. 104

VERY LARGE
*Brown Pelican   p. 82
*American White Pelican   p. 82
*Great Blue Heron   p. 84
*Great Egret   p. 85
*Wood Stork   p. 86
*Glossy Ibis   p. 86
*Roseate Spoonbill   p. 86

Birds That Cling to Tree Trunks

SMALL
Downy Woodpecker   p. 119
White-breasted Nuthatch   p. 129
Red-breasted Nuthatch   p. 129
Brown Creeper   p. 129
Black-and-White Warbler   p. 138

MEDIUM
Red-bellied Woodpecker   p. 118
Red-headed Woodpecker   p. 118
Acorn Woodpecker   p. 118
Northern Flicker   p. 119
Yellow-bellied Sapsucker   p. 119
Hairy Woodpecker   p. 119
Three-toed Woodpecker   p.119

LARGE
Pileated Woodpecker   p. 118

Red-shouldered Hawk   p. 107
Swainson's Hawk   p. 107
*Osprey   p. 108
Marsh Hawk   p. 109
Short-eared Owl   p. 115

VERY LARGE
*Brown Pelican   p. 82
*American White Pelican   p. 82
*Great Blue Heron   p. 84
*Great Egret   p. 85
*Wood Stork   p. 86
Sandhill Crane   p. 87
*Great Black-backed Gull   p. 102
Turkey Vulture   p. 106
Golden Eagle   p. 108
*Bald Eagle   p. 108

Sooty
Shearwater

Greater
Shearwater

Leach's Storm-petrel
Oceanodroma leucorhoa

Length: *7½–8½ in.*
What to look for: *small dark seabird; tail forked; rump white (dark in southern California); butterflylike flight.*
Habitat: *open seas; islands (breeding).*

Storm-petrels are among the smallest and most aquatic oceanic birds. They spend most of the year on the open sea, pattering over the waves with their webbed feet, and approach land only to breed. Leach's Storm-petrels, like the closely related Wilson's Storm-petrels (*Oceanites oceanicus*), nest in colonies. Each female lays a single egg at the end of a tunnel. During incubation one parent stays underground while the other seeks tiny fish and crustaceans at sea.

Greater Shearwater
Puffinus gravis

Length: *17½–19½ in.*
What to look for: *long, narrow wings; dark cap; white on tail; alternately flaps and glides.*
Habitat: *open seas.*

The name shearwater reflects the way these seabirds skim along the waves in search of fish and squid swimming just beneath the surface. They also chase prey underwater, using their long wings to propel themselves. In spring, after nesting more than 2,500 miles south of the equator, thousands of Greater Shearwaters migrate into the northern Atlantic. A second species, the Sooty Shearwater (*Puffinus griseus*), migrates over both the Atlantic and the Pacific.

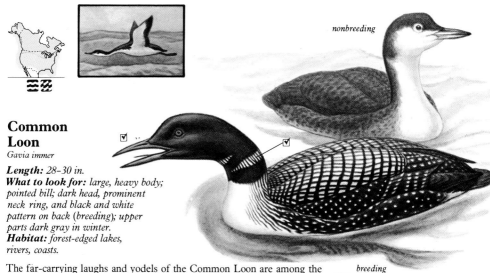

nonbreeding

Common Loon
Gavia immer

Length: *28–30 in.*
What to look for: *large, heavy body; pointed bill; dark head, prominent neck ring, and black and white pattern on back (breeding); upper parts dark gray in winter.*
Habitat: *forest-edged lakes, rivers, coasts.*

breeding

The far-carrying laughs and yodels of the Common Loon are among the most extraordinary sounds in nature. Although this bird is a strong flier, it can take off only from water—and a large body of water at that. Its legs are set so far back that it walks poorly, but once afloat the loon is completely at home. It occasionally rides with bill and eyes dipped below the surface, as if scouting, then dives in the wink of an eye. A loon can swim long distances underwater, now and again poking its bill above the surface for air. Like the Common Loon, the smaller Red-throated Loon (*Gavia stellata*) winters mainly along the coast.

nonbreeding

breeding

Pied-billed Grebe
Podilymbus podiceps

Length: *12–15 in.*
What to look for: *small size; thick neck; white undertail; bill short, with black ring near tip (breeding).* **Habitat:** *ponds, marshes with open water; bays, coves (winter).*

Water Witch and Hell-diver are old-time names for this chunky bird, which can sink underwater with startling swiftness by forcing air out of its body and compressing the feathers. Like the young of other grebes, the soft, striped Pied-billed Grebe chicks are excellent divers from the time of hatching. Chicks riding piggyback on a parent may stay aboard even when the adult dives, perhaps holding on to the parent's feathers with their bills.

Horned Grebe
Podiceps auritus

Length: *12–15 in.*
What to look for: *small size; short neck; thin bill; golden "horns" (breeding); white cheek and neck (nonbreeding).* **Habitat:** *lakes, ponds, marshes; coasts (winter).*

On the waters of its northern breeding grounds, this golden-horned bird is an exquisite sight. (Occasionally, migrating birds occur in full breeding plumage.) Horned Grebes are solitary nesters, one pair to a pond. They feed on small fish, frogs, snails, and insects and, like other grebes, regularly eat feathers. Ornithologists have suggested that the feathers may serve to strain out less digestible bits of shell and fishbones and hold them for further softening.

Western Grebe
Aechmophorus occidentalis

Length: *22–25 in.*
What to look for: *large size; neck long, slender; black cap; bill pointed, greenish.*
Habitat: *lakes with reedy edges; coasts (mainly in winter).*

These elegant "swan grebes" of western lakes and sloughs build floating nests anchored to reeds. Before nesting, Western Grebes perform a variety of courtship dances on the water. Swimming side by side, male and female rhythmically arch their necks, the head of each bird repeatedly touching its back. Also side by side, they race across the surface with heads thrust forward and bodies held upright. Clark's Grebe (*Aechmophorus clarkii*), which occupies the same range as the Western, differs in having the white on the cheek extending above the eye, and in having a yellow bill.

immature

Brown Pelican
Pelecanus occidentalis

Size: *length, 3½–4½ ft.; wingspan, 7 ft.*
What to look for: *large, bulky bird with large,*
bulky bill; gray-brown body; whitish head;
red-brown neck with white stripe (breeding);
flies with alternate flaps and glides.
Habitat: *usually in ocean or brackish water.*

The Brown Pelican sights its prey while in flight, then dives with bill closed and enters the water in a burst of spray. At that moment it lifts its upper mandible and opens its pouch outward, forming a scoop. Once the fish is safe inside—along with water twice the weight of the bird—the bill shuts, and the pelican bobs to the surface. The bird may take less than 2 seconds to make its catch. A minute or so may pass while it floats with bill pointed downward, evidently waiting for water to drain out so it can swallow the fish. Louisiana is sometimes called the Pelican State, although the pelican population in that state has been drastically depleted.

American White Pelican
Pelicanus erythrorhynchos

Size: *length, 4–5 ft.; wingspan, 9 ft.*
What to look for: *plumage white*
except for black on wings; bill and pouch
pinkish orange (gray on immature).
Habitat: *lakes, ponds; when not breeding,*
in coastal bays.

Many observers remark on the seemingly military behavior of pelican flocks. Flying American White Pelicans usually flap their wings and glide in unison. Over long distances they proceed in straight lines or in V's. A group may sun on a sandspit, all facing in the same direction, all bills pointed to the sky. "Should one chance to gape," wrote Audubon, "all, as if by sympathy, in succession open their . . . mandibles, yawning lazily and ludicrously." When fishing, American White Pelicans form a line in the water and swim toward the beach, beating the water with their wings and herding the fish ahead of them. Unlike Brown Pelicans, they do not dive.

BIRDS

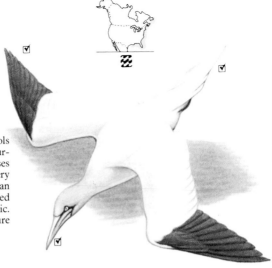

Northern Gannet
Morus bassanus

Size: *length, 3–3½ ft.; wingspan, 6 ft.*
What to look for: *wings long, pointed,*
black-tipped; tail pointed; white
body (gray-brown on immature); head
pale orange; bill long, conical.
Habitat: *oceans, offshore islands.*

This cousin of cormorants and pelicans sights schools
of fish from heights of 80 to 100 feet above the surface. When diving on its prey, a Gannet partly closes
its wings and plunges into the water like an artillery
shell, leaving a geyser behind to mark the spot. It can
reportedly dive deeper than 100 feet. Gannets breed
in centuries-old colonies on both sides of the Atlantic.
The largest one in North America is on Bonaventure
Island, off the Gaspé Peninsula in Quebec.

Double-crested Cormorant
Phalacrocorax auritus

Length: *2½–3 ft.*
What to look for: *large dark bird; thin bill;*
orange on throat; whitish breast and buffy
belly on immature; often stands with
wings outstretched. **Habitat:** *coasts, freshwater.*

Flocks of migrating Double-crested Cormorants can be mistaken for Canada Geese. But instead of flapping steadily and
honking as they fly, cormorants flap for a while and then sail.
They are silent in flight. Like loons and grebes, they fish by diving from the surface. Cormorants breed in colonies, chiefly on
rocky islands and in groves of trees and bushes. Their nests, constructed of sticks and other plant materials, may be garnished
with feathers and sprigs of greenery.

Anhinga
Anhinga anhinga

Length: *about 3 ft.*
What to look for: *neck long, sinuous;*
pointed bill; wings streaked with
white; female browner, with whitish throat.
Habitat: *slow-moving fresh or*
brackish water; occasionally in
protected saltwater areas.

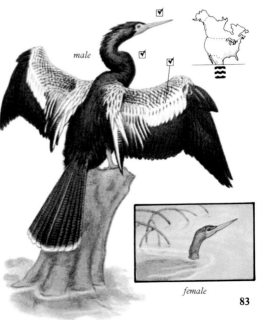

male

The Snakebird, or Water Turkey, frequently assumes
a spread-wing pose when ashore, as do certain other
species. The posture may help some birds to regulate
body temperature or to balance themselves. Anhingas
are believed to hold out their wings to dry—a necessity because of the porous nature of their feathers,
which absorb more water than the oilier plumage of
ducks and grebes. An Anhinga spends much time
swimming with just its snakelike head and neck
above water. It eats everything from frogs' eggs and
insects to fish and small alligators.

female

83

Great Blue Heron
Ardea herodias

Size: *length, 36–40 in.; height, 4 ft.*
(including head and neck); wingspan, 6 ft.
What to look for: *large size; blue-gray*
appearance; long bill and neck; flies with head
and neck folded back. **Habitat:** *freshwater*
areas, salt marshes.

This wary and powerful bird spears fish or catches them by using its bill like scissors. It also feeds on frogs, snakes, mice, and birds. A Great Blue Heron may slowly stalk its prey or stand motionless waiting for something to come within reach. Though bulky, it can float like a goose and take off from the surface of the water. It nests in colonies, usually in tall trees. Ornithologists have recently concluded that the "Great White Heron," found in Florida, the West Indies, and Mexico, is actually an all-white version of the Great Blue Heron, not a separate species.

adult

immature

Green Heron
Butorides
virescens

Length: *18–22 in.*
What to look for: *small size; brownish*
appearance (white streaks on underside of
immature); red-brown neck; sharp-pointed
bill; orange legs. **Habitat:** *lakes, ponds,*
bogs, freshwater and saltwater marshes.

This species is often seen poised motionless at the water's edge. It is a resourceful and even acrobatic fish catcher and also eats small land animals. It has been observed, for example, perched on a post and leaning down until most of its body was below its feet; from that position it snatched a fish, then righted itself to swallow. Occasionally the heron will dart from its perch and dive underwater after prey. And one individual was spotted apparently using a floating feather to attract small fish to the surface.

Black-crowned Night-heron
Nycticorax nycticorax

Length: *23–26 in.*
What to look for: *black crown and back;*
white below; gray wings; bill dark, stout;
short legs; brown-and-white pattern on immature.
Habitat: *tree-edged marshes, bogs, ponds.*

During daylight hours a sharp eye can pick out a stocky night-heron hunched over at the edge of a pond or in a nearby tree. Night-herons do most of their feeding between dusk and dawn. Although they are mainly fish eaters, a group of them nesting near a tern colony may prey on tern chicks and eggs after dark. A young Black-crowned Night-heron looks much like a young Yellow-crowned Night-heron (*Nycticorax violacea*), a less common·species with an eastern range. But in flight part of the legs of the latter bird projects beyond the tail; the Black-crowned Night-heron shows only the feet.

Snowy Egret
Egretta thula

Length: *22–26 in.*
What to look for: *slim, white bird; filmy plumes (breeding); black bill; legs black, with bright yellow feet.* **Habitat:** *tree-edged wetlands near shallow fresh or brackish water.*

Great Egret
Ardea alba

Length: *36–42 in.*
What to look for: *large white bird; neck long, thin, curved in flight; bill orange-yellow; legs and feet black.* **Habitat:** *wetlands, wet pastures.*

Few birds rival the white egrets in the beauty of their breeding plumage—a beauty that nearly caused their extinction. (Both the Snowy Egret and its larger relative, the Great Egret, were shot by the thousands for their filmy plumes.) In spite of the Snowy Egret's quick, darting motions and golden "slippers," it is often confused with the immature Little Blue Heron (*Egretta caerulea*), a white bird with green legs and feet and a bluish bill. The Reddish Egret (*Egretta rufescens*) has a white phase as well.

Egrets and herons nest in trees, frequently in mixed colonies that include cormorants and ibises. When the male Great Egret (also known as the Common or American Egret) is ready to incubate the eggs, he lands on a branch near the nest; as he approaches, he raises his wings and the long nuptial plumes on his back. His mate reacts by raising her back feathers as he caresses her with his head. After the female leaves, the male settles on the eggs, once more raising and flaring his plumes.

American Bittern
Botaurus lentiginosus

Length: *25–30 in.*
What to look for: *brown and white pattern; white throat; black "whiskers"; outer wing areas dark in flight; yellowish bill.*
Habitat: *marshes, bogs, swamps; occasionally in salt marshes.*

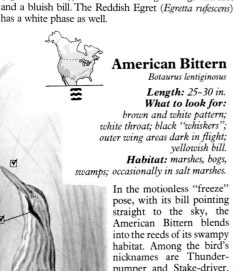

In the motionless "freeze" pose, with its bill pointing straight to the sky, the American Bittern blends into the reeds of its swampy habitat. Among the bird's nicknames are Thunder-pumper and Stake-driver. Both are references to its spring song, which sounds like an old-time water pump or, from a distance, a sledgehammer striking a stake. A bittern swallows air in several gulps, swelling its throat; then it violently constricts its thick neck muscles, expelling the air and producing the pumping sound.

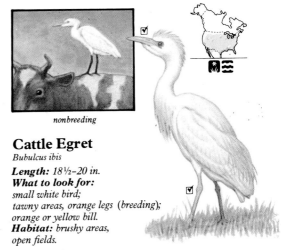

nonbreeding

Cattle Egret
Bubulcus ibis

Length: *18½–20 in.*
What to look for: *small white bird; tawny areas, orange legs (breeding); orange or yellow bill.*
Habitat: *brushy areas, open fields.*

Until late in the 19th century this species was found only in the Old World. Then it began a remarkable range expansion that is still under way. Just how Cattle Egrets crossed the Atlantic (whether by boat or on the wing) is still a question. In any case, they first appeared in South America about 1880, nested in Florida in 1952, and spread rapidly into other states. Often they associate with grazing animals, feeding on insects stirred up by the hooves. They also follow farm tractors, which perform a similar service for these opportunistic birds.

85

Wood Stork
Mycteria americana

Size: *length, 36–42 in.; wingspan, 5½ ft.*
What to look for: *large white bird; head and neck blackish, bare-skinned; bill long, heavy, tapering; black flight feathers.* **Habitat:** *swamps, marshy meadows, shallow freshwater areas.*

This species, formerly called the Wood Ibis, is the only stork in North America. Among the stork's nicknames are Gourdhead and Flinthead, references to the bare, dark skin covering the head and upper neck. Young storks, unlike their parents, are feathered in those areas. Another difference is in voice; although older storks are mostly silent, the young birds produce an unbelievable clamor. One observer heard the grunts, squeals, bleats, and bellows coming from a Wood Stork colony and thought at first that the tremendous uproar was made by Bullfrogs and alligators, for "it hardly seemed credible that birds should make such a noise."

White-faced
Ibis

breeds along coast

in Florida all year

Glossy Ibis

in Florida, western Gulf, and western Mexico

Roseate Spoonbill
Ajaia ajaja

Length: *30–33 in.*
What to look for: *spoon-shaped bill; general pink and white coloration; immature white, with yellowish legs.*
Habitat: *mangrove swamps, coastal islands, shallow lagoons.*

Glossy Ibis
Plegadis falcinellus

Length: *19–26 in.*
What to look for: *overall dark appearance; bill long, curved downward; whitish neck and throat on immature.* **Habitat:** *marshes, shallow ponds, salt or brackish lagoons.*

This handsome bird with bronzy plumage has spread northward in recent years, as have the Cardinal and Northern Mockingbird. For most of this century colonies of Glossy Ibis were confined to Florida and the Gulf states, but now the species breeds along most of the Atlantic coast and strays into Canada. For feeding, the Glossy Ibis prefers a grassy marsh with shallow water. It probes in the mud with its long downward-curved bill, seeking crayfish and mollusks; it also takes insects, frogs, and small fish. A similar species, the less common White-faced Ibis (*Plegadis chihi*), is more western in range; the White Ibis (*Eudocimus albus*) is generally restricted to the Gulf Coast and southeastern states.

A spoonbill moves its partly opened bill from side to side through water or mud, feeling for its prey. When it encounters small fish, shrimp, or shellfish, it snaps its bill shut. If the catch is a fish, the bird may beat it on the water before swallowing. Roseate Spoonbills build stick nests in trees, frequently in company with herons, egrets, cormorants, ibises, and Anhingas. Mainly residents of Florida, the Gulf Coast, and areas to the south, the spoonbills were once much more common than they are today. In the past they were shot for their wings, which were made into fans; today their habitat continues to be reduced. Everglades National Park in Florida and areas near Rockport, Texas, are prime places to see the birds.

Whooping Crane
Grus americana

Size: *length, 4–4½ ft.;*
wingspan, 7–7½ ft.
What to look for: *large*
white bird (immature
tawny); black on wings;
red often visible on head.
Habitat: *northern bogs,*
grasslands, marshes.

This magnificent bird takes its name from its penetrating, bugling voice. The Whooping Crane is a
wary bird, with long legs and neck that permit it to
see long distances across the marshes. Despite its
wariness, it was always an irresistible target for hunters, and fewer than two dozen Whooping Cranes
remained in the wild by the 1940's. Although the
breeding range once included much of central North
America, the species now nests only in a remote area
(Wood Buffalo National Park) in northwestern
Canada. Whooping Cranes are slowly increasing
in number, thanks to intensive conservation efforts.
Since 1993, about 100 juveniles have been released in
central Florida in an attempt to establish a non-
migratory flock. Wintering Whooping Cranes in small
family groups can be readily seen at the Aransas
National Wildlife Refuge in Texas.

Sandhill Crane
Grus canadensis

Size: *length, 3–4 ft.;*
wingspan, 6½–7 ft.
What to look for: *tall gray bird*
(immature pinkish brown);
reddish cap. **Habitat:** *tundra,*
marshes, grasslands; grainfields
(migration, winter).

All of the cranes are spectacular dancers. The Sandhill Crane bows, droops its wings, skips, hops, and
leaps as high as 15 or 20 feet into the air. Pairs perform together during courtship, but dancing is confined neither to the breeding season nor to pairs; hundreds of birds may dance at the same time. Cranes
nest on mounds of vegetation, often surrounded by
water. The female usually lays two eggs, and young
birds stay with their parents for nearly a year. Cranes
eat amphibians, reptiles, insects, and small mammals,
as well as fruits, grain, and other plant material.

Virginia Rail
Rallus limicola

Length: *9–11 in.*
What to look for: *long bill; orange legs; brownish-red breast; flanks barred with white; undertail white.* **Habitat:** *freshwater marshes; salt marshes (mainly in winter).*

North America's rails are elusive birds that generally manage to escape notice. Except in migration, they seldom fly if they can walk. The Virginia Rail usually stays airborne for only a few yards, then drops into the marsh grass and runs into hiding. The King Rail (*Rallus elegans*) of freshwater marshes and the Clapper Rail (*Rallus longirostris*) of salt marshes resemble this species in coloring but are about twice as large.

Sora
Porzana carolina

Length: *9–10 in.*
What to look for: *small trim bird; short bill; black face and throat; flanks barred with white; undertail white; legs yellow-green.* **Habitat:** *wet grasslands, swamps; salt marshes (mainly in winter).*

Though it is seldom seen, the Sora is actually our commonest rail. Like others of its family, it prefers walking to flying; its compressed body enables it to slip between reed stalks without betraying its passage. It feeds on small mollusks, insects, and seeds, notably wild rice. Vocalizations include a rising whistle and a musical descending call.

Mute Swan
Cygnus olor

Length: *4½–5 ft.*
What to look for: *large white bird (immature gray); neck held in S-curve; bill orange, with black tip; black knob at base of upper mandible.* **Habitat:** *lakes, ponds, marshes, sheltered coastal areas.*

Many years ago Mute Swans were brought to North America from Europe. Some escaped from captivity in the New York area and gave rise to a wild population, which has slowly expanded its range. Mute Swans feed on aquatic plants and insects. The nest, built near water or among reeds in the shallows, is a mound of vegetation 3 or 4 feet across. Up to a dozen young (called cygnets) hatch in the depression on top. Mute Swans are not really mute: the cygnets peep, and the adults sometimes hiss or grunt. In flight the stroking of the great wings produces a far-carrying hum.

Tundra Swan
Cygnus columbianus

Length: *4–4½ ft.*
What to look for: *large white bird (immature gray); neck held straight; bill black, usually with yellow spot.* **Habitat:** *tundra lakes, grassland pools; estuaries (winter).*

This stately bird, formerly known as the Whistling Swan, is the most widespread swan in North America. It nests in the Far North, but thousands winter on both the Atlantic and Pacific coasts, as well as on lakes in the interior. During spring and fall its call—not a whistle but a mellow, musical honking—is heard from large flocks as they travel to or from the breeding grounds on the tundra.

Common Moorhen

Gallinula chloropus

Length: *12-14 in.*
What to look for: *dark ducklike bird; frontal shield red (whitish on immature); bill red, yellow-tipped; white along flanks and undertail.* **Habitat:** *weedy edges of rivers, lakes, ponds, marshes.*

The moorhens, along with the rails and coots, belong to the Rallidae, a worldwide family of some 130 species. The Common Moorhen, formerly called the Common Gallinule, has a larger range and is more abundant than the colorful Purple Gallinule (*Porphyrula martinica*) of the southeastern states. Both species swim well, with a characteristic pumping motion of the head. They also move about by walking on floating lily pads.

American Coot

Fulica americana

Length: *13-15 in.*
What to look for: *dark ducklike bird; white bill and frontal shield; whitish undertail.* **Habitat:** *lakes, ponds, marshes, grasslands near water; bays, estuaries (winter).*

Unlike certain kinds of ducks, coots cannot spring into the air from the water's surface. Instead, they patter along on top of the water into the wind until they achieve sufficient lift. Usually, however, they do not bother to take flight; they simply dash to safety farther from shore or disappear into the nearest stand of reeds.

Snow Goose

Chen caerulescens

Length: *24-30 in.*
What to look for: *white bird with black wing tips (white phase); dark body with white head and neck (blue phase).* **Habitat:** *tundra ponds, lakes; grasslands, saltwater (migration).*

From the time they hatch, the two types of Snow Goose are distinct. White-phase goslings are yellowish; blue-phase, olive-green. Audubon believed the blue-phase birds to be immatures; later they were considered a separate species. It was not until 1929 that a nesting area of "Blue Geese" was discovered north of Hudson Bay. By observing nesting birds, scientists learned that the two phases interbreed, and that there is an intermediate phase. They are now considered members of the same species.

blue phase

white phase

Canada Goose

Branta canadensis

Length: *22-40 in.*
What to look for: *white area on cheek; dark neck, back, and tail; white undertail.*
Habitat: *ponds, lakes, bays, estuaries, grasslands.*

North America's commonest goose ranges in size from the small "cackling" race, weighing as little as 2 pounds, to the "giant" race, of up to 18 pounds. Canada Geese nest in all sorts of places. The usual sites are near the water's edge on a moderately elevated platform, such as a small island or muskrat house, but some birds nest on rock ledges in cliffs or in the abandoned tree nests of other large birds. Man's successful efforts at conserving this species have radically changed its migration habits. Wildlife refuges in the central states, for example, now hold many thousands of wintering geese that would previously have traveled much farther south.

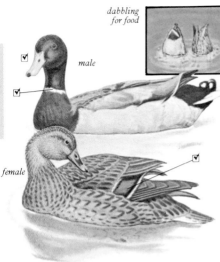

dabbling for food

male

female

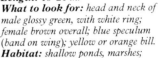

Mallard
Anas platyrhynchos

Length: *16–24 in.*
What to look for: *head and neck of male glossy green, with white ring; female brown overall; blue speculum (band on wing); yellow or orange bill.*
Habitat: *shallow ponds, marshes; sheltered saltwater (winter).*

The commonest duck in the world breeds in Europe, Asia, and North America. Remarkably adaptable to civilization, it will breed in a city park if there is even a small pond. Mallards usually nest near the water's edge, but occasionally they choose a site on higher ground. When the ducks are agitated, they can leap upward from the water into flight and then almost hover in midair before selecting an escape route. Mallards are often seen with just the ends of their tails sticking up out of shallow water as they feed on the plants and small animals found at the bottom. They also eat grain and other foods.

Northern Pintail
Anas acuta

Length: *20–30 in.*
What to look for: *neck long, slim; male with white stripe on neck and long pointed tail; female mottled brown, with shorter tail.*
Habitat: *lakes, ponds, marshes; sheltered saltwater (winter).*

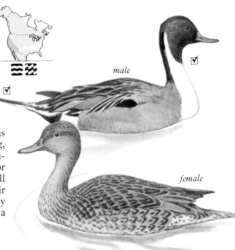

male

female

This slender, graceful duck has as broad a nesting range as the Mallard. Like the Mallard, it is a tip-up, or dabbling, duck. The stripe on the male's neck makes him readily identifiable at a long distance, but females may be mistaken for other kinds of ducks. Between the breeding season and fall migration, the males (drakes) of many species molt their feathers and develop an "eclipse" plumage, in which they look much like the females. The Pintail drake becomes a browner and darker version of his mate.

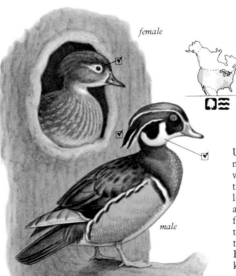

female

male

Wood Duck
Aix sponsa

Length: *18–21 in.*
What to look for: *white throat and facial pattern ("spectacles" on female); crest (not always obvious).*
Habitat: *forest-edged lakes, ponds, swamps, marshes.*

Unless you are on the lookout for this handsome bird, you may hear rather than see it as it flies off quickly through the woods, crying *weep, weep, weep*. Wood Duck females nest in tree cavities or in man-made nest boxes. Up to 15 eggs are laid on a bed of white down and incubated by the female for about four weeks. Soon after hatching, the ducklings jump from the nest hole in response to the call of their mother. If the nesting tree is in an upland area, she then leads her brood to water. Wood Ducks are not the only tree-nesting ducks; Buffleheads, Hooded Mergansers, goldeneyes, and several kinds of whistling (tree) ducks also nest in tree cavities.

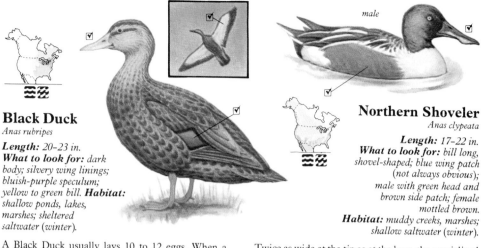

Black Duck
Anas rubripes

Length: *20-23 in.*
What to look for: *dark body; silvery wing linings; bluish-purple speculum; yellow to green bill.* **Habitat:** *shallow ponds, lakes, marshes; sheltered saltwater (winter).*

Northern Shoveler
Anas clypeata

Length: *17-22 in.*
What to look for: *bill long, shovel-shaped; blue wing patch (not always obvious); male with green head and brown side patch; female mottled brown.* **Habitat:** *muddy creeks, marshes; shallow saltwater (winter).*

A Black Duck usually lays 10 to 12 eggs. When a chick is ready to break out of the shell, it chips a row of holes around one end. Eventually the "cap" gives way, and the duckling pushes out—first its head, then one wing, then the other. Finally it lies completely out of the shell, exhausted by the effort. It is wet and appears naked except for a few scattered dark hairs. As the chick dries, these hairs split open; out of each pops a down feather as big as a fingertip. Within a short time a fluffy duckling is ready to follow its mother out of the nest.

Twice as wide at the tip as at the base, the specialized bill of the Shoveler sets it apart from other ducks. As the name implies, the bird uses the bill like a shovel to collect the mud and water from which it strains out its food. Its diet includes snails, water insects, and such small aquatic plants as duckweed. The Shoveler usually nests close to water. In a plant-lined depression the female lays from 8 to 12 eggs at the rate of an egg a day. As the laying goes on, she plucks down from her body and adds it to the nest. She does not start incubating until the last egg is laid.

Blue-winged Teal (*male*)

Green-winged Teal (*male*)

American Wigeon
Anas americana

Length: *18-24 in.*
What to look for: *head of male white on top, with green patch; large white wing patch; white underparts; black tail on male; female brownish above, pale tawny on sides.* **Habitat:** *ponds, lakes, rivers, irrigated land; sheltered saltwater (winter).*

Often called Baldpate because of its snowy cap, the American Wigeon feeds in shallow water, tipping up like the Mallard, Pintail, and other dabbling ducks. Wigeons are sometimes found in the company of coots, scaup, and other diving birds, feeding on the deeper-growing plants that these divers have brought to the surface. As they forage, wigeon may also eat small animals (insects and snails) and young grass. The sounds they make differ according to sex. The male whistles, usually in a quick three-note series— *whew, whew, whew;* the female growls and quacks.

Green-winged Teal
Anas crecca

Length: *12-16 in.*
What to look for: *small size; green eye patch on male; green speculum (not always obvious); vertical white bar on side of male; female mottled brown.* **Habitat:** *shallow ponds, lakes, streams, marshes; sheltered saltwater (occasionally in winter).*

Compact, speeding flocks of little Green-winged Teal turn and twist as if they were controlled by a single force. These birds winter mostly in the southern states and in Mexico, although some remain as far north as Alaska and the Great Lakes. A close relative, the Blue-winged Teal (*Anas discors*), usually winters south of the border; some individuals may cover 7,000 miles as they migrate between northern Canada and southern South America. Blue-winged Teal are generally among the last ducks to arrive on the nesting grounds and the first to leave.

91

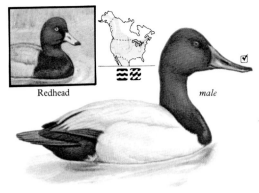

Redhead

male

Canvasback
Aythya valisineria

Length: *19–24 in.*
What to look for: *head with "ski-slope" profile;
male with red-brown head and pale back;
female with brown head, neck, and breast.*
Habitat: *lakes, ponds, marshes;
sheltered saltwater (winter).*

Even at a distance, this handsome duck can be recognized by its long neck and the distinctive profile of its head and bill. The Canvasback is a deep diver, reaching depths of up to 30 feet in its search for small invertebrates and the roots of aquatic plants. Canvasbacks are often found together with Redheads (*Aythya americana*). Though superficially similar, the Redhead has a shorter neck, rounder head, and grayer back.

female

female

male

male

Lesser Scaup
Aythya affinis

Length: *14–18 in.*
What to look for:
*blue bill; white
wing stripe; male with
purple gloss on head;
female with
white at base of bill.*
Habitat: *ponds, lakes,
marshes; sheltered saltwater (winter).*

Ring-necked Duck
Aythya collaris

Length: *15–18 in.*
What to look for: *bill bluish, with
white ring, black tip, and white at base;
male with purple gloss on head, black back,
and white bar on side; female brown,
with white eye-ring and streak to nape.*
Habitat: *forest-edged lakes, ponds, rivers,
marshes; sheltered saltwater (winter).*

On a gray spring morning, when the ice has just melted in a northern pond, a male Ring-necked Duck riding on the dark waters blends into the subtle tints of its setting. The ring on the bird's neck is virtually invisible, and the species might better have been named for the prominent ring around its bill. In flight the Ring-necked Duck can be distinguished from the scaups by its inconspicuous wing stripe.

The Little Bluebill, as old-time hunters called this small diving duck, breeds near small prairie lakes and ponds. Lesser Scaup winter in freshwater or occasionally in protected coastal seas, typically forming dense masses known as rafts. Greater Scaup (*Aythya marila*) are strictly coastal in cold weather. The two scaups look quite similar, but the white wing stripe is more extensive on the Greater Scaup and the head has a green gloss.

Ruddy Duck
Oxyura jamaicensis

Length: *14–17 in.*
What to look for: *dark cap; large white cheek patch (female with
dark slash); blue bill (breeding male); tail short, spiky, usually
erect.* **Habitat:** *lakes, ponds, rivers, marshes; saltwater (winter).*

In the breeding season the richly colored male puts on a remarkable display. He erects the stiff feathers of his tail until they nearly touch the back of his head, flares the feathers over his eyes into "horns," puffs up his neck and breast, and drums on his throat with his bright blue bill. The drumming forces air from his breast feathers so that the water bubbles in front of him. The female usually makes her nest among such standing plants as rushes, which she pulls over to make a sort of roof. The eggs are huge for such a small duck—bigger than those of the Canvasback, which is much larger than a Ruddy Duck.

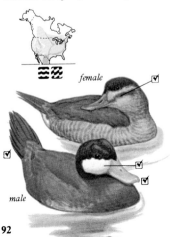

female

male

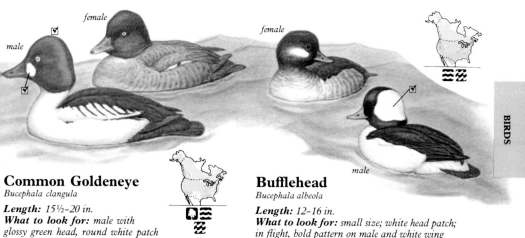

female

male

male

female

female

male

Common Goldeneye
Bucephala clangula

Length: *15½–20 in.*
What to look for: *male with glossy green head, round white patch below eye, black and white back, and white belly; female mottled gray, with tawny head and white neck.*
Habitat: *rivers, lakes; open bays, estuaries (winter).*

The nickname of this strikingly marked diving duck is Whistler, a reference to the ringing sound of its wings in flight. The courtship display of the Common Goldeneye is spectacular. While the male is snapping his head violently back and forth, his mate may lie on the water as if dead. Barrow's Goldeneye (*Bucephala islandica*), common in the West but rare elsewhere, is similar in appearance but is blacker and has a white crescent in front of the eye, and a purplish head. Both goldeneyes nest in cavities in trees.

Bufflehead
Bucephala albeola

Length: *12–16 in.*
What to look for: *small size; white head patch; in flight, bold pattern on male and white wing patch on female.* **Habitat:** *ponds, lakes, rivers; sheltered saltwater (winter).*

The Bufflehead is as lively in courtship as the goldeneye. The male puffs out his snowy crown for extra visibility, snaps his head back and forth, and stands erect with beating wings. When nesting, the female usually chooses a tree cavity excavated by a flicker or other woodpecker. The opening may be only 3 inches in diameter, but somehow the chunky little duck (also known as the Butterball) manages to squeeze in and lay her eggs. The name Bufflehead comes from the little duck's big-headed appearance, which reminded early observers of the buffalo.

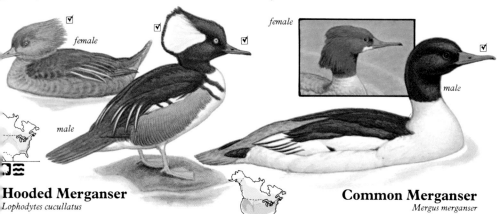

female

male

female

male

Hooded Merganser
Lophodytes cucullatus

Length: *16–20 in.*
What to look for: *narrow, dark bill; male with white breast and black-edged, white crest; female with tawny crest and gray breast.*
Habitat: *forest-edged lakes, rivers, ponds, marshes; occasionally in saltwater.*

Both male and female Hooded Mergansers have rounded, fan-shaped crests. When swimming they hold their crests partly closed (the male fully expands his showy topknot in courtship display). Hooded Mergansers in flight look very different, for their crests are laid completely back. These handsome ducks nest in tree cavities in swampy, woody country, often returning to the nest site of the previous year. They are good divers and feed on the bottom as well as at the surface.

Common Merganser
Mergus merganser

Length: *21–27 in.*
What to look for: *long, slim body; thin reddish bill; male with dark green head and white breast; female with reddish head and shaggy crest.*
Habitat: *lakes, ponds, marshes, rivers in forested areas; open freshwater, sheltered saltwater (winter).*

This fish duck often behaves like a loon or grebe. Hunting for food, it dips its bill and eyes below the surface; it dives well and can ride high or low in the water. Its nickname is Sawbill, a reference to the serrations that help it catch and hold fish. Partial to freshwater, the Common Merganser will remain there in winter as long as fish are plentiful and waters stay open. The Red-breasted Merganser (*Mergus serrator*), or Saltwater Fish Duck, has crests on both sexes and a reddish breast band on the male.

93

BIRDS

Black
Oystercatcher

American
Oystercatcher

American Oystercatcher

Haematopus palliatus

Length: *17–20 in.*
What to look for: *large size; pied pattern;*
long red bill; white wing stripe prominent in flight.
Habitat: *coastal areas.*

Oysters form only part of the diet of this strikingly patterned bird. Both
the American Oystercatcher and its Pacific Coast relative, the Black
Oystercatcher (*Haematopus bachmani*), feed not only on bivalves exposed at low tide but also on barnacles, limpets, snails, and marine
worms. The bills are used to break and pry open shells, to probe
into the sand, and to dislodge small animals clinging to rocks. Oyster
catchers nest in shallow depressions, sometimes lining them with pebbles or bits of shell, plants, or driftwood.

American Avocet

Recurvirostra americana

Length: *15–20 in.*
What to look for: *head and neck cinnamon (gray on*
nonbreeding bird); bill long, upturned; striking
pattern in flight. **Habitat:** *marshes,*
mud flats, beaches, shallow lakes, ponds.

The avocet catches a variety of food with its long, upcurved bill.
Sweeping the bill from side to side along the bottom, it finds some prey
by touch. Aquatic insects are snatched from the surface; flying insects
are caught in midair. Avocets nest in colonies, each female laying an
average of four eggs in a slight hollow. If the sites are flooded, the birds
may quickly build up the nests until they are a foot or more high. The
chicks are long-legged like the adults, but their bills show only a faint
upward turn at first. They are able to swim, dive, and feed themselves
soon after hatching.

Black-necked Stilt

Himantopus mexicanus

Length: *13½–15½ in.*
What to look for: *tall, slim bird; long red legs;*
straight, thin bill; wings, back, and back
of neck black; legs extended well behind when
flying. **Habitat:** *shallow lakes, mud flats,*
marshes, rice fields, other irrigated areas.

Many shorebirds engage in distraction displays when their eggs or
young are threatened. Black-necked Stilts are masters at confusing and
drawing away an intruder. In one type of display the stilt crouches with
its wings spread and quivering. Or it may bob up and down in shallow
water, splashing with its body. It suddenly falls down as if it had broken
a leg, then gets up, takes a few steps, and falls again. Since stilts nest in
colonies, they often perform together, calling loudly in the process.
Ornithologists believe that such displays probably originated in purposeless frenzies caused by the bird's inability to decide whether to run
away or attack.

94

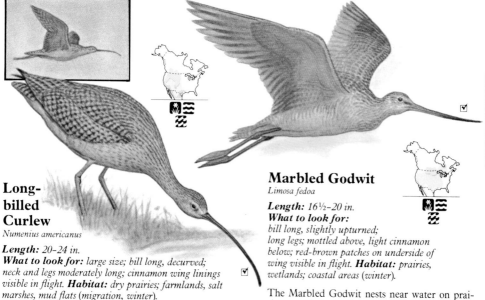

Long-billed Curlew

Numenius americanus

Length: *20-24 in.*
What to look for: *large size; bill long, decurved; neck and legs moderately long; cinnamon wing linings visible in flight.* **Habitat:** *dry prairies; farmlands, salt marshes, mud flats (migration, winter).*

This is the largest North American shorebird, and its sickle-shaped bill is of a size to match. Originally the species nested on the central grasslands, and it suffered when prairies were turned into cropland. In areas that have been returned to grass for grazing purposes, the Long-billed Curlew is returning as well. Flocks of curlews fly high in migration, uttering the melodious whistle that suggests their name. In winter they are indeed shorebirds, for they feed on ocean beaches and salt meadows, where the slightly smaller Whimbrel (*Numenius phaeopus*) is also a common species.

Marbled Godwit

Limosa fedoa

Length: *16½-20 in.*
What to look for:
bill long, slightly upturned; long legs; mottled above, light cinnamon below; red-brown patches on underside of wing visible in flight. **Habitat:** *prairies, wetlands; coastal areas (winter).*

The Marbled Godwit nests near water on prairies, usually laying four eggs in a "saucer" of dry grass. Its food is mainly aquatic—snails, insects, small crustaceans. The species was once much more widespread than it is today. Gunning reduced its numbers, and the conversion of prairies to cultivation drastically restricted the territory available for nesting. The smaller Hudsonian Godwit (*Limosa haemastica*) has a white wing stripe and a broad white band at the base of the tail. It breeds in the Far North, migrates mainly through the middle of the continent, and winters in South America.

Willet

Catoptrophorus semipalmatus

Length: *14-17 in.*
What to look for:
bill long, sturdy; mottled gray plumage; black and white wing pattern visible in flight.
Habitat: *wetlands, moist prairies; salt marshes, beaches (winter).*

Birds often do the unexpected, thereby surprising observers who have only a general familiarity with their habits. Although the Willet is a shorebird and so might not be expected to perch on trees, bushes, and fences, often it does just that. When landing it holds its dramatically marked wings above its head, as if poised for flight. Willets are noisy birds. They often repeat their name—*pill-o-will-o-willet*—but they also have a variety of sharper notes.

Greater Yellowlegs

Tringa melanoleuca

Length: *12-15 in.*
What to look for:
long yellow legs; bill slender, rather long; mottled gray back; white rump and barred tail visible in flight. **Habitat:** *bogs; marshes, streams, ponds, tidal flats (migration, winter).*

With its loud, whistled call (a series of three to five notes), the Greater Yellowlegs is one of the noisiest of the sandpipers. Old-timers called it Tattler or Tell-tale, for its cries signaled the approach of an intruder. During migration this long-legged bird may be seen dashing after minnows in a shallow pool or feeding with other shorebirds on a mud flat. Smaller and with a proportionately shorter, thinner bill, the Lesser Yellowlegs (*Tringa flavipes*) is best identified by the one- or two-syllable call.

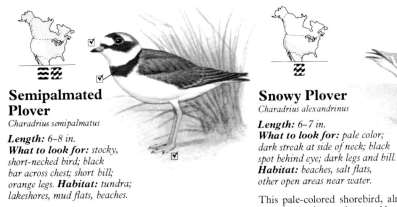

Semipalmated Plover
Charadrius semipalmatus

Length: *6–8 in.*
What to look for: *stocky, short-necked bird; black bar across chest; short bill; orange legs.* **Habitat:** *tundra; lakeshores, mud flats, beaches.*

Despite its bold markings, this shorebird is a fine example of protective coloring. The prominent black band breaks up the plover's outline and makes it virtually invisible against a stony or pebbly background. On beaches where it feeds, its back blends in so well with the wet sand or mud that the bird may escape notice—even at close range—until it moves. The word semipalmated means "half-webbed" and describes the bird's toes, which are webbed for only about half their length.

Snowy Plover
Charadrius alexandrinus

Length: *6–7 in.*
What to look for: *pale color; dark streak at side of neck; black spot behind eye; dark legs and bill.*
Habitat: *beaches, salt flats, other open areas near water.*

This pale-colored shorebird, almost unmarked except for an incomplete neckband, lives mostly on beaches above the high-tide line. Though difficult to spot in such surroundings, it sometimes gives itself away by the plover habit of bobbing its head. On Atlantic beaches the Snowy Plover is replaced by the orange-legged Piping Plover (*Charadrius melodus*). Both species lay speckled eggs in shallow "scrapes," which may be lined with bits of shell or other material. Increasing beach traffic is interfering with the nesting of these small plovers.

breeding

nonbreeding

nonbreeding

breeding

American Golden-plover
Pluvialis dominicus

Length: *9–11 in.*
What to look for: *short neck; upright posture; black below, extending to tail (breeding); speckled with yellow above (breeding); mottled brown (nonbreeding).* **Habitat:** *tundra; mud flats, grasslands (migration).*

Black-bellied Plover
Pluvialis squatarola

Length: *11–15 in.*
What to look for: *black patch under wing; underparts black, except white undertail (breeding); whitish above, with black flecks (breeding); nonbreeding bird grayish.* **Habitat:** *tundra; prairies, wetlands (migration); mud flats, salt marshes (winter).*

Once far more common than today, this trim, fast-flying bird was almost wiped out by market gunners. Audubon, watching near New Orleans in 1821, estimated that the 200 gunners standing within his view would bring down 48,000 birds that day. The species may have been saved by its unusual migration route: in late summer and fall, most Golden-plovers fly nonstop over the Atlantic from Nova Scotia to the South American pampas. Returning in spring, they use a different route: north up the Mississippi Valley.

A shyer bird than the Golden-plover, this species survived the 19th century in greater numbers. Early hunters sometimes wrote admiringly of the Black-bellied Plover's alertness and caution. Its plaintive whistle—*pe-u-eee*—may announce its arrival long before the bird is seen. In marshes and fields it eats grasshoppers, seeds, and berries. But it is more often seen feeding at low tide on mud flats or at the water's edge. Then it will tilt forward to pick up some marine tidbit, run a few steps, and dip again, often pausing with head erect as if listening for danger.

Killdeer
Charadrius vociferus

Length: *8½–11 in.*
What to look for: *2 black bars across upper chest; white collar, forehead, spot behind eye; reddish rump and upper tail; wide white wing stripe visible in flight.*
Habitat: *prairies, meadows, other open areas, coasts, mud flats, irrigated land.*

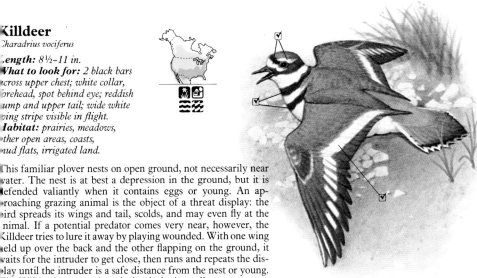

This familiar plover nests on open ground, not necessarily near water. The nest is at best a depression in the ground, but it is defended valiantly when it contains eggs or young. An approaching grazing animal is the object of a threat display: the bird spreads its wings and tail, scolds, and may even fly at the animal. If a potential predator comes very near, however, the Killdeer tries to lure it away by playing wounded. With one wing held up over the back and the other flapping on the ground, it waits for the intruder to get close, then runs and repeats the display until the intruder is a safe distance from the nest or young. The Killdeer's name echoes its loud, ringing call.

Ruddy Turnstone
Arenaria interpres

Length: *7–9 in.*
What to look for: *chunky bird; orange legs; black and white pattern on head and chest; red-brown back (nonbreeder dusky); striking color pattern in flight.*
Habitat: *tundra; coasts (migration, winter).*

Turnstones use their bills to get at animal food under stones, as well as under shells and driftwood. An object too heavy for one bird may be rolled aside by two working together. Or a single bird will put its breast against the object and shove. Ruddy Turnstones also dig in drifts of debris along the tide line, tossing bits of seaweed and shells about in what one observer called a perfect shower. In the process, this stocky shorebird may excavate a hole nearly big enough to furnish a place to hide.

Black Turnstone
Arenaria melanocephala

Length: *about 9 in.*
What to look for: *blackish gray above and on chest, white below; legs and feet blackish; black and white pattern in flight.*
Habitat: *tundra; rocky coasts (migration, winter).*

Unlike the Ruddy Turnstone, which nests in Arctic regions around the world, the Black Turnstone breeds only on the Alaskan coast, where its nest is usually a grass-lined hollow in the mud. Both parents help brood the eggs during the 21-day incubation period. Black Turnstones are the sentinels of the tundra shore. Ever alert, they will pursue even the fiercest predatory birds, uttering high-pitched alarm notes during the chase. When danger threatens the nest, they call sharply *peet, weet, weet*—quite like the call of the familiar Spotted Sandpiper.

nonbreeding

nonbreeding

breeding

breeding

breeds in Alaska and on Canadian islands

breeding

Long-billed Dowitcher
Limnodromus scolopaceus

Length: 9½–10½ in.
What to look for: *bill long, sturdy, held straight down in feeding; mottled above, with rusty breast (breeding); rump and lower back white; tail white, barred with black.*
Habitat: *tundra; pools, marshes, tidal flats (migration, winter).*

Some closely related birds seem designed to confuse people. The two dowitcher species—the Long-billed and the Short-billed (*Limnodromus griseus*)—are such a pair. Even when the two are seen together, the difference in bill length is not easily detected. There is a slight difference in overall size (the Long-billed is larger). And the voices differ: although each species utters a one-syllable note (singly or in a series), the Long-billed's squeaky *keek* contrasts with the low-pitched *tu* of its relative.

Sanderling *Calidris alba*

Length: 7–8 in.
What to look for: *mottled red head, chest, and back (breeding); gray above, white below (nonbreeding); black legs and bill; wide white wing stripe visible in flight.* **Habitat:** *tundra; sandy shores (migration, winter).*

The "little one of the sands" is the shorebird most partial to the outer beach. Sanderlings feed right at the margin of the water, where incoming waves drop their load of food. A line of birds will scamper forward, pecking rapidly, eating on the run, then retreating as the next wave approaches. Large flocks may easily be spooked, but small groups will not take wing when a beach walker approaches.

Red Knot
Calidris canutus

Length: 10–11 in.
What to look for: *plump, short-necked bird; short bill; breast red-brown (whitish on nonbreeding bird).*
Habitat: *tundra; tidal flats, beaches (migration, winter).*

The word "knot" is thought by some to be linked to the Danish king Canute, who, it was said, liked to eat this kind of bird. Others point out that knots often utter a low, clucking *knut*. Red Knots breed in Arctic regions around the globe and migrate as far south as Australia and South America. They travel in tight formations, often making astonishingly synchronized turns, swoops, and upward dashes. On the flats at low tide they feed in close ranks, plodding along in a businesslike fashion as they probe the mud for food.

Dunlin *Calidris alpina*

Length: 8–9 in.
What to look for: *black belly (breeding); bill long, drooping at tip; brownish red above (breeding).* **Habitat:** *tundra; marshes, ponds, tidal areas (migration, winter).*

Sometimes called the Red-backed Sandpiper (a reference to its breeding plumage), this species winters along both coasts. Dunlins feed on wet surfaces, tapping them with slightly open bills. One ornithologist examined a mud flat where Dunlins had recently fed; it was dotted with innumerable shallow dents, "not much larger than those on a thimble," he reported. When the food, often a marine worm, is located, the bird inserts its bill and pulls it out.

nonbreeding

breeding

breeding

nonbreeding

Western Sandpiper
Calidris mauri

Length: *6–7 in.*
What to look for: *bill long (especially on female), drooping at tip; black legs; reddish above, streaked on face and chest (grayer on nonbreeding bird); often feeds in deeper water than other small sandpipers.* **Habitat:** *tundra; marshes, mud flats, coastal areas (migration, winter).*

The small sandpipers are collectively referred to as peeps. Among them are several that cannot easily be told apart, especially when the birds are not in breeding plumage. The different calls are helpful in identification. The Western Sandpiper most often gives a high, squeaky *cheep* or *chireep*, suggesting the call of a young robin. The Semipalmated Sandpiper's call is a lower-pitched *krip, cherk,* or *chrruk.* That of the Least Sandpiper is a soft, high-pitched *breep* or *threep.* Some knowledge of migration routes will also make identification easier. The Western Sandpiper, for instance, migrates mostly down the Pacific Coast, where the Semipalmated is extremely rare.

nonbreeding

breeding

mixed flock
of shorebirds

immature

Least Sandpiper
Calidris minutilla

Length: *5–6 in.*
What to look for: *small size; dark brown back (paler on nonbreeding bird); streaked breast; yellow legs; often feeds in grassy and muddy areas.* **Habitat:** *tundra, northern wetlands; marshes, shores of ponds, mud flats, tidal areas (migration, winter).*

The smallest North American sandpipers are sometimes called mud peeps because of their fondness for oozy tidal flats. Like most other sandpipers, the male of this species performs a courtship flight. He rises with wings bent downward and vibrating, flutters in circles, and trills repeatedly. He may climb as high as 150 feet and often changes altitude during a sustained performance. He also sings from the ground. The songs are variable in sound; one observer noted a particularly lovely series of pure, sweet trills progressing up an octave in a minor key.

Semipalmated Sandpiper
Calidris pusilla

Length: *5–7 in.*
What to look for: *mottled grayish brown above (grayer on nonbreeding bird), white below; black legs and feet.* **Habitat:** *tundra; lakeshores, wetlands, coasts (migration, winter).*

Often seen in large flocks with other peeps, the Semipalmated Sandpiper may be the commonest North American shorebird. Its young, like those of most shorebirds, are able to leave the nest within hours of hatching. Pale below and buffy with light markings above, the chicks blend well with their tundra surroundings and literally disappear once they stop toddling along. In Alaska, a Snowy Owl was seen flying toward a female sandpiper and her brood. They flattened and froze. The owl reached the spot, poised above it, and then flew on, apparently unable to locate its camouflaged prey.

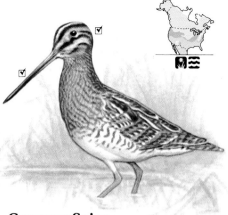

American Woodcock
Scolopax minor
Length: *10–12 in.*
What to look for: *chunky, short-legged bird; long bill; rounded wings; short tail; wings whistle when bird suddenly takes flight.*
Habitat: *moist woodlands near clearings; alder thickets, wet bottomlands.*

The male woodcock's spring courtship display begins with thin, nasal *peenting* at dusk and dawn (sometimes at night). Then the bird takes off, its wings producing a musical flutter as it rises two or three hundred feet in the air. Circling randomly, it begins a bubbly chipping that it continues as it descends. The American Woodcock prefers somewhat drier territory than the Common Snipe, but the two may occur in the same area. At a quick glance they look somewhat alike. A "flushed" woodcock, however, goes off in a straight line instead of zigzagging. Another difference is the barring on the heads, which is crosswise on the woodcock and lengthwise on the snipe.

Common Snipe
Gallinago gallinago
Length: *10–12 in.*
What to look for: *bill long, slender; head, throat, and back streaked; dark rump; moderately long legs.* **Habitat:** *freshwater marshes, swamps, bogs, wet meadows, streamsides.*

Snipe and woodcock are technically sandpipers, though in habitat and range they are vastly different from most of their relatives. Snipe are birds of the marshy meadows. The male is famed for his spectacular courtship flights, often performed at dusk in spring. From high above, where the bird may be out of sight, a humming, winnowing sound filters down to earth. This eerie sound is not vocal. It is produced as air is forced through the bird's fanned-out tail feathers during his successive swoops and dives.

Solitary Sandpiper
Tringa solitaria
Length: *7–9 in.*
What to look for: *white eye ring; barred tail; legs long, dark; no white wing stripe.*
Habitat: *forested wetlands, edges of lakes, streams; occasionally in coastal areas (winter).*

This slim and elegant bird is an unusual sandpiper: it lays its eggs not on the ground but in old tree nests of such birds as robins and grackles. It feeds in marshes and swamps, on mud flats, along slow-moving brooks, and around ponds and puddles. Although it may be confused with the Spotted Sandpiper, the Solitary Sandpiper is not as restless, teeters much less, and shows no wing stripe when it flies. Its *peet-weet, peet-weet-weet* calls, similar to those of the Spotted Sandpiper, have a thinner, higher quality.

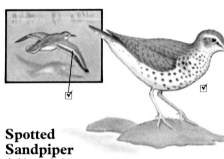

Spotted Sandpiper
Actitis macularia
Length: *7–8 in.*
What to look for: *back dark; underside white with round black spots (breeding); white wing stripe in flight.*
Habitat: *pebbly edges of rivers, streams, lakes, ponds; occasionally in coastal areas (migration, winter).*

The nicknames given the Spotted Sandpiper—Tip-up, Teeter-bob, Teeter-tail—point out the characteristic action by which it can be identified. As the bird moves along, it continually tips forward and backward. When disturbed, it flies low, with wings held at or below the horizontal. Unlike the typical sandpiper, female "Spotties" are not monogamous: they may mate with two or three males. Only the last male gets help from the female in incubating the eggs and caring for the young.

Upland Sandpiper
Bartramia longicauda

Length: *9½–10½ in.*
What to look for: *small head; long neck; brownish above, white below, with mottled breast and flanks; outer wing feathers much darker than rest of wing and back; central tail feathers dark brown, outer ones barred.*
Habitat: *grasslands, prairies, cultivated fields.*

This long-winged bird flies very high on migration and sometimes also during courtship. When it drops to earth it may dive with wings closed and brake only a few feet from the ground. It lands gently and holds its wings open above its back for a moment, then folds them carefully. The Upland Sandpiper's voice can be extremely moving. "Once heard in its perfection it will never be forgotten," promised one ornithologist. The common call is a "sweet, mellow, rolling trill." With some ploverlike habits, this species was once called a sandpiper, then a plover. Recently it has been classified as a sandpiper once again.

Wilson's Phalarope
Phalaropus tricolor

Length: *8–10 in.*
What to look for: *neck long, slender; thin bill; female with black and red stripe on neck; male paler, less reddish; gray above on nonbreeding bird.*
Habitat: *areas with pools of shallow water, including marshes and tidal flats.*

Phalaropes are remarkable birds in several respects. Although technically shorebirds, they spend much time swimming in open water. When they breed, it is the colorful females that do the courting and the drab males that build the nest, incubate the eggs, and raise the young. Wilson's Phalarope is the phalarope most likely to be seen, for it is mainly a freshwater species. It feeds in the middle of shallow prairies lakes and ponds, sinning around in circles and dabbing for floating food with its long slender bill. The Red and the Northern Phalarope (*Phalaropus fulicaria* and *lobatus*) are more marine.

Pectoral Sandpiper
Calidris melanotos

Length: *8–9 in.*
What to look for: *breast buffy, with rows of vertical dashes, sharply separated from white underparts; yellowish legs.* **Habitat:** *tundra; wetlands, ponds, meadows, marshes (migration).*

These far-ranging shorebirds breed from Alaska east to Hudson Bay and winter in South America. On their trip north, made mostly through the central states, they stop over in marshes and grasslands instead of the mud flats and beaches favored by other sandpipers. This species is likely to stand motionless when alarmed, then take off in a zigzag flight. On the Arctic breeding grounds, displaying males puff out an inflatable sac in their throats and utter deep, resounding booms or hoots.

male

Wilson's Phalarope

female

Ring-billed Gull

Larus delawarensis

Length: *17–20 in.*
What to look for: *light gray mantle; wing tips black, with white spots; bill yellow, with black ring near tip; yellow legs; immature with narrow black band on tail.* **Habitat:** *lakes, rivers, coasts, garbage dumps.*

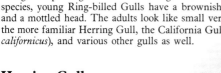

immature

adult

The different kinds of gulls are often difficult to identify. Success depends on sorting out a number of details: relative size; color of the head, of the back and upper wing surface (or mantle), and of the bill and legs; markings on the wing tips and tail. Gulls also undergo both seasonal and growth changes in plumage. Like immature gulls of many other species, young Ring-billed Gulls have a brownish mantle and a mottled head. The adults look like small versions of the more familiar Herring Gull, the California Gull (*Larus californicus*), and various other gulls as well.

Herring Gull

Larus argentatus

Length: *22–26 in.*
What to look for: *mantle light gray; wing tips black, with white spots; yellow bill (red spot near tip); pinkish legs; juvenile (very young) and immature bird brownish, with dark tail.* **Habitat:** *lakes, rivers, coasts, garbage dumps.*

adult

This widespread species plays an important role in cleaning up harbors and beaches. But the Herring Gull is more than a scavenger. It relishes crabs and other marine tidbits, and is well known for cracking clams open by dropping them on rocks and roads. It also preys on the eggs and young of other birds. Herring Gulls nest in colonies, usually in dunes behind the high-tide line. Nests are crude affairs of sticks, seaweed, and other vegetation. The fuzzy, spotted chicks peck at the conspicuous red spot on the adult's bill when they are ready for a meal of regurgitated food.

juvenile

immature

Great Black-backed Gull

Larus marinus

Length: *27–32 in.*
What to look for: *black mantle; bill yellow, with reddish spot near tip; pink legs; immature with dark bill and narrow white tip on tail.* **Habitat:** *coasts, shores of large lakes and rivers, garbage dumps.*

Like the Herring Gull, the world's largest gull is expanding its range to the south. The Great Black-backed Gull is a scavenger and predator. In any mixed gathering of gulls, this impressive bird usually occupies the highest perch, dominating the others and often robbing them of their food. Another dark-backed species is the Western Gull (*Larus occidentalis*). Common along the Pacific Coast, it is a smaller bird, with a slate-colored mantle instead of a black one.

immature

adult

adult

immature

Laughing Gull
Larus atricilla

Length: *15–17 in.*
What to look for: *small size; head black (breeding) or white with gray nape patch (nonbreeding); mantle dark gray; wing tips black; wing with white trailing edge; immature dark above and on breast, with dark band on tail.* **Habitat:** *coasts, estuaries, salt marshes.*

Laughing Gulls are never found far from the coast, though small groups visit freshwater to bathe and drink. They also visit plowed fields in search of earthworms and insects. In southern waters these gulls keep company with Brown Pelicans and steal fish from their pouches. Laughing Gulls sometimes scavenge in dumps, and frequently they follow fishing boats for refuse and handouts. Their name comes from their hearty but wailing *ha-ha-ha*.

Franklin's Gull
Larus pipixcan

Length: *14–16 in.*
What to look for: *all plumages similar to Laughing Gull's, but adult Franklin's Gull has narrow white band separating gray mantle from black wing tips.* **Habitat:** *prairies, marshes, ponds; coasts (winter).*

Although a close relative of the saltwater-loving Laughing Gull, Franklin's Gull breeds far inland, in prairie marshes. Its floating nest is built of dead reeds and anchored to growing vegetation. In summer large bands of these graceful fliers can be seen circling over the grasslands like pigeons, catching flying insects on the wing. The species was named for Sir John Franklin, a 19th-century explorer.

nonbreeding adult

breeding

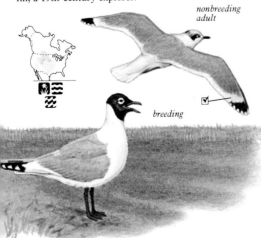

Heermann's Gull
Larus heermanni

Length: *17–20 in.*
What to look for: *only all-dark gull with lighter head; red bill; immature dark brownish gray.* **Habitat:** *coasts, offshore waters (post-breeding, winter).*

This darkest of gulls is an oddity, not only for its color but for its migratory habits. Heermann's Gulls nest on Mexican islands in spring. After breeding, part of the population spends the summer far to the north, then winters off California. Meanwhile, others migrate south to Guatemala for the summer. Heermann's Gulls, like Laughing Gulls, often rob pelicans of their catch, but they also take their own fish by snapping them up from the surface.

Bonaparte's Gull
Larus philadelphia

nonbreeding

Length: *12–14 in.*
What to look for: *small size; black head (nonbreeding white, with black spot behind eye); light gray mantle; white triangle on outer wing; black bill; reddish legs.* **Habitat:** *muskeg; coasts, estuaries (winter).*

winters in Great Lakes

Bonaparte's Gulls breed in boggy, forested areas of the North, where they build stick nests in spruces. Occasionally as high as 20 feet off the ground, the nests are lined with grass and moss. In winter, flocks of Bonaparte's Gulls appear on both coasts. These small gulls fly in a light, bouncy, ternlike fashion and feed on the wing by picking up small fish and crustaceans from the surface of the water. They are named not for the famous emperor Napoleon but for his nephew Charles Lucien Bonaparte, an ornithologist.

nonbreeding

Forster's Tern
Sterna forsteri

Length: *13½–16 in.*
What to look for: *tail deeply forked; mantle gray, with white outer wing; breeding bird with black-tipped reddish-orange bill and black cap; nonbreeding bird with white head, black eye streak, and mostly black bill.*
Habitat: *marshes, lakes, ponds, coasts.*

A typical tern in appearance, with its forked tail and long pointed wings, Forster's Tern is not typical in behavior. It is a bird of the marshes, seldom seen on the beaches where many of its relatives breed. Its nest is often a neat grass-lined cup, not a mere scrape in the sand. And it has the unternlike habit of catching insects on the wing. Where several species of terns occur, Forster's can be recognized by its nasal, low-pitched *zrurr, zreep,* or *tza-aap.*

Common Tern
Sterna hirundo

Length: *13–15 in.*
What to look for: *tail deeply forked; mantle gray, with some black on outer wing; breeding bird with black-tipped red bill, black cap, and reddish legs and feet; nonbreeding bird with white forehead and crown, black eye streak and nape.*
Habitat: *marshes, lakes, coasts.*

Terns on the wing are a pleasure to watch. Graceful, buoyant, and swift, Common Terns are a familiar sight hovering over inland lakes, saltwater harbors, and nesting beaches. The breeding range of the similar Arctic Tern (*Sterna paradisaea*) overlaps the Common Tern's in the Northeast, and there the species are easily confused. Even their calls—a penetrating *kee-arr* and *kip-ki-kip*—sound much alike.

Least Tern *Sterna antillarum*

Length: *8–9 in.* **What to look for:** *small size; tail slightly forked; yellow bill; black cap and eye stripe (breeding); white forehead; mantle gray with black outer wing feathers; feet and legs yellowish.*
Habitat: *mud flats, beaches, rivers, estuaries, coasts.*

Like other terns, the smallest North American species usually breeds in colonies. The female lays two or three speckled eggs in a shallow scrape in the sand, sometimes lined with vegetation, pebbles, or bits of shell. The young birds hatch as sand-colored chicks and can fly in their third week. This species has earned the nickname Little Striker because of the way it hovers above the water and plunges for fish.

Black Skimmer
Rynchops niger

Length: *16–18 in.*
What to look for: *large size; bill heavy, red, black-tipped, with long lower mandible; black above, white below; immature mottled brown above.*
Habitat: *salt marshes, coasts, estuaries, lagoons.*

The Cutwater, as this relative of the gulls and terns was once called, flies along just above the surface, with the tip of its lower bill held submerged. In this position it skims, or scoops up, small fish and crustaceans. The lower jaw may be an inch longer than the upper, and grows about twice as fast because of continual wearing by the water. Skimmers also feed while wading in the shallows—dipping for their prey just like "a chick picking up a worm on dry land," as one observer wrote.

Black Tern

Chlidonias niger

Length: *8½-10 in.*
What to look for: *small size; appears very dark in flight; head and belly black (some white on nonbreeding birds); dark gray mantle, rump, and tail.*
Habitat: *lakes, ponds, marshes; coasts (migration).*

Though the Black Tern is frequently seen along the coast, it breeds on inland lakes and in freshwater or brackish marshes. The nest is built in a slightly elevated situation surrounded by water, such as the top of a muskrat house. The other dark-backed species likely to be seen in North American waters are the Sooty Tern (*Sterna fuscata*) and the Brown Noddy (*Anous stolidus*), which breed in the Dry Tortugas, southwest of the Florida Keys.

Common Murre

Uria aalge

Length: *14-16 in.*
What to look for: *black above, white below; bill long, thin; nonbreeding bird with more white on head; usually seen offshore when not breeding.*
Habitat: *rocky coasts, islands, islets; open seas (winter).*

Common Murres breed in large colonies on ocean cliffs. The female lays a single pear-shaped egg on bare rock (the shape makes it less likely that the egg will roll off a narrow ledge). Before the young can fly, they leave the cliff—by plunging into the sea. In the water they join up with adults (not necessarily their parents), who feed them for several weeks. Murres fish while swimming underwater, and each year many thousands are accidentally killed in commercial salmon nets.

nonbreeding

Caspian Tern

Sterna caspia

Length: *19-22 in.*
What to look for: *large size; heavy red bill; black cap (forehead streaked with white on nonbreeding bird); mantle gray; outer wings blackish on underside; black legs and feet.*
Habitat: *lakes, marshes, estuaries, coasts.*

The Caspian Tern is almost as big as a Herring Gull, and with its soaring flight, it behaves like one. It breeds around the world, nesting along the shores of lakes and oceans; the first description of the species was based on a specimen collected on the Caspian Sea. The Royal Tern (*Sterna maxima*), of our southern coasts, is almost as large, but has a thinner bill, shorter legs, and at most times a white forehead.

Tufted Puffin

Atlantic Puffin

Fratercula arctica

Length: *10-13 in.*
What to look for: *bill large, colorful, flattened at sides; black above, with white face and breast; nonbreeding bird with blackish face and smaller bill; flies with rapid wingbeats.*
Habitat: *rocky coasts; open seas (winter).*

The clown of the Atlantic chases fish by literally flying after them underwater. In the nesting season an adult may bring back to its burrow more than 20 small fish in a single beakful. Young puffins are fed by their parents in their burrows for as long as 50 days; after that, they feed themselves at sea. In the Pacific the Tufted Puffin (*Lunda cirrhata*) breeds on islands from southern California north to Alaska.

105

vulture　　accipiter　　buteo　　eagle　　osprey　　harrier　　falcon

Sorting out the birds of prey. A vulture has broad wings and a small head. An accipiter is a hawk with rounded wings and a long tail; a buteo, a hawk with broad wings and a short tail. The wings of an eagle are very long and broad; those of an osprey are narrow and bent back at the wrist. A harrier (Marsh Hawk) is slim, with long pointed wings and longish tail. A falcon also has pointed wings.

Turkey Vulture
Cathartes aura

Size: *length, 26–32 in.; wingspan, 6 ft.*
What to look for: *large black bird; bare red head (blackish on immature); long tail; holds wings in V when soaring.*
Habitat: *various land habitats, especially around dead trees.*

Turkey Buzzards, as old-timers call them, are magnificent fliers. Alone or by the dozen, they sail for hours high in the sky, rocking slightly from side to side and holding their wings in a shallow V. The Black Vulture (*Coragyps atratus*), a more southern species, holds its wings flat and flaps them frequently; the Turkey Vulture flaps mainly when seeking updrafts at low altitudes. Vultures eat some live prey, but most of their food is carrion. The largest vulture in North America, the endangered California Condor (*Gymnogyps californianus*), has a 10-foot wingspan.

Broad-winged Hawk
Buteo platypterus

Length: *13½–19 in.*
What to look for: *tail broadly barred with black and white; wings mostly whitish below; breast with brownish-red bars; immature with streaks on underside and more finely barred tail.*
Habitat: *deciduous forests.*

Sharp-shinned Hawk
Accipiter striatus

Length: *10–14 in.*
What to look for: *small size; wings short, rounded; tail long, barred; breast finely striped with cinnamon.*
Habitat: *woodlands, brushy areas.*

This is the smallest of the North American accipiters, the dashing hawks that prey on birds and small mammals. Female accipiters are larger than the males. The largest species is the Goshawk (*Accipiter gentilis*) of the northern forests. Cooper's Hawk (*Accipiter cooperii*) resembles the Sharp-shinned Hawk but is a heavier, more deliberate flier. Accipiters fly by flapping their wings a few times, then gliding with wings flat or slightly bowed, then flapping a few more times.

This forest-loving buteo is quiet, almost sedentary in behavior. But in the breeding season the pairs are conspicuous as they soar overhead, whistling *p'deeee, p'deeee*. Their migration is spectacular. The birds proceed by spiraling up on a thermal—a column of warmed, rising air—and then gliding on to the next. As they go, they collect in large groups (kettles) that string out in long lines between thermals, often too high to be seen by the naked eye.

Red-tailed Hawk
Buteo jamaicensis

Size: *length, 19–26 in.; wingspan, 4½ ft.*
What to look for: *bright rufous tail, conspicuous in flight; throat and underparts white, usually with dark belly band; immature with fine barring on brown tail.* **Habitat:** *all types of land habitats, especially open woodlands.*

The distant, soaring buteo that holds its position in a stiff breeze as if "pinned to the sky" is a Red-tailed Hawk. Plumage variations within this species are great; some western birds, for example, are extremely dark; others are very pale. Red-tails hunt from the air and from exposed perches, such as the tops of dead trees. The bulk of their diet is small mammals. Other large buteos include the less common Ferruginous Hawk (*Buteo regalis*) of western grasslands and the Rough-legged Hawk (*Buteo lagopus*), ·an Arctic breeder.

Red-shouldered Hawk
Buteo lineatus

Size: *length, 17–24 in.; wingspan, 3½ ft.*
What to look for: *reddish-brown shoulder patch; rufous below, including underwings near body; tail long, with wide black and narrow white bars; immature lacking patch, streaked with brown below.* **Habitat:** *moist open forests, bottomlands, other wet areas.*

This strikingly marked species is not so conspicuous in its behavior as the Red-tailed Hawk: it soars less frequently and usually perches below the treetops. The nest is built in a big tree, most often in a substantial crotch. The female lays two or three eggs—occasionally more. Incubation lasts about three and a half weeks, with both parents sharing the job (they also raise the chicks together). Five or six weeks after hatching, the young leave the nest. Red-shouldered Hawks eat a wide variety of prey—small mammals, birds, frogs, snakes, lizards, snails, and insects.

Swainson's Hawk
Buteo swainsoni

Length: *19–22 in.*
What to look for: *tail finely barred, with broad band near tip; dark above; underside all dark (dark phase) or mostly white with dark breast band (light phase); immature with heavily streaked breast.* **Habitat:** *brushlands, plains, open forests, foothills.*

A western species common on the Great Plains, Swainson's Hawk travels in groups on migration, as does the Broad-winged Hawk. In flight it holds its wings slightly above the horizontal—a useful identification clue. When a migrating group settles to roost for the night, some of them will rest on the ground if there is a shortage of tree perches. They often feed on the ground as well, hopping after crickets and grasshoppers. They catch gophers by perching on hillocks of earth in front of the rodents' burrows and waiting for an unwary individual to appear.

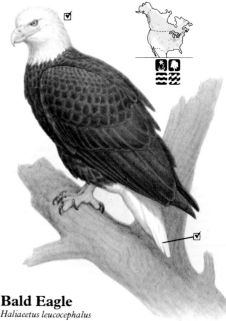

Golden Eagle
Aquila chrysaetos

Size: *length, 30-41 in.; wingspan, to 7½ ft.*
What to look for: *large size; wings held level when soaring; dark brown, with golden-brown crown and nape; immature with white at base of tail and flight feathers.*
Habitat: *remote open areas, mountains, forests.*

Golden Eagles are magnificent fliers and dashing hunters. Fast enough to take grouse and ptarmigan on the wing, they usually prey on ground squirrels, prairie dogs, and rabbits. They will attack mammals up to the size of deer, especially in winter, though they cannot carry off the heavier animals. Golden Eagles build large stick nests on rock ledges or in trees and have been known to defend breeding territories of up to 75 square miles. The young birds, with conspicuous white areas on their wings and tail, look very different from the adults.

Bald Eagle
Haliaeetus leucocephalus

Size: *length, 35–40 in.; wingspan, to 7½ ft.*
What to look for: *large size; head, neck, and tail white; rest of plumage dark brown; immature brown, with whitish wing linings.*
Habitat: *open areas, forests, near water.*

This bird is "bald" not because its head is featherless but because the head of the adult is white—an old meaning of the word. Bald Eagles probably mate for life. They build a nest in a tree, on a cliff, or even on the ground and add to it each year, using such materials as sticks, weeds, and earth, until it may weigh a thousand pounds or more. One observer saw a bird lift and fly away with the top of a muskrat house—presumably as a handy package of nest makings. Bald Eagles eat carrion, waterfowl, and especially fish. Past declines caused by pesticides have been reversed due to environmental clean-ups and programs of re-introduction of eagles.

Osprey
Pandion haliaetus

Size: *length, 21–25 in.; wingspan, to 6 ft.*
What to look for: *white head, with dark stripe through eye; brown above, mostly white below; wings long, crooked in flight, with dark patch below at bend.*
Habitat: *usually near large bodies of water.*

The Osprey, or Fish Hawk, sights its prey while hovering, then plunges feetfirst into the water. Sharp talons pierce and lock into the fish; when the bird rises, it is almost always carrying its catch headfirst. Ospreys nest on dead trees, floating buoys, utility poles and towers, and rarely (if undisturbed) on the ground. The stick nest may contain rope and miscellaneous debris that has washed up on shore, as well as sprigs of greenery—a characteristic also common to hawk and eagle nests. In recent years the Osprey has begun to recover from the disastrous effects of pesticides and other pollutants.

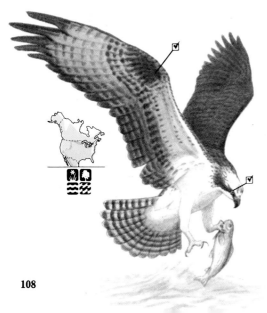

Northern Harrier

Circus cyaneus

Length: *17–24 in.*
What to look for: *long wings and tail; white rump; male gray above, white below; female and immature dark brown above, lighter below.*
Habitat: *prairies, open areas, all types of marshes.*

This species, formerly called the Marsh Hawk, is a relentless hunter. With its long wings held up in a slight V, it pursues—or "harries"—its quarry, zigzagging low over field or marsh. On nesting territory the gray male dives and climbs, dives and climbs, in what one watcher likened to a series of capital U's. Or he may tumble from high up. When he brings food to his brown mate on the ground nest, she flies up, he drops his prey, and she catches it in midair—or they may make the exchange claw to claw, without his alighting.

female

BIRDS

Prairie Falcon

Falco mexicanus

Length: *17–20 in.*
What to look for: *pointed wings; long tail; light brown above, with head pattern; whitish below, with dark streaks on underside and black patch at base of wings.*
Habitat: *open areas in mountains, prairies, deserts.*

Falcons have been admired through the centuries for their powers of flight. The large species, like the Prairie Falcon, prey mostly on birds, which they sometimes pick out of the air in spectacular dives, striking with extended talons. Like most members of its family, this species is not much of a nest builder. The female, somewhat bigger than the male but similar in appearance, lays her eggs on top of a high, isolated rock or on a cliff ledge; or she may take over the abandoned nest of another bird, commonly a raven.

Peregrine Falcon

Falco peregrinus

Length: *15–20 in.*
What to look for: *pointed wings; long tail; bluish gray above, with blackish "mustache" and finely barred whitish breast; immature brown above, with brown "mustache" and brown streaks below.*
Habitat: *open areas from mountains to coasts.*

In North America this worldwide species used to be called the Duck Hawk. Fully capable of taking ducks and other water birds, the Peregrine is an extremely fast flier (one individual was clocked in a dive at 275 miles an hour). In the eastern United States the Peregrine has been wiped out as a breeding species by a combination of pesticides and human disturbance. Now, however, a novel restocking project aims at creating a new population of wild birds.

American Kestrel

Falco sparverius

Length: *9–12 in.*
What to look for: *small size; male rufous, with blue-gray wings, dark facial pattern, and black band near tip of tail; female with rufous wings and blackish bars on rufous back and tail; hovering behavior.* **Habitat:** *open wooded areas, prairies, deserts, farmlands, suburbs, cities.*

female

male

This adaptable little falcon is regularly seen hunting along parkways and in suburban fields. It has two hunting techniques. It may wait on a treetop, pole, or telephone wire until it sights its prey; then it takes off in a dive or glide. Or it may fly out over a field and hover on fast-beating wings before it drops. The American Kestrel used to be called the Sparrow Hawk. It does eat birds, but takes many more insects and small mammals.

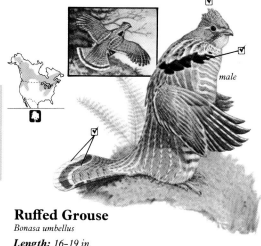

Ruffed Grouse
Bonasa umbellus

Length: *16–19 in.*
What to look for: *small crest; blackish ruff (shorter on female); tail fan-shaped when spread, edged with white and black; mottled brown, gray, or reddish above.*
Habitat: *mixed or deciduous forests.*

Members of the grouse family have a variety of courtship displays. The male Ruffed Grouse stands on a log and drums the air with his wings, slowly at first, then fast, producing a soft, far-carrying *thump, thump, thump-ump-ump-prrrr.* The Spruce Grouse (*Dendragapus canadensis*) of northern forests drums during short flights. The Blue Grouse (*Dendragapus obscurus*) of the western mountains produces booming notes with the colorful air sacs on his neck.

Sharp-tailed Grouse
Tympanuchus phasianellus

Length: *14–20 in.*
What to look for: *tail narrow, pointed, showing white on outer feathers in flight; tawny brown above, with darker barring; lighter below, with chevron markings.* **Habitat:** *prairies, brushy areas.*

Traditional dancing grounds are the setting for the courtship of the Sharp-tailed Grouse. Early on spring mornings the cocks gather. They droop their wings, erect their tails, puff themselves up, and inflate the colorful air sacs on their necks. Then they stamp, run, and leap in a frenzied group dance, competing for dominance and the attention of the hens. Another spectacular dancer is the black-bellied Sage Grouse (*Centrocercus urophasianus*) of western areas.

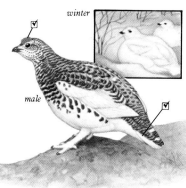

White-tailed Ptarmigan
Lagopus leucurus

Length: *12–13 in.*
What to look for: *mottled brown, with tail, belly, and most of wings white; all white in winter; red patch over eye.* **Habitat:** *mountains above timberline, alpine meadows; lower elevations (winter).*

The source of the word *ptarmigan* is unknown. One authority suggests that it may come from a Gaelic word meaning "mountaineer." The White-tailed Ptarmigan certainly fits that description, for the hardy bird seldom descends to the tree line. Feathered feet help it conserve heat, and it can survive the winter by feeding on nothing more than willow buds. In the breeding season the female's subtly mottled plumage camouflages her on the nest; in winter both sexes match the snowy background.

Northern Bobwhite
Colinus virginianus

Length: *8–10 in.*
What to look for: *small size; short tail; male reddish brown above, with white on head, black necklace, and streaked sides; female duller.* **Habitat:** *brushy areas; open pine woods; farms.*

Both male and female bobwhites help build the nest—sometimes simply a hollow tramped down in a clump of tall grass, but usually a woven cover of pine needles, grass, and nearby vegetation, with an opening on one side. At night a covey of bobwhite roost on the ground in a circle, with heads outward and bodies touching. This arrangement keeps them warm even when they are covered with snow.

Scaled
Quail

California Quail
Callipepla californica
Length: *9–11 in.*
What to look for: *forward-curving plume; back brown,
breast gray-blue, sides streaked with white; scaly pattern
on belly; male with black and white facial pattern.*
Habitat: *brushy areas, meadows, suburbs.*

male

Coveys of plumed California Quail post sentries as they feed.
Although they are not shy, they are easily frightened. When they
dash for cover, they are more likely to run than fly. Gambel's
Quail (*Callipepla gambelii*), a desert bird, also wears a plume.
Another dry-area species, the Scaled Quail (*Callipepla squa-
mata*), is nicknamed Cottontop for its white crest.

male

Ring-necked Pheasant
Phasianus colchicus
Length: *22-35 in.*
What to look for: *large size; tail long, pointed;
male with white collar; female smaller, brownish.*
Habitat: *prairies, brushy areas, fertile croplands.*

The pheasant was named by the ancient Greeks, who
imported this handsome and tasty bird from the region of the River Phasis east of the Black Sea. Ring-
necked Pheasants have been introduced into the wild
around the world. Other game species introduced
into North America are the Chukar (*Alectoris chukar*),
a large partridge established in the West, and the
Gray Partridge (*Perdix perdix*), found here and there
across southern Canada and the northern states.

female

male
displaying

Wild Turkey
Meleagris gallopavo
Length: *3-4 ft.*
What to look for: *very large size;
tail long, with black band near tip;
male glossy brown, with bare, pale bluish head
and red wattles; female smaller, duller.*
Habitat: *oak and mesquite brush,
deciduous woodlands, wooded bottomlands.*

In the breeding period, the male Wild Turkey puts on
a spectacular display. He spreads his tail, swells out
his wattles, and rattles his wings, gobbling and strut-
ting the whole time. Wiped out in many areas by land
development and unrestricted hunting, the species is
making a comeback with the help of reintroductions
and good management. Turkeys roost in trees and
feed on the ground on insects, berries, seeds, and
nuts. The hens nest in leaf-lined hollows in brush or
woodlands; they alone incubate the eggs, sometimes
as many as 20 in a clutch. Wary and difficult to approach, turkeys can fly well for short distances but
prefer to walk or run.

male

BIRDS

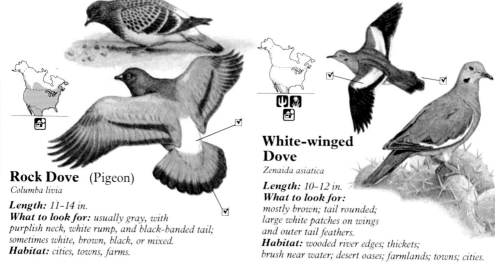

Rock Dove (Pigeon)
Columba livia

Length: *11–14 in.*
What to look for: *usually gray, with
purplish neck, white rump, and black-banded tail;
sometimes white, brown, black, or mixed.*
Habitat: *cities, towns, farms.*

The Rock Dove, originally from Europe and Asia,
nests on cliffs in the wild and has easily adapted to the
ledges of human buildings. Rock Doves breed several
times a year, beginning in March, when the males'
ardent cooing is one of the sounds of spring. A mated
pair shares the incubation and care of the young,
which are fed on regurgitated "pigeon's milk," a secretion from the bird's crop. Breeders have developed several color strains, but free-living flocks usually contain many gray birds with iridescent necks,
similar to the original wild Rock Doves.

White-winged Dove
Zenaida asiatica

Length: *10–12 in.*
What to look for:
*mostly brown; tail rounded;
large white patches on wings
and outer tail feathers.*
Habitat: *wooded river edges; thickets;
brush near water; desert oases; farmlands; towns; cities.*

There are a number of species that beginners may
overlook because they resemble Rock Doves. The
White-winged Dove is one of them. But this bird of
the Southwest, the southern Gulf Coast, and points
south is somewhat smaller than the familiar city Pigeon and has white at the corners of its tail. The
White-winged Dove nests in shrubs, thickets, and
trees, usually at a moderate height and often in colonies. The call is a prolonged series of rough hoots;
though not particularly loud, the sound carries over
long distances.

Mourning Dove
Zenaida macroura

Length: *10–12 in.*
What to look for: *slim body; tail long, pointed,
edged with white; grayish brown above, with
scattered black spots.* **Habitat:** *deserts, brushy
areas, woodlands, farmlands, suburbs, parks.*

The Mourning Dove's mellow, vaguely melancholy
call—*coo-ah, coo, coo, coo*—is repeated again and
again, sliding upward on the second syllable and then
down for the last three notes. Mourning Doves build
a flimsy nest of sticks, usually in an evergreen tree
close to the trunk. Two eggs make a set. The parents
share incubating duties, the male sitting much of the
day and his mate during the night. The young are fed
by regurgitation, then gradually weaned to insects
and the adults' main food, seeds.

Common Ground-dove
Columbina passerina

Length: *5–6½ in.*
What to look for: *small size; tail short,
rounded; wings with brownish-red patches
visible in flight.* **Habitat:** *deserts, dry grasslands,
open woodlands, farmlands.*

The plump little Common Ground-dove is the smallest of our doves, about the size of a House Sparrow.
As it walks along, hunting for seeds, it nods its head
(as do other members of its family). This is a tame
species and will permit a close approach. Usually it
flies for only a short distance, showing bright reddish-brown patches on its wings. In its southern habitat the Ground-dove favors sandy or weedy areas,
cotton fields, and citrus groves. The southwestern
Inca Dove (*Columbina inca*) somewhat resembles the
Ground-dove but has a long, narrow tail edged with
white, like that of a Mourning Dove.

Yellow-billed Cuckoo
Coccyzus americanus

Length: *10½–12½ in.*
What to look for: *long, slim bird; gray-brown above, white below; underside of tail black, with 3 pairs of large white spots; yellow lower mandible; reddish-brown wing patches visible in flight.*
Habitat: *moist second-growth woodlands; brushy areas near water.*

Unlike some cuckoos, the Yellow-billed does not regularly lay its eggs in other birds' nests—but it is not much of a nest maker, either. The structure of sticks, rootlets, grass, and leaves is shallow and loosely built, and often appear to be too small for a sitting bird and her eggs. From the moment the chicks are hatched almost to the day they fly, they are covered with quills, like miniature porcupines. Then the quills burst open and the feathers bloom out. This species and the similar Black-billed Cuckoo (*Coccyzuz erythropthalmus*), common in the East, are as inconspicuous in behavior as in plumage. They slip noiselessly from branch to branch, uttering an occasional *cuk-cuk-cuk*.

Greater Roadrunner
Geococcyx californianus

Length: *20–24 in.*
What to look for: *large size; long tail; rough crest; patch of red and pale blue behind eye; runs rapidly but seldom flies.* **Habitat:** *deserts, semiarid areas with scattered brush and trees.*

The roadrunner is really a ground-dwelling cuckoo, though it neither looks nor behaves like a cuckoo. This long-tailed, long-legged bird is very agile and fast on its feet; one was clocked at 15 miles an hour. The roadrunner is famous for feeding on snakes—poisonous or otherwise—and lizards. It also eats scorpions, spiders, grasshoppers, crickets, small mammals, birds' eggs, and even small birds that it catches in flight by leaping into the air and snatching them with its bill. Most items are simply swallowed, but a big lizard, for instance, is softened by being beaten on a rock. The roadrunner is not a quiet bird. It crows and chuckles. It rolls its mandibles together, producing a clacking sound. And mostly it coos like a dove—a most unusual cuckoo altogether.

female

male

Belted Kingfisher
Ceryle alcyon

Length: *11–14 in.*
What to look for: *shaggy crest; bill heavy, sharp-pointed; blue-gray above, with blue-gray breast band (additional chestnut band on female).*
Habitat: *shores of lakes, ponds, streams; coasts.*

As it leaves a favored perch overlooking a pool or lake, the Belted Kingfisher often utters its rattling call. Still calling, it dashes over the water, keeping its head slightly raised as if it were trying to see just a bit farther. It may fish by swooping close to the surface, dipping for its prey. Or it may climb to a considerable height, hold there on beating wings with head cocked, and then plunge. Kingfishers usually nest in a burrow in a steep bank, preferably near water. The tunnel may be as long as 15 feet, ending in a slightly elevated nest chamber.

113

Common Barn-owl
Tyto alba

Length: *13-19 in.*
What to look for: *face heart-shaped, mostly white; golden brown above, usually white below; legs long, feathered; mothlike flight.* **Habitat:** *forests near open country; farmlands, towns.*

Long before this worldwide species was a "barn" owl, it nested in hollow trees, caves, and burrows. Often it still does. But man's structures furnish it with ideal cover, and the bird can be found in belfries, attics, and abandoned mines as well as barns. This owl is a nocturnal hunter. Experiments have shown that it requires its ears only to locate prey.

Snowy Owl
Nyctea scandiaca

Length: *19-25 in.*
What to look for: *large size; mostly white, with dark flecks; active in daylight.*
Habitat: *tundra; prairies, open fields, marshes, beaches (winter).*

Snowy Owls nest on the tundra around the top of the globe. In winters when food (chiefly lemmings and hares) is scarce, large numbers move south to the northern United States. Snowy Owls show little fear of human activities, and so it is not uncommon to see one perched on the roof of a building or on a highway sign beside an airport. The owls are usually silent in winter, but on their breeding grounds they hoot, whistle, rattle, and bark.

Great Horned Owl
Bubo virginianus

Length: *18-24 in.*
What to look for: *large size; widely spaced ear tufts; mottled brown above, lighter below, with fine dark barring.* **Habitat:** *scrub areas, woodlands, deserts, canyons, bottomlands.*

This daring and adaptable species, found virtually throughout the Americas, will attack any medium-sized mammal or bird—porcupine or skunk, duck or grouse. In North America the Great Horned Owl begins to breed in the cold of winter. Two or three eggs are laid, usually in the old nest of a large hawk or crow, sometimes in a hollow tree or a cave. Calls are many and various, but the common one is a series of muffled hoots—*hoo, hoo-hoo, hoooo-hoo*. The male's voice is higher-pitched than the female's, and a pair in concert seem to harmonize, often in thirds.

Barred Owl
Strix varia

Length: *16-23 in.* **What to look for:** *large round head; no ear tufts; dark eyes; mottled brown, with barred throat and streaked underparts.* **Habitat:** *wet woodlands, wooded swamps, floodplains.*

In the daytime an owl sitting inconspicuously in a tree is frequently mobbed by a noisy flock of scolding small birds—a sure tip-off to an owl watcher. The Barred Owl's far-carrying, rhythmic hooting, heard by day as well as night, is often written as *Who cooks for you? Who cooks for you-all?* The bird also gives a hair-raising catlike scream. The Barred Owl's larger and rarer relative, the Great Gray Owl (*Strix nebulosa*), breeds in northern and mountain forests but occasionally appears farther south and east during the winter.

gray
phase

reddish
phase

Long-eared
Owl

Short-eared Owl

Asio flammeus

Length: *12–16 in.*
What to look for: *head rounded; dark areas on wing; mottled yellowish brown; flight erratic, flapping.* **Habitat:** *tundra, brushy areas, prairies, dunes, marshes.*

This is a bird of the open country. A daytime and twilight hunter, the Short-eared Owl will occasionally perch on a fence post to spot its rodent prey, but usually it is seen coursing over a pasture or marsh. The range of the Short-eared Owl includes much of the Americas and Eurasia. The Long-eared Owl (*Asio otus*) has a similarly wide range. It is nocturnal, however, and nests in trees, not on the ground.

Eastern Screech-owl

Otus asio

Length: *7–10 in.*
What to look for: *small size; ear tufts; reddish, brown, or gray; sometimes perches in tree holes.* **Habitat:** *forests, groves, farmlands, towns, parks.*

The call of this small owl is a series of mellow hoots or, more typically, a quavery, eerie wail. The Screech Owl's wail is not difficult for man to imitate, and such imitations may get dozens of curious or outraged small birds to respond. The Western Screech-owl (*Otus kennicottii*), of the western half of the continent, is almost identical, but its call is a series of soft notes, all on one pitch and speeding up at the end.

Burrowing Owl

Speotyto cunicularia

Length: *8–10½ in.*
What to look for: *round head; long legs; short tail; brown above, spotted with buff and white; paler below.* **Habitat:** *prairies, plains, deserts, other open spaces.*

Typically this owl is seen standing at the entrance to its burrow, bowing and bobbing in a comic way. In the West it nests in the abandoned burrows of prairie dogs. A burrow ordinarily slopes down for about 3 feet, then runs back horizontally to a nesting chamber 10 feet or more from the entrance. The birds line this chamber with feathers, grass, dried mammal dung, and the remains of prey. Five or six eggs make up the set, and both parents incubate and raise the young. These owls feed on insects, reptiles, and rodents, hunting during the day as well as in the evening.

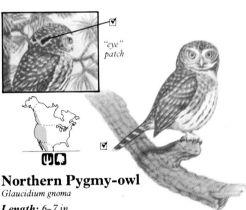

"eye"
patch

Northern Pygmy-owl

Glaucidium gnoma

Length: *6–7 in.*
What to look for: *very small; brownish above, with white-edged black spots on nape; white below, with dark streaks; tail long, barred with white.* **Habitat:** *coniferous and mixed forests; wooded canyons in dry areas.*

The Northern Pygmy-owl is tiny indeed—no bigger than a good-sized sparrow. It has two distinctive features: a long tail, which it often cocks up at an angle, and two black blotches, or "eyes," on the back of its neck. The species nests in tree holes, usually in evergreen forests. The Ferruginous Pygmy-owl (*Glaucidium brasilianum*), a bird of the southwestern deserts, is similar but is usually more rusty, and always has rusty or buffy bars on its tail. The Elf Owl (*Micrathene whitneyi*) of the Southwest is even tinier and very short-tailed.

Whip-poor-will

Caprimulgus vociferus

Length: *9–10 in.*
What to look for:
mottled brown; rounded wings;
white or buff band on throat; white at end of
outer tail feathers (male); most active at dusk.
Habitat: *deciduous and mixed woods with clearings.*

The Whip-poor-will calls its name continually and emphatically from a perch in the dark, but its sound seldom gives away its location. The elusive night bird is equally difficult to locate during the day, when it sleeps among the dried leaves of the woodland floor. The female lays two eggs on the ground, without any nest. The Chuck-will's-widow (*Caprimulgus carolinensis*) is common over much of its relative's range and has a similar call, given at a slower tempo. Both eat moths and other nocturnal insects.

Common Nighthawk

Chordeiles minor

Length: *8–10 in.*
What to look for:
mottled brown;
white
areas on
throat, wings,
and tail
(female with buff
throat and no tail band);
wings long, pointed;
tail slightly forked;
bouncing flight.
Habitat: *grasslands,*
open woods, towns, cities.

Like the Whip-poor-will and others of the family, the Common Nighthawk has a very large mouth, used to capture insects as it flies. The bird does much of its hunting at dusk or in the night, and it calls often in flight (a nasal *beent*). The female lays her eggs on gravel, rock, burned-over ground, or other barren terrain; graveled roofs in urban areas are favorite nesting sites.

Chimney Swift

Chaetura pelagica

Length: *4–5 in.*
What to look for: *small size; dark gray,*
lighter on throat; bow-shaped wings; short tail;
body looks cigar-shaped in flight. **Habitat:** *open air*
over woodlands, farmlands, towns, cities.

Until man provided chimneys, wells, and other alternative sites, this dark little bird nested in hollow trees. Chimney Swifts pass much of their lives in flight, beating their wings rapidly or holding them stiffly as they sail. They utter a distinctive series of high-pitched chips. No one knew where Chimney Swifts wintered until quite recently, when it was discovered that the entire population migrates to a remote part of the upper Amazon.

White-throated Swift

Aeronautes saxatalis

Length: *6–7 in.*
What to look for:
black and white pattern on
underside; long wings; notched tail.
Habitat: *open air over rocky areas,*
especially canyons and mountains.

The fast-flying "rock swift" of the western mountains roosts and nests in crevices of cliffs, especially those overlooking deep canyons. A single crevice may contain a number of roosting swifts; at sunset a procession will stream in and disappear into the face of the cliff with incredible accuracy and speed. Vaux's Swift (*Chaetura vauxi*), another western species, is smaller than the White-throated, with a grayish breast and shorter, unnotched tail.

116

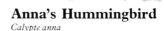

Ruby-throated Hummingbird
Archilochus colubris

Length: *3–3½ in.*
What to look for: *bill long, needlelike; metallic green above; throat metallic red (male) or dingy white (female).* **Habitat:** *deciduous and mixed forests; rural, suburban, and city gardens.*

Of the 15 species of hummingbird that regularly nest north of Mexico, this is the only one breeding east of the Great Plains. The Broad-tailed Hummingbird (*Selasphorus platycercus*) of western mountains is similar in appearance, but the ranges of the two do not overlap. "Hummers," unlike other birds, can fly backwards or straight up and down. They can also hover, and are able to drink flower nectar without actually landing on the blossom. The flowers they drink from are usually long, tubular, and orange or red.

Anna's Hummingbird
Calypte anna

Length: *3–4 in.*
What to look for: *bill long, slender; metallic green above; iridescent dark red crown and throat (male); white-tipped tail (female).* **Habitat:** *open woodlands; chaparral; suburban and city gardens.*

When the female Anna's Hummingbird lays her eggs, her nest may be only half finished; she completes it while incubating. Like most hummingbird nests, it consists of tiny stems and plant down, held together and lashed to a branch with spider silk and often camouflaged with bits of lichen. A female feeds her young without any help from her mate. She collects nectar, tree sap, insects, and spiders, and delivers the meal by thrusting her long bill deep down the nestlings' throats.

Rufous Hummingbird
Selasphorus rufus

Length: *3½–4 in.*
What to look for:
male mostly red-brown, with iridescent orange-red throat and sides of head; female with green back, rufous on flanks and base of tail feathers. **Habitat:** *alpine meadows, edges of woodlands; lowlands (migration).*

The Rufous Hummingbird flies farther north than any other hummingbird. As the birds move south toward Mexico (mainly in July and August) they may be found as high in the mountains as 13,200 feet. Hummingbirds are generally feisty, but this species is particularly pugnacious. Yet at times Rufous Hummingbirds appear to breed in colonies, with some pairs nesting only a few feet from one another. The similar-looking Allen's Hummingbird (*Selasphorus sasin*), which occurs along the West Coast from Oregon south, has a green back and cap.

Black-chinned Hummingbird
Archilochus alexandri

Length: *3–3¾ in.*
What to look for: *back metallic green; throat black, bordered with iridescent purple (male); slightly forked tail.* **Habitat:** *dry scrub, woodlands near streams, wooded canyons, mountain meadows, gardens.*

Hummingbirds are unique to the New World. European explorers were astounded by the tiny glittering creatures that zipped up and down, backwards and sideways, with wings humming and blurred. Hummingbirds perform set figures in courtship flights. The male Black-chinned Hummingbird, for instance, swings in pendulumlike arcs above the female; at the top of each swoop he comes to a dead stop and taps his wings together underneath his body.

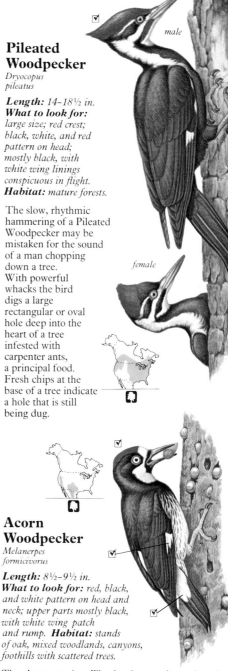

male

female

Pileated Woodpecker

Dryocopus pileatus

Length: *14–18½ in.*
What to look for:
large size; red crest; black, white, and red pattern on head; mostly black, with white wing linings conspicuous in flight.
Habitat: *mature forests.*

The slow, rhythmic hammering of a Pileated Woodpecker may be mistaken for the sound of a man chopping down a tree. With powerful whacks the bird digs a large rectangular or oval hole deep into the heart of a tree infested with carpenter ants, a principal food. Fresh chips at the base of a tree indicate a hole that is still being dug.

Red-bellied Woodpecker

Melanerpes carolinus

Length: *8–10 in.*
What to look for:
fine black and white barring on back; red nape; red crown (male); white patch near end of wings visible in flight.
Habitat: *forests, groves, orchards, farmlands, suburbs.*

This abundant southern species is now expanding its range to the north. In the South the Red-belly occasionally feeds on oranges, but it makes up for this by eating quantities of destructive insects. It most often nests in a dead tree at the edge of a woodland, frequently using the same hole year after year. The female lays unspotted white eggs, usually four or five in a clutch. (This is typical of woodpeckers.) The name Red-bellied Woodpecker is misleading, for the red patch on its belly is rather faint.

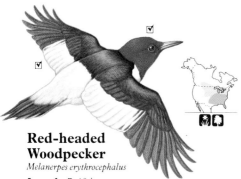

Red-headed Woodpecker

Melanerpes erythrocephalus

Length: *7–10 in.*
What to look for: *red head and neck; mostly black and white, with large white wing patches; immature brownish on head and back.* **Habitat:** *open woods, groves, swamps with dead trees.*

The diet of the Red-headed Woodpecker is notably varied. It includes beechnuts, acorns, corn, fruits, insects, and the eggs and young of small birds. Like several other woodpeckers, this species has the habit of storing food for future use. Grasshoppers are stuffed into crevices in fence posts, and nuts are packed into knotholes and into cracks in buildings. Wherever nut trees are abundant and productive, there is a good chance of seeing this woodpecker and hearing its loud *quee-o, quee-o, queer.*

Acorn Woodpecker

Melanerpes formicivorus

Length: *8½–9½ in.*
What to look for: *red, black, and white pattern on head and neck; upper parts mostly black, with white wing patch and rump.* **Habitat:** *stands of oak, mixed woodlands, canyons, foothills with scattered trees.*

The Acorn-storing Woodpecker, as it used to be called, drills small holes in trees and packs them with nuts (usually acorns), one to each hole. One packed Ponderosa Pine was studded with an estimated 50,000 acorns. The Acorn Woodpecker is remarkable, too, for its breeding habits. Unlike other woodpeckers, it is very social and often nests in colonies of a dozen or so. Several pairs may even share in digging a nest hole and then cooperate in incubating the eggs and raising the young.

red-shafted race

yellow-shafted race

Northern Flicker

Colaptes auratus

Length: *10–13 in.*
What to look for: *white rump; black crescent at throat; yellow or red on underside of wings and tail (in East, yellow only); male with "mustache" of black (East) or red (West).* **Habitat:** *deserts, farmlands, suburbs, parks, open forests.*

This unusual woodpecker is often seen on the ground, searching for ants and licking them up with its long tongue. It does, however, nest in holes in trees—or tree substitutes such as telephone poles. Flickers are conspicuous in fall, when they often travel in loose flocks. In spring their arrival is announced by noisy calls—*wick-a, wick-a, wick-a.*

*Yellow-bellied Sapsucker
S. varius*

eastern species

Yellow-bellied Sapsucker

Sphyrapicus varius

Length: *7–8½ in.*
What to look for: *long white wing stripe; black, white, and red pattern on head and neck; immature brownish, with wing stripe.* **Habitat:** *forests, woodlands, orchards; parks (migration).*

Unlike other woodpeckers, sapsuckers have brushlike tongues, not barbed ones, and cannot extract wood-boring insects from a tree. Instead, they drill neat rows of holes (primarily in birches and orchard trees), remove the nutritious inner bark, and later eat the sap that has run out, as well as the insects trapped in it. There are four species in North America.

*Red-breasted Sapsucker
S. ruber
(a western species)*

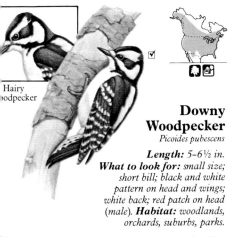

Hairy Woodpecker

Downy Woodpecker

Picoides pubescens

Length: *5–6½ in.*
What to look for: *small size; short bill; black and white pattern on head and wings; white back; red patch on head (male).* **Habitat:** *woodlands, orchards, suburbs, parks.*

The little Downy is probably our most familiar woodpecker. In winter it readily takes suet from bird feeders and often joins the mixed bands of small birds that roam through the woods, each species feeding in a different manner but all deriving protection from the wariness of the flock. The larger Hairy Woodpecker (*Picoides villosus*) is more of a forest dweller than the Downy. Both "Downies" and "Hairies" are named for their feathers, probably the short ones around their nostrils.

Three-toed Woodpecker

Picoides tridactylus

Length: *7–9 in.*
What to look for: *yellow crown (male); back with black and white bars or jagged white patch; barred sides; wings mostly black.* **Habitat:** *coniferous forests.*

The Three-toed Woodpecker is an unusual bird. It is the only woodpecker that lives both in North America and Eurasia. It has two toes pointing forward, one pointing backward. Except for the similar Black-backed Woodpecker, *Picoides arcticus*, other woodpeckers have four toes. Males of both species have yellow head patches, not red. And instead of hammering into trees, as most woodpeckers do, they flake off sheets of bark from dead trees and feed on the wood borers and beetles underneath.

119

attacking a crow

Eastern Kingbird
Tyrannus tyrannus

Length: *7–9 in.*
What to look for:
blackish above, white below;
dark tail, with prominent
white band at tip; flies with stiff,
shallow wingbeats from a high perch.
Habitat: *forest edges,*
woodlands and open areas
with occasional tall trees.

Thoreau called this flycatcher a "lively bird," and wrote that its noisy twittering "stirs and keeps the air brisk." The Eastern Kingbird is not only lively; it is fearless in defense of its territory. It will attack any passing crow or hawk, flying at it from above, pecking at the victim and pulling out feathers; it may even land on the flying intruder. The Gray Kingbird (*Tyrannus dominicensis*) is a slightly larger and paler bird of Florida and nearby coastal areas. Its bill is large, and it has no band on its notched tail.

Western Kingbird
Tyrannus verticalis

Length: *7–9 in.*
What to look for: *outer tail feathers white; cap, nape, and back gray; throat white; underparts yellow.* **Habitat:** *arid open areas with scattered trees or tall brush; wooded stream valleys; farmlands.*

This species, like other flycatchers, hunts from a perch. It flies out, plucks an insect from the air, and then sails back, often to the same spot. Adults teach their young to hunt by catching insects, disabling them, and releasing them for the young to fetch. A similar western species is Cassin's Kingbird (*Tyrannus vociferans*), with a darker breast and no white outer tail feathers.

Scissor-tailed Flycatcher
Tyrannus forficatus

Length: *11–15½ in.*
What to look for: *tail deeply forked, with extremely long feathers; pale gray above, with small rose shoulder patch; whitish below, shading to pink on flanks, belly, and underwings; immature less pink, with shorter tail.* **Habitat:** *open brushy areas with scattered trees, poles, wires, or other high perches.*

The male Scissor-tailed Flycatcher shows off in a remarkable courtship flight. Flying up to perhaps 100 feet above the ground, he begins a series of short, abrupt dives and climbs, ending the sequence by falling into two or three consecutive somersaults. Scissor-tails hunt insects from elevated perches and on the ground, seemingly unencumbered by their long tails. Adults of both sexes have the long, streaming plumes.

Great Crested Flycatcher
Myiarchus crinitus

Length: *7–9 in.*
What to look for: *reddish-brown tail and wing patch; yellow belly; whitish wingbars; slight crest.*
Habitat: *forests, clusters of trees.*

This handsome bird announces its presence with a loud, clear *wheep* or rolling *crrreep*. The Great Crested Flycatcher always nests in a cavity—an abandoned woodpecker hole, a hollow tree, or a nest box. If the hole is too deep, the birds will fill it up from the bottom with debris before beginning the nest of twigs. They may add a cast-off snakeskin or a strip of shiny plastic, which is sometimes left hanging outside the cavity. In dry parts of the West the smaller Ash-throated Flycatcher (*Myiarchus cinerascens*) often nests in a hole in a large cactus.

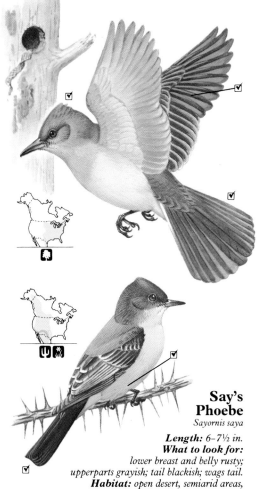

Eastern Phoebe
Sayornis phoebe

Length: *5–7 in.*
What to look for: *brownish olive above, with darker head; whitish below, with gray breast; sits upright on perch and wags tail frequently.* **Habitat:** *woodlands, farmlands, suburbs; usually near water.*

Fibrit, says the Eastern Phoebe emphatically from its perch, wagging its tail in characteristic motion. Phoebes are not shy. Often they are found in or on porches, garages, barns, and bridges, nesting on a ledge or beam. This species made ornithological history in 1803 when Audubon tied silver thread on the legs of nestlings—the first North American experiment in bird banding. The next year he found that two of his marked birds had returned and were nesting nearby.

Say's Phoebe
Sayornis saya

Length: *6–7½ in.*
What to look for: *lower breast and belly rusty; upperparts grayish; tail blackish; wags tail.* **Habitat:** *open desert, semiarid areas, ranchlands, brushy fields, canyon mouths.*

This dry-country flycatcher replaces the Eastern Phoebe in much of the West and has similar habits. It is a tail wagger, and it often nests on or around ranch buildings. Its call, however, is different—a low, plaintive *phee-eur*. Its customary perch is on top of a small bush, a tall weed stalk, or a low rock. In the northern portion of its range, Say's Phoebe is migratory, but it is a year-round resident in warmer areas.

Black Phoebe
Sayornis nigricans

Length: *5½–7 in.*
What to look for: *only flycatcher with black throat and breast; belly and outer tail feathers white; sits erect and wags tail.* **Habitat:** *shaded streams and ponds, wooded or brushy areas, farmlands, suburbs.*

The Black Phoebe breeds near water, often locating its nest on a bridge girder or even down a well; buildings, trees, and cliffs are other nesting sites. A shaded low branch overhanging a pool or stream is a favorite perch. The Black Phoebe's call—*tsip* or *twee*—is repeated frequently, accompanied by flicks of its tail. The song is a plaintive *ti-wee, ti-wee*. Of the three phoebes, this is the only species that usually does not migrate.

Flycatcher identification: some clues. The 10 small *Empidonax* flycatchers—3 of which are shown below—are among the most difficult of our birds to identify. They are all 4 to 6 inches long; most have a dark back, a pale front, a pale eye ring, and two pale wingbars. Slight differences in color can help distinguish some species, and habitat is sometimes a useful clue. But in most cases the only way to tell one *Empidonax* flycatcher from another is by voice; their calls are usually distinctive. However, all of these flycatchers tend to be silent except during the breeding season. At other times of the year most people just give up precise identification and write "*Empidonax*, species?" in their field notebooks.

Yellow-bellied Flycatcher
Empidonax flaviventris

Length: 4½–5½ in.
What to look for: *small size; brownish olive above, yellow below, with yellow throat; yellowish eye ring; whitish wingbars.* **Habitat:** *northern coniferous forests, bogs; alder thickets, mixed woodlands (migration).*

A bird of the wet northern forests, the Yellow-bellied Flycatcher nests on the ground or not far above it, in the side of a moss-covered bank or in the ferndraped earth clinging to the roots of a fallen tree. Its song is an upward-sliding *chee-weep*, sweet and melancholy; it also utters a short *killick*. In breeding plumage this species shows more yellow than any of its relatives in its range—the Least (below), the Willow (*Empidonax traillii*), or the Alder (*Empidonax alnorum*). The Acadian Flycatcher (*Empidonax virescens*) is a southeastern species, but it too is a bird of wet woods and streamsides, and on migration may be found in the same places as the Yellow-bellied.

Least Flycatcher
Empidonax minimus

Length: 4½–5 in.
What to look for: *small size; belly white or pale yellow; head and back olive-gray; whitish eye ring and wingbars.*
Habitat: *open forests, orchards, rural towns, suburbs, parks.*

The Least Flycatcher is noisy during the breeding season. Its curt *chebec* is given as often as 75 times a minute, and it may go on repeating itself for several hours at a time. The male sometimes adds a warble—*chebec-tree-treo, chebec-treee-chou*. Other notes include one-syllable *whit* calls. The species nests in both conifers and deciduous trees, usually quite low but at times as high as 60 feet. The deep little cup is frequently nestled in the crotch of a limb; materials include shreds of bark, plant down, spiderweb, fine woody stems, and grasses. Southerly nesters may raise two broods a year.

Western Flycatcher
Empidonax difficilis/occidentalis

Length: 5–6 in.
What to look for: *yellow throat and belly; olive-brown back; whitish eye ring and wingbars.*
Habitat: *moist coniferous and mixed forests, deciduous groves, wooded canyons.*

Scientists have decided that the Western Flycatcher is actually two species separated by geography, the Pacific-slope (*Empidonax difficilis*) of the coast and Cordilleran (*Empidonax occidentalis*) of the Rockies. The green moss nest of the Western Flycatcher, lined with shredded bark, is always located in damp woods—often near a stream and sometimes even under the lip of a streambank. (It may also build as high as 30 feet up in a tree.) Two close relatives of the Western Flycatcher are best identified by habitat. Hammond's Flycatcher (*Empidonax hammondii*) breeds in high coniferous forests. The Dusky Flycatcher (*Empidonax oberholseri*) is a bird of the foothill chaparral and of brushy mountain slopes.

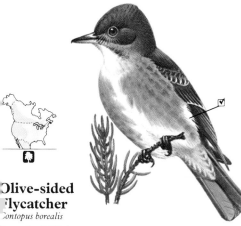

Olive-sided Flycatcher
Contopus borealis

Length: 6-7½ in.
What to look for: *grayish brown above, white below, with brown-streaked sides; white patch below wing sometimes visible.* **Habitat:** *coniferous and mixed woodlands, forest-edged bogs, swamps with dead trees; eucalyptus groves (California).*

Perched on top of a tall tree or dead snag, the Olive-sided Flycatcher whistles a cheery *pip-whee-beer*. The first note, *pip*, is inaudible at a distance, but the rest of the song is high and clear. When alarmed, this husky flycatcher calls *pip-pip-pip-pip*. The Greater Pewee (*Contopus pertinax*) of the southwestern mountains resembles the Olive-sided, but lacks the streaked sides and white patches.

Eastern Wood-pewee
Contopus virens

Length: 5-6 in.
What to look for: *brownish olive above, whitish below; conspicuous white wingbars; no eye ring.* **Habitat:** *mature deciduous forests, other woodlands; especially along rivers.*

Pee-a-wee, this bird whistles, sliding down, then up in pitch. Next it pauses, and adds a downward-slurred *pee-ur*. During daylight a male pewee repeats this song every 5 or 10 seconds. But before dawn and after sunset it sings even more frequently, and adds the phrase *ah-di-day*—three ascending notes. The Western Wood-pewee (*Contopus sordidulus*) also has a "twilight song," ending in a rough *bzew*.

Vermilion Flycatcher
Pyrocephalus rubinus

Length: 5-6 in.
What to look for: *male with brilliant red cap and underparts, dark brown back, wings, and tail; female brown above, light below, with fine streaking and pink wash on sides.* **Habitat:** *wooded streamsides in arid regions; groves near water.*

The courting male is very conspicuous as he circles up on rapidly beating wings, pausing often to give his tinkling song. He may climb as high as 50 feet before swooping down to perch near his mate. The nest, usually built into a horizontal crotch of a willow or mesquite, is a flat saucer of twigs, weeds, hair, and feathers, tied down with spider silk.

female

male

Horned Lark
Eremophila alpestris

Length: 6-7½ in.
What to look for: *chest and head patterned with black and yellow; black tail with white on outside; "horns" not always visible.* **Habitat:** *stony deserts, tundra, grasslands, other open spaces, shore areas.*

The Horned Lark is a bird of the bare earth, where it nests and feeds, and the sky, where it soars, sings, and plummets downward once again. In the fall individuals from the Far North migrate in large flocks, joining the local breeding birds wherever they find their preferred habitat—ground with a minimum of low vegetation to supply the seeds on which they feed. This is North America's only true lark.

prairie race

northern race

123

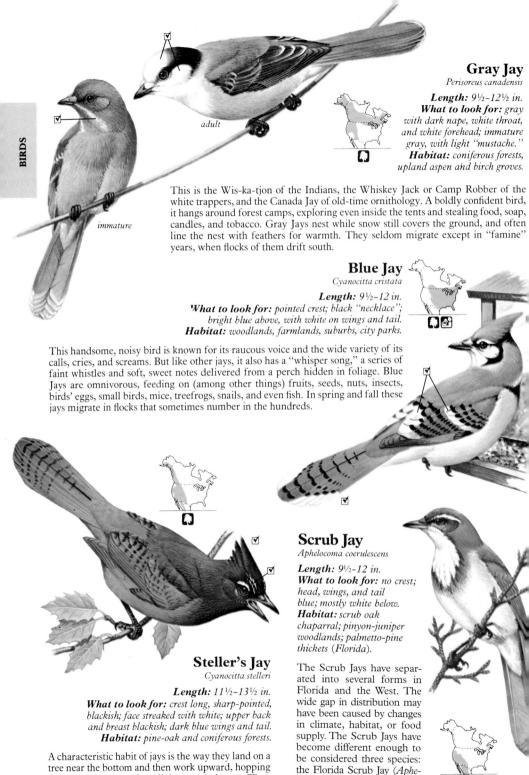

Gray Jay
Perisoreus canadensis

Length: 9½–12½ in.
What to look for: *gray with dark nape, white throat, and white forehead; immature gray, with light "mustache."*
Habitat: *coniferous forests, upland aspen and birch groves.*

adult

immature

This is the Wis-ka-tjon of the Indians, the Whiskey Jack or Camp Robber of the white trappers, and the Canada Jay of old-time ornithology. A boldly confident bird, it hangs around forest camps, exploring even inside the tents and stealing food, soap, candles, and tobacco. Gray Jays nest while snow still covers the ground, and often line the nest with feathers for warmth. They seldom migrate except in "famine" years, when flocks of them drift south.

Blue Jay
Cyanocitta cristata

Length: 9½–12 in.
What to look for: *pointed crest; black "necklace"; bright blue above, with white on wings and tail.*
Habitat: *woodlands, farmlands, suburbs, city parks.*

This handsome, noisy bird is known for its raucous voice and the wide variety of its calls, cries, and screams. But like other jays, it also has a "whisper song," a series of faint whistles and soft, sweet notes delivered from a perch hidden in foliage. Blue Jays are omnivorous, feeding on (among other things) fruits, seeds, nuts, insects, birds' eggs, small birds, mice, treefrogs, snails, and even fish. In spring and fall these jays migrate in flocks that sometimes number in the hundreds.

Scrub Jay
Aphelocoma coerulescens

Length: 9½–12 in.
What to look for: *no crest; head, wings, and tail blue; mostly white below.*
Habitat: *scrub oak chaparral; pinyon-juniper woodlands; palmetto-pine thickets (Florida).*

The Scrub Jays have separated into several forms in Florida and the West. The wide gap in distribution may have been caused by changes in climate, habitat, or food supply. The Scrub Jays have become different enough to be considered three species: the Florida Scrub Jay (*Aphelocoma coerulescens*), the Western Scrub Jay (*Aphelocoma californica*), and the Island Scrub Jay (*Aphelocoma insularis*).

Steller's Jay
Cyanocitta stelleri

Length: 11½–13½ in.
What to look for: *crest long, sharp-pointed, blackish; face streaked with white; upper back and breast blackish; dark blue wings and tail.*
Habitat: *pine-oak and coniferous forests.*

A characteristic habit of jays is the way they land on a tree near the bottom and then work upward, hopping from branch to branch until they reach the top. Then they leave, perhaps to repeat the maneuver. Steller's Jays, like their relatives, build bulky nests of dead leaves and twigs, usually near the trunk of a conifer.

Black-billed Magpie
Pica pica

Length: 17½–21½ in.
What to look for: *tail long, tapering, metallic green; bold black and white pattern in flight.*
Habitat: *open forests; brushy areas of prairies and foothills; bottomland groves; ranches.*

This conspicuous, long-tailed species constructs a particularly strong nest in a bush or low in a tree. Sticks, often thorny, make up the base and walls. Mud or fresh dung mixed with vegetation is packed inside, and the cup is lined with roots, stems, and hair. Over the nest the birds build a dome of sticks—again, often thorny. The Yellow-billed Magpie (*Pica nuttalli*) of California builds the same sort of nest.

American Crow
Corvus brachyrhynchos

Length: 16–20 in.
What to look for:
glossy black, with black bill, legs, and feet; rounded wings and tail.
Habitat: *forests; woods near water; open areas; farmlands; suburbs.*

Judged by human standards, crows are perhaps the most intelligent of birds. They can count at least to three or four; they quickly learn new information; they appear to have a complex language and well-developed social structure. North America has three kinds, the American Crow and two smaller species usually found near the shore—the Northwestern and the Fish Crow (*Corvus caurinus* and *ossifragus*). A Mexican species also visits Texas. The Common and the Chihuahuan Raven (*Corvus corax* and *cryptoleucus*), larger birds with wedge-shaped tails, are sometimes mistaken for crows.

Common Crow

Common Raven

Clark's Nutcracker
Nucifraga columbiana

Length: 12–13 in.
What to look for: *body light gray; wings and tail black, with white patches; bill long, pointed.*
Habitat: *coniferous forests near tree line; lower slopes, isolated groves.*

William Clark, of the Lewis and Clark expedition, thought this bird was a woodpecker, but the leading American ornithologist of the day, Alexander Wilson, called it a crow. Clark's Nutcracker has the woodpecker's bounding flight at times; at other times it flies more directly, like a crow. It pecks at cones and nuts like a woodpecker, and robs the nests of other birds, as crows do.

Bank Swallow

Tree Swallow
Tachycineta bicolor

Length: 4½–5½ in.
What to look for:
glossy blue-black or greenish above
(*immature dark brown*), white below; tail
slightly forked. **Habitat:** open areas with
scattered trees and dead stubs; usually near water.

This is the hardiest swallow, arriving early in spring an
even wintering over in some localities. When insects are u
available, Tree Swallows feed mostly on bayberries; som
wintering birds have also been seen picking seeds from pon
ice. Tree Swallows will nest in birdhouses and mailboxes, a
well as in holes in dead tree stubs, their natural nesting site
In fall the brown-backed immatures can be mistaken fo
Bank Swallows (*Riparia riparia*), which have brown "co
lars," and for Rough-winged Swallows (*Stelgidopteryx serr
pennis*), which have a brown wash on the throat. In the Wes
adult birds can be confused with Violet-green Swallow
(*Tachycineta thalassina*), a species with more white on th
lower back.

Cliff Swallow
Hirundo pyrrhonota

Length: 5–6 in.
What to look for: *mostly dark above; light
forehead; rusty rump and throat; square tail.*
Habitat: *open country cliffs, farmlands with
bridges or buildings for nesting; usually near water.*

After it was reported from Hudson Bay in 1772, no naturalist noticed the Cliff Swallow—or mentioned it, any-
way—until 1815, when Audubon found a few in Kentucky. From then on, the birds were seen in many parts of
North America. Probably they had simply been overlooked all those years. Quite likely, Cliff Swallows began
appearing where people could get a look at them as they
gradually discovered the suitability of nest sites under the
eaves of houses and barns (cliffsides are their natural nest
sites). These are the swallows that return to the Mission
of San Juan Capistrano, in California, on or about March
19 each year.

immature

Barn Swallow
Hirundo rustica

Length: 5½–7 in.
What to look for: *tail deeply
forked; glossy dark blue
above; light rufous below, with
darker throat.* **Habitat:** *open woodlands,
other open areas, farmlands, suburbs.*

Like the Cliff Swallow, this species has benefited
from man's constructions, building its mud nest in
culverts, under wharves and bridges, and inside
sheds, garages, and barns. The Barn Swallow feeds
almost entirely on insects, which it picks out of the air
in its swift, graceful flight; often it will dart close to
the surface of a pond, splashing itself from time to
time. Before the start of the fall migration, Barn
Swallows join with other swallow species to form
huge flocks that rest and preen on telephone wires.

Purple Martin
Progne subis

Length: *7–8 in.*
What to look for: *largest swallow; tail slightly forked; male glossy blue-black; female duller above, with mottled throat and whitish belly.*
Habitat: *open areas, scattered woodlands, farmlands, suburbs; usually near water.*

female

male

Purple Martins have a long history of nesting in shelters supplied by man. In the past they used hollow gourds hung by Indians, and today the species is largely dependent on martin houses. These birds have a strong homing instinct, demonstrated by a colony that returned one spring to find its apartment house gone. The martins hovered and circled at the precise spot in midair where the house had been.

Black-capped Chickadee
Parus atricapillus

Length: *4½–5½ in.*
What to look for: *mostly light gray; black cap and throat; white cheek patch.*
Habitat: *mixed and deciduous forests, suburbs, parks.*

Chickadees that look somewhat alike can often be told apart by their sounds. *Fee-bee,* the Black-capped Chickadee whistles, the first note of the song a full tone higher than the second. Its call is the familiar *chick-a-dee.* In the Middle West and Southeast the Carolina Chickadee (*Parus carolinensis*) whistles a longer, more sibilant *su-fee, su-bee,* ending on a low note. Its *chick-a-dee* calls are more rapid.

Boreal Chickadee
Parus hudsonicus

Length: *4½–5 in.*
What to look for: *brown cap and back; red-brown sides; black throat.*
Habitat: *northern coniferous forests.*

The Boreal Chickadee seldom wanders far from its northern breeding range. But some winters the "brown caps" move southward in great numbers, probably inspired by a dwindling supply of insect eggs, larvae, and conifer seeds. Boreal Chickadees sing their *chick-a-dee* in a drawling, buzzy voice. The Chestnut-backed (*Parus rufescens*), found along the Pacific coast and inland to Idaho and Montana, has a shriller, more explosive call.

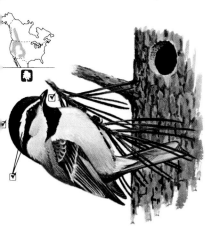

Mountain Chickadee   *Parus gambeli*

Length: *4½–5½ in.*
What to look for: *black line through white cheek patch; black cap and throat.* **Habitat:** *oak-pine and coniferous mountain forests; mixed forests at lower elevations (winter).*

All the chickadees nest in cavities, usually in living trees but occasionally in nest boxes and even in holes in the ground. Some species, like the Black-capped Chickadee, chop out their own holes in rotting wood. The Mountain Chickadee uses natural cavities or old woodpecker holes that need little enlarging. After the young are raised, this high-altitude species, like the other chickadees, joins mixed flocks of small birds that circulate through the forest as they feed.

Tufted Titmouse   *Parus bicolor*

Length: *5½–6 in.*
What to look for: *gray with buffy flanks; gray crest (black in Texas).* **Habitat:** *deciduous forests, cypress swamps, pine woods, wooded bottomlands, orchards, suburbs.*

Long regarded as a southern species, the Tufted Titmouse has been spreading northward in recent years. Now these tame, confiding birds are familiar visitors at feeders from Michigan to New England. Their ringing song varies; usually it is a rapid two-note whistle—*pe-ter, pe-ter.* Titmice are relatives of the chickadees, and this species has a number of chickadeelike calls. In the West, the Plain Titmouse (*Parus inornatus*), which lacks the buffy flanks of the Tufted, actually does call *tsick-a-dee-dee.*

Verdin   *Auriparus flaviceps*

Length: *4–4½ in.*
What to look for: *small size; grayish, with yellow on head (paler on female) and chestnut shoulder patch.* **Habitat:** *semiarid or arid regions with scattered thorny scrub and mesquite.*

A remarkable nest builder, the Verdin weaves a round, long-lasting shell of stout, thorny twigs. The nest is lined with plant down and other plant material, spider silk, and feathers. Inside the entrance is a high "doorstep" that discourages intruders. The Verdin usually locates its nest conspicuously in a cactus, thorny bush, or small tree, choosing a fork at the end of a low branch. These structures are also used for roosting and winter shelter.

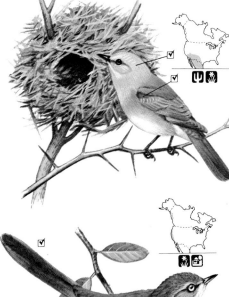

Wrentit
Chamaea fasciata

Length: *5–6 in.*
What to look for: *brown bird with streaked breast; tail long, rounded, often erect; light eye.* **Habitat:** *chaparral, brushy areas, suburbs, parks.*

Once it is located by its loud, whistling song, this little bird is difficult to watch. It seldom flies any distance or perches in the open, but instead moves about stealthily in dense brush. Much of what is known about the Wrentit is due to an observer who studied a population in a California canyon. Among other discoveries, she found that at night roosting pairs sit side by side and shuffle their body feathers so that they become enveloped in a single bundle of plumage.

Bushtit
Psaltriparus minimus

Length: *3–4 in.*
What to look for: *small grayish bird with long tail; brown cap (Rocky Mountain race with gray cap and brown cheeks); male in extreme Southwest with black mask.* **Habitat:** *mixed woodlands; stands of scrub oak, pinyon, or juniper; chaparral.*

Bushtits are small, inconspicuous birds that build elaborate nests. A pair begins by constructing a more or less horizontal rim between adjacent twigs. With this as a frame, the birds weave a small sack and gradually stretch and strengthen it, working mostly from inside. A hood and an entrance hole are added at the top. Materials vary with the locality, but usually the nest is held together with spiderweb and decorated with bits of moss and lichen.

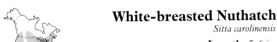

White-breasted Nuthatch

Sitta carolinensis

Length: *5–6 in.*
What to look for: *black crown and nape; blue-gray above, white below; bill long, straight.* ***Habitat:*** *mixed and deciduous forests, woods; groves; suburbs.*

The nuthatches are the only birds that habitually climb down tree trunks headfirst, gathering insects and insect eggs from crevices and under the bark. The name nuthatch derives from *nut-hack,* for the way the birds wedge nuts and other food into crevices and chop them into pieces. The southeastern Brown-headed Nuthatch (*Sitta pusilla*) and the western Pygmy Nuthatch (*Sitta pygmaea*) are smaller species.

Red-breasted Nuthatch

Sitta canadensis

Length: *3½–4½ in.*
What to look for:
white line above eye; black cap; blue-gray back; reddish underparts.
Habitat: *coniferous forests; mixed woodlands (mainly in winter).*

The Red-breasted Nuthatch usually digs its nest hole in dead wood, but it may also use natural cavities, old woodpecker holes, and nest boxes. Whatever site it chooses, it always smears the entrance hole with pitch from spruce, fir, or pine, perhaps to discourage predators. This nuthatch is an active little bird, scurrying over tree trunks and branches, dashing from tree to tree, and calling *yna, yna, yna, yna* in a thin, nasal voice. The White-breasted species has a lower-pitched call.

Brown Creeper

Certhia americana

Length: *4½–5½ in.*
What to look for: *streaked brown above, white below; bill long, slender, curved down.*
Habitat: *mixed and coniferous forests, groves, woods.*

The spring song of the Brown Creeper is a high, sweet phrase, surprisingly different from its usual thin *sssst.* But since the spring song is ventriloquistic, the bird can be difficult to locate. In feeding the Brown Creeper invariably flies to the bottom of a tree and gradually hitches its way up the trunk in its search for insects. Then it drops to the bottom of another tree and begins hitching upward once again.

American Dipper

Cinclus mexicanus

Length: *5½–8 in.*
What to look for: *stocky bird; slate-gray, with white eye ring; legs long, yellowish; short tail; bobs continually.* ***Habitat:*** *fast-flowing mountain streams.*

Dippers are so dependent on water that they are seldom seen flying even short distances over dry land. A dipper collects its food—aquatic insects and small fry—by diving into the water and wading submerged along the bottom. In Alaska dippers have been seen flitting around the icy edges of open water holes and diving when the air temperature was far below zero. The nest is built under a streambank or waterfall.

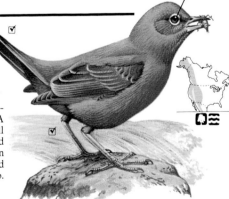

129

House Wren
Troglodytes aedon

Length: *4–5 in.*
What to look for: *gray-brown above, lighter below, with barring on wings and tail; tail often held erect.* **Habitat:** *open woodlands, forest edges, shrubby areas, suburbs, parks.*

House Wrens are aggressive and adaptable nesters. They will build their nests in just about any container left out in the open—flowerpot, empty tin can, pocket of an old coat—as well as tree holes and nest boxes. They often bully other birds, ejecting them from nest sites and even destroying eggs and young. Two broods a season are raised. The male frequently changes partners in mid-season, so that while his original mate is still feeding chicks, another female is sitting on new eggs.

Winter Wren
Troglodytes troglodytes

Length: *3–4 in.*
What to look for: *small size; reddish brown, with dark barring on flanks; very short tail.*
Habitat: *coniferous and mixed forests with heavy undergrowth, often near streams; wooded swamps.*

The song of the Winter Wren is clear, rapid, and very high in pitch, often with notes beyond the range of human ears. The wren sings along at 16 notes a second, stringing beautiful, tinkling passages into long pieces. It sings over the sound of surf on remote Alaskan islands, where it nests on cliffs and rocky slopes near the shore. Elsewhere it is most often a bird of the deep woods, nesting in the earth that clings to the roots of fallen trees, under standing roots, or in crevices between rocks.

Carolina Wren
Thryothorus ludovicianus

Length: *4½–5½ in.*
What to look for: *wide white eye stripe; rufous above, with white throat and tawny sides.*
Habitat: *forests with dense undergrowth; scrubby areas; thickets; brush near water.*

The loud, ringing call of the Carolina Wren is one of the commonest sounds of southeastern woods, where it is heard even in winter. The call is usually a series of double or triple notes, written as *cheery, cheery, cheery* or *tea-kettle, tea-kettle, tea-kettle*. The bird has been called "mocking wren" because it sometimes sounds like a catbird, a kingfisher, or certain other kinds of birds.

Marsh Wren
Cistothorus palustris

Length: *4–5 in.*
What to look for: *brown cap; wide white eye stripe; streaked upper back; reddish lower back; white underparts.*
Habitat: *freshwater and brackish marshes.*

Because of both habits and habitats, some wrens are heard more often than seen. The furtive Marsh Wren may pop out only briefly from thick stands of reeds, cattails, and marsh grasses to give its sputtering song. The Sedge Wren (*Cistothorus platensis*), of sedgy bogs and wet meadows in the East, is very secretive. It sings a thin, dry *tip, tip-tip-trrrrrr*.

Bewick's Wren

Thryomanes bewickii

Length: *4½–5½ in.*
What to look for: *white eye stripe; brown above, white below; tail long, with white spots on outer feathers.* **Habitat:** *woodlands, brushy areas, chaparral, suburbs.*

Audubon named this species for a British friend, Thomas Bewick (pronounced "buick"), whose wood engravings of birds were famous in his day. Though somewhat larger than the House Wren, Bewick's Wren is less aggressive, and it usually loses out when the two species compete for space. Its diet, like that of all wrens, consists almost entirely of insects, spiders, and other small invertebrates; Bewick's Wren in particular is credited with destroying many injurious species such as scale insects and bark beetles.

Rock Wren

Salpinctes obsoletus

Length: *4½–6 in.*
What to look for: *upper parts grayish brown, with rufous rump; throat and breast white, finely streaked with brown.* **Habitat:** *deserts; high, dry meadows; rocky areas.*

The Rock Wren is a loud, rough-voiced, and garrulous singer with the habit of repeating itself. One listener wrote: *"Keree, keree, keree, keree, he says. Chair, chair, chair, chair, deedle, deedle, deedle, deedle, tur, tur, tur, tur, keree, keree, keree, trrrrrrrrr."* The Rock Wren nests in holes in the earth, between boulders, or under loose stones, often on slopes. It usually paves the floor beneath and around its nest with small stones and sometimes also with bones and assorted trash. Another western species of about the same size is the white-breasted Canyon Wren (*Catherpes mexicanus*).

Cactus Wren

Campylorhynchus brunneicapillus

Length: *6–8½ in.*
What to look for: *large size; white eye stripe; throat and breast heavily spotted with black; wings and tail barred with black.* **Habitat:** *brushy desert areas with cactus, yucca, and mesquite.*

The largest wren is a bird of arid, low-altitude country where cacti are plentiful. Its nest is conspicuous—a domed affair with a tunnel entrance 5 or 6 inches long. The whole structure, woven of plant fibers, leaves, and twigs, is shaped rather like a flask lying on its side. Typically, it is placed in the arms of a big cactus or on a branch of a thorny bush or mesquite tree. A pair of Cactus Wrens will maintain several nests at one time and may raise three broods a year, changing nests at the beginning of each cycle. After the young have left, the adults continue to make repairs, since the nests are used as winter roosts.

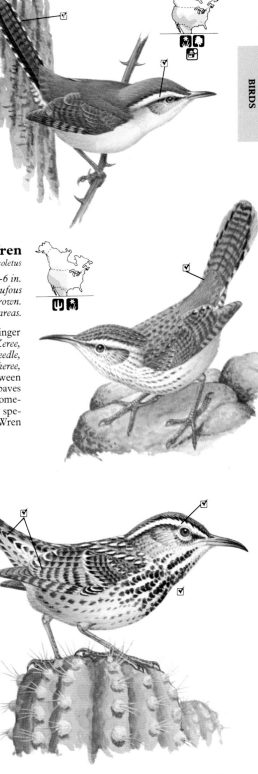

Loggerhead Shrike
Lanius ludovicianus

Length: *7-9½ in.*
What to look for: *gray above, with
black mask; paler below; bill short, heavy;
wings black, with white patches;
outer tail feathers white.* **Habitat:**
open areas with scattered trees and shrubs.

Both the Loggerhead Shrike and the rarer Northern Shrike (*Lanius excubitor*) are nicknamed
"butcher-birds." They kill insects, snakes, rodents, and small birds, then impale them on
thorns or barbed wire or jam them into twig forks.
Often they build up sizable larders. Evidently,
however, the purpose of this habit is more than
storage against lean times. For although the
shrikes have hooked, hawklike bills, they lack
powerful, hawklike feet and apparently must fix
the prey on something firm before tearing it
with the bill.

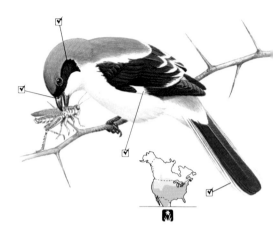

Northern Mockingbird
Mimus polyglottos

Length: *9-11 in.*
What to look for: *gray above,
whitish below; tail long, blackish;
white wing patches; no black eye mask.*
Habitat: *open areas, farmland,
suburbs, parks; scrubby growth
near water (dry areas).*

Within its range the mockingbird is much more
common than the similarly colored shrikes. It is
best known for its song, which may be heard day
or night. Typically the bird repeats a phrase over
and over (perhaps half a dozen times), then drops
that phrase and goes on to another. Often the
phrases are imitations of other birds' songs, and
"mockers" have also been known to sound like
frogs, crickets, and dogs, among others. They do
not need a recent reminder, it seems, but can remember phrases for several months at least.

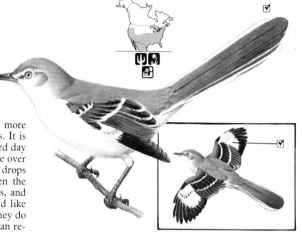

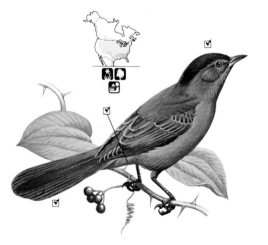

Gray Catbird
Dumetella carolinensis

Length: *7-9 in.*
What to look for: *long tail; dark gray,
with black cap and rusty undertail.*
Habitat: *undergrowth in woodlands, hedgerows,
brushy areas, suburbs, parks.*

Often in the nesting season this trim bird is a close
neighbor of man. Like the mockingbird, the Gray
Catbird is regarded as a mimic, but it is less an actual
imitator than a plagiarist of musical ideas. As one listener put it, the catbird "*suggests* the songs of various
birds—never delivers the notes in their way!" It
burbles along, now loud, now soft, uttering a long run
of squeaky phrases, seldom repeating itself. It gets its
name from its call note—a petulant, catlike *mew*.

Brown Thrasher
Toxostoma rufum

Length: *9½–11 in.*
What to look for: *long tail;*
bright reddish brown above;
2 white wingbars; white below,
streaked with brown.
Habitat: *open brushy areas,*
forest edges, hedgerows,
thickets, suburbs, parks.

Thrashers, like mockingbirds and catbirds, are members of the family Mimidae, or mimic thrushes. (The name thrasher derives from the word *thrush.*) A characteristic of this group is the imitation of sounds. The most notable quality of the thrasher's music, aside from the occasional imitation, is the phrasing. The loud, ringing song has been written in this vein: "Hurry up, hurry up; plow it, plow it; harrow it; chuck; sow it, sow it, sow it; chuck-chuck, chuck-chuck; hoe it, hoe it." The bird is usually seen singing from a high perch out in the open.

California Thrasher
Toxostoma redivivum

Length: *11–13 in.*
What to look for: *bill long, curved down;*
long tail; dark gray-brown above, lighter below;
cinnamon belly and undertail; dark mustache; light
eye stripe. **Habitat:** *dry brushy areas, suburbs, parks.*

Many birds that feed on the ground forage by scratching with their feet, kicking over leaves and other debris. But the California Thrasher uses its long, curved bill, uncovering hidden food and chopping deep into the earth after buried larvae. Its diet includes beetles, ants, bees, and caterpillars. Very strong afoot, this thrasher seems to prefer running to flying except in emergencies. Not all grayish, sickle-billed thrashers are necessarily this species. Three other somewhat similar thrashers are found in California and the Southwest: the Curve-billed (*Toxostoma curvirostre*), Le Conte's (*Toxostoma lecontei*), and the Crissal (*Toxostoma dorsale*).

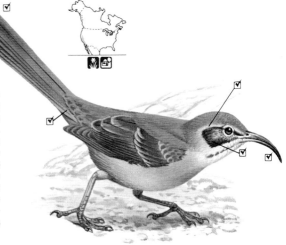

Sage Thrasher
Oreoscoptes montanus

Length: *8–9 in.*
What to look for: *small thrasher; bill short, thin;*
gray-brown above, with 2 white wingbars; white below,
streaked with brown; tail tipped with white.
Habitat: *shrubby areas, brushy slopes, sagebrush;*
deserts (winter).

This small thrasher is a bird of the dry foothills and plains. It nests on the ground or, more usually, low down in sagebrush or other shrubby growth. Nest materials include twigs, plant stems, and bark fibers, with hair and fine roots for lining. Occasionally Sage Thrashers build a twig "awning" in the branches above the nest, as if to provide shade from the hot sun. Their song, a series of trills and warbles somewhat like that of the eastern Brown Thrasher, sounds more fluent because it lacks the pauses between the repeated phrases.

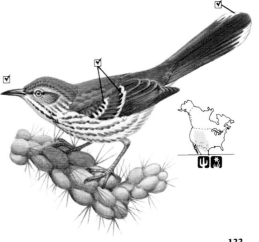

133

American Robin
Turdus migratorius

Length: *9–11 in.*
What to look for: *bright reddish orange below; dark gray above (head paler on female), with broken eye ring and white-tipped tail; immature with light, speckled breast.*
Habitat: *open forests, farmlands, suburbs, parks; sheltered areas with fruit on trees (winter).*

immature

The Robin, a member of the thrush family, is one of the most neighborly of birds. A pair will often build their nest—a neat cup of mud and grasses—on a branch of a dooryard tree or on the ledge of a porch; and they hunt confidently for earthworms on the lawn and in the garden, regardless of human activities nearby. Robins eat insects as well as worms; they also like fruits, both wild and cultivated.

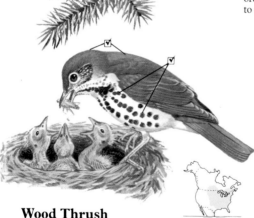

female

male

Varied Thrush
Ixoreus naevius

Length: *8–9½ in.*
What to look for: *dark gray above, with pale orange eye stripe and wingbars; orange below, with black breast band; female paler, browner, with gray breast band.*
Habitat: *damp coniferous and mixed forests, other moist woodlands, wooded canyons.*

The Varied Thrush, though a native of the Pacific Northwest, is famous as a winter wanderer outside its normal range. The species has turned up in many unexpected places, frequently as far east as the Atlantic Coast. Even for a thrush, its song is remarkable. The singer makes use of a "scale" of five or six notes, and—choosing these pitches in no particular order—whistles a series of pure single notes, each note rising to a crescendo and then fading away to a brief pause.

Wood Thrush
Hylocichla mustelina

Length: *7½–8½ in.*
What to look for: *head and upper back reddish brown; white below, with large, dark brown spots from throat to belly.* **Habitat:** *moist deciduous forests, suburbs, parks.*

This thrush nests in dark, damp woods, where it builds a tidy cup of grasses, stems, and dead leaves, usually mixed with mud and lined with roots. Often strips of birch bark, paper, or white cloth are woven into the structure. The Wood Thrush's song is complex and beautiful—a series of brief, liquid phrases often interspersed with a high trill.

Hermit Thrush
Catharus guttatus

Length: *6–7½ in.*
What to look for: *brown above, with reddish rump and tail; white below, with dark spots on throat and breast.* **Habitat:** *moist coniferous or mixed forests; other woodlands, parks (migration).*

The song of this retiring bird is an extraordinary sequence of phrases on varying pitches. Each phrase begins with a single whistle and closes with a jumble of brilliant, bubbly notes. On nesting territory in the northern forests, its song may often be heard with the songs of Swainson's and the Gray-cheeked Thrush (*Catharus ustulatus* and *minimus*), olive-backed birds that lack the Hermit's rusty tail.

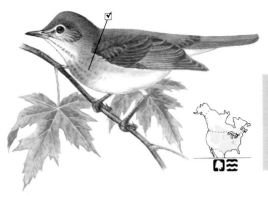

Veery

Catharus fuscescens

Length: 6½–7½ in.
What to look for: *brownish red above; whitish below, with buffy, brown-spotted breast band; in West, darker and less reddish.* **Habitat:** *humid deciduous woodlands, river groves, wooded swamps.*

The name Veery is said to have been coined in imitation of the bird's song, a downward-spiraling series of hollow, liquid phrases best written as *whree-u, whree-u, whree-u,* and so on. Many thrushes—this one in particular—sing far into the dusk and sometimes even after dark. Veeries feed on the ground, hopping along and turning over dead leaves.

Eastern Bluebird

Sialia sialis

Length: 5–7 in.
What to look for: *male bright blue above, with orange-red throat and breast; female paler; immature mostly gray, spotted with white on back and breast.*
Habitat: *open areas with scattered trees and fencerows; farmlands, orchards, suburbs.*

female

male

The sweet chirrup and the flash of blue in garden or orchard or along a rural road have made the Eastern Bluebird a special favorite. But for many years this much-admired bird has been in trouble: introduced House Sparrows and Starlings have taken over its preferred tree holes. Fortunately, bluebirds will nest in birdhouses specially designed to keep out the alien intruders. In many areas, hundreds of these houses have been set up along "bluebird trails"—ambitious projects that have halted the species' decline and even reversed it in some places.

Mountain Bluebird

Sialia currucoides

Length: 6–7½ in.
What to look for: *male sky-blue above, light blue below; female mostly gray, with some blue; immature grayer, with streaked underparts.*
Habitat: *open high-elevation areas with scattered trees and brush; sometimes in lowlands.*

female

male

Both the Eastern and the Western Bluebird (*Sialia mexicana*) hunt for insects by scanning the ground from perches on wires or fence posts and then dropping on the prey. The Mountain Bluebird, which eats a greater proportion of insects than the other two do (seeds and berries are also part of the diet), does more of its hunting in the air. It darts out from a perch to catch a flying insect, or flies over the ground and hovers, then pounces. Like other bluebirds, this one nests in cavities, especially old woodpecker diggings; it also uses birdhouses and holes in cliffs and banks.

135

Cedar Waxwing
Bombycilla cedrorum

Length: 5½–7½ in.
What to look for: *crest; mostly soft brown,
with black face pattern, yellow-tipped tail,
and red spots on wing; immature with brown streaks.*
Habitat: *open forests, areas with scattered trees,
wooded swamps, orchards, suburbs.*

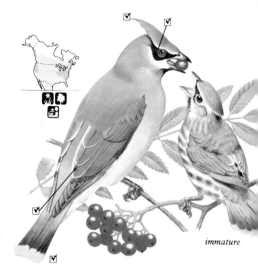

Cedar Waxwings are a particularly sociable species.
It is not unusual to see a row of them perched on a
branch, passing a berry or an insect down the line
and back again, bill to bill, in a ceremony that ends
when one swallows the food. The birds wander in
flocks whose arrivals and departures are unpredictable. Flocks of the northwestern Bohemian Waxwing
(*Bombycilla garrulus*) are also erratic, and may suddenly appear well outside their normal range.

immature

Blue-gray Gnatcatcher
Polioptila caerulea

Length: 4–5 in.
What to look for: *slim, long-tailed bird;
blue-gray above, white below; tail blackish, with white
outer feathers; white eye ring.* **Habitat:** *mixed and
oak forests, chaparral, open pinyon-
juniper forests, thickets and groves along rivers.*

This tiny bird darts from perch to perch, uttering its thin, mewing *spee*,
flicking its long tail, and feeding on tiny insects. In the breeding season the
male has a soft, warbling song. He assists with the building of the nest,
which may be located as low as 3 feet or as high as 80 feet above the
ground. The structure is roughly the shape of an acorn with the top hollowed out, and it consists of various fine materials, including plant down,
petals, feathers, and hair.

female

male

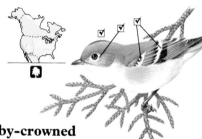

Golden-crowned Kinglet
Regulus satrapa

Length: 3–4 in.
What to look for: *small size; center of crown
orange (male) or yellow (female); greenish above, with
white eye stripe and wingbars.* **Habitat:** *coniferous
forests; other forests, thickets (migration, winter).*

Restless, flitting movements and a very small size are
good signs that the bird you are looking at is a
kinglet. Scarcely pausing to perch, kinglets glean
small insects and their eggs from leaves and bark. In
its fluttering flight the Golden-crowned Kinglet utters a high, thin *ssssst*, which is often repeated several
times as a phrase.

Ruby-crowned Kinglet
Regulus calendula

Length: 3½–4 in.
What to look for: *small size; greenish above,
with white eye ring and wingbars; red crown (male);
often flicks wings.* **Habitat:** *coniferous forests;
other woodlands, thickets (migration, winter).*

The ruby crown of this kinglet is worn only by the
males, and even on them it is not always evident.
(The amount of red that shows seems to depend on
how agitated the kinglet is.) Though a mere mite of a
bird, it has a loud and varied song, and ornithologists
from Audubon on have mentioned how astonished
they were the first time they heard a Ruby-crowned
Kinglet sing.

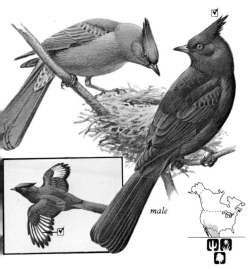

male

Phainopepla
Phainopepla nitens

Length: 6½–7½ in.
What to look for: *crest; male glossy black, with white wing patches conspicuous in flight; female and immature dingy gray, with pale wing patches.*
Habitat: *scrubby arid and semiarid areas with scattered trees; oak groves in canyons.*

The name Phainopepla means "shining robe," a reference to the bright, silky plumage of the male. The species is believed to be related to the waxwings, and like them it is both a fly catcher and a fruit eater. The Phainopepla's shallow nest, made of small twigs, sticky leaves and blossoms, and spiderweb, is usually placed in a fork of a mesquite or other small tree. The male generally begins the project, and his mate does the rest of the job.

Warbling Vireo
Vireo gilvus

Length: 4½–5½ in.
What to look for:
*no conspicuous markings;
grayish green above, white below.*
Habitat: *open mixed and deciduous forests; groves; orchards; shade trees in towns and suburbs.*

Twelve species of vireos nest in North America. The Warbling Vireo and a few others have continent-wide ranges. Others—the eastern White-eyed (*Vireo griseus*) and western Bell's (*Vireo bellii*), for example—are limited to smaller areas. All are noted for the leisurely pace of their activity, compared with that of kinglets and warblers, with which they are often seen on migration. They also have thicker bills.

Red-eyed Vireo
Vireo olivaceus

Length: 5–6½ in.
What to look for: *white eye stripe; gray cap; greenish above, white below; no wingbars.*
Habitat: *deciduous woodlands, open areas with scattered trees, suburbs.*

During the breeding season the male Red-eyed Vireo is a persistent singer, delivering lengthy passages of short, two- to six-note phrases. The bird tends to go on so long that he used to be nicknamed "preacher." Usually he sings at normal volume, but in courtship he also has a "whisper song," sometimes quite different in character from the regular song.

Solitary Vireo
Vireo solitarius

Length: 4½–6 in.
What to look for: *white "spectacles"; white wingbars; gray or bluish head; greenish or gray above, mostly white below.*
Habitat: *mixed or coniferous forests.*

Like all the vireos, the Solitary hangs its nest by the rim in a twiggy fork. As a structure too, the nest is typical of vireos', consisting of bits of bark and moss, leaves, and fine materials such as wool and feathers. The parents sing to each other as they share incubation and early care of the young. The song is bright and measured, not unlike a pure robin song.

137

Identifying warblers. North America has more than 50 species of warblers, distinguished as a group by their small size, thin, sharp bills, active behavior, and bright or contrasting colors in spring. Warblers are usually dimorphic—that is, the sexes differ in plumage. In general, female warblers are paler and duller, lacking the distinctive markings of the males. In the fall many males lose most of these identifying marks; they become as drab as the females, and immature birds looking somewhat like adult females add to the confusion. Unless otherwise noted, all warblers shown here are males in breeding plumage.

Black-and-white Warbler
Mniotilta varia

Length: 4–5½ in.
What to look for: *streaked black and white above, white below; white stripe through crown; female and immature duller.*
Habitat: *forests.*

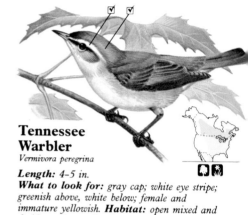

Early ornithologists called this species the Black-and-white Creeper or Creeping Warbler. Constantly in motion, it searches for insects on bark, moving along head up like a creeper or down like a nuthatch. It has a brisk, sibilant song, usually a string of high-pitched double syllables—*weesee, weesee, weesee, weesee.*

Tennessee Warbler
Vermivora peregrina

Length: 4–5 in.
What to look for: *gray cap; white eye stripe; greenish above, white below; female and immature yellowish.* **Habitat:** *open mixed and deciduous forests, brushy areas, forest edges.*

The ornithologist Alexander Wilson discovered this species and the related Nashville Warbler (*Vermivora ruficapilla*) on an 1810 bird-finding trip in the South. Like many birds, these two were named for the places where they were first seen.

Northern Parula
Parula americana

Length: 3½–4 in.
What to look for: *blue above, with greenish-yellow patch on back; white wingbars; throat and breast yellow; darker band across throat (male).*
Habitat: *humid forests, usually near water; other forests (migration).*

The name parula means "little titmouse," a reference to the bird's active behavior as it forages through the foliage for insects. In the South, the parula hollows out a shallow nest in trailing clumps of Spanish Moss; in northern forests, it nests in *Usnea* lichen. Its song is a buzzy trill, sliding upward in pitch and snapping off at the end—*zzzzzzzz-zup.*

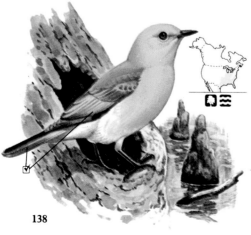

Prothonotary Warbler
Protonotaria citrea

Length: 4½–5 in.
What to look for: *bright orange-yellow head and breast, fading to lighter below; gray wings and tail; female more yellowish.*
Habitat: *wooded bottomlands; lowland swamps; moist, frequently flooded woods.*

Court officers, or prothonotaries, who sometimes wore bright yellow robes inspired the name of this handsome species. The Prothonotary Warbler is a bird of wooded swamps and riverbanks. As a rule it nests in a tree cavity or a deserted woodpecker hole, but in some localities it is tame enough to choose a birdhouse or any other small container.

MacGillivray's Warbler

Oporornis tolmiei

Length: *4½–5½ in.*
What to look for: *slate-gray head, blackish near breast; incomplete white eye ring; olive-green above, yellow below; female and immature duller.*
Habitat: *dense brushy areas, moist thickets.*

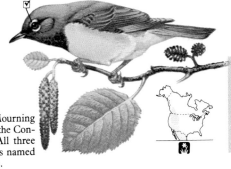

Three warblers have gray hoods—this one, the similar Mourning Warbler (*Oporornis philadelphia*) of the North and East, and the Connecticut Warbler (*Oporornis agilis*), also a northern bird. All three skulk in dense vegetation near the ground. This species was named for a Scottish ornithologist who edited Audubon's writings.

female

male

American Redstart

Setophaga ruticilla

Length: *4–5½ in.*
What to look for: *male black, with white belly and orangish patches on wings and tail; female and immature grayish above, white below, with yellow patches.* **Habitat:** *second-growth deciduous forests, thickets, suburbs, parks.*

One of the commonest warblers, this is also one of the most attractive. Flashes of color on the fanned-out wings and tail ("redstart" means "red-tailed") make the lively birds resemble flitting butterflies as they catch insects on the wing. The variable song is a set of single or double notes on one pitch, which may end with a higher or lower note—*zee-zee-zee-zee-zee-zeeo.*

Ovenbird

Seiurus aurocapillus

Length: *5–6 in.*
What to look for: *olive above, with orange crown bordered by black; white below, with dark streaks; white eye ring; pinkish legs; walks on ground.*
Habitat: *deciduous woodlands.*

Once it has become familiar, the voice of the Ovenbird is one of the most obvious in the woods. The song begins softly and builds to a ringing crescendo—*teacher, teacher, teacher, teacher!* The Ovenbird is a ground-dwelling warbler. Its covered nest, which accounts for its name, is generally hidden on the forest floor.

Northern Waterthrush

Seiurus noveboracensis

Length: *5–6 in.*
What to look for: *pale eye stripe; dark brown above, buffy with dark streaks below; teeters continually.*
Habitat: *wet woodlands; brushy areas (migration).*

Look and listen for this warbler near placid water. The closely related Louisiana Waterthrush (*Seiurus motacilla*) is more likely near fast-flowing streams. Both species bob and teeter along over banks, rocks, and logs. Their looks are similar, but with practice they can be distinguished by their voices. Both build their nests, of moss and other bits of vegetation, near water.

Hooded Warbler
Wilsonia citrina

Length: *4¼–5½ in.*
What to look for:
*male with yellow face,
black hood, black throat;
female with brownish cap;
greenish above, yellow below;
white on tail.*
Habitat: *dense deciduous forests,
wooded swamps, thickets; usually near water.*

Canada Warbler
Wilsonia canadensis

Length: *4½–5½ in.*
What to look for: *gray above,
yellow below; "spectacles";
male with black "necklace";
female duller, with faint "necklace."*
Habitat: *mature deciduous woodlands near
streams or swamps; moist brushy areas;
second-growth forests (migration).*

This distinctively marked species breeds in cool, damp forests in Canada and elsewhere. It is usually a ground-nester, frequently choosing a site in or near a moss-covered log or stump. Its song is a bright, rapid warble on one pitch.

In the East two common warblers have black caps on yellow heads. One is this species; the other is Wilson's Warbler (*Wilsonia pusilla*), which ranges the continent and lacks the Hooded's black bib. The Hooded Warbler is a bird of the undergrowth, nesting low in a bush or sapling. From the outside the nest looks like a wad of dead leaves, but inside it is an impressive construction of bark, plant fibers, down, grass, and spiderweb.

male

female

Common Yellowthroat
Geothlypis trichas

Length: *4–5½ in.*
What to look for: *male
with black mask, edged above
with white; greenish brown above,
with yellow throat, upper breast,
and undertail; female without mask.*
Habitat: *wet brushy areas,
freshwater and saltwater marshes.*

This familiar warbler, black-masked like a little bandit, is usually first seen peering at the intruder from the depths of a shrub or thicket. Sooner or later, the Yellowthroat announces itself with a rhythmic *witchery, witchery, witchery* or variations on that theme. Yellowthroats sometimes nest in loose colonies, but most often breeding pairs are well distributed through brushy or marshy areas.

Yellow-breasted Chat
Icteria virens

Length: *6½–7½ in.*
What to look for: *largest warbler; dark mask;
heavy bill; white "spectacles"; green above; yellow breast.*
Habitat: *dense thickets and tangles, usually near
water; shrubby areas in upland pastures.*

For years ornithologists have been saying that this bird is in all probability not really a warbler. It is half again as big as some species, and much more robust. Its song is loud and varied. One observer who tried to put a passage into syllables got this result: "C-r-r-r-r-r—whirr—that's it—chee—quack, cluck—yit-yit-yit—now hit it—tr-r-r—when—caw, caw—cut, cut—tea-boy—who, who—mew, mew—and so on till you are tired of listening."

Magnolia Warbler
Dendroica magnolia

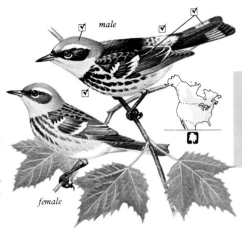

male

Length: *4-5 in.*
What to look for: *black above, yellow streaked with
black below; gray cap; yellow rump; wings and tail
black, with large white patches; female and immature paler.*
Habitat: *coniferous forests; other wooded areas (migration).*

Alexander Wilson first sighted this warbler in magnolia
trees, and the scientific name he gave it included the word
magnolia. Eventually "Magnolia Warbler," being a pretty
way of referring to a beautiful bird, became the common
name. But as one authority remarked, if the warbler had to
be named after a tree, spruce or balsam would have been
more appropriate for this northern forest bird.

female

"myrtle warbler"

"Audubon's warbler"

Yellow-rumped Warbler
Dendroica coronata

Length: *4½-5½ in.*
What to look for: *male with yellow crown, rump, and
shoulder patch, white (East) or yellow (West) throat, black
bib, white tail patches (visible mainly in flight);
female and immature paler, browner.*
Habitat: *coniferous and mixed forests;
other woodlands, thickets (migration, winter).*

This is one of the most abundant of our warblers, and at
times in migration seems to outnumber all the others combined. It has a bright, loud *chip* call that is easily learned, but
recognizing its trilling song takes practice. Audubon's Warbler (the western subspecies) and the eastern Myrtle were
long considered separate species.

female

male

Palm Warbler
Dendroica palmarum

Length: *4-5½ in.*
What to look for: *reddish cap
(breeding); underparts yellow or whitish,
streaked, with yellow undertail; wags tail.*
Habitat: *forest swamps, bogs;
brushy areas (migration, winter).*

Ornithologists first observed this warbler
wintering among the palms of Florida, hence
its common name—surely a misnomer for a
species breeding in northern bogs. During
migration the Palm Warbler is often seen on
the ground or in a low tree, where it flicks its
tail up and down. The Prairie Warbler
(*Dendroica discolor*), common in areas crossed
by migrating Palms, flicks its tail from side to
side. It lacks the red cap and yellow undertail.

Yellow Warbler
Dendroica petechia

Length: *4-5 in.*
What to look for:
*mostly yellow (more greenish
above); male streaked with
reddish on breast; female
duller.* **Habitat:** *riverside
woodlands, wet thickets,
brushy marsh edges,
orchards, suburbs, parks.*

This species has the largest
breeding range of any warbler and
is common not only in most of North America but as far south as Peru. The Yellow Warbler often nests in willows, alders, or other
shrubs along the edge of a swamp or road; its
neat cup of silvery plant fibers is usually built
in a low fork. The male is a persistent singer
with two basic songs: *pip-pip-pip-sissewa-is
sweet* and *wee-see-wee-see-wiss-wiss-u.*

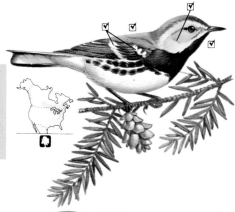

Black-throated Green Warbler
Dendroica virens

Length: *4–5 in.*
What to look for: *yellow face; black throat and breast; green above; white wingbars; female and immature duller, with less black.* **Habitat:** *coniferous forests; other woodlands (migration, winter).*

The Black-throated Green has a preference for pines and other conifers, but during migration it can be seen high up in a deciduous tree or low down in a roadside thicket. This is the only eastern warbler with yellowish cheeks. Other handsome, similar-looking species are Townsend's Warbler (*Dendroica townsendi*) and the Hermit Warbler (*Dendroica occidentalis*), both of the Far West.

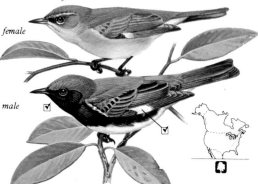

female

male

Black-throated Blue Warbler
Dendroica caerulescens

Length: *5–5½ in.*
What to look for: *male dark blue above, with prominent white wing spot and black face, throat, and sides; female dull olive (paler below), with white wing spot.* **Habitat:** *deciduous and mixed forests with heavy undergrowth.*

The male Black-throated Blue looks the same in spring, summer, and fall, and so it is one of the easiest warblers to recognize. It is easy to spot, too, for it is usually found quite low—in rhododendron, laurel, and similar undergrowth. Observing another blue-backed species, the Cerulean Warbler (*Dendroica cerulea*), may require a lot of neck-craning, since it usually feeds high in a tree.

Black-throated Gray Warbler
Dendroica nigrescens

Length: *4–5 in.*
What to look for: *male with black head and throat, white stripe above and below eye; gray above, white below; female and immature paler, with less black.* **Habitat:** *oak, juniper, and pinyon forests, mixed woodlands with heavy undergrowth.*

Like a number of other *Dendroica* warblers, this species is partial to evergreen trees, at least in the mountains of the Northwest. Farther south, it breeds in the dry scrubby growth of canyon and valley walls. Its nests are not easy to find; they are often located, for example, at the junction of several leafy twigs that hold and screen the structure.

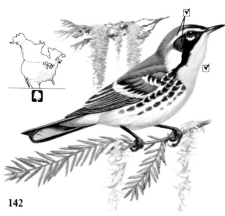

Yellow-throated Warbler
Dendroica dominica

Length: *5–5½ in.*
What to look for:
yellow throat; gray above; black and white pattern on face; female similar but duller.
Habitat: *pine and oak forests, cypress swamps.*

The song of the Yellow-throated Warbler is a clear, bright whistle—*see-wee, see-wee, see-wee, swee, swee, swee, swee*—that speeds up and drops in pitch toward the end. This bird seems less nervous than many other warblers. It forages carefully for insects on tree bark in much the manner of the Brown Creeper or the Black-and-White Warbler.

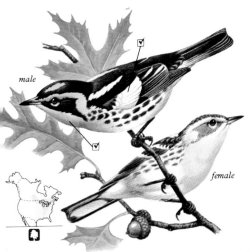

male

female

Blackburnian Warbler
Dendroica fusca

Length: *4–5½ in.*
What to look for: *male with bright orange throat, striped black back, broad white wingbars; female and immature paler, brownish; facial pattern always present.* **Habitat:** *coniferous or mixed forests; other woodlands (migration).*

A bird of the deep woods, the Blackburnian nests in a variety of conifers—spruces, firs, pines, hemlocks. On migration it is a treetop forager and singer, often difficult to spot despite the glowing orange throat. Its song is thin and buzzy, ending with a single high, up-sliding note. The species was named for Anna Blackburn, an 18th-century patron of ornithology.

Blackpoll Warbler
Dendroica striata

Length: *4¼–5½ in.*
What to look for: *male with black cap, white face, black-streaked flanks; female browner, without cap; in fall both sexes greenish, with white wingbars.* **Habitat:** *coniferous woodlands; other woodlands (migration).*

Many birders greet the Blackpolls' arrival each spring with some regret, for it signals the end of the exciting warbler migration. The Blackpoll's song is said to be the highest in pitch of any songbird's (some people can't hear it at all). It is a fast series of single syllables more or less on the same thin note, loudest in the middle.

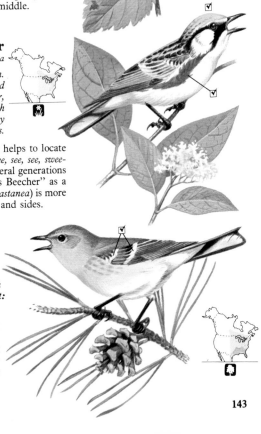

Chestnut-sided Warbler
Dendroica pensylvanica

Length: *4–5 in.*
What to look for: *male with yellow cap and chestnut sides, whitish below; female duller, with spotty chestnut areas; immature yellowish green above, white below.* **Habitat:** *brushy fields, open woodlands, farmlands.*

The distinctive song of the Chestnut-sided Warbler helps to locate the bird. The usual version approximates *tsee, see, see, see, see, swee-BEAT-chew*, with the last note dropping in pitch; several generations of birders have used the words "I wish to see Miss Beecher" as a memory aid. The Bay-breasted Warbler (*Dendroica castanea*) is more richly colored, with deep chestnut on head, breast, and sides.

Pine Warbler
Dendroica pinus

Length: *5–5½ in.*
What to look for: *olive-green above, yellowish with streaks below; white wingbars; female duller.* **Habitat:** *open pine forests; deciduous woodlands (migration).*

The name of this bird is quite appropriate: except when on migration the Pine Warbler "sticks to pine woods as a cockle-bur sticks to a dog's tail." The nest is usually built in a clump of pine needles or on the top of a pine bough between 15 and 80 feet from the ground. The song is a loose, sweet trill.

Bobolink

Dolichonyx oryzivorus

Length: 5½–7½ in.
What to look for: *breeding male black, with back of head yellowish and much white on wings and lower back; other plumages buffy, heavily streaked above.*
Habitat: *moist open fields, meadows, farmlands, marshes.*

The jumbled tinkling of the Bobolink's song seems to come from every quarter of the wet meadow or grainfield where the bird nests. The male may be sitting on a weed stalk or fence post or in a tree along the edge; he may be hovering on beating wings or dashing after a female in courtship. Once the breeding season is over, the singing mostly ceases. The male molts into a plumage like that of his mate, and flocks of Bobolinks fly to South America, calling *pink* from time to time as they go.

Western Meadowlark **Eastern Meadowlark**

Western Meadowlark

Sturnella neglecta

Length: 8–10½ in.
What to look for: *black V across bright yellow underparts; outer tail feathers white; streaked brown above.*
Habitat: *prairies, meadows, open areas.*

Lewis and Clark first noticed the differences between this species and the Eastern Meadowlark (*Sturnella magna*), which look much alike but differ greatly in song. When Audubon rediscovered the Western Meadowlark in 1843, the scientific name he gave it poked fun at the long time between sightings: it means "neglected meadowlark." Many who have heard the songs of both meadowlarks believe that the sweet, melancholy phrases of the eastern bird cannot compare with the rich, flutelike bubblings of the western.

Yellow-headed Blackbird

Xanthocephalus xanthocephalus

Length: 8–10 in.
What to look for: *male black, with yellow head and breast and white wing patches; female brown, with dull yellow on face and breast and white throat.*
Habitat: *freshwater marshes, adjacent open areas.*

This handsome species nests over water 2 to 4 feet deep, and may abandon a nest if the water level drops. The nests are slung between reed stems and are woven of soggy blades of dead grass. When the grass dries, the nest fabric tightens and the reeds are drawn together, improving the nest's stability. The lining is of leaves, grass, and filmy reed plumes.

Red-winged Blackbird

Agelaius phoeniceus

Length: 7–9½ in.
What to look for: *male black, with yellow-bordered red shoulder patch; female dark brown, heavily streaked; immature male like female but with red patch.* **Habitat:** *swamps, marshes, adjacent open areas, farmlands.*

The male Red-winged Blackbird's song is a herald of spring. *Con-ka-ree,* he calls, as if proclaiming victory over winter. Red-wings feed and roost in flocks, but in late summer the flocks vanish. They have retired to some marsh, where the birds hide in the vegetation, molt their flight feathers, and grow new ones. Then the flocks reappear, headed south.

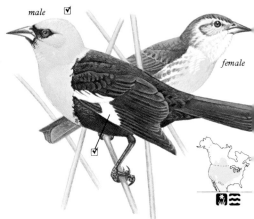

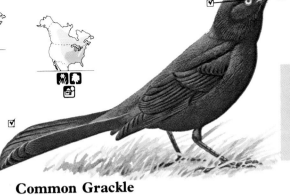

Brown-headed Cowbird
Molothrus ater

Length: *6-8 in.*
What to look for: *conical bill; male glossy black, with dark brown head; female gray, with paler throat.* **Habitat:** *farmlands, groves, forest edges, river woodlands.*

Few birds are as generally disapproved of as the Brown-headed Cowbird, which lays its eggs in the nests of other birds, particularly flycatchers, sparrows, vireos, and warblers. A newly hatched cowbird quickly grows larger than the rightful nestlings and devours most of the food; it may even push the hosts' eggs or young out of the nest. The foster parents feed the huge intruder until it can fly.

Common Grackle
Quiscalus quiscula

Length: *10-12½ in.*
What to look for: *long keel-shaped tail; long pointed bill; light yellow eye; male glossy black, with purple, bronze, or greenish cast; female less glossy.* **Habitat:** *farmlands, groves, suburbs, parks; usually near water.*

Before the trees have begun to leaf out in the North, the Common Grackles arrive. Soon courting males are posturing in the treetops, puffing up their glossy plumage, spreading their long tails, and uttering their rasping *chu-seeck*. Larger species of grackles are the Great-tailed (*Quiscalus mexicanus*) of southern farmlands and the Boat-tailed (*Quiscalus major*), a salt-marsh bird.

Brewer's Blackbird
Euphagus cyanocephalus

Length: *7½-9½ in.*
What to look for: *male black, with yellow eye and purple gloss on head; female grayish brown, darker above, with dark eye; tail proportionately shorter than grackle's.* **Habitat:** *open areas, lakeshores.*

Two medium-sized blackbirds closely resemble one another—this species and the Rusty Blackbird (*Euphagus carolinus*). In winter they may be found in many of the same regions, but Brewer's Blackbird frequents grassy areas and the Rusty swampy woods. Brewer's gives a strong rough whistle or a "whirring gurgle"; the Rusty calls *tickle-EE*, sounding like a mechanical joint that needs oiling.

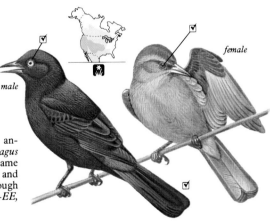

European Starling
Sturnus vulgaris

Length: *7-8½ in.*
What to look for: *long pointed bill; short, square tail; black overall, with greenish and purple gloss (nonbreeding with light spots); immature brownish, darker above.* **Habitat:** *farmlands, open woodlands, brushy areas, towns, cities.*

In 1890 the efforts to introduce this European bird to North America succeeded, and descendants of the 100 birds released in New York City began to spread across the land. The starling's habit of gathering in huge roosts has made it a pest in many areas, and it deprives many hole-nesting species of their homes. It does, however, eat many destructive insects.

145

Baltimore/Bullock's Oriole

Icterus galbula/bullockii

Length: *6–7½ in.*
What to look for: *sharp-pointed bill; male bright orange, with black on head, throat, back, wings, and tail; female and immature pale yellow or orange below, brownish above, with white wingbars.* **Habitat:** *open deciduous woodlands; shade trees in farmlands, towns, cities.*

male
(Baltimore)

female
(Baltimore)

male
(Bullock's)

A liquid, whistled song and a flash of brilliant color at the top of a tall tree signal the presence of an oriole. Scientists have recently returned these orioles to two species having merged them in the 1950s. Where the eastern Baltimore and western Bullock's ranges overlap in mid-continent there is some interbreeding, but not enough to consider them valid species. The Baltimore's nest is the familiar deep pouch swinging at the end of a slender limb; its western cousin's is often tied to twigs at the top and sides.

male

female

Scott's Oriole

Icterus parisorum

Length: *6½–8 in.*
What to look for: *male bright yellow, with black head, upper back, and throat and black on wings and tail; female and immature yellowish green, darker above, with whitish wingbars.* **Habitat:** *deserts; semiarid areas; dry mountain slopes with oaks, pinyons, yucca.*

Like other orioles, this western species feeds on insects, fruits, and probably nectar. Like its relatives, it sings throughout the day in the breeding season. And its nest, like theirs, is woven of plant fibers. Often hidden among the spiky dead leaves of a yucca, the nest varies in structure according to the surroundings.

female

male

first-
year
male

Orchard Oriole

Icterus spurius

Length: *6½–7 in.*
What to look for: *adult male rusty brown, with black head, throat, upper breast, and upper back and black on wings and tail; first-year male greenish, with black throat; female yellowish green, darker above, with white wingbars.* **Habitat:** *farmlands, orchards, suburbs, towns.*

This bird does nest in orchards, where its preference for insects makes it particularly valuable, but it also nests in other habitats. An unusual site was discovered in Louisiana, where nests woven of salt-meadow grasses were suspended from canes in a marsh. The species often seems colonial. On one 7-acre plot in the Mississippi Delta, 114 orchard oriole nests were found in one season. Nearly 20 nests at a time have been noted in a single Louisiana Live Oak.

female

male

Scarlet Tanager
Piranga olivacea

Length: *6-7 in.*
What to look for: *male scarlet, with black wings and tail (in fall, red replaced by yellowish green); female yellowish green, with darker wings and tail.* **Habitat:** *thick deciduous woodlands, suburbs, parks.*

The Scarlet Tanager's song is not hard to pick out: listen to a robin sing for a while, then listen for the same song with a burr in it. The species also has a distinctive, hoarse call—*chick-kurr* in the East, sometimes *chip-chiree* elsewhere. Scarlet Tanagers devour many destructive caterpillars and wood-boring beetles, most often but not exclusively in oaks. Young males may be principally orange or splotched with red and yellow.

Western Tanager
Piranga ludoviciana

Length: *6-7 in.*
What to look for: *male bright yellow, with red head and black on upper back, wings, and tail (no red on nonbreeder); female greenish above, yellowish below (only female tanager with wingbars).* **Habitat:** *open mixed and coniferous woodlands; other forests (migration).*

female

male

The song of the Western Tanager is much the same as that of the Scarlet Tanager—a series of short phrases separated by pauses. Its call is two- or three-syllabled—*pit-ic, pit-it-ic.* On migration, flocks of Western Tanagers pass through valleys, plains, and foothills. They nest mostly in the mountains, in firs and pines, often at high elevations. Like other tanagers, they lay three to five eggs. The female alone incubates, but both parents share the care and feeding of the nestlings.

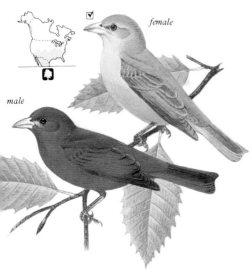

female

male

Summer Tanager
Piranga rubra

Length: *6-7½ in.*
What to look for: *yellowish bill; male red; female yellowish green above, yellow below.* **Habitat:** *woodlands; in uplands, drier forests of oak, hickory, or pine.*

Tanagers are mainly insect eaters, though they do take some buds and fruits. The Summer Tanager is especially fond of beetles and bees, and it will tear wasps' nests apart to get at the larvae. The hard parts of beetles are not digested, but are coughed up as pellets. This species builds a flimsy nest on a horizontal bough. Its song is a more musical version of the Scarlet Tanager's, and its spluttery call is traditionally written as *chicky-tucky-tuck.* A less common species, similar in appearance but with a dark mask, is the Hepatic Tanager (*Piranga flava*) of the mountainous Southwest.

147

Northern Cardinal
Cardinalis cardinalis

Length: *7–8½ in.*
What to look for: *prominent crest;
conical reddish bill; male bright
red, with black around eye and bill;
female brownish yellow, with red
on wings and tail.* **Habitat:** *open woods,
forest edges, thickets, suburbs, parks.*

female

male

The cardinal's rich coloring and its readiness to come to feeders have made it a favorite among birdwatchers. Its varied musical repertoire consists of loud, clear whistles that are usually repeated several times—*wheet, wheet, wheet, wheet, chew, chew, chew, cheedle, cheedle, cheedle.* Male and female may sing alternately, as if in response to each other. Cardinals also have a metallic *pink* note. This species is one of a number of southern birds that have extended their ranges northward during this century. Among the others are the Mockingbird, Tufted Titmouse, Turkey Vulture, and Red-bellied Woodpecker.

female

male

Evening Grosbeak
Coccothraustes vespertinus

Length: *7–8 in.*
What to look for:
*bill large, light-colored,
conical; male yellow-brown,
with black tail and
black and white wings;
female paler, grayish.*
Habitat: *coniferous forests;
other forests and at feeders
(migration, winter).*

The name Evening Grosbeak was given this species by an observer who heard a flock at twilight, at a site northwest of Lake Superior. At that time—1823—the Evening Grosbeak was a western species; since then, it has spread far to the east. One hypothesis is that feeding trays loaded with sunflower seeds may have played a part in this expansion, but reports show that grosbeaks regularly pass up such offerings in favor of boxelder seeds and other wild food.

Blue Grosbeak
Guiraca caerulea

Length: *6–7 in.*
What to look for: *large conical bill;
rusty or buffy wingbars; male blue;
female brownish, with dark wings.*
Habitat: *brushy areas, open woodlands,
forests near rivers.*

male

female

Snakeskins are occasionally woven into the nest of the Blue Grosbeak, sometimes covering the entire outside; other nesting materials include dry leaves, cornhusks, and strips of plastic or newspaper. The female incubates the four eggs for 11 days; the young—fed by both parents, mostly on insects and snails—leave the nest less than two weeks after hatching. For adults, fruits, seeds, and other vegetable matter make up perhaps a third of the diet.

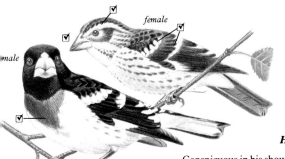

female

male

Rose-breasted Grosbeak
Pheucticus ludovicianus

Length: *7–8 in.*
What to look for: *heavy bill; male with rose breast patch and black and white pattern; female streaked brown, with white eye stripe and wingbars.*
Habitat: *deciduous woodlands, groves, suburbs.*

Conspicuous in his showy plumage, the male Rose-breasted Grosbeak joins the spring chorus in April or early May. His song has a cheery, lyrical quality, with almost the swing of a march. Though the less colorful female is usually the one to build the loosely constructed nest, some pairs will share the work and both male and female incubate. If a pair raises a second brood, the male may take charge of the first while his mate sits on the new eggs.

Black-headed Grosbeak
Pheucticus melanocephalus

Length: *6½–7½ in.*
What to look for: *heavy whitish bill; male orangish yellow, with black head and black and white wings; female brownish, with facial pattern and streaks.*
Habitat: *open mixed or deciduous woodlands, forest edges, chaparral, orchards, parks.*

male

female

This species is the western counterpart of the Rose-breasted Grosbeak, and their clear, whistled songs are similar. The usual song of the Black-headed Grosbeak lasts about five seconds, but may be longer; a male once performed for seven hours.

Indigo Bunting *Passerina cyanea*

Length: *4½–5½ in.*
What to look for: *male indigo-blue, with blackish wings and tail, no wingbars; female brown above, whitish below, with faint streaking on breast.*
Habitat: *brushy areas, scrubby fields, forest edges.*

The male Indigo Bunting is one of the few birds giving full-voiced performances at midday. A typical song has been written down as *sir, chewe, chewe, cheer, cheer, swe, swe, chir, chir, chir, sir, sir, see, see, fish, fish, fish.* The western Lazuli Bunting (*Passerina amoena*), with sky-blue head, rusty breast, and wingbars, interbreeds with the Indigo where their ranges overlap.

female

male

Painted Bunting *Passerina ciris*

Length: *5–5½ in.*
What to look for: *male with blue head, red underparts and rump, and green back; female green above, yellowish below.*
Habitat: *brushy fields, forest edges, shrubby streamsides, fencerows, towns.*

Considered by many to be North America's most beautifully colored bird, the male Painted Bunting justly merits the nickname "nonpareil" (unequaled). Males are very conspicuous as they sing from high, exposed perches, but the species favors thick ground cover and shrubbery for feeding and nesting. The majority of Painted Buntings migrate to Central America, though some may overwinter in Florida.

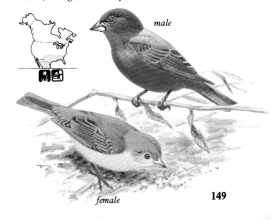

male

female

149

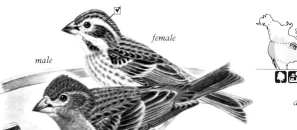

Purple Finch
Carpodacus purpureus

Length: 5¼–6 in.
What to look for: *male with white belly and raspberry-red head, upperparts, and breast; female brown above, heavily streaked below with broad white stripe behind eye.*
Habitat: *mixed woodlands; suburbs and at feeders (migration, winter).*

These handsome finches move erratically from place to place, often in large numbers. In winter an area with few or no Purple Finches one day may have thousands the next. Flocks may consist mostly or solely of brightly colored males or of brown females and immatures. In late summer Purple Finches begin to molt, and in winter plumage the males' reddish areas appear frosted. With wear, the whitish tinge disappears, revealing the rich breeding color.

House Finch
Carpodacus mexicanus

Length: 5–5½ in.
What to look for: *male with bright red head, breast, and rump; female dull brown, with faintly streaked breast and no eye stripe.*
Habitat: *deserts, scrubby areas, open forests, farmlands, towns, suburbs; at feeders.*

The House Finch is an exceptionally adaptable species. Once restricted to the Southwest, it began to extend its range in the 1920's; following the release of caged birds in New York in 1940, House Finches spread in the East. The birds nest in all sorts of sites—in holes in trees, among cactus spines, on the beams of buildings, and in the nests of other birds. In the West, Cassin's Finch (*Carpodacus cassinii*) may be mistaken for this species or for the Purple Finch.

Red Crossbill
Loxia curvirostra

Length: 5½–6 in.
What to look for: *crossed tips of bill; male brick-red, with dark wings and tail; female greenish yellow, lighter below.*
Habitat: *coniferous forests; occasionally in other woodlands.*

The two crossbills—the Red and the White-winged (*Loxia leucoptera*)—are nomads, following the seed crops of conifers or sometimes other forest trees. Their choice of when to nest also seems to depend on the cone supply; they will nest in early spring or even late winter if food is plentiful. A crossbill uses its beak to pry apart the scales of a cone while the tongue extracts the seeds.

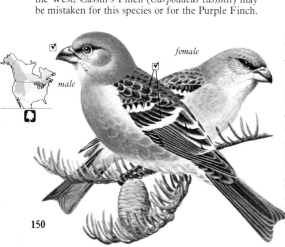

Pine Grosbeak *Pinicola enucleator*

Length: 7½–9½ in.
What to look for: *large size; conical blackish bill; male mostly rosy red, with blackish wings and tail; female greenish brown above, grayer below.* **Habitat:** *coniferous forests; other woodlands (some winters).*

The scientific name of this species translates roughly as "the bird that lives in pines and shells the seeds." But the Pine Grosbeak has a far more varied diet than the name implies—one that includes beechnuts, crab apples, weed seeds, and insects. Pine Grosbeaks breed in the Far North and in mountain areas. In winter they fly to lower latitudes and elevations.

Common Redpoll
Carduelis flammea

Length: *4½–5½ in.*
What to look for:
red forehead; black chin; streaked back and sides; white wingbars; breast and rump pinkish (male).
Habitat: *scrub forests, tundra; brushy areas, birch groves, and at feeders (winter).*

These northern-breeding "winter finches" occasionally appear at feeders farther south. But often redpolls are much more secretive; they chatter high overhead, become visible for an instant as they dive for a thicket, and then vanish. The Pine Siskin (*Carduelis pinus*), which flocks with redpolls, has yellow on the wings and tail and no red anywhere.

nonbreeding male

female

male

American Goldfinch
Carduelis tristis

Length: *4–5 in.*
What to look for: *male bright yellow, with black forehead, wings, and tail; female olive-green above, lighter below; white rump; both sexes yellowish brown in winter; undulating flight.* **Habitat:** *farmlands, weedy fields with scattered trees, river groves, suburbs, parks, at feeders.*

Goldfinches breed late in the summer, when thistledown is available for their tightly woven nests. Feeding flocks can be located by their song, chirps interspersed with *swe-si-iees* or *per-chick-o-rees*, which they also utter in flight. In the West is the Lesser Goldfinch (*Carduelis psaltria*), with a dark back.

female (East)

male (East)

male (West)

Eastern/Spotted Towhee
Pipilo erythrophthalmus/maculatus

Length: *7-8 in.*
What to look for: *male mostly black and white, with rufous flanks and white on wings and tail; white spots on back (West); female with brown instead of black.* **Habitat:** *thickets, open forests, brushy fields, chaparral, suburbs, parks.*

A loud, buzzy *shree* or *shrank* from the underbrush and vigorous scratching in the leaves announce the presence of an Eastern Towhee. Its song is often transcribed as *drink-your-teeeee*. In the West, the Spotted Towhee behaves much the same, and it sounds much like its eastern cousin. There are other towhee species in the West; the California (*Pipilo crissalis*) and the Canyon (*Pipilo fuscus*) were once considered one species. They are common in suburban yards.

Lark Bunting   *Calamospiza melanocorys*

Length: *5½–7 in.*
What to look for: *male black or dark gray, with large white wing patch; female, immature, and winter male brown above, finely streaked below, with light wing patch.* **Habitat:** *prairies, semiarid areas, brushy fields.*

Lark Buntings are gregarious. They winter and travel in flocks, and nest fairly close together. The conspicuously marked breeding males perform song flights in which they rise more or less straight up to a height of 10 to 30 feet and then rock slowly down with stiff wings, butterfly-fashion, singing from start to landing. Often several will do this together.

male

female

Savannah Sparrow
Passerculus sandwichensis

Length: *4–6 in.*
What to look for: *streaked above, heavily streaked below; light stripe above eye; short tail; varies from pale to dark.*
Habitat: *tundra, prairies, meadows, salt marshes, beaches.*

When alarmed, the Savannah Sparrow seems to prefer running through the grass to flying. When it does fly up it usually skims over the grass very briefly, then drops out of sight. Males often sing from a weed-top perch. The song—*tsip-tsip-tsip-seeeee-saaaaay*—ends in a two-part trill that at a distance is all that can be heard. "Savannah" is a fair description of the bird's habitat, but the name actually refers to the Georgia city where the first specimen was found.

Grasshopper Sparrow
Ammodramus savannarum

Length: *4–5 in.*
What to look for: *short-necked appearance; flat head; short tail; buffy, rather unstreaked breast; streaked back.* **Habitat:** *grasslands, meadows, weedy fields, marshes.*

The usual song of the Grasshopper Sparrow consists of a few faint ticks followed by a long, dry trill. The bird sounds like a grasshopper. It also eats grasshoppers, and so the name is doubly appropriate. Grasshopper Sparrows nest in colonies in open grasslands, laying eggs in a slight hollow at the base of a short tuft of vegetation. The nest is difficult to find because the female leaves and approaches it on foot, under cover.

Sharp-tailed Sparrow
Ammodramus caudacutus

Length: *4½–5½ in.*
What to look for: *gray cheek patch on bright buffy face; dark crown; buffy breast with fine streaking; light stripes on back.*
Habitat: *muskeg, reedy margins of swamps, marshes.*

The Sharp-tailed Sparrow occupies the drier parts of salt marshes; the Seaside Sparrow (*Ammodramus maritima*), grayer than the Sharp-tailed and with just a spot of yellow between eye and bill, prefers the wetter terrain. These species, like many grassland sparrows, are skulkers. A useful technique to bring them up to a visible perch is "spishing"—repeating the sound *spsh* over and over. The trick works with other birds, too.

Vesper Sparrow
Pooecetes gramineus

Length: *5–6 in.*
What to look for: *white outer tail feathers; white eye ring; reddish shoulder patch; brown above, with darker streaks; white below, with brown streaks.* **Habitat:** *open fields, grasslands with scattered trees, sagebrush areas.*

This is a ground-nesting species: it makes a small depression in the earth and fills it with grasses, roots, and sometimes hair. The female lays from three to five eggs, which—if they escape predation—hatch within two weeks. The young are ready to leave the nest less than two weeks later. The Vesper Sparrow often sings its sweet song at dusk—hence its name.

"Oregon junco"
(a western race)

"slate-colored junco"
(eastern race)

Black-throated Sparrow
Amphispiza bilineata

Length: *4½–5½ in.*
What to look for: *black throat;
white lines above and below eye patch;
plain gray back; white outer tail feathers.*
Habitat: *brushy deserts, semiarid areas.*

This species sometimes competes for habitat with the Sage Sparrow (*Amphispiza belli*), but the Black-throated Sparrow is more of a true desert bird and is regularly found far from any water hole or stream. Both have nestlings with pale downy plumage, as do other species that nest in hot, open areas. This coloration is believed to help the young survive, by reflecting rather than absorbing light.

Dark-eyed Junco
Junco hyemalis

Length: *5–6½ in.*
What to look for: *white outer tail feathers;
light pink bill; white belly; rest of plumage slate-gray
(with or without white wingbars) or rusty brown
with dark head and pinkish-brown flanks.*
Habitat: *coniferous and mixed forests;
forest edges and at feeders (winter).*

Until recently, the birds shown above were considered separate species. A third form was the White-winged Junco, found in a limited range in the West. All three are now believed to be races of a single species, and have been "lumped" under the name Dark-eyed Junco. A fourth form, the Gray-headed, common in the Southwest, was recently added to this species.

Lark Sparrow   *Chondestes grammacus*

Length: *5½–6½ in.*
What to look for: *facial pattern; clear breast with black
spot (immature with streaked breast); tail with white border.*
Habitat: *prairies, open woodlands, fields, farmlands.*

Lark Sparrows collect in flocks to feed, but the males are extremely pugnacious near their nests. They fight each other on the ground or in the air, and often these battles turn into free-for-alls. One observer reported seeing five or six males fighting together in midair, "so oblivious to their surroundings that [they] nearly hit me in the face."

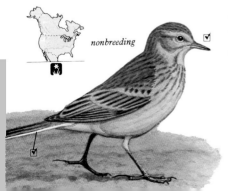

nonbreeding

American Pipit   *Anthus rubescens*

Length: *5–6½ in.*
What to look for: *slim shape; thin bill; dark above,
streaked below (breeding bird paler, less streaked);
white outer tail feathers; frequently wags tail.* **Habitat:** *tundra,
alpine meadows; grasslands, beaches, coasts (migration).*

This is the more widespread of the pipits; the paler-legged Sprague's Pipit (*Anthus spragueii*) occurs in a swath down the center of the continent. Both species walk, instead of hopping like the sparrows they resemble. (Pipits and sparrows actually belong to two very different families.) In courtship, singing males fly almost straight up as high as 200 feet, then float down on fluttering wings.

American Tree Sparrow
Spizella arborea

Length: *5½–6½ in.*
What to look for: *reddish cap and eye streak; dark spot in center of pale gray breast.*
Habitat: *sub-Arctic areas with stunted trees; brushy areas, grasslands, woodland edges, weedy fields, and at feeders (winter).*

Preferring underbrush and shrubs to trees, American Tree Sparrows nest on the ground in dense thickets in the Far North. Whether they appear in large numbers in more southerly regions during winter months depends on the severity of the weather. When the warmth of spring returns, the birds' tinkling song can be heard before they depart for their northern nesting grounds.

Chipping Sparrow
Spizella passerina

Length: *4½–5½ in.*
What to look for: *reddish cap; white stripe above eye; black eye streak; pale grayish below; immature with streaky brown cap.*
Habitat: *open woodlands, forest edges, farmlands, orchards, suburbs, parks.*

immature

The "Chippy" is named for its song—a trill or string of musical *chips*, varying from quite long to very brief. It normally sings from a perch in a tree, often an evergreen. Evergreens are also favorite nesting sites, although the birds may be found raising young in orchard trees, in dooryard vines and shrubbery, and occasionally even on the ground.

Field Sparrow
Spizella pusilla

Length: *5–6 in.*
What to look for: *pinkish bill; reddish cap; buffy below; immature with streaked cap and buffy chest band.* **Habitat:** *brushy and weedy grasslands, meadows, forest edges.*

The sweet song of the Field Sparrow is a series of whistled notes delivered slowly at first and then accelerated into a rapid run. In spring, males establish territories by singing and by chasing their neighbors; once a male is mated, he sings far less than before. Early in the season, nest sites are on the ground or only a short distance above it. As the season advances and the pairs begin second and third families, fewer ground nests are attempted. Nests, however, are seldom more than 3 feet above the ground.

immature

Brewer's Sparrow
Spizella breweri

Length: *4½–5 in.*
What to look for: *finely streaked buffy cap; gray cheek patch; very pale below.*
Habitat: *sagebrush, other brushy areas, alpine meadows; weedy fields (winter).*

A shy bird, Brewer's Sparrow tends to keep out of sight, and its nest is even harder to find. One observer wrote of scaring up an incubating bird; although it flushed about 3 feet in front of his foot and he saw it leave, he had to get down on hands and knees and inspect the ground inch by inch in order to discover the nest. Brewer's Sparrow migrates in flocks with the Clay-colored Sparrow (*Spizella pallida*), a confusingly similar species with a more eastern range.

male

female

House Sparrow (English Sparrow)
Passer domesticus

Length: *5-6 in.*
What to look for: *male with black, whitish, gray, and reddish on head and breast; female brownish above, grayer below.* **Habitat:** *farms, suburbs, cities.*

Most people regret the efforts made in the 19th century to transplant the House Sparrow from Europe. House Sparrows, which belong to a completely different family from our native sparrows, drive bluebirds, wrens, and other songbirds from nesting sites; they tear up nests, destroy eggs, and toss out nestlings. The species reached its peak early in this century. Since then, numbers have declined, probably because of the scarcity of horses and therefore of the waste horse feed eaten by the birds.

immature

Golden-crowned Sparrow
Zonotrichia atricapilla

Length: *6-7 in.*
What to look for: *large size; crown yellow, with black border (immature with duller, brown-bordered crown); breast gray.* **Habitat:** *Arctic and mountain areas with stunted trees; spruce woodlands; brushy slopes; thickets, scrub areas (winter).*

This western sparrow is most often seen during migration or in winter, when it may be common on patios and in gardens. It feeds on seeds, seedlings, buds, and blossoms. This bird is large; the Fox Sparrow and Harris' Sparrow (*Zonotrichia querula*), a black-throated species with a mid-continental range, are the only bigger North American sparrows.

White-crowned Sparrow
Zonotrichia leucophrys

Length: *5½-7 in.*
What to look for: *crown broadly striped with black and white (light and dark brown on immature); gray breast; pink or yellowish bill; pale throat.* **Habitat:** *mountain thickets, areas with scattered brush and trees; roadsides, suburbs (winter).*

The trim, elegant White-crowned Sparrow breeds in brushy, open terrain, whether in the sub-Arctic, in western mountains, or along the Pacific Coast. The nest site is usually on or near the ground. Male and female approach the nest differently: the male flies in directly; the female lands 10 to 15 feet away, then moves in by stages, pausing often to perch.

White-throated Sparrow
Zonotrichia albicollis

Length: *5½-6½ in.*
What to look for: *white throat; gray breast; black and white striped crown, often with yellow patch in front of eye (crown of immature with brown and buff stripes).* **Habitat:** *woodlands with dense brush; brushy areas, forest edges (migration, winter).*

immature

The White-throat is often nicknamed the Canada Bird or the Peabody Bird, in imitation of a typical song, written as "Oh, sweet Canada, Canada, Canada," or "Poor Sam Peabody, Peabody, Peabody." But there are regional dialects among White-throated Sparrows, as well as marked individual variations. And because the White-throat is abundant and whistles its sweet song loudly and not too fast, these variations are especially noticeable.

gray form

red-brown form

Fox Sparrow
Passerella iliaca

Length: *6-7¼ in.*
What to look for: *large size; rusty tail;*
brown, red-brown, or gray above;
streaked below, with large central spot.
Habitat: *scrubby trees of sub-Arctic and*
mountain slopes; forest undergrowth;
thickets, farmlands, parks (migration, winter).

The husky Fox Sparrow scratches vigorously for seeds, small fruits, and insects among fallen leaves, jumping forward and back with both feet and spraying litter in all directions. Its summer food is mostly insects and other animals; Audubon reported seeing Fox Sparrows eat tiny shellfish in coastal Newfoundland and Labrador. Its voice is as distinctive as its appearance. The song is a series of rich, often slurred whistles run together in a short "sentence." Indeed, the general impression is that of a conversation.

Swamp Sparrow
Melospiza georgiana

Length: *4½-5½ in.*
What to look for: *reddish cap; gray face*
and breast; whitish throat; buffy
or pale tawny flanks; rusty wings.
Habitat: *brushy swamps, bogs, marshes;*
fields, weedy edges (migration, winter).

Within its breeding range this is one of the last diurnal birds to fall silent at night and among the first to tune up in the morning, long before daybreak. Sometimes Swamp Sparrows keep singing through the night. Their musical trilling—richer than the Chipping Sparrow's but otherwise quite similar—sounds from all over the northern marshes where they nest. One authority writes that some swamp sparrow phrases are double. The birds sing two different songs on different pitches at once—"the higher notes being slow and sweet . . ., and the lower notes faster and somewhat guttural."

Song Sparrow
Melospiza melodia

Length: *5-7 in.*
What to look for: *heavily streaked below,*
with dark central breast spot;
longish tail; immature more finely streaked.
Habitat: *forest edges, brushy areas,*
thickets, hedgerows, parks, beaches.

Ornithologists recognize more than 30 subspecies of the remarkably adaptable Song Sparrow. The birds vary considerably in size, with the largest races 40 percent bigger than the smallest. The color ranges from reddish or dark brown to pale gray. The song typically begins with several regularly spaced notes, followed by a trill, then a jumble of notes. Because Song Sparrows seem to learn the structure of their music from other Song Sparrows, local "dialects" are common. And each Song Sparrow has a variety of private versions; no two individuals sing the same tune.

immature

nonbreeding male

nonbreeding female

breeding male

male

female

Lapland Longspur
Calcarius lapponicus

Length: 5½–6½ in.
What to look for: *some plumages with chestnut nape; white outer tail feathers; breeding male with black head, throat, and breast; nonbreeding male with white throat and black breast band; female finely streaked.*
Habitat: *tundra; prairies, meadows, beaches (winter).*

The dramatic summer dress of this species is never seen by most people, for the Lapland Longspur nests in the Far North. There, ornithologists have noticed that its breeding activities are remarkably synchronized. Most males start singing at once, most pairs mate at the same time, and most egg laying begins on the same date. Most adults and young also follow a common schedule when they molt before migration.

Chestnut-collared Longspur
Calcarius ornatus

Length: 5½–6½ in.
What to look for: *tail white with black central triangle; breeding male with bold facial pattern, chestnut nape, and black underparts; female and nonbreeding male streaked buffy brown.*
Habitat: *prairies, plains, large fields.*

Loose colonies of Chestnut-collared Longspurs breed in shortgrass prairies or weedy fields. The conspicuous male defends his territory by perching on a stone or weed stalk and by singing in flight. The protectively colored female digs a slight hollow near a grass tuft and lines it, mainly with grass. She alone incubates, but both parents supply the young with food. Though the summer diet includes insects, seeds are the mainstay the rest of the year.

Snow Bunting
Plectrophenax nivalis

Length: 5½–7 in.
What to look for: *mostly white; breeding male with black on back, wings, and tail; nonbreeding male with reddish brown on head and shoulders; female paler.*
Habitat: *tundra; prairies, meadows, beaches (migration, winter).*

The Snowflakes or Snow Birds breed farther north than any other species of songbird. The males arrive on their Arctic breeding grounds by mid-May, three or four weeks earlier than the females. The Eskimos welcome them as harbingers of spring. Snow Buntings nest mainly on rocky terrain, usually building their bulky fur- and feather-lined nests in holes and crannies. In winter they flock along coasts and in open country; they feed on fallen grain in fields and pastures and on weed seeds, as well as on sand fleas and other insects.

breeding male

nonbreeding male

Reptiles
and Amphibians

Appreciating these animals often begins with a fondness for friendly little lizards or long-legged frogs. And as unknowns become knowns, apprehension is transformed into genuine admiration.

When asked why reptiles and amphibians are customarily lumped together, one consultant replied, tongue in cheek, "They're both ugly." We don't—and we hope you won't—share that point of view. Glance through the pages that follow for a glimpse of their beauty—the ornate pattern on a Painted Turtle, the coral snakes' vibrant rings, the sleek lines on the Striped Chorus Frog. Admire the creatures for their survival techniques—the lizard's habit of losing its tail (better than its head!), the wiggling lure of the Alligator Snapper, the skink's ability to see even when its eyes are closed.

Reptiles

Leaping lizards, slithering snakes, torpid turtles, and awesome alligators are all reptiles, despite their profound differences in shape, mobility, and way of life. The typical reptile has a protective covering of scales or plates, five clawed toes on each foot, and lungs instead of gills. Most species eat animals (land tortoises are among the exceptions), and most lay eggs (all poisonous snakes on this continent except the coral snakes produce live young). But no one trait separates the reptiles from all other animals, as feathers do for birds.

Less tied to freshwater than amphibians, reptiles live just about everywhere in the United States and southern Canada—in freshwater, in saltwater, in forests, grasslands, deserts, and suburban places. (At one time they were even found in the air, but the large flying reptiles, like the dinosaurs, have been extinct for millions of years.) The lizard population is especially diverse in the Southwest, and the snake population in the East.

Alligators and Crocodiles
Found in the United States only in the Southeast, these armored reptiles are most easily seen in southern Florida, especially in portions of Everglades National Park. There, from elevated boardwalks, you can observe enormous alligators as they bask on muddy banks or drift in the water like logs. (A refuge for crocodiles, which are rare in the United States, was recently established on Key Largo in Florida. On a springtime visit to the Everglades you may even hear the roar of a courting male—a sound unusual not only for its intensity but also because of its source. Most other reptiles never utter a sound.

Turtles
Just under 50 species of turtles live in Canada and the United States, with Florida an especially turtle-rich state. These reptiles are most often found in or near water, especially on logs that are partially submerged.

A turtle, it has been said, carries its house about on its back. The characteristic bony shell—the upper part is called the carapace and the lower the plastron—is covered with hard shields, known as scutes. Turtles that spend little time on land, such as the softshell turtles, often have reduced shells.

To identify a turtle, you may have to pick it up and look at its plastron. Although turtles are toothless (all other reptiles have teeth), they can still inflict a painful bite, and they should be handled with care—or in the case of the bigger ones, not at all.

Lizards
Although only a small number of the world's lizard species (some 115 out of 3,000) live north of the Mexican border, it is hard to imagine a more diverse group. Most have four legs

The habitat symbols used in this section are: 🌵 *desert* 🐾 *grassland/meadow/brush* 🌲 *fores*

Fondly dubbed the herps or herptiles by their human friends (the name comes from the Greek for "creeping," *herpetos*), these two groups of animals include not only creepers (snakes) but also swimmers (sea turtles, among others), climbers (treefrogs), hoppers (toads), runners (lizards), gliders (certain tropical snakes), and burrowers (just about all groups). They share neither a method of locomotion nor any other trait that is theirs alone.

Like mammals, birds, and fishes, the reptiles and amphibians have backbones; but unlike the other vertebrates, they have neither fur nor feathers nor paired fins. The reptiles and amphibians are cold-blooded, in contrast with mammals and birds: the temperature of their bodies varies with the outside temperature, and their activities come to a halt when the weather gets too cold. As a result, they are most common in the warmer areas of the world—that is, the tropics and subtropics. On this continent they are both relatively small divisions, with fewer than 300 species of reptiles and 200 of amphibians north of Mexico.

The differences between reptiles and amphibians tend to reflect the reptiles' greater independence from water. Their bodies, unlike those of the thin-skinned amphibians, are covered with scales or plates, which furnish general protection and combat water loss. Unlike the eggs of amphibians, theirs have shells (either brittle like a bird's egg or leathery like a pair of moccasins) and are less likely to dry out when laid on land.

For further information about these animals, consult the individual introduction to each group. The one for the reptiles (alligators, turtles, lizards, and snakes) begins below; the one covering the amphibians (salamanders, toads, and frogs) appears on page 181.

---

but the glass and the legless lizards have none at all. Bodies range from slim to massive; tails may be long and slender or short and thick; scales may be smooth or spiny, with scale size as well as texture of some significance in identification. (For example, whiptails and racerunners have large scales on the belly and small ones on the back.) Color is often of little help in identification, since it may vary with region, age, and sex. In certain species the males are brighter in color, and they may be larger and longer-tailed than the females.

Lizards love sunshine, and most kinds are active during the day. Look for little ones basking on stone walls, running along rail fences and logs, hiding in brush piles and heaps of dead leaves; inspect deserted buildings, sawdust piles, rocky slopes, canyon walls, and patches of sandy soil. Only one species in our region, the Gila Monster, is venomous (though others may bite), and that particular one many people would avoid on the basis of size alone.

Snakes

Although some might prefer that snakes not lose their aura of mystery, the human fascination with snakes can to some extent be explained by certain aspects of their biology and behavior. Snakes have no legs (although the Rubber Boa and closely related species have short remnants, known as spurs). They have no eyelids (hence the "unwinking stare").

They rely solely on animals for food (all other groups of reptiles include some plant-eating species). And they can injure and even kill human beings.

Snakes often catch your attention only when they slither away from you. A deliberate search for these animals involves turning over logs and boards, poking through brush piles, and exploring rocky ledges, stone walls, and edges of ponds and streams. Do this with care; don't put your hand where you cannot see, or step over a log or a rock without first checking for snakes on the other side. Nocturnal species, such as the Night Snake, may sometimes be found by walking or slowly driving down a hardtop country road after dark. Occasionally you may encounter not the snakes themselves but their cast-off skins (snakes molt several times a year).

A snake should never be handled unless you are absolutely certain it is not a venomous one. (Even nonvenomous ones, however, may bite.) Although only about a sixth of North America's 115 species are venomous, nearly all parts of the United States and southern Canada have at least one species that is. This book does not picture all of the venomous species (the Arizona Coral Snake and certain rattlesnakes are omitted), nor are all races and color variations of each species shown. Act with discretion in places where there may be snakes, and especially around the snakes themselves.

Alligators *Alligator*

The largest reptiles in North America are also the loudest, the males bellowing lustily during the spring mating season. For a reptile, the female is an extraordinary parent. After mating she builds a nesting mound near water, lays 20 to 60 eggs, covers them with vegetation, and guards them until they hatch, some 10 weeks later. The young may stay with her for a year or more, eating frogs, crustaceans, and aquatic insects; adults prey on fish, turtles, birds, and small mammals. The alligator's close relative, the slender-snouted American Crocodile (*Crocodylus acutus*), is a rare resident of brackish and saltwater swamps in southern Florida.

American Alligator
Alligator mississippiensis

Length: *6–15 ft.*
What to look for: *snout broad, rounded; old adults gray-black; young black, with yellow crossbands.* **Habitat:** *freshwater, brackish marshes; swamps, rivers, bayous.*

Alligator Snapping Turtles
Macroclemys

Weighing up to 200 pounds or more, the Alligator Snapper is the world's largest freshwater turtle. More sedentary than its relative the Snapping Turtle, it lies submerged and half buried in the mud, wiggling the pink wormlike projection on its tongue. When a fish is lured by the "bait," the turtle's jaws snap shut. (Turtles are toothless but have sharp edges on their jaws.) The hefty reptile also feeds on worms, snails, mussels, carrion, and other kinds of turtles.

Alligator Snapping Turtle
Macroclemys temmincki

Shell length: *13–26 in.*
What to look for: *carapace brown or gray, with 3 knobby ridges; head big, with strongly hooked beak; long tail.* **Habitat:** *lakes, sloughs, deep rivers.*

Snapping Turtles
Chelydra

The head and limbs of the Snapping Turtle are so large and its lower shell so small that the animal cannot retreat completely into its shell. Its powerful jaws are its defense. Opportunistic feeders, Snappers eat a wide variety of aquatic plants and animals. They are usually seen floating lazily just below the water's surface. Females occasionally come on land to seek out sites for laying their eggs, and can be very aggressive at that time.

Snapping Turtle
Chelydra serpentina

Shell length: *8–20 in.*
What to look for: *head big, with powerful jaws; carapace brown, often covered with algae or mud; long tail.* **Habitat:** *quiet mud-bottomed waters.*

Stinkpot (Musk Turtle)
Sternotherus odoratus

Shell length: *3-5½ in.*
What to look for: *2 pale stripes on each side of head; carapace smooth, high-domed; plastron with 11 plates.*
Habitat: *streams, bayous, ponds, canals.*

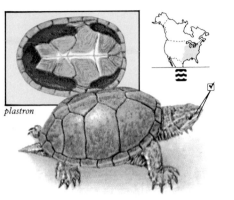

plastron

Loggerhead Musk Turtle
Sternotherus minor

Shell length: *3-5¼ in.*
What to look for: *carapace brown or orange, often with dark border and dashes or streaks; plastron pink or yellow, with 11 plates.*
Habitat: *streams, rivers, sinkholes.*

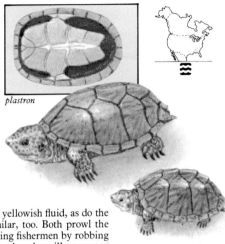

plastron

young turtle, with ridged carapace

Musk Turtles   *Sternotherus*

When annoyed, these small turtles secrete a foul-smelling yellowish fluid, as do the closely related mud turtles. Many of their habits are similar, too. Both prowl the bottom in search of small animal prey, occasionally annoying fishermen by robbing them of their bait. When handled, musk turtles and some mud turtles will attempt to bite. In spring they bask in the sun in shallow water or among floating plants, with only the top of the "dome" protruding above the surface. Sunbathing raises the temperature of turtles and other cold-blooded animals, speeding up their metabolism.

Yellow Mud Turtle
Kinosternon flavescens

Shell length: *3½-6 in.*
What to look for: *carapace smooth, with dark-edged olive to brown plates; plastron yellow to brown, with 11 plates, 2 hinges, and dark seams; jaws and throat white or yellow.*
Habitat: *streams, rivers, ponds, lakes.*

hinges

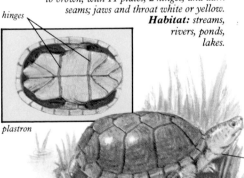

plastron

Eastern Mud Turtle
Kinosternon subrubrum

Shell length: *3-3¾ in.*
What to look for: *carapace smooth, unmarked, olive to dark brown; plastron yellow to brown, with 11 plates and 2 hinges.* **Habitat:** *lakes, swamps, salt marshes, flooded ditches.*

hinges

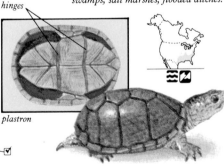

plastron

Mud Turtles   *Kinosternon*

Although these turtles look like musk turtles from above, they are quite distinct when viewed from below. A mud turtle's plastron, or lower shell, covers most of its under-surface and bears two readily visible hinges. The hinges allow the turtle to bend its plastron when it pulls in its head, feet, and tail, thus furnishing added protection for its soft parts. In contrast, a musk turtle has a relatively small plastron with a single inconspicuous hinge.

161

plastron

Wood Turtle
Clemmys insculpta
Shell length: *5–9 in.*
What to look for: *carapace brown,
with pyramidlike plates; plastron yellow,
with black markings; neck and front legs often orange.*
Habitat: *woodland streams; farmlands; swamps, marshes.*

Spotted Turtle
Clemmys guttata
Shell length: *3½–5 in.*
What to look for: *carapace
black, with yellowish spots;
eyes brown (male) or orange
(female).* **Habitat:** *flooded
woodlands, soft-bottomed
streams, wet meadows,
beaver ponds.*

Western Pond Turtle
*Clemmys
marmorata*
Shell length:
3½–7 in.
What to look for:
*carapace smooth,
flattened, olive to
dark brown, usually
with dark lines or
spots that radiate
from plate centers.*
Habitat: *still and
slow-moving water,
including reservoirs;
sometimes in
brackish water.*

Pond Turtles *Clemmys*

All of North America's four kinds of pond turtle
spend some time on land. Although the Wood Turtle
winters in a sheltered spot under water, at other times of
year it may wander through woodlands, meadows, and plowed
fields. The Spotted Turtle likes to bask on grassy tussocks in spring.
"Spotties" also congregate on partially submerged logs, diving into the water
when frightened and digging into the muddy bottom. The Western Pond Turtle, the
only freshwater turtle in most of its range (it overlaps slightly with the Painted Turtle), is the most aquatic member of this group. Often seen basking alone on a favorite
rock, log, or mudbank, it too is quick to dive when disturbed. The fourth pond turtle,
the 4-inch Bog Turtle (*Clemmys muhlenbergi*), lives in scattered areas from New York
to North Carolina. Bright yellow or orange blotches on the sides of its head contrast
sharply with its basically brown shell. Like the other pond turtles, it feeds on mollusks and other small animals as well as on aquatic plants.

Diamondback Terrapin
Malaclemys terrapin
Shell length: *4–9½ in.*
What to look for: *carapace gray to black, often
with deeply incised rings; head and neck gray, with
black flecks.* **Habitat:** *salt marshes, estuaries.*

Diamondback Terrapins *Malaclemys*

Male and female Diamondback Terrapins differ greatly in
size; the female may be twice as long as her mate. (Map turtles exhibit this same trait.) The male's longer, thicker tail
and concave plastron facilitate mating. The female deposits
4 to 18 eggs above the high-tide line, in a cavity dug by her
hind feet and filled in with sand. The eggs hatch in two to
four months, their numbers depleted by marauding Raccoons, skunks, foxes, and gulls.

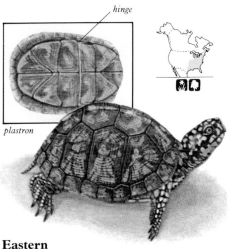

hinge

plastron

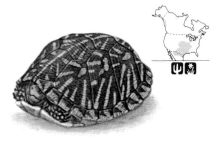

Western Box Turtle
Terrapene ornata

Shell length: *4–5¾ in.*
What to look for: *carapace high-domed, black or brown, with radiating yellow lines; plastron hinged, similarly colored.*
Habitat: *dry prairies, scrub plains, woodlands, mesquite grasslands.*

Eastern Box Turtle
Terrapene carolina

Shell length: *4–8½ in.*
What to look for: *carapace high-domed, brown to black, with yellow, orange, or olive lines or spots; plastron plain or blotched, with hinge.*
Habitat: *damp forests, fields, and floodplains.*

Box Turtles *Terrapene*

Although most kinds of turtles can withdraw into their shells, a box turtle can close up more completely than other species: because its plastron, or lower shell, is hinged, the front and rear sections can be bent upward so that the edges of the two shells meet. Box turtles are basically land-dwelling reptiles, but sometimes cool themselves in woodland pools or puddles. They are renowned for their longevity. Although some individuals have reportedly lived for more than a hundred years, estimates of a turtle's age are not always reliable. Dates scratched into the shell indicate little more than the personality of the person doing the carving. Counting the growth rings that develop on the plates overlying the shell can also be misleading. The rings do not develop equally each year, and after 10 or 15 years they may largely disappear.

Map Turtle
Graptemys geographica

Shell length: *4–10¾ in.*
What to look for: *low central ridge on carapace; carapace greenish, with thin yellow-orange rings; yellow spot (usually shaped like triangle) behind eye.*
Habitat: *rivers and lakes with mud bottoms.*

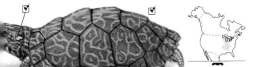

False Map Turtle
Graptemys pseudogeographica

Shell length: *3½–10¾ in.*
What to look for: *carapace brown to olive, often with dark blotches and pale ovals; black-knobbed ridge on carapace; yellow mark behind eye (shape varies from crescent to short bar).*
Habitat: *weedy lakes, rivers, sloughs, reservoirs.*

Map Turtles *Graptemys*

The dozen or so species of map turtle, all native to eastern North America, have a low ridge, or keel, along the midline of the carapace. Certain species, such as the False Map Turtle, have knobs on the keel and are sometimes called sawbacks. As the turtle ages, the knobs tend to wear down. The Ouachita Map Turtle (*Graptemys ouachitensis*), similar in appearance to the False Map Turtle and overlapping much of its range, is distinguished by four large yellow spots or alternating yellow and dark green bars on the underside of the head. Other map turtles are specific to certain river basins in the South. All are gregarious, basking together atop logs or on steep banks and vanishing quickly when an intruder appears. Although some species eat plants, invertebrates make up most of their diet. The female Map Turtle takes freshwater clams and snails, while the smaller male feeds on insects and crayfish.

163

plastron

Painted Turtle
Chrysemys picta

Shell length: *4–9¾ in.*
What to look for: *carapace smooth, olive to black, with red bars or crescents along edge; plastron yellow, sometimes with markings.*
Habitat: *shallow, weedy freshwater areas.*

Slider
Trachemys scripta

Shell length: *5–11½ in.*
What to look for: *red, orange, or yellow stripe or patch behind eye; chin rounded on underside; carapace olive to brown, with yellow stripes and bars.*
Habitat: *shallow, weedy freshwater areas.*

Turtles, tortoises, and terrapins. Any reptile with a bony shell and a toothless beak is a turtle. North America has some 50 species, including 3 that belong to the tortoise family. Adapted to life on land, tortoises usually have short legs, webless feet, and high dome-shaped shells. The word "terrapin" has no specific scientific meaning. Instead, it is used as the popular name for several kinds of edible and formerly commercially valuable freshwater turtles.

Basking Turtles
Chrysemys, Pseudemys, Trachemys

Nearly all turtles bask in the sun, but the sunbathing habit is especially marked among members of this group, who often pile on top of one another on a favorite log. The Slider, said to slide speedily into the water when approached, belongs to this group; so do the Painted Turtle, North America's most wide-ranging turtle, and the cooters *(Pseudemys concinna* and *floridana),* two yellow-bellied southeastern species whose name comes from an African word for turtle. One member of the group, the red-eared turtle (a race of the Slider), was once commonly sold in pet shops. Although the needs for pet turtles vary according to species, most require a varied diet ("turtle food" is not adequate), a clean tank, a basking spot, and an understanding of their habits.

Chicken Turtles *Deirochelys*

A turtle's place in the food chain changes with age. Many of the aquatic species, including the Chicken Turtle, feed on small animals early in life and then switch to a vegetarian diet. As a turtle grows, its enemies also change. Young Chicken Turtles are eaten by Raccoons, otters, and wading birds; alligators and man feed on the adults. (The succulent flesh of the Chicken Turtle was once marketed as food.) The larger species of turtle, such as the tortoises and snappers, have few predators except man.

Chicken Turtle
Deirochelys reticularia

Shell length: *4–10 in.*
What to look for: *neck unusually long, with yellow stripes; carapace with fine incised lines, giving wrinkled look.*
Habitat: *swamps; shallow, weedy ponds and lakes.*

Blanding's Turtles *Emydoidea*

Although the one species in this group is sometimes confused with a box turtle, its long, yellow-throated neck is quite different; and it cannot close its shell as tightly, even though its plastron is hinged. More active in colder weather than most turtles, it has sometimes been seen swimming beneath ice.

Blanding's Turtle
Emydoidea blandingi

Shell length: *5–10½ in.*
What to look for: *carapace high, smooth, black, with yellowish spots, blotches, or lines; plastron hinged; chin and throat yellow.* **Habitat:** *marshes; shallow, weedy creeks, ponds, lakes.*

hinge

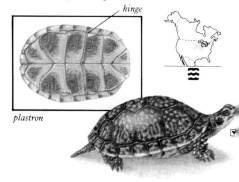

plastron

REPTILES

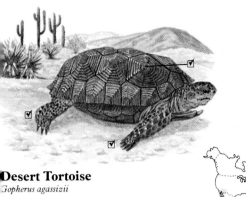

Desert Tortoise
Gopherus agassizii

Shell length: 9-14½ in.
What to look for: *carapace with high dome and deeply incised concentric lines, often with yellow or orange in center; front feet flat, with large scales; hind feet round, stumpy.*
Habitat: *canyon bottoms; slopes, washes, oases.*

Gopher Tortoises *Gopherus*

Named for their gopherlike digging habits, the only tortoises in North America have flattened front limbs used in scooping out the dry soil. Two of the North American species, the Desert Tortoise and the Gopher Tortoise, dig a long tunnel with a resting chamber at the end. The third species, Berlandier's Tortoise (*Gopherus berlandieri*), of Texas and Mexico, has a simpler burrow, often just a sloping hole. All three have the slow gait and vegetarian diet typical of tortoises throughout the world.

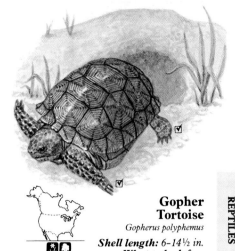

Gopher Tortoise
Gopherus polyphemus

Shell length: 6-14½ in.
What to look for:
carapace with high dome; front feet flat; hind feet round, stumpy; head large, rounded, grayish black.
Habitat: *dry, sandy transition zones between grasslands and forests.*

Softshell Turtles *Trionyx*

Most turtles have two layers of protective armor—a bony shell and an overlying layer of hard plates. A softshell turtle is not truly soft-shelled, for it too has a bony shell; but instead of the hard plates, soft, leathery skin covers the shell. In the young and in most adult males this skin is dotted with dark circles. The males are much smaller than the females. Softshell turtles spend long periods underwater buried in mud, with their tubular snouts just reaching the water's surface. Two species are widespread: the Spiny Softshell and the Smooth Softshell (*Trionyx muticus*), which inhabits the Mississippi and its tributaries.

Spiny Softshell
Trionyx spiniferus

Shell length: 5-18 in.
What to look for: *carapace soft, leathery, thin, flat, with spiny projections along front edge; feet webbed; nose long, tapering.*
Habitat: *fast rivers; lakes, marshy streams, ponds.*

Loggerhead
Caretta caretta

Shell length: 31-48 in.
What to look for: *flipperlike limbs; carapace reddish brown, with 3 knobby ridges; 2 pairs of scales between eyes.* **Habitat:** *open seas, salt marshes, bays.*

Loggerhead Sea Turtles *Caretta*

Sea turtles come ashore (at night and formerly in large numbers) only to lay eggs. The Loggerhead, the species most commonly encountered along the North American coast, follows the typical pattern. After mating in shallow water, the female digs a deep hole in the beach, lays more than a hundred eggs, covers them with sand, and heads out to sea. The eggs hatch about eight weeks later. Sea turtles have been drastically affected by man. Their large size, large number of eggs, and predictable habits have worked against their survival, as has development in coastal areas.

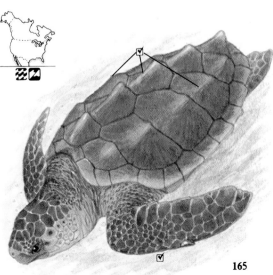

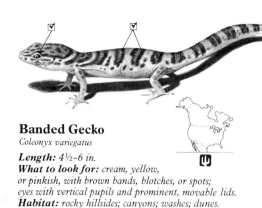

Banded Gecko
Coleonyx variegatus

Length: 4½–6 in.
What to look for: cream, yellow, or pinkish, with brown bands, blotches, or spots; eyes with vertical pupils and prominent, movable lids.
Habitat: rocky hillsides; canyons; washes; dunes.

Banded Geckos *Coleonyx*

Geckos form a large family of tropical and subtropical lizards. Although many geckos can climb, the banded species are ground dwellers, hiding in rock crevices by day and prowling about at night for insects. Most geckos lack functional eyelids, but the three banded geckos, all residents of the Southwest, have eyelids that open and shut.

Leopard Lizards *Gambelia*

During the day these large, agile lizards wait in the shade of a bush for spiders, insects, and smaller lizards, darting to another bush if nothing passes by. Like collared lizards, a leopard lizard raises its front legs and holds them in front of its body while running at high speed on its hind legs. Elusive and pugnacious, it may hiss if cornered and will bite if picked up. The Blunt-nosed Leopard Lizard (*Gambelia sila*), an endangered species, occurs in California's San Joaquin Valley.

Leopard Lizard
Gambelia wislizenii

Length: 8½–15 in.
What to look for: body and tail rounded; gray or tan, with brown, leopardlike spots and white bars.
Habitat: deserts, dry plains.

Green Anole
Anolis carolinensis

Length: 5–8 in.
What to look for: usually green (can become mottled or solid brown); pink throat fan; toe pads enlarged.
Habitat: trees, shrubs, vines, walls, fences.

Anoles *Anolis*

Abundant in the tropics, anoles are the largest group of reptiles in the Western Hemisphere: there are nearly 200 species. Only the Green Anole is native to North America, although several West Indian species have been introduced into southern Florida. Anoles have enlarged toe pads, enabling the lizards to climb with ease. Like African chameleons, anoles change color in response to changes in light, temperature, and emotional state. Males are highly territorial and drive away rivals with a series of head-bobs, followed by a display of the colorful throat fan.

Earless Lizards *Holbrookia*

Unlike snakes and salamanders, most lizards have ear openings through which they hear airborne sounds. Earless lizards do not. Larger than the Lesser Earless Lizard but with a smaller range, the Greater Earless Lizard (*Cophosaurus texanus*) has conspicuous dark bands on the underside of its tail.

Lesser Earless Lizard
Holbrookia maculata

Length: 4–5 in.
What to look for: absence of ear openings; gray to red-brown (similar to soil); 2 rows of dark blotches from neck to tail along each side.
Habitat: sand and gravel areas in shortgrass prairies; cultivated areas; barren deserts.

Night Lizards   *Xantusia*

Despite their name, night lizards are not entirely nocturnal. Although certain species hide under rocks, bark, or decaying plants when the sun is up, the Desert Night Lizard forages for insects during the day and into the evening. Its young are born alive, tailfirst and upside down. Most other lizards hatch from eggs.

Desert Night Lizard
Xantusia vigilis

Length: 3¾–5 in.
What to look for: *eyes with vertical pupils; no eyelids; soft skin; scales on back small, grainy; belly scales large, square; light stripe from eye to neck.*
Habitat: *rock outcrops, debris beneath desert plants.*

back scales

belly scales

REPTILES

Zebra-tailed Lizard
Callisaurus draconoides

Length: *6–9 in.*
What to look for: *2 rows of dusky spots on back; tail white below, with black bars; ear openings.*
Habitat: *open areas with packed soil.*

Zebra-tailed Lizards   *Callisaurus*

Discretely spotted and rather dull overall, the Zebratail blends with its surroundings to an extraordinary extent. When frightened, however, it may take on a different appearance, raising and curling its tail and thus exposing the zebralike stripes on the underside as it runs. It is one of North America's fastest lizards and can reach speeds of more than 15 miles an hour over short distances.

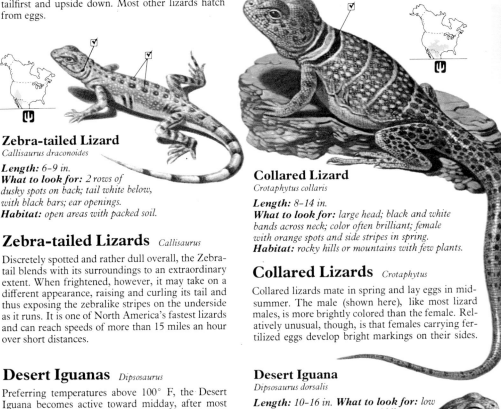

Collared Lizard
Crotaphytus collaris

Length: *8–14 in.*
What to look for: *large head; black and white bands across neck; color often brilliant; female with orange spots and side stripes in spring.*
Habitat: *rocky hills or mountains with few plants.*

Collared Lizards   *Crotaphytus*

Collared lizards mate in spring and lay eggs in midsummer. The male (shown here), like most lizard males, is more brightly colored than the female. Relatively unusual, though, is that females carrying fertilized eggs develop bright markings on their sides.

Desert Iguanas   *Dipsosaurus*

Preferring temperatures above 100° F, the Desert Iguana becomes active toward midday, after most other reptiles in the area have taken refuge from the heat. When the sand becomes unbearably hot, it climbs into a creosote bush to cool itself and eat the vegetation. At night, and also during hibernation, it rests in a rodent burrow whose entrance it has plugged with sand.

Desert Iguana
Dipsosaurus dorsalis

Length: *10–16 in.* **What to look for:** *low crest of enlarged scales down middle of back; round body; head small, short-snouted.* **Habitat:** *creosote-bush desert.*

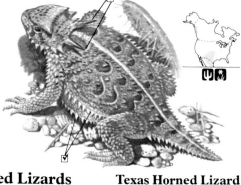

Short-horned Lizard
Phrynosoma douglassi

Length: 2½–5¾ in.
What to look for: *flat body; head armed with short spines; 1 row of pointed scales along flanks; 2 dark blotches at back of neck.*
Habitat: *prairies to high mountain forests.*

Horned Lizards
Phrynosoma

Expanded scales on the head, and sometimes also on the sides, give horned lizards (or "toads") a bizarre appearance and protect them from predators as well. If attacked, a horned lizard may open its mouth, hiss, bite, or even eject blood from the corners of its eyes. Horned lizards can remain active at temperatures above 100° F, but when it gets too hot they dig into loose soil by shuffling the body sideways.

Texas Horned Lizard
Phrynosoma cornutum

Length: 2½–7 in.
What to look for: *flat body; head armed with spines (2 long ones in center); 2 rows of pointed scales along flanks.* **Habitat:** *dry, sparsely vegetated flatlands with loose soil.*

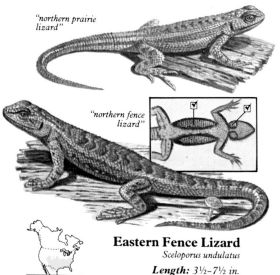

"northern prairie lizard"

"northern fence lizard"

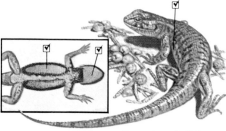

Sagebrush Lizard
Sceloporus graciosus

Length: 5–6 in.
What to look for: *rusty area behind front legs; shoulder usually with black spot; small, grainy scales on back of thigh; males with blue on throat and darker blue on belly.* **Habitat:** *sagebrush flats to mountain forests.*

Eastern Fence Lizard
Sceloporus undulatus

Length: 3½–7½ in.
What to look for: *body with rough, raised scales; gray to brown, with dark, wavy crossbars or dark and light stripes; males with bluish patches on throat and belly.* **Habitat:** *dry woodlands, prairies, brushlands.*

Spiny Lizards *Sceloporus*

The Eastern Fence Lizard is North America's most widespread lizard. The males, like those of other spiny lizards (18 species occur in the United States and Canada), usually have bright blue belly patches, displayed when they flatten their sides to attract a female or warn off an intruder.

Side-blotched Lizards *Uta*

The Side-blotched Lizard, the only representative of this group in the United States, rises early, warms itself by basking on a rock, and then begins searching for food. An insatiable eater, it consumes myriads of insects, spiders, and scorpions. It bobs its head to drive off intruders, a habit shared with the spiny lizards. It also looks somewhat like a spiny lizard, but is distinguished by a dark blotch on each side and a loose fold of skin under the throat.

Side-blotched Lizard
Uta stansburiana

Length: 4–6¼ in. **What to look for:** *blue to black blotch behind front leg; fold of skin across throat; ear openings.* **Habitat:** *deserts to mountains; sandy or rocky areas with low vegetation or scattered trees.*

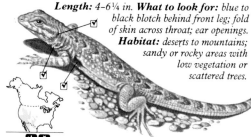

REPTILES

168

Chuckwalla
Sauromalus obesus

Length: *11–16½ in.*
What to look for: *body large, puffy; loose folds of skin at neck and sides; tail thick, blunt-tipped.*
Habitat: *rocky hillsides, outcrops in creosote-bush deserts.*

Chuckwallas *Sauromalus*

In the morning the Chuckwalla basks until its body temperature reaches about 100° F. Then it forages for flowers, fruits, and leaves. When frightened, this large, timid lizard flees into a rock crevice and inflates its body so that it is wedged in place. Chuckwallas vary widely in appearance. For example, the young have crossbands, which fade with time and disappear entirely on the larger males.

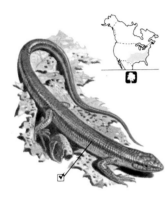

Ground Skink
Scincella lateralis

Length: *3-5 in.* **What to look for:** *brown lizard with dark side stripe running from eye onto tail; small legs; long tail; smooth, shiny scales.* **Habitat:** *humid woods rich in leaf litter.*

Ground Skinks *Scincella*

One difference between lizards and snakes is that most lizards have eyelids. (A snake's eye is covered by a clear scale and can never close.) Although a lizard's eyelids, like human eyelids, are usually opaque, the lower lids of ground skinks and a few others have a transparent "window," permitting the animal to see while its eyes are closed. This is especially advantageous for creatures that live underground or in other places where loose particles of soil or debris could injure their eyes.

Skinks *Eumeces*

Like most lizards in temperate parts of North America, these shiny creatures hibernate in soil in winter, court and mate in spring, and lay eggs that hatch in late summer or early fall. The female skink becomes secretive after mating. She hollows out a depression in moist soil or rotting wood, deposits 2 to 21 eggs in the nest, and protects the eggs until they hatch a month or two later. The hatchlings look different from the adults—so different that people once thought they were another species.

Great Plains Skink
Eumeces obsoletus

Length: *6½-13¾ in.*
What to look for: *rows of scales angling upward on sides between limbs; adult beige or gray, with dark-edged scales; young shiny black, with small white and orange head spots and blue tail.*
Habitat: *grasslands, mesas, canyons, other rocky areas.*

Five-lined Skink
Eumeces fasciatus

Length: *5-8 in.*
What to look for: *adult with faded stripes and gray tail; breeding male with red-orange jaws; young with 5 light stripes and blue tail.*
Habitat: *damp woods with leaf litter, shaded gardens.*

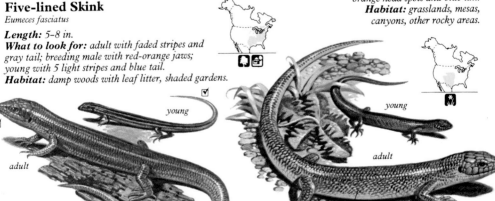

young

young

adult

adult

169

marbled race

Six-lined Racerunner
Cnemidophorus sexlineatus

Length: 6-10½ in.
What to look for: 6 or 7 light stripes, with black between stripes; scales on back tiny, grainy; scales on belly large, rectangular; throat blue to green (male) or white (female).
Habitat: dry woodlands, grasslands.

Great Basin race

Whiptails and Racerunners
Cnemidophorus

As these long-tailed lizards search for insects and spiders, they move in a rapid, jerky manner and nervously turn their heads from side to side. Like other lizards, both species shown here consist of males and females. But certain other species in the group—the New Mexico Whiptail (*Cnemidophorus neomexicanus*), for example—are unisexual: all individuals are females, which lay fertile eggs without mating.

Western Whiptail
Cnemidophorus tigris

Length: 8-12 in.
What to look for: chest with black spots; overall pattern may include light stripes, dark crossbars, or spots; scales on back tiny, grainy; scales on belly large, rectangular.
Habitat: deserts to dry woodlands.

Southern Alligator Lizard
Elgaria multicarinatus

Length: 10-16¾ in. **What to look for:** fold of skin with small scales along lower part of side; back and tail with dark crossbands; dark lines on belly.
Habitat: shrubby grasslands to oak and pine woodlands.

Alligator Lizards
Elgaria

Alligator lizards, like alligators, have a protective armor—in this case, bony plates embedded in the scales. The deep groove along the side of the lizard allows the animal to expand when digesting food or carrying eggs. The glass lizards, which lack legs, have similar plates and grooves.

Slender Glass Lizard
Ophisaurus attenuatus

Length: 22-42 in. **What to look for:** legless body; head with eyelids and ear openings; groove along side, with dark speckling or stripes below. **Habitat:** prairies to woodlands; often near water.

Glass Lizards *Ophisaurus*

The tail of a glass lizard is exceptionally fragile, shattering like glass when under stress. An individual with its original tail (the replacement is shorter and darker) is a rare find. People often mistake glass lizards for snakes, but snakes have neither eyelids nor ear openings.

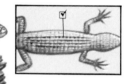

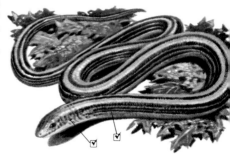

170

Gila Monster
Heloderma suspectum

Length: *18-24 in.*
What to look for: *heavy body; thick, short, blunt tail; black face and feet; scales beadlike, black, with yellow, orange, or pink.* **Habitat:** *rocky, sparsely vegetated areas; canyon bottoms; washes.*

Gila Monsters   *Heloderma*

The world's only venomous lizards, the Gila Monster and its close relative the Mexican Beaded Lizard (*Heloderma horridum*), hold on with bulldog tenacity when they bite. The venom, which is produced in glands along the lower jaw, helps subdue potential predators as well as prey. (The lizards feed on rodents and on the eggs and young of ground-nesting birds.) Gila Monsters are active primarily at dusk and after dark, escaping the heat of day in abandoned burrows, under rocks, or in tunnels they have dug themselves.

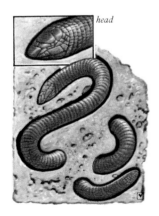

head

Worm Lizard
Rhineura floridana

Length: *7-16 in.*
What to look for: *fuchsia-colored, wormlike body; scales in rings around body; tail flat, with small bumps.* **Habitat:** *dry, sandy soil; pine or hardwood hammocks.*

Worm Lizards   *Rhineura*

These burrowing reptiles, found in the United States only in Florida, are not true lizards. Lacking eyes, ear openings, and limbs, they live a largely underground life, sometimes surfacing after heavy rains. People who encounter them while digging or plowing may confuse them with earthworms, but earthworms lack the distinct head and tail.

California Legless Lizard
Anniella pulchra

Length: *6-9¼ in.*
What to look for: *shovel-shaped snout; no limbs; no ear openings; movable eyelids; shiny scales; back silver or beige, with black lines down middle and along each side; yellow belly.* **Habitat:** *moist sand or loam; beaches to pine-oak woodlands.*

Legless Lizards   *Anniella*

More abundant than is generally believed, legless lizards may sometimes be found by turning over logs or rocks or raking through surface litter in the appropriate habitat. Much of their life is spent moving in serpentine fashion through loose soil. At dusk and at night they occasionally come to the surface or search the leaf litter below bushes for small insects.

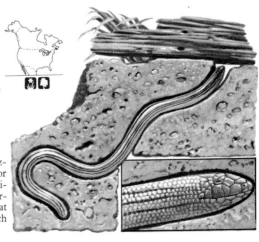

171

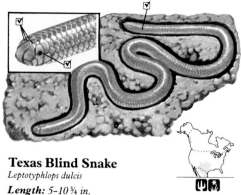

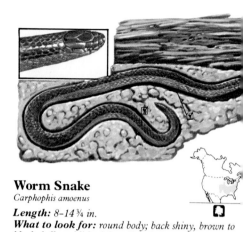

Texas Blind Snake
Leptotyphlops dulcis

Length: *5–10¾ in.*
What to look for: *body wormlike, shiny; head and tail blunt; eyes tiny, black; scales on belly same size as those on back; large translucent scale over eye; 3 small scales between eyes atop head.* **Habitat:** *pockets of moist sand or loam; plains, deserts, rocky hillsides.*

Blind Snakes *Leptotyphlops*

The tiny eyes of these nocturnal snakes are useless for finding prey. Instead, the reptiles use their sense of smell to locate ants and termites. Normally hidden in moist soil beneath a rock or log, they come to the surface in daylight after a heavy rain. Precise identification requires a close look at the head: the Western Blind Snake (*Leptotyphlops humilis*) has only one scale between its eyes.

Worm Snake
Carphophis amoenus

Length: *8–14¾ in.*
What to look for: *round body; back shiny, brown to black; belly reddish pink; tail with sharp spine on tip.* **Habitat:** *moist forests; hillsides near streams.*

Worm Snakes *Carphophis*

Like some three-quarters of the world's 2,700 species of snakes, the Worm Snake belongs to the colubrid family. (*Coluber* is a Latin word for "snake.") Colubrids have well-developed eyes, belly scales as wide as their bodies, and teeth on both jaws. Although a few colubrids are venomous, only two—both African —can inflict fatal bites. Like all colubrids, Worm Snakes are carnivorous; they feed on earthworms.

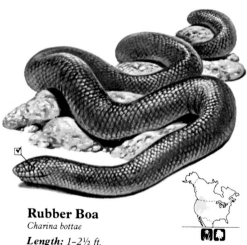

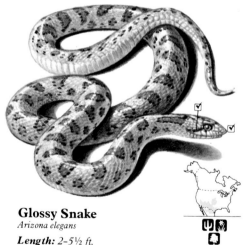

Rubber Boa
Charina bottae

Length: *1–2½ ft.*
What to look for: *rubbery body; tip of tail looks like head; large scales on top of head; other scales small, smooth, shiny; eyes small, with vertical pupils.* **Habitat:** *damp soil, rotting logs; grasslands to forests.*

Rubber Boas *Charina*

The Rubber Boa is closely related to anacondas and pythons. Like its awesome relatives, it constricts its prey (mammals and birds) until the victim suffocates. Most snakes have no outward sign of limbs, but boas have small remnants ("spurs") on their bellies, used by the male to stroke the female during courtship. Females produce live young, not eggs.

Glossy Snake
Arizona elegans

Length: *2–5½ ft.*
What to look for: *scales smooth, shiny; nose slightly pointed; dark line from eye to corner of mouth; belly unmarked.* **Habitat:** *deserts, chaparral, woodlands.*

Glossy Snakes *Arizona*

Faded Snake is another name for the pallid creature that is the sole member of this group. Like many other desert snakes, it is active mainly at night, leaving its burrow after sundown to search for lizards and small rodents, which it kills by constriction. It lacks the dark belly marks of one of the kingsnakes and the ridged scales of gopher and rat snakes.

Scarlet Snake
Cemophora coccinea

Length: *1–2½ ft.*
What to look for: *snout red, pointed; thin black bands, not encircling body; belly white or yellow, unmarked; compare with coral snakes and "scarlet kingsnake."*
Habitat: *forests; nearby fields with loose soil.*

Scarlet Snakes   *Cemophora*

The eggs of other reptiles are the favorite food of the Scarlet Snake, the single species in this group. Small eggs are eaten whole; bigger ones are torn with its enlarged upper teeth. Scarlet Snakes usually hide beneath rocks or logs during the day.

Western Shovel-nosed Snake
Chionactis occipitalis

Length: *10–17 in.* **What to look for:** *white or yellow, with 21 or more dark bands wholly or partially encircling body (may have partial bands of red between the dark); flat snout.* **Habitat:** *mesquite–creosote-bush deserts, sandy washes, dunes, rocky slopes.*

REPTILES

Shovel-nosed Snakes   *Chionactis*

With their spadelike snouts, glossy scales, and flat bellies, these snakes can almost swim through the desert soil. Occasionally abroad during the day, they forage mostly at night for insects, spiders, centipedes, and scorpions.

blue race   *western yellow-bellied race*

Racers   *Coluber*

Active by day, the Racer glides swiftly along the ground, holding its head high above the surface. If chased, it often climbs into bushes or trees. When threatened, it vibrates the tip of its tail in dead vegetation, producing a buzzing sound like a rattler. It kills not by constriction, but by pinning down its victim and swallowing it whole.

northern black race

Racer
Coluber constrictor

Length: *3–6 ft.*
What to look for: *slim body; smooth scales; color variable.* **Habitat:** *woods, grassy and brushy areas, rocky slopes.*

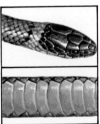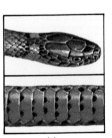

northern race   *prairie race*

Ringneck Snakes   *Diadophis*

Although common in many localities, the Ringneck escapes notice because it rarely prowls in the open. In spring and early summer it hides under flat rocks or bark; later, warm weather forces it into deeper retreats where the soil stays damp. Large numbers may congregate in a single hiding place, and females sometimes lay their eggs in a communal nest. When disturbed, a Ringneck may coil its tail in a tight spiral, exposing the red belly.

southern race

Ringneck Snake
Diadophis punctatus

Length: *1–2½ ft.*
What to look for: *back plain olive, gray, brown, or black; neck ring usually present; belly red, orange, or yellowish, often with black spots; scales smooth.* **Habitat:** *damp areas in forests, grasslands, desert; rocky wooded hillsides.*

173

Mud Snake
Farancia abacura

Length: *3–6¾ ft.*
What to look for: *back bluish black; belly with black and pink or red bars extending onto sides; sharp spine on tail.* **Habitat:** *swampy areas, slow streams, floodplains.*

Indigo Snake
Drymarchon corais   eastern race

Length: *5–8½ ft.*
What to look for: *body stout, smooth-scaled, shiny blue-black; throat, sides of head orange, red, or cream; front part of Texas race brownish, with trace of pattern.* **Habitat:** *woodlands, orange groves, thickets, grasslands; near water.*

Mud and Rainbow Snakes   *Farancia*

According to legend, these snakes can hold their tails in their mouths, roll like hoops, and kill people by stinging with their tails. The tail does in fact have a sharp spine, used to subdue struggling prey. The Mud Snake eats amphibians, and the closely related Rainbow Snake (*Farancia erytrogramma*), eels. Brilliantly striped with red and yellow, the Rainbow Snake occupies much the same habitat as the Mud Snake but has a more restricted range.

Indigo Snakes   *Drymarchon*

The largest snake in North America has an unusual distribution: a gap of hundreds of miles separates the two races, which look quite different from one another. Although at one time the two populations must have been connected, the gap is not of recent origin and should not be attributed to man. But human disturbance has caused the current decline of the eastern race, shown here with its eggs.

"Great Plains rat snake"

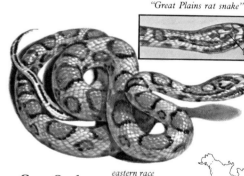

black race

yellow race

gray race

Rat Snake
Elaphe obsoleta

Length: *3–8 ft.*
What to look for:
body fairly stout; belly flat; sides straight (not rounded); belly scales flat in middle, angled where they meet sides; back scales slightly ridged; striped, blotched, or uniformly colored.
Habitat: *swamps; hardwood forests; rocky, wooded hillsides; farms; suburban woods.*

Corn Snake
Elaphe guttata   eastern race

Length: *2–6 ft.*
What to look for: *belly flat; sides straight; belly scales flat in middle, angled where they meet sides; arrow-shaped blotch on head; belly with black squarish blotches; tail striped on underside.* **Habitat:** *pine barrens; rocky, wooded hillsides; groves; farms; abandoned farm buildings.*

Rat Snakes   *Elaphe*

A rat snake, like many other harmless snakes, puts on a show of aggressiveness when cornered. It vibrates its tail, creating a rattling sound in dry vegetation; it hisses and lunges, raising the front part of its body above the ground and drawing its head back in an S-shaped curve. Rat snakes usually crawl on the ground in search of rats and other rodents, thereby earning the friendship of farmers aware of their habits. (They also eat frogs, lizards, birds, and bird eggs.) Rat snakes are superb climbers—an ability enhanced by the special shape of their belly scales. The scales curve upward where they meet the sides, giving the reptiles better traction.

REPTILES

174

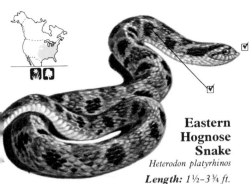

Eastern Hognose Snake
Heterodon platyrhinos

Length: 1½–3¾ ft.
What to look for: *upturned snout; wide neck; thick body; underside of tail lighter than belly; yellow, brown, tan, or reddish, with dark, squarish blotches on back and round ones on sides; may be all black.*
Habitat: *sandy areas, woodland edges, grasslands.*

Hognose Snakes *Heterodon*

Various local names—blow viper, puff adder, hissing adder—stem from the belligerent behavior of the Eastern Hognose Snake. If the hissing, lunging, puffed-up body and flattened neck fail to discourage an interloper, the snake rolls over, playing dead. The Western Hognose (*Heterodon nasicus*), a midwestern species with large black belly blotches, puts on a similar but somewhat less impassioned performance.

Night Snake
Hypsiglena torquata

Length: 1–2 ft.
What to look for: *large, dark blotch on each side of neck (may meet in center); vertical pupils; dark line behind eye; white scales on upper lip.* **Habitat:** *plains, deserts, chaparral, oak-pine woodlands.*

Night Snakes *Hypsiglena*

True to its name, the Night Snake searches after dark for lizards and frogs; during the day it hides in crevices or under plant debris. Night Snakes, like most nocturnally active snakes, usually have vertical pupils; day-active snakes generally have round ones. Although not considered dangerous to man, Night Snakes should be treated with caution: they have enlarged teeth toward the back of the upper jaw.

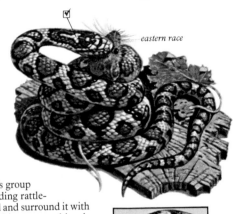

eastern race

Milk Snake
Lampropeltis triangulum

Length: 1½–4 ft.
What to look for: *Y- or V-shaped light mark behind head. or white or yellow collar around neck and black-bordered red bands separated by white or yellow rings that widen on sides; scales smooth, glossy.* **Habitat:** *varied; includes woodlands, rocky hillsides, grasslands, suburbs.*

Milk Snakes and Kingsnakes *Lampropeltis*

Although Milk Snakes supposedly milk cows, the snakes in this group actually feed on rodents, birds, lizards, and other snakes, including rattlesnakes and Copperheads. They seize the victim behind the head and surround it with several coils, constricting the prey until it suffocates. The food is consumed head-first—a typically snakelike way of eating. Loosely joined jaws can stretch, enabling the snake to swallow prey considerably larger than its head. The eastern race of the Milk Snake may be mistaken for a Copperhead, and the scarlet race for a coral snake.

southeastern race
("scarlet kingsnake")

speckled midwestern race

California race

eastern race

Common Kingsnake
Lampropeltis getula

Length: 3–6½ ft.
What to look for: *scales smooth, glossy, with light-colored centers; chocolate-brown to black, with crossbands, chain links, blotches, stripes, or speckles.* **Habitat:** *varied; includes pine woodlands, marshes, swamps, valleys, rocky hillsides, grasslands, deserts, chaparral.*

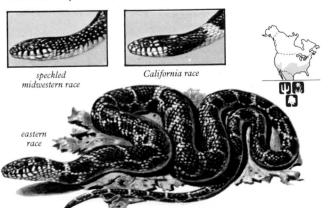

175

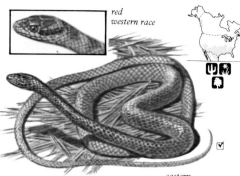

red
western race

eastern
race

Coachwhip
Masticophis flagellum

Length: *3–8½ ft.*
What to look for: *slim, unstriped body; tail long, sometimes pink on underside or paler than body; smooth scales; overall color varying from black to pink, red, tan, or gray.* **Habitat:** *pine woodlands, rocky hillsides, prairies, scrublands, chaparral.*

Coachwhips and Whipsnakes
Masticophis

Alert and agile, North America's fastest snakes undulate in a series of S-shaped curves—the main way that snakes move. Some snakes can crawl like a caterpillar (this is known as rectilinear motion), move by extending and contracting the body (concertina motion), or slip sideways (sidewinding).

Smooth Green Snake
Opheodrys vernalis

Length: *1–2 ft.*
What to look for: *slim body; long tail; bright green above, white to pale yellow below; smooth scales.*
Habitat: *damp grass; fields bordering woodlands; streambanks; marshes.*

Green Snakes *Opheodrys*

The eggs of the Smooth Green Snake hatch in 4 to 23 days, a sharp contrast with the several months that most snakes take. In this species the embryos develop to a relatively advanced stage before the eggs are laid. The Rough Green Snake (*Opheodrys aestivus*), a large southern species, has a longer incubation time.

Northern Water Snake
Nerodia sipedon

Length: *2–4 ft.*
What to look for: *crossbands on neck; dark blotches on back and sides; belly with crescentlike spots, scattered or in 2 rows; stout body; broad head; scales with ridges.*
Habitat: *all types of freshwater; tidal marshes.*

Water and Salt Marsh Snakes *Nerodia*

On sunny days water snakes bask on tree limbs or shrubs overhanging streams and ponds, unnoticed until they slide or drop into the water. Most snakes can swim, but these species are especially adept swimmers and divers, slithering through the water and capturing fish and frogs (both tadpoles and adults). Frequently mistaken for Copperheads or Cottonmouths, they are not venomous but can inflict a painful bite. Snakes use their teeth for holding prey, not for chewing.

Plain-bellied Water Snake
Nerodia erythrogaster

Length: *2½–5 ft.*
What to look for: *belly red, orange, or yellow; back plain or with dark-bordered light crossbars; stout body; head broad, distinct from neck; scales with ridges.*
Habitat: *swamps, forested edges of streams, ponds, lakes.*

Southern Water Snake
Nerodia fasciata

Length: *1½–5 ft.*
What to look for: *back with dark bands; dark line from eye to corner of mouth; belly with squiggles or squarish blotches; stout body; broad head; scales with ridges.*
Habitat: *all types of freshwater; tidal marshes.*

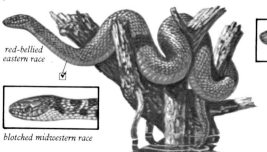

red-bellied
eastern race

blotched midwestern race

broad-banded
midwestern race

banded
eastern race

Pine Snake, Bullsnake, or Gopher Snake
Pituophis melanoleucus

Length: *4–8 ft.*
What to look for: *stout body; head relatively small, pointed; scales with ridges; 4 scales across nose in front of eyes (2 in most other snakes); hisses loudly.*
Habitat: *grasslands, brushlands, pine barrens, rocky deserts.*

Pine Snakes, Bullsnakes, or Gopher Snakes *Pituophis*

All these names refer to the same species, a powerful constrictor that seeks out rodents in their burrows and occasionally climbs trees in search of birds or eggs. Pine snake is the eastern name; bullsnake, the midwestern; gopher snake, the western. There are several races.

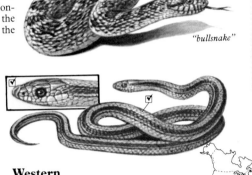

"northern pine snake"

"bullsnake"

Long-nosed Snake
Rhinocheilus lecontei

Length: *2–3 ft.*
What to look for: *snout pointed, jutting beyond lower jaw; black blotches flecked with white, alternating with reddish or pink blotches.*
Habitat: *prairies, brushy deserts, chaparral.*

Long-nosed Snakes *Rhinocheilus*

The single species in this group spends most of its life underground or hidden between rocks. At night it emerges to feed on small mammals, small reptiles, and reptile eggs.

Western Patch-nosed Snake
Salvadora hexalepis

Length: *2–3¾ ft.*
What to look for: *wide triangular scale curved back over tip of snout; beige or yellow back stripe bordered by dark side stripes.* **Habitat:** *deserts, chaparral.*

Patch-nosed Snakes *Salvadora*

Unlike most snakes of the arid West, the patch-nosed snakes tolerate high temperatures and are active at midday. Their prey includes lizards, snakes, and small rodents.

Red-bellied Snake
Storeria occipitomaculata

Length: *8–16 in.*
What to look for: *neck with 3 light spots or collar; belly red, orange, yellow, or black; back brown, with 4 faint dark stripes or 1 wide pale stripe.* **Habitat:** *hilly woodlands, damp meadows, bogs.*

Red-bellied and Brown Snakes *Storeria*

Although common in many parts of their range, these secretive serpents often go unnoticed as they search for worms and slugs beneath rocks, lumber, leaves, and trash. Snakes in this group do not lay eggs. Instead, the female gives birth, in summer and early fall, to some 5 to 18 young, each 3 to 4 inches long.

Brown Snake
Storeria dekayi

Length: *10–20 in.*
What to look for: *wide, pale back stripe, bordered by rows of dark spots; small black dots along edge of belly; scales with ridges.* **Habitat:** *damp woodlands, pond edges, fresh and saltwater marshes, suburban parks, vacant lots.*

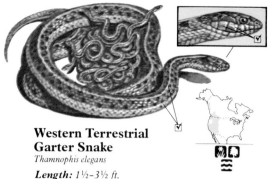

Western Terrestrial Garter Snake

Thamnophis elegans

Length: 1½–3½ ft.
What to look for: *3 stripes, one on back and one on each side; side stripes occupy 2nd and 3rd rows of scales above belly; area between stripes has dark spots or light flecks; overall color variable; 8 upper lip scales (6th and 7th enlarged) on each side.* **Habitat:** *damp meadows; edges of ponds, lakes, streams.*

Garter and Ribbon Snakes

Thamnophis

Garter snakes are familiar to just about everyone. Together the 13 species range over most of the lower 48 states and southern Canada, differing primarily in the pattern of stripes. Snakes in this group produce live young and feed on fish, worms, and other small animals. Like most other reptiles, they molt several times a season. Snakes shed their skins all at once rather than in small pieces. When a snake is about to molt, it loses interest in food. Its eyes cloud over, indicating that new tissue is forming beneath the old. Until its eyes clear, several days before the molt, the snake stays in hiding. Then it begins to move about, rubbing its jaws and snout against rough surfaces. Normally the skin on the head pulls away first. Then the snake winds its way through rock crevices or brush, causing the skin to be pulled away inside-out.

Black-headed and Crowned Snakes *Tantilla*

Though harmless to man, these dark-capped, nocturnal snakes have a saliva that is mildly toxic, helping them subdue such prey as worms and spiders. Of the 13 North American species, only the Plains Black-headed Snake, the Southeastern Crowned Snake (*Tantilla coronata*), and the midwestern Flat-headed Snake (*Tantilla gracilis*) are widespread.

Plains Black-headed Snake

Tantilla nigriceps

Length: 7–14¾ in.
What to look for: *black cap on head, with rounded or pointed edge; belly white, with pink, red, or orange stripe; back tan to gray.* **Habitat:** *rocky hillsides, prairies, brushy areas, open woodlands.*

Eastern Ribbon Snake

Thamnophis sauritus

Length: 1½–3 ft.
What to look for: *slim body; 3 bright (usually yellow) stripes against dark background, one on back and one on each side; side stripes occupy 3rd and 4th rows of scales above belly; belly plain, bordered with dark brown.* **Habitat:** *marshes, damp meadows; weedy edges of ponds, lakes, streams.*

red-sided western race

Common Garter Snake

Thamnophis sirtalis

2 forms of eastern race

Length: 1½–4 ft.
What to look for: *3 stripes, one on back and one on each side; side stripes occupy 2nd and 3rd rows of scales above belly; area between stripes often with double row of black spots or red blotches.* **Habitat:** *grasslands, marshes, woodlands, suburban parks; often near water.*

Earth Snakes *Virginia*

The two earth snakes are small, nondescript burrowers found primarily in the East. As the name implies, the Rough Earth Snake (*Virginia striatula*) has ridged scales instead of the rather even ones of the Smooth Earth Snake. To confirm the identification, scientists count scales. The Smooth Earth Snake has six scales on each side of its upper lip; its cousin, five.

Smooth Earth Snake

Virginia valeriae

Length: 7–13 in.
What to look for: *back gray or brown, with occasional dark flecks; belly white or yellow; scales smooth or with slight ridge.*
Habitat: *moist deciduous forests, suburban woods.*

REPTILES

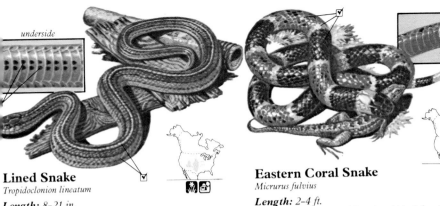

underside

underside

Lined Snake
Tropidoclonion lineatum

Length: 8-21 in.
What to look for: belly with 2 rows of dark semicircles; central back stripe; side stripes on 2nd and 3rd rows of scales above belly; light to dark gray, with stripes of varying color. **Habitat:** woodland edges, prairie slopes, vacant lots, city parks.

Lined Snakes   *Tropidoclonion*

A garter snake look-alike, the single species in this group must be viewed belly-up for positive identification—not an easy chore, for Lined Snakes thrash about and discharge a foul-smelling excretion when handled. (Many other snakes also do this.) No snake should be picked up unless you are familiar with the proper method of handling and can also identify the venomous species.

Eastern Coral Snake
Micrurus fulvius

Length: 2-4 ft.
What to look for: wide red and black bands encircling body, separated by narrow yellow ones (red may be speckled with black); blunt snout; head black to just behind eyes. **Habitat:** dry woodlands to wet subtropical hammocks; rocky hillsides and canyons in Texas.

Eastern Coral Snakes   *Micrurus*

North America's poisonous snakes fall into two categories. The Arizona Coral Snake (*Micruroides euryxanthus*) and the Eastern Coral Snake have two stationary fangs in the upper jaw; the fangs of snakes in the other group (known as pit vipers) fold back against the roof of the mouth. Coral snake venom affects the nervous and respiratory systems; pit viper venom, blood vessels and red blood cells.

REPTILES

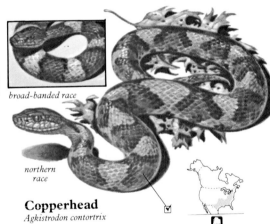

broad-banded race

northern race

Cottonmouth
(Water Moccasin)
Agkistrodon piscivorus

Length: 2-6 ft.
What to look for: stout body; head flat, wider than neck; pit in front of and just below eye; vertical pupils; back plain or with wide, dark, ragged-edged crossbands (young with vivid pattern and yellow tip on tail); mouth white on inside. **Habitat:** swamps, slow streams, shallow lakes, ditches, rice fields.

Copperhead
Agkistrodon contortrix

Length: 2-4½ ft.
What to look for: back copper, orange, or pinkish, with bold red-brown crossbands, often narrowing at center of back; plain-colored head; pit in front of and just below eye; vertical pupils.
Habitat: rock outcrops and ravines in forests; edges of swamps and floodplains.

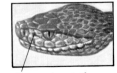

pit   close-up of Copperhead

Cottonmouths and Copperheads   *Agkistrodon*

Cottonmouths, Copperheads, and rattlesnakes are all pit vipers, snakes with a deep sensory pit between each eye and nostril. Temperature-sensitive receptors in the pits allow the snakes to detect and strike at warm-blooded prey. Pit vipers have long, hollow venom-injecting fangs that fold back against the roof of the mouth when the jaws are closed and move into position as the mouth opens to strike. They give birth to live young, which are venomous from the moment of birth.

179

rattlesnake shedding skin

Eastern Diamondback Rattlesnake
Crotalus adamanteus

Length: *3–8 ft.*
What to look for: *rattle on tail; back with dark-edged, diamond-shaped blotches surrounded by row of light scales; 2 pale diagonal stripes on side of head; pale vertical lines on snout.* **Habitat:** *pine and oak woodlands, abandoned farmlands, Saw-palmettos.*

Western Diamondback Rattlesnake
Crotalus atrox

Length: *3–7 ft.*
What to look for: *tail with rattle and encircling black and white bands; back with pale-bordered diamonds or hexagonal blotches, often faded or sprinkled with dark spots; 2 pale diagonal stripes on cheek.* **Habitat:** *dry prairies, brushy deserts, rocky foothills.*

northern form (yellow phase)

"canebrake rattlesnake"

prairie race

southern Pacific race

Timber Rattlesnake
Crotalus horridus

Length: *3–6 ft.*
What to look for: *tail black, with rattle; head wider than neck; northern form all black to predominantly yellow with dark blotches; southern form with tan or red-brown back stripe and dark stripe behind eye.* **Habitat:** *rocky wooded slopes in North; swamps, lowland forests, canebrakes in South.*

Western Rattlesnake
Crotalus viridis

Length: *1¼–5¼ ft.*
What to look for: *rattle on tail; dark blotches of variable shape on neck, becoming bands toward tail; background color pale red, yellow, tan, brown, or blackish.* **Habitat:** *prairies to evergreen forests.*

Rattlesnakes   *Crotalus*

These venomous pit vipers have a warning device at the end of the tail: loosely interlocking segments produce a buzzing noise when the snake is alarmed. Although a new rattle is added each time the snake sheds its skin, the rattles break off frequently and do not indicate age. North America has 13 species, most found west of the Mississippi. One western species, the Sidewinder (*Crotalus cerastes*), has the unusual habit of moving its body sideways in loops, leaving J-shaped tracks in the desert sand.

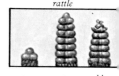

rattle

young   mature   old

Massasauga
Sistrurus catenatus

Length: *1½–3¼ ft.*
What to look for: *light-edged dark stripe behind eye; rows of dark blotches in center of back and on sides; thick tail; small rattle.* **Habitat:** *wetlands to dry woods in East; wet to dry grasslands in Southwest.*

Massasaugas and Pygmy Rattlesnakes   *Sistrurus*

These small rattlers differ from other rattlesnakes in having nine large scales on top of their heads instead of many small ones. The southeastern Pygmy Rattlesnake (*Sistrurus miliarius*) averages only about 1½ feet long.

REPTILES

180

Amphibians

These are the creatures that lead double lives (*amphi* means "both" and *bios* "life"), typically inhabiting freshwater early on and then changing to forms that can live on land. The most pronounced changes—from gills to lungs, from fins to legs, and from a vegetarian diet to an animal one—occur among certain frogs and toads, but many salamanders undergo metamorphosis as well.

Salamanders

North America has more kinds of salamanders (the group that includes the newts) than all the other continents. In the East they live throughout the Appalachians, especially in the Great Smoky Mountains. The West Coast has its own kinds, too. With several exceptions, including the Tiger Salamander, you won't find any in the Rockies, the desert, or the Central Plains; glaciers kept them out of the Rockies, and the other places are just too dry.

Salamanders look much like lizards, but their skin is thin and moist (lizards have hard scales or plates), they have only four toes on their front feet (lizards have five), and they have no claws. Being amphibians, salamanders are more closely tied to water than lizards, which are reptiles. Though most adults live on land, many species lay their eggs in water.

Eggs laid in water hatch into larvae with tufted external gills. (Eggs laid on land, such as those of the woodland salamanders, bypass this stage.) Several salamanders, including the waterdogs and sirens, retain their gills and never leave the water; others, after periods ranging from several months (the Spotted Salamander) to several years (the Two-lined), lose their gills and transform into land-dwelling adults. The adults breathe through their skin or with lungs. Salamanders are carnivorous as both larvae and adults, feeding on fish, insects, crustaceans, worms, and even small mice.

Finding salamanders takes a bit of searching; they are silent creatures, and most are active only at night. The best times of year to look for them are spring and fall; the best places, under stones in streams and under logs and leaves in moist forests. Some kinds, including the Spotted Salamander, spend much of their time underground, where their surroundings are damper and their enemies fewer than above the surface.

Frogs and Toads

More widespread than salamanders, these lively animals are also less secretive. But they too are mostly nocturnal (the Northern Cricket Frog and the Oak Toad are among the exceptions), resting during the day in burrows, in trees, or under leaves, undetected unless they leap out from under your feet. At night during mating time (often in spring), however, groups of singing males loudly announce their presence. A flashlight may help you to locate some of the songsters; and with a little practice, you may be able to identify species by their calls. You can even buy recordings of frog sounds, as you can for birds.

Female frogs and toads tend to be larger than the males. Males attract them with song, then cling to them (sometimes using special clasping pads that develop during the breeding season) and fertilize their eggs as they shed them into the water. The eggs hatch into "polliwogs"—round-bellied, long-tailed larvae that, like those of salamanders, have gills on the outside of the body. In frogs and toads, but not in salamanders, these external gills are soon covered with skin. So most of the tadpoles you catch will have no visible gills.

Eventually, in one of nature's most dramatic transformations, the tadpole metamorphoses into a frog or toad — a tailless terrestrial creature with long hind limbs and lungs instead of gills. How long tadpoles stay tadpoles varies with both species and temperature. Desert-dwelling spadefoot toads may spend a mere two weeks at this stage, whereas North America's biggest frog, the Bullfrog, may not metamorphose for several years in the colder parts of its range.

Tips on Identifying Amphibians

Like other types of animals, this group includes a number of "giveaway" species; recognizing a Spotted Salamander, a Hellbender, or a Spring Peeper is no difficult task. For many of the other amphibians, however, you may need the creatures literally in your hand, to check for special markings or structural details. Among the features important in identifying salamanders are the hind feet and the grooves in the side. Frogs and toads often have characteristic protuberances or markings on the head or back, and their feet may also merit a closer look (toe shape, for example, may be significant).

Mudpuppy
Necturus maculosus

Length: *8–17 in.*
What to look for: *body thick, gray to rusty brown, with irregular black spots; tail flattened from side to side; bushy, dark red gills behind head; 4 toes on both front and hind feet.*
Habitat: *canals, streams, rivers, lakes.*

Lesser Siren
Siren intermedia

Length: *8–26 in.*
What to look for: *eellike body; tail with pointed tip; no hind legs; 4 toes on front feet; stubby or bushy gills just in front of legs.*
Habitat: *weedy ponds; swamps; warm, shallow lakes.*

Mudpuppies and Waterdogs
Necturus

These stubby-tailed salamanders, active mainly at night, hunt small aquatic animals. As is true of most salamanders, males and females look nearly alike. After mating in spring, the female lays dozens of eggs, producing them one by one and placing them under rocks, sticks, or other submerged objects. The Mudpuppy is the most widespread member of this group. Several species known as waterdogs live in different parts of the Southeast.

Sirens
Siren

Waterdogs and sirens have a similar life cycle. Unlike most amphibians, which transform from aquatic larvae to land-dwelling adults, these creatures remain larvae all their lives. They never lose their bushy external gills, they never leave the water, and they reproduce in the larval stage. Although sirens have relatively well-developed front legs, they have no hind legs, which differentiates them from the amphiumas, another group of eellike amphibians of the Southeast.

Hellbenders
Cryptobranchus

The Hellbender is strictly aquatic. Though it has four legs, it does not use them for swimming; instead, it propels itself with its flattened tail. The wrinkles in its skin are believed to supply additional surface for taking in oxygen from the water. Bulkiest of North American salamanders, the Hellbender is dwarfed by its close relative in Japan, the 5½-foot Giant Salamander (*Andrias japonica*). The Hellbender is essentially a river creature, but its Japanese relative inhabits smaller streams.

Hellbender
Cryptobranchus alleganiensis

Length: *12–29 in.*
What to look for: *body stocky, gray or brown, with dark spots or mottling; loose flap of skin along each side; broad, flat head.*
Habitat: *clear rivers and streams with rocky bottoms.*

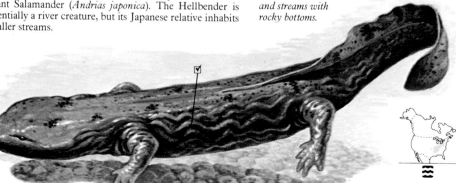

Blue-spotted Salamander
Ambystoma laterale

Length: *3–5 in.*
What to look for: *back and sides dark brown to blue-black, with bluish-white patches, spots, or flecks.* **Habitat:** *moist deciduous woods.*

Spotted Salamander
Ambystoma maculatum

Length: *5½–9¾ in.*
What to look for: *body stout, dark brown to black; 2 irregular rows of orange or yellow spots down back.* **Habitat:** *woods, hillsides; near water.*

Long-toed Salamander
Ambystoma macrodactylum

Length: *4–6¾ in.*
What to look for: *body slender, dark brown to black; orange, yellow, or green stripe on back; long toes.* **Habitat:** *diverse; from sagebrush to moist forests.*

Marbled Salamander
Ambystoma opacum

Length: *3½–5 in.*
What to look for: *body stocky, grayish to black, with white or silvery crossbars; bars may be joined along sides.* **Habitat:** *swampy lowlands to wooded hillsides near temporary ponds.*

Tiger Salamander
Ambystoma tigrinum

Length: *6–13½ in.*
What to look for: *bulky body; broad head; small eyes; highly variable color and pattern (may include light or dark markings); 1 or 2 tubercles on sole of foot.* **Habitat:** *diverse; from arid plains to high-elevation forests.*

tubercles on sole

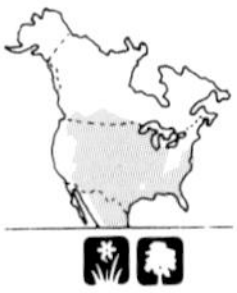

Mole Salamanders
Ambystoma

Mole salamanders burrow into moist ground or leafy debris in a molelike fashion, and they are rarely seen above the surface except on rainy nights or when they congregate around a breeding pond. Their eggs are usually laid in water, though one species, the Marbled Salamander, lays eggs on land. Mole salamanders generally have prominent indentations in their sides, called costal grooves, which mark the spaces between the ribs. The number varies according to species.

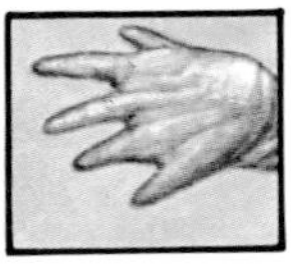

no tubercles on sole

Giant Salamanders
Dicamptodon

These northwestern salamanders lay clumps of eggs in cool lakes and pools. The newly hatched larvae swim into tributary streams and then take up life on land. Some individuals, however, never transform into land-dwelling adults, reproducing instead while they are aquatic larvae. The Pacific Giant Salamander is the world's largest land salamander. It eats the usual salamander fare of insects and other small animals, but it also preys on snakes and mice.

Pacific Giant Salamander
Dicamptodon ensatus

Length: *7–11¾ in.*
What to look for: *body heavy, purplish or brown with black mottlings; no tubercles on feet.* **Habitat:** *rivers; adjacent cool, humid forests.*

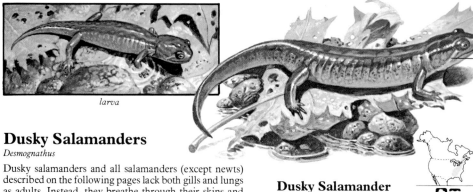
larva

Dusky Salamanders
Desmognathus

Dusky salamanders and all salamanders (except newts) described on the following pages lack both gills and lungs as adults. Instead, they breathe through their skins and the lining of their mouths, sometimes pumping their throats rapidly to increase the flow of air. Commonest in the Appalachian Mountains, the dusky salamanders lay grapelike clusters of eggs in soft dirt or shallow excavations near water. Newly hatched larvae may live on land for several weeks before entering the water and completing their development.

Dusky Salamander
Desmognathus fuscus

Length: 2½–5½ in.
What to look for: tan to dark brown, with dark mottling or pairs of blotches that may be fused to form a ragged-edged stripe; light line from eye to angle of jaw. **Habitat:** springs, rocky streams, floodplains, adjacent moist areas.

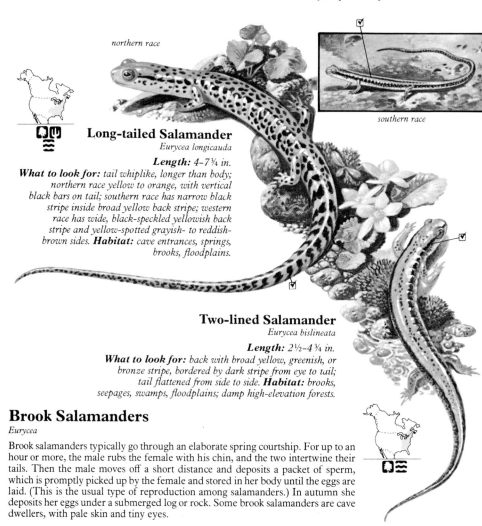

northern race

Long-tailed Salamander
Eurycea longicauda

Length: 4–7¾ in.
What to look for: tail whiplike, longer than body; northern race yellow to orange, with vertical black bars on tail; southern race has narrow black stripe inside broad yellow back stripe; western race has wide, black-speckled yellowish back stripe and yellow-spotted grayish- to reddish-brown sides. **Habitat:** cave entrances, springs, brooks, floodplains.

southern race

Two-lined Salamander
Eurycea bislineata

Length: 2½–4¾ in.
What to look for: back with broad yellow, greenish, or bronze stripe, bordered by dark stripe from eye to tail; tail flattened from side to side. **Habitat:** brooks, seepages, swamps, floodplains; damp high-elevation forests.

Brook Salamanders
Eurycea

Brook salamanders typically go through an elaborate spring courtship. For up to an hour or more, the male rubs the female with his chin, and the two intertwine their tails. Then the male moves off a short distance and deposits a packet of sperm, which is promptly picked up by the female and stored in her body until the eggs are laid. (This is the usual type of reproduction among salamanders.) In autumn she deposits her eggs under a submerged log or rock. Some brook salamanders are cave dwellers, with pale skin and tiny eyes.

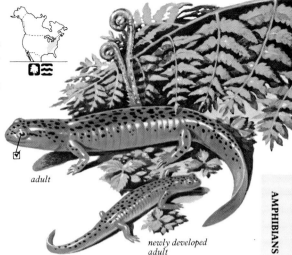

Red Salamander
Pseudotriton ruber

Length: 3¾–7 in.
What to look for: *body stout, red, with uneven black spots; short legs and tail; yellow eyes.*
Habitat: *springs, cool mountain streams, seepages; adjacent woods and lowlands.*

Red Salamanders
Pseudotriton

The Red Salamander and the Mud Salamander (*Pseudotriton montanus*) look much alike and have overlapping ranges. The Mud Salamander, however, has brown eyes and a more snubby snout, and its body is sometimes brownish. In both species the red color is most distinctive in the young and generally fades as the animal matures and develops spots.

adult

newly developed
adult

AMPHIBIANS

Spring Salamander
Gyrinophilus porphyriticus

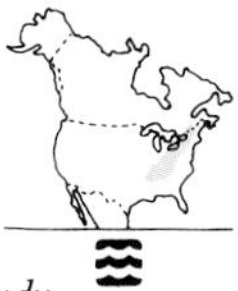

Length: 4–8½ in.
What to look for: *red- or yellow-brown, brownish pink, or salmon; black markings; light bar from eye to nostril; skin often looks cloudy.*
Habitat: *springs, cool mountain streams, caves.*

Spring Salamanders
Gyrinophilus

Like most salamanders, the Spring Salamander (the commonest species in this group) is generally gentle and good-natured but may try to defend itself by biting. Though it is carnivorous and sometimes even cannibalistic, its teeth are not large enough to inflict an impressive bite. The two close relatives of the Spring Salamander are cave dwellers with extremely limited ranges, one in West Virginia and the other in Tennessee.

California Slender Salamander
Batrachoseps attenuatus

Length: 3–5½ in.
What to look for: *body slim, soot-colored, with broad yellow, brownish, or reddish stripe on back; 4 toes on hind feet.* **Habitat:** *grassy meadows to redwood forests.*

Slender Salamanders
Batrachoseps

Eight species of wormlike salamanders make up this group, most of them limited to particular canyons or forests on the West Coast. When hiding under logs or rocks, a slender salamander generally loops or coils its body much like a snake. If the salamander is exposed, it writhes wildly, and its tail commonly breaks off. The females lay about a dozen round eggs on land. The eggs hatch not into larvae but into miniature adults.

185

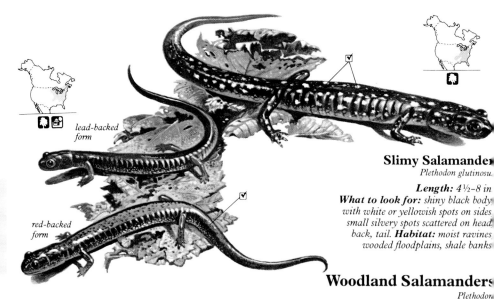

lead-backed
form

red-backed
form

Slimy Salamander
Plethodon glutinosus

Length: 4½–8 in
What to look for: *shiny black body
with white or yellowish spots on sides;
small silvery spots scattered on head,
back, tail.* **Habitat:** *moist ravines,
wooded floodplains, shale banks.*

Red-backed Salamander
Plethodon cinereus

Length: 2½–5 in.
What to look for: *slender body; red-backed form
with wide, straight-edged reddish stripe on back
that extends from head well onto tail; lead-backed
form with light to dark gray back.*
Habitat: *deciduous to coniferous forests.*

Woodland Salamanders
Plethodon

About two dozen species of woodland salamanders,
including some with a range of only a few square
miles, inhabit moist woodlands from coast to coast.
Though usually slow-moving, they can rise on their
legs and run rapidly through the forest. The Red-
backed Salamander is a jumper, leaping along by
slapping its tail against the ground. Most species
exude a white fluid that is distasteful to predators.

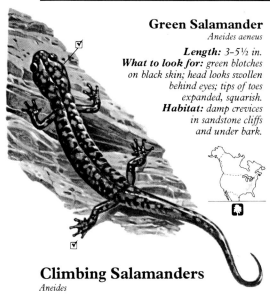

Green Salamander
Aneides aeneus

Length: 3–5½ in.
What to look for: *green blotches
on black skin; head looks swollen
behind eyes; tips of toes
expanded, squarish.*
Habitat: *damp crevices
in sandstone cliffs
and under bark.*

Four-toed Salamander
Hemidactylium scutatum

Length: 2–4 in.
What to look for: *red-brown back;
gray sides; belly white, with black spots;
pinched-in area at base of tail; hind
feet with 4 toes.* **Habitat:** *sphagnum
bogs, adjacent moist hardwood forests.*

Climbing Salamanders
Aneides

With flattened suctionlike tips on their toes, these salamanders can cling to vertical surfaces and climb
trees or rock walls. They are land animals whose eggs
hatch directly into diminutive adults, without going
through an aquatic larval stage. Of the five species,
only the Green Salamander occurs east of the Mississippi. Camouflaged by its color, it is nearly invisible
as it climbs about on plant-covered bark.

Four-toed Salamanders
Hemidactylium

The tail of the Four-toed Salamander breaks off easily at a conspicuous grooved or pinched-in area at its
base. The severed portion continues to wriggle, generally satisfying the attacker (perhaps a Raccoon or
fox) while the salamander makes its escape. A new
tail soon grows to replace the old, but the replacement
has no bones. This species is one of the few salamanders with four rather than five toes on the hind feet.
All salamanders have four toes on their front feet.

Ensatina Salamander

Ensatina eschscholtzi

Length: *3-5¾ in.*
What to look for: *tail constricted at base; 5 toes on hind feet; leg color lighter at base than at end.*
Habitat: *cool damp forests; shaded canyons.*

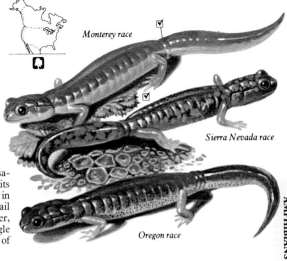

Monterey race

Sierra Nevada race

Oregon race

Ensatina Salamanders

Ensatina

When first exposed from its hiding place, the Ensatina Salamander stands high on its legs, arches its back, and secretes a sticky white fluid from glands in its back and tail. The tail pops off if it is grabbed. Tail length differs between the sexes; the male's is longer, measuring at least the length of the body. The single species in this group shows an astounding range of color and pattern.

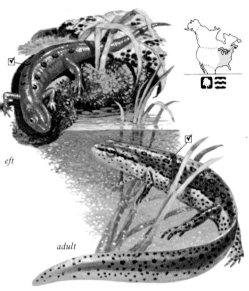

eft

adult

Eastern Newt (Red Eft)

Notophthalmus viridescens

Length: *2½-5½ in.*
What to look for: *aquatic adult olive-green to dark brown, with many black dots on yellow belly; land-dwelling eft varies from bright orange to reddish brown; both may have red markings on back.*
Habitat: *quiet, weedy ponds, lakes, backwaters; moist woodlands.*

Eastern Newts

Notophthalmus

Newts form a family of salamanders that lack the side grooves typical of most salamanders. Their reproductive habits are diverse. Both the Eastern Newt and the southeastern Striped Newt (*Notophthalmus perstriatus*) lay eggs in water in spring. The larvae remain aquatic until late summer, then lose their gills and transform into red land-dwelling creatures known as efts. After one to three years, the efts become drab-looking adults and return to the water to mate. The adults never go back to land. A third species, the Black-spotted Newt (*Notophthalmus meridionalis*) of Texas, has no eft stage.

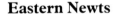

Rough-skinned Newt

Taricha granulosa

Length: *5-8½ in.*
What to look for: *rough, warty skin; dark brown back; yellow or red-orange belly; dark lower eyelids.*
Habitat: *slow-moving streams, ponds, lakes; adjacent grasslands and forests.*

Pacific Newts

Taricha

When attacked by a bird, snake, or other predator, a Pacific newt lifts its head and tail and displays the bright warning colors on its underside. If the predator ignores this warning and puts the newt into its mouth, it receives a further check; the "warts" on the salamander's skin are clumps of glands that give off an irritating secretion. Pacific newts, unlike eastern ones, do not go through a land-dwelling eft stage.

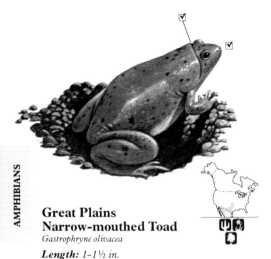

AMPHIBIANS

Frog or toad? With their long legs and tailless bodies, adult frogs and toads are easy to tell from other amphibians. But the distinction between animals commonly called frogs and those called toads is less precise.
• Frogs are generally slim and speedy; toads, fat-bodied and rather sluggish.
• Frog skin is usually smooth. Toads have warts.
• Most frogs usually live in or near water. Adult toads may occur in drier habitats.
• Both frogs and toads usually lay eggs in water. Frog eggs are laid in clumps; toads', in strings (usually double strands).

Great Plains Narrow-mouthed Toad
Gastrophryne olivacea

Length: *1-1½ in.*
What to look for: *tiny head with pointed snout; fold of skin across back of head; white, unmarked belly.* **Habitat:** *deserts, grasslands, woodlands; in moist burrows or under rocks or logs.*

Narrow-mouthed Toads
Gastrophryne

Narrow-mouthed toads spend most of the day in burrows or under rocks, logs, or debris, emerging at night to feed on ants. These secretive creatures have a distinctive shape: their bodies are bulbous, their snouts pointed, and their heads narrow, with a fold of skin across the back. The tadpoles of this species are also relatively easy to recognize: the mouth is surrounded by a soft disk instead of the hard jaws typical of most tadpoles. In general, frog and toad tadpoles are difficult to sort out. Identification usually requires looking not only at the tadpole's mouth but also at its spiracle (the exit hole for water used in breathing) and vent (anal opening).

Eastern Narrow-mouthed Toad
Gastrophryne carolinensis

Length: *1-1½ in.*
What to look for: *tiny head with pointed snout; fold of skin on back of head; color variable; belly spotted with gray.* **Habitat:** *moist areas, including leaf litter, rotting logs, burrows, and under rocks.*

Tailed Frog
Ascaphus truei

Length: *1-2 in.*
What to look for: *small bumps on skin; long, slender front toes; vertical pupils; short "tail" on male; no external eardrum.*
Habitat: *swift, cold, clear mountain streams.*

Tailed Frogs
Ascaphus

The usual pattern among frogs and toads is that the two sexes find one another by sound: the males, often equipped with inflatable vocal sacs, attract the females by singing in chorus. Tailed Frogs, also known as Tailed Toads, inhabit mountain streams, where the noise of the rushing water obscures other sounds. These amphibians are not known to utter any sound, but are believed to crawl along the stream bottom until they find a mate.

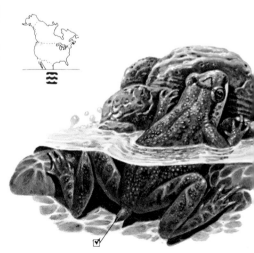

Spadefoot Toads
Scaphiopus, Spea

These fat, relatively smooth-skinned toads use the hard spades on their hind feet to dig burrows in sand or loose dirt. As they dig, they progress backwards into the excavations and shuffle rapidly out of sight. Spadefoots come out at night to hunt insects and other small animals, and to congregate at aquatic breeding sites. The males utter loud, harsh, nasal calls audible over long distances; females grunt more quietly in response. After mating, the female toads lay masses of eggs on submerged vegetation. The entire development—from egg to tadpole to adult—may take as little as two weeks, the shortest time for any North American toad or frog. Spadefoots usually live in dry environments, breeding in pools of rainwater that disappear quickly. Their accelerated development means that the toads spend a minimum of time in the stages that require water for survival.

*sickle-shaped spade
on hind foot*

*wedge-shaped spade
on hind foot*

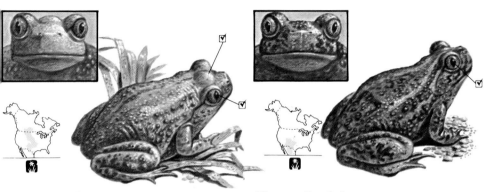

Plains Spadefoot
Spea bombifrons

Length: *1½–2½ in.*
What to look for: *plump body; black, wedge-shaped "spade" on inner side of hind foot; front toes slightly webbed; eyes with vertical pupils; bony hump between eyes.*
Habitat: *sandy or gravelly shortgrass prairies.*

Western Spadefoot
Spea hammondi

Length: *1½–2½ in.*
What to look for: *plump body; black, wedge-shaped "spade" on inner side of hind foot; front toes slightly webbed; eyes with vertical pupils; no bony hump between eyes.* **Habitat:** *dry plains, mountain valleys, floodplains.*

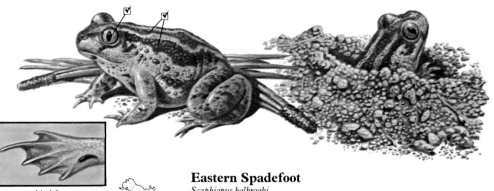

hind foot

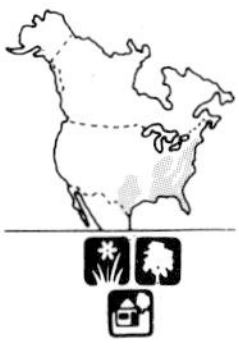

Eastern Spadefoot
Scaphiopus holbrooki

Length: *1¾–3¼ in.*
What to look for: *stout body; sickle-shaped "spade" on inner side of hind foot; front toes slightly webbed; eyes with vertical pupils; irregular pale lines often extend backward from eyes.*
Habitat: *sandy, gravelly, or loamy soils; from farmland to forest.*

189

True Toads *Bufo*

Included in this group are more than a dozen species, ranging in size from the 1-inch Oak Toad to the 9-inch Giant, or Marine, Toad (*Bufo marinus*), a tropical species now well established in Texas and Florida. Most true toads have prominent bony ridges (called cranial crests) on top of their heads, and conspicuous swellings (parotoid glands) behind their eyes. The parotoid glands are a defense against predators, for they secrete fluids that are toxic if taken internally. The warts exude a similar toxin. Despite the prevalent myth, toads do not cause warts in humans and are not poisonous to the touch.

At breeding time (usually spring and summer), large numbers of toads congregate at quiet bodies of water. The males, often distinguished by dark throats and dark pads on some of their toes, call loudly. (The singing of each species is characteristic.) To mate, a male climbs astride a female's back and clasps her firmly, his hold facilitated by the rough pads on his toes. The pair floats together for some time. The female lays strings of eggs, which are fertilized as they pass from her body. After mating, the adult toads may move far from water. Unlike frogs, toads have a thick skin, which reduces water loss and permits survival in dry areas.

True toads, like many other amphibians, eat plants as larvae (tadpoles) and insects as adults. The adult's long tongue, attached at the front of the mouth, can be flipped out to its full length to catch a crawling or flying insect. At times toads also eat fruits and vegetables, and individuals living around houses will feast on dogfood set out for the household pets. As insect eaters, toads in gardens or elsewhere should be valued for their role in pest-control.

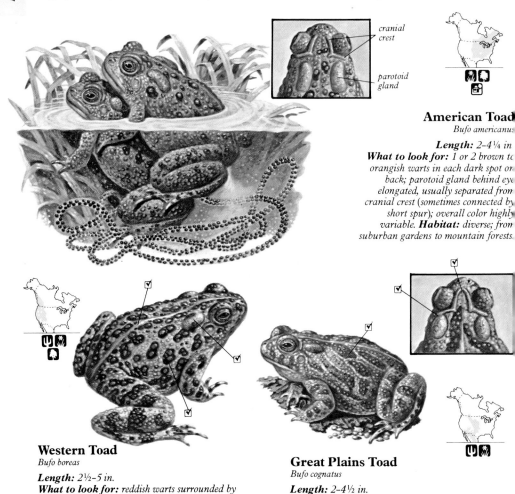

cranial crest

parotoid gland

American Toad
Bufo americanus

Length: *2-4¼ in*
What to look for: *1 or 2 brown to orangish warts in each dark spot on back; parotoid gland behind eye elongated, usually separated from cranial crest (sometimes connected by short spur); overall color highly variable.* **Habitat:** *diverse; from suburban gardens to mountain forests.*

Western Toad
Bufo boreas

Length: *2½-5 in.*
What to look for: *reddish warts surrounded by dark blotches; thin, light line down middle of back; oval parotoid gland behind eye; no cranial crest.* **Habitat:** *diverse; from arid lowlands to woodland mountain meadows.*

Great Plains Toad
Bufo cognatus

Length: *2-4½ in.*
What to look for: *large dark blotches (often paired), with light borders; cranial crests meet at bony hump on snout; oval parotoid glands touch crests behind eyes.* **Habitat:** *grasslands to brushy deserts.*

Red-spotted Toad
Bufo punctatus

Length: 1½–3 in.
What to look for: *warts with yellowish-orange to red tips; head small and flat; round parotoid glands; cranial crests absent or poorly defined.*
Habitat: *grasslands to desert canyons; near water.*

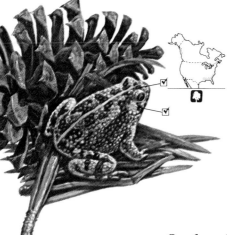

Oak Toad
Bufo quercicus

Length: ¾–1¼ in.
What to look for: *small size; distinct white to orange line down middle of back; 4 or 5 pairs of dark blotches on back; parotoid glands elongated; cranial crests poorly developed.*
Habitat: *scrubby oak forests and pinelands.*

Southern Toad
Bufo terrestris

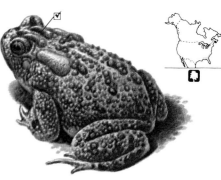

Length: 1½–4¼ in.
What to look for: *usually brown (color ranges from gray to brick-red); warts often with spines; cranial crests high, with prominent knobs.*
Habitat: *sandhills or oak woods.*

eastern race (Fowler's toad)

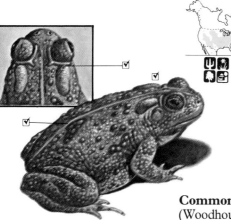

calling male, with inflated vocal sac

a western race

Common Toad
(Woodhouse's Toad)
Bufo woodhousei

Length: 2½–5 in.
What to look for: *light line down middle of back; cranial crests prominent, touching elongated parotoid glands; eastern race has 3 or more warts in each dark spot on back; western races have variable spots and warts.* **Habitat:** *sandy areas near freshwater.*

191

Cricket Frogs

Acris

Like so many sounds of the wilderness, the mating call of a male cricket frog says different things to different people. To some it echoes the melodious chirp of a cricket; to others, the clacking together of stones or pieces of metal. The calls are commonly heard around ponds and lakes from spring through midsummer and sometimes even later in the southern part of the range. After mating, the female lays 200 or more eggs, singly rather than in clumps like most frogs. By autumn the tadpoles have transformed into froglets. Cricket frogs live in plant cover along the water's edge and are active at night as well as during the day. They jump into the water quickly if disturbed, turn while swimming underwater, and come back to shore at some other point.

Southern Cricket Frog

Acris gryllus

Length: ½–1¼ in.
What to look for: rough skin (color variable); dark triangle between eyes; dark, sharp-edged stripe on back of thigh; web on hind foot does not reach tip of first toe or next-to-last joint of longest toe.
Habitat: in vegetation at edges of marshes, swamps, ponds, ditches, and streams.

hind foot

Treefrogs *Hyla*

Equipped with large suction pads at the tips of their toes, treefrogs have the unfroglike ability to climb vertical surfaces. Most of the 10 species are small (2 inches long or less) and even a leaf is strong enough to support the weight of one. Perched on vegetation near water, the males sing loudly at night or on cloudy, rainy days in spring. Their calls are clear and melodius. The females lay eggs that float at the surface in thin films, with several to several dozen eggs in each patch. Within a week, the eggs hatch into tiny tadpoles; within two months, the tadpoles transform into adults. Most adult treefrogs can change their color or pattern in response to variations in temperature, light, or humidity, although the process may take as long as an hour. The color changes occur in captive animals as well as wild ones, adding to the attractiveness of these diminutive creatures as terrarium pets. Prospective owners should be aware, however, that treefrogs require live insect food and a good deal of care to survive for any length of time in an artificial environment.

hind foot of treefrog

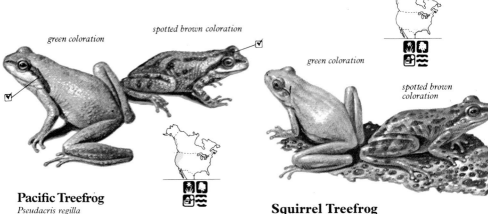

green coloration

spotted brown coloration

green coloration

spotted brown coloration

Pacific Treefrog

Pseudacris regilla

Length: ¾–2 in.
What to look for: skin rough, green, tan, brown, or blackish; back sometimes with dark markings; black eye stripe; dark triangle often present between eyes. **Habitat:** usually in rocks or low plants near water; rarely high above ground.

Squirrel Treefrog

Hyla squirella

Length: 1–1½ in.
What to look for: skin smooth, varying from green to brown; may have poorly defined, light stripe on sides of body. **Habitat:** trees, shrubs; from suburbs to pine flatwoods.

Northern Cricket Frog
Acris crepitans

Length: ½–1½ in.
What to look for: warty skin (color variable); dark triangle between eyes; dark, ragged-edged stripe on back of thigh; fuzzier in midwestern race; web on hind foot reaches tip of first toe and next-to-last joint of longest toe.
Habitat: mudflats; edges of shallow ponds, streams, floodplains.

midwestern race

eastern race

hind foot

hind foot

Striped Chorus Frog
Pseudacris triseriata

Length: ¾–1½ in.
What to look for: smooth skin; 3 dark stripes (may be broken) on back; dark eye stripe; light stripe on upper lip; tips of toes small, round.
Habitat: grasslands to woodland swamps.

Chorus Frogs
Pseudacris

These small, slim-legged frogs are most conspicuous in the breeding season, when the males gather around ponds and produce a near-deafening clamor. The seven species belong to the treefrog family, but they have nearly webless toes and lack the suction pads of their relatives.

AMPHIBIANS

calling male, with inflated vocal sac

Spring Peeper
Pseudacris crucifer

Length: ¾–1¼ in.
What to look for: smooth skin; dark X on back; dark bar between eyes. **Habitat:** usually in low plants near temporary pools in thickets and woodlands.

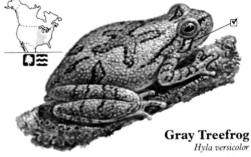

Gray Treefrog
Hyla versicolor

Length: 1¼–2¼ in.
What to look for: warty skin; light, dark-edged mark below eye; inner surface of hind thigh bright orange or yellow, mottled with black.
Habitat: trees and shrubs near woodlands, usually near permanent body of water.

Green Treefrog
Hyla cinerea

Length: 1¼–2½ in.
What to look for: skin smooth, yellow to green; white or yellow stripe usually present on upper jaw and sides of body; back often with tiny gold spots edged with black.
Habitat: in trees and shrubs near lakes, ponds, swamps, streams.

Barking Treefrog
Hyla gratiosa

Length: 2–2¾ in.
What to look for: skin rough, varying in color from green to brown and usually with round dark spots; light stripe from upper jaw extends along sides of body. **Habitat:** in trees or shrubs near pools or ponds, in burrows, or floating on water.

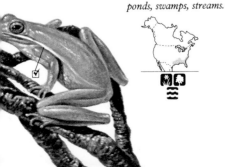

193

True Frogs
Rana

These are the typical pond frogs, once almost unbelievably abundant but now much less common because of widespread pollution and the destruction of wetland habitats. The 26 species are rather similar in appearance, with a greenish or brownish color and irregularly shaded dark spots or splotches on their bodies. One important identifying characteristic is the presence or absence of dorsolateral ridges, a pair of folds that run down the back of certain species. The Green Frog has dorsolateral ridges; the Bullfrog, the largest frog in North America, looks quite similar but lacks these folds. Originally found only in the eastern part of the continent, the Bullfrog has been released in suitable locations throughout North America and has also escaped from "farms" where it has been raised for food or other purposes. The deep, sonorous *jug-o-rum* mating calls of the males are familiar spring sounds, so loud and booming that they drown out the weaker calls of smaller species. Male Bullfrogs sing solos rather than joining in choruses like most frogs. Their larger eardrums, or tympanums (the round area behind each eye), distinguish them from the females.

frog with dorsolateral ridges

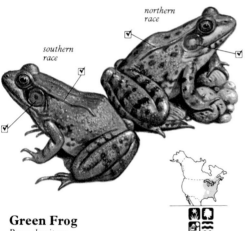

northern race

southern race

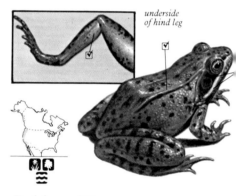

underside of hind leg

Green Frog
Rana clamitans

Length: *2–4 in.*
What to look for: *green or brown; ridges along two-thirds of body; large eardrum; upper lip typically green.* **Habitat:** *wetlands, streams.*

Red-legged Frog
Rana aurora

Length: *2–5¼ in.*
What to look for: *red-brown to gray, with black flecks and blotches; distinct ridges; dark mask; light jaw stripe; underside of leg reddish yellow.* **Habitat:** *ponds, lakes, streams; adjacent woods.*

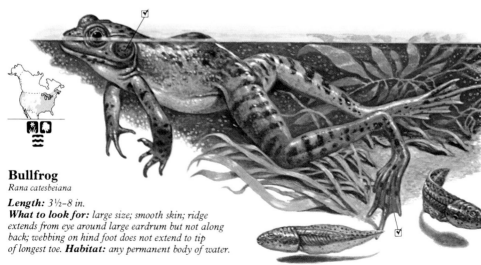

Bullfrog
Rana catesbeiana

Length: *3½–8 in.*
What to look for: *large size; smooth skin; ridge extends from eye around large eardrum but not along back; webbing on hind foot does not extend to tip of longest toe.* **Habitat:** *any permanent body of water.*

tadpole

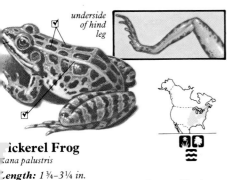

underside
of hind
leg

Pickerel Frog
Rana palustris

Length: 1¾–3¼ in.
What to look for: *parallel rows of square blotches; light stripe on jaws; yellow ridges; inner surface of thigh bright yellow to orange.* **Habitat:** *cool, clear woodland streams, ponds, lakes; adjacent wet meadows; southern swamps.*

Wood Frog
Rana sylvatica

Length: 1¼–3¼ in.
What to look for: *pink, tan, reddish brown, or dark brown; dark mask; light line on upper jaw; prominent ridges.* **Habitat:** *damp shady woodlands; open areas in far north.*

Mink Frog
Rana septentrionalis

Length: 1½–3 in.
What to look for: *large eardrum; hind legs spotted or blotched; web reaches last joint of longest hind toe; musky odor; ridges may be absent.* **Habitat:** *cold lakes, ponds.*

Northern Leopard Frog
Rana pipiens

Length: 2–5 in.
What to look for: *green or brown; large, round, light-bordered spots on back; light-colored ridges; light stripe on upper jaw; no light spot in center of eardrum.* **Habitat:** *damp meadows; weedy edges of streams and lakes; brackish marshes.*

Spotted Frog
Rana pretiosa

Length: 2–4 in.
What to look for: *eyes slightly upturned; dark spots with light centers; light jaw stripe; underside of hind leg yellowish to orange-red; ridges present.* **Habitat:** *permanent bodies of cold water.*

Southern Leopard Frog
Rana sphenocephala

Length: 2–5 in.
What to look for: *green or brown, with dark spots that lack light border; slender head; pointed snout; light-colored ridges; light stripe on upper jaw.* **Habitat:** *shallow freshwater; nearby areas with dense vegetation; slightly brackish marshes.*

Crawfish Frog
Rana areolata

Length: 2¼–4½ in.
What to look for: *fat-bodied; short, wide head and short legs; skin smooth or warty; many dark markings on back and sides.* **Habitat:** *floodplains, wet meadows, sandhills; burrows of crayfish, gopher tortoises, and small mammals.*

underside
of hind leg

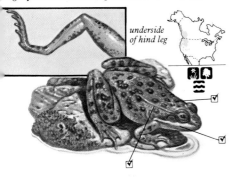

Fish

Don't think "fish are fish" and let it go at that.
Swordfish, barracuda, stingray, flyingfish—once you start
naming names, you begin perceiving differences, wondering
about whys and wherefores, marveling at the intricate
adaptations of these creatures to their watery realm.

Because our realm is a terrestrial one, fish are more mysterious to us than all other vertebrates save perhaps whales, mammalian occupants of the marine world. Most of us know some facts about fish—that they are cold-blooded, that they breathe by means of gills, that they often have fins and scales. But the demands of the environment have molded fish over time, creating a diversity of life-style as well as form. There are blind fish, electric fish, fish that can crawl about on land. Some build nests, some puff themselves up to ward off predators, some change color in essentially a flash (within a few seconds or so).

Of the 2,000-odd species in North American waters, nine-tenths are bony fishes, with skeletons made mostly or solely of bone. (The Largemouth Bass, shown at right, is a bony fish.) On each side of a bony fish a gill cover protects the gills, and often an internal organ called the swim bladder helps the fish stay buoyant. Bony fishes generally spawn rather than mate, the males fertilizing the eggs after the females shed them from their bodies.

Other fishes, including sharks and rays, have skeletons of cartilage rather than bone. As the painting of the Dusky Shark illustrates, sharks have multiple gill slits instead of a single covered opening. (A ray's gill slits are on the underside.) A cartilaginous fish has no swim bladder, so it generally has to keep moving to stay above the bottom (hence the shark's "restless prowl"). Sharks and rays mate rather than spawn, and the females often produce live young, not eggs. More restricted than bony fishes in both habitat and diet, they live primarily in saltwater and feed on animal life.

How to Use This Section
The section begins with the sharks and rays, shown on pages 198 through 203. The bony fishes follow, forming the bulk of the section (pages 204 through 235). A third, smaller

group, the jawless hagfishes and lampreys, is included at the bottom of page 203.

North America has more kinds of fishes than any other vertebrate. To make sure that all the important types are represented in this book, the italicized identification capsules in this section have been written for families of fish rather than species. (For example, an identification capsule describes the needlefish family, not a particular kind of needlefish.) Each family is illustrated by one or more species, and range maps are included for both family (gray) and species (pink). To simplify the maps, the ranges of saltwater fishes have been shown extending a uniform distance from shore. Some species will be found in water deeper than the maps imply.

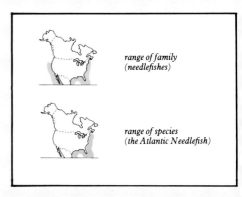

range of family
(needlefishes)

range of species
(the Atlantic Needlefish)

Adult fishes range in size from half an inch long (certain gobies) to more than 40 feet (the Whale Shark), and it is impossible to show all species in the same scale. In this section the species shown on facing pages are in scale with one another, but the scale usually changes when you turn the page. Very small fishes have been painted to a larger scale to show detail. In such cases dark silhouettes of the fishes have been added to show their true size in relation to others on the spread.

The habitat symbols used in this section are: ≋ *freshwater*   ≋ *saltwater*

Tips on Identifying Fish

To identify a fish, you generally need to look at it closely, and that means either catching it or swimming along with it, using scuba or snorkeling gear to see below the surface. Once a fish is at hand, here are some features to observe.

Body shape. Fishes living in open water, such as mackerels and tunas, tend to be streamlined and torpedo-shaped, with bodies that are roundish in cross section. (Seeing a live fish head-on gives a reasonable approximation of its cross-sectional shape.) Is the fish you're watching shaped differently? Flounder and other bottom dwellers are flattened from top to bottom; butterflyfishes, from side to side.

Fins. Even a quick look at the identification capsules in this section reveals the role of fins—their size, shape, structure, and position—in differentiating among groups of fishes. The paintings below show the standard fins (and other structures as well) of a shark and of a bony fish. In sharp contrast are such modifications as the enlarged pectoral fins (and sometimes the pelvic ones too) of the flyingfishes, which they use for gliding over water, and the threadlike pelvic fins of the cusk-eels, used not for motion but for feeling along the bottom. The fins of a bony fish are generally made of thin membranes supported by rods. The rods are either hard, pointed spines or flexible soft rays, and which type (or types) supports a particular fin—especially the dorsal fin—is often important in identification.

Head area. Different types of fishes obtain their food in different ways, and their heads may look different as a result. Check such features as the position of the mouth (is it at the tip of the head or on the underside?), the number and location of the teeth (these may not always be visible), and the presence of such special structures as "whiskers" (on catfishes and goatfishes, for example) and "eyelashes" (greenlings and combtooth blennies).

Scales. Whether a fish has any scales (freshwater catfishes don't) and, if so, where it has them (herrings have them on the body but not on the head) may help separate different groups of fishes. So can the type of scale. Seahorses would look strange even without their equine appearance (their small, hard scales form rings of armor around their bodies), and the bony plates of a sturgeon make it impossible to confuse the creature with any other type of fish.

Color and markings. Some fish you see may have colors different from the ones shown in this book. Color fades rapidly when a fish is taken from water, and color can vary with season, water temperature, and background as well as the sex, age, and mood of the fish. Markings like spots and bars are variable too. A more reliable "marking" in some cases is the lateral line, a stripe (or stripes) visible down the side of such fishes as barracudas and drums. The part you see is formed by a row of special scales and is more than a decoration: it forms part of a sense organ responsive to waterborne vibrations.

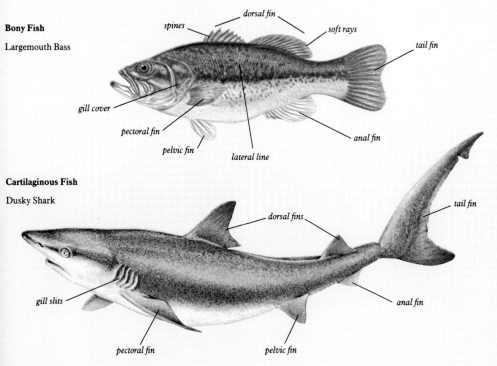

Bony Fish

Largemouth Bass

spines · dorsal fin · soft rays · tail fin · gill cover · pectoral fin · pelvic fin · lateral line · anal fin

Cartilaginous Fish

Dusky Shark

dorsal fins · tail fin · gill slits · anal fin · pectoral fin · pelvic fin

197

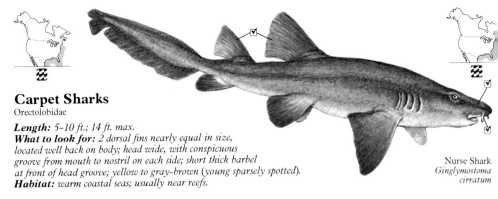

Carpet Sharks
Orectolobidae

Length: *5–10 ft.; 14 ft. max.*
What to look for: *2 dorsal fins nearly equal in size,
located well back on body; head wide, with conspicuous
groove from mouth to nostril on each side; short thick barbel
at front of head groove; yellow to gray-brown (young sparsely spotted).*
Habitat: *warm coastal seas; usually near reefs.*

Nurse Shark
*Ginglymostoma
cirratum*

The sluggish Nurse Shark, the only North American species of carpet shark, is commonly seen close to shore, swimming slowly or lying on the bottom. Although small-toothed and unaggressive, a Nurse Shark will bite in self-defense—as, for example, when being removed from baited hooks intended for other fish. In such close encounters, the sex of a shark can readily be determined, for the male has an elon-

gated clasper on the inner side of each pelvic fin. In mating a male Nurse Shark holds onto a female by grasping one of her pectoral fins with his teeth. As a result, a veteran of several mating seasons can be quickly spotted by her ragged fin. The pups develop inside the body of the female, as they do in most kinds of shark. But unlike mammal embryos, they receive no nourishment from the mother.

Whale Sharks
Rhincodontidae

Length: *15–35 ft.; 45 ft. max.*
What to look for: *huge size;
many white spots on back and sides;
3 distinct ridges on each side of back;
head blunt, with mouth at tip
(not on underside).* **Habitat:** *warm open seas;
usually just below surface.*

The Whale Shark weighs up to 20 tons and is the world's largest fish. Although it has numerous teeth, all are small and nonfunctional. Like the largest whales, the Whale Shark feeds on tiny marine life. It swims along with mouth open, swallowing water and filtering out small animals on the sievelike gill rakers that line its gills. The slightly smaller Basking Shark (*Cetorhinus maximus*) obtains food in similar fashion, straining out food with its stiff gill rakers. Considered part of the mackerel shark family, the Basking Shark has a streamlined shape and a more northerly range than the Whale Shark.

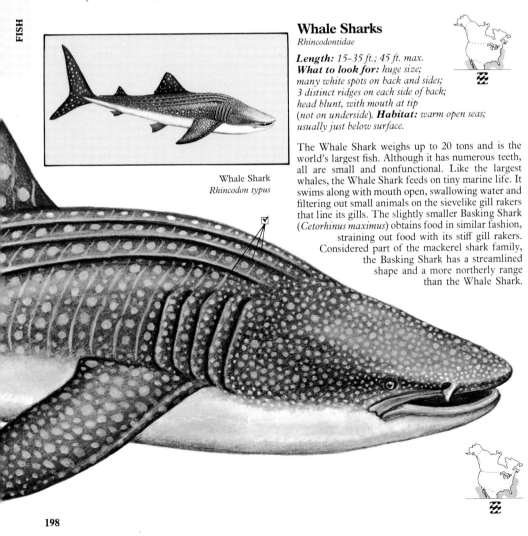

Whale Shark
Rhincodon typus

Sand Tigers Odontaspididae

Length: *4–9 ft.; 10½ ft. max.*
What to look for: *mouth underslung, with many slender protruding teeth; fifth gill slit placed well in front of pectoral fin; anal fin and 2 dorsal fins equal in size.* **Habitat:** *coastal seas.*

Swimming sluggishly but constantly along the bottom, the Sand Tiger preys on fish and shellfish, feeding mainly at night. Although equipped with large teeth and suspected of attacks on humans, it is not considered aggressive or dangerous unless molested in some way. The Sand Tiger does well in captivity and is regularly exhibited in large aquariums. A female Sand Tiger bears her first young when she is about 7 feet long. Although she produces a large number of eggs, only two develop in her body at the same time (one on each side), for the embryos devour any other eggs that are produced during the one-year gestation. (A similar phenomenon occurs in the mackerel shark family.) The pups are nearly 3 feet long at birth. The Sand Tiger is a common Atlantic species; a close relative, the Ragged-tooth Shark *(Odontaspus ferox)*, is the western representative.

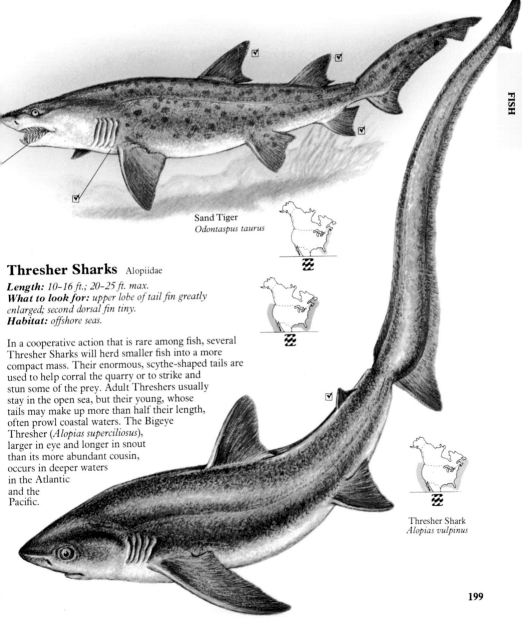

Sand Tiger
Odontaspus taurus

Thresher Sharks Alopiidae

Length: *10–16 ft.; 20–25 ft. max.*
What to look for: *upper lobe of tail fin greatly enlarged; second dorsal fin tiny.*
Habitat: *offshore seas.*

In a cooperative action that is rare among fish, several Thresher Sharks will herd smaller fish into a more compact mass. Their enormous, scythe-shaped tails are used to help corral the quarry or to strike and stun some of the prey. Adult Threshers usually stay in the open sea, but their young, whose tails may make up more than half their length, often prowl coastal waters. The Bigeye Thresher (*Alopias superciliosus*), larger in eye and longer in snout than its more abundant cousin, occurs in deeper waters in the Atlantic and the Pacific.

Thresher Shark
Alopias vulpinus

FISH

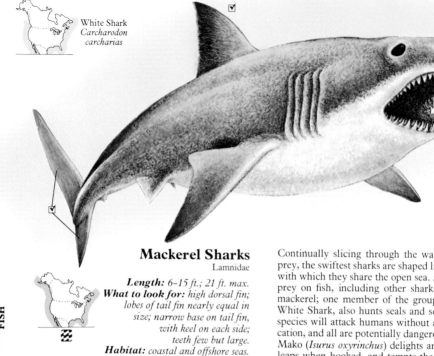

White Shark
*Carcharodon
carcharias*

Mackerel Sharks

Lamnidae

Length: 6–15 ft.; 21 ft. max.
What to look for: high dorsal fin;
lobes of tail fin nearly equal in
size; narrow base on tail fin,
with keel on each side;
teeth few but large.
Habitat: coastal and offshore seas.

Continually slicing through the water in search of prey, the swiftest sharks are shaped like the mackerel with which they share the open sea. Mackerel sharks prey on fish, including other sharks, herrings, and mackerel; one member of the group, the notorious White Shark, also hunts seals and sea turtles. Some species will attack humans without apparent provocation, and all are potentially dangerous to man. The Mako (*Isurus oxyrinchus*) delights anglers with high leaps when hooked, and tempts the palate with the swordfishlike taste of its meat.

Requiem Sharks

Carcharhinidae

Length: 2–13 ft.; 24 ft. max.
What to look for: fifth gill slit
placed farther back than usual
(above base of pectoral fin); base
of first dorsal fin in front of
pelvic fin; pit above base of tail fin.
Habitat: all seas; occasionally
in brackish or fresh water.

Two types of shark occur in this group. The smaller ones, such as the western Leopard Shark and the eastern Smooth Dogfish (*Mustelus canis*), inhabit coastal waters. The larger requiem sharks usually stay in deeper waters, but several large species, including the Dusky Shark, Lemon Shark (*Negaprion brevirostris*), and Tiger Shark (*Galeocerdo cuvieri*), cruise close to shore. Although sharks are usually saltwater creatures, one species in this group, the dangerous Bull Shark (*Carcharhinus leucas*), has ascended the Mississippi River as far as Illinois. It is the only freshwater shark in North America.

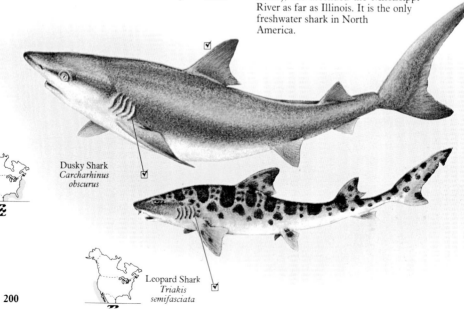

Dusky Shark
*Carcharhinus
obscurus*

Leopard Shark
*Triakis
semifasciata*

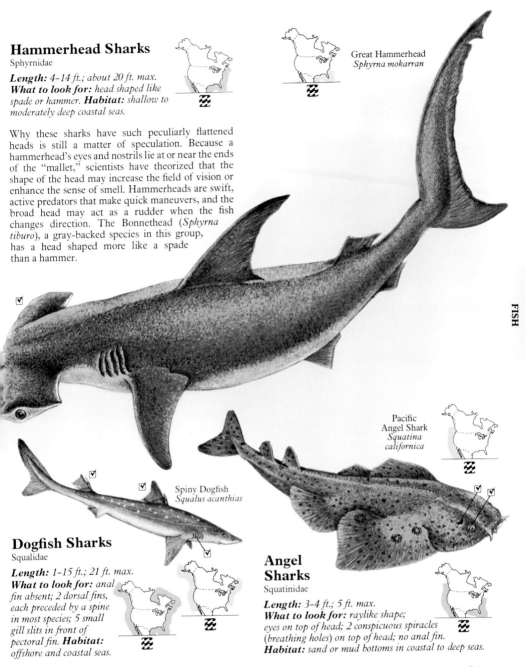

Hammerhead Sharks
Sphyrnidae

Length: *4-14 ft.; about 20 ft. max.*
What to look for: *head shaped like spade or hammer.* **Habitat:** *shallow to moderately deep coastal seas.*

Why these sharks have such peculiarly flattened heads is still a matter of speculation. Because a hammerhead's eyes and nostrils lie at or near the ends of the "mallet," scientists have theorized that the shape of the head may increase the field of vision or enhance the sense of smell. Hammerheads are swift, active predators that make quick maneuvers, and the broad head may act as a rudder when the fish changes direction. The Bonnethead (*Sphyrna tiburo*), a gray-backed species in this group, has a head shaped more like a spade than a hammer.

Great Hammerhead
Sphyrna mokarran

Pacific
Angel Shark
Squatina californica

Spiny Dogfish
Squalus acanthias

Dogfish Sharks
Squalidae

Length: *1-15 ft.; 21 ft. max.*
What to look for: *anal fin absent; 2 dorsal fins, each preceded by a spine in most species; 5 small gill slits in front of pectoral fin.* **Habitat:** *offshore and coastal seas.*

Angel Sharks
Squatinidae

Length: *3-4 ft.; 5 ft. max.*
What to look for: *raylike shape; eyes on top of head; 2 conspicuous spiracles (breathing holes) on top of head; no anal fin.* **Habitat:** *sand or mud bottoms in coastal to deep seas.*

The Spiny Dogfish, the most widespread dogfish shark of North America, prefers cool water (42° to 60° F) and moves offshore or northward as the inshore water temperature rises. The Spiny Dogfish is frequently caught unintentionally on hooks and in nets (the name may relate to its tenacity on hook and line), and fishermen must handle it with care to avoid being stabbed by the venomous spines on its dorsal fins. Other dogfish sharks, such as the sluggish sleeper sharks and the luminescent deepwater species, also possess spines on their fins.

With a slight stretch of the imagination, a fish-watcher can envision the flattened body and broad head of the angel shark as an angel with open wings. Angel sharks, which catch fish, crustaceans, and mollusks on or near the bottom, move close to shore in summer but retreat to deeper waters, which remain warmer, in winter. The location of the gill slits on the sides of the head instead of completely on the undersides, identifies these fish as sharks rather than rays. The Atlantic Angel Shark (*Squatina dumerili*) is the eastern species in this group.

FISH

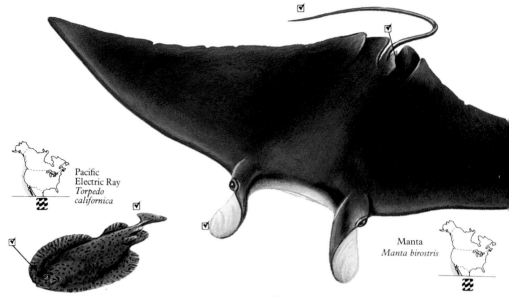

Pacific
Electric Ray
Torpedo
californica

Manta
Manta birostris

Electric Rays Torpedinidae

Length: *1-4 ft.; 5 ft. max.*
What to look for: *round, thick disk,
formed by expanded pectoral fins; eyes
small, on top of head; well-developed
tail fin.* **Habitat:** *sand or mud bottoms
in shallow to moderately deep seas.*

Some electric rays can generate more than 200 volts,
using the large mass of modified muscle on each side.
After producing a number of shocks, each weaker
than the one before, the "batteries" are completely
discharged. Recharging may take several days. Used
mostly to immobilize prey, the electrical discharge
also aids these fish in orientation and defense.

Mantas Mobulidae

Size: *disk width 3-20 ft.; 25 ft. max.*
What to look for: *winglike pectoral fins;
large lobe ("horn") on each side of head;
eyes on sides of head; small dorsal fin;
whiplike tail; no tail fin.*
Habitat: *tropical and warm temperate seas.*

These rays vary dramatically in size. A Manta
captured in the Bahamas measured 22 feet across
and weighed more than 3,000 pounds, but the Devil
Ray *(Mobula hypostoma)*, also an Atlantic species,
only grows to 3 or 4 feet across. Mantas inhabit the
open ocean, feeding near the surface on plankton
and small fish and occasionally jumping completely
out of the sea.

Skates Rajidae

Length: *1½-6 ft.; 8 ft. max.*
What to look for: *flat disk, formed
by head, trunk, and pectoral fins; tail
slender, spiny; 2 small dorsal fins;
tail fin small or absent.*
Habitat: *sand, mud, or gravel bottoms.*

Unlike other rays, which bear live young, a skate produces a tough case ("mermaid's purse") with one or
more eggs inside. The Big Skate's case, which lacks
the corner filaments typical of most, is about a foot
long. Skates and other rays have winglike pectoral
fins. The "wings" of certain species, such as the Big
Skate and the eastern Barndoor Skate *(Raja laevis)*,
are used as food.

Big Skate
Raja binoculata

egg case
of skate

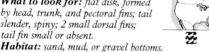

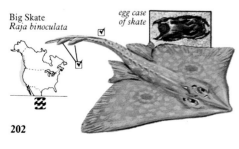

Stingrays Dasyatidae

Size: *disk width 1-5 ft.; 7 ft. max.*
What to look for: *disk formed by head
and expanded pectoral fins; tail slender,
often whiplike, with 1 or more sharp,
barbed spines; no dorsal or tail fins.*
Habitat: *usually in warm, shallow seas.*

Stingrays use their "wings" to excavate the bottom,
exposing shellfish that they crush with flat, powerful
tooth plates. They often lie buried in sand or mud. A
wader stung by the poisonous tail spine experiences
excruciating pain as venom travels down grooves on
each side of the spine and into the wound. The large,
wide butterfly rays, often considered part of this
group, are less dangerous.

Southern Stingray
Dasyatis americana

Sawfishes Pristidae

Length: *8–16 ft.; 18–20 ft. max.*
What to look for: *snout elongated into flat, toothed blade; sharklike body; flattened head.* **Habitat:** *sand or mud bottoms in shallow seas; lower reaches of rivers.*

Smalltooth
Sawfish
*Pristis
pectinata*

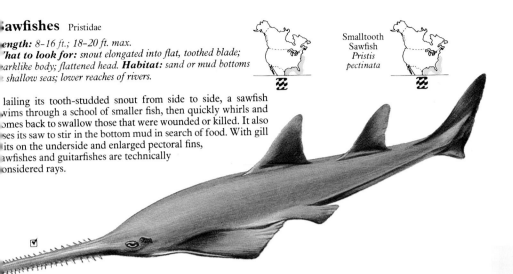

Trailing its tooth-studded snout from side to side, a sawfish swims through a school of smaller fish, then quickly whirls and comes back to swallow those that were wounded or killed. It also uses its saw to stir in the bottom mud in search of food. With gill slits on the underside and enlarged pectoral fins, sawfishes and guitarfishes are technically considered rays.

Shovelnose Guitarfish
Rhinobatos productus

Guitarfishes Rhinobatidae

Length: *1–4 ft.; 5 ft. max.*
What to look for: *head flattened, with wedgelike snout; pectoral fins moderately expanded, continuous with head; 2 small dorsal fins; sharklike tail fin.* **Habitat:** *sand or mud bottoms in shallow seas and brackish water.*

These strange-looking rays swim close to the bottom, hunting small shellfish, and often lie nearly buried in the sand or mud. Like sharks, guitarfishes and sawfishes have a well-developed tail used for propulsion. In contrast, the tail of a typical ray is quite slender, and most rays propel themselves through the water by beating their enlarged pectoral fins.

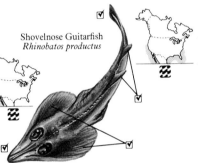

Atlantic Hagfish
Myxine glutinosa

Sea
Lamprey
*Petromyzon
marinus*

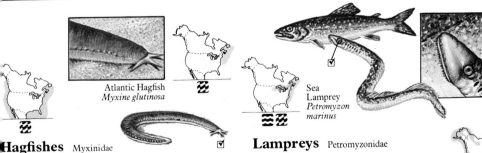

Hagfishes Myxinidae

Length: *16–24 in.; 31 in. max.*
What to look for: *body slender, eellike, without pectoral or pelvic fins; mouth surrounded by small barbels and lacking movable jaws; no visible eyes.* **Habitat:** *marine; usually deeper than 100 ft.*

Hagfishes and lampreys are primitive scaleless fish with a fossil history of nearly 500 million years. Both groups have round mouths and rasping tongues. The slimy hags bore into dead or dying fish (including ones trapped in commercial fishing nets) and feed until only a sack of skin and bones remains. A single victim may be attacked by a number of hags.

Lampreys Petromyzonidae

Length: *6–24 in.; 36 in. max.*
What to look for: *body slender, eellike, without pectoral or pelvic fins; mouth circular, without jaws or barbels; large eyes.* **Habitat:** *clear, cold streams; some species may enter ocean.*

The Sea Lamprey spawns in freshwater, but was not originally native to the upper Great Lakes; it reached them after the opening of a canal. The lampreys, attaching themselves to other fish and sucking out their blood, wreaked havoc in Great Lakes fisheries until they were controlled with selective poisons. Some other lampreys are not parasitic.

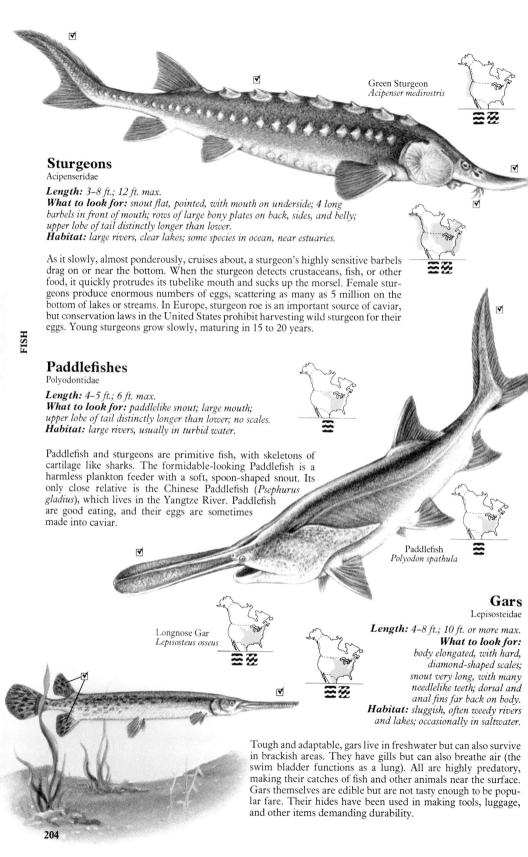

Green Sturgeon
Acipenser medirostris

Sturgeons
Acipenseridae

Length: *3–8 ft.; 12 ft. max.*
What to look for: *snout flat, pointed, with mouth on underside; 4 long barbels in front of mouth; rows of large bony plates on back, sides, and belly; upper lobe of tail distinctly longer than lower.*
Habitat: *large rivers, clear lakes; some species in ocean, near estuaries.*

As it slowly, almost ponderously, cruises about, a sturgeon's highly sensitive barbels drag on or near the bottom. When the sturgeon detects crustaceans, fish, or other food, it quickly protrudes its tubelike mouth and sucks up the morsel. Female sturgeons produce enormous numbers of eggs, scattering as many as 5 million on the bottom of lakes or streams. In Europe, sturgeon roe is an important source of caviar, but conservation laws in the United States prohibit harvesting wild sturgeon for their eggs. Young sturgeons grow slowly, maturing in 15 to 20 years.

Paddlefishes
Polyodontidae

Length: *4–5 ft.; 6 ft. max.*
What to look for: *paddlelike snout; large mouth; upper lobe of tail distinctly longer than lower; no scales.*
Habitat: *large rivers, usually in turbid water.*

Paddlefish and sturgeons are primitive fish, with skeletons of cartilage like sharks. The formidable-looking Paddlefish is a harmless plankton feeder with a soft, spoon-shaped snout. Its only close relative is the Chinese Paddlefish (*Psephurus gladius*), which lives in the Yangtze River. Paddlefish are good eating, and their eggs are sometimes made into caviar.

Paddlefish
Polyodon spathula

Gars
Lepisosteidae

Length: *4–8 ft.; 10 ft. or more max.*
What to look for:
body elongated, with hard, diamond-shaped scales; snout very long, with many needlelike teeth; dorsal and anal fins far back on body.
Habitat: *sluggish, often weedy rivers and lakes; occasionally in saltwater.*

Longnose Gar
Lepisosteus osseus

Tough and adaptable, gars live in freshwater but can also survive in brackish areas. They have gills but can also breathe air (the swim bladder functions as a lung). All are highly predatory, making their catches of fish and other animals near the surface. Gars themselves are edible but are not tasty enough to be popular fare. Their hides have been used in making tools, luggage, and other items demanding durability.

Bowfins
Amiidae

Length: *18–24 in.; 34 in. max.*
What to look for: *long dorsal fin; rounded tail fin, often with dark spot (spot has orange or yellow ring in breeding male); large throat plate; many strong teeth.*
Habitat: *quiet, weedy waters.*

This "living fossil" is the only existing member of an ancient group of fish. Although normally the Bowfin breathes with its gills, in near-stagnant water it will gulp air into its swim bladder, which is supplied with blood vessels and serves as a lung. Even if the water dries up, the Bowfin can survive, so long as the mud at the bottom stays moist. In spring a male Bowfin uses his fins to sweep clear a circular area, then drives one or two females to the nest. He guards the eggs and also protects the young.

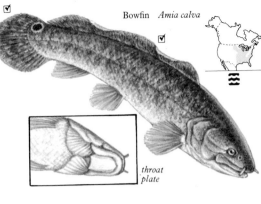

Bowfin *Amia calva*

throat plate

Pacific Herring
Clupea pallasii

FISH

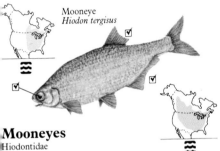

Mooneye
Hiodon tergisus

Mooneyes
Hiodontidae

Length: *12–18 in.; 20 in. max.*
What to look for: *large eyes; body slab-sided, with firmly embedded silvery scales; anal fin long, not joined to tail; no keel as in herrings; dorsal fin short, well behind middle of body.*
Habitat: *lakes, moderately clear to turbid rivers.*

Resembling but not closely related to herrings, the Mooneye and the slightly smaller Goldeye (*Hiodon alosoides*) are the only species in this group. Both are predatory, feeding on other fish as well as insects and mollusks; both are caught commercially and generally sold smoked.

Herrings
Clupeidae

Length: *2–18 in.; 25 in. max.*
What to look for: *head scaleless; body with many silvery scales; body usually flattened from side to side, creating sharp keel on belly; fins without spines.*
Habitat: *coastal and offshore seas; estuaries, rivers, ponds, lakes.*

These silvery, schooling fish include not only the species called herrings but also menhaden, sardines, shads, alewives, and pilchards. Most live in saltwater, although shad and some other marine species migrate long distances to spawn in freshwater. Nearly all are filter feeders; extensions on their bony gill arches (called gill rakers) form a sieve that traps plankton from the water. The family is of extraordinary value as a source of food, fish meal, and oil.

Anchovies
Engraulidae

Length: *1½–6 in.; 9 in. max.*
What to look for: *mouth overhung by tip of snout; large eyes; upper jaw extends well behind eye; body with silvery stripe and scales that fall off easily; fins without spines.*
Habitat: *shallow seas; several species in brackish or (occasionally) fresh water.*

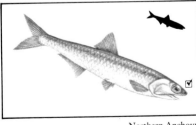

Northern Anchovy
Engraulis mordax

Traveling in huge, shimmering schools, the little anchovies are an important food of predatory fish, and they serve as fishermen's bait as well. Anchovies, like herrings, feed on plankton filtered from the water by numerous long, slender gill rakers. The females lay nearly transparent oval eggs that float near the surface (most fish lay round eggs).

For species illustrated with both a color painting and a silhouette, the silhouette, not the color painting, is in scale with other species on the spread.

205

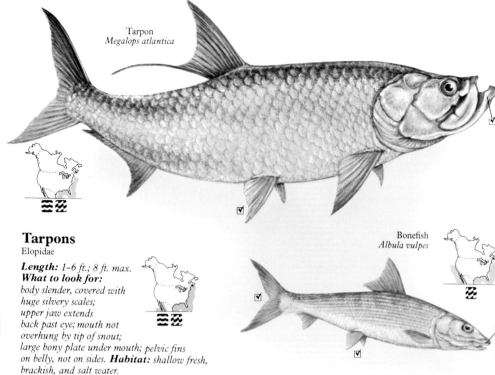

Tarpon
Megalops atlantica

Tarpons
Elopidae

Length: *1-6 ft.; 8 ft. max.*
What to look for:
*body slender, covered with
huge silvery scales;
upper jaw extends
back past eye; mouth not
overhung by tip of snout;
large bony plate under mouth; pelvic fins
on belly, not on sides.* **Habitat:** *shallow fresh,
brackish, and salt water.*

The bullish Tarpon, which usually weighs less than
50 pounds but may tip the scales at 300, ranks high as
a game fish because of its fast runs and twisting leaps
when hooked. In the United States, most hooked
Tarpons are released alive, but those of exceptional
size or battling spirit may be kept as trophies. The
Tarpon feeds mainly on small fish but also eats some
shrimp and crabs. Noisily and regularly, it rolls at the
surface, taking gulps of air into its swim bladder.
Tarpons lay eggs (as many as 12 million) in estuaries
in spring. The fish grow very slowly, and a 100-
pound individual is 13 years old or older. The
Tarpon's cousins, the Ladyfish *(Elops saurus)* in the
Atlantic and the Machete *(Elops affinis)* in the Pacific, are equally energetic fighters. But these two
species rarely reach a length of 3 feet or weigh more
than 5 pounds.

Lizardfishes
Synodontidae

Length: *6-12 in.; 18 in. max.*
What to look for:
*head somewhat flattened;
cigar-shaped body; head and body covered
with scales; mouth well toothed; small
fleshy fin between dorsal fin and tail.*
Habitat: *bottom of coastal and offshore seas.*

A lizardfish spends most of its time propped up by its large
pelvic fins, waiting for small fish or other prey to swim overhead. Then it darts forward in a flash to seize the prey. Lizardfish, like most other fish, propel themselves by body undulation
and movement of the tail fin. Pelvic and pectoral fins aid in
climbing, banking, diving, stopping, and turning, while the tail
fin functions as a rudder. The anal and dorsal fins serve mainly
as stabilizers.

Bonefish
Albula vulpes

Bonefishes
Albulidae

Length: *1-2 ft.; 3½ ft. max.*
What to look for: *upper jaw stops
short of eye; lower jaw overhung by
tip of snout; small throat plate under
mouth; pelvic fins on belly; body
moderately rounded in cross section and
covered with silvery scales; tail fin
deeply forked.* **Habitat:** *shallow mud
and sand flats.*

Fishermen stalk the wary Bonefish (the only North
American representative of this group) in shallow
flats, watching for swirls of water as the fish probes
head down in the mud for shellfish. It also preys on
small fish. A hooked Bonefish makes a lightning-fast
run through the water. As its name indicates, the
Bonefish is extremely bony, and so most hooked individuals are returned alive to the sea.

Inshore Lizardfish
Synodus foetens

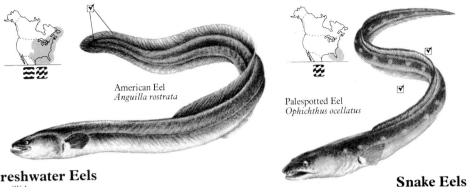

American Eel
Anguilla rostrata

Palespotted Eel
Ophichthus ocellatus

Freshwater Eels
Anguillidae

Length: *2-3 ft.; 4 ft. max.*
What to look for: *body long, slender; dorsal, pectoral, and anal fins well developed; dorsal and anal fins continuous around tail; large mouth.*
Habitat: *rivers, creeks, lakes, and bays (often under rocks or logs); spawning adults and larvae in sea.*

Freshwater eels spawn far out in the Atlantic, in the Sargasso Sea. Each female produces as many as 20 million eggs. Then the males spread milt over the eggs, and the adults die. The eggs hatch into thin, transparent larvae (called leptocephali) that drift with the currents. In one to three years, transformed into elvers (young eels), they reach the coast. Females swim up streams, sometimes squirming over mud or wet grass to reach lakes or ponds. Males stay close to the sea. In about eight years, the eels begin their journey back to the Sargasso.

Snake Eels
Ophichthidae

Length: *1-4 ft.; 6 ft. max.*
What to look for: *body long, slender, scaleless, with dorsal fin extending almost full length and anal fin starting halfway back, both usually stopping short of tail tip; tail tip usually hard; 2 pairs of nostrils, rear ones within or piercing upper lip.*
Habitat: *sand or mud bottoms (occasionally reefs) in coastal and offshore areas.*

In the daytime snake eels stay in hiding, burrowing tailfirst into the bottom. At night large numbers may be attracted to fishermen's lights; divers report seeing them crawling over the bottom in snakelike fashion. Snake eels are fast and slippery, and though most are docile, a few species are quick to bite if handled. Like other eels, they are predatory, making their meals of fish, crab, shrimp, and octopus.

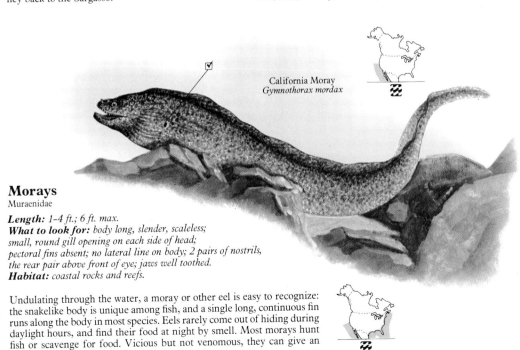

California Moray
Gymnothorax mordax

Morays
Muraenidae

Length: *1-4 ft.; 6 ft. max.*
What to look for: *body long, slender, scaleless; small, round gill opening on each side of head; pectoral fins absent; no lateral line on body; 2 pairs of nostrils, the rear pair above front of eye; jaws well toothed.*
Habitat: *coastal rocks and reefs.*

Undulating through the water, a moray or other eel is easy to recognize: the snakelike body is unique among fish, and a single long, continuous fin runs along the body in most species. Eels rarely come out of hiding during daylight hours, and find their food at night by smell. Most morays hunt fish or scavenge for food. Vicious but not venomous, they can give an inquisitive diver a severe bite.

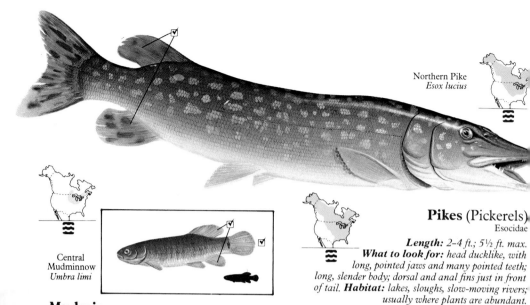

Northern Pike
Esox lucius

Central
Mudminnow
Umbra limi

Mudminnows Umbridae

Length: *3-6½ in.; 8 in. max.*
What to look for: *tail rounded;
snout short, somewhat rounded;
dorsal and anal fins far back on body.*
Habitat: *small lakes, ponds,
sloughs, sluggish streams;
usually where plants are abundant.*

These fishes have a remarkable capacity to survive on little oxygen, burrowing into the mud for extended periods of time during cold weather. They feed mostly on aquatic invertebrates and small fish.

Pikes (Pickerels)
Esocidae

Length: *2-4 ft.; 5½ ft. max.*
What to look for: *head ducklike, with
long, pointed jaws and many pointed teeth;
long, slender body; dorsal and anal fins just in front
of tail.* **Habitat:** *lakes, sloughs, slow-moving rivers;
usually where plants are abundant.*

Pikes are solitary and carnivorous, stalking other fish from beneath logs and overhanging banks and from other protected areas. The spoon-shaped lures that fishermen use to attract the larger pikes—the Northern Pike, the Chain Pickerel (*Esox niger*), and the Muskellunge (*Esox masquinongy*)—are believed to move and glitter like the living prey. The Northern Pike occurs in North America, Europe, and Asia, one of only two freshwater fishes definitely known to live on these three continents.

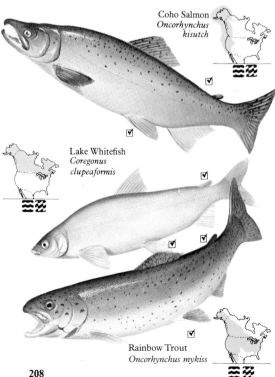

Coho Salmon
*Oncorhynchus
kisutch*

Lake Whitefish
*Coregonus
clupeaformis*

Rainbow Trout
Oncorhynchus mykiss

Trout, Salmon, Whitefishes, and Graylings
Salmonidae

Length: *1-3 ft.; 5 ft. max.*
What to look for: *adipose
(fleshy) fin on rear of back;
body usually moderately slender,
round in cross section; no spines
in fins; scales smooth, small; pelvic fins
on belly; some species lack teeth.*
Habitat: *cold, clear lakes and streams,
especially in turbulent areas;
some species spend part of life in sea.*

Common and widespread in Canada and the northern United States, these fishes range south in mountain areas. The Atlantic Salmon *(Salmo salar)* and the various kinds of Pacific salmon *(Oncorhynchus)* spend most of their lives in the ocean, returning to fresh water to spawn. Because a salmon's appearance is molded by the environment to an extraordinary degree, scientists do not know the precise number of species in the group. Among the 40 or so in North America are these:
• the Brown Trout *(Salmo trutta)*, a golden brown species introduced from Europe;
• the Cutthroat Trout *(Oncorhynchus clarki)*, a red-jawed western species that somethings migrates to the sea;
• the Brook Trout *(Salvelinus fontinalis)*, an elaborately patterned eastern species introduced throughout the continent;
• the Chinook Salmon *(Oncorhynchus tshawytscha)*, the largest member of the salmon family.

FISH

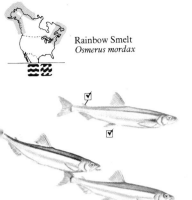

Rainbow Smelt
Osmerus mordax

Smelts Osmeridae

Length: *4–8 in.; 12 in. max.*
What to look for: *adipose (fleshy) fin on rear of back; body slender, elongated; mouth large, with well-developed teeth; no spines in fins; scales smooth, small; pelvic fins on belly.* **Habitat:** *lakes, streams, coastal seas.*

These abundant fishes look like small salmon and have a similar life history: most live in the sea and swim into freshwater to spawn. Certain smelts, such as the western Pond Smelt (*Hypomesus olidus*) and some Rainbow Smelts, remain in freshwater all their lives. Most of the nine North American species are commercially important—some as food (the cold-water Capelin, *Mallotus villosus*, for example) and others as a source of oil. The western Eulachon (*Thaleichthys pacificus*), or Candlefish, was dried by Indians and used as a torch.

Minnows and Carps Cyprinidae

Length: *1½–36 in.; 72 in. max.*
What to look for: *teeth in throat only; no adipose fin; usually no spines in fins; smooth scales; fleshy barbels occasionally present around mouth; mouth rarely underslung and suckerlike.* **Habitat:** *varied; ranges from weedy lakes to rapid rivers.*

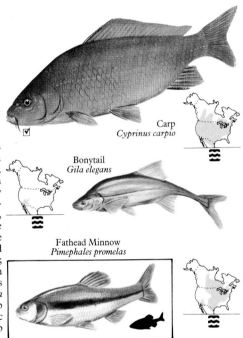

Carp
Cyprinus carpio

Bonytail
Gila elegans

Fathead Minnow
Pimephales promelas

Not all small fish are minnows, nor are all minnows small fish. Our largest native species, the four western squawfishes *(Ptychocheilus)*, grow to 3 feet or more; the bewhiskered Carp, and Asian import thriving in polluted waters, attains a similar size. The minnow family in North America includes some 240 species—among them, the various kinds of shiners, dace, and chubs. One shared characteristic is the presence of teeth in the pharynx, or throat (these cannot be observed without killing the fish). The minnow and the sucker families have teeth in the pharynx only; other species with pharyngeal teeth also have teeth in the mouth or on the jaw. Although most minnows feed on small animals, the Stoneroller *(Campostoma anomalum)* scrapes algae from rocks, the Grass Carp *(Ctenopharyngodon idella)* eats other types of aquatic plants (it was brought to North America to gobble up weeds), and the squawfishes prey on other large fish.

Suckers Catostomidae

Length: *6–30 in.; 40 in. max.*
What to look for: *mouth underslung, suckerlike, usually with thick lips; no adipose fin; teeth in throat only; no spines in fins; smooth scales; no barbels.* **Habitat:** *varied; ranges from sluggish sloughs to swift streams.*

Northern
Hog Sucker
*Hypentelium
nigricans*

Suckers are bottom feeders, locating worms and other soft-bodied invertebrates with their lips and sucking up the food into their distended mouths. Several of the red-finned species called redhorses *(Moxostoma)* feed on clams and snails. In spring many species, including the abundant White Sucker *(Catostomus commersoni)*, migrate into small tributary streams and spawn in large numbers over rubble or gravel riffles. Suckers are good eating but are riddled with many small bones.

FISH

For species illustrated with both a color painting and a silhouette, the silhouette, not the color painting, is in scale with other species on the spread.

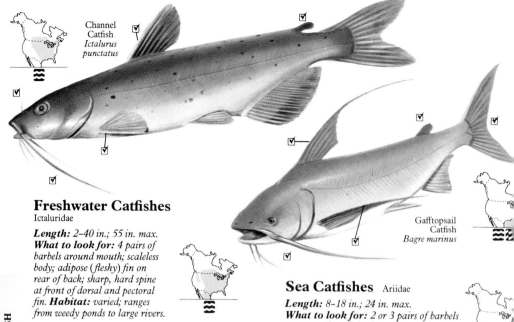

Channel
Catfish
*Ictalurus
punctatus*

Gafftopsail
Catfish
Bagre marinus

Freshwater Catfishes
Ictaluridae

Length: *2–40 in.; 55 in. max.*
What to look for: *4 pairs of
barbels around mouth; scaleless
body; adipose (fleshy) fin on
rear of back; sharp, hard spine
at front of dorsal and pectoral
fin.* **Habitat:** *varied; ranges
from weedy ponds to large rivers.*

Like other catfishes, members of this family locate
food (fish and aquatic invertebrates) by probing the
bottom with sensitive, whiskerlike barbels. Although
many species, including the Channel Catfish and
Brown Bullhead *(Ameiurus nebulosus)*, are important
to sport and commercial fishermen, the catfish with
the greatest fame belongs to a different group. The
Walking Catfish *(Clarias batrachus)*, a member of the
family Clariidae, is an aggressive species capable of
breathing air and walking on land. Brought from Asia
to North America for the aquarium trade, it now
breeds in the wild in southern Florida.

Trout-
Perch
*Percopsis
omiscomaycus*

Trout-Perches
Percopsidae

Length: *2–4 in.; 6 in. max.*
What to look for: *adipose (fleshy)
fin on rear of back; lateral line
running along entire length of body;
body scaled, head naked; short dorsal
and anal fins, each with 1 or 2 spines.*
Habitat: *lakes, rivers, streams.*

As fish developed over time, their brains became
more complex and their bodies more capable of precise maneuvers. Trout and other members of the
salmon family represent an early stage; perches are
more advanced. Trout-perches fall somewhere in
between. For example, their pelvic fins lie midway
between the primitive position (on the belly) and the
advanced (just behind the throat). The adipose fin is a
primitive trait; spines in the fins are a more recent
development. Significant to scientists because of their
in-between status, these fishes are important ecologi-
cally, serving as "forage" for larger species.

Sea Catfishes Ariidae

Length: *8–18 in.; 24 in. max.*
What to look for: *2 or 3 pairs of barbels
near mouth; tail fin forked; sharp, hard spine
at front of dorsal and pectoral fin; adipose
(fleshy) fin on rear of back; scaleless body.*
Habitat: *shallow seas and brackish areas;
occasionally in lower reaches of rivers.*

Male sea catfishes are good parents. They incubate
the eggs in their mouths for several weeks and do the
same with the hatchlings, protecting the offspring
during the critical phase of development. They do
not feed during this time. Sea catfishes have poisonous sheaths around their spines. Active and often
found in large schools, they move offshore in winter
and return in early spring. The Sea Catfish *(Arius
felis)*, an Atlantic species, may swim into freshwater.

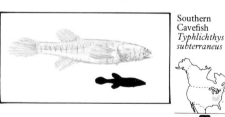

Southern
Cavefish
*Typhlichthys
subterraneus*

Cavefishes Amblyopsidae

Length: *1½–3 in.; 3½ in. max.*
What to look for: *eyes absent or very
small; body white or brown; rows of tiny
swellings on head, body, and tail; pelvic
fins absent or very small; tail rounded.*
Habitat: *limestone caves, cave outlets;
secluded areas in streams and ditches
(the Swampfish, Chologaster cornuta).*

The fishes found solely in caves are blind and have an
enhanced ability to detect vibration and odor (their
tiny swellings are sense organs). Requiring little food,
they can survive on animal matter washed into the
cave. Though few people come upon cavefishes in the
wild, visitors to Kentucky's Mammoth Cave can view
them in tanks along the trail.

FISH

Pacific Hake
Merluccius productus

Atlantic
Cod
*Gadus
morhua*

Codfishes Gadidae

Length: *1-4 ft.; 6 ft. max.* ***What to look for:*** *pelvic fins ahead of pectoral fins;
no spines in fins; chin barbel often present.* ***Habitat:*** *shallow to deep seas;
occasionally in lower reaches of rivers; lakes, rivers (the Burbot,* Lota lota).

These are fish-eating, bottom-dwelling, phenomenally fertile fishes: 9 million eggs were
recorded from a single Atlantic Cod. The family includes these, among others:

• the Haddock (*Melanogrammus aeglefinus*), an
Atlantic species with three dorsal fins, a dark lateral
line, and a dark blotch above each pectoral fin;
• the Red, or Squirrel, Hake (*Urophycis chuss*),
an Atlantic species with a long filament trailing
from the first of the two dorsal fins;

• the Pollock (*Pollachius virens*), an Atlantic
species with a projecting lower jaw, a forked tail,
three dorsal fins, and a pale lateral line;
• the Atlantic and the Pacific Tomcod (*Microgadus
tomcod* and *proximus*), which have three dorsal fins
and a filament extending from each pelvic fin.

Cusk-Eels
and Brotulas Ophidiidae

Length: *1-24 in.; 36 in. max.*
What to look for: *eel-shaped, with head
broader than body; dorsal, tail, and anal fins
often forming one continuous fin; filamentous pelvic fins
usually present under jaw or throat.* ***Habitat:*** *reef crevices
or sand burrows in shallow to very deep seas.*

Spotted
Cusk-Eel
*Chilara
taylori*

With some species living in shallow coral reefs and others at depths of
23,000 feet or more, this group is believed to have the greatest depth
range of any fish family. Shallow-water species forage over the bottom, locating invertebrate food by dragging their "feelers" (highly
modified pelvic fins) like mine detectors. They are rather secretive and
often back into rock crevices or burrow into mud by using their tails.
The eelpouts (Zoarcidae) resemble this group but generally have less
highly modified pelvic fins.

Pearlfishes Carapidae

Length: *2-6 in.; 7 in. max.*
What to look for: *body elongated, tapering toward
tail; dorsal and anal fins very long; pelvic and tail
fins absent; body scaleless, nearly transparent.*
Habitat: *often inside invertebrates; one North American
species inside sea cucumber in shallow tropical seas.*

Pearlfish
*Carapus
bermudensis*

Unique among fish, these secretive creatures may live inside other
animals, including sea urchins, starfish, and mollusks (where they
sometimes become embedded in a layer of pearl). Certain species nibble away at the internal organs of their hosts, although some will roam
along the bottom in search of food.

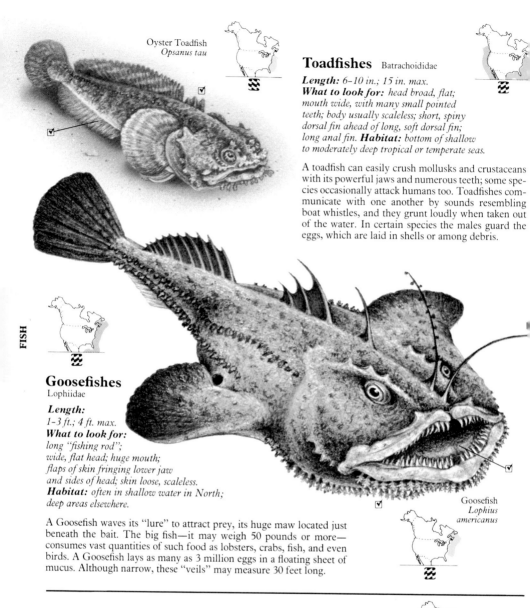

Oyster Toadfish
Opsanus tau

Toadfishes Batrachoididae

Length: *6–10 in.; 15 in. max.*
What to look for: *head broad, flat; mouth wide, with many small pointed teeth; body usually scaleless; short, spiny dorsal fin ahead of long, soft dorsal fin; long anal fin.* **Habitat:** *bottom of shallow to moderately deep tropical or temperate seas.*

A toadfish can easily crush mollusks and crustaceans with its powerful jaws and numerous teeth; some species occasionally attack humans too. Toadfishes communicate with one another by sounds resembling boat whistles, and they grunt loudly when taken out of the water. In certain species the males guard the eggs, which are laid in shells or among debris.

Goosefishes
Lophiidae

Length:
1–3 ft.; 4 ft. max.
What to look for:
long "fishing rod"; wide, flat head; huge mouth; flaps of skin fringing lower jaw and sides of head; skin loose, scaleless.
Habitat: *often in shallow water in North; deep areas elsewhere.*

A Goosefish waves its "lure" to attract prey, its huge maw located just beneath the bait. The big fish—it may weigh 50 pounds or more—consumes vast quantities of such food as lobsters, crabs, fish, and even birds. A Goosefish lays as many as 3 million eggs in a floating sheet of mucus. Although narrow, these "veils" may measure 30 feet long.

Goosefish
Lophius americanus

Needlefishes Belonidae

Length: *1–3 ft.; 4 ft. max.* **What to look for:** *slim body; large mouth; jaws elongated, with many needlelike teeth; dorsal, anal, and pelvic fins toward rear.*
Habitat: *near surface of inshore waters and over continental shelves; Atlantic Needlefish enters freshwater.*

With their bodies almost vertical and only the tails submerged, the silvery needlefishes skitter across the surface as they vibrate their tails. At night they may jump toward lights. The needlefish known as the Houndfish (*Tylosurus crocodilus*) is notorious for this habit; and because it can grow to 4 feet long, it can be a hazard to fishermen in boats or on shore along the southeastern coast. Needlefishes travel in small schools and feed on smaller fish that swarm just beneath the surface, catching them with sudden bursts of speed. Although edible, they are seldom used as human food because of their small size and greenish flesh.

Atlantic Needlefish
Strongylura marina

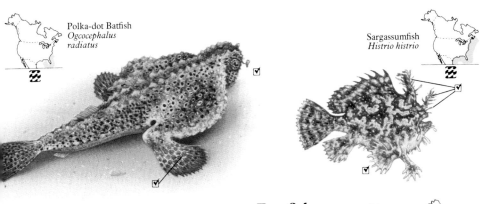

Polka-dot Batfish
*Ogcocephalus
radiatus*

Sargassumfish
Histrio histrio

Batfishes Ogcocephalidae

Length: *2–10 in.; 12 in. max.*
What to look for: *flattened body
covered with bony tubercles; armlike
pectoral fins; single spine forms
"fishing rod"; snout often long.*
Habitat: *bottom of tropical or subtropical
seas; occasionally farther north.*

Like the closely related frogfishes and goosefishes,
the stubby-finned batfishes are better walkers than
swimmers. They attract small fish or other prey with
a "fishing rod" that is extended from a small tube
beneath the snout and vibrated vigorously. They are
most prevalent in deep offshore waters.

Frogfishes Antennariidae

Length: *1–8 in.; 15 in. max.*
What to look for: *first 3 dorsal spines
separate, with 1 or 2 modified as "lures";
body balloon-shaped, with loose, scaleless
skin; armlike pectoral fins.*
Habitat: *usually on bottom of warm seas.*

The most specialized frogfish is the Sargassumfish, a
well-camouflaged resident of floating sargassum. It
rarely swims away from the algae, where it climbs
about, stalking small fish and other creatures that are
part of the sargassum community. A Sargassumfish
can inflate its body by swallowing air or water—possibly a means of preventing predators from pulling it
out of the seaweed.

FISH

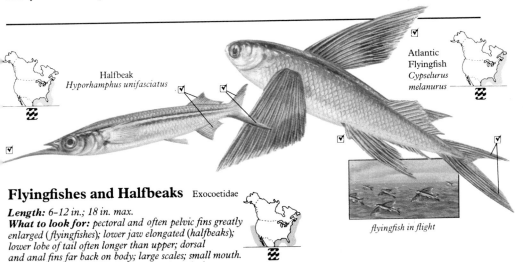

Halfbeak
Hyporhamphus unifasciatus

Atlantic
Flyingfish
*Cypselurus
melanurus*

flyingfish in flight

Flyingfishes and Halfbeaks Exocoetidae

Length: *6–12 in.; 18 in. max.*
What to look for: *pectoral and often pelvic fins greatly
enlarged (flyingfishes); lower jaw elongated (halfbeaks);
lower lobe of tail often longer than upper; dorsal
and anal fins far back on body; large scales; small mouth.*
Habitat: *near shore in tropical and subtropical
regions; near surface in open sea.*

Flyingfishes eat smaller fish and are eaten in turn by
tuna, mackerel, and other large surface feeders. In
escaping these attackers, or when otherwise disturbed, they swim rapidly, then turn upward suddenly and shoot into the air. Though usually airborne
for only 50 yards or less, they may occasionally
glide for hundreds of yards, now and then dipping

the tail into the water to get an additional boost of
power. The close relationship between flyingfishes
and halfbeaks is illustrated by the Smallwing Flyingfish (*Oxyporhamphus micropterus*), whose pectoral
fins are barely larger than those of the halfbeaks, and
by juvenile flyingfishes, which have the elongated
lower jaw of the halfbeaks.

California Killifish
Fundulus parvipinnis

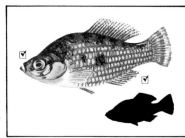

Flagfish
Jordanella
floridae

Killifishes Cyprinodontidae

Length: *1-5 in; 7 in. max.* **What to look for:** *small size; upturned mouth; anal fin never elongated (compare with males in livebearer family).*
Habitat: *shallow waters of all types.*

Killifishes, or topminnows, generally feed at the surface, using their upturned mouths to snatch vast quantities of mosquito larvae and other insects. (Unlike true minnows, with which they are often confused, topminnows have teeth in their mouths.) Some extraordinary species belong to this group. The Salt Creek Pupfish (*Cyprinodon salinus*) and other desert species can survive water temperatures greater than 100°F. Among the other North American species are the Mummichog (*Fundulus heteroclitus*), a popular bait fish on the Atlantic coast, and the Pygmy Killifish (*Leptolucania ommata*) of inland Florida, a brightly colored aquarium fish. The Rivulus (*Rivulus marmoratus*), a relative found in southern Florida and the West Indies, functions as both a male and a female, and fertilizes its own eggs inside its body.

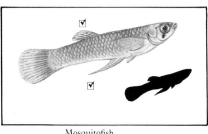

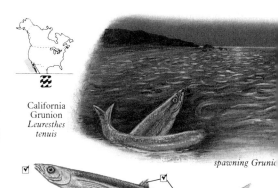

California
Grunion
Leuresthes
tenuis

spawning Grunio

Mosquitofish
Gambusia affinis

Livebearers

Poeciliidae

Length: ¾-2½ in.;
6 in. max.
What to look for:
stubby body; spineless dorsal fin located far back on body; male with long, modified anal fin.
Habitat: *still or slow-moving waters, including brackish areas, in warm regions.*

A male livebearer uses his long anal fin to transfer sperm to the female, who gives birth to live young. Their reproductive habits and hardiness make our native mollies (*Poecilia*) and platyfishes (*Xiphophorus*)—as well as the Guppy (*Poecilia reticulata*) and other livebearers from Central and South America—especially popular with aquarium hobbyists. The Mosquitofish has been introduced throughout the world to control mosquitoes (it eats the larvae and pupae). Like other livebearers, it can survive in stagnant water by extracting oxygen from the surface film. Its mouth is upturned, like the killifishes'.

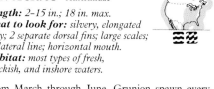

Silversides Atherinidae

Length: *2-15 in.; 18 in. max.*
What to look for: *silvery, elongated body; 2 separate dorsal fins; large scales; no lateral line; horizontal mouth.*
Habitat: *most types of fresh, brackish, and inshore waters.*

From March through June, Grunion spawn every two weeks on southern California beaches, coming in on the waves of the highest tides. Huge numbers of females wriggle into the wet sand and lay their eggs in pockets several inches deep; the males swarm over them and quickly fertilize the eggs. Two weeks after the eggs are laid, the tiny fry squirm out of the sand and into the sea. The 11 other North American silversides, including the western Jacksmelt (*Atherinopsis californiensis*) and the Atlantic Silverside (*Menidia menidia*), spawn in the water, in smaller congregations. Silversides typically have very small teeth.

FISH

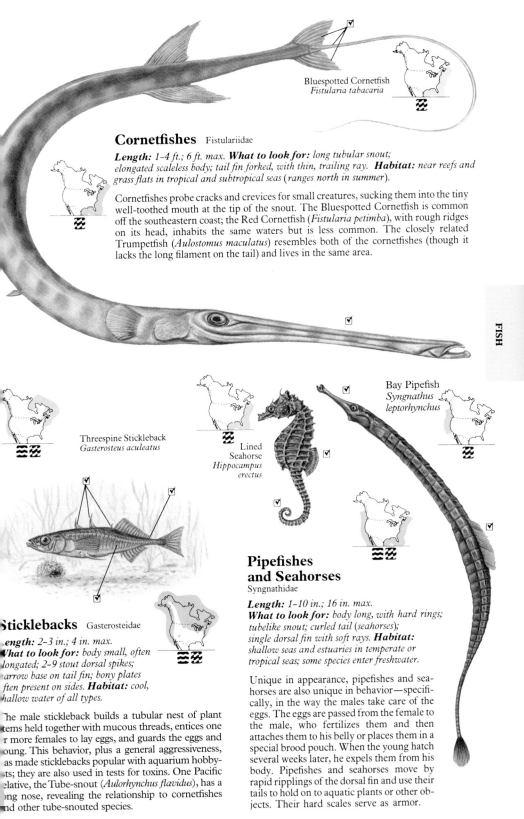

Bluespotted Cornetfish
Fistularia tabacaria

Cornetfishes Fistulariidae

Length: *1–4 ft.; 6 ft. max.* **What to look for:** *long tubular snout; elongated scaleless body; tail fin forked, with thin, trailing ray.* **Habitat:** *near reefs and grass flats in tropical and subtropical seas (ranges north in summer).*

Cornetfishes probe cracks and crevices for small creatures, sucking them into the tiny well-toothed mouth at the tip of the snout. The Bluespotted Cornetfish is common off the southeastern coast; the Red Cornetfish (*Fistularia petimba*), with rough ridges on its head, inhabits the same waters but is less common. The closely related Trumpetfish (*Aulostomus maculatus*) resembles both of the cornetfishes (though it lacks the long filament on the tail) and lives in the same area.

Bay Pipefish
Syngnathus leptorhynchus

Threespine Stickleback
Gasterosteus aculeatus

Lined
Seahorse
Hippocampus erectus

Pipefishes and Seahorses
Syngnathidae

Length: *1–10 in.; 16 in. max.*
What to look for: *body long, with hard rings; tubelike snout; curled tail (seahorses); single dorsal fin with soft rays.* **Habitat:** *shallow seas and estuaries in temperate or tropical seas; some species enter freshwater.*

Unique in appearance, pipefishes and seahorses are also unique in behavior—specifically, in the way the males take care of the eggs. The eggs are passed from the female to the male, who fertilizes them and then attaches them to his belly or places them in a special brood pouch. When the young hatch several weeks later, he expels them from his body. Pipefishes and seahorses move by rapid ripplings of the dorsal fin and use their tails to hold on to aquatic plants or other objects. Their hard scales serve as armor.

Sticklebacks Gasterosteidae

Length: *2–3 in.; 4 in. max.*
What to look for: *body small, often elongated; 2–9 stout dorsal spikes; narrow base on tail fin; bony plates often present on sides.* **Habitat:** *cool, shallow water of all types.*

The male stickleback builds a tubular nest of plant stems held together with mucous threads, entices one or more females to lay eggs, and guards the eggs and young. This behavior, plus a general aggressiveness, has made sticklebacks popular with aquarium hobbyists; they are also used in tests for toxins. One Pacific relative, the Tube-snout (*Aulorhynchus flavidus*), has a long nose, revealing the relationship to cornetfishes and other tube-snouted species.

For species illustrated with both a color painting and a silhouette, the silhouette, not the color painting, is in scale with other species on the spread.

215

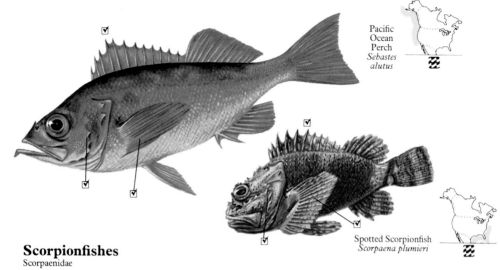

Pacific
Ocean
Perch
*Sebastes
alutus*

Spotted Scorpionfish
Scorpaena plumieri

Scorpionfishes
Scorpaenidae

Length: *6–24 in.; 36 in. max.* **What to look for:** *body compressed, usually scaled; head usually with ridges and spines; most species with single, many-spined dorsal fin; broad pectoral fins.* **Habitat:** *on or near bottom.*

Scorpionfishes produce venom at the base of spines in certain fins, usually the one (or ones) on the back. The venom, presumably produced as a defense against predators, is mild in North American species, but the stonefishes and other Indo-Pacific species are the most poisonous fishes in the sea. Many scorpionfishes have bright colors (deepwater species are typically red), and sport complex assemblages of spines and fleshy protuberances on the head. All are carnivorous bottom dwellers that generally lurk among rocks or in other protected places and are often called rockfish. Some live in shallow water, others to depths as great as 1,000 feet. Certain species—for example, the Redfish (*Sebastes marinus*), or Ocean Perch, of the Atlantic and the Bocaccio (*Sebastes paucispinis*) of the Pacific—are important commercially.

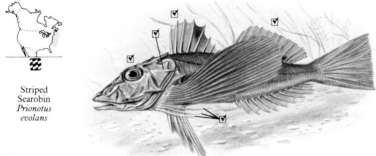

Striped
Searobin
*Prionotus
evolans*

Searobins
Triglidae

Length: *3–12 in.; 18 in. max.* **What to look for:** *head with bony plates; 2 or 3 pectoral rays enlarged and separate, the others joined and winglike; 2 dorsal fins; eyes high on head.* **Habitat:** *shore areas to edge of continental shelf in tropical or temperate seas.*

The separate, individually movable rays on a searobin's pectoral fins are believed to be sensitive to touch and taste, helping the fish to locate food. They are also used for walking slowly along the bottom. Most searobins live in shallow water, many of them close to shore, but those in the group called armored searobins are found only at 500 feet or deeper. As the name indicates, hard plates (modified scales) cover and protect most of the body. Searobins are rarely eaten in North America, but in some parts of the world they are considered a fine food.

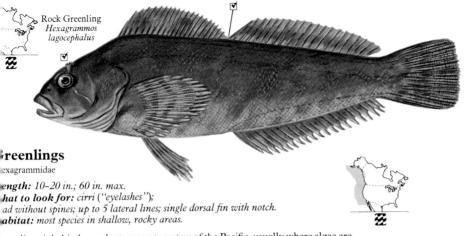

Rock Greenling
*Hexagrammos
lagocephalus*

Greenlings

Hexagrammidae

Length: *10-20 in.; 60 in. max.*
What to look for: *cirri ("eyelashes");
head without spines; up to 5 lateral lines; single dorsal fin with notch.*
Habitat: *most species in shallow, rocky areas.*

Greenlings inhabit the cooler temperate waters of the Pacific, usually where algae are abundant. They make their meals of fish and of shrimp, clams, and other invertebrates, and they attach their masses of eggs to rocks. Most are too small to be harvested commercially. An exception is the Lingcod (*Ophiodon elongatus*), which reaches a length of 5 feet and weighs as much as 70 pounds; it is also a popular sport fish. Its tasty flesh is greenish, as is the flesh of most greenlings.

Fourhorn Sculpin
*Myoxocephalus
quadricornis*

Banded
Sculpin
*Cottus
carolinae*

Sculpins   Cottidae

Length: *2-30 in.; 40 in. max.* **What to look for:** *stout body; head large,
often somewhat flattened; big eyes near top of head; 2 dorsal fins.*
Habitat: *bottom of cool or cold seas, springs, and headwater streams.*

Though the Cabezon (*Scorpaenichthys marmoratus*) of the Pacific may weigh 25 pounds, most sculpins are much smaller. Sculpins lack protective scales but often have spines or fleshy frills of skin, particularly around the head. Some lift their spines menacingly if approached. Almost exclusively bottom dwellers, sculpins walk on their leglike fins, usually slowly but sometimes in quick rushes. Nearly all hide in rocks or vegetation during the day. Some, notably the Sea Raven (*Hemitripterus americanus*), can inflate themselves with air or water as a protective device.

Poachers

Agonidae

Warty Poacher
Occella verrucosa

Length: *2-10 in.; 12 in. max.*
What to look for: *body covered with bony,
often sawtooth-edged plates; 1 or 2 dorsal fins.*
Habitat: *on bottom in open sea;
some species in tide pools.*

These armored fishes are bottom dwellers, feeding on other fish and invertebrates. The species called alligatorfishes have one rather than two dorsal fins. Most poachers are found in the northern Pacific.

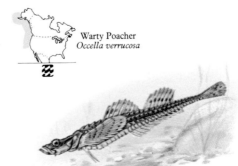

*For species illustrated with both a color painting and a silhouette,
the silhouette, not the color painting, is in scale with other species on the spread.*

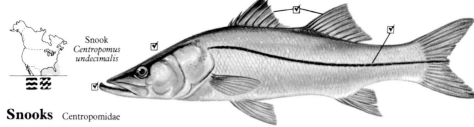

Snooks Centropomidae

Length: *1–3½ ft.; 4½ ft. max.*
What to look for: *long body; protruding lower jaw; sloping forehead; 2 separate dorsal fins, the first spiny; lateral line extends onto tail.*
Habitat: *near river mouths and mangrove thickets in warm regions.*

The wary, unpredictable Snook, largest and most common of the four North American snooks, usually feeds at night, and it often exasperates sport fishermen by refusing bait or lures put directly in front of its snout. But when a bigmouthed Snook does feel the bite of a hook, it fights ferociously and leaps high out of the water. The Snook, very tolerant of freshwater, is a popular game fish as far inland as Lake Okeechobee in Florida.

Temperate Basses Percichthyidae

Length: *8–60 in.; 7 ft. max.*
What to look for: *2 dorsal fins, usually well separated; body silvery, often with horizontal stripes; gill cover with 2 rounded spines; lateral line continuous from gill cover to base of tail fin.*
Habitat: *usually in temperate fresh and coastal waters.*

The 2-foot-long Striped Bass is by nature anadromous (that is, it lives in the sea but swims upriver to spawn), and its natural range is only in the East. But upstream from dams, some strictly freshwater populations have developed, and transplants in the West have perpetuated themselves for more than a hundred years. Other temperate basses include the freshwater White Bass (*Morone chrysops*) and California's quarter-ton Giant Sea Bass (*Stereolepis gigas*).

Striped Bass
Morone saxatilis

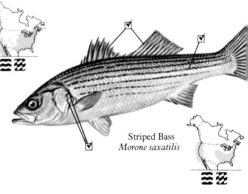

Kelp Bass
Paralabrax clathratus

Sea Basses
Serranidae

Length: *2–72 in.; 8 ft. max.*
What to look for: *dorsal fin not completely divided; large mouth; gill cover with 3 spines; small scales; 3 spines on anal fin; no axillary scale on pelvic fin.*
Habitat: *tropical and temperate seas; often near reefs, rocks, or kelp.*

Most sea basses are hermaphroditic: a single individual has both male and female reproductive organs. In such species as the Snowy Grouper, eggs are produced by the smaller individuals, which become functional males as they increase in size. In others, such as the Belted Sandfish (*Serranus subligarius*) of the Atlantic, a mature individual can produce eggs and sperm at the same time.

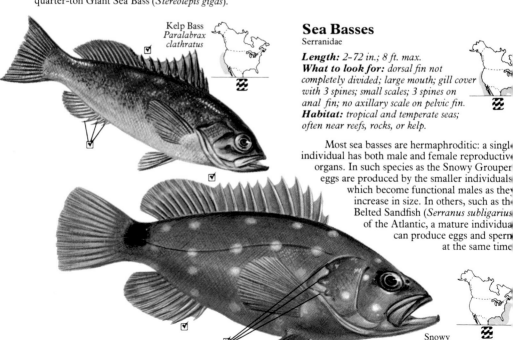

Snowy Grouper
Epinephelus niveatus

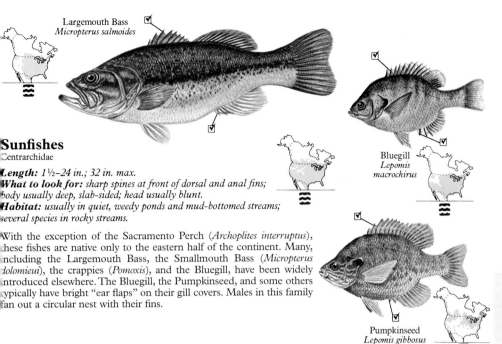

Largemouth Bass
Micropterus salmoides

Bluegill
*Lepomis
macrochirus*

Sunfishes
Centrarchidae

Length: *1½–24 in.; 32 in. max.*
What to look for: *sharp spines at front of dorsal and anal fins;
body usually deep, slab-sided; head usually blunt.*
Habitat: *usually in quiet, weedy ponds and mud-bottomed streams;
several species in rocky streams.*

With the exception of the Sacramento Perch (*Archoplites interruptus*),
these fishes are native only to the eastern half of the continent. Many,
including the Largemouth Bass, the Smallmouth Bass (*Micropterus
dolomieui*), the crappies (*Pomoxis*), and the Bluegill, have been widely
introduced elsewhere. The Bluegill, the Pumpkinseed, and some others
typically have bright "ear flaps" on their gill covers. Males in this family
fan out a circular nest with their fins.

Pumpkinseed
Lepomis gibbosus

FISH

Bigeyes
Priacanthidae

Length: *8–15 in.; 24 in. max.*
What to look for: *large eyes; red color;
anal fin with 3 spines; rough scales.*
Habitat: *usually near bottom in warm seas,
usually near reefs or other obstructions.*

The combination of large eyes and red color suggests
that a fish is nocturnal, and with the bigeyes, the
squirrelfishes (reef creatures that look much like the
bigeyes but belong to the family Holocentridae), and
the cardinalfishes (right), that is indeed the case.
Bigeyes hunt at night for fish and large invertebrates,
including crabs and shrimps. Though generally too
small and found too far from shore to be of much
commercial importance, bigeyes are salted, dried,
and eaten in parts of Asia. They are also called
catalufas, from the name of a variegated carpet cloth.

Cardinalfishes
Apogonidae

Length: *1–4 in.; 8 in. max.*
What to look for: *small size; large eyes;
2 separate dorsal fins, the first with many
spines; anal fin with 2 spines and many rays;
often reddish.* **Habitat:** *usually near corals
and rocks in warm seas.*

A small fish finds refuge in places where larger fish
cannot follow in pursuit—rock crevices, burrows,
and even local animal life. The Sponge Cardinalfish
(*Phaeoptyx xenus*), for example, lives in tube sponges;
another Atlantic cardinalfish uses the large sea snails
called conchs and is, appropriately enough, known
as the Conchfish (*Astrapogon stellatus*). These two
species are brownish, though the colors of most
cardinalfishes bear out their name.

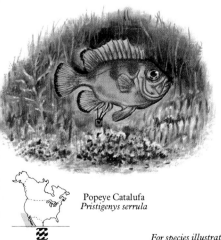

Popeye Catalufa
Pristigenys serrula

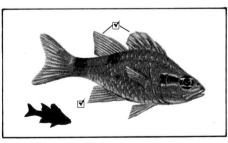

Flamefish
Apogon maculatus

*For species illustrated with both a color painting and a silhouette,
the silhouette, not the color painting, is in scale with other species on the spread.* **219**

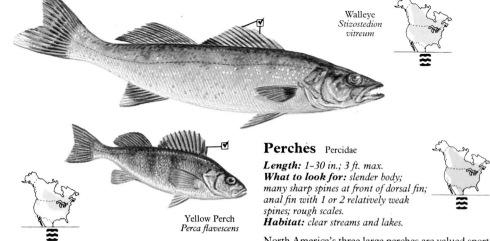

Walleye
*Stizostedion
vitreum*

Perches Percidae

Length: *1–30 in.; 3 ft. max.*
What to look for: *slender body;
many sharp spines at front of dorsal fin;
anal fin with 1 or 2 relatively weak
spines; rough scales.*
Habitat: *clear streams and lakes.*

North America's three large perches are valued sport
and commercial fish. The 2-foot-long Walleye sometimes weighs 20 pounds or more; the Yellow Perch
and the Sauger (*Stizostedion canadense*) rarely weigh
more than a pound. The perch family also includes
the minnowlike, often brightly colored darters, most
abundant in the East. Darters generally inhabit
streams, where they rest on the bottom and dart forward to a new position every now and then. Although
some species have wide ranges, others are extremely
limited in distribution. The Snail Darter (*Percina
tanasi*), whose endangered status nearly stopped the
completion of a dam in Tennessee, lives only in certain parts of that state; the Maryland Darter (*Etheostoma sellare*), in an area only 75 to 150 feet long in a
northeastern Maryland creek. Darters require clean
water, and their presence or absence can therefore be
used to assess pollution in a stream.

Yellow Perch
Perca flavescens

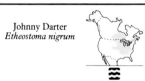

Johnny Darter
Etheostoma nigrum

Tilefishes Malacanthidae

Length: *1–2 ft; 3 ft. max.* **What to look for:** *body usually long, flattened
from side to side; long single dorsal fin, with many spines and soft rays; head
blunt; mouth nearly horizontal.* **Habitat:** *moderately deep waters; near bottom.*

Abundant for the first time in a century, the Tilefish is once again being sold in East
Coast markets. This mild-flavored fish, said to taste like lobster, became popular
soon after the 1879 discovery of commercially harvestable numbers. Three years
later, billions of them floated to the surface, killed by an unusual combination of
temperature conditions along the upper Atlantic coast. For many years the species
was believed to be extinct, but its population is slowly building along the edge of the
continental shelf, where the ocean floor drops steeply into the depths.

Tilefish
*Lopholatilus
chamaeleonticeps*

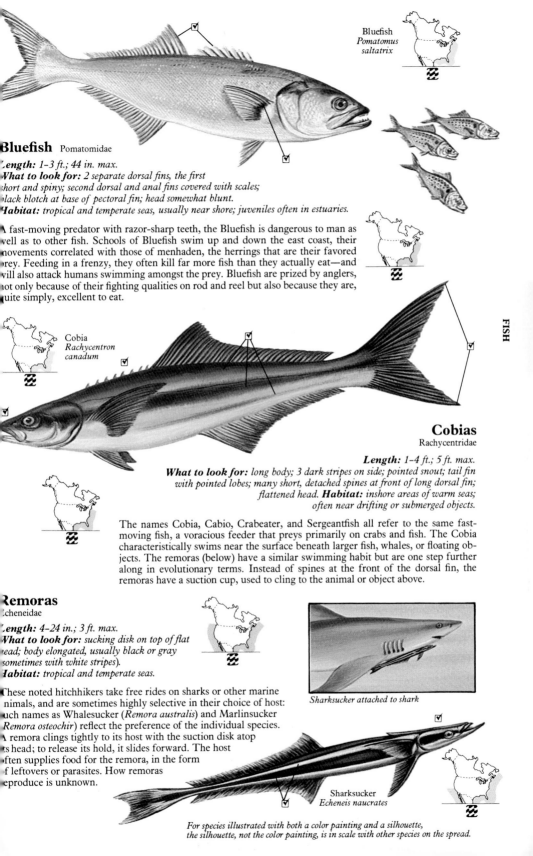

Bluefish
*Pomatomus
saltatrix*

Bluefish Pomatomidae

Length: 1-3 ft.; 44 in. max.
What to look for: 2 separate dorsal fins, the first
short and spiny; second dorsal and anal fins covered with scales;
black blotch at base of pectoral fin; head somewhat blunt.
Habitat: tropical and temperate seas, usually near shore; juveniles often in estuaries.

A fast-moving predator with razor-sharp teeth, the Bluefish is dangerous to man as
well as to other fish. Schools of Bluefish swim up and down the east coast, their
movements correlated with those of menhaden, the herrings that are their favored
prey. Feeding in a frenzy, they often kill far more fish than they actually eat—and
will also attack humans swimming amongst the prey. Bluefish are prized by anglers,
not only because of their fighting qualities on rod and reel but also because they are,
quite simply, excellent to eat.

Cobia
*Rachycentron
canadum*

Cobias
Rachycentridae

Length: 1-4 ft.; 5 ft. max.
What to look for: long body; 3 dark stripes on side; pointed snout; tail fin
with pointed lobes; many short, detached spines at front of long dorsal fin;
flattened head. Habitat: inshore areas of warm seas;
often near drifting or submerged objects.

The names Cobia, Cabio, Crabeater, and Sergeantfish all refer to the same fast-
moving fish, a voracious feeder that preys primarily on crabs and fish. The Cobia
characteristically swims near the surface beneath larger fish, whales, or floating objects. The remoras (below) have a similar swimming habit but are one step further
along in evolutionary terms. Instead of spines at the front of the dorsal fin, the
remoras have a suction cup, used to cling to the animal or object above.

Remoras
Echeneidae

Length: 4-24 in.; 3 ft. max.
What to look for: sucking disk on top of flat
head; body elongated, usually black or gray
(sometimes with white stripes).
Habitat: tropical and temperate seas.

These noted hitchhikers take free rides on sharks or other marine
animals, and are sometimes highly selective in their choice of host:
such names as Whalesucker (*Remora australis*) and Marlinsucker
(*Remora osteochir*) reflect the preference of the individual species.
A remora clings tightly to its host with the suction disk atop
its head; to release its hold, it slides forward. The host
often supplies food for the remora, in the form
of leftovers or parasites. How remoras
reproduce is unknown.

Sharksucker attached to shark

Sharksucker
Echeneis naucrates

*For species illustrated with both a color painting and a silhouette,
the silhouette, not the color painting, is in scale with other species on the spread.*

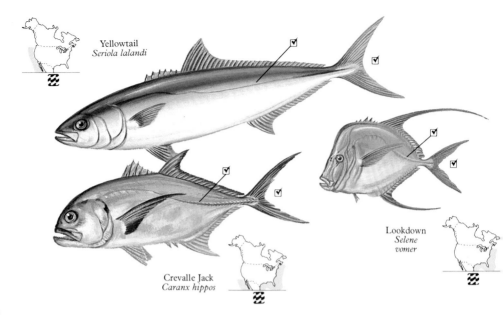

Yellowtail
Seriola lalandi

Lookdown
*Selene
vomer*

Crevalle Jack
Caranx hippos

Jacks and Pompanos Carangidae

Length: *6–36 in.; 5 ft. max.*
What to look for: *body cigar-shaped or flattened from side to side; scales on lateral line often greatly enlarged toward tail; tail fin forked, with narrow base.*
Habitat: *tropical and temperate seas.*

Although all of these strong, fast swimmers prey on other marine animals, precisely what they eat varies with the species, and sometimes with circumstances as well. Jacks (*Caranx*) and amberjacks (*Seriola*) feed exclusively on fish; pompanos (*Trachinotus*), only on invertebrates. Young Leatherjackets (*Oligoplites saurus*) eat parasites on the skin of other fishes but switch to a fish diet as they mature. The Pilotfish (*Naucrates ductor*) swims in front of sharks and other large creatures, in excellent position to feed on leftovers.

Dolphins Coryphaenidae

Length: *1-4 ft.; 6 ft. max.*
What to look for: *long dorsal fin (extends from head to tail); long anal fin; radiant colors when alive; tail fin deeply forked.*
Habitat: *open ocean in tropical and temperate regions.*

To the delight of sport fishermen, the surface-feeding Dolphin strikes hard, then makes a fast run with frequent rocketing aerial leaps. Fishermen usually leave the first catch on a line to keep the rest of the school following the boat. Dolphins weigh up to 75 pounds or more and make excellent eating. Despite their large size, their maximum life span is probably only 2 or 3 years (such fishes as trout may live 5 to 10 years), which indicates a remarkably fast rate of growth. Dolphin males, or bulls, have a high, blunt forehead; the female's head slants, in typical fish fashion.

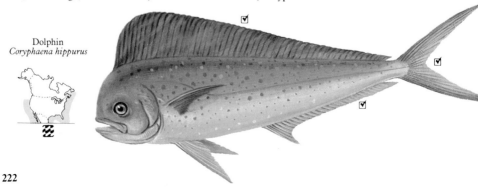

Dolphin
Coryphaena hippurus

222

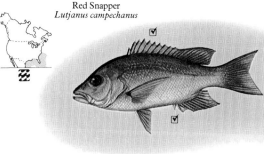

Red Snapper
Lutjanus campechanus

Yellowtail Snapper
Ocyurus chrysurus

Snappers
Lutjanidae

Length: *10–30 in.; 3½ ft. max.*
What to look for: *first and second dorsal fins joined, sometimes with shallow notch in between; anal fin with 3 spines; big well-toothed mouth, often with pointed canine teeth; pelvic fin with transparent axillary scale at base (not always visible).*
Habitat: *warm seas (usually near reefs or submerged objects); some species enter freshwater.*

Snappers generally swim near the bottom, feeding on fish, crabs, shrimps, and mollusks. Unlike most other big carnivorous fish, they often travel in large schools. Those that live in shallow waters are caught regularly by sport fishermen, and all kinds are good to eat. The most sought-after commercially is the Red Snapper, a market and restaurant delicacy found in relatively deep water. Fishermen use hand lines with heavy weights to get the bait quickly to the right depth.

FISH

Tripletails
Lobotidae

Length: *1–2 ft.; 3 ft. max.*
What to look for: *body flattened from side to side; many heavy scales; yellow to brown, often mottled; 3-tailed appearance.*
Habitat: *temperate and subtropical seas; usually near flotsam or pilings.*

Tripletails have only one tail, of course; enlarged portions of the dorsal and anal fins give them their three-tailed appearance. Until a Tripletail is about 3 inches long, it floats and swims on its side, looking deceptively like a dead leaf. (The young are more likely than the adults to occur in places with floating leaves—that is, near shore.) Plantlike disguises conceal a number of fishes in other families from predators or prey. For example, the Sargassumfish and the Giant Kelpfish look somewhat like seaweed; various gars resemble floating sticks; and in certain areas young Atlantic Spadefish are said to look much like the seeds of mangrove trees.

Mojarras
Gerreidae

Length: *4–10 in.; 15 in. max.*
What to look for: *greatly extendable mouth; body and head heavily scaled, usually silvery; bases of dorsal and anal fins covered by scaly sheath; tail deeply forked.* **Habitat:** *near sandy bottoms in shallow seas and estuaries; occasionally in freshwater.*

Mojarras, or moharras, typically travel in schools, probing the bottom for small animals in the sediments and sucking them into their extendable, tube-like mouth. The name is akin to the Spanish for "spear head." Most species are too small to be eaten by man, but meals are sometimes made of the larger ones, such as the Irish Pompano (*Diapterus auratus*). The Spotfin Mojarra and the Striped Mojarra (*Diapterus plumieri*) regularly range into freshwater.

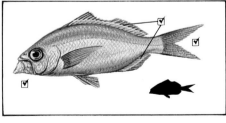

Tripletail
Lobotes surinamensis

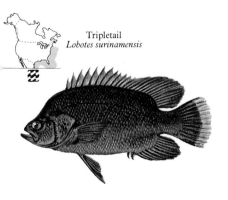

Spotfin Mojarra
Eucinostomus argenteus

For species illustrated with both a color painting and a silhouette, the silhouette, not the color painting, is in scale with other species on the spread.

White Grunt
Haemulon plumieri

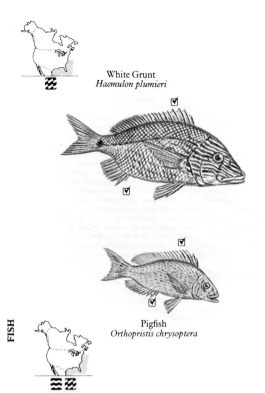

Pigfish
Orthopristis chrysoptera

Grunts
Haemulidae

Length: *6–18 in.; 2 ft. max.*
What to look for: *single dorsal fin with 10 spines and 8 or 9 soft rays; anal fin with 3 spines; feeble teeth in jaws; often striped or spotted.* **Habitat:** *near reefs or weeds in warm seas; one species enters freshwater.*

Grunts grunt continually, not only when they are underwater but also after they have been taken out. The Spanish name for the group, *ronco*, means "hoarse," and such specific English names as Pigfish also allude to the sound. In grunts a drumlike swim bladder amplifies the sounds made by the grinding throat (pharyngeal) teeth. Squirrelfishes also produce sounds in this way, but in most of the other sound-producing species throat teeth are not involved.

Grunts feed mainly on bottom-dwelling invertebrates—not just the predictable mollusks and crabs but also, in some cases, long-spined sea urchins. Various species, especially the French Grunt (*Haemulon flavolineatum*), have a curious kissing behavior. With mouths wide open (the inside is often brightly colored), two grunts rush toward one another, make contact in the form of a kiss, and separate after pushing one another back and forth. This may be courtship behavior or perhaps some form of territorial defense.

Sheepshead
Archosargus probatocephalus

Pinfish
Lagodon rhomboides

Porgies
Sparidae

Length: *6–18 in.; 2 ft. max.*
What to look for: *deep body; front teeth like incisors or pegs, side ones low and flattened; anal fin with 3 spines.*
Habitat: *temperate and tropical seas; usually near reefs, wrecks, or grass beds; 2 species enter freshwater.*

Porgies, like grunts, are small, schooling fishes, most of them weighing less than a pound. (The Sheepshead, reaching 30 pounds, is a giant within the group.) Porgies are in general warmwater fishes, though several species range northward to New York and beyond. One of these, the Scup (*Stenotomus chrysops*), spawns in shallow water in spring and summer; after spawning it moves into deeper water, which is warmer in winter. Fishes from a number of other families, such as mackerels and drums, make a similar migration; the cold-loving codfishes do just the reverse.

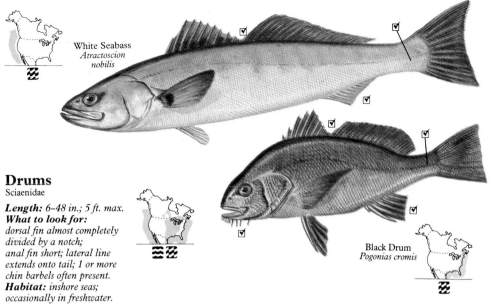

White Seabass
*Atractoscion
nobilis*

Drums
Sciaenidae

Length: *6–48 in.; 5 ft. max.*
What to look for:
*dorsal fin almost completely
divided by a notch;
anal fin short; lateral line
extends onto tail; 1 or more
chin barbels often present.*
Habitat: *inshore seas;
occasionally in freshwater.*

Black Drum
Pogonias cromis

Drums and the closely allied croakers produce sound by contracting special muscles adjacent to the swim bladder, which acts as an amplifier. In certain species only the males have the muscles, suggesting that the sounds are involved in breeding activities; in others, neither sex has a swim bladder, so the sounds cannot be produced. A number of popular edible species belong to this group, including the kingfishes (*Menticirrhus*) and also the weakfishes (*Cynoscion*).

FISH

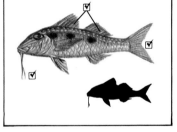

Spotted
Goatfish
*Pseudupeneus
maculatus*

Bermuda Chub
Kyphosus sectatrix

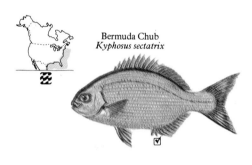

Goatfishes Mullidae

Length: *6–12 in.; 13 in. max.*
What to look for: *2 long barbels
on chin; forked tail fin; body long,
heavily scaled; 2 separate dorsal
fins, the first with 6–8 spines.*
Habitat: *shallow warm seas with
sand or mud bottoms.*

Fishes, like humans, have specialized taste buds. Though some species (the freshwater catfishes, for example) have taste buds all over the body, taste buds are usually concentrated in the lining of the mouth, in the throat, on the lips, or in sensitive structures called barbels. Goatfishes use their barbels, said to resemble the beard of a goat, to probe the bottom for invertebrate food. Most goatfishes are gregarious, swimming with other species or with their own kind.

Sea Chubs
Kyphosidae

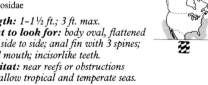

Length: *1–1½ ft.; 3 ft. max.*
What to look for: *body oval, flattened
from side to side; anal fin with 3 spines;
small mouth; incisorlike teeth.*
Habitat: *near reefs or obstructions
in shallow tropical and temperate seas.*

Sea chubs browse on seaweeds, but experiments with two Atlantic species (including the one shown) demonstrate that they eat more than just the plants: they require the small animals living on the seaweeds as part of their diet. Similar evidence shows that this may also be true of the Opaleye (*Girella nigricans*), a blue-eyed Pacific member of this group. Opaleyes frequent offshore kelp beds but move into shallow water to spawn. Though the eggs sometimes drift out to sea, the fishes swim into tide pools when about an inch long. Eventually they move into deeper water.

Atlantic Spadefish
Chaetodipterus faber

Spadefishes
Ephippidae

Length: *6–24 in.; 36 in. max.*
What to look for: *body deep,
flattened from side to side; vertical bars
on sides (except in large adults);
dorsal fin with distinct spiny and soft parts;
small horizontal mouth.* **Habitat:** *near
pilings, reefs, and outcrops in warm seas.*

Shaped much like a butterflyfish, the Atlantic Spadefish and its Pacific counterpart (*Chaetodipterus zonatus*) are more somberly colored and much more likely to swim about in schools. Small mouths limit their diet to water plants and small invertebrates. Caught regularly on hook and line, spadefishes put up a stubborn (but unspectacular) fight and make excellent eating.

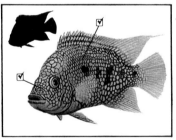

Barred
Surfperch
*Amphistichus
argenteus*

Surfperches   Embiotocidae

Length: *4–15 in.; 19 in. max.*
What to look for: *body flattened from side to side,
well scaled; single dorsal fin; anal fin with spines
and many soft rays.* **Habitat:** *tide pools, kelp forests,
and inshore areas; one species exclusively in freshwater.*

The surfperches, or sea perches, are viviparous, giving birth to six or eight (sometimes more) live young—an unusual mode of reproduction for a saltwater fish. Equally unusual is their capacity to reproduce at a very early age, sometimes as young as a day or two. As their name implies, surfperches generally occur in the surf zone. Many species, however, will enter bays, and one, the Tule Perch (*Hysterocarpus traski*), occurs only in streams draining into San Francisco Bay.

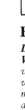

Rio Grande
Perch
*Cichlasoma
cyanoguttatum*

Spotfin
Butterflyfish
*Chaetodon
ocellatus*

Cichlids   Cichlidae

Length: *4–8 in.; 12 in. max.*
What to look for: *body usually deep,
flattened from side to side; one nostril
on each side of snout; lateral line broken
in center of body; 3 or more anal spines.*
Habitat: *usually in mud- or sand-
bottomed lakes and slow streams.*

Cichlids are popular aquarium fish. They are pretty, many species never grow very big, and they have at least one trait of interest to those who can get them to breed: most species incubate their eggs in their mouths (some also hold their young there). The fish shown here is the only cichlid native to the United States, though several introduced species breed in a few warm places.

Butterflyfishes   Chaetodontidae

Length: *2–6 in.; 8 in. max.*
What to look for: *body disk-shaped,
very compressed, heavily scaled, usually
with bright colors and distinct markings;
mouth small, extendable; dorsal and
anal fins scaled, enlarged near tail.*
Habitat: *near rocks and reefs in warm seas.*

Butterflyfishes and the closely related angelfishes illustrate well the relationship between form and function. Their deep, compressed bodies help them maneuver through reefs; their rounded, sometimes highly extended lips help them pluck coral polyps and other small bits of food; and their conspicuous eyespots deflect a predator's attention from the head to a less vital area.

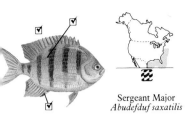

Sergeant Major
Abudefduf saxatilis

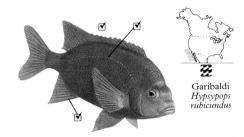

Garibaldi
*Hypsypops
rubicundus*

Damselfishes
Pomacentridae

Length: 2-12 in.; 14 in. max.
What to look for: body relatively deep, flattened from side to side,
with many large scales; lateral line absent toward rear of body or broken
in center; small mouth; anal fin with 2 spines; single dorsal fin.
Habitat: usually near reefs or rocky shores in warm seas.

Highly aggressive on their "home turf," these little fishes will chase—and sometimes
even nip—animals far larger than themselves. The females lay clusters of eggs on the
bottom; the males chase any intruders away from the nest. Damselfishes have a single
nostril in front of each eye (most other fishes have two). As a fish moves or breathes,
water passes into its nostril, reaches the smell receptors on the inside, and then flows
out. (On fishes with double nostrils, water goes in one nostril and out the other.)
Sensations transmitted from the smell receptors to the brain are used in navigation
and in finding food.

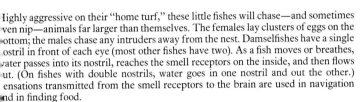

Mullets Mugilidae

Length: 1-2 ft.; 2½ ft. max.
What to look for: round, silvery body;
head somewhat flattened; dorsal fins
widely spaced; fatty eyelids cover all
but narrow slit. **Habitat:** inshore seas
and estuaries; 2 species enter freshwater.

Striped Mullet
Mugil cephalus

The torpedo-shaped mullets leap high out
of the water, though not to capture food; they feed
on algae and detritus, grubbing it from along the bottom
and then grinding it in their small, highly muscular,
gizzardlike stomachs. Mullets are closely related to barracudas—
a surprising fact indeed, considering the extreme differences in diet.

Barracudas Sphyraenidae

Length: 1-5 ft.; 10 ft. max.
What to look for: pointed head, with large mouth and many knifelike teeth;
projecting lower jaw; elongated body; lateral line extends onto tail fin.
Habitat: shallow to moderately deep areas in warm seas.

Barracudas are attracted to shiny objects—perhaps mistaking them for fish—
and will often follow swimmers, waders, or boats. Though this behavior
may be disconcerting to those being followed, barracudas are not
nearly as dangerous as their reputation would make them.
Popular with sport fishermen, these
strong fighters have been clocked
at more than 25 miles an hour.

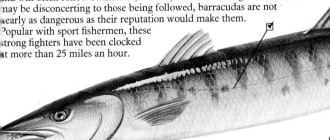

Great Barracuda
Sphyraena barracuda

FISH

227

Barbu
Polydactylus virginicus

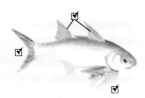

Threadfins
Polynemidae

Length: *6-15 in.; 18 in. max.*
What to look for: *underslung mouth; threadlike rays on pectoral fin; 2 dorsal fins, the first spiny and the second soft-rayed; tail fin deeply forked; body usually silvery.*
Habitat: *sand bottoms in warm, shallow seas.*

With the exception of the Littlescale Threadfin (*Polydactylus oligodon*), which inhabits clear water near reefs, these schooling fishes live in turbid places. Threadfins locate invertebrate prey (mainly shrimp) with the tactile threads that dangle from their pectoral fins. Each of the threads—the number varies according to species—can be moved independently.

Wrasses   Labridae

Length: *3-24 in.; 36 in. max.*
What to look for: *body often cigar-shaped, brightly colored; front teeth usually project outward; dorsal fin continuous, with many spines in front.*
Habitat: *near reefs, rocks, or other submerged objects in sea.*

The gaily colored wrasses grow to very different sizes, ranging from 3 inches (the Bluehead) to 10 feet (giants that live only in the Indo-Pacific region). Shapes differ too: although the typical wrasse has a narrow body and a pointed head, blunter foreheads are characteristic of such species as the California Sheephead. Most wrasses are tropical, but certain species prefer cooler waters, and the slim Cunner (*Tautogolabrus adspersus*) extends north to Labrador.

As might be expected in such a diverse group, eating habits also vary. Many species seek out such hard-shelled invertebrates as sea urchins and crabs, crushing them with their large pharyngeal (throat) teeth. Others school over reefs, eating plankton in mid-water. Still others, the famed "cleaner fish," nibble on the skin parasites of larger species.

Bluehead
Thalassoma bifasciatum

Tautog
Tautoga onitis

California Sheephead
Semicossyphus pulcher

FISH

228

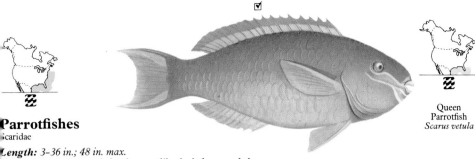

Parrotfishes
Scaridae

Length: *3–36 in.; 48 in. max.*
What to look for: *teeth fused, parrotlike; body large-scaled, often brightly colored; dorsal fin with many spines and soft rays.*
Habitat: *shallow warm seas; near reefs and grass flats.*

Should a parrotfish's beauty fail to impress the snorkeler, surely its slow, stately motions will. As the fish swims about through the reef, it scrapes off algae growing on the coral, using its fused, beak-forming teeth and breaking off bits of coral in the process. At night parrotfishes sleep on the bottom, sometimes secreting a mucous cocoon—a "blanket" believed to be unique in the fish world. They are among the largest reef fish; the species shown here grows to about 20 inches long.

Queen
Parrotfish
Scarus vetula

Jawfishes
Opistognathidae

Length: *1½–5 in.; 6½ in. max.*
What to look for: *large mouth; scaleless head; large eyes; long body; long dorsal fin; lateral line high on body, ending near middle.*
Habitat: *sand and mud bottoms in warm seas.*

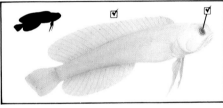

The jawfish is a burrower, generally spending most of its time with only its head exposed, venturing forth to attack an intruder or to grab at a passing bit of food. (The species shown here hovers just above its burrow instead of remaining inside.) Most jawfishes, particularly males, have brightly colored mouth linings, which function in species and sexual recognition. Certain species brood their eggs inside the unusually large mouth.

Yellowhead
Jawfish
*Opistognathus
aurifrons*

*burrowing
jawfish*

Stargazers
Uranoscopidae

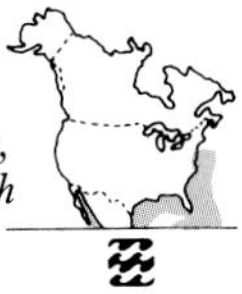

Length: *5–15 in.; 17 in. max.*
What to look for: *small eyes atop large, squarish head; mouth nearly vertical, with fringed lips; pelvic fins close together under throat.* **Habitat:** *sand or mud bottoms in temperate and subtropical seas.*

Almost completely buried in sand, a stargazer attracts small animals by waving a filamentlike lure in its mouth, then leaps up to capture the prey. Stargazers can discharge electricity—as much as 50 volts—to discourage attack and stun or kill their victims, and some species have poison glands as well (just above their pectoral fins). Unique among fish, stargazers can use water taken in through their nostrils for breathing (the nostrils and gills are connected) and can breathe when their gills are covered with sand.

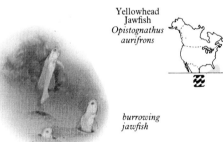

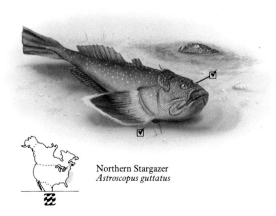

Northern Stargazer
Astroscopus guttatus

*For species illustrated with both a color painting and a silhouette,
the silhouette, not the color painting, is in scale with other species on the spread.*

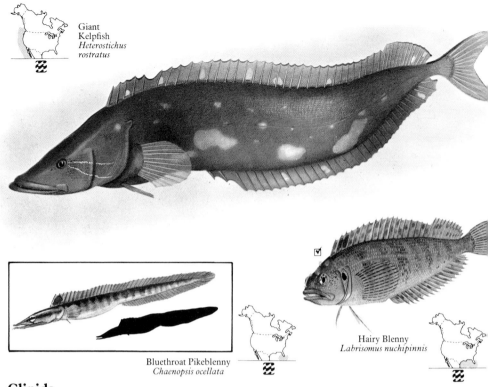

Giant
Kelpfish
*Heterostichus
rostratus*

FISH

Bluethroat Pikeblenny
Chaenopsis ocellata

Hairy Blenny
Labrisomus nuchipinnis

Clinids
Clinidae

Length: *4–20 in.; 24 in. max.*
What to look for: *body usually elongated, scaled; head usually pointed,
often with small, fleshy projections between eye and dorsal fin; patches of conical teeth.*
Habitat: *shallow areas (often in tide pools) in tropical and temperate seas.*

Most clinids, or klipfishes, are small and occur close to shore. One big exception is
the Giant Kelpfish, which reaches a length of 2 feet and has been observed by divers
more than 100 feet below the surface. Its color varies with the color of the surrounding seaweed (it is usually green or brown). The Hairy Blenny, its head bedecked with
conspicuous "hairs," grows to 9 inches; a Pacific fish of about the same length, the
Sarcastic Fringehead (*Neoclinus blanchardi*), is said to have the largest mouth, relative to total size, of any fish. Lean and pike-shaped, the Bluethroat Pikeblenny grows
to 5 inches long.

Combtooth Blennies
Blenniidae

Length: *1–4 in.; 6 in. max.*
What to look for: *body elongated,
flattened from side to side, scaleless; head usually
blunt, often with "eyelashes"; comblike teeth.*
Habitat: *shallows; often in tide pools.*

Combtooth blennies "comb" algae from rocks and
coral with their teeth, and use their fins like limbs in
crawling along the bottom. Some regularly emerge
from the water to bask on rocks, remaining there as
long as they are kept moist by spray and waves.
Blennies of both sexes spread apart their fringes and
crests in a pre-spawning courtship display. Females
attach their eggs to the underside of coral or rocks;
males guard them until they hatch.

Bay Blenny
*Hypsoblennius
gentilis*

*For species illustrated with both a color painting and a silhouette,
the silhouette, not the color painting, is in scale with other species on the spread.*

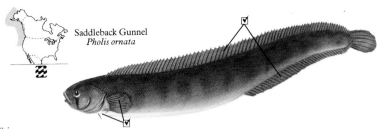

Saddleback Gunnel
Pholis ornata

Gunnels
Pholidae

Length: *3–10 in.; 18 in. max.*
What to look for: *eellike body; dorsal fin twice as long as anal fin; pectoral and pelvic fins small or absent.*
Habitat: *around rocks in tide pools and shallow, cool seas.*

The slender, blennylike gunnels are most abundant in cool waters of the Pacific, hiding in crevices or under rocks. The eastern Rock Gunnel (*Pholis gunnellus*), a warmer brown than the Saddleback Gunnel and more distinctly marked on the back, shelters among kelp plants, in the lowest part of the intertidal zone. Both species have minuscule pelvic fins; the wolffishes, of a separate but closely related family (Anarhichadidae), have none. Much bigger than gunnels (up to 5 feet in length), wolffishes are much more formidable—and not only because of size. With powerful jaws, doglike teeth at the front of their mouths, and crushing teeth elsewhere, they crush clams and other mollusks, and will attempt to do the same to the hands of fishermen removing them from hooks or nets.

FISH

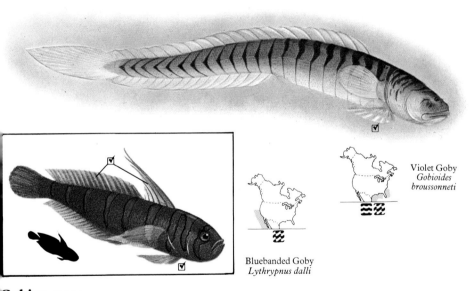

Violet Goby
Gobioides broussonneti

Bluebanded Goby
Lythrypnus dalli

Gobies Gobiidae

Length: *1–3 in.; 20 in. max.*
What to look for: *small size; pelvic fins usually united, often forming adhesive disk; usually 2 separate dorsal fins; body usually scaled.* ***Habitat:*** *tropical and temperate seas, usually in shallows offering cover; some in freshwater.*

This is the largest group of predominantly marine fish, with at least 800 species worldwide and many more, scientists are convinced, remaining to be discovered. Some species burrow in mud or crawl over wet rocks; others cling to the wave-pounded shore with a suction disk beneath the throat; still others live in sponges or the burrows of shrimps and crabs. Male gobies perform an elaborate courtship ritual, spreading their fins to attract the females, and they will fight to protect selected nest sites. The group includes the smallest of all fishes: one Philippine goby is fully mature when just a quarter inch long.

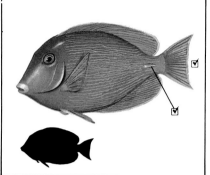

Surgeonfishes
Acanthuridae

Length: *4–8 in.; 12 in. max.*
What to look for: *body oval, flattened from side to side; horizontal spine at base of tail; concave tail fin.* **Habitat:** *shallow tropical seas; usually around reefs or submerged structures.*

A carelessly handled surgeonfish can inflict a painful cut if it unsheaths its switchblade spine, but it is precisely this defensive weaponry that makes these fishes popular in aquariums. Surgeonfishes are actually algae eaters, scraping their food from rocks and coral. Very young ones have hollow, bony spines that keep them buoyant as ocean currents carry them long distances.

Blue Tang
Acanthurus coeruleus

Albacore
Thunnus alalunga

Mackerels and Tunas Scombridae

Length: *1–6 ft.; 14 ft. max.*
What to look for: *streamlined body; 2 dorsal fins, fitting into grooves; finlets behind anal and second dorsal fins; tail fin deeply forked narrow at base, with 1 or 2 keels on base.*
Habitat: *open seas in tropical and temperate areas.*

Atlantic Mackerel
Scomber scombrus

Swift, schooling fishes, with torpedo-shaped bodies that are typically dark blue or green above and silvery white elsewhere, these top predators are among the most important of all sport and commercial species. All are excellent eating (their flesh ranges from white to reddish, depending on the species), and their livers are a rich source of vitamin A. Among the several dozen in North American waters (some are found worldwide) are these:
• the Bluefin Tuna (*Thunnus thynnus*), a giant among tunas (up to 1,800 pounds);
• the King Mackerel (*Scomberomorus cavalla*) of the Atlantic, averaging about 10 pounds, identified by a lateral line that drops sharply at the middle of the body;
• the various bonitos (*Sarda*), similar to tunas but with oilier flesh.

Butterfishes
Stromateidae

Length: *6–10 in.; 12 in. max.*
What to look for: *soft, silvery skin; oval, compressed body; long dorsal and anal fins; deeply forked tail fin; no scales.*
Habitat: *shallow to moderately deep seas in temperate and tropical regions.*

Living amongst the tentacles of jellyfishes and Portuguese Men-of-war, two members of this group—the western Medusafish (*Icichthys lockingtoni*) and the eastern Man-of-war Fish (*Nomeus gronovii*)—gain some protection, but are not totally immune to the stings. Some young Harvestfish and Butterfish (*Peprilus triacanthus*) also take refuge there.

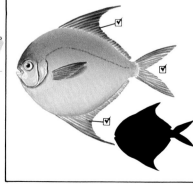

Harvestfi
*Peprilu.
alepidotu*

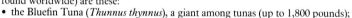

FISH

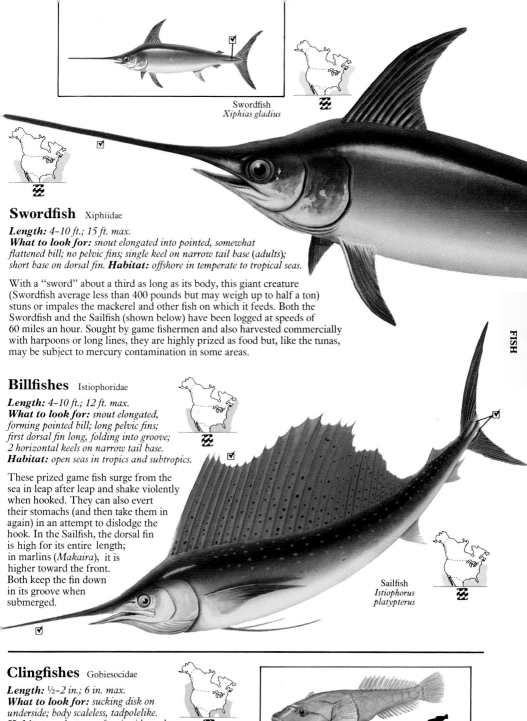

Swordfish
Xiphias gladius

Swordfish   Xiphiidae

Length: *4–10 ft.; 15 ft. max.*
What to look for: *snout elongated into pointed, somewhat flattened bill; no pelvic fins; single keel on narrow tail base (adults); short base on dorsal fin.* **Habitat:** *offshore in temperate to tropical seas.*

With a "sword" about a third as long as its body, this giant creature (Swordfish average less than 400 pounds but may weigh up to half a ton) stuns or impales the mackerel and other fish on which it feeds. Both the Swordfish and the Sailfish (shown below) have been logged at speeds of 60 miles an hour. Sought by game fishermen and also harvested commercially with harpoons or long lines, they are highly prized as food but, like the tunas, may be subject to mercury contamination in some areas.

Billfishes   Istiophoridae

Length: *4–10 ft.; 12 ft. max.*
What to look for: *snout elongated, forming pointed bill; long pelvic fins; first dorsal fin long, folding into groove; 2 horizontal keels on narrow tail base.* **Habitat:** *open seas in tropics and subtropics.*

These prized game fish surge from the sea in leap after leap and shake violently when hooked. They can also evert their stomachs (and then take them in again) in an attempt to dislodge the hook. In the Sailfish, the dorsal fin is high for its entire length; in marlins (*Makaira*), it is higher toward the front. Both keep the fin down in its groove when submerged.

Sailfish
Istiophorus platypterus

FISH

Clingfishes   Gobiesocidae

Length: *½–2 in.; 6 in. max.*
What to look for: *sucking disk on underside; body scaleless, tadpolelike.* **Habitat:** *on bottom; often in tide pools and on rocky shores.*

With pelvic fins modified into suction disks, giving them a tight hold on rocks, shells, and other hard objects, the peculiar little clingfishes have no close relatives anywhere in the world. The most common Atlantic species is the Skilletfish (*Gobiesox strumosus*), which reaches a length of about 4 inches.

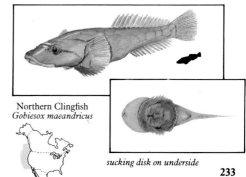

Northern Clingfish
Gobiesox maeandricus

sucking disk on underside

California Halibut
Paralichthys californicus

Starry Flounder
Platichthys stellatus

Lefteye Flounders
Bothidae

Length: *4–36 in.; 60 in. max.*
What to look for: *very flat body; both eyes on left side; lower jaw usually prominent.* **Habitat:** *bottoms of all seas; 2 species enter freshwater.*

The flatfishes—that is, the members of the two floun-der (fluke) families plus the tonguefishes and the soles—represent the ultimate degree of compression as well as an extraordinary adjustment to a bottom-dwelling way of life. Young flatfishes swim upright, like other fish. As they grow, they begin to lie on their sides. Slowly the eye on the lower side migrates up-ward. The underside loses its color; sometimes the mouth twists upward. In the lefteye flounders, which include the Summer, Gulf, and Southern flounders (*Paralichthys dentatus, albigutta,* and *lethostigma*), the right eye migrates and the left side is up.

Righteye Flounders
Pleuronectidae

Length: *1–5 ft.; 6 ft. max.*
What to look for: *very flat body; both eyes on right side; lower jaw usually prominent.* **Habitat:** *bottoms of temperate seas; 1 species enters freshwater.*

To tell whether a particular flatfish is right-eyed, hold it with the pigmented side toward you; if the fish is now facing right, it is a right-eyed fish. Righteye flounders include the various kinds of turbot (*Pleuronichthys*), halibut (*Hippoglossus*), the Dover Sole (*Microstomus pacificus*), and the Winter Floun-der (*Pseudopleuronectes americanus*); members of the sole family are also right-eyed. Curiously, certain species, including the Starry Flounder, have a high percentage of "mavericks"—that is, many individu-als belonging to a typically right-eyed species may become left-eyed, or vice versa.

Boxfishes Ostraciidae

Length: *6–12 in.; 19 in. max.*
What to look for: *bony "shell"; no pelvic or spiny dorsal fins.* **Habitat:** *warm coastal seas.*

Encased in its coat of armor, a boxfish, or trunkfish, cannot wiggle its body like other fish; it swims by fluttering its small fins and tail. Boxfishes feed mainly on small animals sucked into their mouths, and some-times they will squirt jets of water onto sand or mud to flush out prey. Dried, their "boxes" are commonly sold as novelties.

Scrawled Cowfish
Lactophrys quadricornis

Triggerfishes
and Filefishes Balistidae

Length: *4–24 in.; 39 in. max.*
What to look for: *strong spine or spines in first dorsal fin; body flattened from side to side; pelvic spine (but no fin) on belly; small mouth; 2 rows of protruding teeth in upper jaw.* **Habitat:** *warm seas.*

When the strong spines on the dorsal fin of a trigger-fish or filefish snap upright, they protect the fish in one of two ways: by preventing a predator from pull-ing it out from between rocks or coral, or by making the fish difficult to swallow. In triggerfishes, the sec-ond, shorter spine locks the first one into position.

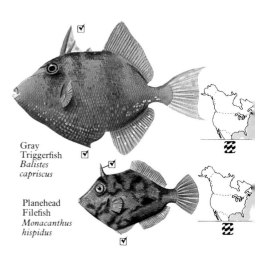

Gray
Triggerfish
Balistes capriscus

Planehead
Filefish
Monacanthus hispidus

FISH

Porcupinefishes
Diodontidae

Length: *6–12 in.; 36 in. max.*
What to look for: *sharp spines covering body; no pelvic fins; jaw beaklike, with fused teeth; inflates when agitated.*
Habitat: *warm coastal seas.*

Most North American species in this group are known as burrfishes, and their spines are in a fixed upright position. But in the Porcupinefish, the spines ordinarily lie close against the body, standing out stiffly only when the fish inflates. All members of the family are solitary and active both day and night. Their fused teeth, forming one big tooth in the upper jaw and another in the lower, are used to crush the shells of mollusks and crustaceans.

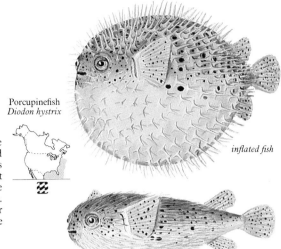

Porcupinefish
Diodon hystrix

inflated fish

Puffers
Tetraodontidae

Length: *2–18 in.; 24 in. max.*
What to look for: *body scaleless, sometimes with prickles; dorsal and anal fins small, spineless, far back; jaw beaklike, with 4 fused teeth; no pelvic fins; inflates when agitated.*
Habitat: *nearly all temperate and tropical seas.*

Gulping in air, a puffer, or blowfish, inflates its body and floats upside down. It may become twice the normal size—a definite discouragement to most predators. To turn right side up again, it deflates. Puffers also puff up by taking in water. Many species are so poisonous that eating them is not advised, though in some countries they are ranked as delicacies.

inflated fish

Northern Puffer
Sphoeroides maculatus

Molas
Molidae

not in scale with other species

Length: *4–8 ft.; 11 ft. max.*
What to look for: *large size; no pelvic fins; large, erect dorsal and anal fins; looks chopped in half.*
Habitat: *near surface offshore; in warm seas.*

Seen only in the open sea and not at all common, the Ocean Sunfish is included in this book because of the excitement generated when one of these giants—they weigh up to 600 pounds—is discovered. Ocean Sunfish generally lie on their side near the surface, as if sunning, but can move slowly by slapping their dorsal and anal fins in alternation. To feed, they siphon in other fishes, squid, jellyfishes, and other creatures. Young Ocean Sunfish have numerous spiny projections and drift long distances in ocean currents.

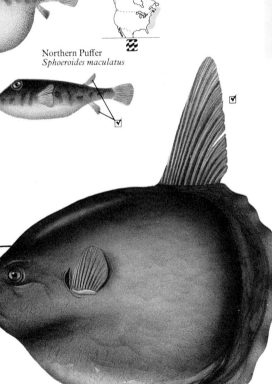

Ocean Sunfish
Mola mola

Invertebrates

*Flickering fireflies, burrowing clams, armored crabs,
and flowerlike sea anemones—the invertebrates are
a motley crowd indeed. Whether small and lively
or large and ponderous, they are difficult to ignore.*

A rather solemn and technical word, "invertebrates" is used here not to signify a change in the popular nature of this book but because no other expression works as well. Little creatures, one might call them (most are under a few inches long), except that the giant squid can top 40 feet. Nor can they all be considered primitive; some have brains, and some an elaborate social structure.

Zoologists have divided the animal kingdom into two groups—vertebrates and invertebrates—according to the location of the animals' hard parts. A vertebrate (mammal, bird, reptile, amphibian, or fish) has its skeleton inside its body; a lobster, beetle, or other invertebrate generally has its skeleton on the outside, if it has one at all. Invertebrates have no single positive feature in common; that is, there is no

---

Mollusks

Seaside vacationers never seem to stop searching for shells. Fascinated by a scallop's fluted beauty, the smooth roundness of a moon snail, an abalone's pearly iridescence, we transport our treasures far and wide, memories of the ocean lingering in those natural souvenirs.

Although seashells are the most commonly found mollusks (even if many people don't think of them as mollusks), a mollusk is not necessarily either shelled or connected with the sea. The word *mollusk* comes from the Latin for "soft" and refers to the living animal's inner parts (the edible portion of a clam, for instance). Though most species live in or near the ocean, some occur in freshwater or on land; and though most species have a shell or pair of shells, some, like octopuses and slugs, have none at all.

Univalves

Snails form by far the largest group of mollusks, once you have accepted the scientists' designation of whelks, periwinkles, and limpets as snails. What defines a snail is its single shell, or valve, usually spiral in form but occasionally cap-shaped (as in a limpet). Slugs are snails that have "lost" their shells. Most snails have a discernible head with a pair of tentacles, a pair of eyes, and a special toothed "tongue" that helps them in scraping off algae or tearing or drilling into prey.

Often active at night, snails creep about on their flat solelike foot, which in some species has a hard plate, called the operculum, attached toward the end. When the snail withdraws into its shell, the operculum acts as a trapdoor and seals the opening. So as you search the beach for shells, keep your eye out for any loose opercula. They are small, flat, hard objects, usually oval or roundish and some shade of brown or white. Different types of snails often have opercula that look very different, and this book shows some of the many forms they take.

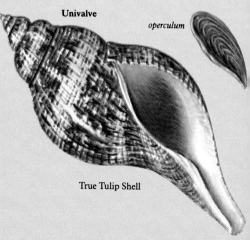

Univalve

operculum

True Tulip Shell

The habitat symbols used in the last part of this section are: 🏜 *desert* 🌱 *grassland/meadow/brush*

ructure that all invertebrates have and all of
e vertebrates don't have.

Ours is a vertebrate-centered world. Human
ings are vertebrates; the animals dearest to
are vertebrates; the biggest and most con-
icuous creatures are vertebrates. Though
any books about animals completely ignore
vertebrates, they are just too important and
o widespread to be left out here. They are ex-
aordinarily common (the group includes
me 95 percent of all known animal species),
ey can be found just about anywhere (though
u may have to get down on your hands and
ees), and they have enormous impact on
an and the natural world (where would we
—and where would flowers be—without in-
ct pollinators?).

Primary in importance, in nature and in this
ook, are the mollusk and insect divisions of
e invertebrate world. The section on mol-

lusks, which begins with the introduction below, covers seashells, octopuses and squid,
and various species that live in freshwater or on
land. The insect coverage begins with the introduction on page 263, then moves from
butterflies and moths through beetles and bees
to dragonflies and mayflies. (Many other insects are also included.) Following the insects
are their close relatives (spiders, scorpions,
and centipedes) and the water invertebrates—
aquatic insects, crabs and other crustaceans,
and such assorted marine creatures as jellyfish,
starfish, and coral.

Because the invertebrates form such a large,
diverse group, the coverage of them in this
book is by necessity less comprehensive than it
is for the other animals. Although you are sure
to find some creatures that aren't illustrated
here, chances are that some of their close relatives are indeed pictured in this book.

---

ivalves

lams, mussels, and other bivalves have no
eed of an operculum; their two shells gener-
lly close tightly around the animal's soft body.
ivalves feed by filtering out small organisms
om water taken in through the siphon (popu-
rly known as the "neck," as in the neck of a
lam). When a clam detects footsteps or other
ibrations, it retracts its siphon and shuts its
alves. Sometimes it hurriedly digs deeper, us-
g its extended muscular foot.

Living bivalves are often more difficult to
bserve than freely moving snails. Clams may

lie deeply buried in the bottom; oysters stay cemented to submerged rocks or other hard objects. Although both bivalves and univalves
are more familiar as shells (or items to eat) than
as living creatures, they are fascinating animals
indeed. Some lay peculiar "collars" of eggs;
some change from males to females as they
grow; some drill holes in their prey and suck
out the meat. We urge you to read about their
lives—their feeding habits, their breeding
habits, their weapons and defenses—in the
section that follows.

How to Use This Section

Snails and other univalves, which generally
have a single spiraling shell, are shown on
pages 238 through 250 and again on page 262
(page 262 shows land species, and 250 freshwater ones). Clams and other bivalves are
shown on pages 251 through 260 (the first page
covers freshwater bivalves). On page 261 are
representatives of three smaller groups: the
chitons, whose shell is divided into eight overlapping plates; the aptly named tusk, or tooth,
shells; and the cephalopods, the group that includes the octopuses and squids.

In this section, as in the others, the habitats
described in the identification capsules are
those of the living animals. Seashells, of
course, can be found far from the homes of the
living mollusks, especially after storms.

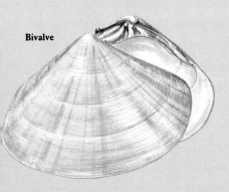

Bivalve

Pismo Clam

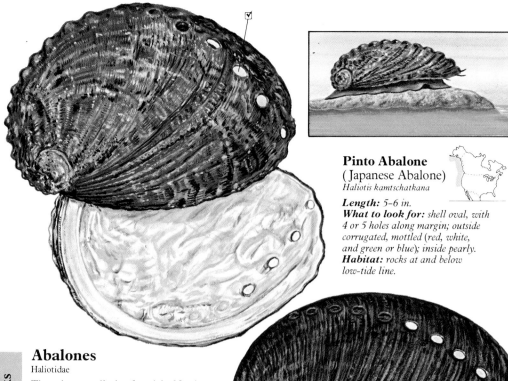

Pinto Abalone
(Japanese Abalone)
Haliotis kamtschatkana

Length: 5-6 in.
What to look for: *shell oval, with 4 or 5 holes along margin; outside corrugated, mottled (red, white, and green or blue); inside pearly.*
Habitat: *rocks at and below low-tide line.*

Abalones
Haliotidae

These large mollusks, found in North America only along the Pacific coast, grow from tiny, free-swimming larvae called veligers. After a week or so of swimming about, the larva settles on a rock or other hard object and develops into an adult. A mature abalone remains in the same vicinity all its life, creeping across neighboring rocks as it feeds on algae and microscopic organisms. Along the edge of the shell are open holes through which it expels wastes and water used in breathing. The iridescent shell of the abalone has long been used for jewelry and inlaid work, and the large muscular foot with which the animal clings to rocks is a culinary delicacy. Most abalone sold as food is the Red Abalone (*Haliotis rufescens*), a species obtained by divers.

Black Abalone
Haliotis cracherodii

Length: 6-7 in.
What to look for: *shell nearly circular, with about 8 holes along margin; outside smooth, black or green-black; inside pearly.* **Habitat:** *rocks at and below low-tide line.*

Keyhole Limpets Fissurellidae

A keyhole limpet usually has a hole near the top of the shell, where water taken in at the rim of the shell and circulated over the gills is expelled. Many keyhole limpets, as well as the true limpets (which have no hole), hollow out a slight depression in their home rock. The depression fits the animal's contours and prevents evaporation when the tide is out. Both groups feed by scraping algae off rocks with the band of small teeth, called a radula, found in the mouth of most types of snails.

Rough Keyhole Limpet
Diodora aspera

Length: 1½-2 in.
What to look for: *hole oval, surrounded by callus and radiating ridges; off-white or striped.*
Habitat: *rocks at and below low-tide line.*

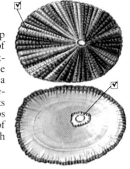

inside view

Top Shells Trochidae

Most snails can retreat inside the shell and close the entrance with the operculum, a hard object attached to the foot of the living animal and often found detached on shore. The operculum helps distinguish top shells from turban shells. That of a typical top shell is round, thin, whorled, and made of a horny material; the turban shell's is thick, oval, and chalklike.

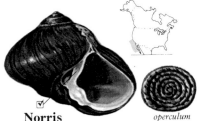

Western Ribbed Top Shell
Calliostoma ligatum

Length: *1 in.*
What to look for: *shell conical, dark brown, with encircling raised ribs; pearly opening.* **Habitat:** *stones and rubble on shore.*

Black Tegula
Tegula funebralis

Length: *1–1½ in.*
What to look for: *shell thick, smooth, with circular opening; outside black or blackish; base pale; inside pearly.* **Habitat:** *shore rocks.*

Norris Top Shell
Norrisia norrisi

Length: *2–2¼ in.*
What to look for: *shell squat, heavy, glossy, chestnut-brown; last whorl constitutes most of shell; greenish slit in lip.* **Habitat:** *kelp beds.*

operculum

True Limpets Acmaeidae

A limpet is a seashore snail whose shell is uncoiled, rather flat (but with a peak), and often ribbed. Like the keyhole limpets, true limpets occur in great diversity along the Pacific coast. There the most common species is the mottled Fingered Limper (*Collisella digitalis*), named for its fingerlike peak.

Atlantic Plate Limpet
Lottia testudinalis

Length: *1–1½ in.*
What to look for: *apex near center; outside speckled brown and cream; inside blue to white, with brown center.* **Habitat:** *rocks along shore.*

Wavy Turban
Astraea undosa

Length: *4–5 in.*
What to look for: *shell triangular, wider than tall; outside corrugated, brown, with white-edged whorls; operculum thick, ridged.* **Habitat:** *rocks and algae along shore.*

operculum

Turban Shells Turbinidae

Many turban shells have wavy-edged whorls, giving them a starlike appearance when viewed from the top. Typically found in tropical seas, turbans generally range only to Florida on the Atlantic coast. On the Pacific coast, the Red Turban (*Astraea gibberosa*) extends north to British Columbia.

exposed areas   *protected areas*   *inside view*

inside view

Volcano Limpet
Fissurella volcano

Length: *1 in.*
What to look for: *shell volcano-shaped, gray, brown, or maroon, with dark rays.* **Habitat:** *algae-covered rocks.*

Great Keyhole Limpet
Megathura crenulata

Length: *3–4 in.*
What to look for: *shell somewhat flat; hole large, edged with white; outside tan; inside white, smooth.* **Habitat:** *rocks along shore.*

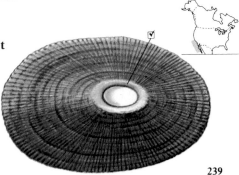

Nerites Neritidae

Found mainly in the tropics and subtropics, nerites occur in North America only in Florida and along the Gulf coast. Some species cling to surf-swept rocks; others prefer quiet, brackish waters; still others (but none on this continent) live in freshwater lakes, rivers, and streams. Most species have toothlike projections around their openings and only a few whorls on their conical shells.

Bleeding Tooth
Nerita peloronta

Length: *1–1½ in.*
What to look for: *lip with red stain and white teeth; oval shape.*
Habitat: *wave-washed rocks.*

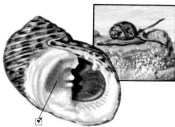

Olive Nerite
Neritina reclivata

Length: *½ in.*
What to look for: *shell smooth, oval, green or olive, with pattern of fine dark lines.* **Habitat:** *mud flats in brackish water; occasionally in rivers.*

operculum

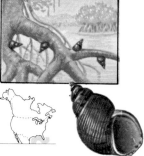

Angulate Periwinkle
Littorina angulifera

Length: *1–1¼ in.*
What to look for: *shell tall, tapered, thin, with fine spiral lines; color variable.*
Habitat: *brackish water; mangrove roots and pilings, usually well above waterline.*

Periwinkles Littorinidae

Rocks, piers, seawalls, mangrove roots, and splash pools are all home to these rounded snails. But different species occupy different regions of the shore and vary in their dependence on the sea. The Northern Rough Periwinkle, for example, is almost a landlubber: it lives high on shore, breathes with lunglike gills, and gives birth to live, shelled young. Most other periwinkles hatch from eggs laid in water or on algae. The Common European Periwinkle, a circumpolar species, lays a floating egg capsule, which may have helped it spread southward to Maryland.

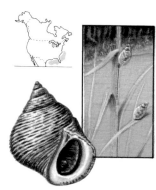

Marsh Periwinkle
Littorina irrorata

Length: *1 in.*
What to look for: *shell pointed, with pronounced spiral lines broken into dashes.*
Habitat: *marsh grasses and reeds in estuaries.*

Common European Periwinkle
Littorina littorea

Length: *1–1¼ in.*
What to look for: *shell oval, thick, smooth, with fine spiral lines; dull brown to gray.*
Habitat: *rocks and algae along shore.*

Checkered Periwinkle
Littorina scutulata

Length: *½ in.*
What to look for: *pointed spire; thin lip; surface smooth, red-brown, with small bluish-white spots.* **Habitat:** *high on rocks along shore.*

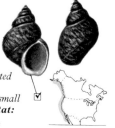

Northern Rough Periwinkle
Littorina saxatilis

Length: *½ in.*
What to look for: *shell oval, with flange on lip; spiral cords; color variable.*
Habitat: *high on rocks in splash zone.*

Northern Yellow Periwinkle
Littorina obtusata

Length: *½ in.*
What to look for: *low spire; shell smooth, globular, often bright yellow or orange; young may be banded.*
Habitat: *rockweed.*

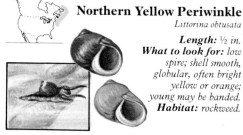

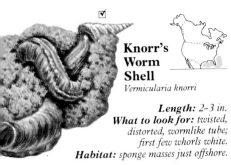

Knorr's Worm Shell
Vermicularia knorri

Length: *2-3 in.*
What to look for: *twisted, distorted, wormlike tube; first few whorls white.*
Habitat: *sponge masses just offshore.*

Florida Cerith
Cerithium atratum

Length: *1¼-1½ in.*
What to look for: *shell long, tapered, rough, tan, with opening oblique to main axis; operculum oval.* **Habitat:** *shallow water along sandy or muddy shores.*

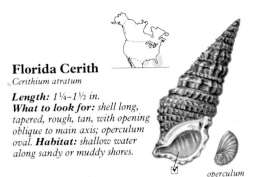

operculum

Turret Shells Turritellidae

Early in their lives, all of the mollusks in this group have tall, tightly twisted shells. In some species the shell retains its turretlike shape as it grows. But in others the twisting gradually becomes looser, producing a wormlike shell with a turret at only one end. Turret shells live on rocks, in sand and mud, or in sponges and coral.

Ceriths Cerithiidae

The name cerith comes from the Greek word for "little horn," and these shells do indeed somewhat resemble the horns used by shepherds or goatherds. Most species live in shallow waters of warm seas, generally in grassy areas. No true ceriths occur on the Pacific coast north of Mexico, although some small relatives may wash ashore.

False Cerith
(Black Horn Shell)
Batillaria minima

Length: *¾ in.*
What to look for: *shell small, pointed, rough; color variable (white to black), often with bands; operculum like tiny bull's-eye.* **Habitat:** *mud flats.*

operculum

California Horn Shell
Cerithidea californica

Length: *1-1½ in.*
What to look for: *shell very tapered, pointed, blackish, with raised riblets on each whorl.* **Habitat:** *mud flats along shore and in estuaries.*

False Ceriths and Horn Shells Potamididae

Similar to the true ceriths in size and shape, the false ceriths and horn shells live in brackish water, mostly on mud flats in estuaries and mangrove swamps. As a rule, the shells in this group are dull colored, although often distinctly banded. The operculum, or "trapdoor," sealing the opening distinguishes these mollusks from the true ceriths. Among false ceriths the operculum is circular, with a central nucleus and many whorls. The operculum of a true cerith is oval, with a nucleus near the edge and only a few whorls.

Wentletraps Epitoniidae

Wentletraps are carnivorous snails that often live in association with sea anemones, and have been known to eat them at times. When disturbed, wentletraps exude a bright pink-purple dye. Their name has nothing to do with trapping prey, but comes instead from the Dutch words for "turning" and "stairs." (They are also known as staircase shells.) The Brown-banded Wentletrap is one of the few wentletraps whose shell is not pure white. Its ribbons of egg capsules are typical of the group.

egg capsules

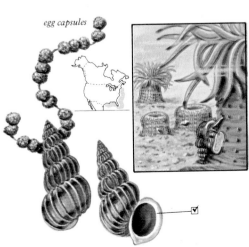

Brown-banded Wentletrap
Epitonium rupicola

Length: *¼-1 in.*
What to look for: *shell delicate, with fine raised riblets on whorls; spiral bands of brown on tan shell; lip rounded, white.*
Habitat: *shallow water; sandy shores.*

Slipper Shells Crepidulidae

All the mollusks in this group have an inside platform that helps support the animal's soft parts. Slipper shells usually attach themselves to other shells (living or dead), rocks, or submerged plants. Many species, including the Atlantic Slipper Shell, live one atop another in piles of up to a dozen or more individuals. The larger shells at the bottom of the pile are the females. The males, smaller and on top, change to females as they grow.

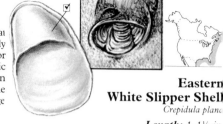

Eastern White Slipper Shell
Crepidula plana

Length: *1-1½ in.*
What to look for: *raised platform at one end; white inside and out; shape variable.*
Habitat: *shallow water; inside larger shells*

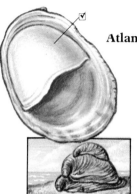

Atlantic Slipper Shell
Crepidula fornicata

Length: *1¼-2 in.*
What to look for: *white platform in brown interior; shape variable.* **Habitat:** *attached to objects in shallow water.*

Spiny Cup-and-Saucer
Crucibulum spinosum

Length: *1-1½ in.*
What to look for: *white cup attached to shiny brown interior; outside rough, with irregular spines; circular outline.* **Habitat:** *on rocks and shells in bays.*

Cowries Cypraeidae

Unfortunately for North American collectors, these highly prized shells—smooth, glossy, and toothed around the openings—are mainly tropical, with only 5 of the 200 or so species found in local waters. Cowries generally hide under rocks or coral by day and creep forth at night to feed. When in motion, the animal extends its mantle, or fleshy layer, over its back, concealing part or all of its shell.

"zebra" (immature)

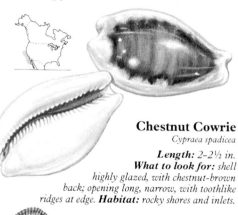

Chestnut Cowrie
Cypraea spadicea

Length: *2-2½ in.*
What to look for: *shell highly glazed, with chestnut-brown back; opening long, narrow, with toothlike ridges at edge.* **Habitat:** *rocky shores and inlets.*

Measled Cowrie
Cypraea zebra

Length: *3-4½ in.*
What to look for: *shell highly glazed, with spotted brown back (light brown bands on immature); opening long, narrow, with toothlike ridges.* **Habitat:** *bays, inlets.*

Coffee-bean Trivia
Trivia pediculus

Length: *½ in.*
What to look for: *shell bean-shaped, covered with tiny ribs and looking wrinkled; pink or pinkish brown, with brown blotches.* **Habitat:** *tidal areas.*

Trivias Eratoidae

Trivias resemble miniature, wrinkled cowries and may be white, pink, or brown, sometimes with darker spots. These little mollusks generally live with and feed on sea squirts, stationary animals that squirt out water when touched.

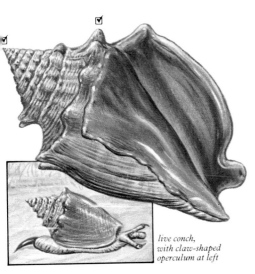

Florida Fighting Conch
Strombus alatus

Length: *3-4 in.*
What to look for: *shell conical, with pointed spire; regularly spaced knobs around spire; area around opening highly glazed; color variable.*
Habitat: *shallow water, especially sand flats.*

Conchs Strombidae

Far from being aggressive, the conchs are peaceful plant eaters. The sobriquet "fighting conch" stems instead from the animal's active nature, particularly its ability to somersault away from danger. A conch moves rapidly with the aid of its claw-shaped operculum. The large Pink, or Queen, Conch (*Strombus gigas*) occurs off southern Florida, but most shells in gift shops are imports from the Caribbean.

live conch, with claw-shaped operculum at left

Moon Snails Naticidae

A moon snail plows the sand rapidly, leaving a wide, meandering trail. When it finds a buried clam, it envelops the clam with its large powerful foot, drills a hole near the hinge, and sucks out the meat. Moon snails deposit thousands of eggs within a collar of sand and mucus. Strong when wet, the collar becomes extremely fragile when dry and collapses when the eggs hatch. People who find living moon snails can distinguish the various types by their opercula—chalky in the naticas, horny in the polinices, and nonexistent in the baby's ears.

Common Baby's Ear
Sinum perspectivum

Length: *1½-2 in.*
What to look for:
shell white, very flat, with large ear-shaped opening; fine ribs.
Habitat: *sand in shallow water.*

Common Northern Moon Snail
Lunatia heros

Length: *3-4½ in.*
What to look for: *shell globular, brown or gray, with deep depression near large opening.*
Habitat: *sandy shallows.*

sand collar

Atlantic Moon Snail
Polinices duplicatus

Length: *2½-3 in.*
What to look for: *shell thick, oval, either gray, blue-gray, or tan; large brown callus near opening; operculum pliable, brown.* **Habitat:** *shallows; sand.*

operculum

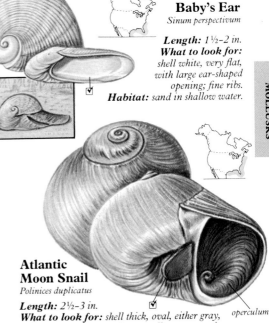

Colorful Atlantic Natica
Natica canrena

Length: *1½-2 in.*
What to look for: *shell globular, with large opening; pale brown with dark markings; operculum chalky, grooved.*
Habitat: *sandy shallows.*

operculum

243

female laying eggs

Scotch Bonnet
Phalium granulatum
Length: *3–3½ in.*
What to look for: *shell oval, with fine spiral grooves; lip flared, with thick, toothed edge; white with brown markings.* **Habitat:** *offshore.*

Bonnet and Helmet Shells
Cassidae

Bonnet and helmet shells typically have a thick, shiny inner lip. The largest North American species, the Emperor Helmet (*Cassis madagascariensis*), can measure 12 inches or more, while the Atlantic Wood-louse (*Morum oniscus*) is only about an inch long. No species occur on the Pacific coast. These mollusks live on sandy bottoms or coral reefs, feeding on sea urchins and sand dollars. The females of certain species, such as the Scotch Bonnet, lay their egg capsules in towering columns.

Rock Shells   Muricidae

Rock shells are active carnivores that prey on barnacles, mussels, and other shellfish. In fact, the Oyster Drill is a serious threat to oyster beds. A rock shell obtains its food by using its small teeth and a shell-softening secretion to bore a hole into the victim's shell. Most species also produce a yellowish substance that apparently anesthetizes the prey. Upon exposure to light and air, this secretion turns red and then purple, furnishing a dye that has been widely used since ancient times. The shells in this group vary greatly. Some are smooth, others ribbed or spiny. Even members of the same species may differ according to locale: rock shells living in quiet waters tend to be frillier and spinier than their cousins in rougher seas.

Oyster Drill
Urosalpinx cinerea
Length: *1–1½ in.*
What to look for: *shell thick, spindle-shaped, with rounded ribs and thin, wide lip; gray or dirty white, with brown opening.* **Habitat:** *oyster beds.*

Apple Murex
Phyllonotus pomum
Length: *3–5 in.*.
What to look for: *shell rough, heavy; inner lip extends over shell and has dark blotch at upper end; color variable (brown, pink, or yellow).* **Habitat:** *sandy shallows.*

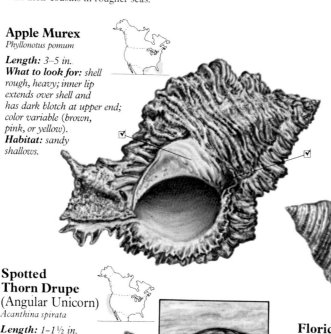

Spotted Thorn Drupe
(Angular Unicorn)
Acanthina spirata
Length: *1–1½ in.*
What to look for: *lip with large tooth (thorn) near bottom; interrupted spiral lines.* **Habitat:** *rocks, breakwaters.*

Florida Rock Shell
Thais haemastoma floridana
Length: *2–3 in.*
What to look for: *flesh-colored mouth; largest whorl with shoulder and spiral row of knobs; grayish, blotched.* **Habitat:** *just offshore, especially near oyster beds.*

MOLLUSKS

Fig Shells
Ficidae

There are only about a dozen species of fig shells, most in the tropical Pacific and Indian oceans. Although the lightweight shells of the Paper Fig sometimes wash ashore on beaches in the southeastern United States, the mollusks in this group usually live in sand below the tide line and are seldom seen alive. Fig shells hunt sea urchins and other marine animals. They move by gliding along the bottom on their large foot, extending the fleshy mantle so that it almost covers the shell.

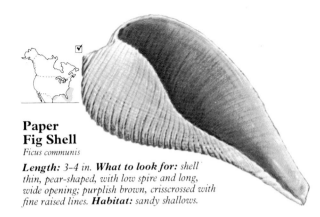

Paper Fig Shell
Ficus communis

Length: *3-4 in.* **What to look for:** *shell thin, pear-shaped, with low spire and long, wide opening; purplish brown, crisscrossed with fine raised lines.* **Habitat:** *sandy shallows.*

Emarginate Dogwinkle
Nucella emarginata

Length: *1-1½ in.*
What to look for: *low spire; wide opening (more than half shell length); dark purplish brown; sometimes with alternating large and small spiral cords.* **Habitat:** *rocky shores; near mussel beds.*

Atlantic Dogwinkle
Nucella lapillus

Length: *1-2 in.*
What to look for: *shell oval; opening thickened within lip; color variable, usually white or off-white.* **Habitat:** *rocks near shore.*

Poulson's Dwarf Triton
Ocenebra poulsoni

Length: *1-2 in.*
What to look for: *shell spindle-shaped; evenly spaced ribs; gray with fine brown lines; white opening.* **Habitat:** *rocks, pilings.*

Frilled Dogwinkle
Nucella lamellosa

Length: *1½-5 in.*
What to look for: *shell somewhat spindle-shaped, but variable in shape, color, and sculpturing.* **Habitat:** *rocky shores (smoother shells), bays, inlets.*

Thick-lipped Drill
Eupleura caudata

Length: *½-1 in.*
What to look for: *shell tapered; outer lip toothed; usually dirty white with darker opening.* **Habitat:** *oyster beds, rocky shores.*

MOLLUSKS

Dove Shells   Columbellidae

Of the several hundred species in this family (several dozen occur in North America), few measure more than half an inch long. Whether smooth or ribbed, plain or spotted, dove shells are easily recognized by their weakly toothed and somewhat spotted outer lip. Usually they live below the tide line, clinging to rocks or algae.

Greedy Dove Shell
Anachis avara

Length: *½-1 in.*
What to look for: *shell spindle-shaped, yellow to tan, with raised ribs; opening long, narrow; teeth on inner edge of outer lip.* **Habitat:** *eelgrass beds, pilings, breakwaters.*

Whelks Buccinidae

Whelks prey on other animals or scavenge dead material. When feeding on clams or other bivalves, a whelk uses its strong foot to force the valves just far enough apart for the outer lip of its shell to enter. Eventually a hole big enough to permit the whelk to feed is chipped away. Although the North American species in this group tend to have a northerly distribution, the inch-long Dire Whelk (*Searlesia dira*) is common in tide pools south to central California, and certain species occur only in Florida and the West Indies. The foot of the larger whelks is sometimes used as food.

Common Northern Whelk
Buccinum undatum

Length: *2–4 in.*
What to look for: *shell rather globular, white to buff, with high spire; ribs slanted, wavy, evenly spaced; opening white, nearly half length of shell.* **Habitat:** *offshore; often trapped in lobster pots or trawling nets.*

egg mass

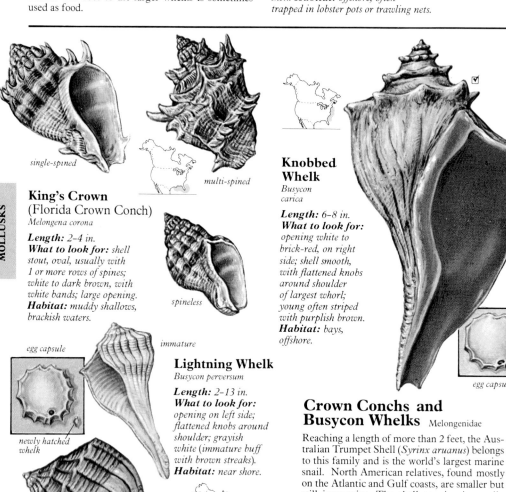

single-spined

multi-spined

King's Crown
(Florida Crown Conch)
Melongena corona

Length: *2–4 in.*
What to look for: *shell stout, oval, usually with 1 or more rows of spines; white to dark brown, with white bands; large opening.* **Habitat:** *muddy shallows, brackish waters.*

spineless

immature

egg capsule

newly hatched whelk

Lightning Whelk
Busycon perversum

Length: *2–13 in.*
What to look for: *opening on left side; flattened knobs around shoulder; grayish white (immature buff with brown streaks).* **Habitat:** *near shore.*

Knobbed Whelk
Busycon carica

Length: *6–8 in.*
What to look for: *opening white to brick-red, on right side; shell smooth, with flattened knobs around shoulder of largest whorl; young often striped with purplish brown.* **Habitat:** *bays, offshore.*

egg capsule

Crown Conchs and Busycon Whelks Melongenidae

Reaching a length of more than 2 feet, the Australian Trumpet Shell (*Syrinx aruanus*) belongs to this family and is the world's largest marine snail. North American relatives, found mostly on the Atlantic and Gulf coasts, are smaller but still impressive. The shell opening is usually large, the siphonal canal long, and the shoulder well defined. The Lightning, or Left-handed, Whelk is, as its name implies, often left-handed: when the shell is held with its spire up and its opening facing the observer, the opening lies to the left. (Most other snails are right-handed.) Mollusks in this group often prey on clams. Long strings of sturdy egg capsules, sometimes with young snails inside, are frequently found by beachcombers.

MOLLUSKS

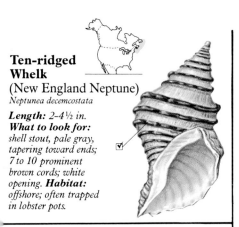

Ten-ridged Whelk
(New England Neptune)
Neptunea decemcostata

Length: 2–4½ in.
What to look for: shell stout, pale gray, tapering toward ends; 7 to 10 prominent brown cords; white opening. **Habitat:** offshore; often trapped in lobster pots.

egg capsule

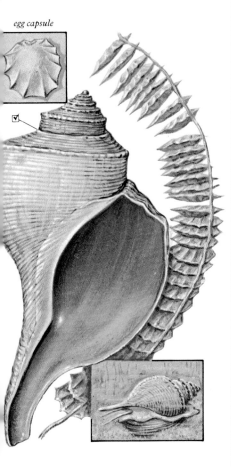

Channeled Whelk
Busycon canaliculata

Length: 2–8 in.
What to look for: shell pear-shaped, gray, with deep channel around spire; opening purplish brown, on right side; fuzzy tan coating. **Habitat:** muddy shallows, bays.

operculum

Common Eastern Nassa
Nassarius vibex

Length: ½–⅔ in.
What to look for: shell small, chunky, gray-brown, with sharply pointed spire; nubby surface; inner lip thick, glossy; outer lip with teeth. **Habitat:** sand or mud in shallow water.

Giant Western Nassa
Nassarius fossatus

Length: 1½–2 in.
What to look for: shell fat, sharply pointed, buff to red-brown; spiral cords and small beadlike bumps on surface; outer lip flared, cords showing within. **Habitat:** near shore; bays, lagoons.

operculum

New England Nassa
Nassarius trivittatus

Length: ¾ in.
What to look for: shell small, sharply pointed, light buff; surface neatly beaded; each whorl with squared shoulder; inner lip white. **Habitat:** offshore, on sand.

Eastern Mud Nassa
Ilynassa obsoleta

Length: ¾–1 in.
What to look for: shell stout, black or purplish brown, usually worn and battered-looking; blunt spire; inner lip shiny, folded back. **Habitat:** tidal mud flats, especially in bays.

Mud Snails Nassariidae

These small conical snails generally stay buried in the mud, with only the siphon extending up into the water. When they find a dead fish or other creature (they sense its presence through chemicals in the water), they may emerge in great numbers to feed. The typical mud snail seen up close looks rather bizarre, with a very long snout and a foot described as having a "ridiculously small operculum, two horns in front, and two tails behind." Some mud snails produce vase-shaped capsules of eggs; in other species the eggs are retained within the female's body until they hatch.

operculum

egg capsules

Florida Horse Conch
Pleuroploca gigantea

Length: *1–24 in.*
What to look for: *shell huge, with bumps, spiral cords, and pointed spire; long canal beyond opening; dirty white to brown (young are orange), with orange or brown opening; brown coating.* **Habitat:** *sand or weed beds; shallows or offshore.*

True Tulip Shell
Fasciolaria tulipa

Length: *5–8 in.*
What to look for: *shell spindle-shaped, fairly smooth, usually buff with bands of brown, orange, or red; opening paler within.* **Habitat:** *offshore, on sand flats, bays.*

Tulips and Horse Conchs
Fasciolariidae

Generally strong and spindle-shaped, the shells in this group taper to a high spire at one end and a long canal at the other. The canal accommodates the animal's siphon, the spoutlike organ that takes in water for breathing. All these mollusks are predators on other mollusks. To feed on a clam, a tulip shell wedges its outer lip between the two valves. If the prey is a large snail, the tulip grabs its operculum to prevent the victim from retreating into its shell.

operculum

attachment side of operculum

Lettered Olive
Oliva sayana

Length: *2½–3 in.*
What to look for: *shell smooth, thick, glazed, cylindrical; usually beige with brown markings; opening long, narrow.* **Habitat:** *sandy shallows.*

Olive, Dwarf Olive, and Rice Shells Olividae

All of these mollusks are carnivores that burrow into the sand, occasionally emerging to seize prey. (They are believed to smother victims with the foot.) Small species sometimes serve as food for their larger relatives. When disturbed, a small individual may flap its wide-spreading mantle and swim, though its movements are erratic and of limited success.

Purple Dwarf Olive
Olivella biplicata

Length: *1–1¼ in.*
What to look for: *shell stout, glossy, usually blue-gray with purple at base and spire.* **Habitat:** *sandy shallows.*

Atlantic Auger
Terebra dislocata

Length: *1½-2 in.*
What to look for: *shell thin, tapering, gray or buff; whorls ribbed, bordered by bumpy spiral cord; center column twisted at base.*
Habitat: *sandy shallows.*

Auger Shells   Terebridae

These slender shells can be distinguished from worm and horn shells by the elongated opening and central column, which is somewhat twisted at the base. Only a few species live in North American waters, some in shallows and others in fairly deep water. Certain species possess a poison gland, which is probably used to paralyze small prey.

California Bubble
Bulla gouldiana

Length: *1½-2½ in.*
What to look for:
shell thin, globular, smooth; opening flared, with white inner lip; gray- to purple-brown, with dark spots.
Habitat: *bays and lagoons at low tide.*

Bubble Shells
Bullidae

Buried in grassy flats by day, bubble shells sometimes emerge by the thousands at night. Even seen singly, the living animal has a startling appearance. Far too large for its shell, the fleshy creature envelops the shell rather than vice versa. The shell itself has an unusual feature. The spire is sunken, hiding the earliest whorls and creating a depression where most other shells have the spire.

Sea Hares   Aplysiidae

The ancient Greeks and Romans believed that these soft-bodied creatures caused premature births and were deadly to touch. Even today they may create alarm, especially when a stranded one exudes its red-purple dye. Sea hares commonly browse for algae on intertidal grass flats but can also propel themselves slowly and gracefully on the surface. Some species have a rudimentary internal shell.

Common Marsh Snail
Melampus bidentatus

Length: *½ in.*
What to look for: *shell small, smooth, often badly worn; tan or brown, often with encircling dark bands.*
Habitat: *salt marshes.*

Marsh Snails   Ellobiidae

Although more closely related to land snails than to the typical seashell, these air-breathing snails cannot reproduce without the sea: their eggs develop into free-swimming larvae. The eggs of certain species hatch only when covered with water during the high spring tides. Representatives of the group live on the Atlantic, Pacific, and Gulf coasts.

Striped False Limpet
Siphonaria pectinata

outside

Length: *1 in.*
What to look for:
nearly circular shape, with bulge in margin and peak in center; gray or brown, with fine raised lines; glossy inside.
Habitat: *rocks near high-tide line.*

inside

False Limpets
Siphonariidae

These air-breathing mollusks look remarkably like the true limpets except for the bulge on one side of the shell and the corresponding groove underneath. Typically, false limpets live on wave-washed rocks, and the eggs of many species hatch as free-swimming larvae. They do not extend north of Mexico on the Pacific coast or north of Georgia on the Atlantic.

Willcox's Sea Hare
Aplysia willcoxi

Length: *5-9 in.*
What to look for: *fleshy animal with no visible shell; flaplike lobe on each side of body; 2 large tentacles; dark brown, blackish, or mottled brown and green.*
Habitat: *shallow water, especially in eelgrasses.*

snail with eggs

Florida Apple Snail
Pomacea paludosa

Length: *2–2½ in.*
What to look for: *shell globular, smooth, with large opening (closed by operculum in living animal); olive-brown, with encircling brown bands.*
Habitat: *still or slow freshwater.*

Apple Snails Ampullariidae

Although sometimes found in stagnant water, apple snails are more common in lakes and rivers where the water is clear and high in oxygen. These large, herbivorous snails usually breathe with their gills, but they can also obtain oxygen from the air through a lunglike structure in the mantle. After mating, a female apple snail lays masses of ¼-inch eggs on plant stems and low branches near water. The young snails drop into the water after hatching.

Eastern Mystery Snail
Viviparus georgianus

Length: *1½–1¾ in.*
What to look for: *shell glossy, with round opening and rather high spire; rounded whorls; olive-green, usually with brown bands.*
Habitat: *ponds, lakes, rivers.*

Mystery Snails Viviparidae

These rather large snails are unusual in that they give birth to living, shelled young. (Most other freshwater snails lay eggs.) The largest species in North America, the Chinese Mystery Snail (*Viviparus malleatus*), was brought to the United States in the 19th century for use as an aquarium cleaner (it eats algae) and has become well established in the Northeast.

Stagnant Pond Snail
Lymnaea stagnalis

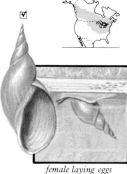

Length: *1¾–2 in.*
What to look for: *shell cornucopialike, thin, with sharp spire; lip large, flaring; tan or pink.*
Habitat: *lakes, ponds.*

female laying eggs

Pond Snails Lymnaeidae

Despite their watery surroundings, these thin-shelled snails generally breathe oxygen from the air. How frequently they come to the surface depends to a great extent on the temperature and oxygen content of the water. Although the usual breathing interval ranges from 15 seconds to a few hours, the Stagnant Pond Snail has been known to survive for several months without surfacing.

Three-whorled Ram's Horn
Helisoma trivolvis

Length: *½–1¼ in.*
What to look for: *shell flat, with whorls coiled in same plane; flared opening; thin lip; buff, brown, or chestnut.*
Habitat: *lakes, ponds, slow streams.*

Ram's Horn Snails Planorbidae

These air-breathing snails, sometimes called wheel snails, are distributed worldwide in ponds or slow-moving streams with abundant plant life. They are hermaphrodites: each has both male and female reproductive organs. In spring they can sometimes be seen in a chain, with individuals mating simultaneously as male and female.

Common Tadpole Snail
Physa heterostropha

Length: *½–1 in.*
What to look for: *shell with large, flared opening on left side; pointed spire; color variable (yellow to brown).*
Habitat: *ponds, lakes, streams.*

Tadpole Snails Physidae

Because their shells open on the left side, tadpole snails, or pouch snails, are easy to recognize. They live in rivers, streams, ponds, and even stagnant pools, feeding primarily on plants and obtaining oxygen from the air through a saclike cavity in the mantle. They rise to the surface fairly often to breathe, moving on a mucous thread spun from the foot.

MOLLUSKS

Looking at bivalves. The shell of a clam or other bivalve often washes ashore with its two valves intact, held together by a ligament at the hinge. A thin coating, called the periostracum, may cover the outside, but in beached shells this has frequently worn away. Concentric growth lines similar to tree rings are often apparent on the surface. Rings laid down during periods of food scarcity tend to be narrower and thicker than rings produced at other times.

On the inside of the shell, in the hinge area, are one or more toothlike projections, called hinge teeth, that fit into corresponding hollows in the other valve. Below the hinge some shells have a triangular depression that held cartilage when the mollusk was alive. One or two flat oval scars (the number varies according to species) occur on the inside of the shell. An adductor muscle, which closes the two valves of a living mollusk, was attached to the shell in the region of the scar. A thin line connecting the scars shows where the mantle was attached. If the line has a pronounced inward curve, the animal had a siphon that could be withdrawn fully into the shell. If the two valves gape when closed, the siphon or the foot extended outside the shell in the living animal.

Asiatic Clam
Corbicula manilensis

Length: *1–2½ in.*
What to look for:
shell triangular,
pointed in hinge area;
concentric ridges;
outside brown, with
blackish coating;
inside purple or
blue. **Habitat:** *rivers.*

Marsh and Little Freshwater Clams Corbiculidae

Introduced accidentally to western states in the late 1930's, the Asiatic Clam has multiplied and become a major nuisance, clogging irrigation ditches and pipes. Eggs of this clam receive an unusual degree of care: instead of being shed into the water, they are brooded inside the parent's gills until they hatch. The Carolina Marsh Clam (*Polymesoda caroliniana*) and the Florida Marsh Clam (*Polymesoda maritima*) are native species that occur in brackish water.

Pearl Mussel
Margaritifera margaritifera

Length: *3–6 in.*
What to look for: *shell*
elongate, elliptical,
flat; outside smooth,
with black coating;
inside pearly white,
pink, or purplish.
Habitat: *streams,*
brooks; usually in
fast water.

Pearl Mussels Margaritiferidae

Both pearl and river mussels need fish to survive. Instead of leading an independent life, the newly hatched mussels attach themselves to the gills, fins, or skin of fish and feed for several weeks on their tissues. (This does not directly harm the fish, although it may cause infection.) Then the mussels drop off, sink to the bottom, and develop into adults. A few species use hosts other than fish.

Filter Mussel
Elliptio complanata

Length: *3–4 in.*
What to look for:
shell elliptical; outside rough,
sometimes with rays; brown
coating (may be buff to black);
ridge from top to edge; inside pearly.
Habitat: *ponds, lakes, rivers, streams.*

River Mussels Unionidae

River mussels vary in shape according to their surroundings—that is, whether they are growing on a hard or soft bottom and in still or running water. A favorite food of Muskrats, they have been and in some areas are still eaten by man. They are also harvested for their pearly shells, as are pearl mussels. The shells are cut into mother-of-pearl buttons or into the tiny pellets used in making cultured pearls.

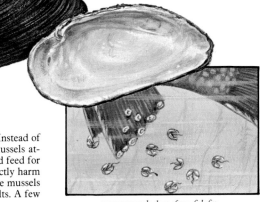

young mussels drop from fish fin

251

Ark Shells Arcidae

The ark shell's ark is a sturdy, rather rectangular shell whose hinge is long and straight and bears many small teeth. Such teeth, which occur on most bivalves, help keep the two valves locked together. Some living arks attach themselves in mussel fashion to rocks; others burrow into the sand. Several species, most notably the Blood Ark, have red blood—a rarity among mollusks, whose blood is usually colorless or slightly blue. Ark shells are abundant in warm, shallow seas; the few North American species are found mainly on the Atlantic and Gulf coasts.

Blood Ark
Anadara ovalis

Length: *2–2½ in.*
What to look for:
*shell thick, oval,
with broad ribs;
dirty white, with brown
coating.* **Habitat:**
in sand near shore.

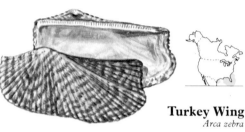

Turkey Wing
Arca zebra

Length: *3–3½ in.*
What to look for: *shell roughly rectangular,
winglike, with fine ribs; white to buff,
with irregular reddish-brown stripes.*
Habitat: *on rocks near shore.*

Ponderous Ark
Noetia ponderosa

Length: *2–3 in.*
What to look for:
*shell deeply concave,
very thick, with sturdy
ribs split by thin
incised line; dirty white,
with black coating.*
Habitat: *in sandy
mud near shore.*

Pen Shells Pinnidae

Pen shells produce a large clump of hairy threads called a byssus, with which they attach themselves to buried stones or pieces of shell. The wide part of the shell extends a half-inch or more above the mud surface, occasionally presenting a hazard to barefoot waders along the southeastern coast. For centuries the byssus of the Mediterranean Pen Shell (*Pinna nobilis*) was woven into a fine fabric and made into stockings, gloves, caps, and collars.

inside   outside

Saw-toothed Pen Shell
Atrina serrata

Length: *6–12 in.*
What to look for: *shell large,
thin, brittle; one end pointed;
ribs with small raised scales;
greenish olive to tan.*
Habitat: *in sandy mud near shore.*

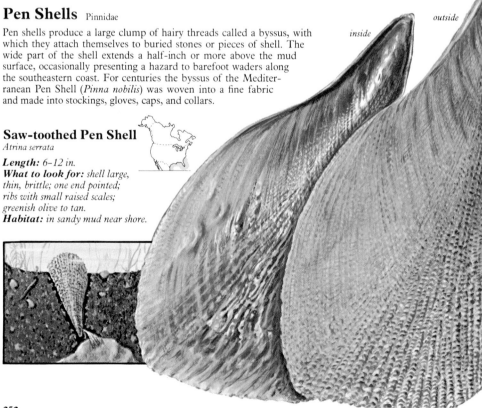

Mussels Mytilidae

The thin-shelled mussels are generally sedentary animals, attached to rocks or other hard objects by strong threads. When laying down these threads, collectively called the byssus, the mussel presses its foot against the rock. A gland at the base of the foot secretes a sticky substance, which hardens into the threads upon contact with seawater.

Like most other bivalves, mussels feed by filtering particles from seawater. Mussels in turn are eaten by such animals as starfish and predatory snails (and also man). But mussel eaters are not the only additional residents of mussel colonies. Since algae thrive on the shells and associated rocks, limpets and other algae eaters browse in their midst. Because organic debris is trapped by the byssus (and also in the spaces between the mussels), small crabs and other debris-feeders frequent mussel beds.

Northern Horse Mussel
Modiolus modiolus

Length: *3–6 in.*
What to look for: *shell thick, deeply concave; outside white to mauve, with shaggy blackish coating and faint concentric ridges; inside bluish white.* **Habitat:** *on rocky bottoms in deep water.*

Common Blue Mussel
Mytilus edulis

Length: *2–3 in.*
What to look for: *shell long, rather pear-shaped; outside blue-black, with shiny coating and irregular concentric ridges; inside bluish, with dark edge and 4 fine teeth at narrow end.* **Habitat:** *shallow water; in colonies attached to rocks, piers, pilings, jetties.*

starfish feeding on mussels

Atlantic Ribbed Mussel
Geukensia demissa

Length: *3–4 in.*
What to look for: *shell long, rather pear-shaped; outside brown, often rough, with fine ribs running lengthwise; inside pearly white.* **Habitat:** *in mud in bays and salt marshes.*

Hooked Mussel
Ischadium recurvum

Length: *1–2½ in.*
What to look for: *shell flatter than in other mussels; narrow end curved; outside gray, finely ribbed, with black between ribs; inside purplish or red-brown, glossy.* **Habitat:** *shallow water; on rocks, pilings, breakwaters.*

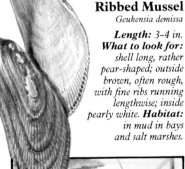

MOLLUSKS

A warning note on collecting mollusks for food. Before gathering clams, mussels, or other mollusks for eating, check with local health and conservation departments. Some states require licenses for certain species and have strict laws regulating the time and place of harvest as well as the number harvested. Obviously, mollusks from polluted waters are undesirable as human food. Outbreaks of red tide occasionally bring a halt to the collecting of edible mollusks. The minute organisms that discolor the water produce a poison that accumulates in clams and other filter-feeders and also in their predators. The poison is not destroyed by cooking and can cause serious illness. Edible mollusks should be taken and kept alive. Properly refrigerated, most will survive for several days. Discard any that do not.

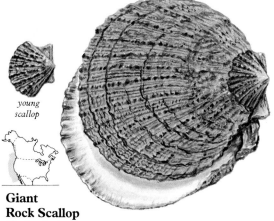

young scallop

Giant Rock Scallop
Hinnites giganteus

Length: *3-6 in.* **What to look for:** *shell large, massive, variable in shape; outside rough, red-brown to brown; inside white, often with purplish blotch.* **Habitat:** *attached to rocks, pilings below low-tide line; young are free-swimming.*

Kelp-weed Scallop
Leptopecten latiauratus

Length: *¾-1 in.*
What to look for: *shell thin, flattened, with 12-16 slightly raised ribs; orange-brown, with white zigzag markings.* **Habitat:** *kelp and eelgrasses near shore.*

swimming scallop

Pacific Calico Scallop
Argopecten circularis

Length: *2½-3 in.*
What to look for: *shell circular, deeply concave, with 19-22 surface ribs; white to yellow-orange, with brown markings.*
Habitat: *mud bottoms in bays, lagoons.*

Atlantic Bay Scallop
Argopecten irradians

Length: *2-3 in.*
What to look for: *shell circular, slightly flattened, with about 18 raised ribs; usually gray (lower valve often lighter than upper).* **Habitat:** *bays with muddy bottoms, usually in eelgrasses.*

Atlantic Deep-sea Scallop
Placopecten magellanicus

Length: *5-8 in.*
What to look for: *shell flattened, pinkish, almost circular; ribbed with fine lines.* **Habitat:** *deep water.*

Scallops Pectinidae

Although some scallops are permanently attached to underwater objects, others jet-propel themselves in zigzags through the water, snapping their valves open and shut in a motion controlled by the adductor muscle. (Scallops have a single adductor, which is the part eaten by man; most other bivalves have two.) Protruding between the valves, at the edge of the mantle, are tentacles responsive to touch. Dozens of tiny eyes shine near the base of the tentacles. Alerted by these sense organs to an enemy's presence, a scallop can often outmaneuver starfish and other potential predators.

ingle Shells Anomiidae

These little mollusks, sometimes mistaken for young oysters, pass most of their lives firmly attached to underwater objects by the byssus threads, which pass through a hole in the lower valve. The threads hold the animal so firmly that the lower valve flattens and takes on the shape of the object to which it is anchored. The stronger upper valve, said to make jingling sounds on pebbly beaches, is collected to make jewelry and wind chimes.

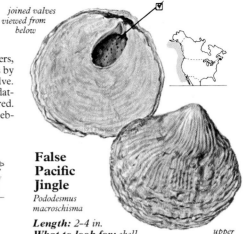

joined valves viewed from below

Atlantic Jingle
Anomia simplex

Length: *1–2 in.*
What to look for: *shell thin, translucent; lower valve flat, usually off-white, with large hole; upper valve convex, orange or yellow (occasionally gray or black).* **Habitat:** *bays.*

False Pacific Jingle
Pododesmus macroschisma

Length: *2–4 in.*
What to look for: *shell similar to Atlantic Jingle's but larger, thicker; outside rough, usually white; inside green, pearly.*
Habitat: *rocks and pilings near shore.*

upper valve

Oysters Ostreidae

Renowned as a delectable taste treat, oysters have been imported to areas far from their natural homes by oyster-farming enterprises. (Living oysters are usually transported as spat, the young free-swimming stage.) The Eastern Oyster is raised on the West Coast, and the Giant Pacific Oyster is actually a native of Japan. Other native North American species include the Native Pacific Oyster *(Ostrea lurida)*, a small mollusk with a green interior, and the Coon Oyster *(Dendrostrea frons)*, frequently found attached to mangrove roots. None of the edible oysters produces commercially valuable pearls.

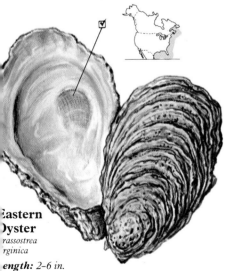

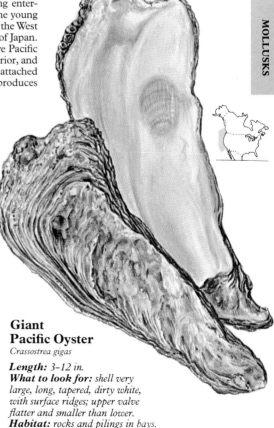

Eastern Oyster
Crassostrea virginica

Length: *2–6 in.*
What to look for: *lower valve usually deep, upper one flattened; outside dirty white or gray; inside white, with purple scar near center.* **Habitat:** *bays, estuaries, offshore areas; attached to hard objects.*

Giant Pacific Oyster
Crassostrea gigas

Length: *3–12 in.*
What to look for: *shell very large, long, tapered, dirty white, with surface ridges; upper valve flatter and smaller than lower.*
Habitat: *rocks and pilings in bays.*

255

Jackknife Clams · Solenidae

The elongated jackknife clams, which usually live in tidal areas or just below the low-tide line, evade would-be captors by swiftly burrowing into the sand. When vibrations warn of danger, the clam's foot protrudes from the lower opening between the valves, swells with blood, and contracts, pulling the clam deeper. It repeats this action many times in rapid succession. Considered by some to be the most delicious clams, jackknife clams include several species that are taken commerically.

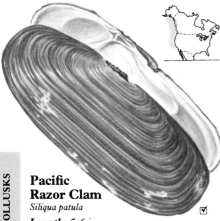

Pacific Razor Clam
Siliqua patula ☑

Length: 5–6 in.
What to look for: *shell long, thin, oval, with rounded ends; white with glossy brown coating; inside with reinforcing rib.*
Habitat: *sand flats in tidal areas.*

Atlantic Jackknife Clam
Ensis directus

Length: 6–10 in.
What to look for: *shell long, narrow, slightly curved, tubelike, open at both ends; white with greenish-brown coating.* **Habitat:** *sand or mud in shallow bays.*

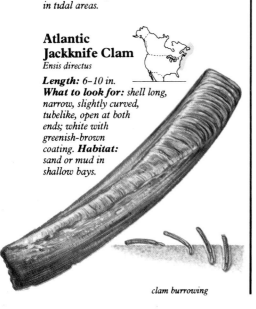

clam burrowing

Lucines · Lucinidae

These circular, usually fat shells take their name from Lucina, the Roman goddess of childbirth. Lucine shells may be smooth or concentrically ridged. Some species, such as the western Nuttall's Lucine (*Lucina nuttalli*), also have ribbed lines radiating from the hinge.

Cross-hatched Lucine
Divaricella quadrisulcata

surface detail

Length: ¾–1 in.
What to look for: *shell round, white, fat, with chevronlike grooves.*
Habitat: *deep water.*

Jewel Boxes · Chamidae

These frilly shells grow in colonies on rocks or other hard objects below the tide line in warm waters, and often wash ashore after a storm. The Florida Spiny Jewel Box (*Arcinella cornuta*) is white with delicate ribs and slender spines.

Clear Jewel Box
Chama arcana

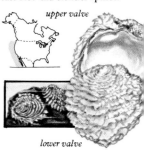
upper valve

Length: 1½–3 in.
What to look for: *lower valve deep, circular; upper valve flat, with leafy scales; white or tinged with pink.*
Habitat: *bays, offshore.*

lower valve

Macomas and Tellins · Tellinidae

These mollusks live buried in sand or mud and use their long siphons to sweep the water above them for organic debris. The tellins, often called sunrise shells, are the more colorful members of the group.

Baltic Macoma
Macoma balthica

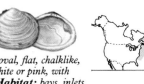

Length: ¾–1 in.
What to look for: *shell oval, flat, chalklike, often worn-looking; off-white or pink, with remnants of tan coating.* **Habitat:** *bays, inlets.*

Bent-nose Macoma
Macoma nasuta

Length: 2½–3½ in.
What to look for: *shell rounded, thin, smooth, with twist in one end; off-white with thin tan coating.*
Habitat: *muddy areas of quiet bays.* ☑

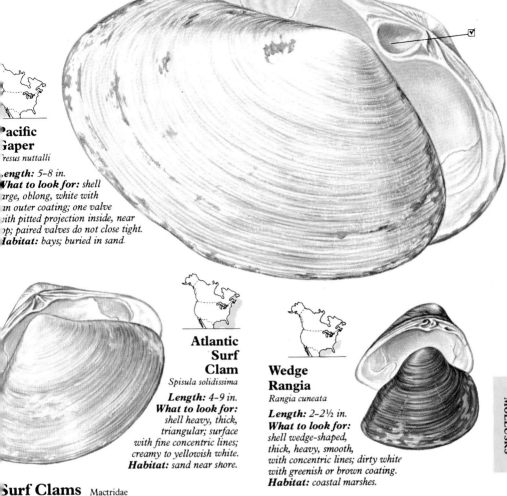

Pacific Gaper
Tresus nuttalli

Length: *5–8 in.*
What to look for: *shell large, oblong, white with an outer coating; one valve with pitted projection inside, near top; paired valves do not close tight.*
Habitat: *bays; buried in sand.*

Atlantic Surf Clam
Spisula solidissima

Length: *4–9 in.*
What to look for: *shell heavy, thick, triangular; surface with fine concentric lines; creamy to yellowish white.*
Habitat: *sand near shore.*

Wedge Rangia
Rangia cuneata

Length: *2–2½ in.*
What to look for: *shell wedge-shaped, thick, heavy, smooth, with concentric lines; dirty white with greenish or brown coating.*
Habitat: *coastal marshes.*

Surf Clams Mactridae

Often only partially embedded in sand, surf clams are easily dislodged and tumbled ashore by the waves. These shells tend to be triangular in shape, usually with one rounded end. The hinge contains a large spoon-shaped depression called a chondrophore, which, in the living animal, holds the elastic portion of the ligament. The shells vary in thickness. Rangia shells are so thick and strong that they have been used as roadbed fill, but the Channeled Duck Clam (*Raeta plicatella*) has a shell thin enough for a gull to peck a hole in. Atlantic Surf Clams are dredged annually by the millions; most are canned as minced clams.

Donax Clams
Donacidae

Most of these diminutive clams, also called butterfly clams, travel up and down the hard-packed sand of surf-washed beaches, sometimes leaping up out of the sand on an incoming wave and burrowing rapidly as the wave recedes. Sparkling with color, the Florida Coquina contrasts sharply with the somber-hued Pacific species—the Bean Clam (*Donax gouldi*) and the California Donax (*Donax californicus*), both with purple inside.

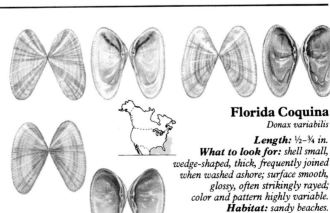

Florida Coquina
Donax variabilis

Length: *½–¾ in.*
What to look for: *shell small, wedge-shaped, thick, frequently joined when washed ashore; surface smooth, glossy, often strikingly rayed; color and pattern highly variable.*
Habitat: *sandy beaches.*

Venus Clams Veneridae

The clams bearing the name of the goddess of beauty and love are rather strong, heavy shells, usually with a pronounced beak. Perhaps the best known of the group is the Northern Quahog, the various sizes of which are known as Littlenecks and Cherrystones. Indians made hollow, cylindrical beads from quahog shells. Called wampum, the beads were strung together and used as money, with the greatest value given to the ones made from the dark purple inner edge. The larger Southern Quahog (*Mercenaria campechiensis*) looks like the northern species but rarely has a purple stain.

Cross-barred Venus
Chione cancellata

Length: 1-1¾ in.
What to look for: shell small, heavy, with latticework of concentric ridges on top of radiating ribs; outside gray to brown; inside purplish.
Habitat: shallow water near shore.

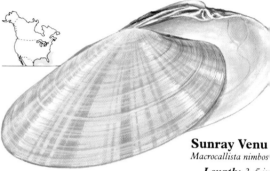

Pacific Littleneck
Protothaca staminea

Length: 1½-2 in.
What to look for: shell circular to oval, with radiating ribs on top of fine concentric lines; outside tan or whitish, sometimes with brown mottling; inside white to purple. **Habitat:** sandy bays.

Pismo Clam
Tivela stultorum

Length: 3-6 in.
What to look for: shell thick, heavy, triangular, smooth; outside buff, often with brown rays and varnishlike coating. **Habitat:** sand at low-tide line.

Calico Clam
(Checkerboard Clam)
Macrocallista maculata

Length: 2½-3 in.
What to look for: shell smooth, nearly circular; squarish brown markings in checkerboard pattern. **Habitat:** sand near shore.

Sunray Venu
Macrocallista nimbos

Length: 3-5 in
What to look for: shell elongated, oval, smooth outside buff, with brown rays and glossy coating inside white. **Habitat:** sandy mud near low-tide line

Disk Dosinia
Dosinia discu

Length: 2½-3 in
What to look for: shell circular, flat, with fine ridges; white with pale brown coating. **Habitat:** sand just offshore

Northern Quahog
(Hard-shelled Clam)
Mercenaria mercenaria

Length: 3-5 in.
What to look for: shell oval, heavy, thick, with fine lines; rounded area near top twisted off-center; outside dirty white to gray; inside white, with purple at edge. **Habitat:** bays and near shore.

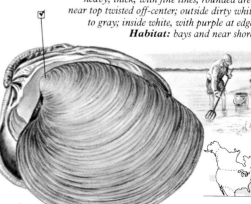

Cockles Cardiidae

Because the two valves look heart-shaped from the side, cockles are also known as heart clams. Their siphons are short, and they do not burrow deeply. They can, however, use their strong foot to hop several inches off the bottom and move about. Cockles are harvested and eaten in Europe, but not usually in North America; this leaves all the more for the diving ducks that use them as food. The Common Pacific Egg Cockle (*Laevicardium substriatum*) closely resembles Morton's Egg Cockle.

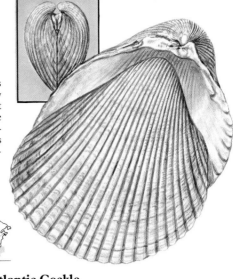

Morton's Egg Cockle
Laevicardium mortoni

Length: ½–1 in.
What to look for: *shell small, puffy, thin; outside smooth, glossy, cream-colored; inside egg-yolk yellow (fades with exposure).* **Habitat:** *bays, muddy shallows.*

Giant Atlantic Cockle
Dinocardium robustum

Length: 4–5 in. **What to look for:** *shell heavy, deeply concave, with about 35 broad ribs; outside light buff; inside pale mahogany-red; joined valves heart-shaped in side view.* **Habitat:** *sandy mud just offshore.*

Carditas Carditidae

Though all carditas are strongly ribbed, most are more circular in outline than the Broad-ribbed Cardita. Some species brood their eggs. The ¼-inch Kelsey's Milner Clam (*Milneria kelseyi*) of California even has a special exterior chamber on the shell where this takes place.

Broad-ribbed Cardita
Carditamera floridana

Length: 1–1½ in. **What to look for:** *shell elongate, thick, with about 15 strong ribs; outside white to gray; inside white.* **Habitat:** *sandy mud in shallow water.*

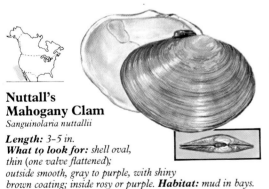

Nuttall's Mahogany Clam
Sanguinolaria nuttallii

Length: 3–5 in.
What to look for: *shell oval, thin (one valve flattened); outside smooth, gray to purple, with shiny brown coating; inside rosy or purple.* **Habitat:** *mud in bays.*

Stout Tagelus
Tagelus plebeius

Length: 2–3½ in.
What to look for: *shell oblong, rounded at ends; outside off-white with yellowish-brown coating; joined valves form tube open at both ends.*
Habitat: *sand in shallow water.*

Sanguin Clams Psammobiidae

Sanguin comes from the Latin word for blood. The rare Atlantic Sanguin (*Sanguinolaria sanguinolenta*), more evocatively known as the Blood-stained Sand Clam, is tinted red near the beak. Though glossy brown on the outside, Nuttall's Mahogany Clam sometimes has a rosy or purplish wash on the inside of the shell. Sanguin clams generally occur in tropical waters, and the eastern species range no farther north than Florida.

Razor Clams Solecurtidae

The rather drab razor clams are rectangular in shape and vary in size from the 3½-inch yellowish California Tagelus (*Tagelus californianus*) to the 1-inch-long Purplish Tagelus (*Tagelus divisus*), common on sandy mud flats of the Atlantic coast. Certain species that are known in the vernacular as razor clams belong to another family—the Solenidae, or jackknife clams.

259

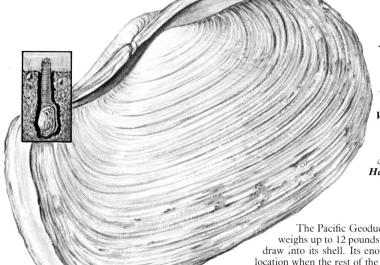

Pacific Geoduck
Panopea generosa

Length: *7–9 in.*
What to look for: *shell huge, dirty white; joined valves do not meet at ends; tough 2-ft.-long siphon on living clam looks like elephant trunk.*
Habitat: *mud flats, sandy bays.*

Geoduck Clams
Hiatellidae

The Pacific Geoduck (pronounced goo′ey-duck), weighs up to 12 pounds and cannot completely withdraw into its shell. Its enormous siphon gives away its location when the rest of the animal lies deep in the mud. The Atlantic Geoduck (*Panopea bitruncata*) is smaller and seldom seen, because it lives in deep water.

Soft-shelled Clams Myidae

Buried deep in mud or sand, soft-shelled clams, or steamers, extend their siphons up to the bottom of the bay to feed. When danger nears, the clam expels a squirt of water and retracts the siphon, leaving a hole that reveals its location.

Soft-shelled Clam *Mya arenaria*

Length: *4–5½ in.* **What to look for:** *shell large, oval, dull white with wrinkled surface and thin brown coating; one valve flatter, with spoon-shaped projection inside; joined valves do not meet at ends.* **Habitat:** *mud or sand in bays.*

Piddocks Pholadidae

A young piddock slowly bores its way into rock, wood, or other materials (the choice varies with the species), carving out a depression by etching and abrasion. The rough end of the shell is used for boring; the siphon extends from the smoother end. The mud-dwelling Angel Wing contracts violently when disturbed and often cracks its delicate shell. The smaller False Angel Wing (*Petricola pholadiformis*) has much the same range, living in bays and tidal marshes in clay, peat, or wood.

Scale-sided Piddock
Parapholas californica

Length: *2–4 in.*
What to look for: *shell arched, wedge-shaped, dirty white; diagonal line from top divides shell; bulbous section with fine raised scales and rasplike edge; other end elongated, with heavy brown coating.*
Habitat: *soft rock at low-tide line.*

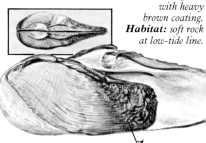

Angel Wing
Cyrtopleura costata

Length: *5–8 in.*
What to look for: *shell long, thin, arched, winglike; ribs beaded, evenly spaced; white with gray coating.*
Habitat: *bays, inlets; in mud and clay.*

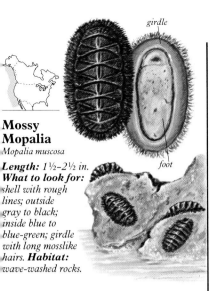

girdle

foot

Mossy Mopalia
Mopalia muscosa

Length: *1½–2½ in.*
What to look for: *shell with rough lines; outside gray to black; inside blue to blue-green; girdle with long mosslike hairs.* **Habitat:** *wave-washed rocks.*

Chitons Polyplacophora

Little changed from the shells of 400 million years ago, a chiton shell is actually eight overlapping valves, or plates, held together by a leathery girdle. Chitons occur along the Pacific, Atlantic, and Gulf coasts, although the greatest diversity is found on Pacific shores. During the day the primitive mollusk clings to rocks. At night it creeps about on the muscular foot, feeding on algae and microscopic life.

Tusk Shells Scaphopoda

The narrow end of a tusk shell projects up into the water when the mollusk burrows in sand or mud. Filaments called captacula extend from the other end into the sand, catching tiny particles of food and bringing them into the mouth. Tusk shells occur along most North American shores, though the mollusks usually live in deep water. Indians used the western species as currency.

Indian Money Tusk
Dentalium pretiosum

Length: *1½–2 in.*
What to look for: *slender, curved tube, open at both ends (tapering at one end); resembles tiny elephant tusk in shape and color.* **Habitat:** *sandy mud near shore.*

Octopuses and Squids Cephalopoda

North America has several kinds of octopus. The wide-ranging Pacific species occurs from Mexico to Alaska, the Common Atlantic Octopus (*Octopus vulgaris*) extends north to New England, and several other species live on southern shores. Squids have a similarly wide distribution. Both octopuses and squids belong to the group of mollusks called cephalopods, predatory creatures that lack an outer shell. (Cuttlefish and nautiluses are also cephalopods.) Their arms are their most notable feature. An octopus has 8 and a squid 10, including 2 longer tentacles. Equipped with suction disks, the arms hold fish and other prey. Both octopuses and squids can swim, although the octopus crawls more, using its suckers to hold on to rocks.

Atlantic Long-finned Squid
Loligo pealei

Length: *1–2 ft.*
What to look for: *body long, narrow; head with 2 large eyes and 10 arms; triangular fins at other end; color variable.* **Habitat:** *offshore; sometimes in large schools.*

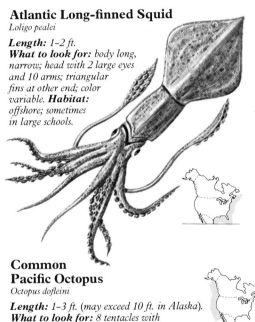

Common Pacific Octopus
Octopus dofleini

Length: *1–3 ft. (may exceed 10 ft. in Alaska).*
What to look for: *8 tentacles with suction disks; oval body; color variable (usually red- or purple-brown).*
Habitat: *rock crevices from shore to deep sea.*

swimming octopus

Banded Forest Snail
Monadenia fidelis

Length: 1–1 ¾ in. **What to look for:** *spire raised or flat; upper part tawny, ocher, or yellow; band around middle dark brown, visible inside; brown base; white lip and interior.* **Habitat:** *forests, woodlands.*

Tree Snails   Helminthoglyptidae

Although land snails generally require humid conditions, this group has some desert-dwelling species. During dry spells they seal the shell opening with mucus, which hardens and prevents evaporation. Land snails, unlike periwinkles and most other saltwater species, have no operculum.

Striped Forest Snail
Anguispira alternata

Length: ¾–1 ¼ in.
What to look for: *shell somewhat flat, with large depression in base; lip thin, flared; light tan, with neatly spaced chestnut blotches.* **Habitat:** *forests, woodlands, urban areas.*

Forest Snails   Endodontidae

Land snails can move several inches a minute (small ones are generally faster), but they cannot move at all without secreting slime as a lubricant. The Striped Forest Snail, one of the larger species in this group, deposits a trail of orange slime as it moves along.

Seven-whorled Land Snail
Polygyra septemvolva

Length: ¼–½ in.
What to look for: *shell flat, very small, with 6 to 10 coiled whorls; opening small, round; buffy brown (weathered shell is white).* **Habitat:** *forests to open areas.*

Litter Snails   Polygyridae

These tiny flattened snails, whose shells often have narrow toothed openings, feed on decaying leaves and other plant materials, as do most other land snails. Although land snails generally live only a year or two, some desert species in this group may survive for 15 years.

White-lipped Forest Snail
Triodopsis albolabris

Length: ¾–1 ¾ in.
What to look for: *shell rotund, with flattened spire; opening with white rolled-over lip; edge of lip covers center of whorls at base; pale tan or straw.* **Habitat:** *wooded and urban areas.*

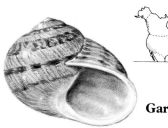

Speckled Garden Snail
Helix aspersa

Length: 1 ½–1 ¾ in.
What to look for: *shell globular, thin, with round opening; thin lip; creamy yellow, with brown bands.* **Habitat:** *farms, urban areas.*

Garden Snails   Helicidae

No garden snail is native to North America (most are European), but several introduced species now breed in the wild. Although an individual garden snail, like other land snails, is both male and female, snails usually mate before laying eggs. A hard, stimulatory "love dart" is shot into the partner before mating.

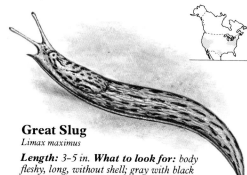

Great Slug
Limax maximus

Length: 3–5 in. **What to look for:** *body fleshy, long, without shell; gray with black spots.* **Habitat:** *urban and suburban areas.*

Slugs   Limacidae

Slugs have a small remnant of a shell embedded in their bodies. They generally stay in moist places by day and emerge at night to feed, a pattern typical of most land snails. The imported Great Slug, once believed to have magical and medicinal powers, is considered a pest in gardens.

MOLLUSKS

Insects

Chirping crickets, spectacularly patterned butterflies, and round little ladybird beetles need no kind words to enhance their appeal. But the world of insects has attractions beyond these familiar favorites. The very number and diversity—more than a hundred thousand species in North America alone—are astounding. Though often small in size, insects are no easy prey, their defenses ranging from near-perfect camouflage (try to spot a walkingstick, a treehopper, a caddisfly larva *before* it moves) to the stink of the stink bugs and certain caterpillars' stinging nettlelike hairs. Nor are insects simple creatures. Consider the dragonfly's astonishing eyes, each a glittering mosaic of thousands of tiny facets; watch the activities of ants or bees, "lowly" animals cooperating in ways so incredibly complex. Above all, keep in mind the fascinating relationship between insects and flowers, the role that insects play in the pollination and perpetuation of flowering plants.

Remarkable too is the way insects develop. Instead of just growing bigger, some undergo a metamorphosis even more dramatic than a tadpole's turning into a frog. Such insects as beetles and butterflies go through what scientists call complete metamorphosis, with four very different life stages: egg, larva (caterpillar, grub, or "worm"), pupa (the "resting" stage, sometimes covered by a cocoon), and adult. Insects with incomplete metamorphosis, such as grasshoppers and dragonflies, lack the pupal stage; their young, called nymphs, frequently resemble the adults except that they are smaller and wingless. Usually, insects stop growing when they reach adulthood, and some, such as the giant silk moths, never feed as adults.

Because there are so many different kinds of insects, identifying them, especially the smaller ones, is often a matter of determining the group to which they belong instead of pinpointing the exact species. So in this section of *North American Wildlife*, the italicized identification capsules are at the group rather than the species level. Each group is illustrated by one or more species, shown approximately life-size. Enlarged views of very small insects are also provided.

Tips on Identifying Insects

Our word "insect" comes from the creatures' Latin name, insectum, *meaning "notched" and referring to the indented or divided body. An insect body has three major divisions: the head, the thorax, and the abdomen. Another characteristic is the six jointed legs. (Spiders, which are also included in this section, have eight.) Most insects have two pairs of wings as adults and a single pair of antennae.*

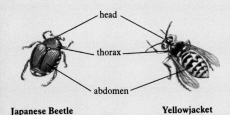

head

thorax

abdomen

Japanese Beetle   **Yellowjacket**

Head. Antennae and mouthparts are the important features to look at here. The antennae may be long (as in long-horned grasshoppers) or short (short-horned grasshoppers); they sometimes show such special details as feathering (in tussock moths, on one side only) or protuberances at the tip (stag beetles). The mouthparts vary with the type of food. Weevils generally have hole-boring snouts; nectar-drinking butterflies have long sucking tubes, kept coiled when not in use; female mosquitoes have stilettolike mouthparts, used to pierce skin and then draw blood.

Thorax. The middle division, the thorax, carries the legs and wings. Note leg length (grasshoppers have very long hind legs) and texture (the front legs of a mantid are armed with spines). Although the typical insect has two pairs of wings, flies and certain others have one and most walkingsticks none. If wings are present, their texture, markings, and vein pattern may be important in identification, especially among butterflies and moths, whose wings are covered with scales.

Abdomen. Any external reproductive structures are located on the abdomen. Female ichneumons (wasps) and sawflies have a long egg-laying appendage at the rear; female wasps and bees have them too, but beware: they also act as stingers.

Monarch
*Danaus
plexippus*

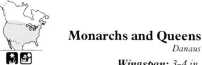

Monarchs and Queens
Danaus

Wingspan: *3–4 in.*
What to look for: *brown to orange-
brown butterfly; wings with white-spotted
black borders and dark veins (lighter on Queen);
male with dark scent patch along fifth vein of hindwing.*
Habitat: *fields, grasslands, gardens; groves (winter).*

Milkweed Butterflies Danaidae

As the name suggests, these butterflies are often associated with milkweeds. The larvae (caterpillars) feed on the leaves, ingesting substances that make them toxic to birds and other predators; the adults, which retain the poisons, sip the flower nectar, inadvertently pollinating the flowers as they do so. The Monarch winters in Mexico, California, and the Caribbean; the smaller, darker Queen (*Danaus gilippus*) is a southeastern stay-at-home. One member of the brush-footed butterfly family, the Viceroy, looks like the Monarch, and predators avoid it, too.

larva

pupa

Buckeyes
Junonia

Wingspan: *2–2½ in.*
What to look for:
brown butterfly;
6 large eyespots
(1 on each forewing,
2 on each hindwing).
Habitat: open fields,
desert washes, thin
brush; beaches
(migration).

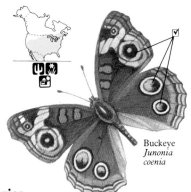

Buckeye
*Junonia
coenia*

Pearl
Crescent
*Phyciodes
tharos*

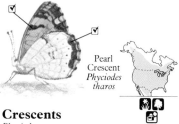

Crescents
Phyciodes

Wingspan: *1¼–1¾ in.*
What to look for: small orange-brown
butterfly; sharply contrasting black
markings on top of wings; underside orange
to creamy, with black markings on
forewing and brown ones on hindwing.
Habitat: meadows, grasslands,
open woodlands.

Greater Fritillaries
Speyeria

Wingspan: *2–3¾ in.*
What to look for: orange- to tan-brown butterfly;
silvery spots on underside of hindwing. **Habitat:** open
woodlands; occasionally in grasslands, scrub, or deep forests.

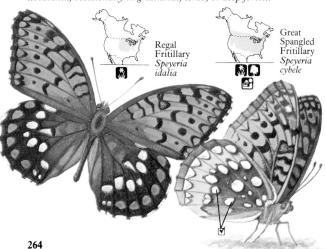

Regal
Fritillary
*Speyeria
idalia*

Great
Spangled
Fritillary
*Speyeria
cybele*

Chalcedon
Checkerspot
*Euphydryas
chalcedona*

Checkerspots
Euphydryas

Wingspan: *1½–3 in.*
What to look for: black to dark red-
brown butterfly; checkerboard pattern
(black or red and pale yellow on top
of wings, red and white outlined in
black below). **Habitat:** marshy
meadows; grasslands; chaparral;
dry, scrubby woodlands.

INSECTS

264

Question Mark
Polygonia interrogationis

Mourning Cloak
Nymphalis antiopa

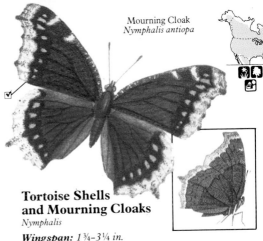

Angle Wings
Polygonia

Wingspan: *1½–2¾ in.*
What to look for: *ragged edges on wings; red-orange with black spots above, mottled brown, gray, and black (resembling bark) below; silvery C-shaped mark on underside of hindwing.*
Habitat: *woodlands; occasionally in fields.*

Brush-footed Butterflies

Nymphalidae

Like other insects, butterflies have three pairs of legs, but the front pair is generally reduced in size. In this particular group (which includes the species at left as well as those on this page), the front legs are too short to be useful for walking and are kept folded against the chest. Brush-footed butterflies have hairy front legs—hence their name.

Before they can fly, butterflies must warm their bodies to 81° F or more. In so doing they hold their wings in characteristic positions. Most brush-footed butterflies open their wings at a 45-degree angle when basking and fold them above the body when they feed. Milkweed butterflies also bask in this position; swallowtails spread their wings wider. Other basking positions are with wings closed and undersides perpendicular to the sun's rays (sulphurs bask this way) and with wings held slightly open so that the sun's rays strike the body directly (blues, coppers, and hairstreaks).

Ladies and Red Admirals
Vanessa

Wingspan: *1¾–2¼ in.*
What to look for: *bright color; tip of forewing black with white spots and smooth (not ragged) edge.*
Habitat: *open woods, meadows, deserts.*

Tortoise Shells and Mourning Cloaks
Nymphalis

Wingspan: *1¾–3¼ in.*
What to look for: *underside of wings tan to dark gray (resembling bark), without silvery mark; inner edge of forewing straight; top of wings variously marked.* **Habitat:** *forests, woodlands; occasionally in open fields.*

Viceroys and Admirals
Limenitis

Wingspan: *2½–3½ in.*
What to look for: *large blue- to brown-black butterfly; most species with wide white bands (some with red spots); Viceroy resembles Monarch but has prominent black line across veins of hindwing.*
Habitat: *forests, brushy areas, meadows, desert washes; near willows.*

INSECTS

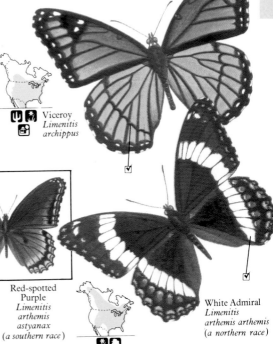

Viceroy
Limenitis archippus

Red
Admiral
Vanessa atalanta

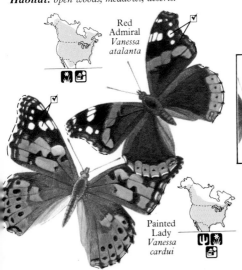

Painted
Lady
Vanessa cardui

Red-spotted
Purple
Limenitis arthemis astyanax
(a southern race)

White Admiral
Limenitis arthemis arthemis
(a northern race)

Wood Nymphs
Cercyonis

Wingspan: *1¾–2¾ in.*
What to look for: *brown butterfly; black, often white-pupiled eyespots on forewing (sometimes also on hindwing); patch around forewing eyespots often yellow-brown.*
Habitat: *moist to dry grasslands and open woodlands.*

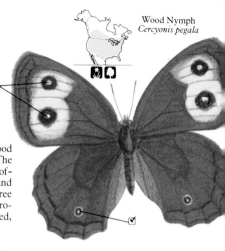

Wood Nymph
Cercyonis pegala

Satyrs and Wood Nymphs   Satyridae

Though generally drab and brown overall, satyrs and wood nymphs usually have conspicuous eyespots on their wings. The veins of the forewing are swollen at the base. Butterflies are often thought of as nectar feeders, but some wood nymphs and other species are attracted to other substances, including tree sap, animal remains, rotting fungi, and the sticky honeydew produced by aphids. Larvae of this group—usually green, striped, and fork-tailed—feed on grasses and sedges.

Spring Azure
Celastrina ladon

Coppers, Blues, and Hairstreaks   Lycaenidae

Easy to distinguish from other butterflies, the jewel-like creatures in this family are small and iridescent. Two species, the Western and the Eastern Pygmy Blue *(Brephidium exilis* and *isophthalma)*, measure scarcely more than half an inch across and are the smallest butterflies in North America.

Although blues occur throughout the continent, many of the species are especially abundant on mountains or in the Far North. Butterflies living in cold climates tend to be on the wing with less frequency than their southern or lowland relatives. For example, the Arctic Blue *(Agriades aquilo)* appears as an adult butterfly only once every two to four years (it spends most of the rest of that time in the larval stage, eating low-growing heaths and becoming dormant during cold weather). Other species may be on the wing year after year, and even throughout the year in the southern part of their range—not the same individuals, of course, but successive generations.

Blues
Polyommatinae

Wingspan: *½–1¼ in.*
What to look for: *small blue butterfly; underside with rows of darker spots (occasionally dark with white spots).*
Habitat: *tidal marshes, fields, bogs, woodlands, deserts.*

Gray Hairstreak
Strymon melinus

White-M Hairstreak
Parrhasius m-album

underside

adult

pupa

larva

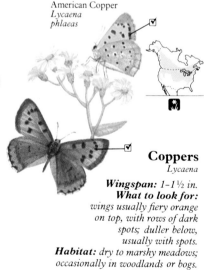

American Copper
Lycaena phlaeas

Coppers
Lycaena

Wingspan: *1–1½ in.*
What to look for: *wings usually fiery orange on top, with rows of dark spots; duller below, usually with spots.*
Habitat: *dry to marshy meadows; occasionally in woodlands or bogs.*

Hairstreaks
Theclinae

Wingspan: *¾–1½ in.*
What to look for: *pattern of lines (occasionally spots) on underside; "tail" usually present at edge of hindwing.*
Habitat: *forests, woodlands, fields, gardens.*

INSECTS

Snout Butterflies
Libytheana

Wingspan: *1¾ in.*
What to look for: *medium-sized, warm brown butterfly; extended mouthparts.*
Habitat: *grasslands, desert washes, woodlands along watercourses; beaches (migration).*

Snout Butterfly
Libytheana bachmanii

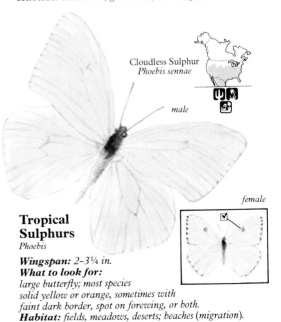

Snout Butterflies   Libytheidae

The snout of a snout butterfly is formed by elongations of the lower jaw, called palpi. Between the palpi is the typical butterfly "tongue," which stays coiled except when the insect is sucking up liquids. Like many species, snout butterflies often obtain moisture from muddy soil, congregating near lakes, streams, and other water sources for that purpose. The larvae feed mainly on the leaves of hackberries.

Whites and Sulphurs   Pieridae

Although color alone separates these butterflies from most other groups, members of the same species vary in appearance. Males often differ from females in color and pattern; butterflies emerging from their pupae in summer tend to be lighter in color and larger than cold-weather forms.

Larvae in this group are often green, striped, and destructive to crops. The accidentally imported European Cabbage Butterfly eats cabbages and related plants; the Alfalfa Butterfly, Alfalfa and other legumes; the western, black-fronted Pine White (*Neophasia menapia*), pines. When the larvae transform into pupae, they spin two structures to attach themselves to twigs or leaves: a silken girdle around the waist as well as the usual button at the anal end.

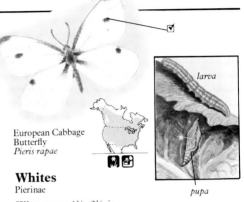

European Cabbage Butterfly
Pieris rapae

larva

pupa

Whites
Pierinae

Wingspan: *1¼–2½ in.*
What to look for: *white butterfly; forewings usually with black checkered markings or spots.*
Habitat: *woodlands, grasslands, deserts, gardens.*

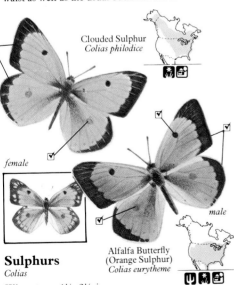

Clouded Sulphur
Colias philodice

female

male

Sulphurs
Colias

Alfalfa Butterfly
(Orange Sulphur)
Colias eurytheme

Wingspan: *1¼–2½ in.*
What to look for: *medium-sized, yellow to orange butterfly; black margins on both wings; forewing often with black spot; hindwing often with deeper orange or yellow spot.* **Habitat:** *woodlands, meadows, tundra, alpine summits.*

Cloudless Sulphur
Phoebis sennae

male

female

Tropical Sulphurs
Phoebis

Wingspan: *2–3¼ in.*
What to look for:
large butterfly; most species solid yellow or orange, sometimes with faint dark border, spot on forewing, or both.
Habitat: *fields, meadows, deserts; beaches (migration).*

267

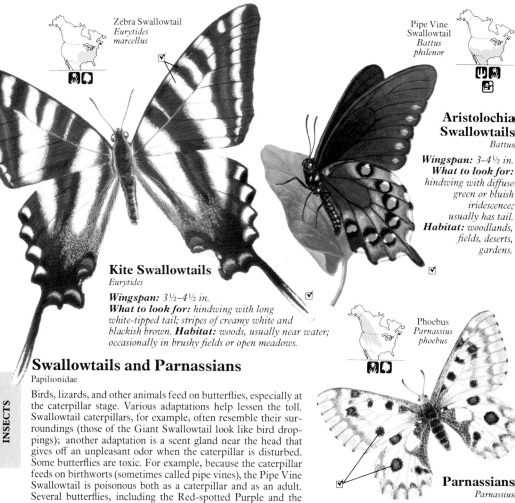

Zebra Swallowtail
Eurytides
marcellus

Pipe Vine
Swallowtail
Battus
philenor

Aristolochia Swallowtails
Battus

Wingspan: *3-4½ in.*
What to look for:
hindwing with diffuse green or bluish iridescence; usually has tail.
Habitat: *woodlands, fields, deserts, gardens.*

Kite Swallowtails
Eurytides

Wingspan: *3½-4½ in.*
What to look for: *hindwing with long white-tipped tail; stripes of creamy white and blackish brown.* **Habitat:** *woods, usually near water; occasionally in brushy fields or open meadows.*

Swallowtails and Parnassians
Papilionidae

Birds, lizards, and other animals feed on butterflies, especially at the caterpillar stage. Various adaptations help lessen the toll. Swallowtail caterpillars, for example, often resemble their surroundings (those of the Giant Swallowtail look like bird droppings); another adaptation is a scent gland near the head that gives off an unpleasant odor when the caterpillar is disturbed. Some butterflies are toxic. For example, because the caterpillar feeds on birthworts (sometimes called pipe vines), the Pipe Vine Swallowtail is poisonous both as a caterpillar and as an adult. Several butterflies, including the Red-spotted Purple and the dark form of the female Tiger Swallowtail, look like the Pipe Vine Swallowtail and gain some measure of protection thereby.

The parnassians are among the butterflies in this group that lack tails. They have another unusual characteristic: after the female mates, she develops a hard pouch called the sphragis, which prevents other males from implanting their sperm.

Phoebus
Parnassius
phoebus

Parnassians
Parnassius

Wingspan: *2¼-3½ in.*
What to look for: *white to cream-colored butterfly with irregular black blotches and red spots, especially on hindwing; no tail.* **Habitat:** *alpine meadows, tundra, mountain woodlands.*

Skippers   Hesperiidae

Lightly skipping from flower to flower in search of nectar, many skippers seem to appear and disappear with lightning speed. There are nearly 300 North American species, and even the lepidopterists have difficulty telling them apart. Skippers' bodies are large in proportion to the wings, and their antennae have a hook at the end. A butterfly antenna is a sense organ responsive to odor, touch, and possibly sound. Other sense organs include the taste receptors, located near the mouth and on the feet, and the eyes, relatively large structures made up of thousands of individual facets. Butterflies lack the complex hearing organs of many moths but can nonetheless perceive sound.

Silver-spotted
Skipper
Epargyreus
clarus

Silver-spotted Skippers
Epargyreus

Wingspan: *1¾-2¼ in.*
What to look for: *large silver blotch usually on underside of hindwing; gold spots on both sides of forewing; hooked antennae.*
Habitat: *woodlands, fields, gardens.*

INSECTS

Giant
Swallowtail
*Papilio
cresphontes*

Tiger
Swallowtail
*Papilio
glaucus*

*dark
phase
of Tiger
Swallowtail*

Fluted Swallowtails
Papilio

Wingspan: *2¾–6½ in.*
What to look for: *large butterfly; usually dark, with pale to bright yellow spots near edge of wings; usually has tail.*
Habitat: *deserts, grasslands, forests, gardens.*

Black
Swallowtail
*Papilio
polyxenes*

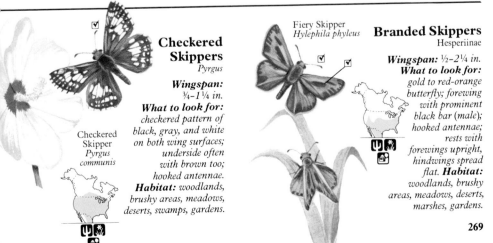

Checkered Skippers
Pyrgus

Wingspan:
¾–1¼ in.
What to look for:
checkered pattern of black, gray, and white on both wing surfaces; underside often with brown too; hooked antennae.
Habitat: *woodlands, brushy areas, meadows, deserts, swamps, gardens.*

Checkered
Skipper
*Pyrgus
communis*

Fiery Skipper
Hylephila phyleus

Branded Skippers
Hesperiinae

Wingspan: *½–2¼ in.*
What to look for:
gold to red-orange butterfly; forewing with prominent black bar (male); hooked antennae; rests with forewings upright, hindwings spread flat. **Habitat:** *woodlands, brushy areas, meadows, deserts, marshes, gardens.*

269

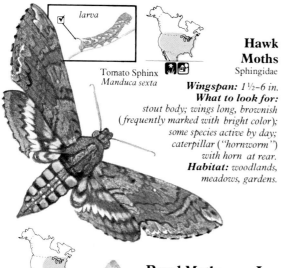

larva

Tomato Sphinx
Manduca sexta

Hawk Moths
Sphingidae

Wingspan: *1½–6 in.*
What to look for:
*stout body; wings long, brownish
(frequently marked with bright color);
some species active by day;
caterpillar ("hornworm")
with horn at rear.*
Habitat: *woodlands,
meadows, gardens.*

egg
case

Gypsy Moth
*Lymantria
dispar*

Tussock Moths
Lymantriidae

larva

Wingspan: *½–1¾ in.*
What to look for: *wings broad, held like a tent
over abdomen at rest; antennae feathered on one side;
larva with tufts of hair.* **Habitat:** *woodlands,
brushy meadows, backyards.*

Royal Moths
Citheroniinae

Wingspan: *1½–7 in.*
What to look for:
*long-winged moth,
often patterned
in reds, yellows, and
browns; antennae
feathered near base.*
Habitat: *woodlands;
occasionally in open
country; near lights.*

Rosy Maple Moth
Dryocampa rubicunda

Larger Moths Macroheterocera

Moths are best separated from butterflies on the basis of their
antennae: those of a moth are feathery or threadlike, lacking
the clublike swelling of a butterfly antenna. Most moths are
active at night, fly by rapid wingbeats, and do without food
during their adult life.

Moth caterpillars look and behave much like butterfly
caterpillars. They are often furred or armed with spines, and
some have fewer than the normal eight pairs of legs, causing
them to loop or inch along. Many spin silk cocoons as they
develop into pupae, but royal moths and certain other species
form cocoonless pupae in the ground.

Woolly Bear
(Isabella Tiger Moth)
Pyrrarcti isabella

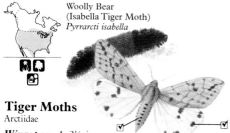

Tiger Moths
Arctiidae

Wingspan: *1–2½ in.*
What to look for: *usually dull-colored moth with
spots or lines on forewing; hindwing often whitish
to bright yellow or pinkish, with dark blotches;
abdomen often red, orange, or yellow, with black
spots; larva with long, thick hair.* **Habitat:**
fields, marshes, woodlands; occasionally in deserts.

Spring Cankerworm
*Paleacrita
vernata*

Loopers, Cankerworms, and Relatives Geometridae

Wingspan: *½–2 in. (certain females wingless).*
What to look for: *wings broad, usually with
zigzags of black, brown, yellow, or white;
wings held flat or upright (not held like a tent);
larva with legs at head and tail only, walks in loops.*
Habitat: *nearly all land habitats.*

Smaller Moths Microlepidoptera

Very fine structural differences separate the
"micros" from the "macros," but usually size
is enough to distinguish between the two
groups: a moth with a wingspan of less than
three-quarters of an inch is probably a "micro."
Especially for the smaller species, the common
name may reflect a characteristic of the pesky
caterpillars rather than of the inconspicuous
adults. The larvae often bore into their food
plants, roll themselves in the foliage, or walk
about in cases of leaves and other plant material.

Bagworms
Psychidae

Wingspan: *½–1 in.*
What to look for:
*male dark, hairy,
with clear wings;
female wingless;
larva, pupa, and female
adult in "bag."*
Habitat: *woodlands,
brushy areas, gardens.*

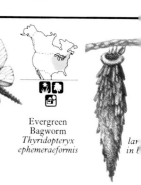

Evergreen
Bagworm
*Thyridopteryx
ephemeraeformis*

lar
in l

American Tent Caterpillar
Malacosoma americana

larvae

Tent Caterpillars and Relatives
Lasiocampidae

Wingspan: *½–3 in.*
What to look for: *dull brown moth, often with scalloped wings; wings held like a tent when at rest; larva hairy, usually in swarms, some making tents.* ***Habitat:*** *woodlands, hedgerows, orchards.*

Army Worm
Pseudaletia unipuncta

Darling Underwing
Catocala cara

Noctuid Moths
Noctuidae

Wingspan: *½–7 in.*
What to look for: *forewing usually with brown, black, and gray spots and lines; hindwing more simply patterned, sometimes brightly colored; threadlike antennae; larva usually hairless, often with reduced number of legs.* ***Habitat:*** *woodlands, deserts, swamps, meadows, gardens; often at lights.*

Pyralid Moths
Pyralidae

Wingspan: *½–1 in.*
What to look for: *narrow forewing; fairly broad hindwing; wings in tentlike position or encircling abdomen at rest.* ***Habitat:*** *nearly all land habitats; certain larvae in ponds.*

larva inside cornstalk

European Corn-borer
Ostrinia nubilalis

Luna Moth
Actias luna

Giant Silk Moths
Saturniidae

Wingspan: *3–7½ in.*
What to look for: *spectacularly colored, broad-winged moth, usually with dark-outlined light spots; featherlike antennae; spiny larva; pupa with cocoon.* ***Habitat:*** *nearly all land habitats with trees; often near lights.*

pupa

larva

Cecropia Moth
Hyalophora cecropia

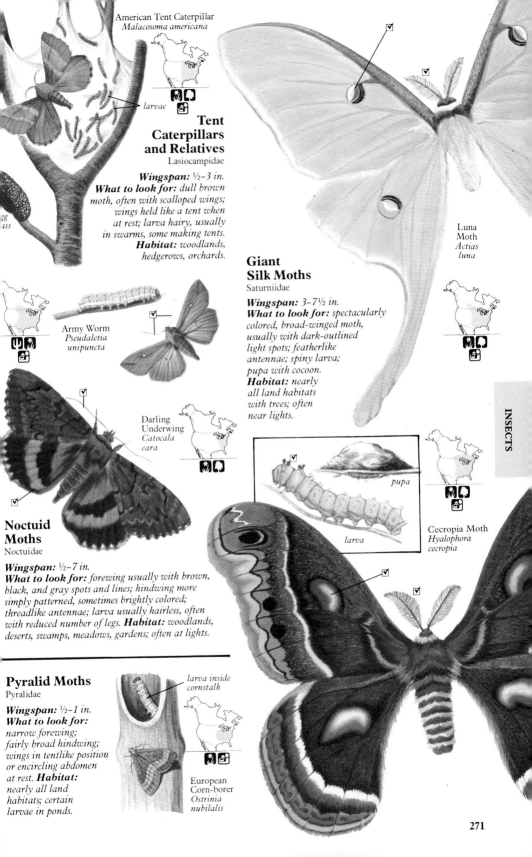

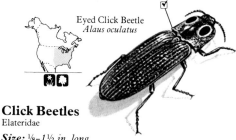

Click Beetles
Elateridae

Eyed Click Beetle
Alaus oculatus

Size: ⅛–1½ in. long.
What to look for: *long, narrow beetle; head loosely hinged to body; triangular projections at rear corners of head (part of click mechanism); clicks and jumps at same time; larva (wireworm) thin, shiny.* **Habitat:** *all land habitats.*

Carrion Beetles
Silphidae

Say's Carrion Beetle
Nicrophorus sayi

Size: ⅛–1½ in. long.
What to look for: *somewhat flat beetle; usually black, often with red or yellow blotches; antennae with bead at tip.* **Habitat:** *forests, meadows, occasionally near houses; near carrion.*

Metallic Wood Borers
Buprestidae

Brassy Metallic Wood Borer
Dicerca divaricata

Size: ⅛–4 in. long.
What to look for: *body similar to click beetle's but slightly more robust; underside and back usually metallic; no click mechanism.* **Habitat:** *woods, brushy areas, deserts; occasionally in fields.*

Fireflies
Lampyridae

Pennsylvania Firefly
Photuris pennsylvanicus

Size: ¼–⅞ in. long.
What to look for: *flashing, luminescent tail (night); soft-bodied beetle with beadlike antennae (day); female wingless.* **Habitat:** *woods, brushy areas, meadows, lawns.*

Black Blister Beetle
Epicauta pennsylvanica

Blister Beetles
Meloidae

Size: ⅛–1¼ in. long.
What to look for: *soft-bodied beetle; thorax narrower than head and abdomen; head bent down; long legs.* **Habitat:** *deserts, grasslands, brushy areas; usually on flowers or foliage.*

Long-horned Beetles
Cerambycidae

Sugar Maple Borer
Glycobius speciosus

Size: ⅛–6 in. long.
What to look for: *long, narrow beetle; long antennae (from half body length to longer than body).* **Habitat:** *woods, brushy areas, deserts, grasslands, along beaches; on plants.*

Two-spotted Ladybird Beetle
Adalia bipunctata

Ladybird Beetles
Coccinellidae

Size: less than ⅜ in. long.
What to look for: *usually red or black with contrasting spots; abdomen and head often hidden (by forewings and front of thorax), making beetle look round.* **Habitat:** *forests, brushy areas, meadows; occasionally in deserts.*

INSECTS

Advanced Beetles Polyphaga

If every plant and animal species sent a representative to a convention, one out of every five delegates would be a beetle. Beetles have chewing mouthparts. Their forewings, called elytra, are hard structures that protect the abdomen and the hindwings (the hindwings are folded under the elytra when the beetle is at rest). Beetles undergo a complete metamorphosis—from egg to larva to pupa to adult.

The largest group of beetles, the advanced beetles (so called because structurally they are more highly developed), numbers some 24,000 species in North America alone. Feeding habits vary widely, although most beetles consume plant material. Few species are entirely harmful or beneficial throughout their life cycle. One exception is the Japanese Beetle, which feeds on plant roots as a larva and on flowers, fruits, and foliage as an adult. In contrast, the insect-eating ladybird beetles are beneficial in both stages.

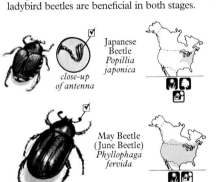

Japanese
Beetle
*Popillia
japonica*

*close-up
of antenna*

May Beetle
(June Beetle)
*Phyllophaga
fervida*

Scarab Beetles
Scarabaeidae

Size: 1/10–5 in. long.
What to look for: wide beetle; often brightly colored; sections at end of antennae can be spread open like a fan. *Habitat:* nearly all land habitats; not in cold areas.

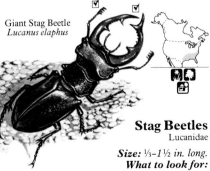

Giant Stag Beetle
Lucanus elaphus

Stag Beetles
Lucanidae

Size: 1/3–1 1/2 in. long.
What to look for:
rather large beetle; pincerlike mouthparts;
antennae clublike, with 3 or 4 sections at tip.
Habitat: forests, brushy areas,
grasslands, beaches; often at lights.

Ground Beetles
Carabidae

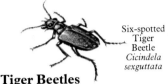

Imported
Calosoma
*Calosoma
sycophanta*

Size: 1/8–3 1/2 in. long.
What to look for:
head narrower than thorax;
thorax narrower than abdomen;
long legs; prominent mouthparts.
Habitat: nearly all land habitats,
especially moist areas; often at lights.

Six-spotted
Tiger
Beetle
*Cicindela
sexguttata*

Tiger Beetles
Cicindelidae

Size: 1/2–2 in. long.
What to look for: brightly colored,
nervously active beetle; large eyes; long, hairy legs.
Habitat: beaches, streambeds, roads, deserts.

Predatory Beetles Adephaga

Although the whirligig beetles (shown on page 282) and certain other species are aquatic, most of the 3,000 or so North American beetles in this group live on land. All of the land dwellers prey on insects, and the group includes some of the fastest runners among beetles. Many of the group—the ground beetles, for example—appear frantically active, running to and fro in search of prey.

Snout Beetles Rhynchophora

The 2,600 or more North American species in this group live in or on plants and are among the most destructive beetles. The European Elm Bark Beetle (*Scolytus multistriatus*) carries Dutch elm disease; the Boll Weevil (*Anthonomus grandis*) ruins cotton crops. Most adults have a long, thin snout with chewing mouthparts at the end.

Snout Beetles (Weevils)
Curculionidae

Size: less than 1/10–1 1/2 in. long.
What to look for: hard-shelled beetle; snout long,
with mouthparts at tip; antennae clubbed,
growing from sides of snout. *Habitat:* all
land habitats; in or on plants.

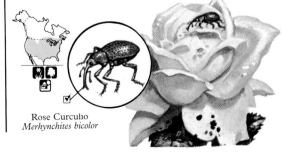

Rose Curculio
Merhynchites bicolor

INSECTS

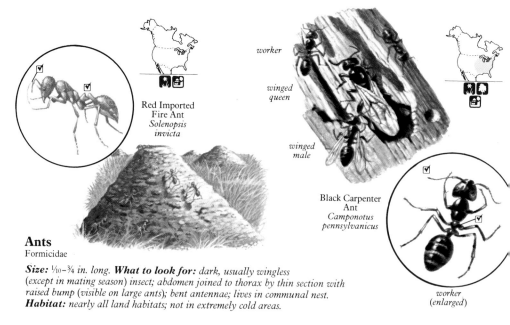

worker

winged queen

winged male

Red Imported
Fire Ant
*Solenopsis
invicta*

Black Carpenter
Ant
*Camponotus
pennsylvanicus*

worker
(enlarged)

Ants
Formicidae

Size: 1/10–3/4 in. long. **What to look for:** *dark, usually wingless (except in mating season) insect; abdomen joined to thorax by thin section with raised bump (visible on large ants); bent antennae; lives in communal nest.* **Habitat:** *nearly all land habitats; not in extremely cold areas.*

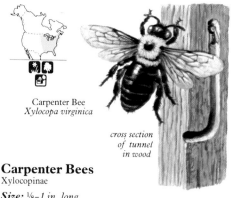

Carpenter Bee
Xylocopa virginica

cross section
of tunnel
in wood

Carpenter Bees
Xylocopinae

Size: 1/8–1 in. long.
What to look for: *robust, sparsely haired bee; metallic blackish or dark blue-green; slight narrowing at waist.* **Habitat:** *woods, fields; often near houses and barns; nests in wood.*

Ants, Bees, and Wasps Apocrita

Many of these insects have a social organization that is among the most elaborate in the animal world. Hundreds, even thousands, of individuals live in a communal nest, each with a task to perform. A queen lays eggs, and the short-lived males (or drones) do nothing but impregnate the queen. Workers gather, make, and store food (honey in the case of bees) for the adults and the wormlike larvae.

Most ants are rather easy to tell apart from other insects. Bees and wasps are distinguished from flies by the two (not one) pairs of wings, and from sawflies by the narrow connection between the thorax and the abdomen (the "wasp waist"). An unseen characteristic is the sting. Only some females have this sharp, hollow, sometimes barbed organ connected to a poison gland inside the abdomen. If disturbed, the insect protrudes the stinger, stabs the victim, and injects poison into the wound, resulting in painful itching or worse. Couple this result with an injection of formic acid, and you get the intense reaction caused by a fire ant, which both stings and bites.

Common
Bumblebee
*Bombus
americanus*

Bumblebees
Bombini

Size: 1/2–1 1/8 in. long.
What to look for:
large, robust, hairy bee; usually yellow and black (occasionally with rust). **Habitat:** *nearly all land habitats, including the Arctic.*

Honeybee
*Apis
mellifera*

Honeybees
Apini

Size: 1/2–1 1/4 in. long.
What to look for: *slender, hairy bee; tawny overall, with some black; pollen baskets on hind legs.* **Habitat:** *hollow trees, man-made hives; usually seen at flowers.*

INSECTS

274

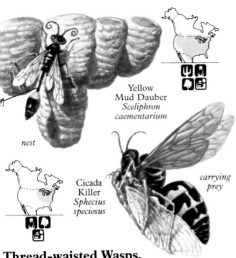

Yellow
Mud Dauber
*Sceliphron
caementarium*

nest

nest

Cicada
Killer
*Sphecius
speciosus*

*carrying
prey*

Thread-waisted Wasps, Digger Wasps, and Mud Daubers
Sphecidae

Size: ¼–1¼ in. long.
What to look for: shiny body; some species with bright color and pattern; abdomen often joined to thorax by thin "thread"; body with little or no hair; wings folded parallel to body at rest.
Habitat: nearly all land habitats.

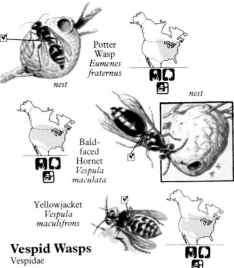

Potter
Wasp
*Eumenes
fraternus*

nest

nest

Bald-
faced
Hornet
*Vespula
maculata*

Yellowjacket
*Vespula
maculifrons*

Vespid Wasps
Vespidae

Size: ⅜–1 in. long.
What to look for: robust, apparently hairless insect; narrow waist; usually black with yellow bands; wings folded parallel to body when at rest. Habitat: all land habitats.

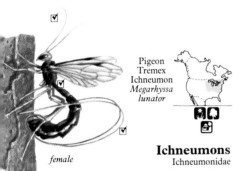

Pigeon
Tremex
Ichneumon
*Megarhyssa
lunator*

female

Ichneumons
Ichneumonidae

Size: ¼–1¾ in. long.
What to look for: slender insect; "wasp waist"; long antennae and legs; female with long, often curved egg-laying apparatus.
Habitat: nearly all land habitats.

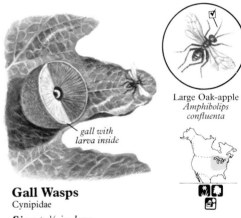

*gall with
larva inside*

Large Oak-apple
*Amphibolips
confluenta*

Gall Wasps
Cynipidae

Size: to ¼ in. long.
What to look for: small, dark wasplike insect; long antennae; larva in swollen deformity (gall) on leaf or stem. Habitat: nearly all land habitats with vegetation.

Sawflies and Horntails Symphyta

Adults in this group resemble flies but have a second pair of wings. Female sawflies lay eggs in plants after cutting a hole with their "saw"; horntails drill holes with a stiletto-like extension at the rear. The larvae of both resemble caterpillars but lack the hindmost pair of legs. When disturbed, a larva raises its rear section into a curled position, ready to spray the potential attacker.

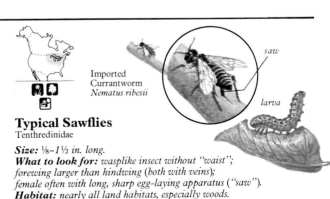

Imported
Currantworm
Nematus ribesii

saw

larva

Typical Sawflies
Tenthredinidae

Size: ⅛–1½ in. long.
What to look for: wasplike insect without "waist"; forewing larger than hindwing (both with veins); female often with long, sharp egg-laying apparatus ("saw").
Habitat: nearly all land habitats, especially woods.

275

Crane Fly
*Holorusia
rubiginosa*

Yellow
Fever
Mosquito
*Aedes
aegypti*

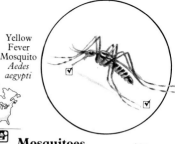

Crane Flies Tipulidae

Size: 1/8–2 in. long.
What to look for: *long, slender insect;
long legs; single pair of long wings; body pale to
dark brown; wings often patterned in dull brown.*
Habitat: *moist woods, fields, yards; often at lights.*

Long-horned Flies Nematocera

All the creatures shown on this page, except the Snow Flea, are flies,
insects with but a single pair of wings. The long-horned flies form a
subgroup that includes many small but bothersome pests, such as
mosquitoes, midges, gnats, punkies, blackflies, and no-see-ums. They
have a delicate build, long, fragile legs, and antennae with numerous
segments. Feeding habits vary: some adults do not eat, some feed on
nectar, and some females suck blood. Most larvae are aquatic.

Mosquitoes
Culicidae

Size: *to 1/2 in. long.*
What to look for:
*small, soft-bodied insect;
long legs; single pair of wings;
female with stilettolike mouthparts,
usually pointed down when at rest.*
Habitat: *all land habitats,
especially near water.*

Robber Flies
Asilidae

Size: *1/2–2 in. long.*
What to look for: *usually long, slender;
head large; legs short, spiny; some species mimic
bumblebees.* **Habitat:** *fields, marshes, deserts.*

Common Gray
Robber Fly
*Efferia
apicalis*

Black Horsefly
*Tabanus
atratus*

Short-horned Flies Brachycera

Many of these flies are large and aggressive.
Robber flies often perch conspicuously at
the end of a twig, ready to ambush other insects. Female horseflies and deerflies feed
on blood, making larger incisions in the victim than mosquitoes do.

Horseflies and Deerflies
Tabanidae

Size: *1/4–1 in. long.*
What to look for: *robust, big-headed fly; eyes often iridescent;
wings plain, dark (may be patterned light and dark).* **Habitat:**
forests, fields; near lakes, streams; around man and livestock.

Circular-seamed Flies
Cyclorrhapha

Most flies, including the Housefly (*Musca domestica*),
belong to this group. Flies have four developmental
stages: egg, larva ("maggot"), pupa, and adult. Adults
of this group emerge from the pupa by cutting a circular seam. Pomace flies pass through the stages so
rapidly that they are often used in genetic studies.

Springtails
Collembola

Springtails have a unique jumping organ. When not
in use it is folded beneath the abdomen, ready to snap
out and propel the insect 3 or 4 inches into the air.
Common though often unnoticed, springtails frequent decaying leaves and moist soil.

Fruit Fly
(Pomace Fly)
*Drosophila
melanogaster*

Pomace Flies
Drosophilidae

Size: *to 1/4 in. long.*
What to look for:
*fragile fly; wings
short, transparent,
with few veins; body
black to yellow-tan,
with black stripes;
eyes prominent, red
to brown.* **Habitat:**
*around rotting fruit
or vegetables.*

Snow Flea
*Hypogastrura
nivicola*

Springtails
Hypogastrurida

Size: *to 1/5 in. long.*
What to look for:
*wingless insect;
furcula (catapultlike
structure at hind end)*
Habitat: *in plant
debris; on snow;
at water's edge.*

Grasshoppers, Crickets, and Relatives
Orthoptera

Heard more often than they are seen, many of these insects produce sounds by rubbing two parts of the body together—forewing against hindwing, for example. The loudest songsters are usually courting males. On many species the front or hind legs are bizarrely modified, usually for jumping but also for digging or, in the case of the mantids, for seizing insect prey. Most species are vegetarian. There is no larval or pupal stage, and adults differ from the immatures (called nymphs) mainly in size. Cockroaches (Blattidae) belong to this group.

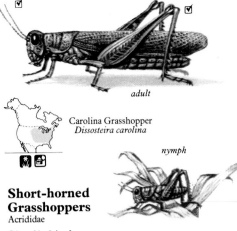

adult

Carolina Grasshopper
Dissosteira carolina

nymph

Short-horned Grasshoppers
Acrididae

Size: ½–2 in. long.
What to look for: large, dull-colored insect; very long hind legs; antennae short; forewings straight, pressed close to body at rest; in flight, may display brightly colored hindwings.
Habitat: grasslands, fields, deserts.

House Cricket
Acheta domesticus

Crickets
Gryllidae

Size: ½–1 in. long.
What to look for: most species dark brown to black; long antennae; very long hind legs; forewing often leathery (*female*) or with thin, transparent areas (*male*).
Habitat: deserts, fields, brushy areas, gardens.

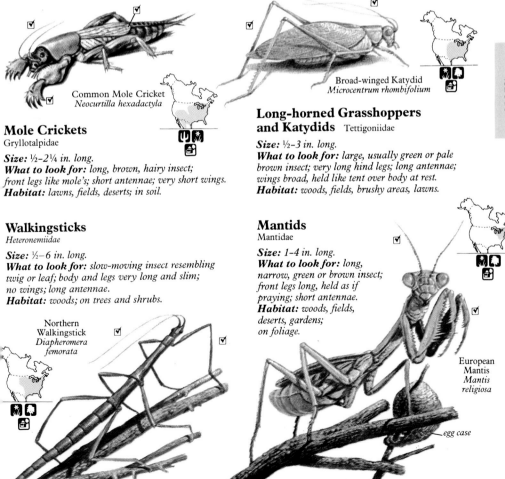

Common Mole Cricket
Neocurtilla hexadactyla

Mole Crickets
Gryllotalpidae

Size: ½–2¼ in. long.
What to look for: long, brown, hairy insect; front legs like mole's; short antennae; very short wings.
Habitat: lawns, fields, deserts; in soil.

Broad-winged Katydid
Microcentrum rhombifolium

Long-horned Grasshoppers and Katydids   Tettigoniidae

Size: ½–3 in. long.
What to look for: large, usually green or pale brown insect; very long hind legs; long antennae; wings broad, held like tent over body at rest.
Habitat: woods, fields, brushy areas, lawns.

Walkingsticks
Heteronemiidae

Size: ½–6 in. long.
What to look for: slow-moving insect resembling twig or leaf; body and legs very long and slim; no wings; long antennae.
Habitat: woods; on trees and shrubs.

Northern Walkingstick
Diapheromera femorata

Mantids
Mantidae

Size: 1–4 in. long.
What to look for: long, narrow, green or brown insect; front legs long, held as if praying; short antennae.
Habitat: woods, fields, deserts, gardens; on foliage.

European Mantis
Mantis religiosa

egg case

277

Stink Bugs
Pentatomidae

Spined Soldier Bug
Podisus maculiventris

Size: ¼–1 in. long.
What to look for: shield-shaped insect, sometimes brightly colored; hard covering on thorax and base of forewing; foul odor when disturbed.
Habitat: nearly all land habitats.

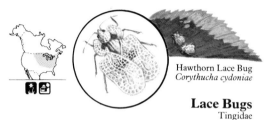

Hawthorn Lace Bug
Corythucha cydoniae

Lace Bugs
Tingidae

Size: ⅛–¼ in. long.
What to look for: wide, flat-bodied insect; forewing and covering over head and body lacy.
Habitat: woods, brushy areas, deserts, gardens.

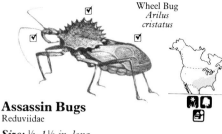

Wheel Bug
Arilus cristatus

Assassin Bugs
Reduviidae

Size: ½–1½ in. long.
What to look for: abdomen boat-shaped, often wider than wings; beak short, stout, curved; some species with "cogwheel" on thorax. **Habitat:** all land habitats, especially warm areas; often at lights.

True Bugs   Hemiptera

All "bugs" are insects, but not all insects are bugs. Whereas the mouthparts of a typical insect are designed for biting and chewing, a true bug's have a tube that pierces plants (occasionally animals) and sucks out their juices. The forewings also set true bugs apart from other insects: in true bugs they are thickened near the base and thin and transparent or smoky toward the tip. Some true bugs that inhabit freshwater are shown on page 282.

INSECTS

Buffalo Treehopper
Strictocephala bubalus

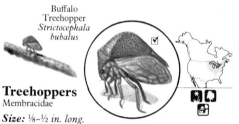

Treehoppers
Membracidae

Size: ⅛–½ in. long.
What to look for: insect wide at head, tapering to rear; hard extension of thorax over abdomen, often with hump; some species look like thorns.
Habitat: woods, brushy areas, fields, deserts, gardens; on leaves.

Aphids, Cicadas, Hoppers, and Relatives   Homoptera

The sucking tube in these insects is shorter than a true bug's and extends from the rear underside of the head. Their forewings, entirely thin and transparent or smoky, are usually held over the body like a tent when the insect is at rest. Whiteflies, scale insects (which seldom have wings), and spittlebugs are part of this group. Young spittlebugs conceal themselves in a white spittlelike substance, popularly known as "snake spit." The adults are called froghoppers because of their shape and jumping ability.

Aphids
Aphididae

Size: ¹⁄₁₆–⅛ in. long.
What to look for: oval soft-bodied insect; wings, if present, usually held above body at rest; antennae long, straight. **Habitat:** all vegetated land habitats.

Grapevine Leafhopper
Erythroneura comes

Leafhoppers
Cicadellidae

Size: ⅛–½ in. long.
What to look for: most species colorfully striped; head triangular (viewed from above); wings tapering to rear; legs spiny. **Habitat:** nearly all temperate land habitats.

Cicadas
Cicadidae

Size: ½–2 in. long.
What to look for: large broad-headed insect; transparent or smoky wings. **Habitat:** woods, brushy areas, deserts, yards.

Periodical (17-year) Cicada
Magicicada septendecim

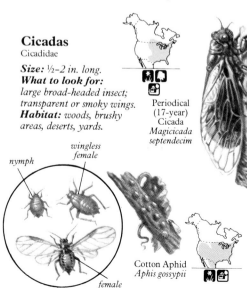

nymph

wingless female

female

Cotton Aphid
Aphis gossypii

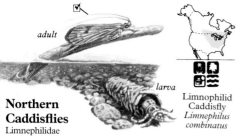

adult

larva

Limnophilid
Caddisfly
*Limnephilus
combinatus*

Northern Caddisflies
Limnephilidae

Size: *adult ¼–1 in. long; larva ⅓–1 ¾ in. long.*
What to look for: *adult mothlike, with long antennae
and hairy wings marked with light and dark brown;
larva caterpillarlike.* **Habitat:** *adult in woods,
fields; larva in ponds, slow-moving streams.*

Caddisflies Trichoptera

A moving bundle of twigs, pebbles, shells, or sand on the
bottom of a pond, lake, or stream is probably a caddisfly
larva. Encased in materials from its environment, it is camouflaged from fish and other predators. The caddisfly pu-
pates in the case, after fastening it to an underwater object.

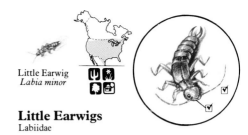

Little Earwig
Labia minor

Little Earwigs
Labiidae

Size: *⅙–1 in. long.*
What to look for: *brown insect; forcepslike pincers;
forewing usually very short, leathery; long antennae.*
Habitat: *woods, brushy fields,
deserts, houses; under litter.*

Earwigs Dermaptera

Contrary to folklore, the fierce-looking pincer-
bearing earwigs do not creep into the ears of
sleeping people. These insects can pinch
sharply if handled, but they are vegetarians or
scavengers that do no harm.

nymph

Dragonflies
Anisoptera

Size: *1½–4 in. long.*
What to look for: *body long, slender, usually
brown or black and often with bright markings;
wings transparent, held straight out from body
at rest; hindwing wider at base than forewing.*
Habitat: *marshes, fields near lakes,
streams, ponds; nymph in water.*

Widow
Skimmer
*Libellula
luctuosa*

Damselflies
Zygoptera

Black-winged
Damselfly
*Calopteryx
maculatum*

Size: *1¼–3 in. long.*
What to look for: *body
needlelike, often jewel-colored;
wings transparent, nearly equal in size,
held folded above abdomen or open and slightly
uptilted at rest.* **Habitat:** *near freshwater.*

Dragonflies and Damselflies Odonata

As they fly, these hunters catch mosquitoes and other insects by making a basketlike trap of their legs. Pairs often
fly together, the male flying in front of the female and
grasping her with an appendage on his abdomen. The
eggs hatch into aquatic nymphs.

Mayflies
Ephemeroptera

As the name Ephemeroptera
suggests, adult mayflies live
but a day or two, eating
nothing during that time.
Young mayflies (nymphs) live
underwater and feed on plants.
Huge numbers may transform
into adults at the same time.

Burrowing Mayflies
Ephemeridae

Size: *body ½–1¼ in. long.*
What to look for: *fragile
insect; 3 long "tails"; wings
triangular, transparent,
held above body at rest;
hindwing small.* **Habitat:**
*forests, fields, yards;
nymphs in water.*

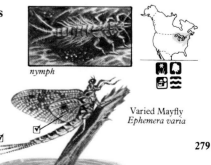

nymph

Varied Mayfly
Ephemera varia

Arachnids Arachnida

The arachnids, whose name recalls the mythological woman who was changed into a spider (*arachne*) by the goddess Athena for challenging her to a weaving contest, differ from the insects in the number of legs—eight rather than six. Their mouthparts differ microscopically, and they have two appendages, called pedipalps, near the mouth. In the scorpions and whip scorpions the pedipalps are claws; among spiders, the males use the pedipalps in mating.

The arachnids include some of the best architects in the animal world—the spiders, whose silken webs, spun from fingerlike glands in the abdomen, trap insects and are thus beneficial to man. For example, the funnel-shaped cobweb of the brown Grass Spider (*Tegenaria domestica*) may annoy the homeowner, but it does reduce the insect population of a house. Instead of building an aerial web, the trap-door spiders dig a tunnel, line it with silk, and close the entrance with a movable door. Some spiders kill their prey with venom, which in certain species (the Black Widow, the Brown Recluse, and the tarantulas) is harmful or even fatal to humans.

Scorpions are menacing-looking animals that use their venom-laden tail to defend themselves and disable prey; the Arizona Scorpion is one species whose sting can be fatal to humans. The whip scorpions, formidable in appearance but sluggish and harmless, have a long tail with no known function. The harvestmen look like long-legged spiders, but their bodies do not show the two-part division of spiders. Mites and ticks also are arachnids.

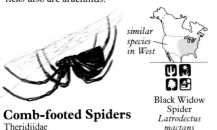

similar species in West

Comb-footed Spiders
Theridiidae

Black Widow Spider *Latrodectus mactans*

Size: *body ¹⁄₁₆–¹⁄₂ in. long.*
What to look for: *large abdomen; front of body small; thin legs; hangs upside down on ragged web.*
Habitat: *nearly all land habitats, including houses.*

Daddy Longlegs *Leiobunum vittatum*

Harvestmen
Opiliones

Size: *body ¹⁄₈–¹⁄₄ in. long.*
What to look for: *small body supported by 8 long, stiltlike legs; head not separate from body.*
Habitat: *most land habitats with vegetation.*

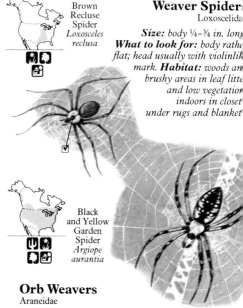

Brown Recluse Spider *Loxosceles reclusa*

Sedentary Weaver Spiders
Loxoscelidae

Size: *body ¹⁄₄–³⁄₄ in. long.*
What to look for: *body rather flat; head usually with violinlike mark.* **Habitat:** *woods and brushy areas in leaf litter and low vegetation; indoors in closets under rugs and blankets.*

Black and Yellow Garden Spider *Argiope aurantia*

Orb Weavers
Araneidae

Size: *body ¹⁄₁₆–1³⁄₄ in. long.*
What to look for: *body generally hairless, often patterned; hairy legs; web formed radially and suspended vertically in trees, bushes, and the like; spider hangs head down at web's center or hides nearby.* **Habitat:** *all land habitats.*

Centipedes and Millipedes
Chilopoda and Diplopoda

Although they can be valuable in controlling household insects, centipedes are often viewed as pests, largely because of the painful (but seldom serious) sting that the poison-bearing claws on the first pair of legs can inflict. While their name means "hundred-legged," the actual number of legs varies from 15 pairs in some species to as many as 173 in others. Even more misnamed is the millipede ("thousand-legged"), which generally has fewer than 50 pairs of legs. Lacking the centipede's ability to sting, a millipede protects itself by releasing an odor unpleasant enough to discourage most predators.

Banded Millipede *Narceus americanus*

Millipedes Diplopoda

Size: *1–5 in. long.*
What to look for: *slow-moving wormlike animal; body in segments, with 2 pairs of legs per segment; short antennae.* **Habitat:** *damp, dark places; beneath rocks, wood, and leaves or in soil.*

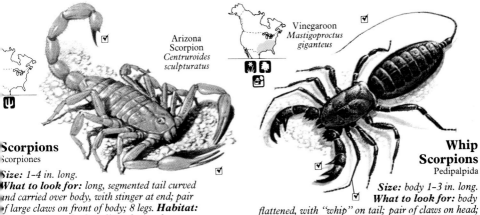

Scorpions
Scorpiones

Size: 1–4 in. long.
What to look for: *long, segmented tail curved and carried over body, with stinger at end; pair of large claws on front of body; 8 legs.* ***Habitat:*** *deserts; under rocks, logs, litter during day.*

Arizona Scorpion
Centruroides sculpturatus

Vinegaroon
Mastigoproctus giganteus

Whip Scorpions
Pedipalpida

Size: body 1–3 in. long.
What to look for: *body flattened, with "whip" on tail; pair of claws on head; first pair of legs threadlike, longer than the others.* ***Habitat:*** *warm, humid areas; under logs or litter or in crevices.*

Wolf Spiders
Lycosidae

Size: body ¹⁄₁₀–1½ in. long.
What to look for: *body somewhat elongated, often dark brown and patterned; usually no web; female carries white egg sac beneath abdomen; young ride on top.* ***Habitat:*** *nearly all land habitats, especially warm areas.*

Wolf Spider
Lycosa punctulata

female with young on back

California Trap-door Spider
Bothriocyrtum californicum

Trap-door Spiders
Ctenizidae

Size: body ⅝–1¼ in. long.
What to look for: *body robust, somewhat hairy, and yellow-brown, brown, gray, or black; makes nest in soil, with trapdoor.* ***Habitat:*** *damp woods to deserts; on or in soil.*

American Tarantula
Dugesiella hentzi

Tarantulas
Theraphosidae

Size: body 1½–1¾ in. long.
What to look for: *body large, hairy, and brown or black or both; legs very hairy; mouthparts fierce-looking; often rears up on hind legs if disturbed.* ***Habitat:*** *arid to semiarid areas; in ground or beneath bark.*

OTHER INVERTEBRATES

Common House Centipede
Scutigera coleoptrata

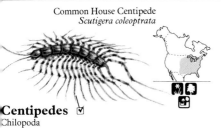

Centipedes
Chilopoda

Size: 1–5 in. long.
What to look for: *fast-moving animal; 1 pair of legs per segment (all segments not always obvious); long antennae.* ***Habitat:*** *nearly all land habitats, including houses; under litter, bark, rocks during day.*

Flat-tailed Night Crawler
Lumbricus terrestris

Earthworms and Freshwater Worms Oligochaeta

In the opinion of Charles Darwin, earthworms may have played a more important role on this planet than any other animal. Ubiquitous in moist soil, they aerate it with their burrows and fertilize it with their castings.

Earthworms
Lumbricidae

Size: ¾–8 in. long.
What to look for: *long, segmented, soft-bodied animal; no legs.* ***Habitat:*** *moist soil.*

281

Black
Whirligig
Beetle
*Dineutus
nigrior*

Water
Strider
*Gerris
conformis*

Whirligig Beetles
Gyrinidae

Size: ⅛–¾ in. long.
What to look for: *oval beetle, usually black
or dark metallic green or both; front legs long
(other legs hidden); swims in circles on surface.*
Habitat: *freshwater ponds, slow-moving streams.*

Water Striders
Gerridae

Size: ½–¾ in. long.
What to look for: *long, thin bug;
front legs shorter than others; curved antennae; skates
at surface.* **Habitat:** *ponds, lakes, slow-moving streams.*

Common
Backswimmer
*Notonecta
undulata*

Water
Boatman
*Arctocorisa
alternata*

Water Boatmen
Corixidae

Size: ¼–½ in. long.
What to look for: *brown bug with
dark lines; front legs short, middle and hind legs longer;
swims on belly on surface or clings to submerged plants.*
Habitat: *ponds, lakes, slow-moving streams;
occasionally in brackish water.*

Backswimmers
Notonectidae

Size: ¼–½ in. long.
What to look for: *yellow-white with black markings
above; dull black below; back legs longer than
front 4; swims or rests on back at or just below
surface.* **Habitat:** *in or near sluggish freshwater.*

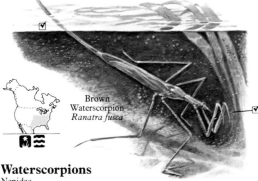

Giant
Water Bug
*Lethocerus
americanus*

Brown
Waterscorpion
Ranatra fusca

Waterscorpions
Nepidae

Size: 1–2 in. long.
What to look for: *sticklike bug,
green to brown; threadlike breathing
tubes at rear; front legs resembling claws,
other legs long, thin.* **Habitat:** *ponds, lakes,
slow-moving streams; sometimes on land.*

Freshwater Insects
Hemiptera and Adephaga

Many insects live in freshwater during the early part of their
lives. Those shown here, all true bugs save the beetle, also live
in freshwater as adults. The larvae breathe underwater with
their gills, but the adults lack gills and must find other ways to
breathe. Some have a breathing tube at the rear, which protrudes above the water's surface while they feed. Others carry
air below the surface; for example, the water boatmen store
bubbles of air under their wings.

Giant Water Bugs
Belostomatidae

Size: ¾–2½ in. long.
What to look for: *oval bug; middle
and hind legs flattened, front legs like
claws; some males carry eggs on back.*
Habitat: *ponds, lakes; often at lights.*

Pistol Shrimps
Alpheidae

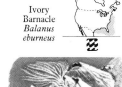

Size: 1–2 in. long.
What to look for: small crustacean; 1 claw (right or left) greatly enlarged; long "thumb" on claw makes loud clicking noise. **Habitat:** near shore, especially in tide pools; under rocks.

Pistol Shrimp
Alpheus dentipes

Crustaceans Crustacea

Best known for such delectable creatures as lobsters and shrimp, this group includes some 26,000 species worldwide, many very small. Most live in or near saltwater. A typical crustacean has jointed legs, two pairs of antennae, and an external skeleton, or "crust," that in some species contains a large amount of calcium and is therefore quite hard. The skeleton is periodically cast off (molted) and replaced by a larger one; the soft-shelled crabs offered by restaurants have just molted. Male crustaceans often have special appendages that clasp the female. The eggs usually hatch in the water and develop into free-swimming larvae.

Hermit Crabs
Paguridae

Blue-clawed Hermit Crab
Pagurus samuelis

Size: 1–1½ in. long.
What to look for:
soft crab living in empty snail shell; 1 claw slightly enlarged; tail soft, curved; 2 pairs of walking feet. **Habitat:** near shore; in tide pools or on mud or sand.

Acorn Barnacles
Balanidae

Ivory Barnacle
Balanus eburneus

Size: to 1 in. tall.
What to look for:
volcanolike shape formed by 6 shelly plates cemented in place; feathery "arms" extend from top when submerged.
Habitat: estuaries to oceans; usually on rocks, pilings, boats.

Ghost Crab
Ocypode quadrata

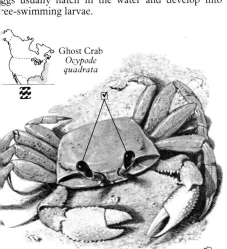

Eastern Crayfish
Cambarus bartonii

Crayfishes
Astacidae

Size: 2–5 in. long.
What to look for: miniature lobsterlike animal in freshwater. **Habitat:** streams, ponds, lakes; under rocks or in mud.

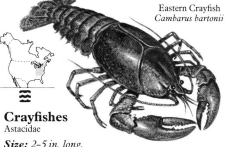

Blue Crab
Callinectes sapidus

Swimming Crabs
Portunidae

Size: 3–9 in. wide.
What to look for:
swimming crab with oval shell, often pointed at sides; last pair of legs paddle-shaped; eyes on short stalks.
Habitat: bays, estuaries, offshore.

Mud Fiddler Crab
Uca pugnax

Shore Crabs
Ocypodidae

Size: ¾–4 in. wide.
What to look for: fast-moving crab with squarish shell; eyes far apart, on long stalks; 4 pairs of walking legs; males of some species with one claw greatly enlarged. **Habitat:** beaches, tidal marshes; in burrows.

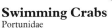

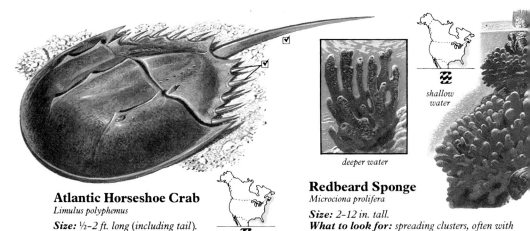

Atlantic Horseshoe Crab
Limulus polyphemus

Size: ½–2 ft. long (including tail).
What to look for: shell dull brown; front horseshoe-shaped; rear spiny, with spikelike tail.
Habitat: near shore in bays, estuaries; deeper water.

Horseshoe Crabs   Xiphosura

These harmless animals enter shallow water for breeding, the male riding atop the larger female. More closely related to spiders than to crabs, they are "living fossils" that have remained essentially unchanged for several hundred million years. All but the Atlantic Horseshoe Crab live in Asian waters.

shallow water

deeper water

Redbeard Sponge
Microciona prolifera

Size: 2–12 in. tall.
What to look for: spreading clusters, often with bumps or cups (clumps with upright branching fingers in deeper water); red to orange (brown when dried).
Habitat: along shores, in bays; on rocks, pilings.

Sponges   Porifera

Only in the 19th century was it firmly established th these sedentary creatures—which cannot synthesiz their own food—actually are animals, not plant Sponges feed by taking in water and filtering ou small organisms and debris. They occur in all sea and occasionally in freshwater as well.

OTHER INVERTEBRATES

Sea Anemones, Corals, and Relatives
Anthozoa

These are fleshy, often colorful creatures with petallike tentacles that sting small prey and carry it into the mouth at the center. Sea anemones have a muscular foot, used to hold on to rocks or move slowly about. Most reef-building corals, such as the Star Coral, live in colonies, with each minute anemonelike animal inhabiting a stony cup. Sea Whips and related species are colonial animals whose fleshy mass covers a hard skeleton.

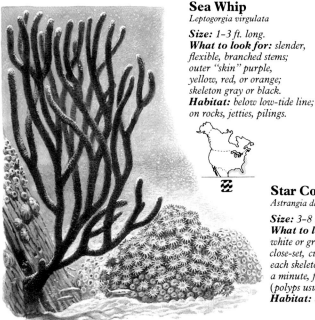

Sea Whip
Leptogorgia virgulata

Size: 1–3 ft. long.
What to look for: slender, flexible, branched stems; outer "skin" purple, yellow, red, or orange; skeleton gray or black.
Habitat: below low-tide line; on rocks, jetties, pilings.

Frille
Sea Anemon
Metridium sen

Size: 2–4 in. ta
What to look for: soft anima body columnar, orange to whit attached at base; top with many fin feathery tentacles, usually whit
Habitat: near shore or in deep water; on rocks, pilin

Star Coral
Astrangia danae

Size: 3–8 in. across.
What to look for: white or gray clusters of close-set, cuplike, stony skeletons, each skeleton containing a minute, fleshy, tentacled polyp (polyps usually retract during the day).
Habitat: below low-tide line; on rocks, pilings.

Moon Jelly
Aurelia aurita

Size: *8–10 in. across.*
What to look for:
pale, jellylike disk;
4-leaf-clover pattern in center
(sex organs); fringe of tentacles at edge.
Habitat: *bays, offshore; floating on surface.*

Jellyfishes and Relatives   Hydrozoa and Scyphozoa

Along the coast of North America these gelatinous creatures often appear in great numbers—not a welcome sight, for the tentacles with which they poison prey can sting humans too. The tropical Portuguese Man-of-war (*Physalia physalia*), which occasionally drifts northward, has tentacles up to 50 feet long; those of the Moon Jelly and the By-the-wind Sailor are relatively short.

By-the-wind Sailor
Velella velella

Size: *2–4 in. long.*
What to look for: *oval,*
gray or purple jellylike float;
translucent triangular "sail";
short tentacles under float.
Habitat: *offshore; warm seas.*

Sea Stars   Asteroidea

Though some sea stars, or starfish, may have 30 arms, 5 is the usual number. If an arm is severed, a new one grows in its place. Sea stars have rows of tube feet on the underside. Tipped with suction cups, they help the animal to move along and to pry open the shells of clams and other bivalves. Some eat sea urchins, carrion, or even other sea stars.

Ocher Sea Star
Pisaster ochraceus

Size: *6–12 in. across.*
What to look for: *leathery, star-shaped animal*
with 5 arms; can be purple, ocher, brown, or orange;
lacy pattern of small, raised, light-colored bumps on
upper surface. **Habitat:** *tidal areas; on rocks, especially in tide pools.*

test

Green Sea Urchin
Strongylocentrotus droebachiensis

Size: *2½–3 in. across.*
What to look for: *globular animal*
with green or purple spines; empty skeleton
(test) usually green, with rows of small bumps.
Habitat: *in tide pools and offshore.*

test

Sand Dollar
Echinarachnius parma

Size: *2½–3 in. across.*
What to look for: *pancake-shaped animal*
with minute fuzzy brown spines; upper surface
with 5-petal design; empty skeleton (test)
bleached white. **Habitat:** *deep water; in sand.*

Sea Urchins and Sand Dollars   Echinoidea

Usually sharp but rarely poisonous, a sea urchin's spines are its defense against predators. The sea urchin itself feeds mainly on algae. Sand dollars, which are flat relatives of sea urchins (and of sea stars, as witnessed by the five-pointed pattern), lie buried or half buried in the sand and feed on small pieces of organic material.

Trees and Shrubs

Trees dominate many of our landscapes—not just in height, but also in the area they cover. The natural vegetation of more than half the continent is trees.

North America has the world's tallest trees, the most massive trees, and the oldest trees. It has nearly 60 kinds of oaks, some 35 pines, and more than a dozen maples. About 750 species of trees grow wild north of the Mexican border.

Exactly how many kinds of trees there are depends to a great extent on which plants are considered trees. One generally accepted definition of a tree is a woody plant with one erect stem (the trunk) reaching a height of at least 12 feet. Shrubs are usually shorter, with multiple stems springing directly from the ground.

Just as most people know instinctively what a tree is, so too are they aware that some trees have needles and others leaves. This is a useful starting point in tree identification, but one that requires refinement. For needles are actu-ally leaves—long narrow ones that, like other leaves, contain chlorophyll, the green pigment required for photosynthesis. Trees with needles belong to the group of plants called conifers, which produce their seeds in cones. (Cedars, junipers, and other trees with scalelike leaves are also conifers.) Nearly all conifers are evergreen—that is, they are never totally without leaves.

Unlike most conifers, the majority of broad-leaved trees (such as maples and oaks) are deciduous in temperate regions, shedding their leaves before winter sets in. Another difference between the two groups is their mode of reproduction. Broad-leaved trees propagate by means of flowers and bear their seeds in fruits. Some broad-leaved species have separate male and female flowers, either on the same tree or on different ones.

Where the Forests Are

North America has seven major types of forest, according to one generally accepted scheme. The species listed below are typical members of their community.

Northern Forest: *Black Spruce, Tamarack, Balsam Fir, Paper Birch, Quaking Aspen*

Pacific Coast Forest: *Western Hemlock, Redwood, Douglas-fir, Western Redcedar*

Western Mountain Forest: *Ponderosa Pine, Lodgepole Pine, Englemann Spruce, Douglas-fir*

Northeastern Forest: *Eastern Hemlock, American Beech, Northern Red Oak, American Basswood, Sugar Maple*

Central Forest: *Tuliptree, Sycamore, Shagbark Hickory, White Oak, Ohio Buckeye*

Southeastern Forest: *Loblolly Pine, Shortleaf Pine, Longleaf Pine, Mockernut Hickory, Live Oak*

Subtropical Forest: *Red Mangrove, Black-mangrove, Cabbage Palmetto*

Unforested Areas: *desert, grassland, tundra*

Different Environments, Different Trees

Conifers and broad-leaved trees have different distributions across the land. Conifers prevail in northern and western forests and in the South and Southwest. Regions with more temperate climates, richer soils, and (to some extent) greater rainfall support forests with a preponderance of broad-leaved trees. Mixed forests, with roughly equal numbers of conifers and broad-leaved trees, occur in intermediate areas.

Trees may belong to the same group yet have different growth requirements. Among the conifers, spruces are at home in cold, moist regions; firs can tolerate somewhat higher temperatures; pines do well in coarse, dry soils in sunny locations, especially where fires have reduced competition from other plants.

Although certain pines and other species often grow in pure stands, trees are more frequently found in associations; that is, if one species is present, so are its "partners," which do well under similar conditions. Oaks and hickories make up an association in several southern and central states; junipers and pinyons, in arid parts of the West. Similarly, certain understory plants are characteristic of one type of forest. Vine Maple grows in the shade of northwestern conifers; Hobblebush, in mixed northeastern forests.

Such associations extend to birds and other animal life. Sapsuckers tap out holes in birch trees; Red Crossbills eat the seeds of various conifers. Relationships like these point out an additional benefit of sharpening your skills in tree identification: if you know which trees are in the vicinity, you can predict what other forms of life are likely to be around.

How to Use This Section

This section is divided into two parts. Species that usually grow as trees are covered on pages 288 through 322, with conifers preceding broad-leaved trees. Shrubs are on pages 323 through 329. (Some low-growing shrubs are included in the wildflower section of this book.) Unless otherwise indicated, the range map for each species shows only the area where it reproduces without cultivation.

The measurements provided are for average-sized mature (fruiting) plants. Since growing conditions influence size, taller or shorter specimens should be expected. Most leaves and twigs are pictured at one-quarter natural size. Exceptions include compound leaves, usually shown at one-eighth.

Tips on Identifying Trees

Certain species—Giant Sequoias, Weeping Willows—can be recognized at a glance. Identifying others is a matter of narrowing down the possibilities.

Leaves. First determine the general type of leaf—needlelike, scalelike, or flat and broad. Then look at the size, shape, texture, color, and arrangement. Most broad-leaved trees have leaves that alternate on the twig. (The maples, with paired leaves, are a major exception.) Some trees, such as hickories and the Boxelder, have compound leaves, with each leaf divided into leaflets. A key to conifer leaves is provided on page 288.

Boxelder

Pitch Pine

Flowers. Large showy blossoms, such as those of the magnolias, often lead to precise identification of a broad-leaved tree. Such unflowerlike blossoms as birch catkins can tell you to which group a particular tree belongs.

Fruits. Closely related trees bear similar fruits, and so fruits can help you place a tree in a group or in a particular species. Oak fruits, for example, are acorns and vary, according to species, in size, shape, and cup texture. Conifer "fruits"—cones—are also surprisingly varied. Check the size and look at the fine details of cones lying on the ground; also look at their orientation on the branches. Fir cones grow upright; spruces' hang down.

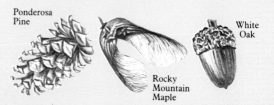

Ponderosa Pine

Rocky Mountain Maple

White Oak

Bark. Precise identification of a tree, especially in winter, may require a look at bark color, pattern, or texture, especially on the mature part of the trunk. If a tree has been identified as to general type, the bark may suggest its specific name: Red Pine, Shagbark Hickory, Paper Birch.

Shape. The shape of a tree involves consideration of height, crown width, the arrangement of branches, and other characteristics. The American Elm is usually called vase-shaped; it has a sturdy trunk dividing into several major limbs, a broad crown, and arching outer branches. Shape varies with location. A forest tree, for example, will be taller and its crown narrower than the same species grown out in the open.

Pacific Yew
Taxus brevifolia

Size: *20-40 ft. tall; needles 1 in. long.*
What to look for: *needles dark green above, pale yellow-green below, growing all around branch but appearing to be in 2 rows; fruits scarlet, fleshy; bark thin, scaly, purple-brown.*
Habitat: *moist soils near water.*

Yews *Taxus*

Red berrylike fruits distinguish the yews from other conifers. Tolerant of shade, yews are often the only shrubs or low trees growing beneath a dense forest canopy. Canada Yew (*Taxus canadensis*), a low shrub, is heavily browsed by winter-feeding Moose and deer; the succulent fruits of various species are favored by grouse. Once prized for archery and hunting bows, yews are valued today as ornamental plants, especially on the north sides of buildings.

Identifying needle-leaved trees. The chart below is a guide to conifers with needlelike leaves. Conifers with short, scalelike leaves are shown on pages 295–297.

Needle Arrangement	Needle Length	Needle in Cross Section	Tree Group
clusters of 5 (pinyons with fewer)	1–5 in.	usually triangular	white pines *pp. 288–289*
clusters of 2–4	1–18 in.	semicircular to triangular	yellow pines *pp. 289–291*
brushlike clusters of 20 or more	up to 2 in.	flat to triangular	larches *p. 292*
single, appearing to be on sides of branch	½–1 in.	flat	yews *p. 288*
single, all around branch	up to 2 in.	square or flattened	spruces *pp. 292–293*
single, on sides of branch or all around	up to 1 in.	flat	hemlocks *p. 293*
single, on top and sides of branch	up to 3 in.	flattened	true firs *p. 294*
	up to 1½ in.	flattened	Douglas-firs *p. 295*
single, on side of branch	up to 1 in.	flat	redwoods, baldcypresses *p. 295*

TREES

Western White Pine

Eastern White Pine

Eastern White Pine
Pinus strobus

Size: *80-100 ft. tall; needles 3-5 in. long.*
What to look for: *needles in 5's; cones resinous; bark smooth, dark green (young) or deeply cracked, dark brown (mature).*
Habitat: *sandy loam, rock ridges, bogs.*

mature

Sugar Pine
Pinus lambertiana

Size: *160-200 ft. tall; needles 2-4 in. long.*
What to look for: *needles in 5's, twisted; cones very long (10-26 in.).*
Habitat: *cool, moist mountain slopes.*

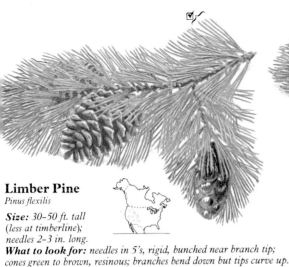

Limber Pine
Pinus flexilis

Size: *30-50 ft. tall (less at timberline); needles 2-3 in. long.*
What to look for: *needles in 5's, rigid, bunched near branch tip; cones green to brown, resinous; branches bend down but tips curve up.*
Habitat: *dry, rocky mountain slopes and peaks.*

Bristlecone Pine
Pinus aristata

Size: *30-40 ft. tall (10 ft. at timberline); needles 1-1½ in. long.*
What to look for: *needles in 5's, bright blue-green, with white resin droplets; cone scales with sharp prickles.*
Habitat: *dry, rocky slopes to ridges.*

Pines *Pinus*

Although pines tend to have a more southerly distribution than spruces and firs, their natural range includes all of North America except the extreme North and some parts of the Midwest. Thirty-six species are native to this continent. Certain ones, such as the Eastern White Pine and the shorter-needled Western White Pine *(Pinus monticola)*, grow almost everywhere, from wet bogs to dry ridges. Even such species as the Monterey Pine *(Pinus radiata)*, naturally restricted to a small area, flourish in other areas when cultivated in tree plantations.

Foresters classify the pines into two groups—the white, or soft, pines and the yellow, or hard, pines—according to the characteristics of the heartwood, the central portion of the trunk. Although the heartwood is not visible on a living tree, other differences between the two groups can be more readily observed. Needles on white pines usually grow in clusters of five; on yellow species, in clusters of two or three. Cones on most yellow pines have prickles; those on a white pine are prickleless, with the notable exception of the Bristlecone Pine, a tree famed for its longevity (some specimens are the oldest trees in North America). Except for the Jack Pine, the trees shown on these two pages are white pines; the Jack Pine and the species on the next two pages are yellow pines.

*ancient
Bristlecone Pines*

Pinyon
Pinus edulis

Size: *20-40 ft. tall; needles ¾-1½ in. long.*
What to look for: *needles in 2's, dark green (Singleleaf Pinyon, Pinus monophylla, has solitary needles); cones egg-shaped; seeds wingless, ½ in. long.* **Habitat:** *dry foothills, mesas, canyons.*

Jack Pine
Pinus banksiana

Size: *30-70 ft. tall; needles ¾-1½ in. long.*
What to look for: *needles in 2's, curved, spread in V; cones usually closed, pointing toward branch tip; bark scaly, red-brown; tree often leaning or with distorted branches.* **Habitat:** *dry, sandy plains to moist soils.*

289

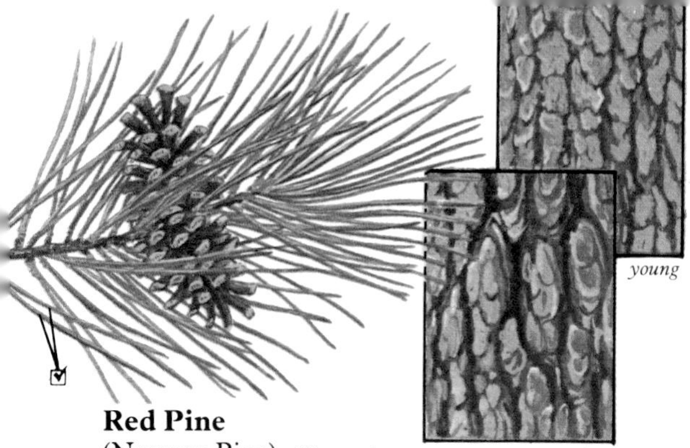

Red Pine
(Norway Pine) *Pinus resinosa*

Size: 50–80 ft. tall; needles 4–6 in. long.
What to look for: needles in 2's, flexible, bunched near branch tips; cone scales without prickles; bark flaky, pink to red-brown (young) or with large, flat plates (mature).
Habitat: sandy soils, rocky slopes.

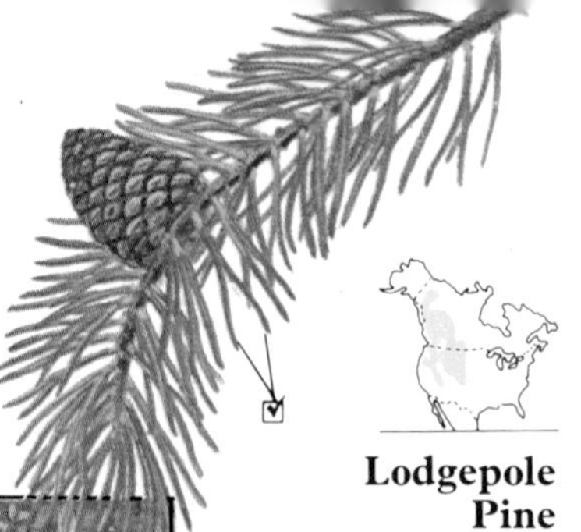

young

mature

Lodgepole Pine
Pinus contorta

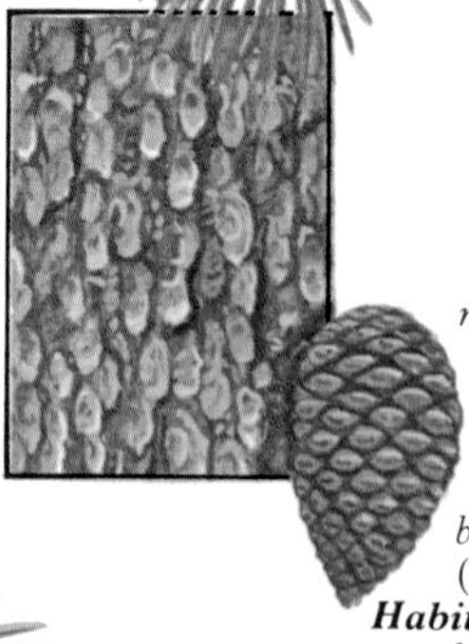

Size: 70–80 ft. tall (shorter near sea); needles 1–3 in. long.
What to look for: needles in 2's, twisted; cones usually closed, prickly, pointing away from branch tip; bark with small plates (larger ones near sea). *Habitat:* mountain slopes, beaches, bogs near sea.

Ponderosa Pine
(Western Yellow Pine)
Pinus ponderosa

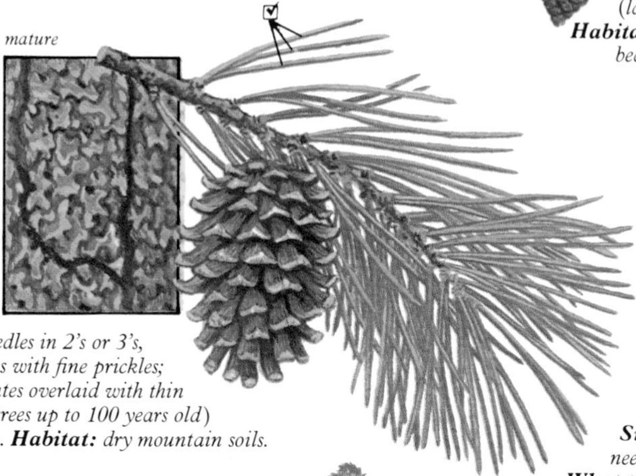

mature

Size: 150–180 ft. tall; needles 4–7 in. long.
What to look for: needles in 2's or 3's, dark yellow-green; cones with fine prickles; bark with large, flat plates overlaid with thin scales, brown to black (trees up to 100 years old) or yellow-brown (older). *Habitat:* dry mountain soils.

Shortleaf Pine
Pinus echinata

Size: 80–100 ft. tall; needles 2½–5 in. long.
What to look for: needles in 2's or 3's, dark green; cones with small prickles; bark almost black, scaly (young) or red-brown with large, flat plates (mature); young twigs green, with purplish tinge. *Habitat:* sandy to dry, gravelly upland soils.

Loblolly Pine
Pinus taeda

Size: 90–110 ft. tall; needles 6–9 in. long.
What to look for: needles in 3's, stiff, yellow-green; cones red-brown, with sharp triangular prickles; bark scaly, nearly black (young) or red-brown (mature); crown open, broad. *Habitat:* sandy river bottoms and swamps to upland clay soils.

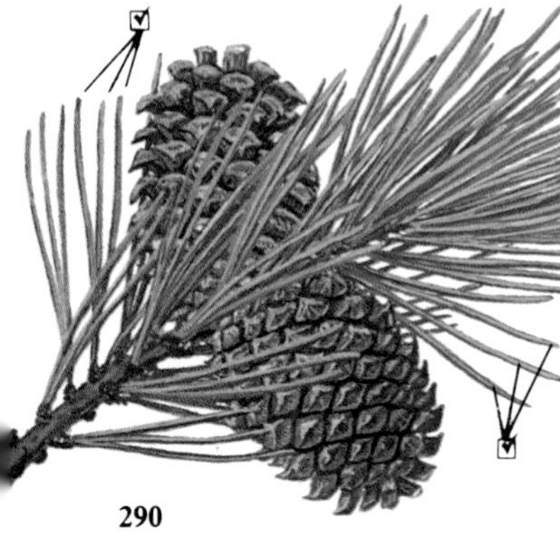

mature

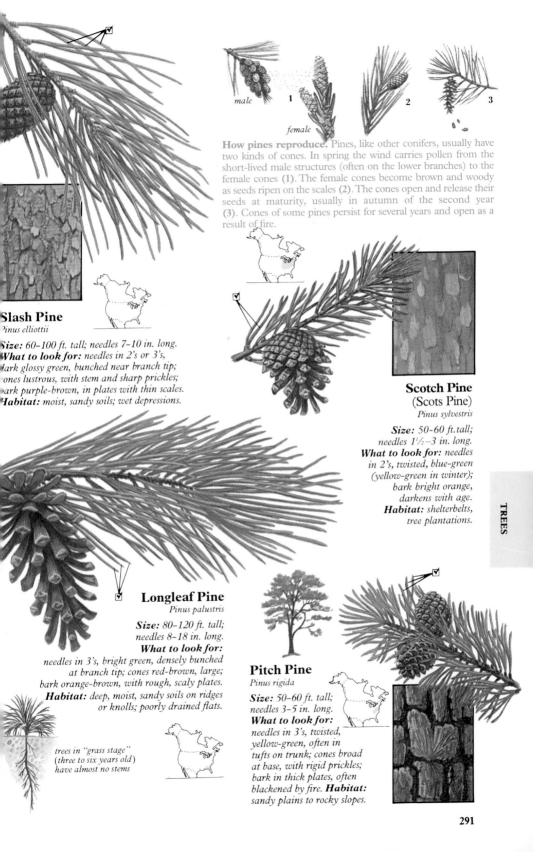

How pines reproduce. Pines, like other conifers, usually have two kinds of cones. In spring the wind carries pollen from the short-lived male structures (often on the lower branches) to the female cones (1). The female cones become brown and woody as seeds ripen on the scales (2). The cones open and release their seeds at maturity, usually in autumn of the second year (3). Cones of some pines persist for several years and open as a result of fire.

Slash Pine
Pinus elliottii

Size: *60–100 ft. tall; needles 7–10 in. long.*
What to look for: *needles in 2's or 3's, dark glossy green, bunched near branch tip; cones lustrous, with stem and sharp prickles; bark purple-brown, in plates with thin scales.*
Habitat: *moist, sandy soils; wet depressions.*

Scotch Pine
(Scots Pine)
Pinus sylvestris

Size: *50–60 ft. tall; needles 1½–3 in. long.*
What to look for: *needles in 2's, twisted, blue-green (yellow-green in winter); bark bright orange, darkens with age.*
Habitat: *shelterbelts, tree plantations.*

Longleaf Pine
Pinus palustris

Size: *80–120 ft. tall; needles 8–18 in. long.*
What to look for: *needles in 3's, bright green, densely bunched at branch tip; cones red-brown, large; bark orange-brown, with rough, scaly plates.*
Habitat: *deep, moist, sandy soils on ridges or knolls; poorly drained flats.*

trees in "grass stage" (three to six years old) have almost no stems

Pitch Pine
Pinus rigida

Size: *50–60 ft. tall; needles 3–5 in. long.*
What to look for: *needles in 3's, twisted, yellow-green, often in tufts on trunk; cones broad at base, with rigid prickles; bark in thick plates, often blackened by fire.* **Habitat:** *sandy plains to rocky slopes.*

TREES

291

Spruces *Picea*

Most of the world's 30 species of spruce share certain characteristics. Generally the needles are sharp and four-sided, and when crushed release a pungent odor. The woody base of the needle remains on the twig when the needle falls, making the twig feel rough to the touch. The mature cones hang down from the branch, in contrast with the erect cones of a fir. And each of the thin, papery scales making up the cone has two seeds, readily eaten by squirrels, crossbills, and other small mammals and birds.

Spruces are typically tall and conical, but soil and climate may alter their pattern of growth. In Alaska and northern Canada frost, wind, and a short growing season stunt the development of Black Spruce; trees more than a hundred years old may measure only 10 feet tall. In the southern Rockies, an Engelmann Spruce may hug the ground, its buds abraded by wind-borne particles.

Often associated in people's minds with northern forests, spruces penetrate south along mountain America–the Engelmann Spruce and the Blue Spruce (*Picea pungens*)–almost reach the Mexican border. (The Blue Spruce is also widely planted as an ornamental.) On eastern mountains the Red Spruce (*Picea rubens*) extends south to the Carolinas.

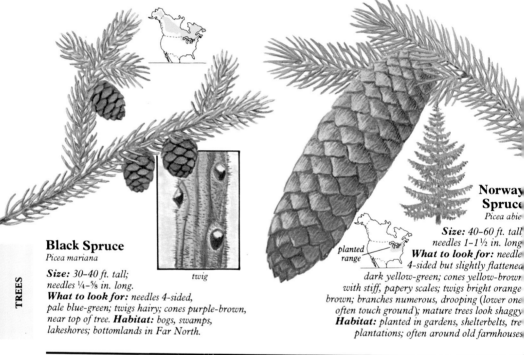

Black Spruce
Picea mariana

Size: 30–40 ft. tall; needles ¼–⅝ in. long.
What to look for: needles 4-sided, pale blue-green; twigs hairy; cones purple-brown, near top of tree. **Habitat:** bogs, swamps, lakeshores; bottomlands in Far North.

twig

Norway Spruce
Picea abie

Size: 40–60 ft. tall needles 1–1½ in. long
What to look for: needle 4-sided but slightly flattened dark yellow-green; cones yellow-brown with stiff, papery scales; twigs bright orange brown; branches numerous, drooping (lower one often touch ground); mature trees look shaggy
Habitat: planted in gardens, shelterbelts, tre plantations; often around old farmhouses

planted range

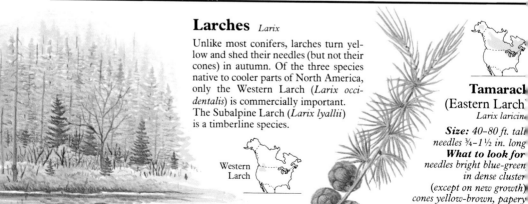

Larches *Larix*

Unlike most conifers, larches turn yellow and shed their needles (but not their cones) in autumn. Of the three species native to cooler parts of North America, only the Western Larch (*Larix occidentalis*) is commercially important. The Subalpine Larch (*Larix lyallii*) is a timberline species.

Western Larch

Tamarack (Eastern Larch)
Larix laricin

Size: 40–80 ft. tall needles ¾–1½ in. long
What to look for needles bright blue-green in dense cluster (except on new growth) cones yellow-brown, papery
Habitat: swamps; bogs upland forests in North

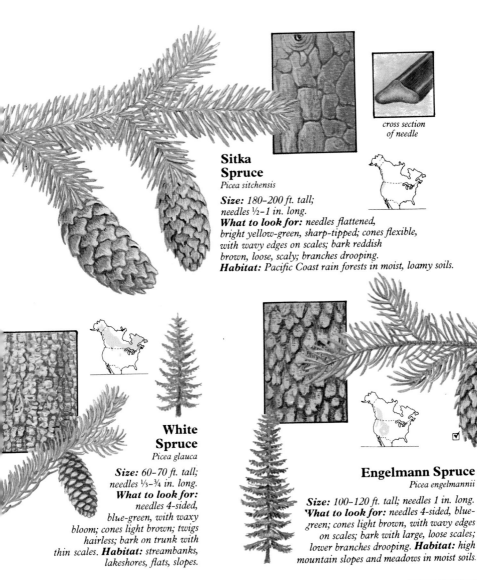

cross section
of needle

Sitka Spruce
Picea sitchensis

Size: *180–200 ft. tall; needles ½–1 in. long.*
What to look for: *needles flattened, bright yellow-green, sharp-tipped; cones flexible, with wavy edges on scales; bark reddish brown, loose, scaly; branches drooping.*
Habitat: *Pacific Coast rain forests in moist, loamy soils.*

White Spruce
Picea glauca

Size: *60–70 ft. tall; needles ⅓–¾ in. long.*
What to look for: *needles 4-sided, blue-green, with waxy bloom; cones light brown; twigs hairless; bark on trunk with thin scales.* **Habitat:** *streambanks, lakeshores, flats, slopes.*

Engelmann Spruce
Picea engelmannii

Size: *100–120 ft. tall; needles 1 in. long.*
What to look for: *needles 4-sided, blue-green; cones light brown, with wavy edges on scales; bark with large, loose scales; lower branches drooping.* **Habitat:** *high mountain slopes and meadows in moist soils.*

TREES

Hemlocks *Tsuga*

The long-lived hemlocks develop slowly in the shade of their forest companions, but in maturity produce such dense shade that few other species can grow beneath the graceful boughs. In the 19th century great forests of Eastern Hemlock were destroyed for the tannin in their bark, but now some of the forests are developing anew. Western Hemlock (*Tsuga heterophylla*) has longer cones and thrives on cool, moist slopes. The Carolina and Mountain hemlocks (*Tsuga caroliniana* and *mertensiana*), species of eastern and western mountains, respectively, have still longer cones.

Western Hemlock

Eastern Hemlock

Eastern Hemlock
Tsuga canadensis

Size: *60–70 ft. tall; needles ⅓–⅔ in. long.*
What to look for: *needles flat, dark green above, whitish below, with short stem; cones small, on tip of branch; crown tip bent away from prevailing wind.*
Habitat: *shady ravines and north-facing slopes in cool, moist soils.*

twig with needle

293

Twigs can help to identify conifers.

• A spruce needle grows from a woody base, which makes the bare twig feel rough.

• Needles on a Douglas-fir narrow at the base, leaving a small, slightly raised scar.

• The stemless needle of a true fir makes a slight depression in the twig, but the twig feels smooth.

True Firs *Abies*

These graceful evergreens, worshipped by ancient Germanic tribes, were the inspiration for the Yuletide song "O Tannenbaum" ("O Christmas Tree"). Indeed, lights on a Christmas tree are thought to be imitations of the snow-covered cone stalks on a fir—the pencillike structures that remain near the tips of branches after the scales have fallen away from the cones. All 40 species of true firs (9 are native to North America) bear upright cones, in contrast with the hanging ones characteristic of most other conifers. True firs grow in cool, moist soils in northern lowland forests, reaching higher elevations farther to the south. The Fraser Fir (*Abies fraseri*) replaces the Balsam Fir in the southern Appalachians; in the West, the purple-coned Subalpine Fir (*Abies lasiocarpa*) grows south to New Mexico and Arizona.

Balsam Fir *Abies balsamea*

Size: *40–60 ft. tall; needles ¾–1½ in. long.*
What to look for: *needles flattened, dark shiny green, all around branch but appearing to be in 2 rows; cones upright, purple-green, resinous; bark dull green, smooth, with resin blisters.* **Habitat:** *swamps to well-drained soils.*

cone stalk

Grand Fir
(Lowland White Fir)
Abies grandis

Size: *140–160 ft. tall; needles 1–2 in. long.*
What to look for: *needles flattened, dark shiny green above, silvery below, in 2 rows; branches bend down slightly but tips curve up.* **Habitat:** *stream valleys, gentle mountain slopes.*

needle length varies on lower branches

White Fir *Abies concolor*

Size: *130–150 ft. tall; needles 2–3 in. long.*
What to look for: *needles flattened, silvery blue turned up like hairbrush; cones upright in top of tree; lower branches slant down.* **Habitat:** *high mountain slopes (usually north facing) in well drained soils.*

mature

young

California Red Fir
Abies magnifica

Size: *150–180 ft. tall; needles ¾–1½ in. long.*
What to look for: *needles flattened, silvery blue to dark green, curved upward; cones upright, purple-brown; bark smooth, whitish (young) or deeply furrowed and red-brown (mature).* **Habitat:** *ravines, high mountain slopes.*

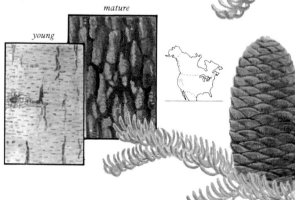

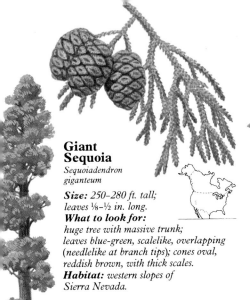

Giant Sequoia
Sequoiadendron giganteum

Size: *250–280 ft. tall; leaves ⅛–½ in. long.*
What to look for: *huge tree with massive trunk; leaves blue-green, scalelike, overlapping (needlelike at branch tips); cones oval, reddish brown, with thick scales.*
Habitat: *western slopes of Sierra Nevada.*

Giant Sequoias
Sequoiadendron

Although some sequoias are more than 3,000 years old, some Bristlecone Pines are still older. Redwoods are taller. But no trees grow more massive than the Giant Sequoias, or Bigtrees, which can measure more than 100 feet around at the base.

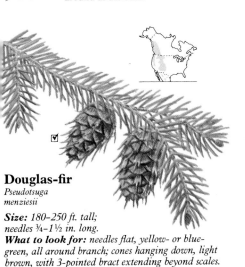

Douglas-fir
Pseudotsuga menziesii

Size: *180–250 ft. tall; needles ¾–1½ in. long.*
What to look for: *needles flat, yellow- or blue-green, all around branch; cones hanging down, light brown, with 3-pointed bract extending beyond scales.*
Habitat: *sea level to mountain slopes in moist, well-drained loam.*

Douglas-firs *Pseudotsuga*

Rivaling the Redwood in height, the Douglas-fir grows tall and straight in moist coastal areas but occurs elsewhere in a very different form. Trees in the Rockies grow only about a third as tall, and their needles usually have a blue rather than a yellow cast. The *Douglas* in the name refers to David Douglas, a 19th-century botanical explorer.

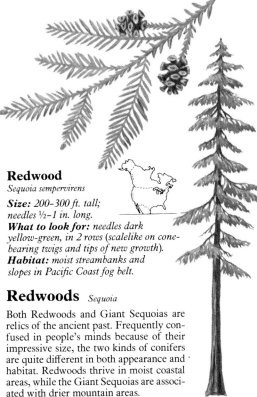

Redwood
Sequoia sempervirens

Size: *200–300 ft. tall; needles ½–1 in. long.*
What to look for: *needles dark yellow-green, in 2 rows (scalelike on cone-bearing twigs and tips of new growth).*
Habitat: *moist streambanks and slopes in Pacific Coast fog belt.*

Redwoods *Sequoia*

Both Redwoods and Giant Sequoias are relics of the ancient past. Frequently confused in people's minds because of their impressive size, the two kinds of conifers are quite different in both appearance and habitat. Redwoods thrive in moist coastal areas, while the Giant Sequoias are associated with drier mountain areas.

Baldcypresses *Taxodium*

Typically festooned with Spanish Moss, the Baldcypress has "knees" arising from the root system. Their function remains a matter of speculation. The tree is unusual in habit as well as appearance; though a conifer, it sheds its leaves in autumn. Its close relative, the Montezuma Baldcypress (*Taxodium mucronatum*), is evergreen.

Baldcypress
Taxodium distichum

Size: *100–120 ft. tall; needles ½–¾ in. long.*
What to look for: *needles in 2 rows, flat, yellow-green (summer) or red-brown (fall); trunk broad at base, often surrounded by bark-covered "knees."*
Habitat: *swamps to seasonally flooded bottomlands.*

Western Redcedar
(Giant Arborvitae)
Thuja plicata

Size: *150–200 ft. tall; leaves about 1 in. long.*
What to look for:
leaves scalelike, overlapping, shiny, dark yellow-green, in drooping fernlike sprays; cones light brown, with opposing leathery scales.
Habitat: *moist flats and slopes, riverbanks, bogs, swamps.*

Thujas *Thuja*

Sometimes called arborvitae ("tree of life"), thujas are known to live for several hundred years, their lacy boughs and scalelike foliage supplying deer with shelter and browse. Both North American species, as well as their Oriental relatives, are widely cultivated as ornamentals. Northern White-cedar supplies lumber for fences, rustic furniture, and planking for small boats; Western Redcedar, shingles and siding.

Northern White-cedar
(Eastern Arborvitae)
Thuja occidentalis

Size: *40–50 ft. tall; leaves ⅛–¼ in. long.*
What to look for:
leaves scalelike, overlapping, dull green, in flat fanlike sprays, with raised resin glands on underside; cones tan, with opposing woody scales. **Habitat:** *limestone bluffs and outcrops; fields, bogs, swamps.*

Junipers *Juniperus*

Junipers are a diverse group, as their shapes and sizes suggest; the 13 North American species range from the ground-hugging Creeping Juniper (*Juniperus horizontalis*) to the pyramidal Eastern Redcedar. Capable of growing almost anywhere except in wet soil, junipers often thrive in areas where other trees cannot grow or have not yet become established. Such species as the Utah Juniper and the Oneseed Juniper (*Juniperus monosperma*) supply welcome visual relief on dry western slopes; the Eastern Redcedar and Common Juniper invade abandoned fields and serve as pioneers, creating an environment hospitable to the growth of broad-leaved trees. Cedar chests are made from the fragrant wood of the Eastern Redcedar; the "berries" (technically considered cones) of the Common Juniper are used as flavoring in gin.

Common Juniper
(Dwarf Juniper)
Juniperus communis

Size: *1–3 ft. tall; leaves ⅓ in. long.*
What to look for:
leaves in whorls of 3, needlelike, whitish above; fruits berrylike, dark blue, with whitish powder; occasionally tree-size, but usually a sprawling shrub.
Habitat: *abandoned fields; sandy to rocky flats and slopes.*

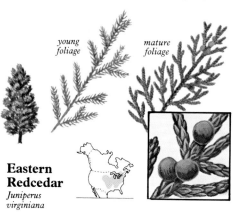

young foliage   *mature foliage*

Eastern Redcedar
Juniperus virginiana

Size: *40–50 ft. tall; leaves 1/16–¼ in. long.*
What to look for: *leaves overlapping, dark green, scalelike (*mature*) or needlelike (*young*); cones berrylike, dark blue, with waxy bloom; crown may be narrowly or broadly pyramidal.*
Habitat: *abandoned fields in poor, dry soils.*

Utah Juniper
(Bigberry Juniper)
Juniperus osteosperma

Size: *10–30 ft. tall; leaves 1/16 in. long.*
What to look for: *leaves overlapping, scalelike, yellow-green, on stout twigs; cones berrylike, brownish, with waxy bloom; trunk short,.often with many branches.*
Habitat: *flats, slopes, mesas in poor, dry soils.*

White-cedars *Chamaecyparis*

As the qualifying adjective "white" suggests, these trees are not considered true cedars. (True cedars, closely related to the pines, are not native to North America.) White-cedars are also called false cypresses—an example of the confusing nomenclature within the cypress family, which includes all the trees on this page and the one opposite except the Ginkgo.

Atlantic White-cedar
(Southern White-cedar)
Chamaecyparis thyoides

Size: 80–85 ft. tall; leaves about ⅛ in. long.
What to look for: leaves scalelike, overlapping, dark blue-green, with raised resin glands; cones round, bluish purple, with waxy bloom; bark gray, with narrow, flat-topped ridges.
Habitat: peat swamps, bogs.

Port-Orford-cedar
(Lawson Cypress)
Chamaecyparis lawsoniana

Size: 140–180 ft. tall; leaves ¹⁄₁₆ in. long.
What to look for: leaves overlapping, scalelike, bright yellow- to blue-green; branches lacy, pendulous; cones red-brown, with waxy bloom.
Habitat: moist valleys and slopes to dry ridges.

Cypresses *Cupressus*

In southern California and other arid regions of the West, seven species of this drought-resistant group endure fires, parched soil, and, in some cases, saltwater spray. Their leaves are tiny, coated with wax, and composed of thickened cells with sunken stomates (breathing pores)—all adaptations to a dry environment.

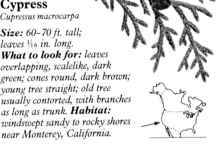

Arizona Cypress
Cupressus arizonica

Size: 50–60 ft. tall; leaves ¹⁄₁₆ in. long.
What to look for: leaves overlapping, scalelike, pale blue-green; cones round, reddish brown, with 6 or 8 pointed scales.
Habitat: canyons and mountain slopes in moist to dry soils.

Monterey Cypress
Cupressus macrocarpa

Size: 60–70 ft. tall; leaves ¹⁄₁₆ in. long.
What to look for: leaves overlapping, scalelike, dark green; cones round, dark brown; young tree straight; old tree usually contorted, with branches as long as trunk. **Habitat:** windswept sandy to rocky shores near Monterey, California.

TREES

Ginkgoes *Ginkgo*

Fossils reveal that many different kinds of ginkgoes existed in the geological past. Today only one species remains, and it too might have become extinct had it not been planted in the temple gardens of China and Japan. Native to the Orient, the Ginkgo is a popular ornamental tree because of its resistance to insects, disease, and pollution.

Ginkgo
(Maidenhair Tree)
Ginkgo biloba

Size: 30–50 ft. tall; leaves 2–3 in. wide.
What to look for: leaves fan-shaped, leathery, yellow to dark green, with veins fanning from narrow end; fruits fleshy, yellow.
Habitat: city streets and parks.

Asiminas *Asimina*

Large fleshy fruits, showy flowers, and pungent leaves and twigs characterize the asiminas. They belong to the chiefly tropical custard-apple family, whose name aptly describes the edible fruit of the Pawpaw. The other seven native asiminas are low shrubs or small trees that grow in the shade of taller hardwoods, mostly in the Southeast and Gulf Coast regions.

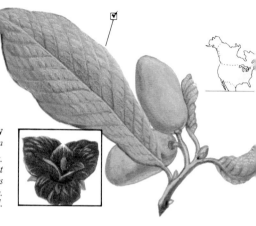

Pawpaw
Asimina triloba

Size: *10–30 ft. tall; leaves 5–10 in. long.*
What to look for: *leaves narrow at base, widest at midpoint; flowers with 6 purplish petals; fruits fleshy, greenish yellow to brown; tree may be shrubby.*
Habitat: *bottomlands in rich, moist soil.*

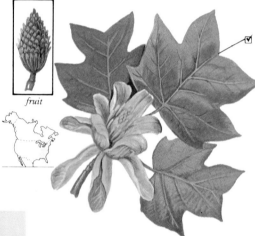

fruit

Yellow-poplars *Liriodendron*

The Tuliptree is one of the tallest, straightest eastern broad-leaved trees, and its trunk is among the largest in diameter. Its tulip-shaped blossoms, borne high above the ground, are camouflaged by the green on the outer petals; only when the blossoms fall prematurely are the bright inner petals revealed. The tree has one living relative, the Chinese Tuliptree (*Liriodendron chinense*).

Tuliptree
(Yellow-poplar)
Liriodendron tulipifera

Size: *100–120 ft. tall; leaves 4–6 in. long.*
What to look for: *leaves 4-lobed, with deeply notched tip, shiny, bright green; flowers tuliplike, green and orange; fruits conelike, tan, remaining on tree after leaves drop.*
Habitat: *moist but well-drained sandy to stony loam.*

Magnolias
Magnolia

Magnolialike fossils more than 70 million years old indicate the ancient lineage of these beautiful trees. In fact, one major classification system for plants is based on the premise that magnolias were the ancestors of all other flowering plants. According to this theory, they were the first plants to bear seeds in a protective ovary, or fruit (pine and other conifer seeds are "naked"). Magnolias cultivated for their pinkish blossoms in early spring are a hybrid of two Chinese species.

Southern Magnolia
(Evergreen Magnolia)
Magnolia grandiflora

Size: *60–80 ft. tall; leaves 5–8 in. long.*
What to look for: *leaves oval, leathery, evergreen, with dense rusty hairs on underside; flowers large, fragrant, with 6–12 white petals.*
Habitat: *rich, well-drained bottomlands.*

underside of leaf

Sassafras
Sassafras albidum

Size: *30–40 ft. tall;*
leaves 3–5 in. long.
What to look for: *leaves*
oval, 3-lobed, or mitten-
shaped; twigs bright green, aromatic
when crushed; fruits blue, berrylike;
stump and roots sprout readily.
Habitat: *well-drained old fields*
and woods; often in hedgerows.

Sassafrases   *Sassafras*

The one North American tree in this group (often a shrub in the North) has aromatic twigs and leaves. The root bark makes a spicy tea, once imbibed as a tonic. Bees favor the nectar of the blossoms, and birds the glossy fruits.

California-laurels   *Umbellularia*

A large tree in Oregon, the single species in this group is a low-growing shrub in southern California, where it is flattened by wind and salt spray. Like other members of the aromatic laurel family, including Sassafras and Spicebush, it produces highly volatile oils with a pleasing odor.

California-laurel
(Oregon-myrtle)
Umbellularia californica

Size: *40–80 ft. tall;*
leaves 2–5 in. long.
What to look for: *leaves*
elliptical, evergreen,
with odor of camphor when
crushed; fruits yellow-green.
Habitat: *rich bottomlands*
to dry rocky slopes and bluffs.

Sycamore
(Planetree)
Platanus occidentalis

Size: *80–100 ft. tall;*
leaves 4–7 in. wide.
What to look for: *leaves*
wide, large-toothed, with
3–5 shallow lobes; fruits
round, bristly; bark mottled,
peeling in irregular flakes.
Habitat: *bottomlands in*
rich, moist soil.

Sycamores   *Platanus*

With their buttonball fruits and mottled bark, sycamores attract attention wherever they grow. In nature they usually prosper along a stream; for example, the California Sycamore (*Platanus racemosa*) thrives on mountain streambanks. But cities also have their sycamore—the London Planetree, a cross between the Sycamore and the Oriental Planetree (*Platanus orientalis*). The seed balls of the Sycamore hang singly from the twig; the London Plane's often occur in twos and threes; and the California Sycamore has up to seven on a threadlike stem.

Cucumbertree
(Cucumber Magnolia)
Magnolia acuminata

Size: *80–90 ft. tall;*
leaves 6–10 in. long.
What to look for: *leaves broadly*
elliptical, pointed at tip, yellow-
green above, light green below;
flowers pale yellow-green; seeds red,
hanging by slender threads from fruit.
Habitat: *gentle slopes and stream*
valleys in moist, rich soil.

fruit

Sweetbay
(Swamp Magnolia)
Magnolia virginiana

Size: *40–60 ft. tall;*
leaves 3–5 in. long.
What to look for: *leaves elliptical,*
shiny bright green above, whitish
below, persisting through winter in
South; flowers creamy white.
Habitat: *edges of swamps*
and moist lowlands
on coastal plain.

TREES

299

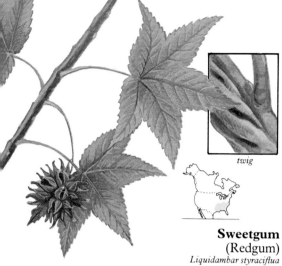

twig

Hackberry
Celtis occidentalis

Size: *30–40 ft. tall; leaves 2½–4 in. long.*
What to look for: *leaves oval, toothed, with curved tip and lopsided base; bark gray, with corky ridges; fruits dark purple; clusters of distorted twigs near branch tips.*
Habitat: *rich bottomlands to limestone outcrops.*

witches' brooms

Sweetgum
(Redgum)
Liquidambar styraciflua

Size: *80–120 ft. tall; leaves 6–7 in. wide.*
What to look for: *leaves star-shaped, with 5–7 points; fruits round, woody, with stout spines, remaining on tree in winter; twigs with corky projections.* **Habitat:** *rich bottomlands, swamps.*

Sweetgums *Liquidambar*

Oozing from wounds in the trunk of a Sweetgum is a fragrant but bitter-tasting resin, used in times past as a chewing gum and a treatment for skin disorders and dysentery. The leaves of the single North American species yield a pleasant odor when crushed, and they turn a spectacular red in fall. Although they might be mistaken for maple leaves, they do not grow in pairs.

Hackberries *Celtis*

The Hackberry has one very conspicuous feature distorted clusters of short twigs ("witches' brooms" caused by mites that inject a growth-retarding sub stance into the leaf buds. The Sugarberry (*Celt laevigata*), a tree of the Mississippi River valley an the Southeast, closely resembles the Hackberry ex cept for its sweet reddish-orange or yellow fruit.

Elms *Ulmus*

In the 1920's a fungus believed to have originated in Asia (Asian species are resistant) killed millions of elms in northern Europe. Carried by bark beetles, Dutch elm disease struck eastern North America in the 1930's. Sweeping westward, it has affected all six native elms. The graceful, vaseshaped American Elm is the most widespread species. The other wide-ranging species, the Slippery Elm (*Ulmus rubra*), has a similar appearance when viewed from a distance, but its twigs and fruits are distinctly different.

Winged Elm
(Wahoo)
Ulmus alata

Size: *30–40 ft. tall; leaves 2 in. long.*
What to look for: *leaves elliptical, toothed, in 2 rows in same plane; twigs with corky projections (wings).*
Habitat: *dry, gravelly uplands to rich, moist bottomlands.*

American Elm
(White Elm)
Ulmus americana

Size: *50–60 ft. tall; leaves 4–6 in. long.*
What to look for: *leaves broadly elliptical, with parallel veins and toothed edges; seed surrounded by thin, hairy collar notched at tip; twigs gray, with chestnut-brown buds (winter); crown arched, spreading.*
Habitat: *bottomlands to moist uplands.*

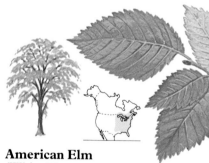

American Elm

twig with buds

fruit

Slippery Elm

twig with buds

fruit

Osage-orange
Maclura pomifera

Size: *30–40 ft. tall; leaves 3–5 in. long.*
What to look for: *leaves broadly lance-shaped, shiny dark green above; stout spines on twigs; fruits yellow-green, nubbly; bark furrowed, shreddy.*
Habitat: *rich bottomlands; planted in hedgerows and shelterbelts.*

Osage-oranges *Maclura*

Native to the south-central states, the Osage-orange was widely planted in the 1930's as a shelterbelt and hedge tree, and now grows wild in many parts of the East. Many people consider it a pest because of its thorny twigs and messy (but attractive) fruit, which exudes a milky sap when bruised.

Red Mulberry
Morus rubra

Size: *20–30 ft. tall; leaves 3–5 in. long.*
What to look for: *leaves oval, mitten-shaped, or 3-lobed, coarsely toothed, hairy below; fruits dark red to purple.* **Habitat:** *bottomlands and gentle slopes in rich, moist soil.*

Mulberries *Morus*

With fruits and leaves relished by man and silkworms respectively, these rapidly growing, drought-resistant trees have been transplanted around the world. Crusaders took the Black Mulberry (*Morus nigra*) from the eastern Mediterranean to the British Isles; the Pilgrims brought it to the New World, where it now reproduces in the wild. White Mulberry (*Morus alba*) is also an escape; Red Mulberry is a native tree. All are named for the commonest color of their fruit.

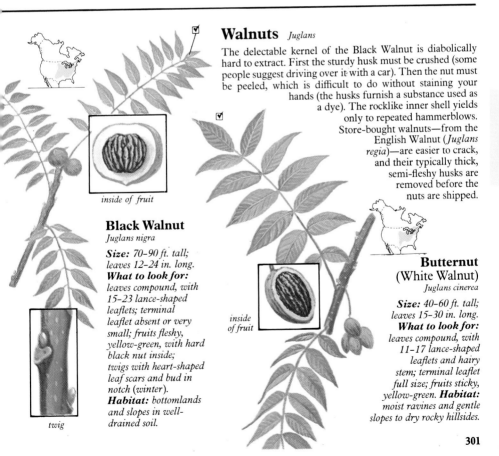

inside of fruit

Walnuts *Juglans*

The delectable kernel of the Black Walnut is diabolically hard to extract. First the sturdy husk must be crushed (some people suggest driving over it with a car). Then the nut must be peeled, which is difficult to do without staining your hands (the husks furnish a substance used as a dye). The rocklike inner shell yields only to repeated hammerblows. Store-bought walnuts—from the English Walnut (*Juglans regia*)—are easier to crack, and their typically thick, semi-fleshy husks are removed before the nuts are shipped.

TREES

Black Walnut
Juglans nigra

Size: *70–90 ft. tall; leaves 12–24 in. long.*
What to look for: *leaves compound, with 15–23 lance-shaped leaflets; terminal leaflet absent or very small; fruits fleshy, yellow-green, with hard black nut inside; twigs with heart-shaped leaf scars and bud in notch (winter).*
Habitat: *bottomlands and slopes in well-drained soil.*

twig

inside of fruit

Butternut
(White Walnut)
Juglans cinerea

Size: *40–60 ft. tall; leaves 15–30 in. long.*
What to look for: *leaves compound, with 11–17 lance-shaped leaflets and hairy stem; terminal leaflet full size; fruits sticky, yellow-green.* **Habitat:** *moist ravines and gentle slopes to dry rocky hillsides.*

Hickories *Carya*

Close relatives of the walnuts, hickories have fewer leaflets per leaf, slimmer twigs, catkins hanging three from a stem, and husks that split in four sections when the nuts are ripe. (Walnut catkins are single or in pairs; the fruit husks do not split at maturity.) Hickory nuts are smooth (sometimes with four or six ribs) and generally edible, although some are bitter and others so small as to be hardly worth the trouble of cracking. In the wild, the various kinds of hickory hybridize quite freely, resulting in a wide variety of growth forms that challenge even the expert at identification. Hickory wood is tough, making excellent tool handles and firewood.

twig with buds

inside of fruit

male catkins at base of unfolding leaves

fruit

Shagbark Hickory
Carya ovata

Size: *70–80 ft. tall; leaves 10–14 in. long.*
What to look for: *leaves compound, with 5 elliptical, finely toothed leaflets (upper 3 are much larger than lower 2); bark with long, loose strips curving away from trunk; fruits nearly round, green, with thick, woody husk and thin-shelled nut.*
Habitat: *moist bottomlands to upland slopes.*

Bitternut Hickory
Carya cordiformis

Size: *50–60 ft. tall; leaves 7–13 in. long.*
What to look for: *leaves compound, with 7–11 leaflets in pairs gradually decreasing in size from apex; buds yellow hairy; fruits with thin, scaly husks splitting part way into 4 sections, and gray- or red-brown bitter tasting nuts.* **Habitat:** *bottomlands with well drained soil; streambanks, swamps, dry uplands.*

Mockernut Hickory
Carya tomentosa

Size: *40–60 ft. tall; leaves 9–14 in. long.*
What to look for: *leaves compound, with 7–9 finely toothed leaflets, densely haired below; fruits nearly round, with thick brown husk and small nuts.* **Habitat:** *moist uplands to dry, sandy slopes and ridges.*

Pecan
Carya illinoensis

Size: *110–140 ft. tall; leaves 12–20 in. long.*
What to look for: *leaves compound, with 9–17 broadly lance-shaped, finely toothed leaflets; nuts in clusters of 3–12, dark brown, surrounded by thin husks that split in 4.* **Habitat:** *bottomlands in rich, well-drained soil.*

fruit

inside of fruit

Beeches *Fagus*

Patriarch of the eastern hardwood forest, the American Beech is the only North American plant in this primarily Eurasian group, whose thin gray bark and papery leaves are unmistakable. A peculiarity of this tree is that the dead leaves may stay on it all winter, twisting and rustling in the wind.

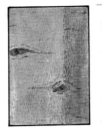

fruit

American Beech *Fagus grandifolia*

Size: *70-80 ft. tall; leaves 2½-5 in. long.*
What to look for: *leaves elliptical, with sharp, widely spaced teeth; bark smooth, light gray; fruits with spiny husk and 2-3 triangular nuts; buds long, slender.*
Habitat: *bottomlands and gentle slopes.*

bud

Chinkapins *Castanopsis*

The Giant Chinkapin is only occasionally giant-size (it is a shrub in Washington); the Sierra Chinkapin (*Castanopsis sempervirens*) is a low-growing timberline species. Neither should be confused with the Allegheny Chinkapin, which is a chestnut.

Giant Chinkapin
Castanopsis chrysophylla

Size: *60-80 ft. tall; leaves 2-6 in. long.*
What to look for: *leaves lance-shaped, evergreen, leathery, yellow below, with edges rolled under; fruits spiny, with 1-2 nuts.* **Habitat:** *moist valleys to dry slopes.*

Tanoaks *Lithocarpus*

Although tanoaks have oaklike leaves and fruits, their blossoms resemble those of chestnuts and chinkapins (the flower clusters are upright rather than hanging). The single North American species was formerly used as a source of tannin.

acorn

Tanoak
Lithocarpus densiflorus

Size: *70-90 ft. tall; leaves 3-5 in. long.*
What to look for: *leaves evergreen, leathery, rusty below (turning white toward fall), sometimes with widely spaced teeth; acorn with hairy cup.* **Habitat:** *bottomlands to gentle slopes in moist soil.*

Chestnuts *Castanea*

Today's chestnuts roasting on an open fire are from Spanish Chestnut trees (*Castanea sativa*). The once common American Chestnut was virtually exterminated by a fungus blight, which is believed to have been brought from Asia about 1900. Although sprouts still develop from tree stumps, nearly all die before bearing fruit.

sprouts from stump

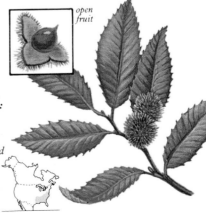

open fruit

American Chestnut
Castanea dentata

Size: *10 ft. tall (formerly 70-90 ft.); leaves 5½-8 in. long.*
What to look for: *leaves lance-shaped, with sharp, incurved teeth; 1-5 sprouts from old stump.* **Habitat:** *gently rolling country with sandy loam to rocky hillsides.*

Allegheny Chinkapin
Castanea pumila

Size: *5-15 ft. tall; leaves 3-5 in. long.*
What to look for: *leaves elliptical, whitish and hairy below, with widely spaced bristle-tipped teeth; fruits spiny, with single nut.*
Habitat: *dry woods and thickets.*

303

Northern Red Oak

Quercus rubra

Size: *60–80 ft. tall; leaves 5–8 in. long.*
What to look for: *leaves lustrous green above and below, with 7–11 evenly spaced, bristle-tipped lobes; acorns oval, with shallow, hairy cup; bark gray to reddish brown, with vertical fissures and flat-topped ridges.* **Habitat:** *bottomlands, slopes, and uplands on well-drained loam.*

Oaks *Quercus*

Of all the broad-leaved trees in North America, oaks are the most widespread, occupy the greatest variety of habitats, and comprise the largest number of species (58 trees and 10 shrubs). The leaves on a single tree may come in many shapes, and the species hybridize freely, adding to the complexity of identification. Pinpointing the species of oak is easiest if the tree is first classified into one of two groups—the red oaks (pages 304–305) or the white oaks (page 306). Red oaks bear tiny bristles at the tip of the leaf, at the ends of the lobes, or both. Their bitter acorns require two years to mature (they therefore remain on the trees in winter), and woolly hairs line the cup. The leaves of white oaks have rounded lobes devoid of bristles. Their sweet acorns mature in six months (and are gone by winter), and the inner wall of the cup is smooth.

Individual species of oak can be identified by their leaves (shape and sometimes color) and fruits, or acorns. The acorns are shown here life-size. In winter, when little other food is available, acorns are a staple in the diet of many birds and mammals—among others, ducks, grouse, quail, Turkeys, jays, titmice, woodpeckers, and bears, Raccoons, squirrels, and deer. Such animals may help propagate oaks by dispersing, storing, and then never reclaiming the acorns. A sprouting acorn develops full-sized leaves and unusually long roots, giving the seedling an advantage in the race toward maturity.

autumn leaf

acorn

old bark

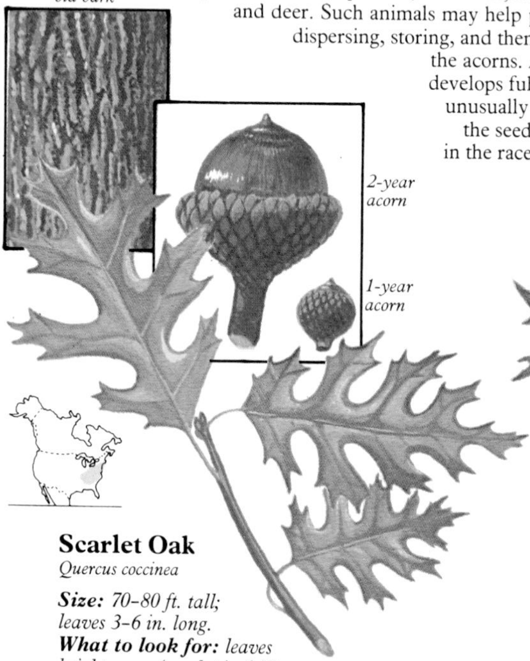

2-year acorn

1-year acorn

hairs on underside

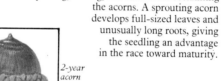

Scarlet Oak

Quercus coccinea

Size: *70–80 ft. tall; leaves 3–6 in. long.*
What to look for: *leaves bright green (scarlet in fall), with 7–9 deeply cut (almost to midvein) bristle-tipped lobes; acorns oval, with deep cup and concentric rings around tip; bark light gray-brown and smooth (young) or dark brown to black with shallow fissures and irregular ridges (mature).*
Habitat: *dry sandy to gravelly soils.*

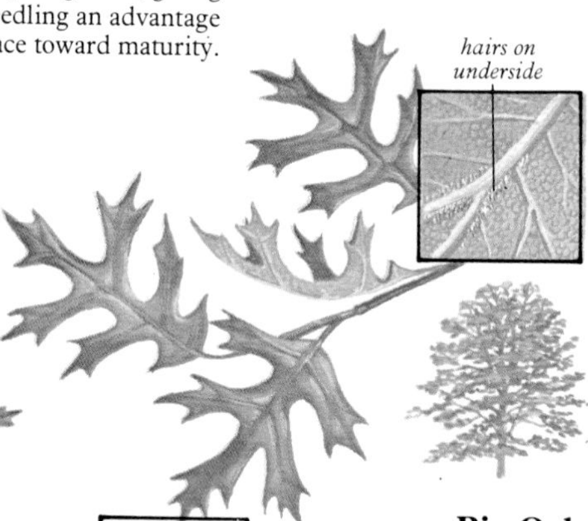

Pin Oak
(Swamp Oak)

Quercus palustris

acorn

Size: *70–80 ft. tall; leaves 3–5 in. long.*
What to look for: *leaves 5-lobed (occasionally 7 or 9), deeply cut, bristle-tipped, with tufts of hair on underside; acorns round, with shallow cup; tree with many small branches and downward-hanging lower limbs.*
Habitat: *wet bottomlands.*

Willow Oak
(Peach Oak)
Quercus phellos

Size: *80–100 ft. tall; leaves 2–5 in. long.*
What to look for: *leaves narrowly lance-shaped, shiny light green above, gray-green below; acorns almost round, with thin cups.* **Habitat:** *rich bottomlands; poorly drained flats; moist uplands.*

acorn

acorn

Blackjack Oak
(Barren Oak)
Quercus marilandica

Size: *20–30 ft. tall; leaves 3–7 in. long.*
What to look for: *leathery, wedge-shaped, 3-lobed leaves, with brownish to rusty hairs on underside; cup covers half of acorn.*
Habitat: *dry sandy flatlands to barren rocky slopes.*

Coast Live Oak
Quercus agrifolia

Size: *60–90 ft. tall; leaves ¾–3 in. long.*
What to look for: *leaves evergreen, elliptical, leathery, with spiny teeth and edges that tend to roll under; acorns slender, with scaly cup.* **Habitat:** *dry valleys, canyons, slopes.*

acorn

California Black Oak
Quercus kelloggii

Size: *50–60 ft. tall; leaves 4–10 in. long.*
What to look for: *leaves yellow-green, with 7 (occasionally 9) bristle-tipped lobes; acorns elongated, with deep cup.*
Habitat: *dry lower mountain slopes, canyons, and grasslands.*

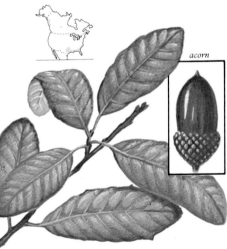

acorn

Live Oak
Quercus virginiana

Size: *40–50 ft. tall; leaves 2–5 in. long.*
What to look for:
leaves elliptical, without lobes, semi-evergreen, leathery, glossy dark green above, pale green and hairy below; acorns shiny, dark brown (almost black); tree often wider than it is tall (shrubby near coast).
Habitat: *coastal sand plains and dunes to inland sand flats in dry to wet soil.*

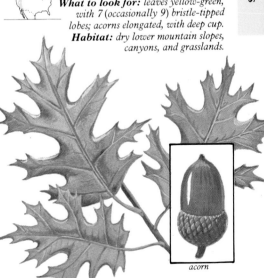

acorn

305

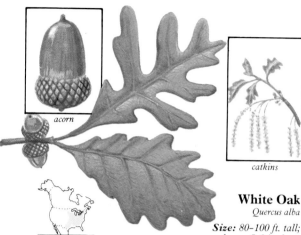

acorn

catkins

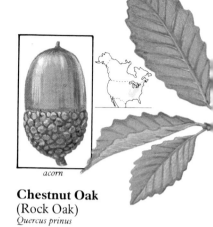

acorn

White Oak
Quercus alba

Size: *80–100 ft. tall;
leaves 5–9 in. long.*
What to look for: *leaves bright green above, pale
green below, with 7–9 rounded major lobes (clefts between
lobes may be deep or shallow); acorn cup shallow, with
knobby scales.* **Habitat:** *riverbanks; moist valleys
to sandy plains and dry hillsides.*

Chestnut Oak
(Rock Oak)
Quercus prinus

Size: *50–60 ft. tall; leaves 4–8 in. long.*
What to look for: *leaves elliptical, with
17–21 shallow lobes, lustrous yellow-green
above, pale green and finely haired below;
acorns shiny, with thin cup and long stem.*
Habitat: *dry sandy uplands to rocky ridges;
valleys with well-drained soil.*

Valley Oak
(California
White Oak)
Quercus lobata

acorn

Size: *70–100 ft. tall;
leaves 2½–4 in. long.*
What to look for: *leaves dark
green above, gray-green and hairy
below, with 7–11 rounded, deeply cut
lobes; acorns long, tapering to point,
with bowllike knobby cup; tree massive.*
Habitat: *rich valleys to dry
gravelly hillsides.*

Bur Oak
(Mossycup Oak)
Quercus macrocarpa

Size: *70–80 ft. tall; leaves 6–12 in. long.*
What to look for: *leaves large, wedge-shaped, with
deep (almost to midrib) indentations near center;
acorn cup deep, fringed with stout hairs.* **Habitat:**
moist bottomlands (East) to dry grasslands (Midwest).

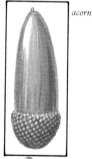

Post Oak *Quercus stellata*

Size: *40–50 ft. tall; leaves 4–6 in. long.*
What to look for: *leaves broadly
cross-shaped,
leathery, dark
green, with gray
to yellow hairs
on underside.*
Habitat:
*dry sandy or
gravelly uplands
and plains; rocky
ridges and hills;
riverbanks in
loam.*

acorn

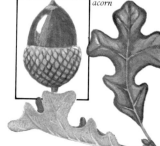

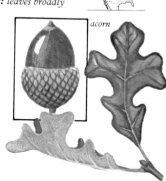

Bur
Oak

Overcup Oak
(*Quercus lyrata*)
has similar leaves

Birches *Betula*

Thin, often shreddy bark and fine-toothed oval leaves mark the 12 birch representatives (7 trees and 5 shrubs) in North America. Birches are a special delight in winter, when their decorative bark adds color and texture to the snowy landscape. Wintertime birches have another conspicuous feature—dangling clusters of flowers (catkins), which will open and release pollen in spring. After pollination, the female flowers develop into conelike fruits with winged nutlets. Scattered by the wind, the seeds do especially well if they land on mineral soils exposed by fire or deposited by a stream or glacier. Many birches are pioneer trees—species that grow rapidly on bare soil, offer shade to the next wave of invaders (often conifers), and die at an early age. The silvery barked Yellow Birch (*Betula alleghaniensis*) is an exception. It is tolerant of shade and thrives among the beeches and maples of eastern forests.

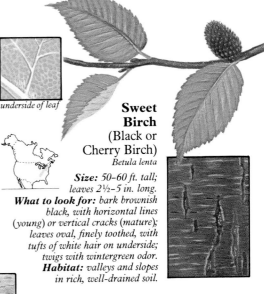

underside of leaf

Sweet Birch
(Black or Cherry Birch)
Betula lenta

Size: 50–60 ft. tall; leaves 2½–5 in. long.
What to look for: bark brownish black, with horizontal lines (young) or vertical cracks (mature); leaves oval, finely toothed, with tufts of white hair on underside; twigs with wintergreen odor.
Habitat: valleys and slopes in rich, well-drained soil.

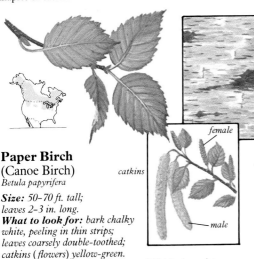

Paper Birch
(Canoe Birch)
Betula papyrifera

female

catkins

male

Size: 50–70 ft. tall; leaves 2–3 in. long.
What to look for: bark chalky white, peeling in thin strips; leaves coarsely double-toothed; catkins (flowers) yellow-green.
Habitat: streambanks, lakeshores, hillsides in moist, sandy soil; often grows in burned-over areas.

River Birch
(Red Birch)
Betula nigra

Size: 70–80 ft. tall; leaves 1½–3 in. long.
What to look for: leaves oval, with coarsely double-toothed edges and wedge-shaped base; bark pale red-brown with papery scales and horizontal lines (young) or dark red-brown to gray with thick scales (mature).
Habitat: streambanks, wet woods.

TREES

Alders *Alnus*

Alders add fertility to soils, for bacteria living on their roots "fix" nitrogen from the air and turn it into nutrients for other plants. Red Alder is the only large tree of the group in North America; others are shrubs or small trees. Alders commonly form tangled thickets along the water's edge. Even in winter they are recognizable by their fleshy buds and miniature woody cones.

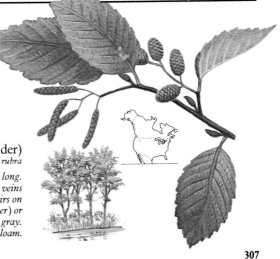

Red Alder (Oregon Alder)
Alnus rubra

Size: 80–130 ft. tall; leaves 3–6 in. long.
What to look for: leaves oval, with sunken veins on upper surface, gray-green with reddish hairs on underside; fruits conelike, green (summer) or red-brown (fall); bark gray.
Habitat: bottomlands and gentle slopes in moist loam.

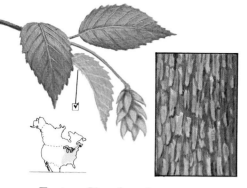

Eastern Hop-hornbeam
Ostrya virginiana

Size: *30–40 ft. tall; leaves 2½–4½ in. long.*
What to look for: *leaves oval, double-toothed, with tufts of yellow hair on lower midrib; fruits bladderlike, light brown, in clusters; mature bark in narrow strips curling away from trunk.* **Habitat:** *hillsides and ridges with gravelly soils.*

Hop-hornbeams   *Ostrya*

Small bladderlike fruits resembling the hops used by brewers characterize the hop-hornbeams. The Eastern Hop-hornbeam, the only widespread North American species in this small group, is also known as Ironwood or Leverwood. Its tough, resilient wood has been used in farm implements.

American Hornbeam   (Blue-beech)
Carpinus caroliniana

Size: *10–30 ft. tall; leaves 2–4 in. long.*
What to look for: *leaves oval, double-toothed; fruits triangular, papery, with single nutlet; bark smooth, fluted, blue-gray.* **Habitat:** *streambanks, bottomlands.*

Hornbeams   *Carpinus*

Within the three-dimensional green space of a mature hardwood forest, small shade-tolerant trees thrive beneath the upper canopy. The American Hornbeam is one such understory tree. It reveals its kinship with the birches when catkins develop along with the leaves in spring. Like its relative the Eastern Hop-hornbeam, it is sometimes called Ironwood.

Loblolly-bay
Gordonia lasianthus

Size: *40–50 ft. tall; leaves 4–5 in. long.*
What to look for: *leaves shiny, evergreen, shallowly toothed; flowers white, with 5 petals; fruits woody, split into 5.* **Habitat:** *moist areas.*

Gordonias   *Gordonia*

The fragrant flowers of the Loblolly-bay perfume southern verandas during summer. This fast-growing tree is the only North American gordonia—a group belonging to the tea family and named for the British horticulturalist James Gordon.

TREES

bract with fruit

American Basswood
Tilia americana

Size: *70–80 ft. tall; leaves 5–6 in. long.*
What to look for: *straplike bracts with hanging flowers or nutlets; leaves heart-shaped, coarsely toothed, smooth on both surfaces.* **Habitat:** *bottomlands in damp loam.*

Basswoods   *Tilia*

The basswoods, or lindens, supply welcome shade on city streets. Their soft, light-colored wood is a carver's delight. And their pale, fragrant flowers yield nectar that bees transform into a most flavorsome honey. All three North American species have heart-shaped leaves and straplike bracts.

fruit

Saguaro (Giant Cactus)
Cereus giganteus

Size: *50–60 ft. tall; spines 1½ in. long.*
What to look for: *leaves spinelike, in clusters; trunk and branches fluted, bright green; flowers white, atop trunk and branches; fruits red.* **Habitat:** *desert valleys, slopes, and rocky hills.*

Cereuses   *Cereus*

Highly resistant to drought, the 200-odd species in this group have a thick, rubbery "skin," spongy, water-storing tissues, and moisture-conserving needles instead of leaves. The only common North American tree in the group is the Saguaro.

Willows *Salix*

Most willows share certain characteristics—lance-shaped leaves, a single caplike scale on the bud, separate male and female catkins (flower clusters), and conspicuous projections at the bases of the leaves. New species, especially shrubby forms in the Arctic, are continually being discovered, and so the world-wide total of three to four hundred is only an estimate. In North America four imports, including the Weeping Willow from Asia, now reproduce in the wild, hybridizing with our native species. Willows never grow far from moist ground. Quick to colonize newly formed sandbars, they help reduce erosion by retaining soil in their fibrous, matted roots. Before the age of plastics, certain low-growing species were commonly harvested for basketmaking—and sometimes still are, in certain parts of the world.

planted range

Weeping Willow
Salix babylonica

Size: 30–40 ft. tall; leaves 3–5 in. long.
What to look for: long branches and lance-shaped leaves that hang down; leaves green above, gray-green below; twigs bright yellow.
Habitat: planted along watercourses, in wet lawns.

Black Willow
Salix nigra

Size: 50–80 ft. tall; leaves 3–6 in. long.
What to look for: leaves lance-shaped, with curved tips, light green below; twigs surrounded by short, scalelike leaves (stipules).
Habitat: along watercourses in wet soils; swamps.

Peachleaf Willow
Salix amygdaloides

male catkin

Size: 30–40 ft. tall; leaves 2½–5 in. long.
What to look for: leaves broadly lance-shaped, shiny green above, whitish green below, with yellow or orange midrib; twigs orange to red-brown. **Habitat:** along watercourses; swamps; poorly drained slopes.

Pussy Willow
(Glaucous Willow)
Salix discolor

Size: 10–20 ft. tall; leaves 2–5 in. long.
What to look for: furry white catkins on twigs in spring; leaves narrow, with widely spaced rounded teeth, dark green above, with whitish bloom below.
Habitat: stream margins, swamps, wet meadows.

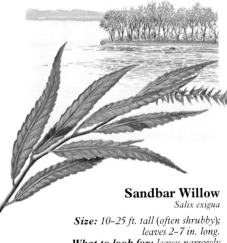

Sandbar Willow
Salix exigua

Size: 10–25 ft. tall (often shrubby); leaves 2–7 in. long.
What to look for: leaves narrowly lance-shaped, with widely spaced teeth; stems gray-green, upright; seed capsules hairy, in clusters. **Habitat:** along watercourses on new sandbars and beaches.

bud of male catkin   *female catkin*   *fruit*

TREES

309

Poplars *Populus*

Like the closely related willows, poplars are pioneer trees. In northern and mountain forests, they colonize burned-over land and areas of new soil in swathes that turn brilliant gold in fall. The poplars known as cottonwoods prefer streambanks, where they help prevent erosion. All poplar leaves have long stems, but those of the aspens are flattened, making the leaves flutter with the merest breeze. A third group of poplars, known as the balsam poplars, is characterized by sticky, resinous buds that smell like Balsam Fir.

Quaking Aspen
Populus tremuloides

Size: *50–60 ft. tall; leaves 1½–3 in. long.*
What to look for: *leaves nearly round, shiny green above, dull green below, with fine, rounded teeth; leafstalks long, flattened (leaves quake in wind); bark pale gray-green, with dark scars.* **Habitat:** *variable; in logged- or burned-over areas.*

Bigtooth Aspen
Populus grandidentata

Eastern Cottonwood *Populus deltoides*

Size: *80–100 ft. tall; leaves 3–6 in. wide.*
What to look for: *leaves triangular, with coarse, rounded teeth; leafstalks flattened; end buds sticky (not aromatic); fruit capsules green, with cottony seeds.*
Habitat: *bottomlands.*

Balsam Poplar
Populus balsamifera

Size: *60–80 ft. tall; leaves 3–6 in. long.*
What to look for: *leaves oval, sharply pointed, finely toothed, dark green above, rusty to golden brown or whitish below; leafstalks usually round; buds long, pointed, sticky, aromatic.*
Habitat: *bottomlands and along watercourses.*

Sweetleaves *Symplocos*

Most of the 350 species of sweetleaves are native to Asia and Australia. Several other groups—for example, beeches and sassafrases—occur mainly in Asia and are represented in the Americas by only one or two species. This distribution has led scientists to speculate that the plants within such a group share an ancestor that existed when, as geologists believe, the continents were united.

Sweetleaf (Horse-sugar)
Symplocos tinctoria

Size: *15–20 ft. tall; leaves 5–6 in. long.*
What to look for: *leaves semi-evergreen, elliptical, dark green above, pale green and hairy below; flowers yellow, close to twig; fruits red-brown; bark gray, with warts and fissures.* **Habitat:** *deciduous forests in rich, moist soils; edges of swamps; grows as understory tree or shrub.*

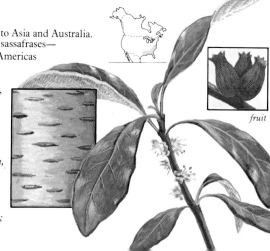

fruit

TREES

Sourwoods
Oxydendrum

The name Sourwood derives from the tree's acid-tasting leaves. Another name, Lily-of-the-valley Tree, refers to its bell-shaped blossoms. The Sourwood belongs to the heath family, and many other heaths, including the madrones and blueberries, have flowers of similar form.

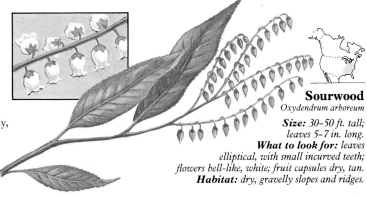

Sourwood
Oxydendrum arboreum

Size: *30–50 ft. tall; leaves 5–7 in. long.*
What to look for: *leaves elliptical, with small incurved teeth; flowers bell-like, white; fruit capsules dry, tan.*
Habitat: *dry, gravelly slopes and ridges.*

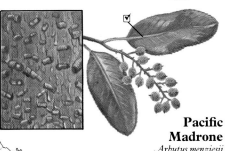

Pacific Madrone
Arbutus menziesii

Size: *70–100 ft. tall; leaves 3–5 in. long.*
What to look for: *leaves oval, leathery, semi-evergreen, with conspicuous midrib; bark red-brown, curling on branches and young trunks; fruits berrylike, orange-red.*
Habitat: *sea level to slopes in well-drained soils.*

Madrones *Arbutus*

Reddish fruits and loosely curling dark red bark make the three North American madrones, all native to the West, rather easy to identify. Adapted to hot, dry summers, they are usually small and crooked, but the Pacific Madrone grows tall and straight in sheltered areas near sea level.

Common Persimmon
Diospyros virginiana

Size: *30–50 ft. tall; leaves 2½–6 in. long.*
What to look for: *leaves oval, shiny dark green above, pale green and hairy below; flowers green-yellow; fruits fleshy.*
Habitat: *bottomlands, old fields, hedgerows.*

Persimmons *Diospyros*

Common Persimmon colonizes old fields, its seeds spread by Raccoons and Opossums feeding on the fruit. Until frost colors it purple-orange, the fruit is paler in color; the equally delectable fruit of Texas Persimmon (*Diospyros texana*) is black. Both trees have fine-grained, ebony-black heartwood.

Oregon Crab Apple
Malus fusca

Size: *25–35 ft. tall; leaves 1–4 in. long.*
What to look for: *leaves elliptical, sharply toothed, dark green above, pale green below; flowers white, fragrant; fruits oval, yellow tinged with red.*
Habitat: *bottomlands.*

Sweet Crab Apple
Malus coronaria

Size: *25–30 ft. tall; leaves 2–3 in. long.*
What to look for: *leaves oval, with coarse teeth, dark green above, pale green below; thornlike twigs; flowers pink to white, fragrant; fruits yellow-green.*
Habitat: *old fields, edges of woods.*

Apples *Malus*

Native to Europe and western Asia, the familiar orchard Apple (*Malus sylvestris*) seeds itself readily on this continent and hybridizes with our four native species, all of which are crab apples. Once planted for their tart fruit (an ingredient in jellies and cider), crab apples now serve primarily as ornamental trees.

fruit

fruit

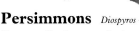

TREES

Mountain-ashes *Sorbus*

The tree most people know by this name is the European species (*Sorbus aucuparia*), sometimes called the Rowan-tree. Widely planted in North America, it reproduces without human help in northern parts of the continent. The orange-red fruits of both the European and the larger-leaved American Mountain-ash are prized by such birds as thrushes, waxwings, and grosbeaks.

fruit

Eu
Mou

America
Mountain-asl
Sorbus american

Size: *20–30 ft. tall*
leaves 6–8 in. long
What to look for: *leav*
compound, with 13–17 lance-shaped, sharp-toothe
leaflets; flowers white, in broad clusters; fruits flesh
orange-red. **Habitat:** *swamp borders to mountainside*

Chokecherr
Prunus virginian

Size: *20–25 ft. ta*
(usually shrubby
leaves 2–4 in. long
What to look for
leaves elliptica
(widest above midpoint
finely toothed, hairless belov
fruits dark purple-re
Habitat: *rich woods, hedgerow*
roadsides, riverbank

Cherries and Plums
Prunus

With glorious spring blossoms, fruits favored by animals and humans alike, and wood exceptionally well-suited for cabinetmaking, this group is one of the more valuable members of the rose family. (Apples belong to the rose family too.) Certain species, such as Chokecherry, the most widespread of the 18 native species, form large thickets, benefiting the land by stabilizing the soil. Black Cherry has a poor reputation with dairy farmers. When its leaves fall off in autumn, a normally harmless substance in them decomposes into glucose and cyanic acid. The latter is highly toxic, and poisons cattle that eat the leaves.

underside

Black Cherry
Prunus serotina

Size: *50–60 ft. tall;*
leaves 2–6 in. long.
What to look for: *leaves elliptical, with long tapered tip, rounded teeth, and rusty hairs along midrib on underside; flowers in long clusters; fruits black when ripe; mature bark peeling, with vertical splits.*
Habitat: *old fields; moist sites in woods.*

Pin Cherr
(Fire Cherry
Prunus pensylvanic

Size: *10–30 ft. ta*
(often shrubby
leaves 3–4½ in. long
What to look for: *leave lance-shaped, curved inwar toward apex, finely toothe bark thin, with fissure flowers in clusters of 5– fruits bright re*
Habitat
variable; ofte
in burned-ove
area

American Plum
Prunus americana

Size: *20–30 ft. tall;*
leaves 3–4 in. long.
What to look for: *leaves oval, thick, leathery, with fine double teeth; flowers malodorous; fruits with bright red skin, yellow flesh; trunk distorted, many-branched.*
Habitat: *edges of streams, swamps, and fields in East; dry uplands and mountain slopes in West.*

TREES

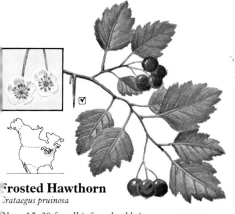

Frosted Hawthorn
Crataegus pruinosa

Size: *15–20 ft. tall (often shrubby); leaves 1–2 in. long.*
What to look for: *leaves dark blue-green, with 6–8 finely toothed lobes; stout thorns; flowers white; fruits green, ripening to purplish with waxy coat.* **Habitat:** *old fields, rocky woods.*

Hawthorns *Crataegus*

Their seeds spread by birds and deer, the hawthorns colonize abandoned fields. Their thorny, zigzagging branches form impenetrable barriers that protect newly rooted seedlings of other species, which eventually overtop and replace the small, bright-fruited hawthorns. The 35 North American species hybridize readily and are difficult to tell apart.

Downy Serviceberry
Amelanchier arborea

Size: *30–40 ft. tall; leaves 2–4 in. long.*
What to look for: *leaves elliptical, coarsely toothed, hairy when young; flowers white, in drooping clusters (very early spring); fruits berrylike, red to dark purple.* **Habitat:** *hillsides, ravines, edges of streams and moist woods.*

Serviceberries (Shadbushes)
Amelanchier

Found throughout the continent but scarcely noticeable most of the year, the delicately flowered serviceberries are harbingers of spring, blooming about the same time that shad swim upriver. The fruits, miniature apples with tiny seeds and sweet flesh, disappear rapidly in midsummer, eaten by Raccoons, chipmunks, squirrels, and songbirds.

Cercocarpus
(Mountain-mahoganies)
Cercocarpus

Members of the rose family, these trees and shrubs of dry mountain slopes of the West are unrelated to true mahoganies. The leaves of the Curlleaf Cercocarpus (*Cercocarpus ledifolius*) curl at the edges and have a white or rusty wool below.

Birchleaf Cercocarpus
Cercocarpus betuloides

Size: *10–25 ft. tall; leaves 1–1¼ in. long.*
What to look for: *leaves evergreen, margin ⅔-toothed, dark green above, pale green and hairy below, with sunken veins; flowers yellow, with 5 sepals; seed capsules with feathery tail.* **Habitat:** *dry open slopes, hillsides.*

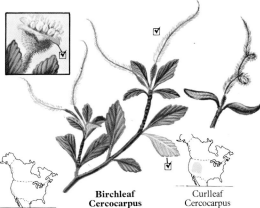

Birchleaf
Cercocarpus

Curlleaf
Cercocarpus

TREES

Eucalyptuses *Eucalyptus*

The eucalyptuses are native to Australia, but several kinds have been introduced successfully into southern Florida and coastal California. At least one species, the Bluegum, now grows in the wild in California.

Bluegum Eucalyptus
Eucalyptus globulus

Size: *80–120 ft. tall; leaves 4–7 in. long.*
What to look for: *leaves evergreen, lance-shaped, curved, gray-green, leathery, aromatic when crushed; bark peeling in long strips; fruit capsules woody, cone-shaped.* **Habitat:** *streets, parks, tree farms.*

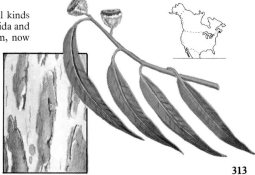

313

Eastern Redbud
Cercis canadensis

Size: *10–20 ft. tall; leaves 3–4½ in. wide.*
What to look for: *leaves heart-shaped, thick, leathery; flowers in clusters of 4–8, pink, developing before leaves; pods dark brown, with brown seeds.*
Habitat: *stream borders, mountain slopes.*

Redbuds *Cercis*

According to legend, the betrayer of Jesus Christ hanged himself from a branch of a Eurasian redbud, hence the alternative name Judas-tree. California Redbud (*Cercis occidentalis*), the only native species besides Eastern Redbud, sprouts pinkish-purple flowers from the bark.

Daleas *Dalea*

The Smokethorn's sparse foliage appears with the spring rains and remains on the tree only a few weeks. When the leaves fall, the tree takes on a smoky look, because of its velvety gray bark. The Smokethorn, the only tree form among the daleas, is one of the few legumes with simple rather than compound leaves.

Smokethorn
(Smoketree, Indigobush)
Dalea spinosa

Size: *15–20 ft. tall; leaves ¾–1 in. long.*
What to look for: *leaves sparse or absent; sharp spines; bark pale gray, velvety when young; flowers blue; pod with single brown bean.*
Habitat: *desert washes.*

fruit

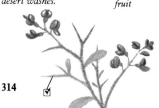

Kentucky Coffeetree
Gymnocladus dioicus

Size: *40–60 ft. tall; leaves 1–3 ft. long.*
What to look for: *leaves doubly compound, with pair of single leaflets at base of stem; pods thick, leathery, with seeds resembling coffee beans.* **Habitat:** *bottomlands, ravines, in rich soils.*

Coffeetrees *Gymnocladus*

Typical members of the legume family (which includes all the trees on this page and the next), coffeetrees have pealike fruits, compound leaves, and nitrogen-fixing bacteria on the roots. Their hard seeds have a flavor reminiscent of coffee. Only one species is North American; three others occur in Asia.

Black Locust *Robinia pseudoacacia*

Size: *40–60 ft. tall; leaves 8–14 in. long.*
What to look for: *leaves compound, with oval leaflets notched at apex; pair of spines at leaf base; pods brown, flat, with orange-red seeds.*
Habitat: *variable; in rich, moist or limestone soils; planted in hedgerows.*

Locusts *Robinia*

The Black Locust was taken to Europe about 1600, one of the first North American trees to be introduced into the Old World. Its decay-resistant wood makes excellent fence posts, railroad ties, and grapevine stakes. In late spring, clusters of its white blossoms, resembling Sweet Peas, perfume the air.

fruit

Mesquites *Prosopis*

Once forming only isolated groves, mesquite now grows in vast thickets, its spread aided by deer, livestock, and other animals feeding on the sweet pods and dispersing the seeds. Overgrazing and fire prevention have also helped the spread of this southwestern plant.

Honey Mesquite
Prosopis glandulosa

Size: *5–30 ft. tall; leaves 8–10 in. long.*
What to look for: *leaves compound, with leaflets in opposite pairs; pods fat, constricted between seeds; trunk branching from base.* **Habitat:** *arid to semi-arid flatlands and foothills.*

TREES

Acacias *Acacia*

Their name possibly influenced by the Greek word for "thorn," the acacias number about 800 species. Most are native to Africa and Asia, where they are an important source of firewood. The species native to North America occur in the Southwest, where they often form impenetrable thickets.

Gregg Catclaw (Catclaw Acacia)
Acacia greggii

Size: *10–30 ft. tall; leaves 1–3 in. long.* **What to look for:** *leaves doubly compound, with hairy leaflets; spines stout, curved; trunk distorted, with low branches; flowers yellow, fragrant; pods narrow, twisted.* **Habitat:** *canyons, mesas, mountain slopes.*

fruit

fruit

Southeastern Coralbean
Erythrina herbacea

Size: *15–20 ft. tall; leaves 6–8 in. long.* **What to look for:** *leaves compound, semi-evergreen, with 3 diamond-shaped leaflets; spines short, curved; flower spikes scarlet, showy; pods with red seeds.* **Habitat:** *coastal areas in sand.*

Coralbeans
Erythrina

This is primarily a tropical group, and the Southeastern Coralbean becomes a shrub or an herb north of Florida. The other North American representative, the Southwestern Coralbean (*Erythrina flabelliformis*), is an inhabitant of canyons in southern Arizona and New Mexico. Its red seeds, sometimes used in jewelry, are poisonous, as are all coralbean seeds.

thorns on bark

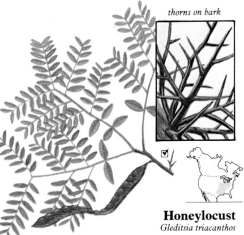

Honeylocust
Gleditsia triacanthos

Size: *70–80 ft. tall; leaves 5–9 in. long.* **What to look for:** *leaves compound or doubly compound, with elliptical, round-tipped leaflets; twigs with 3-branched thorns; bark dark gray-brown, often thorny; pods flat, twisted, with many seeds.* **Habitat:** *bottomlands in moist soils.*

Honeylocusts *Gleditsia*

In the wild the two North American honeylocusts are easily recognized by the clusters of branching thorns on their trunks. (Some cultivated varieties are thornless.) The Waterlocust (*Gleditsia aquatica*) of southern swamps has smaller leaves and short, oval pods with one to three brown seeds.

TREES

Yellow Paloverde
Cercidium microphyllum

Size: *10–15 ft. tall; leaves 2–4 in. long.* **What to look for:** *leaves compound, appearing after rain; branchlets ending in thorns; bark smooth, yellow-green; flowers brilliant yellow, profuse; pods fat, constricted between seeds.* **Habitat:** *desert foothills and plateaus.*

Paloverdes *Cercidium*

Green bark that can photosynthesize compensates for the early loss of leaves on these sometimes shrubby trees. Blue Paloverde (*Cercidium floridum*), which often hybridizes with the Yellow, has blue-green leaflets and flattened, unconstricted pods.

315

Red Mangrove
Rhizophora mangle

Size: *15–20 ft. tall; leaves 3½–5 in. long.*
What to look for: *trunk branching into aerial roots; leaves evergreen, elliptical, with thick edges; flowers pale yellow, in clusters of 2–3; mature fruits with tubelike tail.* **Habitat:** *coastal swamps, estuaries.*

White-mangrove
Laguncularia racemosa

Size: *20–40 ft. tall; leaves 1½–2½ in. long.*
What to look for: *leaves evergreen, oval, leathery, shiny dark green, with red-brown stem; flowers greenish white; fruits oval, berrylike, red-brown; no aerial roots.* **Habitat:** *muddy shores of tidal lagoons, bays, and freshwater outflows.*

Mangroves *Rhizophora*

Mangrove fruits germinate on the tree, then drop into the water and take root in the mud. The sturdy, arching prop roots bind the nutrient-rich silt in tidal marshes and build new land. They also act as a nursery for mollusks, crustaceans, young fish, and algae.

White-mangroves *Laguncularia*

The White-mangrove occupies higher ground than the other mangroves: it lives above the high-tide line and along the banks of freshwater streams. After dropping from the tree, the flask-shaped fruits float to new areas and sprout.

Tupelos *Nyssa*

Both the common and scientific names of these eastern trees refer to their swampy habitat: "tupelo" comes from Indian words for "swamp tree," and Nyssa was a water nymph in Greek legend. The Water Tupelo (*Nyssa aquatica*) has purple fruit.

Black Tupelo
(Sourgum, Blackgum)
Nyssa sylvatica

Size: *60–80 ft. tall; leaves 2–5 in. long.*
What to look for: *leaves oval, dark green, often hairy below; bark gray, blocky; fruits deep blue, berrylike.* **Habitat:** *bottomlands, slopes.*

American Holly
Ilex opaca

Size: *40-50 ft. tall; leaves 2-4 in. long.*
What to look for: *leaves evergreen, stiff, with spiny teeth; fruits berrylike, bright red; flowers greenish white.* **Habitat:** *coastal plains in sandy soil; bottomlands with moist, rich soil.*

Hollies *Ilex*

Whether evergreen or deciduous, tree-shaped or shrubby, the hollies are most prominent in autumn, when the female plants bear bright red fruits beloved by song and game birds. Eastern North American forests include 14 species, found most often in moist places. Some have marvelous names—Possumhaw, Dahoon (*Ilex cassine*), Yaupon (*Ilex vomitoria*), and Common Winterberry (*Ilex verticillata*).

Possumhaw
Ilex decidua

Size: *20-25 ft. tall (often shrubby); leaves 2-3 in. long.*
What to look for: *leaves deciduous, wavy-edged, rounded at tip, on short shoots; fruits berrylike, orange-red.* **Habitat:** *stream and swamp borders; bottomlands.*

TREES

Flowering Dogwood
Cornus florida

Size: 20-30 ft. tall; leaves 3-5 in. long.
What to look for: leaves oval, with veins curving toward pointed tip; flowers with 4 showy white petallike bracts; fruits red, berrylike, in clusters.
Habitat: deciduous forests in well-drained soils.

Carolina Buckthorn
Rhamnus caroliniana

Size: 20-30 ft. tall; leaves 2-6 in. long.
What to look for: leaves elliptical, sparsely toothed, shiny dark green above, paler and often hairy below; fruits berrylike, black; form may be shrubby. **Habitat:** streambanks, rich bottomlands, limestone ridges.

Dogwoods *Cornus*

The 15 species of North American dogwoods range from medium-sized trees to small wildflowers. Most are large shrubs. The petals of two trees, Flowering Dogwood and Pacific Dogwood (*Cornus nuttallii*), are actually modified leaves, with the true flowers, greenish yellow in color, clustered in the center.

Buckthorns *Rhamnus*

The 100-plus globally dispersed buckthorns include a number of trees and shrubs with ornamental or medicinal value: the bark of the western Cascara Buckthorn (*Rhamnus purshiana*), for example, is used to make a mild laxative. Thorny branch tips replace the terminal buds on some species, including the European Buckthorn (*Rhamnus cathartica*), which has escaped from cultivation in North America.

Buckeyes *Aesculus*

The most widely known buckeye in North America is the Eurasian Horsechestnut. Its six native relatives share certain characteristics: palmately compound leaves (the leaflets radiating from the end of the stem), showy pyramidal flower clusters, and large, green-husked fruit. The Yellow Buckeye (*Aesculus octandra*) of the Appalachian Mountains has smooth fruit.

Horsechestnut
Aesculus hippocastanum

Size: 40-60 ft. tall; leaves 8-10 in. wide.
What to look for: leaves palmately compound, with 7-9 wedge-shaped leaflets; flowers white, in showy spikes; fruits with thorny husk and 2-3 shiny brown nuts.
Habitat: streets, parks.

TREES

Ohio Buckeye
(Stinking Buckeye) *Aesculus glabra*

Size: 40-60 ft. tall; leaves 7-9 in. wide.
What to look for: leaves palmately compound, with 5 elliptical leaflets; flowers yellow, malodorous, in spikes; fruits with spiny husk and shiny round nut. **Habitat:** streambanks, bottomlands.

Western Soapberry
Sapindus drummondii

Size: 30-40 ft. tall; leaves 6-7 in. long.
What to look for: leaves compound, with 8-18 lance-shaped leaflets (hairy below); fruits yellow, turning black; bark scaly, red-brown. **Habitat:** canyons, streambanks, dry limestone outcrops.

Soapberries
Sapindus

In warm water the fruits of this mainly tropical group of 12 produce a soapy lather; the smooth bony seed inside is poisonous. One of the two North American species is the Wingleaf Soapberry (*Sapindus saponaria*), native to Florida but widely planted elsewhere.

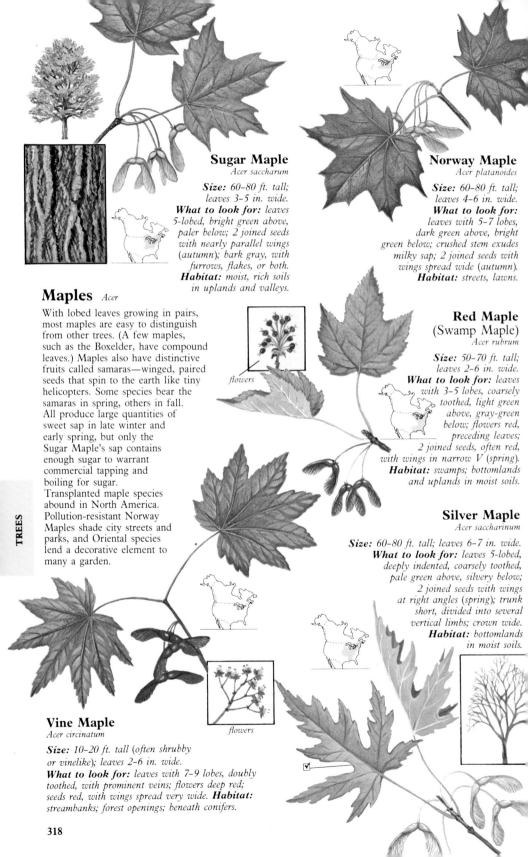

Sugar Maple
Acer saccharum

Size: *60–80 ft. tall; leaves 3–5 in. wide.*
What to look for: *leaves 5-lobed, bright green above, paler below; 2 joined seeds with nearly parallel wings (autumn); bark gray, with furrows, flakes, or both.*
Habitat: *moist, rich soils in uplands and valleys.*

Norway Maple
Acer platanoides

Size: *60–80 ft. tall; leaves 4–6 in. wide.*
What to look for: *leaves with 5–7 lobes, dark green above, bright green below; crushed stem exudes milky sap; 2 joined seeds with wings spread wide (autumn).*
Habitat: *streets, lawns.*

Maples *Acer*

With lobed leaves growing in pairs, most maples are easy to distinguish from other trees. (A few maples, such as the Boxelder, have compound leaves.) Maples also have distinctive fruits called samaras—winged, paired seeds that spin to the earth like tiny helicopters. Some species bear the samaras in spring, others in fall. All produce large quantities of sweet sap in late winter and early spring, but only the Sugar Maple's sap contains enough sugar to warrant commercial tapping and boiling for sugar.

Transplanted maple species abound in North America. Pollution-resistant Norway Maples shade city streets and parks, and Oriental species lend a decorative element to many a garden.

flowers

Red Maple
(Swamp Maple)
Acer rubrum

Size: *50–70 ft. tall; leaves 2–6 in. wide.*
What to look for: *leaves with 3–5 lobes, coarsely toothed, light green above, gray-green below; flowers red, preceding leaves; 2 joined seeds, often red, with wings in narrow V (spring).*
Habitat: *swamps; bottomlands and uplands in moist soils.*

Silver Maple
Acer saccharinum

Size: *60–80 ft. tall; leaves 6–7 in. wide.*
What to look for: *leaves 5-lobed, deeply indented, coarsely toothed, pale green above, silvery below; 2 joined seeds with wings at right angles (spring); trunk short, divided into several vertical limbs; crown wide.*
Habitat: *bottomlands in moist soils.*

Vine Maple
Acer circinatum

Size: *10–20 ft. tall (often shrubby or vinelike); leaves 2–6 in. wide.*
What to look for: *leaves with 7–9 lobes, doubly toothed, with prominent veins; flowers deep red; seeds red, with wings spread very wide.* **Habitat:** *streambanks; forest openings; beneath conifers.*

flowers

Autumn leaves.
Leaves are green because they have chlorophyll, the substance that enables them to manufacture food. Other pigments—red, orange, yellow—are also present but are masked by the green. As the days shorten in fall, chlorophyll synthesis ceases, the green color disappears, and other pigments begin to dominate. The leaves of certain species typically turn a uniform color (yellow on aspens and birches, scarlet on the Red Maple); others are more variable.

Boxelder
(Ashleaf Maple)
Acer negundo

flowers

Size: *30-40 ft. tall; leaves 6-15 in. long.*
What to look for: *leaves compound, with 3-7 irregularly lobed, coarse-toothed leaflets; flowers yellow-green; seeds elongated, with wings in narrow V (autumn).*
Habitat: *along watercourses; swamp edges.*

Striped Maple
(Moosewood)
Acer pensylvanicum

Size: *20-30 ft. tall; leaves 5-6 in. long.*
What to look for: *leaves 3-lobed, finely toothed, pale below; young bark smooth, bright green with white stripes; flowers bright yellow, on long drooping stalk.*
Habitat: *wooded valleys and slopes in moist soils.*

TREES

Bigleaf Maple
(Oregon Maple)
Acer macrophyllum

Size: *40-50 ft. tall; leaves 8-12 in. wide.*
What to look for: *leaves with 5 round, deeply cut lobes; flowers yellow; seeds hairy, with wings in V (autumn).*
Habitat: *bottomlands to rocky slopes in moist soils.*

flowers

Rocky Mountain Maple
(Dwarf Maple)
Acer glabrum

Size: *20-30 ft. tall; leaves 5-7 in. long.*
What to look for: *leaves 3-lobed (sometimes 5), double-toothed, often deeply cut, with bright red stalks; seeds green to pink-red.*
Habitat: *along mountain streams; rock ledges, cliffs.*

319

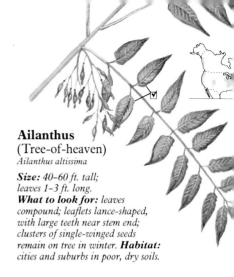

Staghorn Sumac
Rhus typhina

Size: *10–20 ft. tall;
leaves 16–24 in. long.*
What to look for: *leaves compound,
with narrowly lance-shaped, sharply toothed leaflets;
leafstalk hairy; twigs covered with velvety hairs;
dense clusters of dark red, hairy seeds.*
Habitat: *old fields, borders of woodlands.*

Ailanthus
(Tree-of-heaven)
Ailanthus altissima

Size: *40–60 ft. tall;
leaves 1–3 ft. long.*
What to look for: *leaves
compound; leaflets lance-shaped,
with large teeth near stem end;
clusters of single-winged seeds
remain on tree in winter.* **Habitat:**
cities and suburbs in poor, dry soils.

Sumacs *Rhus*

Although these small trees and shrubs belong to the
same family as Poison Sumac and Poison Ivy, they
are not poisonous. In fact, the fruits of Staghorn
Sumac and Lemonade Sumac (*Rhus integrifolia*), a
California shrub, can be brewed into a lemony tea.

Ailanthuses *Ailanthus*

The tree that "grows in Brooklyn" was a Tree-o
heaven, hardiest of the seven or so ailanthuses of tl
Orient and Australia. A rapid grower, even und
urban stress, it has been planted in most major citi
of the world, and now grows wild in many place

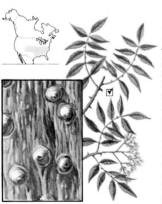

Prickly-ashes
Zanthoxylum

Related to lemons, limes, and oranges, the prickly-ashes and the
hoptrees (below) are among the few
nontropical members of the citrus
family. Plants in this family have
aromatic oil-containing glands in the
bark, fruit, and leaves (in the leaves,
the glands show as translucent dots).
Prickly-ash bark is a component of
certain folk medicines. It was once
chewed to relieve toothache, and
both species shown here are known
as toothache trees.

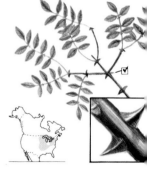

Common Prickly-as
Zanthoxylum american

Size: *4–20 ft. tall (often shrubb
leaves 3–5 in. lor*
What to look for: *twigs gray, w
pair of stout spines at leafstalk joi
leaves compound, with oval leafl
and weak spines on stalks; leaflets and tw
with lemony odor when crushe*
Habitat: *rock-strewn woodlands, riverban*

Hercules-club *Zanthoxylum clava-herculis*

Size: *25–30 ft. tall; leaves 5–8 in. long.*
What to look for: *leaves compound, with spiny stalk
and toothed leaflets; twigs and (often) bark with stout
½-in.-long spines; flowers green, in clusters.*
Habitat: *riverbanks, bluffs, coastal plains; in sandy soils.*

Hoptrees *Ptelea*

Brewers occasionally used the fruit of
the Common Hoptree as a substitute
for hops. Another name, Skunkbush,
comes from the pungent odor of the
twigs and leaves, and a third, Wafer-ash,
from the waferlike fruit and the ashlike
compound leaves. The California Hoptree (*Ptelea crenulata*) grows in the canyons and foothills of that state.

Common Hoptre
Ptelea trifolia

Size: *10–15 ft. ta
leaves 4–6 in. lon*
What to look for: *leaves compoun
with 3 oval leaflets; flowe
tiny, greenish white; fru
pale green wafers with sing
dark seed.* **Habitat:** *roc
strewn woods, forest edge*

TREES

Devils-walkingstick
Aralia spinosa

Size: *15–25 ft. tall (sometimes shrubby); leaves 3–4 ft. long.*
What to look for: *leaves large, doubly compound, with slender prickles on leafstalk; leaflets paired except for 1 at tip and 1 at base of stalk; trunk and branches with many stout spines.* **Habitat:** *woodlands, streambanks.*

Aralias *Aralia*

Devils-walkingsticks sprout rapidly from shallow roots to produce thickets of shoots with just the right appearance for Mephistophelean canes. Other aralias in North America include the shrub Bristly Sarsaparilla (*Aralia hispida*) and two woodland herbs shown in the wildflower section.

Black Ash
Fraxinus nigra

Size:
40–50 ft. tall; leaves 12–16 in. long.
What to look for: *leaves compound, with 7–11 lance-shaped, finely toothed, stemless leaflets; fruits winged, with flattened seed; bark scaly, with shallow fissures.* **Habitat:** *streambanks, floodplains, swamp borders.*

fruit

White Ash
Fraxinus americana

Size: *70–80 ft. tall; leaves 8–12 in. long.*
What to look for: *leaves compound, with 7 oval, sparsely toothed leaflets; fruits narrow, winged, with seed at stem end; bark with diamond-shaped furrows.* **Habitat:** *uplands in rich soils.*

Ashes *Fraxinus*

The typical ash has a compound leaf and a one-seeded fruit with an elongated wing. Only the western Singleleaf Ash (*Fraxinus anomala*) has simple leaves. The White Ash is the most abundant North American species, and the Green Ash (*Fraxinus pennsylvanica*) the most widespread. The Green Ash, which thrives near streams and in moist soil, takes its name from the color of the young twigs.

Black-mangroves *Avicennia*

The name mangrove is used for trees belonging to several groups. The Black-mangrove often grows intermingled with the Red Mangrove or slightly closer to shore. It too helps build and retain shoreline soil.

Black-mangrove
Avicennia germinans

Size: *10–30 ft. tall; leaves 2–3 in. long.*
What to look for: *leaves evergreen, leathery, with gray fuzz below; fruits pale green, podlike; numerous projecting rootlets at base of tree.* **Habitat:** *tidal shores, swamps.*

Fringetrees *Chionanthus*

Common in European gardens, the beautiful, fast-growing Fringetree deserves wider use as a landscape plant in its native land. Fringetrees and ashes belong to the olive family.

Fringetree   (Old-mans-beard)
Chionanthus virginicus

Size: *15–25 ft. tall (sometimes shrubby); leaves 4–8 in. long.*
What to look for: *leaves elliptical, with prominent veins; flowers white, fragrant, in feathery clusters of 3; fruits olive-shaped, dark blue, often with waxy bloom.* **Habitat:** *streambanks, swamp borders.*

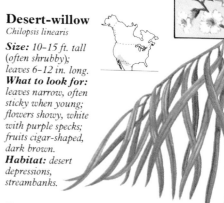

Northern Catalpa
Southern Catalpa

Northern Catalpa
Catalpa speciosa

Size: *40–50 ft. tall; leaves 6–12 in. long.*
What to look for: *leaves heart-shaped, dark green above, hairy below; flowers showy, white with purple and yellow specks; fruits cigar-shaped, green to brown.* **Habitat:** *bottomlands.*

Catalpa   *Catalpa*

Widely planted in the East, both the Northern Catalpa and its southern relative (*Catalpa bignonioides*) have spread far beyond their original ranges. The Southern Catalpa has smaller flowers, densely packed into pyramidal clusters.

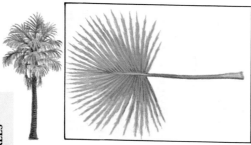

Cabbage Palmetto   *Sabal palmetto*

Size: *30–50 ft. tall; leaves 7–8 ft. wide.*
What to look for: *leaves fan-shaped, sprouting from crown, deeply divided into drooping, bristle-tipped segments; dried leafstalk bases often on upper half of trunk.* **Habitat:** *near ocean.*

Palms   Palmae

Palm leaves are either featherlike, as on the Florida Royalpalm, or fan-shaped, as on the Cabbage Palmetto and also the Saw-palmetto (in the shrub section). They sprout from a cabbagelike head at the top of the trunk, which is pithy throughout and does not develop annual growth rings. The bark is fibrous. Unlike all other North American trees except yuccas, palms are monocotyledons: that is, their seedlings have only one leaf (dicotyledons have two). A more conspicuous difference is in the leaf veins. Monocots have parallel veins; dicots are net-veined.

Desert-willow
Chilopsis linearis

Size: *10–15 ft. tall (often shrubby); leaves 6–12 in. long.*
What to look for: *leaves narrow, often sticky when young; flowers showy, white with purple specks; fruits cigar-shaped, dark brown.*
Habitat: *desert depressions, streambanks.*

Desert-willows   *Chilopsis*

The fragrant blossoms and cigar-shaped fruits of the single species in this group show its close relationship to the catalpas. The long, narrow leaves of the "Desert-catalpa" are better able to resist drought.

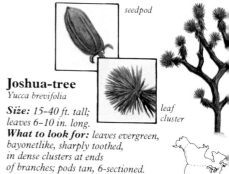

seedpod

Joshua-tree
Yucca brevifolia

Size: *15–40 ft. tall; leaves 6–10 in. long.*
What to look for: *leaves evergreen, bayonetlike, sharply toothed, in dense clusters at ends of branches; pods tan, 6-sectioned.*
Habitat: *desert flats and foothills.*

leaf cluster

Yuccas   *Yucca*

Many people associate yuccas with deserts, but these trees and shrubs of the lily family occur in dry soils elsewhere as well. Because of the sharp, narrow leaves, several species are known as Spanish-bayonet.

Florida Royalpalm
Roystonea elata

Size: *30–50 ft. tall; leaves 12–15 ft. long.*
What to look for: *leaves evergreen, compound, dark green; bark gray; upper part of trunk bright green.*
Habitat: *sandy beaches; planted along streets.*

TREES

Trees, shrubs, and wildflowers. This is the first of nine pages on shrubs—woody plants that are usually smaller than trees and have several stems instead of a trunk. Shrubs may occasionally develop into trees, and chances are that a shrub has close relatives that are trees. Some shrubs are so low-growing that they are shown in the wildflower section of this book. Vines are also in that section.

Sweetshrubs
Calycanthus

With showy flowers and aromatic leaves, the four North American sweetshrubs make attractive landscape plants. The leaf of the Smooth Allspice (*Calycanthus fertilis*) is hairless below.

fruit

Carolina Allspice
Calycanthus floridus

Size: *3-9 ft. tall; leaves 2-5 in. long.*
What to look for: *leaves oval, gray-green, densely hairy below, with camphorlike odor when crushed; flowers red-brown, with strawberry odor; fruits leathery brown capsules.* **Habitat:** *streambanks, wooded hillsides in moist soils.*

Witch-hazels *Hamamelis*

The scraggly Witch-hazel puts forth its curious yellow flowers in fall, after most deciduous plants have lost their leaves. The woody fruit is unusual too: when mature, it ejects its seed a distance of 15 feet or more. The lotion called witch hazel is made from the bark.

Witch-hazel
Hamamelis virginiana

Size: *5-15 ft. tall; leaves 4-6 in. long.*
What to look for: *leaves asymmetrical at base, with coarse rounded teeth; flowers yellow, clustered, with narrow, twisted petals (late fall); fruits hard brown capsules.* **Habitat:** *bottomlands, forests, streambanks.*

flower and fruit

Spicebushes *Lindera*

In bare winter woods spicebush blossoms are a first and welcome sign of spring. The only other North American species in this mainly Asian group is the Hairy Spicebush (*Lindera melissaefolium*) of southern swamps.

Spicebush
Lindera benzoin

Size: *6-10 ft. tall; leaves 3-4 in. long.*
What to look for: *leaves oval, aromatic when crushed; flowers small, close to twig, opening before leaves; berries bright red or yellow.* **Habitat:** *swamps, wet woodlands.*

flowers

Sweet-ferns *Comptonia*

Though its leaves are fernlike, the Sweet-fern is not a fern at all but a flowering plant. Like its relatives the bayberries, it has petalless catkins as flowers; its fruit is a nut with bristly scales.

Sweet-fern
Comptonia peregrina

Size: *1-4 ft. tall; leaves 3-5 in. long.*
What to look for: *leaves narrow, fernlike, hairy below, fragrant when crushed; twigs brown, hairy.* **Habitat:** *fields, logged-over forests.*

close-up of leaf

Bayberries *Myrica*

When bayberry fruits are submerged in boiling water, their waxy coating rises to the surface. Candles can be made from the wax of both the Waxmyrtle and the Northern Bayberry (*Myrica pensylvanica*), but do be forewarned: one candle requires several bushels of fruit.

Waxmyrtle
(Southern Bayberry)
Myrica cerifera

Size: *10-30 ft. tall; leaves 1½-3 in. long.*
What to look for: *leaves lance-shaped, evergreen, dotted with resin; fruits gray, coated with whitish wax.* **Habitat:** *swamps; pine and oak woodlands.*

fruit

SHRUBS

323

Beaked Hazel
(Beaked Filbert)
Corylus cornuta

Size: *3–9 ft. tall
(tree size in California);
leaves 2–5 in. long.*
What to look for:
*leaves oval, sharply
toothed, downy below; twigs
hairless; fruits with
tubular husks.* **Habitat:**
*old fields, margins of
woodland clearings.*

Four-wing Saltbush
Atriplex canescens

Size: *2–4 ft. tall;
leaves 1–2 in. long.*
What to look for:
*leaves narrow, thick,
scaly, gray-green; stems
whitish; fruits with pale tan,
4-winged husk.* **Habitat:**
*salt flats; semideserts
to arid foothills.*

Hazels *Corylus*

Lucky is the forager who finds
the tasty hazelnuts before the
squirrels and other rodents do.
The sweet nuts marketed as
filberts come from Eurasian
hazels, not from either of the
two native species.

American
Hazel
(*Corylus
americana*)

Saltbushes
Atriplex

In dry, nearly barren parts
of the West, wild animals and
livestock alike browse on the Four-wing
Saltbush and its spiny relative the Shad-
scale (*Atriplex confertifolia*), or Sheep-fat.
Saltbushes do well in seashore gardens.

Ocotillo
Fouquieria splendens

Size: *6–20 ft. tall,
leaves ½–1 in. long*
What to look for: *branches
with stout thorns; fleshy
leaves following rain;
showy red flowers after
winter rain.*
Habitat: *deserts*

Ocotillos
Fouquieria

Much of the year ocotillos look like thorny dead
sticks, but a rain at any time will bring forth the
leaves. When the leaves on new growth fall, their
sharp-pointed stalks remain to become the thorns.

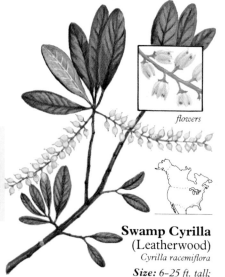

flowers

Swamp Cyrilla
(Leatherwood)
Cyrilla racemiflora

Size: *6–25 ft. tall;
leaves 2–4 in. long.*
What to look for: *leaves semi-evergreen,
elliptical, shiny above, with netlike veins below;
flowers white to pink; pods yellow;
may develop into a tree.* **Habitat:** *swamps,
streambanks of coastal plains.*

Cyrillas *Cyrilla*

In Virginia the Swamp Cyrilla's leaves turn orange
and scarlet in autumn, but farther south the green
leaves persist. The plant occurs not only in the Southeast but also throughout the West Indies and in the
swamps of northern South America. One of its
names, He-huckleberry, alludes to the belief that
Cyrillas are male huckleberry plants.

Labrador Tea
Ledum groenlandicum

Size: *1–3 ft. tall;
leaves 1–2 in. long.*
What to look for:
*leaves evergreen,
narrow, edges rolled
under, white or rusty and
woolly below; flowers white,
5-petaled.* **Habitat:** *bogs,
high mountaintops.*

Ledums *Ledum*

These low shrubs are typical members of
the acid-tolerant heath family. The thick,
leathery leaves conserve moisture, and the
root system carefully buffers the acidic
water entering the plant.

Bog Rosemary
Andromeda glaucophylla

Size: ½–1½ ft. tall;
leaves 1–1½ in. long.
What to look for: leaves
evergreen, very narrow,
with edges rolled under,
white below; flowers
urn-shaped, white to pink;
fruits brown capsules.
Habitat: bogs;
acid, peaty to
sandy soils.

Bog Rosemarys *Andromeda*

Usually growing with other heath plants on
mountaintops or in cool northern bogs, these
plants do well in rock gardens if they have full
sun and acid, peaty soil. A number of shrubs
sold as "andromeda" belong to other groups.

Leatherleaf
Chamaedaphne calyculata

Size: 1–3½ ft. tall;
leaves ½–2 in. long.
What to look for: leaves
semi-evergreen, elliptical,
leathery, with yellowish
scales below; flowers urn-
shaped, white, each
opposite a small leaf;
fruits tan capsules.
Habitat: bogs, tundra.

Leatherleaves *Chamaedaphne*

In North America, Europe, and Asia, the Leatherleaf, or
Cassandra, forms matted tangles that add a bit of a bounce
to a bog-walker's step. The plant blooms in early spring.

Bigberry
Manzanita
Arctostaphylos glauca

Size: 6–12 ft. tall;
leaves 1–2 in. long.
What to look for:
leaves evergreen, oval,
dull green with waxy bloom;
fruits berrylike, juicy,
with single stone;
bark dark red-purple.
Habitat: dry mountain slopes.

Manzanitas *Arctostaphylos*

Numbering 50 or more species, the manzanitas occur
mainly in warm, dry areas of the American West and
in Central America. Some species are occasionally
small trees. The Bearberry (*Arctostaphylos uva-ursi*),
which lives as far north as the Arctic Circle, is shown
in the wildflower section of this book.

Rosebay Rhododendron
(Great Laurel)
Rhododendron maximum

Size: 10–20 ft. tall; leaves 4–12 in. long.
What to look for: leaves evergreen, oval, thick,
leathery, dark green; flowers white to pink,
in large, dense clusters. **Habitat:** moist
mountain slopes, streambanks.

Rhododendrons *Rhododendron*

Asia claims the major share of the 800-odd rhododendron species; only 20 shrubs and 3 small
trees are native to North America. Some species
are evergreen, conserving moisture and warmth
in winter by rolling their leaves lengthwise as
temperatures drop. (The lower the temperature,
the tighter the leaf roll.) The Flame Azalea
(*Rhododendron calendulaceum*), which brightens southeastern woodlands with orange flowers
in May, is a deciduous species.

Mountain
Laurel
Kalmia latifolia

Size: 10–20 ft. tall;
leaves 3–4 in. long.
What to look for:
leaves evergreen,
elliptical, thick, bunched
near branch tips; flowers
delicate pink, in showy
clusters. **Habitat:** hills,
mountain slopes; in all soils
except those with lime.

Laurels *Kalmia*

A laurel blossom has 10 pollen-bearing stamens, each
tucked into a pouch. When triggered by an insect, the
stamens snap toward the center, and pollination occurs. The six native laurels include Lambkill (*Kalmia
angustifolia*) and Bog Laurel (*Kalmia polifolia*), both
poisonous to livestock if eaten in quantity.

Blueberries and Cranberries *Vaccinium*

From Alaska to the Andes and from Norway to the Transvaal, the 300 species of blueberries and cranberries are remarkable for their ability to thrive in a variety of environments. Of the 30 North American species, only the Tree Sparkleberry (*Vaccinium arboreum*) of upland forests in the South gets beyond the shrub stage. The American Cranberry is shown in the wildflower section.

close-up of teeth

Highbush Blueberry
Vaccinium corymbosum

Size: 5–10 ft. tall; leaves 1½–3 in. long.
What to look for: leaves elliptical, smooth, green; flowers white to pink, urn-shaped; berries blue to blue-black, with slight waxy bloom. **Habitat:** swamps, moist woodlands, dry uplands.

Lowbush Blueberry
Vaccinium angustifolium

Size: 3–15 in. tall; leaves ¼–¾ in. long.
What to look for: leaves lance-shaped, shiny, bright green, with fine bristle-tipped teeth; flowers white to pink-tinged, urn-shaped; fruits blue-black, with waxy bloom. **Habitat:** bogs, tundra, dry sandy flats, rocky slopes.

Carolina Silverbell
Halesia carolina

Size: 10–30 ft. tall; leaves 3–4 in. long.
What to look for: leaves elliptical, toothed, somewhat hairy below; flowers white, with shallow lobes; fruits woody, 4-winged; can be shrub or small tree. **Habitat:** streambanks, slopes.

Bigleaf Snowbell
Styrax grandifolius

Size: 3–12 ft. tall; leaves 2½–5 in. long.
What to look for: leaves elliptical to oval, with white hairs below; flowers bell-shaped, white; fruits with pointed tips.
Habitat: swamp and stream edges, wet woods.

Silverbells *Halesia*

The bells of a silverbell are delicate white flowers that dangle from the twigs in spring. Carolina Silverbell grows mainly in the mountains; the other two native species grow on the southeastern coastal plain.

Snowbells *Styrax*

Snowbells have wider-flaring flowers and rounder fruits than the closely related silverbells. The bark of some Asian species is the source of benzoin, a resin used in medicines and perfumes.

Currants and Gooseberries *Ribes*

Generally, currant branches lack prickles, and the flowers and fruits grow in elongated clusters. In contrast, most gooseberries are prickly, with flowers and fruits in short clusters of one to five. Both groups have maple-shaped leaves.

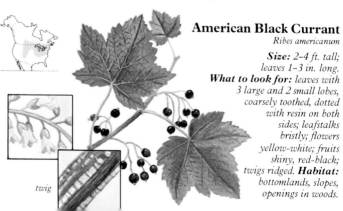

American Black Currant
Ribes americanum

Size: 2–4 ft. tall; leaves 1–3 in. long.
What to look for: leaves with 3 large and 2 small lobes, coarsely toothed, dotted with resin on both sides; leafstalks bristly; flowers yellow-white; fruits shiny, red-black; twigs ridged. **Habitat:** bottomlands, slopes, openings in woods.

twig

Highbush Blackberry

Rubus allegheniensis

Size: *3–7 ft. tall; leaves 3–5 in. long.*
What to look for: *leaves compound, with 3 or 5 doubly toothed leaflets, hairy below; leafstalks spiny; fruits black when ripe; canes red-green, with straight thorns.*
Habitat: *old fields, roadsides.*

Brambles *Rubus*

Blackberries, raspberries, dewberries—these delectable fruits all come from closely related species in the rose family. Their leaves are usually compound, and their thorny branches, called canes, often arch toward the ground. A cane leafs out during its first year; the second year it flowers, fruits, and dies. Bramble patches furnish food and shelter for wildlife and protection for seedlings of trees and other shrubs.

leaf cluster

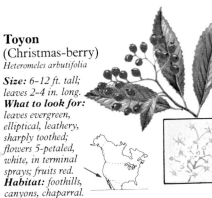

Toyon
(Christmas-berry)

Heteromeles arbutifolia

Size: *6–12 ft. tall; leaves 2–4 in. long.*
What to look for: *leaves evergreen, elliptical, leathery, sharply toothed; flowers 5-petaled, white, in terminal sprays; fruits red.*
Habitat: *foothills, canyons, chaparral.*

Chamise
(Greasewood)

Adenostoma fasciculatum

Size: *2–8 ft. tall; leaves ¼–½ in. long.*
What to look for: *leaves evergreen, needlelike, leathery, clustered; flowers 5-petaled, white, in dense terminal clusters.* **Habitat:** *chaparral, mountain slopes.*

Toyons *Heteromeles*

The Toyon, like other plants of the chaparral and adjacent woodlands, sprouts readily after fire or cutting. Often planted as an ornamental, the fruiting Toyon offers a vivid display of red and green, certain to call holly to mind. Birds eat its small "apples."

Chamises *Adenostoma*

Like other resinous plants of the California chaparral, the chamises are highly flammable. "Chamise" comes from the Spanish word for half-burned wood. One species, Redshank (*Adenostoma sparsifolium*), is named for its peeling red bark.

Multiflora Rose

Rosa multiflora

Size: *3–6 ft. tall; leaves 3–5 in. long.*
What to look for: *leaves compound, with 7 oval, toothed leaflets; fringed stipules at leafstalk base; twigs bright green, with stout thorns; flowers 5-petaled, white; fruits red; branches arching.*
Habitat: *old fields, roadsides.*

Roses *Rosa*

So familiar is the rose that hardly any explanation is needed beyond Gertrude Stein's: "Rose is a rose is a rose is a rose." But botanists have so transformed roses that one tends to forget that wild ones have only five simple petals, most often pink. Among the other distinguishing traits are the arching or climbing form, the stipules (winglike structures at the base of the leafstalk), the thorns, and the bright hips (fruits).

Prairie Rose

Rosa setigera

Size: *4–6 ft. tall; leaves 2–4 in. long.*
What to look for: *leaves compound, with 3 (rarely 5) oval, toothed leaflets; twigs with small thorns; flowers 5-petaled, pale to deep pink; fruits red; branches arching or climbing.*
Habitat: *prairies, woodland thickets.*

327

Red-osier Dogwood
Cornus stolonifera

Size: *3–7 ft. tall; leaves 2–5 in. long.*
What to look for: *leaves oval, dark green above, whitish below; flowers white, in rounded clusters; fruits berrylike, white; stems crimson in winter, white inside.*
Habitat: *near swamps and bogs; wet sites in forests.*

Dogwoods *Cornus*

Tree, shrub, wildflower—this group has representatives in all three sections of this book. Dogwood leaves usually grow in pairs (opposite one another on the twig); an exception is the Alternate-leaf Dogwood. The leaf veins characteristically curve away from the central vein and then bend to follow the edge of the leaf. The small clustered flowers of dogwood shrubs lack the showy petallike bracts of the Flowering Dogwood tree and the Bunchberry wildflower.

Alternate-lea Dogwoo
*Cornu
alternifoli*

*Size
5–10 ft. tall
leaves 3–5 in. long
What to look for
leaves oval, brigh
yellow-green above
pale green below
arranged alternatel
on twig; flower.
white, in broa
clusters; fruit.
berrylike, dark blue
with red stems; stem.
and twigs dark red-brown
Habitat: mixed wood.
in moist, rich soils.*

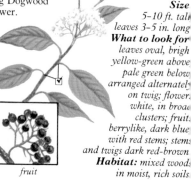

fruit

fruit

Ceanothuses *Ceanothus*

Although the 60 or so species are concentrated in California (some are known as California-lilacs), ceanothuses have been planted around the world for their beautiful blossoms. One of the few eastern species, the white-flowered New Jersey Tea (*Ceanothus americanus*), was reputedly used as a tea substitute during the Revolutionary War. The roots of New Jersey Tea and some other species yield a red dye and also substances used in the past to congeal blood.

Buckbrush
Ceanothus cuneatus

Size: *3–8 ft. tall; leaves ½–1 in. long.*
What to look for: *leaves evergreen, narrow at base, dull gray-green above; wartlike bumps at bases of twigs; flowers white, lavender, or blue; fruit capsules with 3 horns.* **Habitat:** *dry mountain slopes.*

Blueblossom
Ceanothus thyrsiflorus

Size: *5–15 ft. tall; leaves ¾–2 in. long.*
What to look for: *leaves evergreen, broadly oval, with 3 main veins; flowers blue, in branching clusters; fruits with 3 lobes; may be treelike or a creeping mat.* **Habitat:** *dry slopes of foothills and mountains.*

fruit

fruit

Creosote Bushes
Larrea

Creosote bushes are adapted to desert living. Where they are the dominant plants, they often grow in evenly spaced rows—a "self-imposed" method of rationing water. A strong-smelling resin coats the leaves, reducing moisture loss.

Creosote Bush
Larrea tridentata

Size: *3–9 ft. tall; leaves ⅜ in. long.*
What to look for: *leaves evergreen, compound, with 2 semicircular olive-green leaflets; flowers yellow; fruits hairy, white; branches jointed, with dark ring at joint.*
Habitat: *deserts.*

fruit

Burningbushes *Euonymus*

Though concentrated in eastern Asia, the burningbushes have four North American representatives, including one western species. The typical fruit is a brightly colored capsule with a brightly colored coat (bittersweets have similar fruit). The name, however, derives from the scarlet autumn leaves.

Eastern Burningbush (Wahoo)
Euonymus atropurpureus

Size: 10-15 ft. tall; leaves 2-5 in. long.
What to look for: leaves elliptical, finely toothed, narrow at tip; flowers purple; fruits bladderlike, opening to reveal red seeds; may be tree in South.
Habitat: woodland edges in moist soils.

flower

Bladdernuts
Staphylea

With inflated fruit capsules containing large bony seeds, the two North American species in this group are easy to identify. The Sierra Bladdernut (*Staphylea bolanderi*) grows in the mountains of California.

American Bladdernut
Staphylea trifolia

Size: 6-12 ft. tall; leaves 6-8 in. long.
What to look for: leaves compound, with 3 finely toothed leaflets; flowers bell-shaped, in drooping clusters; fruits papery, lantern-shaped, with brown seeds rattling inside.
Habitat: forest edges.

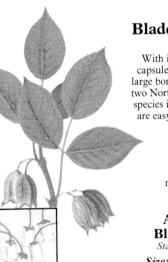

Forestieras
Forestiera

These shrubs and small trees belong to the olive family and have small olivelike fruits; indeed, some species, such as the Florida-privet (*Forestiera segregata*), are even called Wild-olive. The privets used in hedges belong to a different part of the olive family.

flowers

Swamp-privet
Forestiera acuminata

Size: 3-9 ft. tall (tree form to 30 ft.); leaves 2-4½ in. long.
What to look for: leaves elliptical, with pointed apex and base; flowers clustered on twigs, opening before leaves; fruits fleshy, dark purple. *Habitat: stream and swamp edges.*

Poison Sumacs *Toxicodendron*

Sumacs and poison sumacs differ in at least one major detail: only the latter are poisonous (*Toxicodendron* means "poison tree"). The two most notorious poison sumacs are shown in the wildflower section of this book; the sumacs are with the trees.

Poison Sumac *Toxicodendron vernix*

Size: 6-10 ft. tall; leaves 7-14 in. long.
What to look for: leaves compound, with 7-13 oval untoothed leaflets; leafstalks often red; fruits white, hanging in loose clusters (may remain in winter); twigs gray-brown, dotted; may be shrub or tree. *Habitat: bogs, swamps.*

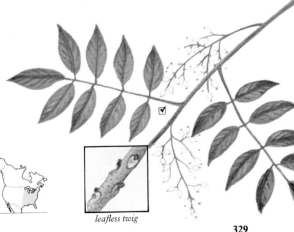

leafless twig

Buttonbush
(Honey-balls)
Cephalanthus occidentalis

Size: *5-15 ft. tall; leaves 2-7 in. long.*
What to look for: *leaves oval, shiny, dark green above; flowers fragrant, whitish, in globe-shaped clusters; fruits round, warty, red-brown.* **Habitat:** *swamps, pond and stream borders.*

fruit

Buttonbushes *Cephalanthus*

Viewed through a magnifying glass, a buttonbush flower cluster shows exquisite detail. Each of the tiny blossoms has petals fused into a narrow tube, a long and wispy pistil, and nectar glands at the base. Bees are a primary pollinator.

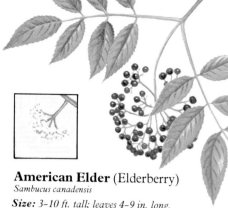

American Elder (Elderberry)
Sambucus canadensis

Size: *3-10 ft. tall; leaves 4-9 in. long.*
What to look for: *leaves compound, usually with 7 elliptical, sharply toothed leaflets; flowers creamy white, in broad clusters; fruits berrylike, purple-black; twigs pithy, white inside.* **Habitat:** *swamp edges; along fences and roads.*

Elders *Sambucus*

Pithy and easily hollowed out, elder twigs make excellent whistles and drinking straws. Though wine is made from the fruits of some species, others, such as the Pacific Red Elder (*Sambucus callicarpa*), have inedible or even poisonous fruit.

Viburnums *Viburnum*

Common in shady forests, the viburnums are treasured ornamental plants. On many species the leathery, opposite leaves assume brilliant fall colors; the flower clusters are showy and often delightfully scented; and the eye-catching fruits may decorate the shrubs well into winter. The American Cranberrybush (*Viburnum trilobum*), or Highbush Cranberry, retains its fruit long after it has lost its maplelike leaves.

Nannyberry
Viburnum lentago

Size: *10-30 ft. tall; leaves 2-4 in. long.*
What to look for: *leaves oval, curved in at tip, sharply toothed; flowers in broad clusters; fruits berrylike, long-stalked, dark blue when ripe, with pointed tips; may be small tree.* **Habitat:** *swamp and forest edges.*

twig with buds

Hobblebush
Viburnum alnifolium

Size: *3-9 ft. tall; leaves 4-6 in. long.*
What to look for: *leaves broadly oval to heart-shaped, rusty-haired below, with fine irregular teeth; flowers in broad clusters, large at edge of cluster; fruits berrylike, purple-black when ripe; branches horizontal, often rooted at tip.* **Habitat:** *cool, moist forests.*

Honeysuckles *Lonicera*

Some honeysuckles are shrubs and others vines (two vines are shown in the wildflower section). One common shrub, the Tatarian Honeysuckle (*Lonicera tatarica*), is not a native species. An escape from gardens, it grows wild in the woods, shading out native plants.

Fly Honeysuckle *Lonicera canadensis*

Size: *2-4 ft. tall; leaves 1½-3 in. long.*
What to look for: *leaves oval, with long fine hair on margins and stalks; flowers tubular, yellowish (often red-tinged), in pairs; berries red, in pairs.* **Habitat:** *forests in rich, moist soils.*

fruit

SHRUBS

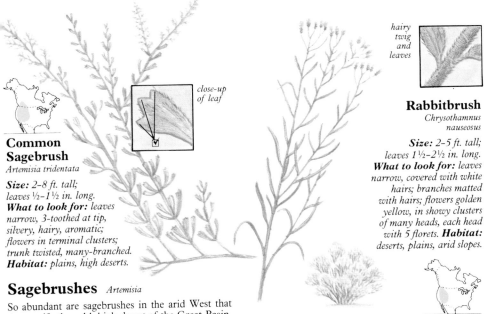

close-up of leaf

hairy twig and leaves

Common Sagebrush
Artemisia tridentata

Size: *2-8 ft. tall; leaves ½-1½ in. long.*
What to look for: *leaves narrow, 3-toothed at tip, silvery, hairy, aromatic; flowers in terminal clusters; trunk twisted, many-branched.*
Habitat: *plains, high deserts.*

Sagebrushes *Artemisia*

So abundant are sagebrushes in the arid West that they typify the cold, high desert of the Great Basin. But species in this group occur across the continent. For example, the Dusty-miller (*Artemisia stelleriana*), a perennial herb from Asia with gray, hairy leaves and stems, has colonized eastern beaches.

Baccharises *Baccharis*

The Groundsel-tree is most conspicuous in autumn, when it blossoms and produces fluffy white fruit similar to a dandelion's. In the West several species with similar flowers and fruit but narrower leaves grow in stream valleys and washes.

Groundsel-tree
Baccharis halimifolia

Size: *3-12 ft. tall; leaves 1-3 in. long.*
What to look for: *leaves diamond-shaped, roughly toothed or shallowly lobed, gray-green, dotted with resin; flowers tiny, in fall; fruit capsules bristling with white hairs.* ***Habitat:*** *seashores, tidal marshes, banks of estuaries.*

flower

fruit

Rabbitbrush
Chrysothamnus nauseosus

Size: *2-5 ft. tall; leaves 1½-2½ in. long.*
What to look for: *leaves narrow, covered with white hairs; branches matted with hairs; flowers golden yellow, in showy clusters of many heads, each head with 5 florets.* ***Habitat:*** *deserts, plains, arid slopes.*

Rabbitbrushes *Chrysothamnus*

Not only rabbits but also deer and other large mammals browse these common desert and high-plain shrubs. The species shown owes the second part of its scientific name to the disagreeable odor of its leaves.

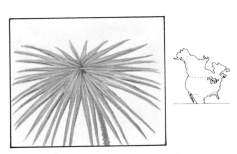

Saw-palmetto
Serenoa repens

Size: *3-6 ft. tall; leaves 1-3 ft. wide.*
What to look for: *leaves fan-shaped, slit more than halfway to base; leafstalks with stout recurved spines; stems often creeping.* ***Habitat:*** *pine barrens, hammocks, sand dunes.*

Saw-palmettos *Serenoa*

Saw-palmettos commonly grow in dense thickets beneath pines, their stems creeping along the ground. Rarely does the stem become tall and the plant tree-like. Creamy white flowers bloom amongst the fans, and the small fruit is black and olivelike.

Wildflowers

Beauty is only part of a blossom's allure. From "ordinary" dandelions to rare orchids, each wildflower is an intricate living jewel with a complex and fascinating life story.

What are wildflowers? If you say native plants with attractive blossoms, you exclude immigrants like the common Dandelion and ugly ducklings like Pokeweed. If you limit the category to herbaceous plants—those that die back every year—you rule out woody vines like the Trumpet Honeysuckle as well as low-growing shrubs. For the purposes of this book, a wildflower is any flowering plant that grows outside cultivation and is neither a tree nor a tall shrub. More than 15,000 such species grow north of the Mexican border.

The incredible variety of flower colors, shapes, textures, and scents serves only one function: to produce the seed for a new generation. Every flower contains ovule- ("egg-") producing female organs (pistils), pollen-producing male organs (stamens), or both. In order to set seed, the ovule, or ovules, at the base of the pistil must be fertilized by a grain of pollen. Like most rules, this one has exceptions; hawkweeds and dandelions are among plants that set seed without pollination.

Since flowers seldom pollinate themselves, most species need the help of an outside agent to transfer pollen from the stamen of one blossom to the pistil of another. For grasses, ragweeds, and many other drab-flowered plants, the agent is the wind. Other plants depend on such animals as hummingbirds and butterflies to perform the service, attracting them with color or smell. The various parts of a blossom are arranged to encourage pollination, and the flower frequently offers its animal allies nectar in return.

How to Use This Section

Plants in this section are arranged according to botanical family, a scheme that involves consideration of both flower and fruit. This arrangement may take some getting used to, and the chart that begins on the next page will help you during the transition.

Maps in this section show the zone, or zones, where each species is most likely to occur. The plant, of course, is not necessarily found throughout that zone. Similarly, plants growing in a particular area may bloom for a shorter time than the blossoming period indicated for the species as a whole.

Throughout history, wildflowers have furnished food and medicine for those knowledgeable enough to use them. Although many such uses are mentioned in this section as items of interest, they can be dangerous, and we advise *against* trying any of them.

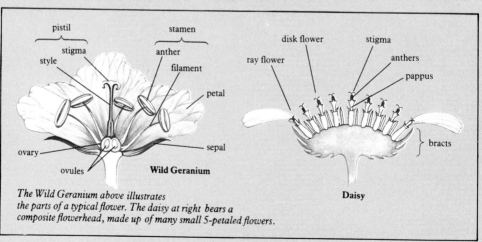

The *Wild Geranium above illustrates the parts of a typical flower. The daisy at right bears a composite flowerhead, made up of many small 5-petaled flowers.*

332   *The habitat symbols for this section are:* *desert* *grassland/meadow/brush* *forest* *roadside* *urban/suburban* *freshwater* *saltwater*

Wildflower Identification Chart

To help you use this section, most of the species shown in it are listed below, arranged by color (yellow to orange, white, red, pink to lavender, blue to purple, and green to brown) and then by overall structure (either small flowers in clusters or a certain number of petals or petallike parts). The symbols used to define flower shapes are explained at right.

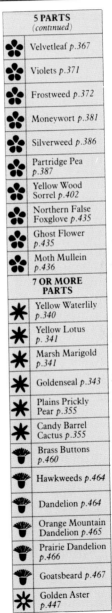

clusters: ✿ rounded   ⁑ elongated   ♉ flat-topped

spreading petals: ✿ 3   ✿ 4   ✿ 5   ✳ 7 or more

🌷 bell- or urnlike   🌼 flaring (lilylike)

🔨 tubular   ✴ orchidlike

👄 bowl- or cuplike   ◖ arumlike

★ 5-pointed star   🌿 thistle- or dandelionlike

✦ 6-pointed star   ❋ daisylike

🐚 miscellaneous odd shapes

CLUSTERS	CLUSTERS (continued)	4 PARTS	5 PARTS (continued)
Cushion Buckwheat *p.363*	Common Mullein *p.436*	California Poppy *p.351*	Velvetleaf *p.367*
Black Mustard *p.374*	Goldenrods *p.449*	Evening primroses *p.396*	Violets *p.371*
Western Wallflower *p.375*	Golden Club *p.480*	Greater Celandine *p.351*	Frostweed *p.372*
Tufted Loosestrife *p.381*	California Bog Asphodel *p.490*	St. Peterswort *p.365*	Moneywort *p.381*
Wall Pepper *p.383*	Cypress Spurge *p.399*	Wild Radish *p.374*	Silverweed *p.386*
Gordon's Ivesia *p.385*	Golden Alexanders *p.406*	**5 PARTS**	Partridge Pea *p.387*
Round-headed Bush Clover *p.393*	Common Tansy *p.460*	Yellow Columbine *p.345*	Yellow Wood Sorrel *p.402*
Orange Milkwort *p.403*	**3 OR 6 PARTS**	Trumpets *p.368*	Northern False Foxglove *p.435*
Butterfly Weed *p.412*	Yellow Mandarin *p.486*	Pinesap *p.379*	Ghost Flower *p.435*
Desert Milkweed *p.413*	Dogtooth violets *p.487*	Virginia Ground Cherry *p.415*	Moth Mullein *p.436*
Navarretia *p. 420*	Big Merrybells *p.487*	Carolina Jessamine *p.404*	**7 OR MORE PARTS**
Spotted Horsemint *p.429*	Yellow Bell *p.491*	Trumpet Creeper *p.439*	Yellow Waterlily *p.340*
Birdbeak *p.434*	Bluebead *p.492*	Yellow Pondlily *p.340*	Yellow Lotus *p. 341*
Alpine Goldenrod *p.449*	Mariposa lilies *p.486*	American Globeflower *p.343*	Marsh Marigold *p.341*
Desert Plume *p.375*	Twisted Yellow-eyed Grass *p.470*	Buttercups *p.347*	Goldenseal *p.343*
Swamp Candles *p.381*	Stinking Benjamin *p.488*	Flower-of-an-hour *p.366*	Plains Prickly Pear *p.355*
Canyon Dudleya *p.383*	Marsh Marigold *p.341*	Scarlet Pimpernel *p.382*	Candy Barrel Cactus *p.355*
Wild Senna *p.387*	Yellow False Garlic *p.481*	St. Johnswort *p.365*	Brass Buttons *p.460*
Milk Vetch *p.389*	Pretty Face *p.483*	Beach Heather *p.372*	Hawkweeds *p.464*
Yellow Lupine *p.391*	Goldenstars *p.490*	Giant Blazing Star *p.372*	Dandelion *p.464*
Wild Indigo *p.392*	Yellow Stargrass *p.490*	Wild Pumpkin *p.373*	Orange Mountain Dandelion *p.465*
Hoary Puccoon *p.422*	Crag Lily *p.496*	Whorled Loosestrife *p.381*	Prairie Dandelion *p.466*
Horse Balm *p.429*	Orange Daylily *p.484*	Buffalo Bur *p.414*	Goatsbeard *p.467*
Downy Paintbrush *p.431*	Lilies *p.485*	Rose Moss *p.360*	Golden Aster *p.447*

333

7 PARTS	
(continued)	
Common Gumweed *p.448*	
Yellow Fleabane *p.450*	
Elecampane *p.452*	
Rosinweeds *p.454*	
Black-eyed Susan *p.455*	
Prairie Coneflower *p.455*	
Sunflowers *p.456*	
Bur Marigold *p.456*	
Tickseeds *p.457*	
Navajo Tea *p.457*	
Mule Ears *p.457*	
Tidy Tips *p.458*	
Mountain Sunflower *p.458*	
Desert Marigold *p.458*	
Goldfields *p.459*	
Bitterweed *p.459*	
Firewheel *p.459*	
Coltsfoot *p.461*	

ODD SHAPES	
Japanese Honeysuckle *p.445*	
Yellow Lady's Slipper *p.500*	
Striped Coralroot *p.502*	
Orange Fringed Orchid *p.503*	
Dingy Dancing Lady *p.506*	
Crested Coralroot *p.506*	
Vanilla Orchid *p.507*	
Longspur Columbine *p.345*	
Birdfoot Trefoil *p.390*	
Rattlebox *p.390*	
Golden Pea *p.390*	
Jewelweed *p.402*	

ODD SHAPES	
(continued)	
Yellow Monkey Flower *p.432*	
Towering Lousewort *p.437*	
Wood Betony *p.437*	
Butter and Eggs *p.437*	
Squawroot *p.438*	
Bladderworts *p.440*	
Yellow Flag *p.497*	

CLUSTERS	
Virgin's Bower *p.342*	
Red Baneberry *p.345*	
Whitlow Grass *p.376*	
Watercress *p.376*	
Early Saxifrage *p.384*	
Prairie Mimosa *p.387*	
White Clover *p.392*	
Snow-on-the-mountain *p.399*	
Wild Sarsaparilla *p.404*	
Ginsengs *p.405*	
Harbinger of Spring *p.405*	
Rattlesnake Master *p.407*	
Great Angelica *p.407*	
Water Pennywort *p.407*	
Whorled Milkweed *p.413*	
White forget-me-nots *p.423*	
Virginia Mountain Mint *p.425*	
Common Horehound *p.428*	
Climbing Boneset *p.447*	
Stinking Fleabane *p.450*	
Pearly Everlasting *p.452*	
Field Pussytoes *p.453*	
Hatpins *p.470*	

CLUSTERS	
(continued)	
Wild Leek *p.489*	
Beargrass *p.493*	
Lizard's Tail *p.338*	
Vanilla Leaf *p.349*	
Miner's Lettuce *p.360*	
Shinleaf *p.378*	
Wandflower *p.379*	
Bishop's Cap *p.384*	
Allegheny Foam-flower *p.384*	
American Burnet *p.385*	
Wild Licorice *p.389*	
Prairie False Indigo *p.392*	
White Sweet Clover *p.393*	
Allegheny Spurge *p.398*	
Seneca Snakeroot *p.403*	
Culver's Root *p.437*	
Silverrod *p.449*	
Fly Poison *p.481*	
Corn Lily *p.493*	
Fairy Wand *p.494*	
Alkali Grass *p.495*	
Canada Mayflower *p.495*	
Solomon's Zigzag *p.495*	
Adam's Needle *p.499*	
Rattlesnake plantains *p.504*	
Ladies' tresses *p.505*	
Phantom Orchid *p.507*	
Queen Anne's Lace *p.406*	
Poison Hemlock *p.407*	
Thoroughwort *p.446*	
Common Yarrow *p.461*	

3 OR 6 PARTS	
Mayapple *p.350*	
White Dogtooth Violet *p.487*	
Asparagus *p.489*	
White Mandarin *p.492*	
Soapweed *p.498*	
Matilija Poppy *p.350*	
Creamcups *p.351*	
Mariposa lilies *p.486*	
Wapato *p.468*	
Trilliums *p.488*	
Goldthread *p.344*	
Anemones *p.348*	
Northern Inside-out Flower *p.349*	
Star-of-Bethlehem *p.482*	
Alp Lily *p.482*	
Soap Plant *p.490*	
Sand Lily *p.494*	
White Blue-eyed Grass *p.496*	
Lilies *p.484*	
Atamasco Lily *p.491*	
Desert Lily *p.496*	

4 PARTS	
Partridgeberry *p.443*	
Prairie Evening Primrose *p.396*	
Cutleaf Toothwort *p.375*	
Springcress *p.376*	
Bunchberry *p.397*	

5 PARTS	
Checkerberry *p.377*	
White Heather *p.377*	
Indian Pipe *p.379*	

5 PARTS (continued)

- Heart's Delight p.354
- Angel's Trumpet p.354
- Devil's Potato p.410
- Jimsonweed p.415
- Wild Potato Vine p.416
- Bindweeds p.417
- Moonflower p.417
- Water Crowfoot p.347
- Anemones p.348
- Swamp Rose p.366
- Fivespot p.421
- Rock Sandwort p.356
- Common Chickweed p.357
- Starry Campion p.358
- Star Cucumber p.373
- One-flowered Wintergreen p.378
- Grass of Parnassus p.384
- Buckbean p.409
- Black Nightshade p.414
- Horse Nettle p.414
- Bladder Campion p.358
- Bouncing Bet p.359
- White Campion p.359
- Leadwort p.364
- Roundleaf Sundew p.369
- Venus Flytrap p.369
- Violets p.371
- Pipsissewas p.378
- Wild Strawberry p.385
- Tall Cinquefoil p.386
- Quail Plant p.423

7 OR MORE PARTS

- Yerba Mansa p.338
- White Waterlily p.340
- Elkslip p.341
- Rue Anemone p.343
- Goldthread p.344
- Carolina Anemone p.348
- Twinleaf p.350
- Bloodroot p.351
- Ice Plant p.362
- Starflower p.382
- Desert Chicory p.466
- Glyptopleura p.467
- Daisy Fleabane p.450
- Easter Daisy p.450
- White Heath Aster p.451
- Oxeye Daisy p.460

ODD SHAPES

- Foxglove Beardtongue p.433
- Japanese Honeysuckle p.455
- Lady's slippers p.500
- Showy Orchis p.503
- Prairie Fringed Orchid p.503
- Palm Polly p.507
- Water Arum p.479
- Dutchman's Breeches p.352
- Squirrel Corn p.352
- Prairie False Indigo p.392
- Yerba Buena p.424
- Bladder Sage p.429
- White Turtlehead p.434
- Water Willow p.439

CLUSTERS

- Four O'Clock p.354
- Crimson Clover p.392
- Trumpet Honeysuckle p.445
- Firecracker Flower p.483
- Snow Plant p.379
- Canyon Dudleya p.383
- Cardinal Spear p.390
- Indian Pink p.404
- Indian paintbrushes p.431
- Leafless Beaked Orchid p.505

3 OR 6 PARTS

- Red Prickly Poppy p.350
- Mariposa lilies p.486
- Wood Lily p.485

4 PARTS

- Scarlet Clematis p.342
- Hummingbird Trumpet p.395
- Trompetilla p.443

5 PARTS

- Wild Columbine p.345
- Prairie Smoke p.386
- Indian Pink p.404
- Cypress Vine p.417
- Standing Cypress p.419
- Cross Vine p.439
- Trumpet Creeper p.439
- Poppy Mallow p.366
- Scarlet Globe Mallow p.367
- Scarlet Pimpernel p.382
- Fire Pink p.358
- Round-leaved Catchfly p.358

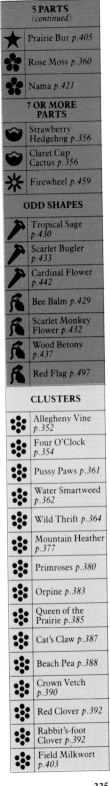

5 PARTS (continued)

- Prairie Bur p.405
- Rose Moss p.360
- Nama p.421

7 OR MORE PARTS

- Strawberry Hedgehog p.356
- Claret Cup Cactus p.356
- Firewheel p.459

ODD SHAPES

- Tropical Sage p.430
- Scarlet Bugler p.433
- Cardinal Flower p.442
- Bee Balm p.429
- Scarlet Monkey Flower p.432
- Wood Betony p.437
- Red Flag p.497

CLUSTERS

- Allegheny Vine p.352
- Four O'Clock p.354
- Pussy Paws p.361
- Water Smartweed p.362
- Wild Thrift p.364
- Mountain Heather p.377
- Primroses p.380
- Orpine p.383
- Queen of the Prairie p.385
- Cat's Claw p.387
- Beach Pea p.388
- Crown Vetch p.390
- Red Clover p.392
- Rabbit's-foot Clover p.392
- Field Milkwort p.403

335

	CLUSTERS *(continued)*
	Milkweeds *p.412*
	Rose Vervain *p.424*
	Field Mint *p.425*
	Mountain Monardella *p.427*
	Stonemint *p.428*
	Wild Bergamot *p.429*
	Bluets *p.443*
	Swamp Pink *p.481*
	Onions *p.489*
	Pale Larkspur *p.346*
	Pinkweed *p.362*
	Sea Lavender *p.364*
	Steeplebush *p.385*
	Showy Locoweed *p.388*
	Showy Tick Trefoil *p.393*
	Kudzu *p.394*
	Spearmint *p.425*
	American Germander *p.426*
	Purple Paintbrush *p.431*
	Water Speedwell *p.436*
	Blazing Stars *p.448*
	Sweet Joe-pye-weed *p.446*

	3 or 6 PARTS
	Rose Mandarin *p.492*
	Pasqueflower *p.348*
	Mariposa lilies *p.486*
	Coast Trillium *p.488*
	Round-lobed Hepatica *p.344*
	Snake Lily *p.483*
	Onions *p.489*
	Swamp Lily *p.491*

	4 PARTS
	Farewell-to-spring *p.395*
	Showy Evening Primrose *p.396*
	Dame's Rocket *p.375*
	American Cranberry *p.377*
	Fireweed *p.395*
	Deerhorn *p.395*
	Meadow beauties *p.397*

	5 PARTS
	Bearberry *p.377*
	Purple-tipped Gentian *p.408*
	Spreading Dogbane *p.411*
	Harebell *p.441*
	Twinflower *p.445*
	Heart's Delight *p.354*
	Morning glories *p.416*
	Naked Broomrape *p.438*
	Musk Mallow *p.366*
	Marsh Mallow *p.367*
	Lilac Sunbonnets *p.419*
	Deptford Pink *p.359*
	Mayflower *p.377*
	Shooting Star *p.380*
	Rose Pink *p.410*
	Rosita *p.410*
	Common Pink *p.358*
	Bouncing Bet *p.359*
	Corn Cockle *p.359*
	Spring Beauty *p.360*
	Rose Moss *p.360*
	Red Maids *p.361*
	Fameflower *p.361*

	5 PARTS *(continued)*
	Dewthread *p.369*
	Violets *p.370*
	Pipsissewa *p.378*
	Mountain Douglasia *p.380*
	Sea Milkwort *p.382*
	Geraniums *p.401*
	Common Wood Sorrel *p.402*
	Phlox *p.418*
	Ground Pink *p.420*
	Purple Gerardia *p.430*
	Dwarf Monkey Flower *p.432*

	7 OR MORE PARTS
	Sacred Lotus *p.341*
	Round-lobed Hepatica *p.344*
	Carolina Anemone *p.348*
	Peyote *p.355*
	Pincushion Cactus *p.357*
	Fishhook Cactus *p.357*
	Bitterroot *p.361*
	Ice Plant *p.362*
	Maypop *p.372*
	Large Marsh Pink *p.410*
	Skeleton Plant *p.465*
	Dusty Maiden *p.459*
	Spotted Knapweed *p.462*
	Nodding Thistle *p.462*
	Thistles *p.463*
	Daisy Fleabane *p.450*
	Easter Daisy *p.450*
	Asters *p.451*
	Pale Purple Coneflower *p.455*

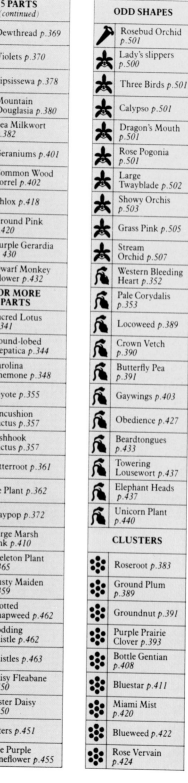

	ODD SHAPES
	Rosebud Orchid *p.501*
	Lady's slippers *p.500*
	Three Birds *p.501*
	Calypso *p.501*
	Dragon's Mouth *p.501*
	Rose Pogonia *p.501*
	Large Twayblade *p.502*
	Showy Orchis *p.503*
	Grass Pink *p.505*
	Stream Orchid *p.507*
	Western Bleeding Heart *p.352*
	Pale Corydalis *p.353*
	Locoweed *p.389*
	Crown Vetch *p.390*
	Butterfly Pea *p.391*
	Gaywings *p.403*
	Obedience *p.427*
	Beardtongues *p.433*
	Towering Lousewort *p.437*
	Elephant Heads *p.437*
	Unicorn Plant *p.440*

	CLUSTERS
	Roseroot *p.383*
	Ground Plum *p.389*
	Groundnut *p.391*
	Purple Prairie Clover *p.393*
	Bottle Gentian *p.408*
	Bluestar *p.411*
	Miami Mist *p.420*
	Blueweed *p.422*
	Rose Vervain *p.424*

CLUSTERS *(continued)*			
Heal-all *p.425*			
Gill-over-the-ground *p.427*			
Chia *p.430*			
Blue-eyed Mary *p.431*			
Escobita *p.434*			
Tall Ironweed *p.447*			
Lupines *p.391*			
American Wisteria *p.394*			
Spiked Loosestrife *p.397*			
Purple Fringe *p.420*			
Hoary Vervain *p.424*			
Woundwort *p.426*			
Carpet Bugleweed *p.426*			
Mountain Kittentails *p.435*			
Louisiana Broomrape *p.438*			
Venus' Looking Glass *p.441*			
Great Blue Lobelia *p.442*			
Blazing Stars *p.448*			
Pickerelweed *p.480*			
Camases *p.494*			
Mistflower *p.446*			

3 or 6 PARTS

- Toadshade *p.488*
- Mariposa lilies *p.486*
- Spiderwort *p.470*
- Stinking Benjamin *p.488*
- Water Shield *p.340*
- Blue Cohosh *p.349*
- Water Hyacinth *p.480*
- Blue-dicks *p.483*
- Blue-eyed Grass *p.496*

3 or 6 PARTS *(continued)*

- Prairie Iris *p.496*
- Brodiaea lilies *p.482*
- Chaparral Lily *p.484*

4 PARTS

- Leatherflower *p.342*
- Fringed Gentian *p.408*
- Desert Candle *p.374*
- Winecup Clarkia *p.395*
- Birdseye Speedwell *p.436*
- Quaker Ladies *p.443*

5 PARTS

- Northern Pitcher Plant *p.368*
- Prairie Smoke *p.386*
- Explorer's Gentian *p.408*
- Greek Valerian *p.419*
- Virginia Bluebells *p.422*
- Southern Harebell *p.441*
- Desert Four O'Clock *p.354*
- Morning glories *p.416*
- Pale Trumpets *p.419*
- Ruellia *p.439*
- Blue Columbine *p.345*
- Bluebells *p.409*
- Baby Blue-eyes *p.421*
- Marsh Cinquefoil *p.386*
- Downy Gentian *p.408*
- Bluestar *p.411*
- Bittersweet Nightshade *p.414*
- Tall Bellflower *p.441*
- Larkspurs *p.346*
- Rose Moss *p.360*

5 PARTS *(continued)*

- Violets *p.370*
- Violet Wood Sorrel *p.402*
- Common Flax *p.403*
- Running Myrtle *p.411*
- Phlox *p.418*
- Nama *p.421*
- Forget-me-not *p.422*

7 OR MORE PARTS

- Strawberry Hedgehog *p.356*
- Maypop *p.372*
- Thistles *p.463*
- Common Chicory *p.466*
- Asters *p.451*

ODD SHAPES

- Spotted Coralroot *p.502*
- Showy Orchis *p.503*
- Purple Fringed Orchid *p.503*
- Cranefly Orchid *p.504*
- Stream Orchid *p.507*
- Jack-in-the-pulpit *p.479*
- Monkshoods *p.344*
- Downy Skullcap *p.427*
- Blue Curls *p.428*
- Bladder Sage *p.429*
- Blue Sage *p.430*
- Allegheny Monkey Flower *p.432*
- Towering Lousewort *p.437*
- Butterwort *p.440*
- Downingias *p.442*
- Asiatic Dayflower *p.470*
- Irises *p.497*

CLUSTERS

- Snow-on-the-mountain *p.399*
- American Spikenard *p.404*
- Green Milkweed *p.413*
- Lamb's Quarters *p.359*
- One-sided Pyrola *p.378*
- Deertongue *p.409*
- Common Plantain *p.424*
- Common Ragweed *p.453*
- Cattails *p.477*
- Indian Poke *p.493*
- Bunchflower *p.495*

3 OR 6 PARTS

- Wild gingers *p.338*
- Indian Cucumber-root *p.487*
- Toadshade *p.488*
- Solomon's Seal *p.492*

5 PARTS

- Cobra Plant *p.368*

7 OR MORE PARTS

- Teddy Bear Cholla *p.355*
- Hen and Chickens Cactus *p.356*

ODD SHAPES

- Heartleaf Twayblade *p.502*
- Puttyroot *p.504*
- Butterfly Orchid *p.506*
- Vanilla Orchid *p.507*
- Skunk Cabbage *p.478*
- Green Dragon *p.479*
- Green Arrow *p.480*
- Dutchman's Pipe *p.339*
- Indian Root *p.339*

Lizard's Tail
Saururus cernuus

Size: *1–3 ft. tall;
flower plume 3–6 in. long.*
What to look for: *flowers
tiny, cream-colored, in drooping
plumes; leaves heart-shaped,
leathery.* **Habitat:** *pond edges,
swampy forests.*
In bloom: *June–Sept.*

Lizard's Tails   *Saururus*

The Lizard's Tail takes its name from the graceful
plumes of delicately scented flowers that have
made it a popular plant for pools and water gardens.
(It is sometimes sold under the less picturesque name
of Swamp Lily.) Spreading by means of branches
that form just above the roots, it occasionally escapes
from cultivation and is therefore found growing in
wetlands well outside its native range.

Yerba Mansa   *Anemopsis*

The alkaline soil of the New Mexico section of
the Rio Grande Valley is bound tightly together by
the spreading root systems of clusters of Yerba
Mansa. Bricks cut from this soil are more waterproof
than plain mud adobe, and so they were preferred as
building material—first by the Indians and later by
the Spanish, who christened the plant *yerba del
manso,* or plant of the farmhouse. The plant group
contains only one species.

Yerba Mansa
Anemopsis californica

Size: *2–6 in. tall;
flower head 1–2 in. wide.*
What to look for: *flower
heads white or pinkish,
composed of many tiny flowers
clustered above petallike
bracts; leaves long-stalked,
oval.* **Habitat:** *wet
meadows, streambanks.*
In bloom: *Mar.–Aug.*

Wild Gingers   *Asarum*

The sharply acrid taste of these plants, reminiscent of
the unrelated tropical spice for which they are
named, protects them against most plant eaters.
Humans, however, dig the spreading underground
stems (called rhizomes), boil the pieces in sugar
water, and use the decoction in place of true ginger.
The ground-hugging flowers have a fetid odor, like
rotting meat, and attract pollinating flies. After
the seeds have formed, ants carry them away but eat
only the seed coats, thus spreading the plant.

Wild Ginger
Asarum canadense

Size: *4–7 in. tall; flower ½–1½ in. wide.*
What to look for: *leaves large, hairy, kidney-shaped;
flowers red-brown to purple, urn-shaped, each borne
on short stem between 2 leaves.* **Habitat:** *rich woods.*
In bloom: *Mar.–June.*

Western
Wild Ginger
Asarum caudatum

Size: *4–8 in. tall; flower 2–5 in. wide.*
What to look for: *leaves slightly hairy, heart-shaped;
flowers brownish purple, urn-shaped, with 3 thin
"tails."* **Habitat:** *rich woods.* **In bloom:** *Apr.–July.*

Birthworts *Aristolochia*

According to the Doctrine of Signatures, a concept prevalent in the 17th century, plants proclaimed their medicinal values by some aspect of their appearance. Because the flowers of birthwort seemed to resemble pregnant wombs, women in labor were advised to chew the roots to ease the pain of childbirth. But the birthwort flower is in fact a flytrap that ensures cross-pollination. In the depths of each blossom is the pistil, or female organ, which matures before the stamens (male organs). The pistil is located at the end of a narrow passageway lined with downward-pointing hairs. Attracted by the fetid-smelling nectar, a fly enters the flower but cannot escape. While imprisoned it feeds on nectar and deposits any pollen it may have carried from another blossom. Later, when the pollen-producing stamens have matured, the flower opens fully. On the way out, the fly picks up fresh pollen to carry to another flower.

Indian Root
Aristolochia watsonii

Size: *vine 1–3 ft. long; flower ¾–1½ in. long.*
What to look for: *stems trailing; flowers tubular with narrow opening, brown to greenish purple; leaves hairy, triangular, lobed at base.*
Habitat: *warm deserts, mountain scrublands.*
In bloom: *Apr.–Aug.*

Virginia Snakeroot
Aristolochia serpentaria

Size: *6–30 in. tall; flower ½–¾ in. long.*
What to look for: *flowers brownish purple, S-shaped, borne on stalks near ground; leaves arrow- to heart-shaped.*
Habitat: *dry to wet forests; often in leaf litter.*
In bloom: *May–July.*

Dutchman's Pipe
Aristolochia durior

Size: *vine to 60 ft. high; flower 1–1½ in. long.*
What to look for: *flowers pipe-shaped, purple to greenish yellow; leaves heart-shaped, to 1 ft. wide.* **Habitat:** *rich woods, swampy forests.*
In bloom: *May–July.*

White Water–Lily
Nymphaea odorata

Size: *flower 2–6 in. wide; leaf 3–20 in. across.*
What to look for: *flowers white, floating; leaves shiny green, oval, notched, floating.* **Habitat:** *still freshwater to 8 ft. deep.*
In bloom: *Mar.–Oct.*

Yellow Water–Lily
Nymphaea mexicana

Size: *flower 3–4 in. wide; leaf 4–8 in. across.*
What to look for: *flowers yellow, floating or slightly above water surface; leaves green blotched with brown, notched, floating.* **Habitat:** *still freshwater to 4 ft. deep.*
In bloom: *Mar.–Sept.*

Water–Lilies *Nymphaea*

Among the many plants that grow rooted to the bottoms of ponds, lakes, and sluggish rivers, these are best beloved, with their bright, floating blossoms and deeply notched pads. When the flower fades, its stalk shrinks, submerging the hard-cased fruit while the edible seeds mature. Then the case opens, and the seeds float free until they finally become waterlogged, sink, and take root.

Yellow Pond–Lily
Nuphar luteum

Size: *flower ½–2½ in. wide; leaf 2–18 in. across.*
What to look for: *flowers cup-shaped, held above water; heart-shaped leaves submerged, floating, or above water.* **Habitat:** *still freshwater to 15 ft. deep.*
In bloom: *May–Oct.*

Water–Shield
Brasenia schreberi

Size: *flower ½ in. wide; leaf 2–4 in. across.*
What to look for: *flowers dull reddish purple, held slightly above water on stout stems; leaves medium green, elliptical, floating on surface.*
Habitat: *still freshwater to 10 ft. deep.*
In bloom: *June–Sept.*

Water–Shields *Brasenia*

The single species of Water Shield grows wild on every continent except Antarctica, known by such names as Deerfood, Frogleaf, Little Waterlily, Purple Dock, and Water Target. The hard round seeds are eaten by ducks the world over, and people of many lands eat the roots and leaves. The undersides of the leaves, stems, and other submerged parts are protected from snails, insect larvae, and many other water animals by a gelatinous coating.

Pond–Lilies *Nuphar*

These plants, also known as spatterdocks, grow so rampantly that they are often eradicated as weeds. Where wildlife is abundant, however, this vigor is of value. Ducks eat the seeds. Moose and deer graze on the greens. Muskrats and beavers relish the sweet rootstocks, storing caches of them for winter. (Indians and frontiersmen, who cooked and ate the rootstocks like potatoes or pounded them into flour, sometimes raided the animal stockpiles.)

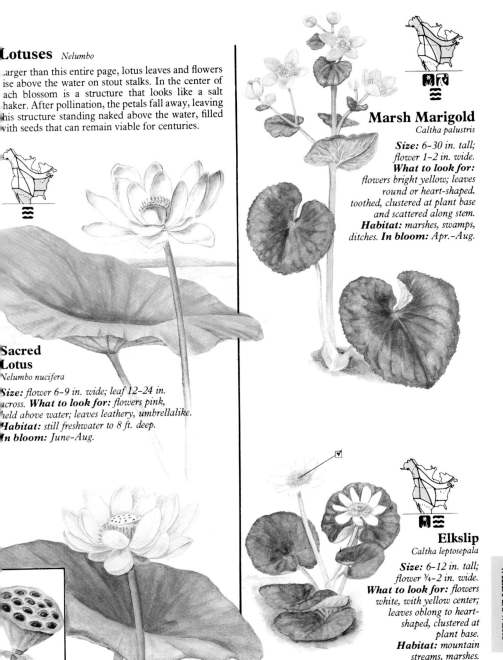

Lotuses *Nelumbo*

Larger than this entire page, lotus leaves and flowers rise above the water on stout stalks. In the center of each blossom is a structure that looks like a salt shaker. After pollination, the petals fall away, leaving this structure standing naked above the water, filled with seeds that can remain viable for centuries.

Sacred Lotus
Nelumbo nucifera

Size: *flower 6–9 in. wide; leaf 12–24 in. across.* **What to look for:** *flowers pink, held above water; leaves leathery, umbrellalike.* **Habitat:** *still freshwater to 8 ft. deep.* **In bloom:** *June–Aug.*

Yellow Lotus
Nelumbo lutea

Size: *flower 6–8 in. wide; leaf 12–24 in. across.* **What to look for:** *flowers yellow, held up to 10 ft. above surface; leaves umbrellalike.* **Habitat:** *still freshwater to 8 ft. deep.* **In bloom:** *June–Sept.*

Marsh Marigold
Caltha palustris

Size: *6–30 in. tall; flower 1–2 in. wide.* **What to look for:** *flowers bright yellow; leaves round or heart-shaped, toothed, clustered at plant base and scattered along stem.* **Habitat:** *marshes, swamps, ditches.* **In bloom:** *Apr.–Aug.*

Elkslip
Caltha leptosepala

Size: *6–12 in. tall; flower ¾–2 in. wide.* **What to look for:** *flowers white, with yellow center; leaves oblong to heart-shaped, clustered at plant base.* **Habitat:** *mountain streams, marshes.* **In bloom:** *May–Aug.*

Marsh Marigolds *Caltha*

Although these plants are called marigolds, they actually belong to the buttercup family. Crowds of their cheery flowers and glistening leaves brighten wetlands throughout the Northern Hemisphere. The leaves are often eaten cooked, but are poisonous to humans and most animals if eaten raw. Elk and moose, however, fed with impunity on the Elkslip.

WILDFLOWERS

341

Leatherflower
Clematis viorna

Size: *vine 3-6 ft. high; flower ¾ in. wide.*
What to look for: *flowers pinkish purple with creamy tips, urn-shaped, nodding; leaves divided into several large egg-shaped leaflets.* **Habitat:** *rich woods; rich thickets.* **In bloom:** *May-Aug.*

Scarlet Clematis
Clematis texensis

Size: *vine 1-6 ft. high; flower ½-¾ in. wide.*
What to look for: *flowers red, urn-shaped, single or clustered; leaves divided into 3-5 pairs of rounded leaflets; stems sprawling or climbing.* **Habitat:** *cliffs, wooded slopes near streams in Texas.* **In bloom:** *May-June.*

Clematises *Clematis*

These plants are unique among the buttercup family in that they are twining vines. They climb trees, arbors, and other supports by what seem to be leafy, coiling branches. To a botanist, each of these climbing tendrils is the central stalk of a single compound leaf, which is divided into several small leaflets growing in pairs along its length. When Charles Darwin studied the Virgin's Bower, he found that each new leafstalk revolves as it grows, making a full circle every five or six hours until it finds a solid object to climb. The technical term for this searching pattern of growth is thigmotropism.

Virgin's Bower
Clematis virginiana

Size: *vine 3-15 ft. high; flower ½-¾ in. wide.*
What to look for: *flowers white, profuse, on dense, tangled vine; leaves divided into 3 leaflets, fruit white, feathery.* **Habitat:** *thickets, fencerows, roadsides.* **In bloom:** *July-Sept.*

fruit

Curlflower
Clematis crispa

Size: *vine 1-10 ft. high; flower 1-2 in. wide.*
What to look for: *flowers bluish purple, bell-shaped, with 4 upcurved lips; leaves divided into 5-9 lance-shaped leaflets.* **Habitat:** *swamps, wet woods, clearings.* **In bloom:** *Apr.-Aug.*

WILDFLOWERS

342

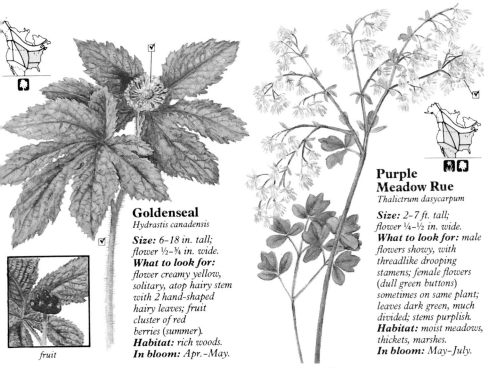

Goldenseal
Hydrastis canadensis

Size: 6–18 in. tall;
flower ½–¾ in. wide.
What to look for:
flower creamy yellow,
solitary, atop hairy stem
with 2 hand-shaped
hairy leaves; fruit
cluster of red
berries (summer).
Habitat: rich woods.
In bloom: Apr.–May.

fruit

Goldenseals *Hydrastis*

Once abundant, the only American goldenseal is
rare now because its thick yellow roots have had great
commercial value. They were used to treat dyspepsia,
skin eruptions, and hemorrhage, and were also a
source of yellow dye and an insect repellent. Lewis
and Clark described Goldenseal to Thomas Jefferson
as a "sovereign remidy [*sic*] for sore eyes."

Purple
Meadow Rue
Thalictrum dasycarpum

Size: 2–7 ft. tall;
flower ¼–½ in. wide.
What to look for: *male
flowers showy, with
threadlike drooping
stamens; female flowers
(dull green buttons)
sometimes on same plant;
leaves dark green, much
divided; stems purplish.
Habitat: moist meadows,
thickets, marshes.
In bloom: May–July.

Meadow Rues *Thalictrum*

Several of these stately perennials bear the male
(pollen-producing) flowers on one plant and the seed-
producing female flowers on the other, and thus depend on wind and—to a lesser extent—on insects to
carry pollen from plant to plant. Most other species
bear both kinds of flowers on one plant, and a few
high mountain species bear "perfect" flowers (each
bloom has both male and female parts).

Rue Anemone
Anemonella thalictroides

Size: 2–8 in. tall;
flower ½–¾ in. wide.
What to look for:
flowers white, in 2's or
3's, surrounded by
whorl of leaflets atop
wiry black stem; leaves
from base much divided.
Habitat: rich woods.
In bloom: Apr.–May.

Rue Anemones *Anemonella*

Neither a rue nor an anemone, the one species in this
group gets its compound name from its ruelike leaves
and anemonelike flowers. The False Rue Anemone
(*Isopyrum biternatum*) resembles this plant (its flowers are smaller), and it has a similar range.

American
Globeflower
Trollius laxus

Size: 4–20 in. tall;
flower ¾–1½ in. wide.
What to look for:
flowers greenish
yellow, cup-shaped,
scattered on plants;
leaves sharply
segmented, toothed.
Habitat: marshes,
swampy woods, streams.
In bloom: Apr.–June.

Globeflowers *Trollius*

Occasionally seen in cultivation, globeflowers are
rather rare in the wild. There is only one species in
North America; a white-flowered variety of this
species is found high in the Rocky Mountains. Its
flowers appear in profusion after the snow melts.

WILDFLOWERS

Goldthreads *Coptis*

Coming across these brilliant white blossoms above a bed of lustrous green leaves in a shady mountain wood is like finding a patch of diamonds aglitter in an emerald setting. The leaves and flowers both arise from the plant's threadlike yellow underground stem, or rhizome—the inspiration for the name.

Goldthread
Coptis trifolia

Size: 2½–5 in. tall; flower ¼–½ in. wide.
What to look for: flowers solitary, on slender, leafless stalks; leaves evergreen, clustered at base, with 3 toothed leaflets.
Habitat: mossy woods, boggy places.
In bloom: May–July.

Hepaticas *Hepatica*

Two forms of hepatica grow in the same general range (though seldom together) and look very much alike except for their leaf shapes. The Round-lobed Hepatica, also called Liverleaf, grows in acid soil; the Sharp-lobed Hepatica flourishes in soil with a limestone base. The flowers of both open in spring before new leaves appear, above a flat blanket of last year's foliage.

Sharp-lobed Hepatica

Hepatica
Hepatica nobilis

Size: 2–5 in. high; flower ½–¾ in. wide.
What to look for: flowers blue, purple, pinkish, or white, on hairy stalks; leaves leathery, 3-lobed.
Habitat: rich woods.
In bloom: Mar.–Apr.

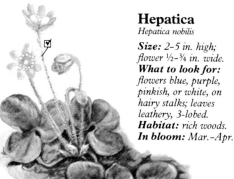

Blue Monkshood
Aconitum columbianum

Size: 1–7 ft. tall; flower ¾–1 in. wide.
What to look for: flowers blue or purple (occasionally white), hooded, on tall stalk; leaves lobed, toothed.
Habitat: streambanks, moist woods, meadows.
In bloom: June–Aug.

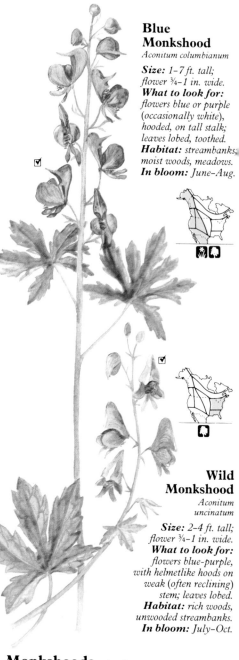

Wild Monkshood
Aconitum uncinatum

Size: 2–4 ft. tall; flower ¾–1 in. wide.
What to look for: flowers blue-purple, with helmetlike hoods on weak (often reclining) stem; leaves lobed.
Habitat: rich woods, unwooded streambanks.
In bloom: July–Oct.

Monkshoods *Aconitum*

The "hood" of the monkshood is technically a sepal that covers the true petals. In some species it more nearly resembles a crested helmet, inspiring such names as Thor's Hat and Helmetflower. Monkshoods are pollinated mainly by bumblebees, which are among the few insects strong enough to enter the hood. The plants are hazardous to both humans and livestock; they contain a deadly substance called aconite, which has been used as arrow poison.

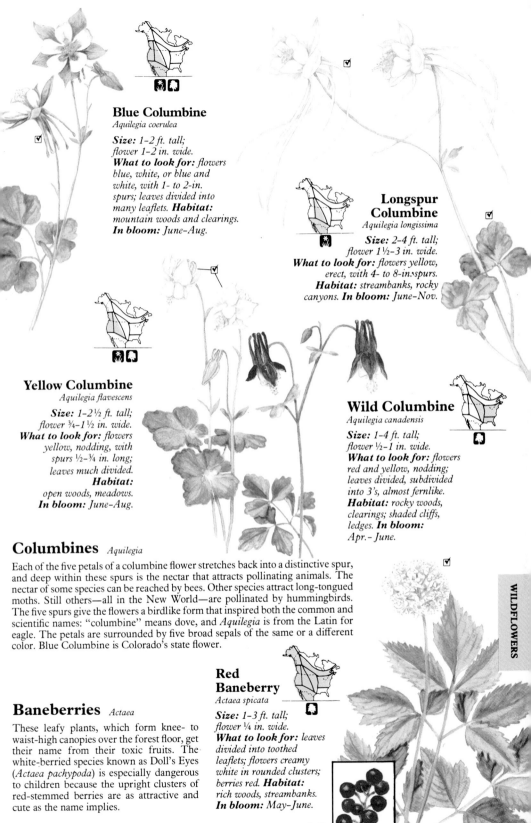

Blue Columbine
Aquilegia coerulea

Size: *1–2 ft. tall; flower 1–2 in. wide.*
What to look for: *flowers blue, white, or blue and white, with 1- to 2-in. spurs; leaves divided into many leaflets.* **Habitat:** *mountain woods and clearings.* **In bloom:** *June–Aug.*

Longspur Columbine
Aquilegia longissima

Size: *2–4 ft. tall; flower 1½–3 in. wide.*
What to look for: *flowers yellow, erect, with 4- to 8-in. spurs.* **Habitat:** *streambanks, rocky canyons.* **In bloom:** *June–Nov.*

Yellow Columbine
Aquilegia flavescens

Size: *1–2½ ft. tall; flower ¾–1½ in. wide.*
What to look for: *flowers yellow, nodding, with spurs ½–¾ in. long; leaves much divided.* **Habitat:** *open woods, meadows.* **In bloom:** *June–Aug.*

Wild Columbine
Aquilegia canadensis

Size: *1–4 ft. tall; flower ½–1 in. wide.*
What to look for: *flowers red and yellow, nodding; leaves divided, subdivided into 3's, almost fernlike.* **Habitat:** *rocky woods, clearings; shaded cliffs, ledges.* **In bloom:** *Apr.– June.*

Columbines *Aquilegia*

Each of the five petals of a columbine flower stretches back into a distinctive spur, and deep within these spurs is the nectar that attracts pollinating animals. The nectar of some species can be reached by bees. Other species attract long-tongued moths. Still others—all in the New World—are pollinated by hummingbirds. The five spurs give the flowers a birdlike form that inspired both the common and scientific names: "columbine" means dove, and *Aquilegia* is from the Latin for eagle. The petals are surrounded by five broad sepals of the same or a different color. Blue Columbine is Colorado's state flower.

Baneberries *Actaea*

These leafy plants, which form knee- to waist-high canopies over the forest floor, get their name from their toxic fruits. The white-berried species known as Doll's Eyes (*Actaea pachypoda*) is especially dangerous to children because the upright clusters of red-stemmed berries are as attractive and cute as the name implies.

Red Baneberry
Actaea spicata

Size: *1–3 ft. tall; flower ¼ in. wide.*
What to look for: *leaves divided into toothed leaflets; flowers creamy white in rounded clusters; berries red.* **Habitat:** *rich woods, streambanks.* **In bloom:** *May–June.*

fruit

Larkspurs *Delphinium*

Shakespeare knew them as lark's heels. Their modern name describes the same characteristic spur, which is formed by the upper sepal of the flower. (There are five sepals, all of the same color.) In the center of each flower are four small petals. The upper two petals extend back to line the inside of the spur, where nectar awaits those insects that can reach it—long-tongued butterflies and moths, and strong, aggressive bumblebees. Because all parts of the plants are poisonous to livestock, as well as to humans, they are among the many plants known in western cattle country as locoweeds, staggerweeds, or cow poisons. The Hopi Indians extracted a blue dye from the flowers of larkspur, and settlers later mixed this extract with a fixative to make blue ink.

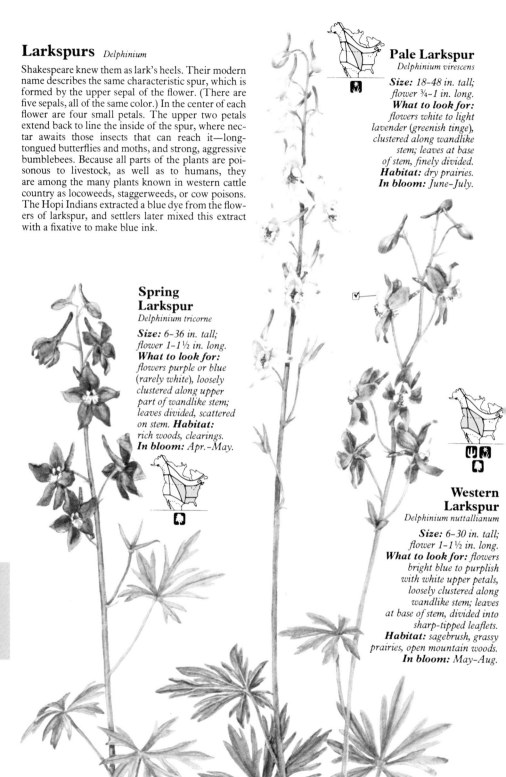

Pale Larkspur
Delphinium virescens

Size: 18–48 in. tall;
flower ¾–1 in. long.
What to look for:
flowers white to light
lavender (greenish tinge),
clustered along wandlike
stem; leaves at base
of stem, finely divided.
Habitat: dry prairies.
In bloom: June–July.

Spring Larkspur
Delphinium tricorne

Size: 6–36 in. tall;
flower 1–1½ in. long.
What to look for:
flowers purple or blue
(rarely white), loosely
clustered along upper
part of wandlike stem;
leaves divided, scattered
on stem. **Habitat:**
rich woods, clearings.
In bloom: Apr.–May.

Western Larkspur
Delphinium nuttallianum

Size: 6–30 in. tall;
flower 1–1½ in. long.
What to look for: flowers
bright blue to purplish
with white upper petals,
loosely clustered along
wandlike stem; leaves
at base of stem, divided into
sharp-tipped leaflets.
Habitat: sagebrush, grassy
prairies, open mountain woods.
In bloom: May–Aug.

Buttercups *Ranunculus*

There are more than 300 species of buttercups. Some grow on land, some in water, and the majority in the moist and marshy places that lie between. Most are notable for their splayed leaves—for which some species are called crowfoot—and cupped flowers. Many contain an acrid juice that can poison cattle and blister human skin. Beggars once used the Tall Buttercup and the aptly named Cursed Crowfoot (*Ranunculus sceleratus*) to induce ulcerous sores on their bodies and faces. Among botanists, buttercups are believed to represent a primitive, nonspecialized stage of evolution. Many species have petals and similar-looking sepals that open to reveal a central mound of multiple stamens and pistils crowded together; a disturbance will shake pollen from one to the other. In more highly evolved plants, the parts are adapted to perform special functions in the process of cross-pollination.

Swamp Buttercup
Ranunculus hispidus

Size: 1–3 ft. long; flower ¾–1 in. wide.
What to look for: flowers bright yellow, with 5 petals much longer than sepals; stems usually sprawling; leaves divided into 3 stalked leaflets.
Habitat: marshes, ditches; wet woods, meadows.
In bloom: Apr.–June.

Prairie Buttercup
Ranunculus rhomboideus

Size: 2–7 in. tall; flower ½–¾ in. wide.
What to look for: flowers light yellow, with 5 narrow petals and 5 short, lavender-tinged sepals around spherical center clusters; stems hairy; leaves lobed near flower, spoon-shaped near base of plant.
Habitat: grasslands, dry prairies. **In bloom:** Apr.–May.

Tall Buttercup
Ranunculus acris

Size: 1–3 ft. tall; flower ¾–1 in. wide.
What to look for: flowers waxy, bright yellow or white, on slender, branched stems; leaves divided into 5–7 toothed leaflets.
Habitat: meadows, fields, roadsides.
In bloom: May–Sept.

Bristly Crowfoot
Ranunculus pensylvanicus

Size: 1–2 ft. tall; flower ¼–½ in. wide.
What to look for: flowers pale yellow, with petals shorter than sepals; stems bristly; leaves hairy, cleft into 3 sharp-pointed lobes. **Habitat:** marshes, ditches, wet meadows.
In bloom: July–Aug.

Water Crowfoot
Ranunculus trichophyllus

Size: 1–3 ft. long; flower ½ in. wide.
What to look for: flowers white with yellow centers, held just above water; leaves round-lobed on surface, hairlike underwater. **Habitat:** ponds, marshes.
In bloom: May–July.

347

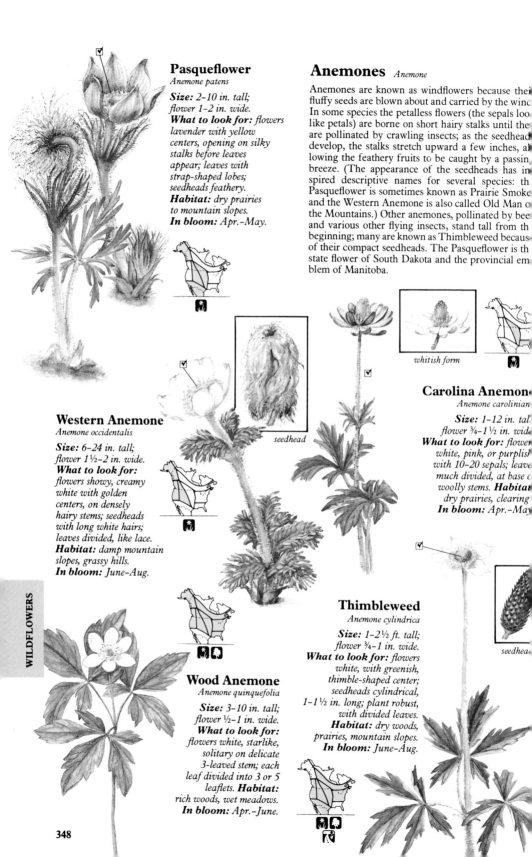

Pasqueflower
Anemone patens

Size: *2–10 in. tall; flower 1–2 in. wide.*
What to look for: *flowers lavender with yellow centers, opening on silky stalks before leaves appear; leaves with strap-shaped lobes; seedheads feathery.*
Habitat: *dry prairies to mountain slopes.*
In bloom: *Apr.–May.*

Anemones *Anemone*

Anemones are known as windflowers because their fluffy seeds are blown about and carried by the wind. In some species the petalless flowers (the sepals look like petals) are borne on short hairy stalks until they are pollinated by crawling insects; as the seedheads develop, the stalks stretch upward a few inches, allowing the feathery fruits to be caught by a passing breeze. (The appearance of the seedheads has inspired descriptive names for several species: the Pasqueflower is sometimes known as Prairie Smoke, and the Western Anemone is also called Old Man of the Mountains.) Other anemones, pollinated by bees and various other flying insects, stand tall from the beginning; many are known as Thimbleweed because of their compact seedheads. The Pasqueflower is the state flower of South Dakota and the provincial emblem of Manitoba.

whitish form

Western Anemone
Anemone occidentalis

Size: *6–24 in. tall; flower 1½–2 in. wide.*
What to look for: *flowers showy, creamy white with golden centers, on densely hairy stems; seedheads with long white hairs; leaves divided, like lace.*
Habitat: *damp mountain slopes, grassy hills.*
In bloom: *June–Aug.*

seedhead

Carolina Anemone
Anemone caroliniana

Size: *1–12 in. tall; flower ¾–1½ in. wide.*
What to look for: *flowers white, pink, or purplish with 10–20 sepals; leaves much divided, at base of woolly stems.* **Habitat:** *dry prairies, clearings.*
In bloom: *Apr.–May.*

Thimbleweed
Anemone cylindrica

Size: *1–2½ ft. tall; flower ¾–1 in. wide.*
What to look for: *flowers white, with greenish, thimble-shaped center; seedheads cylindrical, 1–1½ in. long; plant robust, with divided leaves.*
Habitat: *dry woods, prairies, mountain slopes.*
In bloom: *June–Aug.*

seedhead

Wood Anemone
Anemone quinquefolia

Size: *3–10 in. tall; flower ½–1 in. wide.*
What to look for: *flowers white, starlike, solitary on delicate 3-leaved stem; each leaf divided into 3 or 5 leaflets.* **Habitat:** *rich woods, wet meadows.*
In bloom: *Apr.–June.*

WILDFLOWERS

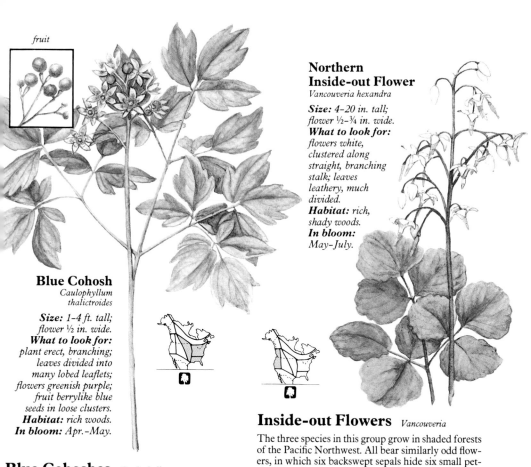

fruit

Blue Cohosh
Caulophyllum thalictroides

Size: *1-4 ft. tall; flower ½ in. wide.*
What to look for: *plant erect, branching; leaves divided into many lobed leaflets; flowers greenish purple; fruit berrylike blue seeds in loose clusters.*
Habitat: *rich woods.*
In bloom: *Apr.–May.*

Northern Inside-out Flower
Vancouveria hexandra

Size: *4-20 in. tall; flower ½–¾ in. wide.*
What to look for: *flowers white, clustered along straight, branching stalk; leaves leathery, much divided.*
Habitat: *rich, shady woods.*
In bloom: *May-July.*

Blue Cohoshes   *Caulophyllum*

Indians gave the name cohosh to several unrelated plants with two things in common: they serve medicinal purposes, and they bear poisonous berries. The Blue Cohosh, which is the only species of *Caulophyllum*, is also called Papoose Root because Indians used it to hasten childbirth.

Inside-out Flowers   *Vancouveria*

The three species in this group grow in shaded forests of the Pacific Northwest. All bear similarly odd flowers, in which six backswept sepals hide six small petals. The Northern Inside-out Flower dies back in autumn; the Redwood Inside-out Flower (*Vancouveria planipetala*) and the Golden Inside-out Flower (*Vancouveria chrysantha*) are evergreen.

Vanilla Leaves   *Achlys*

There are two kinds of vanilla leaf in North America. The California Vanilla Leaf (*Achlys californica*), found only along the Pacific Coast, looks very much like this one, but its leaves are divided into more segments. Both are named for the pleasant fragrance of the leaves when dried, and both grow in dense groups on the moist floors of shady forests.

Vanilla Leaf
Achlys triphylla

Size: *1-2 ft. tall; flower ¼ in. wide.*
What to look for: *leaves large, with 3 fan-shaped leaflets on slim stalk; flowers white, petalless, clustered in dense spike atop leafless stalk.* **Habitat:** *dense to open woods.*
In bloom: *Apr.–June.*

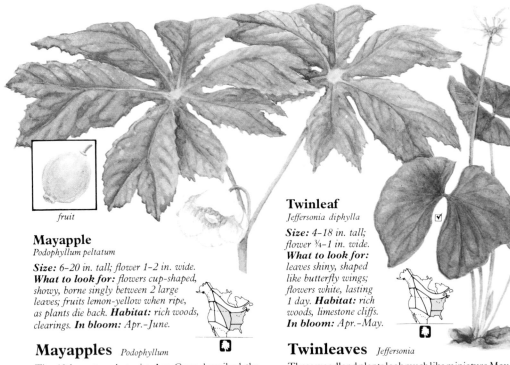

Mayapple
Podophyllum peltatum

Size: *6–20 in. tall; flower 1–2 in. wide.*
What to look for: *flowers cup-shaped, showy, borne singly between 2 large leaves; fruits lemon-yellow when ripe, as plants die back.* **Habitat:** *rich woods, clearings.* **In bloom:** *Apr.–June.*

fruit

Twinleaf
Jeffersonia diphylla

Size: *4–18 in. tall; flower ¾–1 in. wide.*
What to look for: *leaves shiny, shaped like butterfly wings; flowers white, lasting 1 day.* **Habitat:** *rich woods, limestone cliffs.* **In bloom:** *Apr.–May.*

Mayapples *Podophyllum*

The 19th-century botanist Asa Gray described the flavor of the Mayapple's ripe fruit as "somewhat mawkish, beloved of pigs, raccoons, and small boys." Immature fruits, seeds, and all other plant parts are poisonous. In the past, mild infusions have been used medicinally as a powerful purgative.

Twinleaves *Jeffersonia*

These woodland plants look much like miniature May-apples and were, in fact, first included in the same group. The scientist who decided that they belonged in their own category was a friend and colleague of Thomas Jefferson's—himself a botanist of note—and so he called the new group *Jeffersonia*.

Red Prickly Poppy
Argemone sanguinea

Size: *1–4 ft. tall; flower 2–3 in. wide.*
What to look for: *flowers red-purple to pinkish white; leaves lobed, with prickly tips; stems spiny.* **Habitat:** *chaparral, deserts, roadsides, disturbed areas.* **In bloom:** *Feb.–Apr.*

Matilija Poppy
Romneya coulteri

Size: *2–8 ft. tall; flower 4–8 in. wide.*
What to look for: *flowers profuse, with 6 peculiarly crimped white petals around yellow center; leaves divided.* **Habitat:** *chaparral, scrubland, desert canyons.* **In bloom:** *May–July.*

Prickly Poppies *Argemone*

Such impressive armaments as the prickly poppies' coats of stiff spines are not unusual among plants of the desert, where growth is slow, conditions are harsh, and the least palatable plants are often the most likely to survive. When the plants are grown in moist climates, the spines tend to be sparser.

Matilija Poppies *Romneya*

Hikers in the gorges, canyons, and dry washes of southern California's arid mountains—and even occasionally in Arizona's Grand Canyon—may chance upon a fragrant cluster of this spectacular member of the poppy family. Standing shrublike up to 8 feet tall, it is often covered with huge white flowers.

WILDFLOWERS

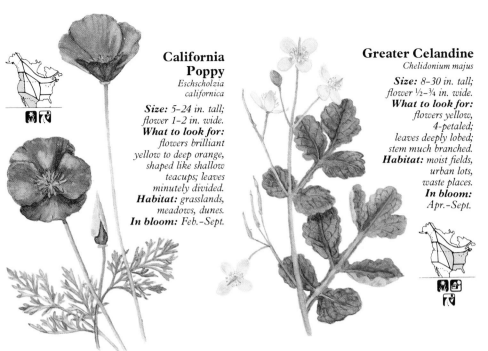

California Poppy
Eschscholzia californica

Size: *5–24 in. tall; flower 1–2 in. wide.*
What to look for: *flowers brilliant yellow to deep orange, shaped like shallow teacups; leaves minutely divided.*
Habitat: *grasslands, meadows, dunes.*
In bloom: *Feb.–Sept.*

Greater Celandine
Chelidonium majus

Size: *8–30 in. tall; flower ½–¾ in. wide.*
What to look for: *flowers yellow, 4-petaled; leaves deeply lobed; stem much branched.*
Habitat: *moist fields, urban lots, waste places.*
In bloom: *Apr.–Sept.*

California Poppies *Eschscholzia*

At night and on cloudy days, California's state flower remains closed, its blossom nightcap-shaped. At the first touch of sunlight, vast fields and hillsides blaze with open poppies. California Poppies are low-growing annuals on the southern coast and in sand dunes. Farther north they are tall perennials.

Celandines *Chelidonium*

European colonists brought this tough poppy with its fragile-looking flowers to these shores because of its medicinal properties. They used its caustic yellow juice in eyedrops and in the treatment of such skin disorders as warts—hence the alternative name of Wartwort. It is often grown in gardens.

Creamcups
Platystemon californicus

Size: *3–12 in. tall; flower ½–1 in. wide.*
What to look for: *flowers usually cream-colored (ranging from yellow to white), 6-petaled; leaves hairy, lance-shaped; stems often branching, hairy.*
Habitat: *dunes, chaparral, grasslands, oak woods.*
In bloom: *Mar.–May.*

Bloodroot
Sanguinaria canadensis

Size: *2–8 in. tall; flower 1–2 in. wide.*
What to look for: *flowers white with golden centers, each on a single stem enfolded in a blue-green leaf; roots and stems filled with red latex.*
Habitat: *rich woods.*
In bloom: *Mar.–May.*

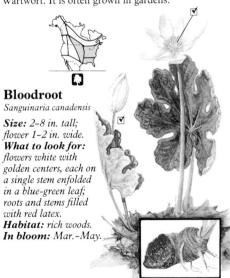

root

Creamcups *Platystemon*

Botanists debate whether there are as many as 60 creamcups species or only one. Those who say that the tiny plants along clay cliffs, the taller, hairy ones of sand dunes, and the gangly ones in shady woods are examples of separate species are known as "split-ters." "Lumpers" say that all are mere variations.

Bloodroots *Sanguinaria*

Algonquian Indians called this member of the poppy family *puccoon*, as they did almost any plant that was a source of dye. They used its copious red latex to color clothing and baskets, and applied it to their bodies and faces as ceremonial paint. In the latter capacity, it also served as an insect repellent.

351

Wild
Bleeding
Heart

Squirrel Corn
Dicentra canadensis

Size: *4–12 in. tall;
flower ½–¾ in. long.*
What to look for:
*flowers white, heart-
shaped, nodding;
leaves springing
from stem
base, much divided.*
Habitat: *rich woods.*
In bloom: *Apr.–May.*

Dutchman's Breeches
Dicentra cucullaria

Size: *4–12 in. tall;
flower ½–¾ in. long.*
What to look for:
*flowers white, waxy,
with 2 spurred petals
like baggy trouser legs;
leaves springing from stem
base, much divided.*
Habitat: *rich woods,
shaded moist ledges.*
In bloom: *Apr.–May.*

Western Bleeding Heart
Dicentra formosa

Size: *8–15 in. tall;
flower ½–¾ in. long.*
What to look for:
*flowers pinkish purple,
heart-shaped, with
spreading lower lobes;
leaves springing from
stem base, divided.*
Habitat: *dense woods,
redwood forests.*
In bloom: *Mar.–July.*

Bleeding Hearts *Dicentra*

The shapes of their flowers have inspired names for these plants that range
from poetic (Bleeding Heart) to humorous (Dutchman's Breeches). An exception is Squirrel Corn, named not for the flowers but for the kernel-
sized yellow corms, or swellings in the stem, that develop beneath the soil.
Practical-minded ranchers call them all staggerweeds because cattle are
poisoned by their toxic juices. The eastern Wild Bleeding Heart (*Dicentra
eximia*) is similar to the western species, but its flowers are a softer pink.

Allegheny Vine
Adlumia fungosa

Size: *to 12 ft. high;
flower ½–¾ in. long.*
What to look for: *flowers
pale pink, bottle-shaped,
hanging in loose clusters;
stems viny, climbing by
means of divided leaves.*
Habitat: *mountain
woodlands, open hillsides.*
In bloom: *June–Oct.*

Allegheny Vines *Adlumia*

Although the only species in this group was first
found in the Allegheny Mountains, it is not restricted
to that area. The plant has become even more widespread since gardeners have adopted it as an ornamental climbing vine, often sold under the name of
Mountain Fringe or Climbing Fumitory.

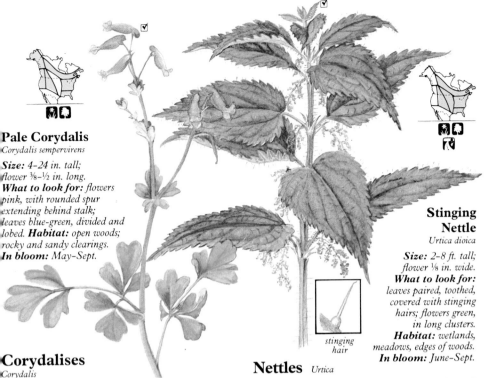

Pale Corydalis
Corydalis sempervirens

Size: *4-24 in. tall; flower ⅜-½ in. long.*
What to look for: *flowers pink, with rounded spur extending behind stalk; leaves blue-green, divided and lobed.* **Habitat:** *open woods; rocky and sandy clearings.*
In bloom: *May-Sept.*

Stinging Nettle
Urtica dioica

Size: *2-8 ft. tall; flower ⅛ in. wide.*
What to look for: *leaves paired, toothed, covered with stinging hairs; flowers green, in long clusters.*
Habitat: *wetlands, meadows, edges of woods.*
In bloom: *June-Sept.*

stinging hair

Corydalises
Corydalis

There are several species of corydalis native to North America. Only the Pale Corydalis has pink flowers; the others, including the Golden Corydalis (*Corydalis aurea*) and the small-flowered Yellow Harlequin (*Corydalis flavula*), bear bright yellow blossoms. These plants are closely related to the bleeding hearts but differ in that only one petal has a spur.

Nettles *Urtica*

The scientific name of this group comes from the Latin *uro* ("I burn")–an apt description of the result of handling the leaves and stems. The downy hairs that cover the plant are actually hollow tubes through which a severe irritant is injected. The young shoots and tender top leaves, however, make a good soup or cooked green. Boiling takes out the sting.

Pokeweed
Phytolacca americana

Size: *1-10 ft. tall; flower ⅛-¼ in. wide.*
What to look for: *flowers greenish white, in upright spikes; berries purple, hanging downward; stems reddish; leaves oval, pointed.*
Habitat: *waste places, edges of woods, fields.*
In bloom: *June-Sept.*

fruit cluster

Pokeweeds *Phytolacca*

"Useful but dangerous" best characterizes these weedy plants. In pioneer days the purple berries of North America's only species were used for ink, and so the plant came to be known as Inkweed. Young shoots and leafy tips are edible if boiled in at least two changes of water, but children have died from eating the berries. The seeds and roots are also quite poisonous, and so are the mature stems and leaves.

353

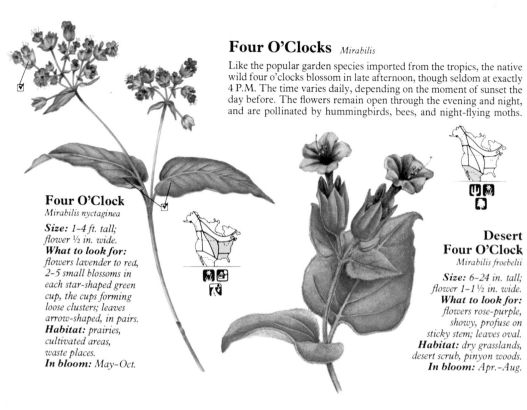

Four O'Clocks *Mirabilis*

Like the popular garden species imported from the tropics, the native wild four o'clocks blossom in late afternoon, though seldom at exactly 4 P.M. The time varies daily, depending on the moment of sunset the day before. The flowers remain open through the evening and night, and are pollinated by hummingbirds, bees, and night-flying moths.

Four O'Clock
Mirabilis nyctaginea

Size: 1–4 ft. tall; flower ½ in. wide.
What to look for: flowers lavender to red, 2–5 small blossoms in each star-shaped green cup, the cups forming loose clusters; leaves arrow-shaped, in pairs.
Habitat: prairies, cultivated areas, waste places.
In bloom: May–Oct.

Desert Four O'Clock
Mirabilis froebelii

Size: 6–24 in. tall; flower 1–1½ in. wide.
What to look for: flowers rose-purple, showy, profuse on sticky stem; leaves oval.
Habitat: dry grasslands, desert scrub, pinyon woods.
In bloom: Apr.–Aug.

Sand Verbenas *Abronia*

The fragrant sand verbenas, like the rest of the four o'clock family, have no petals. The sepals look remarkably like petals and also attract pollinating insects as petals would, but they retain more moisture. The juicy stems and leaves of sand verbenas are adapted to minimize water loss, helping these creepers to blanket the dry sandy areas where they flourish.

Heart's Delight
Abronia fragrans

Size: 4–10 in. tall; flower ½–1 in. long.
What to look for: flowers tubular with lacy white or pale lavender sepals, in caplike clusters; leaves oval; stem covered with sticky hairs. **Habitat:** dry grasslands.
In bloom: Apr.–Aug.

Angel's Trumpets *Acleisanthes*

Each elegant "trumpet" lasts but a single night. During the day, the bud is a dull green tube arising from the base of a leaf. The petallike sepals spread at dusk to attract night-flying moths, which sip the nectar with their long tongues and often pollinate the flower in the process. By the first light of dawn, the flower has collapsed into a limp heap.

Angel Trumpets
Acleisanthes longiflora

Size: to 3 ft. long; flower 4–6 in. long.
What to look for: flowers trumpetlike, white-belled on dull green tubes; leaves triangular to long and thin; stems sprawling on ground.
Habitat: dry rocky soil, sand, deserts.
In bloom: Apr.–Aug.

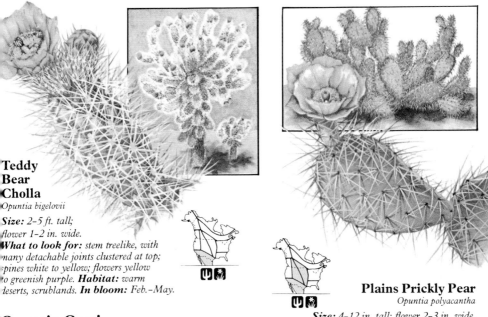

Teddy Bear Cholla
Opuntia bigelovii

Size: 2-5 ft. tall; flower 1-2 in. wide.
What to look for: stem treelike, with many detachable joints clustered at top; spines white to yellow; flowers yellow to greenish purple. **Habitat:** warm deserts, scrublands. **In bloom:** Feb.–May.

Plains Prickly Pear
Opuntia polyacantha

Size: 4-12 in. tall; flower 2-3 in. wide.
What to look for: stems flattened into 3- to 6-in.-long oval pads, sprawling in dense mats; flowers pale yellow; spines in clusters of 5-11.
Habitat: deserts, dry grasslands, dry mountain slopes.
In bloom: May-July.

Opuntia Cacti   *Opuntia*

The upright, cylindrical plants in this group are called chollas; those with flat stems are known as prickly pears because of their edible fruit. Although chollas are densely covered with formidable barbed spines, Cactus Wrens nest among their branches, and a pack rat may protect its burrow with broken-off joints. The stiff spines of prickly pears are grouped in bunches. Peccaries, deer, and cattle feed on the plants, and the pulp of the pads is used to make candy and syrup.

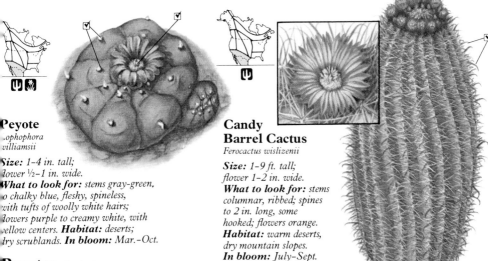

Peyote
Lophophora williamsii

Size: 1-4 in. tall; flower ½-1 in. wide.
What to look for: stems gray-green, to chalky blue, fleshy, spineless, with tufts of woolly white hairs; flowers purple to creamy white, with yellow centers. **Habitat:** deserts; dry scrublands. **In bloom:** Mar.-Oct.

Peyotes   *Lophophora*

The ancient Indians of Mexico and Texas called these soft cacti *mezcal*, or mushrooms. The "buttons" were cut from the turniplike taproots, dried, and eaten for their intense hallucinatory effect. The cacti are still valued by mystics and thrill-seekers, although their use is now illegal except as part of the religious rites of the Native American Church.

Candy Barrel Cactus
Ferocactus wislizenii

Size: 1-9 ft. tall; flower 1-2 in. wide.
What to look for: stems columnar, ribbed; spines to 2 in. long, some hooked; flowers orange.
Habitat: warm deserts, dry mountain slopes.
In bloom: July-Sept.

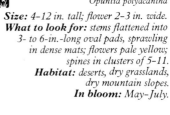

Barrel Cacti   *Ferocactus*

These slow-growing giants (an 8-foot plant may be more than 500 years old) are legendary emergency water sources. But it is hard work to cut off the top and to pound juice from the inner pulp—and the result is less than pleasant tasting. Because barrel cacti lean southward toward the sun, they are also known as compass cacti.

WILDFLOWERS

355

Strawberry Hedgehog
Echinocereus engelmannii

Size: *1-12 in. tall;
flower 1-2½ in. wide.*
What to look for: *stems upright,
in large clumps; flowers showy,
red to maroon; spines in clusters
of 10-12 (about half long, slightly
curved), spines of different colors
(white, yellow, tan, gray) on the
same plant.* **Habitat:** *rocky slopes,
cliffs, deserts, scrublands.*
In bloom: *Feb.-June.*

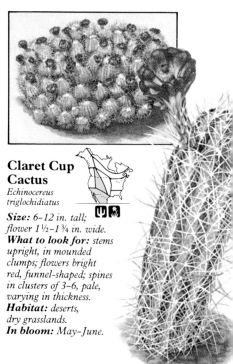

Claret Cup Cactus
*Echinocereus
triglochidiatus*

Size: *6-12 in. tall;
flower 1½-1¾ in. wide.*
What to look for: *stems
upright, in mounded
clumps; flowers bright
red, funnel-shaped; spines
in clusters of 3-6, pale,
varying in thickness.*
Habitat: *deserts,
dry grasslands.*
In bloom: *May-June.*

Hen and Chickens Cactus
*Echinocereus
viridiflorus*

Size: *1-10 in. tall;
flower 1-1½ in. wide.*
What to look for: *stems
sharply ribbed, sometimes
spiraling; flowers green,
long, many-petaled; spines
white or brown, short,
flattened against stem, in
clusters of 10-20.*
Habitat: *deserts, dry
grasslands, rocky hillsides.*
In bloom: *Apr.-July.*

Hedgehog Cacti *Echinocereus*

Cacti have developed a unique set of water-hoarding traits, typified by the hedgehog cacti. The thick pulpy stems are ribbed or segmented, expanding quickly when water is available and shrinking slowly in dry times. Photosynthesis takes place in the tough skin of the stems, close to the water source. The spines are actually modified leaves, shaped and arranged differently in each species. Not only do they protect the plants from browsing animals; they also prevent water loss by shading the stem. Each spine, in fact, collects a little water from the morning dew.

WILDFLOWERS

Sandworts *Arenaria*

There are more than 150 species of these small, sand-loving members of the pink family. Most of them are, like the Rock Sandwort, low-growing, with creeping stems that form dense mats. Several, including the delicate Creeping Sandwort (*Arenaria humifusa*) and the wiry Mountain Sandwort (*Arenaria capillaris*), are common high in the northern Rockies.

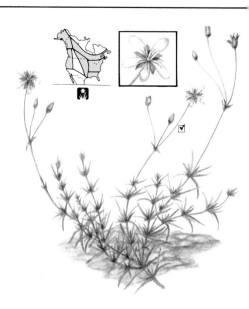

Rock Sandwort
Arenaria stricta

Size: *stem 4-16 in. long; flower ½ in. wide.*
What to look for: *flowers white, 5-petaled,
on threadlike stalks; leaves small, needlelike, in clusters along creeping stem; plant
forms bushy mats.* **Habitat:** *rocky or sandy
prairies, meadows, shores.* **In bloom:** *June-July.*

incushion Cacti
ryphantha

hese miniature cacti, their
ems all but hidden by overlap-
ng spines that radiate from
isters like spokes from a wheel
ib, are favorites of those
10 collect and cultivate desert
ants. Like most cacti, they do
st in neutral to somewhat alka-
ie soil. Because their fine roots
read thirstily near the surface,
re must be taken not to disturb
e soil around them.

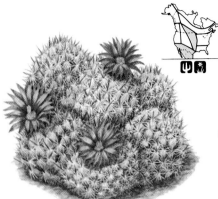

Pincushion Cactus
Coryphantha vivipara

Size: *1-3 in. tall;*
flower 1-1½ in. wide.
What to look for: *stems*
spherical or barrel-shaped,
densely covered with
spines; flowers rose to
purplish, many-petaled;
spines to 1 in. long, in
clusters of 3-10, surrounded
by 12-40 short white
hairlike spines. **Habitat:**
dry prairies, rocky slopes.
In bloom: *May-July.*

Fishhook Cactus
Mammillaria microcarpa

Size: *1-6 in. tall; flower 1-1½ in. wide.*
What to look for: *stem fleshy, knobby,*
barrel-shaped, alone or part of dense
clumps; flowers pink with yellow centers,
forming crown at top of stems; spines in
clusters, with 1-2 hooked spines at
center and many short ones radiating outward.
Habitat: *deserts, scrublands.* **In bloom:** *Apr.-May.*

Nipple Cacti
Mammillaria

Botanists classify cacti according to the way the
spines are clustered, the exact points on the stem
where the flowers grow, and the placement of the stamens in the flowers. The most notable feature of the
nipple cacti is that the spines are clustered, not along
ribs or ridges as in the hedgehogs, but at the tips of
small bumps arranged in rows along the stems.

Chickweeds *Stellaria*

hese delicate-looking edible weeds are bespangled
om early spring to late fall with white, five-petaled
iwers. Each petal is so deeply cleft, however, that
iere seem to be 10 of them. The weak, reclining
ems and tender leaves may be added raw to salads,
it they taste best when boiled briefly in salted water
id served in place of spinach. Because chickweeds
ay green beneath the snow, they can be important
ir winter survival—both for animals and humans.

Common Chickweed
Stellaria media

Size: *stem to 2½ ft. long; flower ¼ in. wide.*
What to look for: *flowers profuse, small, white,*
with 5 deeply cleft petals; stems sprawling,
forming large tangles; leaves oval to elongate.
Habitat: *lawns, meadows, pastures.*
In bloom: *Feb.-Dec.*

Starry Campion
Silene stellata

Size: *1–3 ft. tall;
flower ¾–1 in. wide.*
What to look for:
*flowers white, with 5
fringed petals; leaves
lance-shaped, usually
in 4's.* **Habitat:** *open
woods, clearings.*
In bloom: *July–Sept.*

Round-leaved Catchfly
Silene rotundifolia

Size: *stem 6–24 in. long;
flower ¾–1¼ in. wide.*
What to look for:
*flowers scarlet, with
5 deeply notched
petals; leaves spoon-
shaped; stems weak,
reclining.* **Habitat:**
rocky cliffs, open slopes.
In bloom: *May–July.*

Fire Pin
Silene virgin

Size: *6–30 in. ta
flowers 1–1½ in. wid*
What to look fo
*flowers bright re
with 5 notch
petals; stems a
leaves hairy, stick*
Habitat: *open woo
clearings, roc
slopes.* **In bloor
Apr.–Ju

Common Pink
Silene caroliniana

Size: *2–10 in. tall;
flower ¾–1 in. wide.*
What to look for:
*flowers pink, with 5
wedge-shaped petals;
leaves spatula-shaped to
oblong, clustered at base.*
Habitat: *clearings, open
woods, rocky slopes.*
In bloom: *Apr.–June.*

Catchflies *Silene*

The plants of this diverse group are known by a variety of names, nearly all of which are misleading.
Many are called campions because they look like
members of the genus *Lychnis*. Bright-flowered species are often called pinks, although that name properly belongs to the genus *Dianthus*. The many species
known as catchflies are so called because small flying
insects do indeed find themselves stuck in the spittlelike secretion that coats the hairy stems, flower tubes,
and leaves. However, these plants are not insect eaters like sundews. Their stickiness keeps crawling
insects from the flowers, and thus facilitates cross-
pollination by airborne insects.

Bladder Campion
Silene cucubalus

Size: *8–20 in. tall;
flower ½–1 in. wide.*
What to look for:
*flowers white, with 5
deeply notched petals
emerging from
melonlike swelling;
leaves oblong, pointed.*
Habitat: *roadsides,
open fields.*
In bloom: *Apr.–Aug.*

Bouncing Bet
Saponaria officinalis

Size: *1-2 ft. tall;
flower ¾-1 in. wide.*
What to look for: *flowers white
or pinkish, 5-petaled, in dense
clusters; leaves elliptical to
lance-shaped.* **Habitat:** *streets,
roadsides, railways, pastures.*
In bloom: *July-Sept.*

Soapworts   *Saponaria*

When mixed with water, the bruised leaves
of these European weeds produce a soapy
lather that has been used since ancient times
for laundry and bathing. Bouncing Bet
came to North America with the
colonists and went west with the
pioneers, spreading quickly from
their gardens along the way. Its
cleansing action makes it a useful
home remedy for Poison Ivy.

Corn Cockle
Agrostemma githago

Size: *1-3 ft. tall;
flower 1-1½ in. wide.*
What to look for:
*flowers pink, with pale
centers; stems and
slender paired leaves
covered with silky
hairs.* **Habitat:**
*grainfields, waste
places, roadsides.*
In bloom: *July-Sept.*

Corn Cockles   *Agrostemma*

Despite its pretty pink flower, the one
Corn Cockle species is more often
cursed than admired because it is a
dangerous weed around winter wheat.
Its poisonous seeds mature along with
the grain, and because they are the
same size and weight they cannot easily be winnowed out.

Deptford Pink
Dianthus armeria

Size: *6-24 in. tall;
flower ½ in. wide.*
What to look for: *flowers
bright pink, starlike,
loosely clustered;* **Habitat:**
fields, waste places.
In bloom: *June-Aug.*

Pinks   *Dianthus*

The flowers in this group were
not named for their color, but for
the frilled, or pinked, appearance
of their petals. The color was
later named for the flowers. The
name of the Deptford Pink cele-
brates bygone days when its
blossoms blanketed the open
fields near Deptford, England
—now part of urban London.

White Campion
Lychnis alba

Size: *1-4 ft. tall;
flower ¾-1¼ in. wide.*
What to look for: *flowers white,
with 5 notched petals emerging from
swollen pouch; leaves in pairs,
downy.* **Habitat:** *waste places,
fields.* **In bloom:** *May-Sept.*

Campions   *Lychnis*

The campions include such popular garden
flowers as Scarlet Maltese Cross (*Lychnis
chalcedonica*) and Rose of Heaven (*Lychnis
coeli-rosa*). The night-blooming White
Campion differs from its close relatives the
catchflies in that its male and female flowers
are borne on separate plants.

Goosefoots
Chenopodium

These widespread, leafy weeds,
relatives of beets, spinach, and
Swiss chard, are prized by outdoorsmen for their young leaves
and shoots. When boiled until
tender and served like spinach,
they are a tasty substitute for
garden-grown greens and are rich
in vitamins A and C. Indians
ground the seeds into flour.

Lamb's Quarters
*Chenopodium
album*

Size: *6-72 in. tall;
flower minute.*
What to look for: *leaves
diamond-shaped, toothed,
with white to pink mealy
coating when young; flowers
in dense clusters.* **Habitat:**
fields, yards, waste places.
In bloom: *June-Oct.*

Spring Beauties *Claytonia*

These dainty heralds of spring form large colonies, spreading underground by means of bulblike swellings just above the roots. The swellings, called corms, look like small new potatoes and taste like sweet chestnuts when boiled, earning at least two species the nickname Fairy Spuds. Gathering them is tedious, however, and it takes a great many to make a satisfying meal.

Spring Beauty
Claytonia virginica

Size: *2–10 in. tall; flower ½ in. wide.*
What to look for: *flowers pink to white with dark pink veins, in loose clusters; 2 narrow, slightly succulent leaves on each slender stem.*
Habitat: *meadows, streambanks, woods.*
In bloom: *Mar.–June.*

Montias *Montia*

Of the several edible montias, none is more easily recognized than Miner's Lettuce—so called because it was a dietary staple of the forty-niners in California's gold rush days. What appears to be a single leaf pierced by the stem is actually two leaves fused together. This is the choice part for salads, but the entire plant—flowers included—is edible and flavorsome, whether eaten raw or lightly steamed.

Miner's Lettuce
Montia perfoliata

Size: *3–12 in. tall; flower ¼–½ in. wide.*
What to look for: *flowers cream-colored, loosely clustered on stalk arising from center of umbrellalike, leafy collar; lower leaves narrow.* **Habitat:** *forests, streambanks, meadows, grasslands.*
In bloom: *Feb.–May.*

Purslanes *Portulaca*

The weedy Common Purslane, despised by gardeners for its tenacity, can be a rich source of iron and of vitamins A and C. The tender, leafy tips are a quickly renewed and very tasty salad green, and the entire plant makes a good potherb when simmered for a few minutes in salted water. The thick stems can be cut into chunks and pickled like cucumbers, and the seeds can be ground into flour.
The Rose Moss is an imported garden plant that has spread to the wild.

Common Purslane
Portulaca oleracea

Size: *1–2 in. tall; flower ¼–½ in. wide.*
What to look for: *stems reddish, creeping, covered with fleshy, wedge-shaped leaves; flowers small, yellow.*
Habitat: *lawns, fields, waste places.*
In bloom: *Apr.–Oct.*

yellow form

Rose Moss
Portulaca grandiflora

Size: *3–6 in. tall; flower 1–2 in. wide.*
What to look for: *flowers red, pink, white, yellow, or purple; leaves narrow, succulent, on creeping or ascending reddish stems.*
Habitat: *fields, waste places.*
In bloom: *Apr.–Sept.*

Pussy Paws

Calyptridium umbellatum

Size: *2–10 in. tall; flower cluster 1½–2½ in. wide; leaf 1–3 in. long.*
What to look for: *flowers white to pink, in dense fuzzy clusters at ends of reddish stalks; leaves fleshy, spoon-shaped, in flat rosettes.*
Habitat: *mountain tundra, meadows, pine forests.* **In bloom:** *May–Aug.*

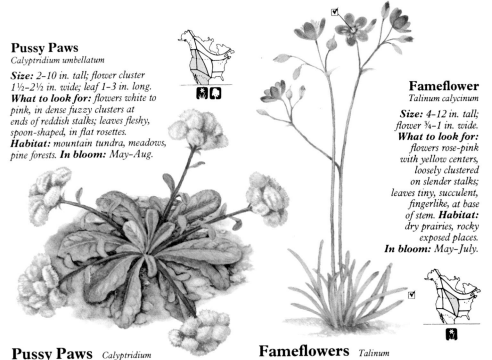

Fameflower

Talinum calycinum

Size: *4–12 in. tall; flower ¾–1 in. wide.*
What to look for: *flowers rose-pink with yellow centers, loosely clustered on slender stalks; leaves tiny, succulent, fingerlike, at base of stem.* **Habitat:** *dry prairies, rocky exposed places.* **In bloom:** *May–July.*

Pussy Paws *Calyptridium*

These ground-huggers are ideally suited to the well-drained and windswept places where they grow, including the steep ridges between glaciers high on the peaks of the Pacific Northwest. The succulent leaves radiate in a flat rosette from the top of a taproot that may delve 12 feet deep for water. The flowering stalks may also lie flat; and the petals, instead of falling, form a protective cap over the seedpods.

Fameflowers *Talinum*

Though not strictly desert plants, fameflowers grow in rocky or sandy places where a few rainless days constitute a drought. They store water in their thick, succulent leaves, which are almost round in cross section. The small five-petaled flowers are short-lived—they open about noon and fade before sunset—but their bright colors attract enough pollinating insects to perpetuate the species.

Red Maids

Calandrinia ciliata

Size: *4–16 in. long; flower ¾–1 in. wide.*
What to look for: *flowers red to rose-purple with pale starlike centers, on spreading, leafy stalks; leaves narrow, spreading from base.*
Habitat: *gravelly ground, moist grasslands.*
In bloom: *Feb.–May.*

leafy rosette

Bitterroot

Lewisia rediviva

Size: *1–3 in. tall; flower 1–2 in. wide.*
What to look for: *flowers rose to creamy white, in showy bunches at or near ground level; leaves narrow, dying back early.* **Habitat:** *dry rocky slopes, open areas.* **In bloom:** *Mar.–July.*

Rock Purslanes *Calandrinia*

Most rock purslanes are relatively large-flowered natives of Australia and South America. (The spectacular rock-garden plant *Calandrinia grandiflora* is in this category.) Red Maids, however, are among California's most abundant spring wildflowers. Their short-lived blossoms, which last but a single sunny day, produce masses of shiny black seeds that are eaten by many kinds of songbirds and rodents.

Lewisias *Lewisia*

Montana's official flower, the Bitterroot, was first collected in 1806 by Capt. Meriwether Lewis from what is now called the Bitterroot Valley. (A mountain range is also named for the plant.) Its rosette of narrow, succulent leaves, which die back as the flowers appear, crowns the starchy edible root for which the plant is named. The bitterness is mostly in the husk, which can be stripped off after boiling.

361

Carpetweed
Mollugo verticillata

Size: *stem to 1 ft. long; flower 1/8 in. wide.*
What to look for: *stems prostrate, spreading; leaves in whorls; flowers white, on short stalks.*
Habitat: *roadsides, cultivated ground, sandy places.* **In bloom:** *June–Nov.*

Carpetweeds *Mollugo*

If you have ever wielded a hoe, you have probably met up with these low-growing weeds, which quickly carpet newly cultivated ground from coast to coast. At each fork in the stem is a whorl of leaves. The small flowers rise from the center of the whorl.

Ice Plant
Mesembryanthemum crystallinum

Size: *2½–3 in. high; stem to 3 ft. long; flower 1 in. wide.*
What to look for: *plant creeping, covered with shiny beads; flowers white to pink.* **Habitat:** *beaches, dunes, roadsides.* **In bloom:** *Mar.–Oct.*

Midday Flowers
Mesembryanthemum

A few species of these African succulents now grow wild in California and Mexico. The flowers open around midday, not by a time clock but in response to the sun's warmth. The Ice Plant's glistening beads are swollen droplets of stored water.

Water Smartweed
Polygonum amphibium

Size: *stem to 8 ft. long; flower 1/8 in. wide.*
What to look for: *flowers pink, in dense spikes; stems spreading underwater or on banks.*
Habitat: *lakes, ponds, swamps.*
In bloom: *June–Sept.*

Pinkweed
Polygonum pensylvanicum

Size: *1–6 ft. tall; flower 1/8 in. wide.*
What to look for: *flowers pink, in dense spikes; stems branched, with knotlike joints.*
Habitat: *fields, roadsides, clearings.*
In bloom: *June–Aug.*

Knotweeds
Polygonum

Although knotweeds are named for their knotlike stem joints, some are also called smartweeds—an allusion to the sharp taste of the foliage. Knotweeds range from open waters to deep forests, supplying food for songbirds, waterfowl, and mammals.

Alligator Weed
Alternanthera philoxeroides

Size: *6–24 in. tall; flower ¼–½ in. wide.*
What to look for: *flowers silvery to pinkish green, in rounded clusters from spreading, matted stems.*
Habitat: *wet meadows, ditches, swamps, waterways, lakeshores.*
In bloom: *all year.*

Copperleaves
Alternanthera

Several of these spreading tropical plants are used by gardeners as summer ground covers that die back in autumn. One species, the aquatic Alligator Weed, has found a home in the Deep South, where it is rapidly choking bayous, streams, and other waterways. It spreads by means of horizontal stems as well as seeds.

flowering stems rising above water

Wild Buckwheats *Eriogonum*

With hairy, densely matted leaves well adapted for retaining moisture, these plants inhabit dry, open areas from deserts to mountain tundra. Wild buckwheats have little in common with the cultivated grain (*Fagopyrum*). Although their seeds are of value only to birds and rodents, bees make wild buckwheat nectar into an excellent honey. There are about 200 wild buckwheat species in North America, many of which are hard to tell apart without a magnifying glass.

Desert Trumpet
Eriogonum inflatum

Size: *4–40 in. tall; flower ⅛ in. wide.*
What to look for: *flowers cream-yellow, in flaring clusters at ends of branches; stem swollen just below branches; leaves at base.* **Habitat:** *deserts, scrublands.*
In bloom: *Mar.–Oct.*

Skeletonweed
Eriogonum deflexum

Size: *3–25 in. tall; flower ⅛ in. wide.*
What to look for: *flowers white or pink, hanging in clusters from leafless, branching stem; leaves oval, at base of stem.*
Habitat: *deserts, mountain slopes.*
In bloom: *all year.*

Cushion Buckwheat
Eriogonum caespitosum

Size: *2–7 in. tall; flower ⅛ in. wide.*
What to look for: *flowers yellow (turning orange), in dense, round clusters on leafless stalks; leaves small, woolly, white, in cushiony mats.*
Habitat: *deserts; dry, rocky slopes.*
In bloom: *Apr.–July.*

Docks *Rumex*

There are few places where docks do not grow. Their rhubarblike leaves have been prized as cooked greens since antiquity, and their wandlike clusters of brown seeds were gathered, hand-winnowed, and stone-ground into flour by Indians and settlers. The bitter taste of the young leaves is not unpleasant, but older leaves must be boiled in at least two changes of water to make them palatable.

flower

fruit

Curly Dock
Rumex crispus

Size: *1–5 ft. tall; flower minute.*
What to look for: *leaves large, dark green, crisped and curled; flowers green and red, in upright clusters; fruits brown, heart-shaped, winged.*
Habitat: *ditches, roadsides, fields, waste places.* **In bloom:** *May–Sept.*

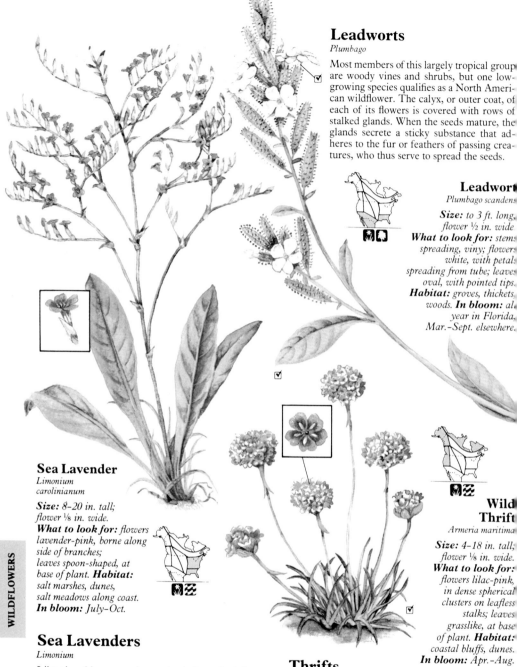

Leadworts
Plumbago

Most members of this largely tropical group are woody vines and shrubs, but one low-growing species qualifies as a North American wildflower. The calyx, or outer coat, of each of its flowers is covered with rows of stalked glands. When the seeds mature, the glands secrete a sticky substance that adheres to the fur or feathers of passing creatures, who thus serve to spread the seeds.

Leadwort
Plumbago scandens

Size: *to 3 ft. long, flower ½ in. wide.*
What to look for: *stems spreading, viny; flowers white, with petals spreading from tube; leaves oval, with pointed tips.*
Habitat: *groves, thickets, woods.* **In bloom:** *all year in Florida, Mar.–Sept. elsewhere.*

Sea Lavender
Limonium carolinianum

Size: *8–20 in. tall; flower ⅛ in. wide.*
What to look for: *flowers lavender-pink, borne along side of branches; leaves spoon-shaped, at base of plant.* **Habitat:** *salt marshes, dunes, salt meadows along coast.* **In bloom:** *July–Oct.*

Sea Lavenders
Limonium

Like a low, blue-gray mist moving in from the Atlantic, dense colonies of these shrubby perennials cover coastal salt marshes and alkaline meadows with their lavender-pink bloom in late summer. The thick rootstocks yield an astringent that was once a popular mouthwash. Some cultivated species, known as statice ("stopping"), were used in ancient times to treat dysentery, hemorrhage, and other ailments.

Wild Thrift
Armeria maritima

Size: *4–18 in. tall; flower ⅛ in. wide.*
What to look for: *flowers lilac-pink, in dense spherical clusters on leafless stalks; leaves grasslike, at base of plant.* **Habitat:** *coastal bluffs, dunes.* **In bloom:** *Apr.–Aug.*

Thrifts
Armeria

Wild Thrift thrives in North America on rocky western cliffs and salt-sprayed bluffs overlooking the Pacific. The English have, over the centuries, known it by such names as Cliff Rose, Sea Pink, Ladies' Cushion, and Midsummer Fairmaid. The plant also grows along the coast of northern Europe and in Iceland, where it is eaten boiled in milk. Like the sea lavenders, thrifts are often sold under the name statice.

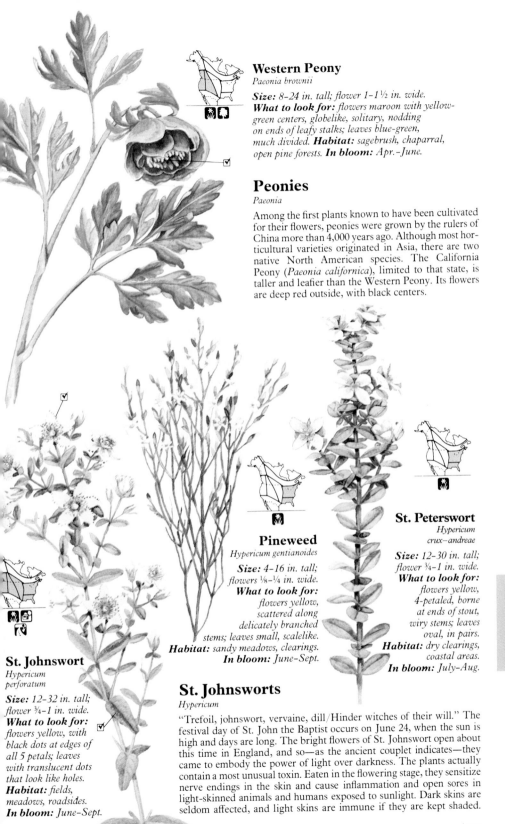

Western Peony
Paeonia brownii

Size: *8–24 in. tall; flower 1–1½ in. wide.*
What to look for: *flowers maroon with yellow-green centers, globelike, solitary, nodding on ends of leafy stalks; leaves blue-green, much divided.* **Habitat:** *sagebrush, chaparral, open pine forests.* **In bloom:** *Apr.–June.*

Peonies
Paeonia

Among the first plants known to have been cultivated for their flowers, peonies were grown by the rulers of China more than 4,000 years ago. Although most horticultural varieties originated in Asia, there are two native North American species. The California Peony (*Paeonia californica*), limited to that state, is taller and leafier than the Western Peony. Its flowers are deep red outside, with black centers.

St. Peterswort
Hypericum crux–andreae

Size: *12–30 in. tall; flower ¾–1 in. wide.*
What to look for: *flowers yellow, 4-petaled, borne at ends of stout, wiry stems; leaves oval, in pairs.* **Habitat:** *dry clearings, coastal areas.* **In bloom:** *July–Aug.*

Pineweed
Hypericum gentianoides

Size: *4–16 in. tall; flowers ⅛–¼ in. wide.*
What to look for: *flowers yellow, scattered along delicately branched stems; leaves small, scalelike.* **Habitat:** *sandy meadows, clearings.* **In bloom:** *June–Sept.*

St. Johnswort
Hypericum perforatum

Size: *12–32 in. tall; flower ¾–1 in. wide.*
What to look for: *flowers yellow, with black dots at edges of all 5 petals; leaves with translucent dots that look like holes.* **Habitat:** *fields, meadows, roadsides.* **In bloom:** *June–Sept.*

St. Johnsworts
Hypericum

"Trefoil, johnswort, vervaine, dill/Hinder witches of their will." The festival day of St. John the Baptist occurs on June 24, when the sun is high and days are long. The bright flowers of St. Johnswort open about this time in England, and so—as the ancient couplet indicates—they came to embody the power of light over darkness. The plants actually contain a most unusual toxin. Eaten in the flowering stage, they sensitize nerve endings in the skin and cause inflammation and open sores in light-skinned animals and humans exposed to sunlight. Dark skins are seldom affected, and light skins are immune if they are kept shaded.

**Swamp
Rose Mallow**
Hibiscus moscheutos

Size: *2-8 ft. tall;
flower 4-8 in. wide.*
What to look for:
*flowers white, with burgundy
centers (entirely pink in
north); leaves toothed,
heart-shaped; stems canelike.*
Habitat: *salt and freshwater
marshes; lakeshores.*
In bloom: *July-Sept.*

Halberdleaf
Rose Mallow
Hibiscus militaris

Size: *2-5 ft. tall;
flower 4-6 in. wide.*
What to look for: *flowers pink,
with wine-red centers;
leaves 3-lobed, like blades of a halberd.*
Habitat: *marshes, shallow freshwater.*
In bloom: *Aug.-Sept.*

Flower-of-an-hour
Hibiscus trionum

Size: *6-20 in. tall;
flower 1-2½ in. wide.*
What to look for:
*flowers yellow
with brown centers,
open briefly in morning;
leaves with
fingerlike lobes;
stems erect or sprawling.*
Habitat: *yards, waste places.*
In bloom: *July-Sept.*

Rose Mallows *Hibiscus*

These leafy, stout-stemmed plants are marked as
members of the mallow family by the odd cylinder,
called a stamen column, that projects from the center
of the flower. In the rose mallows, this column, fuzzy
with pollen from base to tip, completely surrounds
the seed-producing pistil. The five rounded tips of
the pistil, called the stigmas, emerge from the end of
the column. A bee or butterfly, making its rounds in
search of nectar, touches the stigmas with pollen
from another flower, then burrows deeper into the
blossom and picks up a new load of pollen.

Poppy Mallows *Callirhoë*

The showy poppy mallows are also known as wine-
cups for the shape and color of their flowers. Unlike
the rose mallows, these flowers have stamen columns
that become pollen-covered only about halfway
down from the tip. It takes a magnifying glass to see
that the long, threadlike stigmas emerge, not from the
end of the column but along its length.

Poppy Mallow
Callirhoë involucrata

Size: *1-3 ft. long;
flower 1-2½ in. wide.*
What to look for:
*flowers wine-red,
saucer-shaped; stems spreading;
leaves with fingerlike lobes.*
Habitat: *dry prairies,
deserts.* **In bloom:**
June-Aug.

Musk Mallow
Malva moschata

Size: *1-3 ft. tall;
flower 1½-2 in. wide.*
What to look for:
*flowers pink, lavender,
or white, with notched
petals; leaves with
fingerlike lobes.* **Habitat:**
grasslands, waste places.
In bloom: *June-Sept.*

Musk Mallows *Malva*

These European natives were imported for gardens,
but long ago escaped to the wild in the New World.
Their flowers differ from those of American mallows
in that the petals are scalloped and the stamen column
is rounder. The stamens completely enclose the pistil
until they have finished producing pollen. Then they
roll back to allow the stigmas at the tip of the pistil to
receive pollen from another blossom.

Scarlet Globe Mallow
Sphaeralcea coccinea

Size: *1–2 ft. tall; flower 1 in. wide.*
What to look for: *flowers brick-red with pale centers, clustered atop slender stalks; leaves hairy, divided into narrow lobes.* **Habitat:** *dry grasslands, scrub.*
In bloom: *May–Aug.*

Globe Mallows
Sphaeralcea

Among Spanish-speaking Americans, globe mallows are sometimes known as *plantas muy malas* ("very bad plants"), for they are densely covered with detachable hairs that irritate the eyes. These hairs also tend to discourage many animals from eating the plants. The several kinds of globe mallow are often difficult to tell apart because the plants hybridize.

Checker Mallow
Sidalcea neomexicana

Size: *8–36 in. tall; flower ¾–1 in. wide.*
What to look for: *flowers rose-colored, with petals slightly fringed; upper leaves hand-shaped, lower leaves rounded.*
Habitat: *streambanks, moist meadows.*
In bloom: *June–Sept.*

basal leaf

Checker Mallows
Sidalcea

The 20 species of checker mallow, all native to western North America, are commonly known as wild hollyhocks, for at first glance they do indeed look like miniature versions of the garden Hollyhock (*Alcea rosea*). The stamen column in the center of the flowers, unlike that of most other mallows, has two separate groups of pollen-bearing heads.

Marsh Mallow
Althaea officinalis

Size: *2–4 ft. tall; flower 1–1½ in. wide.*
What to look for: *flowers lavender to pink, in clusters along stem; leaves toothed, slightly lobed, with soft hairs.* **Habitat:** *brackish or freshwater marshes near coast.*
In bloom: *July–Sept.*

Marsh Mallows
Althaea

The roots of these Old World plants were the original source of the gummy confection now synthesized from sugar, gelatin, and other ingredients. It was made from the white core of the root; first the rind was peeled away, and then the core was cut into small pieces and boiled in sugar water until it was thick enough to form blobs. Its use was medicinal—as a laxative and as a treatment for sore throat.

Velvetleaf
Abutilon theophrasti

Size: *1–5 ft. tall; flower ½–1 in. wide.*
What to look for: *leaves heart-shaped, velvety; flowers yellow; fruits crownlike.* **Habitat:** *fields, waste places.*
In bloom: *July–Aug.*

Velvetleaves
Abutilon

These aggressive weeds are the bane of corn and soybean farmers across the continent. Although they do not appear until the crop plants have started to grow, they then flourish, flower, and bear fruit with amazing speed, consuming much of the soil's nutrients. The seeds are released from the crimped capsules gradually over the winter, and can remain viable in the soil for as long as 60 years.

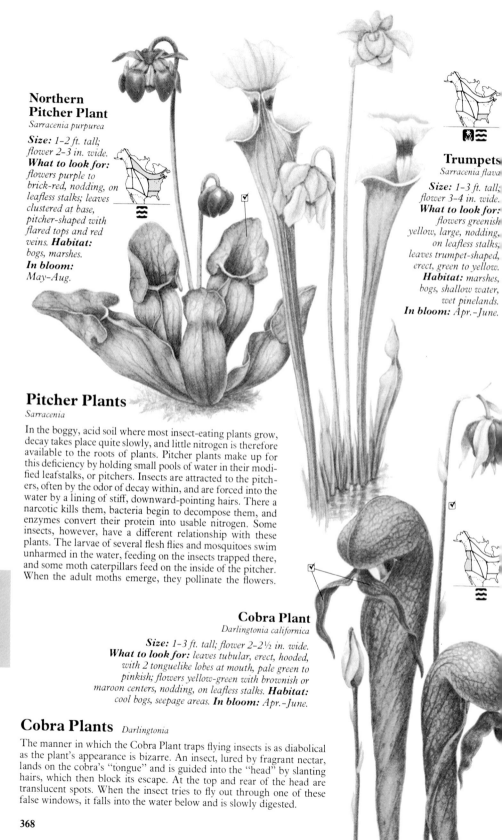

Northern Pitcher Plant
Sarracenia purpurea

Size: *1–2 ft. tall; flower 2–3 in. wide.* **What to look for:** *flowers purple to brick-red, nodding, on leafless stalks; leaves clustered at base, pitcher-shaped with flared tops and red veins.* **Habitat:** *bogs, marshes.* **In bloom:** *May–Aug.*

Trumpets
Sarracenia flava

Size: *1–3 ft. tall; flower 3–4 in. wide.* **What to look for:** *flowers greenish yellow, large, nodding, on leafless stalks; leaves trumpet-shaped, erect, green to yellow.* **Habitat:** *marshes, bogs, shallow water, wet pinelands.* **In bloom:** *Apr.–June.*

Pitcher Plants
Sarracenia

In the boggy, acid soil where most insect-eating plants grow, decay takes place quite slowly, and little nitrogen is therefore available to the roots of plants. Pitcher plants make up for this deficiency by holding small pools of water in their modified leafstalks, or pitchers. Insects are attracted to the pitchers, often by the odor of decay within, and are forced into the water by a lining of stiff, downward-pointing hairs. There a narcotic kills them, bacteria begin to decompose them, and enzymes convert their protein into usable nitrogen. Some insects, however, have a different relationship with these plants. The larvae of several flesh flies and mosquitoes swim unharmed in the water, feeding on the insects trapped there, and some moth caterpillars feed on the inside of the pitcher. When the adult moths emerge, they pollinate the flowers.

Cobra Plant
Darlingtonia californica

Size: *1–3 ft. tall; flower 2–2½ in. wide.* **What to look for:** *leaves tubular, erect, hooded, with 2 tonguelike lobes at mouth, pale green to pinkish; flowers yellow-green with brownish or maroon centers, nodding, on leafless stalks.* **Habitat:** *cool bogs, seepage areas.* **In bloom:** *Apr.–June.*

Cobra Plants *Darlingtonia*

The manner in which the Cobra Plant traps flying insects is as diabolical as the plant's appearance is bizarre. An insect, lured by fragrant nectar, lands on the cobra's "tongue" and is guided into the "head" by slanting hairs, which then block its escape. At the top and rear of the head are translucent spots. When the insect tries to fly out through one of these false windows, it falls into the water below and is slowly digested.

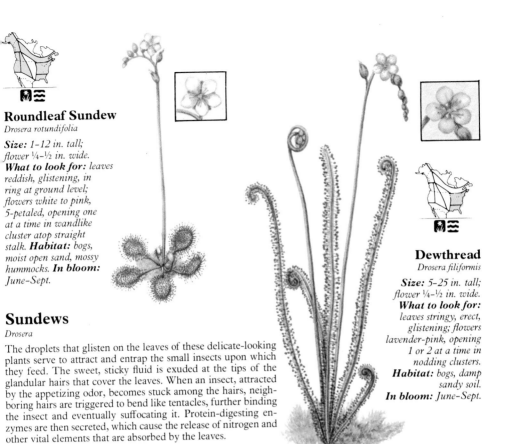

Roundleaf Sundew
Drosera rotundifolia

Size: *1-12 in. tall;
flower ¼-½ in. wide.*
What to look for: *leaves
reddish, glistening, in
ring at ground level;
flowers white to pink,
5-petaled, opening one
at a time in wandlike
cluster atop straight
stalk.* **Habitat:** *bogs,
moist open sand, mossy
hummocks.* **In bloom:**
June-Sept.

Sundews
Drosera

The droplets that glisten on the leaves of these delicate-looking plants serve to attract and entrap the small insects upon which they feed. The sweet, sticky fluid is exuded at the tips of the glandular hairs that cover the leaves. When an insect, attracted by the appetizing odor, becomes stuck among the hairs, neighboring hairs are triggered to bend like tentacles, further binding the insect and eventually suffocating it. Protein-digesting enzymes are then secreted, which cause the release of nitrogen and other vital elements that are absorbed by the leaves.

Dewthread
Drosera filiformis

Size: *5-25 in. tall;
flower ¼-½ in. wide.*
What to look for:
*leaves stringy, erect,
glistening; flowers
lavender-pink, opening
1 or 2 at a time in
nodding clusters.*
Habitat: *bogs, damp
sandy soil.*
In bloom: *June-Sept.*

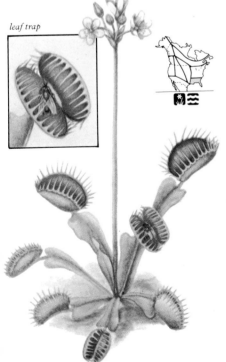

leaf trap

Venus Flytrap
Dionaea muscipula

Size: *4-12 in. tall; flower ¾-1 in. wide.*
What to look for: *leaves traplike,
green outside and often red inside;
flowers white, 5-petaled, in rounded cluster
atop straight stalk.* **Habitat:** *sandy bogs, low
pinelands, savannas in North and South Carolina.*
In bloom: *May-June.*

Venus Flytraps
Dionaea

This most dramatic of all carnivorous plants—the only one of its kind on earth—traps and digests its prey in hinged leaves. Near the central vein of each leaf are several sensitive hairs that, in response to slight pressure, trigger the leaf to fold shut in less than a second. Bristles along the edges interlock, trapping the unwary insect. The leaf remains closed for about a week while antibacterial substances prevent putrefaction, and enzymes dissolve all but the external skeleton. Then the leaf reopens and readies itself for another visitor. The Venus Flytrap has become an endangered species in its native bogs and savannas, a victim of overzealous admirers.

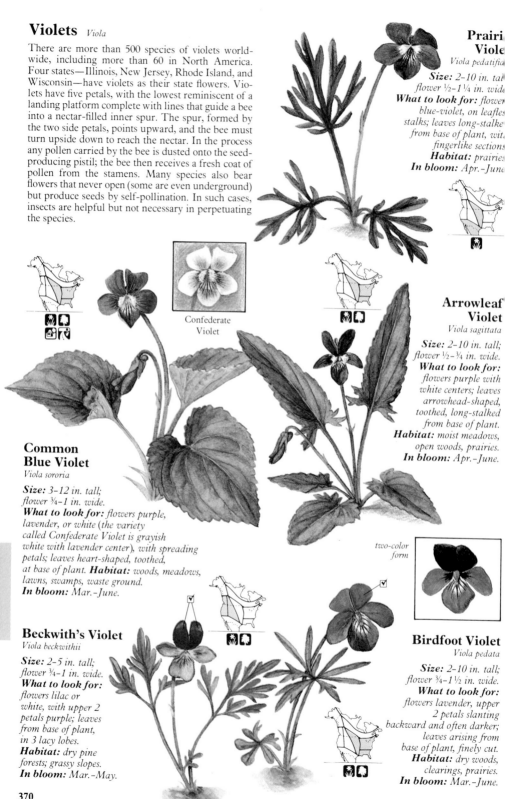

Violets *Viola*

There are more than 500 species of violets world-wide, including more than 60 in North America. Four states—Illinois, New Jersey, Rhode Island, and Wisconsin—have violets as their state flowers. Violets have five petals, with the lowest reminiscent of a landing platform complete with lines that guide a bee into a nectar-filled inner spur. The spur, formed by the two side petals, points upward, and the bee must turn upside down to reach the nectar. In the process any pollen carried by the bee is dusted onto the seed-producing pistil; the bee then receives a fresh coat of pollen from the stamens. Many species also bear flowers that never open (some are even underground) but produce seeds by self-pollination. In such cases, insects are helpful but not necessary in perpetuating the species.

Prairie Violet
Viola pedatifida

Size: 2–10 in. tall;
flower ½–1¼ in. wide.
What to look for: flowers blue-violet, on leafless stalks; leaves long-stalked from base of plant, with fingerlike sections.
Habitat: prairies.
In bloom: Apr.–June.

Confederate Violet

Arrowleaf Violet
Viola sagittata

Size: 2–10 in. tall;
flower ½–¾ in. wide.
What to look for: flowers purple with white centers; leaves arrowhead-shaped, toothed, long-stalked from base of plant.
Habitat: moist meadows, open woods, prairies.
In bloom: Apr.–June.

Common Blue Violet
Viola sororia

Size: 3–12 in. tall;
flower ¾–1 in. wide.
What to look for: flowers purple, lavender, or white (the variety called Confederate Violet is grayish white with lavender center), with spreading petals; leaves heart-shaped, toothed, at base of plant. **Habitat:** woods, meadows, lawns, swamps, waste ground.
In bloom: Mar.–June.

two-color form

Beckwith's Violet
Viola beckwithii

Size: 2–5 in. tall;
flower ¾–1 in. wide.
What to look for: flowers lilac or white, with upper 2 petals purple; leaves from base of plant, in 3 lacy lobes.
Habitat: dry pine forests; grassy slopes.
In bloom: Mar.–May.

Birdfoot Violet
Viola pedata

Size: 2–10 in. tall;
flower ¾–1½ in. wide.
What to look for: flowers lavender, upper 2 petals slanting backward and often darker; leaves arising from base of plant, finely cut.
Habitat: dry woods, clearings, prairies.
In bloom: Mar.–June.

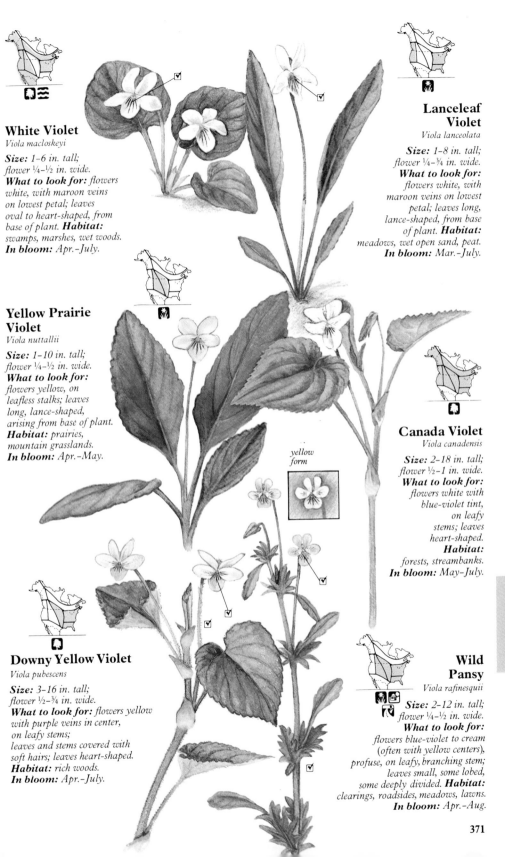

White Violet
Viola macloskeyi

Size: *1–6 in. tall;
flower ¼–½ in. wide.*
What to look for: *flowers
white, with maroon veins
on lowest petal; leaves
oval to heart-shaped, from
base of plant.* **Habitat:**
swamps, marshes, wet woods.
In bloom: *Apr.–July.*

Lanceleaf
Violet
Viola lanceolata

Size: *1–8 in. tall;
flower ¼–¾ in. wide.*
What to look for:
*flowers white, with
maroon veins on lowest
petal; leaves long,
lance-shaped, from base
of plant.* **Habitat:**
meadows, wet open sand, peat.
In bloom: *Mar.–July.*

Yellow Prairie
Violet
Viola nuttallii

Size: *1–10 in. tall;
flower ¼–½ in. wide.*
What to look for:
*flowers yellow, on
leafless stalks; leaves
long, lance-shaped,
arising from base of plant.*
Habitat: *prairies,
mountain grasslands.*
In bloom: *Apr.–May.*

*yellow
form*

Canada Violet
Viola canadensis

Size: *2–18 in. tall;
flower ½–1 in. wide.*
What to look for:
*flowers white with
blue-violet tint,
on leafy
stems; leaves
heart-shaped.*
Habitat:
forests, streambanks.
In bloom: *May–July.*

Downy Yellow Violet
Viola pubescens

Size: *3–16 in. tall;
flower ½–¾ in. wide.*
What to look for: *flowers yellow
with purple veins in center,
on leafy stems;
leaves and stems covered with
soft hairs; leaves heart-shaped.*
Habitat: *rich woods.*
In bloom: *Apr.–July.*

Wild
Pansy
Viola rafinesquii

Size: *2–12 in. tall;
flower ¼–½ in. wide.*
What to look for:
*flowers blue-violet to cream
(often with yellow centers),
profuse, on leafy, branching stem;
leaves small, some lobed,
some deeply divided.* **Habitat:**
clearings, roadsides, meadows, lawns.
In bloom: *Apr.–Aug.*

371

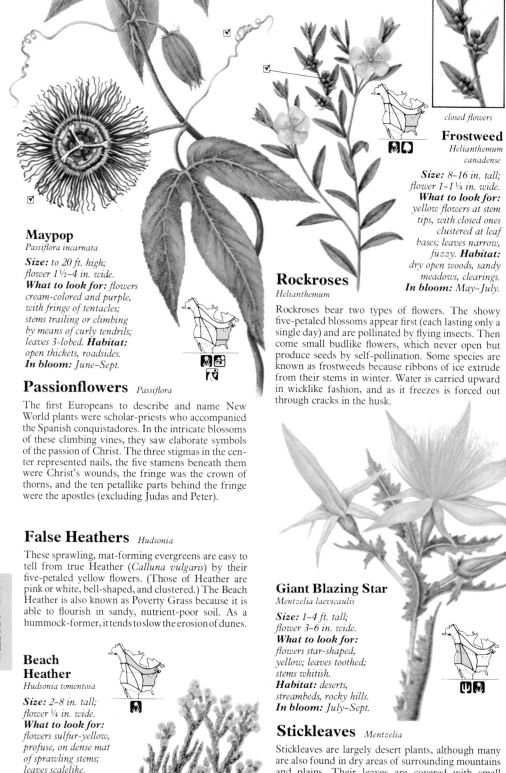

closed flowers

Frostweed
*Helianthemum
canadense*

Size: *8–16 in. tall;
flower 1–1¼ in. wide.*
What to look for:
*yellow flowers at stem
tips, with closed ones
clustered at leaf
bases; leaves narrow,
fuzzy.* **Habitat:**
*dry open woods, sandy
meadows, clearings.*
In bloom: *May–July.*

Maypop
Passiflora incarnata

Size: *to 20 ft. high;
flower 1½–4 in. wide.*
What to look for: *flowers
cream-colored and purple,
with fringe of tentacles;
stems trailing or climbing
by means of curly tendrils;
leaves 3-lobed.* **Habitat:**
open thickets, roadsides.
In bloom: *June–Sept.*

Rockroses
Helianthemum

Rockroses bear two types of flowers. The showy
five-petaled blossoms appear first (each lasting only a
single day) and are pollinated by flying insects. Then
come small budlike flowers, which never open but
produce seeds by self-pollination. Some species are
known as frostweeds because ribbons of ice extrude
from their stems in winter. Water is carried upward
in wicklike fashion, and as it freezes is forced out
through cracks in the husk.

Passionflowers   *Passiflora*

The first Europeans to describe and name New
World plants were scholar-priests who accompanied
the Spanish conquistadores. In the intricate blossoms
of these climbing vines, they saw elaborate symbols
of the passion of Christ. The three stigmas in the center represented nails, the five stamens beneath them
were Christ's wounds, the fringe was the crown of
thorns, and the ten petallike parts behind the fringe
were the apostles (excluding Judas and Peter).

False Heathers   *Hudsonia*

These sprawling, mat-forming evergreens are easy to
tell from true Heather (*Calluna vulgaris*) by their
five-petaled yellow flowers. (Those of Heather are
pink or white, bell-shaped, and clustered.) The Beach
Heather is also known as Poverty Grass because it is
able to flourish in sandy, nutrient-poor soil. As a
hummock-former, it tends to slow the erosion of dunes.

Giant Blazing Star
Mentzelia laevicaulis

Size: *1–4 ft. tall;
flower 3–6 in. wide.*
What to look for:
*flowers star-shaped,
yellow; leaves toothed;
stems whitish.*
Habitat: *deserts,
streambeds, rocky hills.*
In bloom: *July–Sept.*

Beach Heather
Hudsonia tomentosa

Size: *2–8 in. tall;
flower ¼ in. wide.*
What to look for:
*flowers sulfur-yellow,
profuse, on dense mat
of sprawling stems;
leaves scalelike.*
Habitat: *beaches,
shifting sands.*
In bloom: *May–July.*

Stickleaves   *Mentzelia*

Stickleaves are largely desert plants, although many
are also found in dry areas of surrounding mountains
and plains. Their leaves are covered with small
barbed hairs, causing them to stick to clothing and
animal fur. Several species are also known as blazing
stars for their bright, distinctive blossoms.

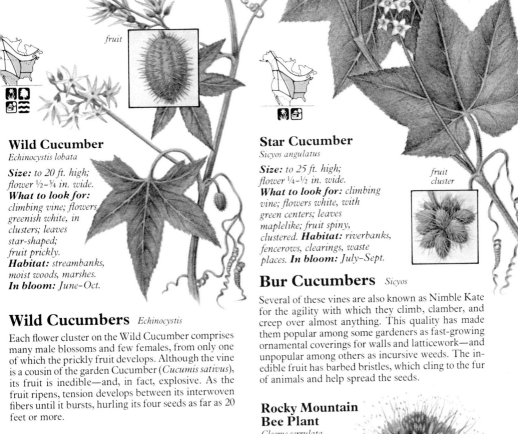

fruit

Wild Cucumber
Echinocystis lobata

Size: to 20 ft. high; flower ½-¾ in. wide.
What to look for: climbing vine; flowers greenish white, in clusters; leaves star-shaped; fruit prickly.
Habitat: streambanks, moist woods, marshes.
In bloom: June-Oct.

Wild Cucumbers *Echinocystis*

Each flower cluster on the Wild Cucumber comprises many male blossoms and few females, from only one of which the prickly fruit develops. Although the vine is a cousin of the garden Cucumber (*Cucumis sativus*), its fruit is inedible—and, in fact, explosive. As the fruit ripens, tension develops between its interwoven fibers until it bursts, hurling its four seeds as far as 20 feet or more.

Squashes *Cucurbita*

This valuable group of plants includes garden squashes as well as the familiar jack-o'-lantern pumpkin. Although the fruit of the Wild Pumpkin is inedible, it is not useless; it contains a lathery substance that can be used as a substitute for soap.

Stinking Gourd
Cucurbita foetidissima

Size: to 20 ft. long; flower 3-4 in. wide.
What to look for: trailing vine; flowers yellow; fruit striped; leaves triangular.
Habitat: dry prairies, grasslands. **In bloom:** May-Aug.

fruit

Star Cucumber
Sicyos angulatus

Size: to 25 ft. high; flower ¼-½ in. wide.
What to look for: climbing vine; flowers white, with green centers; leaves maplelike; fruit spiny, clustered. **Habitat:** riverbanks, fencerows, clearings, waste places. **In bloom:** July-Sept.

fruit cluster

Bur Cucumbers *Sicyos*

Several of these vines are also known as Nimble Kate for the agility with which they climb, clamber, and creep over almost anything. This quality has made them popular among some gardeners as fast-growing ornamental coverings for walls and latticework—and unpopular among others as incursive weeds. The inedible fruit has barbed bristles, which cling to the fur of animals and help spread the seeds.

Rocky Mountain Bee Plant
Cleome serrulata

Size: 1-5 ft. tall; flower ½ in. wide.
What to look for: flowers pink to white, clustered, with long stamens; seedpods long, thrust from center of flowers; leaflets in 3's.
Habitat: riverbanks, prairies, roadsides.
In bloom: May-Aug.

Spiderflowers *Cleome*

These tall plants of the plains have two sets of names describing very different qualities. The flower clusters, with their leggy-looking stamens and protruding pistils and seedpods, evoke the name spiderflowers; the rich nectar within earns the name bee plants. (The odor of the crushed leaves, however, inspires additional epithets like stinkweed, skunkweed, and stinking clover.)

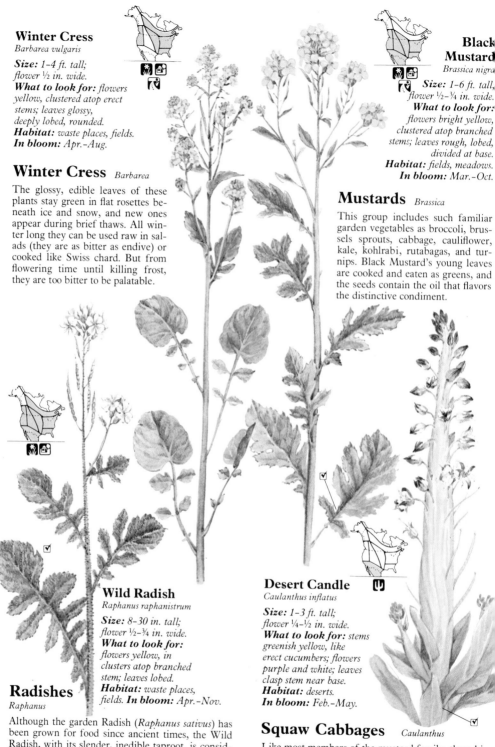

Winter Cress
Barbarea vulgaris

Size: *1-4 ft. tall; flower ½ in. wide.*
What to look for: *flowers yellow, clustered atop erect stems; leaves glossy, deeply lobed, rounded.*
Habitat: *waste places, fields.*
In bloom: *Apr.-Aug.*

Winter Cress   Barbarea

The glossy, edible leaves of these plants stay green in flat rosettes beneath ice and snow, and new ones appear during brief thaws. All winter long they can be used raw in salads (they are as bitter as endive) or cooked like Swiss chard. But from flowering time until killing frost, they are too bitter to be palatable.

Black Mustard
Brassica nigra

Size: *1-6 ft. tall; flower ½-¾ in. wide.*
What to look for: *flowers bright yellow, clustered atop branched stems; leaves rough, lobed, divided at base.*
Habitat: *fields, meadows.*
In bloom: *Mar.-Oct.*

Mustards   Brassica

This group includes such familiar garden vegetables as broccoli, brussels sprouts, cabbage, cauliflower, kale, kohlrabi, rutabagas, and turnips. Black Mustard's young leaves are cooked and eaten as greens, and the seeds contain the oil that flavors the distinctive condiment.

Wild Radish
Raphanus raphanistrum

Size: *8-30 in. tall; flower ½-¾ in. wide.*
What to look for: *flowers yellow, in clusters atop branched stem; leaves lobed.*
Habitat: *waste places, fields.* **In bloom:** *Apr.-Nov.*

Radishes
Raphanus

Although the garden Radish (*Raphanus sativus*) has been grown for food since ancient times, the Wild Radish, with its slender, inedible taproot, is considered a noxious weed. Its small seeds remain viable in the ground for decades, sprouting only when they work their way to the surface. In some areas the young leaves are cooked as a potherb, and immature seedpods are diced into salads for sharp flavor.

Desert Candle
Caulanthus inflatus

Size: *1-3 ft. tall; flower ¼-½ in. wide.*
What to look for: *stems greenish yellow, like erect cucumbers; flowers purple and white; leaves clasp stem near base.*
Habitat: *deserts.*
In bloom: *Feb.-May.*

Squaw Cabbages   Caulanthus

Like most members of the mustard family, these bizarre desert plants start out as dense leafy clusters produced from seeds. Then a stout stem arises, and four-petaled flowers appear at its tip. They become long seedpods as the stem grows beyond them and more blossoms are produced.

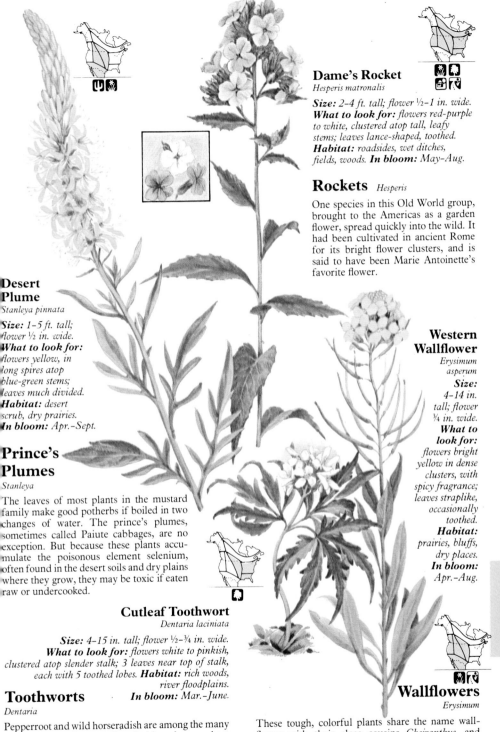

Dame's Rocket
Hesperis matronalis

Size: *2-4 ft. tall; flower ½-1 in. wide.*
What to look for: *flowers red-purple to white, clustered atop tall, leafy stems; leaves lance-shaped, toothed.*
Habitat: *roadsides, wet ditches, fields, woods.* **In bloom:** *May-Aug.*

Rockets   *Hesperis*

One species in this Old World group, brought to the Americas as a garden flower, spread quickly into the wild. It had been cultivated in ancient Rome for its bright flower clusters, and is said to have been Marie Antoinette's favorite flower.

Desert Plume
Stanleya pinnata

Size: *1-5 ft. tall; flower ½ in. wide.*
What to look for: *flowers yellow, in long spires atop blue-green stems; leaves much divided.*
Habitat: *desert scrub, dry prairies.*
In bloom: *Apr.-Sept.*

Prince's Plumes
Stanleya

The leaves of most plants in the mustard family make good potherbs if boiled in two changes of water. The prince's plumes, sometimes called Paiute cabbages, are no exception. But because these plants accumulate the poisonous element selenium, often found in the desert soils and dry plains where they grow, they may be toxic if eaten raw or undercooked.

Western Wallflower
Erysimum asperum

Size: *4-14 in. tall; flower ¾ in. wide.*
What to look for: *flowers bright yellow in dense clusters, with spicy fragrance; leaves straplike, occasionally toothed.*
Habitat: *prairies, bluffs, dry places.*
In bloom: *Apr.-Aug.*

Cutleaf Toothwort
Dentaria laciniata

Size: *4-15 in. tall; flower ½-¾ in. wide.*
What to look for: *flowers white to pinkish, clustered atop slender stalk; 3 leaves near top of stalk, each with 5 toothed lobes.* **Habitat:** *rich woods, river floodplains.*
In bloom: *Mar.-June.*

Toothworts
Dentaria

Pepperroot and wild horseradish are among the many names given to these small, early-blooming members of the mustard family. The names refer to the ivory-colored underground stems, or rhizomes. These root-like parts bear sharp knobs like little teeth, and their peppery taste has made them popular snack foods for children, campers, and long-distance hikers.

Wallflowers
Erysimum

These tough, colorful plants share the name wallflower with their close cousins *Cheiranthus*, and plants of both groups are listed interchangeably in many garden catalogs. Both are sun-lovers, known for pushing their way between the rocks of old dry-walls and for brightening the bases of rocky cliffs throughout the Northern Hemisphere.

WILDFLOWERS

375

Fringepod
Thysanocarpus curvipes

Size: *8–20 in. tall; fruit ¼ in. wide; flower minute.*
What to look for: *fruits brownish, with gearlike green pattern; flowers tiny, greenish to white.*
Habitat: *dry mountain grasslands, sagebrush, open oak woods.*
In bloom: *Mar.–June.*

fruit

Fringepods   *Thysanocarpus*

Like many in the mustard family, fringepods are hard to recognize by their flowers. But when fruits begin forming from the bottom of the flowering stalk, there is no mistaking them. In some species the lacy effect of the seedpods is heightened by small holes between the coglike rays.

Shepherd's Purse
Capsella bursa-pastoris

Size: *3–20 in. tall; fruit to ¼ in. long; flower minute.*
What to look for: *fruits heart-shaped; flowers cream-colored, clustered atop straight stem; much-divided leaves at base.* **Habitat:** *fields, lawns, disturbed areas.*
In bloom: *Feb.–Dec.*

fruit

Shepherd's Purses
Capsella

The little white flowers that are tightly clustered atop the stems of these weedy plants begin to form fruit from the bottom up. As each seedpod forms, its stalk elongates and the stem above it continues to grow. When the plant has gone completely to seed, it looks like a coat tree with small heart-shaped purses or pouches on its arms.

Whitlow Grass   *Draba verna*

Size: *3–12 in. tall; flower ¼ in. wide.*
What to look for: *flowers white, with yellow centers and 4 deeply notched petals; leaves spatula-shaped, clustered at base.*
Habitat: *dry grasslands.* **In bloom:** *Mar.–June.*

*bas
lea*

Whitlow Grasses   *Draba*

In old England, a whitlow was an inflammation under or around the fingernails or toenails. The sharply acidic juices of the whitlow grasses were said to be a remedy for the affliction, although it is unlikely they did much good. Like some others of the mustard family, these plants are known as winter annuals because they sprout in the fall, survive the winter, and begin to grow again in early spring.

Watercresses   *Nasturtium*

Watercress grows almost everywhere in the world that freshwater runs, and its leaves and stems are prized for salads and fresh greens wherever it grows. It must be washed carefully before being eaten; it can survive in polluted water, and its leaves are a favored browsing place for tiny snails and water insects.

Watercress
Nasturtium officinale

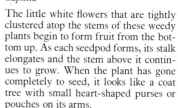

Size: *to 10 ft. long; flower ¼ in. wide.*
What to look for: *stems matted in water, creeping on bank; leaves shiny, divided into many leaflets; flowers white, in clusters.*
Habitat: *cold water; banks of springs and streams.* **In bloom:** *Mar.–Nov.*

Bittercresses   *Cardamine*

Only the older bittercress leaves are bitter enough to be truly unpalatable. The young leaves of most species are so sharply flavored that they rival Watercress as a pungent salad green. The bulbous rootstock of Springcress can be grated and mixed with vinegar to make a substitute for horseradish.

Springcress
Cardamine bulbosa

Size: *4–20 in. tall; flower about ½ in. wide.*
What to look for: *flowers white, loosely clustered at top of slender stem; leaves lance-shaped along stem, rounded at base.* **Habitat:** *moist woods, wet meadows, shallow freshwater.*
In bloom: *Mar.–June.*

Bearberry
Arctostaphylos
uva-ursi

Size: stem to 10 ft. long;
flower about ¼ in. wide.
What to look for: leaves
glossy; flowers white to
pink, urn-shaped;
red to purple berries
last all winter.
Habitat: dry, sandy soils.
In bloom: Apr.-June.

American Cranberry
Vaccinium macrocarpon

Size: 8-12 in. high;
flower ½ in. wide.
What to look for: stems wiry, trailing;
leaves small, oval, leathery;
flowers pink, with swept-back petals;
berries red, about ¾ in. long.
Habitat: bogs; moist, sandy
meadows. **In bloom:** June-Oct.

Manzanitas   *Arctostaphylos*

Among this group of evergreen shrubs (a typical species is represented in the shrub section of this book) the low-growing Bearberry is unique. It occurs in northern Europe and Asia as well as in colder areas of North America, where its berries are more valuable as winter food for birds and deer than for bears.

Cranberries and Blueberries   *Vaccinium*

Wild cranberries—so named because their flower resembles the head of a crane—were among the first native foods that the Pilgrims learned to relish, and soon became one of the first North American crops grown commercially for export. Blueberries are shown in the shrub section of this book.

Checkerberry
Gaultheria procumbens

Size: 2-6 in. tall;
flower ¼ in. wide.
What to look for:
flowers white, nodding;
leaves leathery, oval;
berries red; plant aromatic.
Habitat: sandy woods,
clearings. **In bloom:** July-Aug.

White Heather
Cassiope mertensiana

Size: 2-10 in. tall;
flower about ¼ in. wide.
What to look for: flowers
white, nodding; leaves
scalelike. **Habitat:**
tundra; moist, stony soils.
In bloom: July-Aug.

Wintergreens   *Gaultheria*

The evergreen leaves of wintergreens were the original source of wintergreen oil, also found in the inner bark of some birches. Because a ton of wintergreen leaves is required to produce a pound of oil, commercial producers now rely on birch twigs and synthetic compounds for this familiar flavoring.

Cassiopes   *Cassiope*

Most of these dwarf shrubs are native to high northern mountains around the globe, and others grow in the Arctic. With one exception—*Cassiope stelleriana* of the American Northwest—they bear tiny leaves that overlap like shingles to protect against the drying effect of the wind.

Mayflower
Epigaea repens

Size: stem to 5 ft. long;
flower ¼-½ in. wide.
What to look for: leaves
in pairs; stems trailing on
ground; flowers pink
and white, trumpet-shaped.
Habitat: sandy or peaty
woods, clearings.
In bloom: Mar.-July.

Mountain Heather
Phyllodoce breweri

Size: 4-12 in. high;
flower ½ in. wide.
What to look for:
flowers pink, bowl-
shaped, clustered at
ends of stems; leaves
needlelike, with blunt tips.
Habitat: tundra; open,
moist, rocky soil.
In bloom: July-Aug.

Trailing Arbutuses
Epigaea

North America's single species of trailing arbutus is the state flower of Massachusetts. (The only other species is native to Japan.) Its fragrant spring flowers are so tempting that picking them is forbidden by law in many parts of its range.

Mountain Heathers
Phyllodoce

Like Europe's true Heather (*Calluna vulgaris*), these high-altitude beauties of the tundra and northern mountain ranges are low, mat-forming shrubs whose dense covering of fine foliage forms a textured backdrop for clustered masses of bell-like blossoms.

Pipsissewa
Chimaphila umbellata

Size: *3-10 in. tall; flower ¾ in. wide.*
What to look for: *flowers white to pink, fragrant, nodding, in clusters atop stems; leaves evergreen, toothed, broad near tips, borne in whorls.*
Habitat: *dry woods, often in acid soil.*
In bloom: *July-Aug.*

Spotted Wintergreen
Chimaphila maculata

Size: *4-10 in. tall; flower ¾ in. wide.*
What to look for: *flowers white to pink, nodding, fragrant; leaves evergreen, striped white along midvein, in whorls.*
Habitat: *dry woods.*
In bloom: *May-Aug.*

Pipsissewas
Chimaphila

The Cree Indians called these plants *pipsisikweu*, which means "it-breaks-into-small-pieces," because they believed the leaves were effective in breaking down kidney stones and gallstones. Pipsissewa tonic was still a popular home remedy in the early part of this century, but today this leaf extract is used merely to flavor candy and soft drinks. In Colonial times, the leathery leaves were also used to make a poultice to apply to bruises and skin irritations.

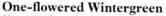

One-flowered Wintergreen
Moneses uniflora

Size: *1-6 in. tall; flower about ¾ in. wide.*
What to look for: *flowers white, nodding, fragrant; leaves round, leathery, clustered at base of plant.* **Habitat:** *cool, mossy forests.* **In bloom:** *June-Aug.*

One-flowered Wintergreens   *Moneses*

There is only one species in this group, which is sometimes included amon the shinleafs. Each delicate plant produces a single small and surprisingl fragrant flower, borne on a slender stalk above a few evergreen leaves. Al though these flowers grow in many places, they were never abundant and ar now becoming rare, even in the northern coniferous woods and bogs.

Shinleaf
Pyrola elliptica

Size: *4-12 in. tall; flower ¾ in. wide.*
What to look for: *flowers white, waxy, nodding, along slender stalk; leaves shiny green, oval, clustered at base of plant.* **Habitat:** *dry to moist woods, usually in acid soil.* **In bloom:** *June-Aug.*

Shinleafs   *Pyrola*

These small plants carpet the floors of coniferous for ests throughout North America, their stalks of waxy fragrant flowers rising from rosettes of glossy, ever green leaves. Shinleafs differ from most flowers i that their anthers (the pollen-bearing tips of the mal organs) do not split lengthwise to release pollen. In stead, the pollen comes out through a small pore a the end of each anther.

One-sided Pyrol
Pyrola secund

Size: *2-8 in. tal flower ¼ in. wide*
What to look for *flowers greenish yellow along one side o arching stalk; leave oval or rounded, i clusters at base* **Habitat:** *moist to dr woods, clearings, tundra* **In bloom:** *June-Aug*

WILDFLOWERS

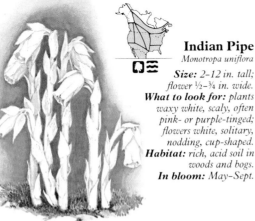

Indian Pipe
Monotropa uniflora

Size: *2–12 in. tall; flower ½–¾ in. wide.*
What to look for: *plants waxy white, scaly, often pink- or purple-tinged; flowers white, solitary, nodding, cup-shaped.*
Habitat: *rich, acid soil in woods and bogs.*
In bloom: *May–Sept.*

Pinesap
Monotropa hypopithys

Size: *4–16 in. tall; flower ¼–½ in. wide.*
What to look for: *plants yellow to red, fleshy, scaly; flowers yellow, often highlighted with red, in nodding clusters.*
Habitat: *open woods.*
In bloom: *June–Oct.*

Indian Pipes *Monotropa*

The Indian pipes are unusual among flowering plants (as opposed to mushrooms and other fungi, which they somewhat resemble) in that they contain no chlorophyll. They do not manufacture their own food by photosynthesis, depending instead on small wood-rotting fungi in the soil to free nutrients for their use.

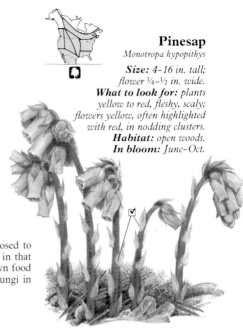

Snow Plant
Sarcodes sanguinea

Size: *4–12 in. tall; flower ½–¾ in. long.*
What to look for: *plants bright red, fleshy; leafless but with leaflike red scales to 4 in. long; flowers urn-shaped.*
Habitat: *deep humus in forests.* **In bloom:** *May–June.*

Snow Plants *Sarcodes*

Red is invisible to bees and most other pollinating insects, but it attracts carrion insects. The Snow Plant, which looks like a chunk of meat left on the ground, is believed to be pollinated by beetles and other such carrion eaters. Snow plants were once thought to be root parasites, but in fact, like the Indian pipes, they subsist on nutrients freed by fungi from decaying matter in the soil.

Wandflower
Galax rotundifolia

Size: *3–24 in. tall; flower about ¼ in. wide.*
What to look for: *leaves heart-shaped, shiny, dark green (bronze in fall and winter), in clusters near ground; flowers small, white, at top of wandlike stalk.* **Habitat:** *rich woods and streambanks in mountain areas.*
In bloom: *May–July.*

Wandflowers *Galax*

The single species of wandflower is one of the few plants for which a town—Galax, Virginia—has been named. Its round, glossy evergreen leaves are a familiar sight in the forests of the southern Appalachians, where they often form continuous ground covers beneath such woodland plants as Mountain Laurel. Wandflowers now grow in the wild as far north as Massachusetts, having escaped from gardens where they are cultivated for their distinctive flower spikes.

Primroses *Primula*

These denizens of mountain slopes, northern stream-banks, and other cool, moist places take their name from the Latin word for "first." Wherever they grow, they are likely to be among the earliest bloomers. Their small, brilliant flowers appear in clusters atop naked stalks that rise from rosettes of leaves. Each bloom's yellow center attracts bees and other pollinators to the nectar within. Humans are not always similarly attracted: the lovely Mountain Primrose, for example, has a foul odor.

Bird's-eye Primrose
Primula mistassinica

Size: *1-6 in. tall; flower ¼-½ in. wide.* **What to look for:** *flowers pink or lilac, with yellow centers; leaves clustered at base of stalk.* **Habitat:** *moist cliffs, meadows.* **In bloom:** *Apr.-Aug.*

Mountain Primrose
Primula parryi

Size: *4-16 in. tall; flower ½-1 in. wide.* **What to look for:** *flowers rose-purple, with yellow centers; leaves fleshy, clustered at base of stalk.* **Habitat:** *high mountain meadows, streambanks.* **In bloom:** *June-Aug.*

Sierra Primrose
Primula suffrutescens

Size: *1-4 in. tall; flower ¼-½ in. wide.* **What to look for:** *flowers pink or purple, with yellow centers; leaves in tufts at base of downy stalks.* **Habitat:** *cliffs, ledges.* **In bloom:** *July-Aug.*

Mountain Douglasia
Douglasia montana

Size: *1-3 in. tall; flower ¼-½ in. wide.* **What to look for:** *flowers pink, in clusters at stem tips; leaves tiny, narrow, forming tufted mats.* **Habitat:** *dry, rocky soil; mountaintops.* **In bloom:** *May-July.*

Douglasias *Douglasia*

These humble plants, whose small flowers are so profuse that they all but blot out the leaves, share a distinction with the lordly Douglas-firs growing in the same parts of the Pacific Northwest. Both are named for the Scottish explorer David Douglas, who found them while on a plant-hunting expedition from Oregon to Hudson Bay. The Mountain Douglasia is one of several species popular among rock gardeners.

Shooting Star
Dodecatheon meadia

Size: *4-20 in. tall; flower ¾-1 in. wide.* **What to look for:** *flower petals white to pink, swept back like trailing flames; leaves spatula-shaped, at base of stalk.* **Habitat:** *prairies, meadows, open woods.* **In bloom:** *Apr.-June.*

Shooting Stars
Dodecatheon

Legend has it that wherever a star falls to earth these flowers appear with their swept-back petals. The plants are quite versatile, flourishing in sunny grasslands and shady woods. The Sierra Shooting Star (*Dodecatheon jeffreyi*) thrives from the mountains of Alaska to California's Sierra Nevada. Like most kinds of shooting stars, it is able to produce seeds by self-pollination, thus assuring species survival even where insects are scarce.

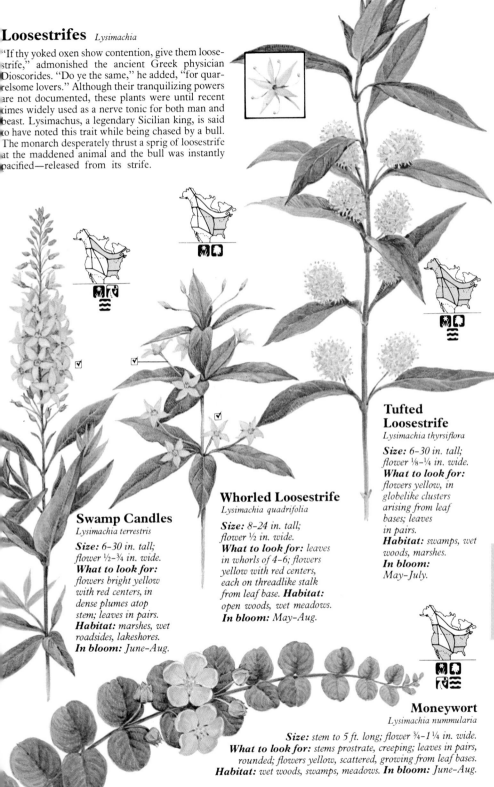

Loosestrifes *Lysimachia*

"If thy yoked oxen show contention, give them loosestrife," admonished the ancient Greek physician
Dioscorides. "Do ye the same," he added, "for quarrelsome lovers." Although their tranquilizing powers
are not documented, these plants were until recent
times widely used as a nerve tonic for both man and
beast. Lysimachus, a legendary Sicilian king, is said
to have noted this trait while being chased by a bull.
The monarch desperately thrust a sprig of loosestrife
at the maddened animal and the bull was instantly
pacified—released from its strife.

Tufted Loosestrife
Lysimachia thyrsiflora

Size: *6-30 in. tall;
flower ⅛-¼ in. wide.*
What to look for:
*flowers yellow, in
globelike clusters
arising from leaf
bases; leaves
in pairs.*
Habitat: *swamps, wet
woods, marshes.*
In bloom:
May-July.

Swamp Candles
Lysimachia terrestris

Size: *6-30 in. tall;
flower ½-¾ in. wide.*
What to look for:
*flowers bright yellow
with red centers, in
dense plumes atop
stem; leaves in pairs.*
Habitat: *marshes, wet
roadsides, lakeshores.*
In bloom: *June-Aug.*

Whorled Loosestrife
Lysimachia quadrifolia

Size: *8-24 in. tall;
flower ½ in. wide.*
What to look for: *leaves
in whorls of 4-6; flowers
yellow with red centers,
each on threadlike stalk
from leaf base.* **Habitat:**
open woods, wet meadows.
In bloom: *May-Aug.*

Moneywort
Lysimachia nummularia

Size: *stem to 5 ft. long; flower ¾-1¼ in. wide.*
What to look for: *stems prostrate, creeping; leaves in pairs,
rounded; flowers yellow, scattered, growing from leaf bases.*
Habitat: *wet woods, swamps, meadows.* **In bloom:** *June-Aug.*

WILDFLOWERS

381

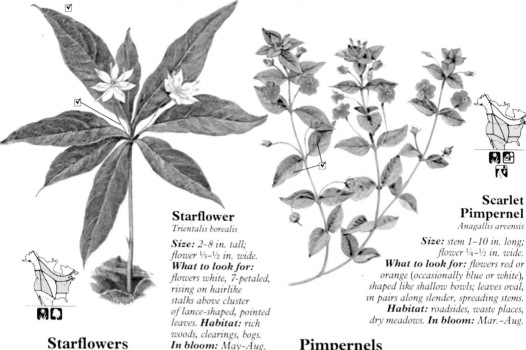

Starflower
Trientalis borealis

Size: *2-8 in. tall; flower ⅓-½ in. wide.*
What to look for: *flowers white, 7-petaled, rising on hairlike stalks above cluster of lance-shaped, pointed leaves.* **Habitat:** *rich woods, clearings, bogs.* **In bloom:** *May-Aug.*

Scarlet Pimpernel
Anagallis arvensis

Size: *stem 1-10 in. long; flower ¼-½ in. wide.*
What to look for: *flowers red or orange (occasionally blue or white), shaped like shallow bowls; leaves oval, in pairs along slender, spreading stems.* **Habitat:** *roadsides, waste places, dry meadows.* **In bloom:** *Mar.-Aug.*

Starflowers
Trientalis

Many flowers are starlike in form, but these fragile shade-lovers have a special right to their name: the astral effect of their blossoms is repeated in an underlying collar of pointed leaves. Like many other spring bloomers, the starflowers store nutrients through the winter in fleshy underground tubers. Because of these tubers, one pink-flowered western species, *Trientalis latifolia*, is commonly known as Indian Potato.

Pimpernels
Anagallis

The Scarlet Pimpernel is a European native that is now widespread in North America and around the world. In England it is known as the Poor Man's Weather Glass because of its great sensitivity to atmospheric change. Not only do its blossoms close at the first hint of approaching dusk and fail to open on overcast days, but—in response to rising humidity—they close when stormy weather threatens.

Sea Milkworts
Glaux

Although it lives where water is abundant, this seaside plant (the only sea milkwort species in the world) is similar in many ways to some desert succulents. The common denominator is the ability of the small, fleshy leaves to withstand the drying effect of salt. The root membranes supply added protection by regulating the movement of water, thus allowing the plants to grow even where water is quite salty.

Featherfoils
Hottonia

When conditions are right, the seeds of these water plants sprout in late summer and grow underwater throughout fall and winter. In spring, buoyed by air-filled cells, the hollow stems surface and bloom, surrounded by a submerged wreath of feathery leaves. Conditions are seldom right, however, and so the plants may bloom profusely one season, then disappear for several years before blooming again.

Sea Milkwort
Glaux maritima

Size: *1-12 in. long; flower ⅛ in. wide.*
What to look for: *flowers white, pink, or purple, borne singly at leaf bases; leaves oblong, in pairs along gray-green, sprawling stems.* **Habitat:** *beaches, salt marshes.* **In bloom:** *May-July.*

Featherfoil
Hottonia inflata

Size: *3-12 in. tall; flower ⅛-¼ in. wide.*
What to look for: *stems protruding above water; flowers white, clustered at stem joints; leaves below surface, feathery.* **Habitat:** *still freshwater.* **In bloom:** *Apr.-June.*

Stonecrops
Sedum

Stonecrops can survive in arid locales—including deserts, rocky shores, tundra, and dry spots in otherwise congenial climates—because their fleshy leaves store water. In addition, the pores of their leaves follow an unusual schedule of opening and closing, one that is the reverse of the general rule: they open at night to admit the carbon dioxide needed for growth, then close during the day to prevent water loss. So effective is this system of conservation that many species are known as live-forevers: the leaves stay fresh long after the plants have been picked.

Orpine
Sedum telephium

Size: *10–22 in. tall;*
flower ¼–½ in. wide.
What to look for:
flowers yellow-green
or reddish lavender, in dense cluster
atop stem; leaves fleshy, toothed, oval.
Habitat: *fields, meadows.*
In bloom: *July–Sept.*

Roseroot
Sedum rosea

Size: *1–12 in. tall;*
flower ¼–½ in. wide.
What to look for:
stems matted, turning
up at ends; flowers
red-purple, clustered at
stem tips; leaves fleshy,
oval. **Habitat:** *tundra,*
mountains, rocky coasts.
In bloom: *July–Sept.*

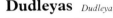

Wall Pepper
Sedum acre

Size: *1–3 in. tall;*
flower ⅓–½ in. wide.
What to look for:
stems creeping, matted;
leaves succulent,
evergreen; flowers
yellow, star-shaped,
in small clusters
atop short stalks.
Habitat: *rocks, walls,*
dry clearings.
In bloom: *June–July.*

Ditch Stonecrops
Penthorum

Though they look a great deal like stonecrops and belong to the same botanical family, the ditch stonecrops are not succulent. They are wetland plants that usually grow in ditches and other low spots where water collects. Of the group's three species, the one shown here is the only North American native; the others originated in Asia.

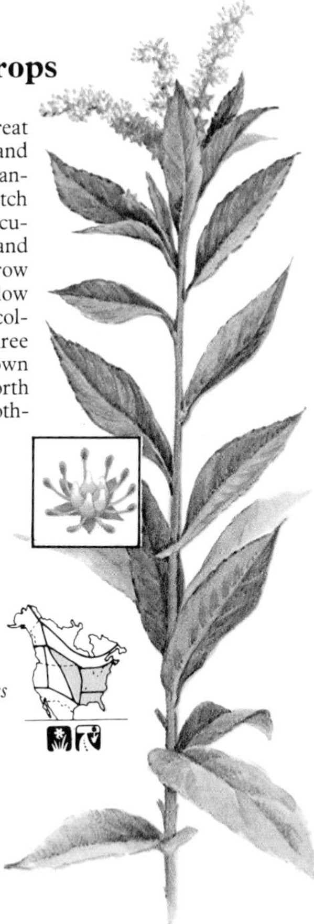

Ditch Stonecrop
Penthorum sedoides

Size: *6–36 in. tall;*
flower ¼–½ in. wide.
What to look for:
flowers greenish with
creamy white tips,
densely borne on leafless
stalks; leaves
lance-shaped, along
upright stem.
Habitat: *marshes,*
ditches, streambanks.
In bloom: *June–Oct.*

Dudleyas *Dudleya*

These western plants are closely related to the stonecrops (many species in each group are known as liveforevers) and thrive in the same arid conditions. The most obvious difference is the way the flowers are borne. Those of the dudleyas appear on stalks that arise from among a cluster of leaves, while the stonecrops' are borne at the ends of leafy stems.

Canyon Dudleya
Dudleya cymosa

Size: *4–8 in. tall;*
flower ¼–½ in. wide.
What to look for: *flowers*
yellow to bright red, bell-
shaped, clustered atop nearly
leafless stalks; leaves broad,
oblong, densely clustered at
base of plant. **Habitat:** *rocky*
cliffs, sagebrush, open woods.
In bloom: *Mar.–July.*

383

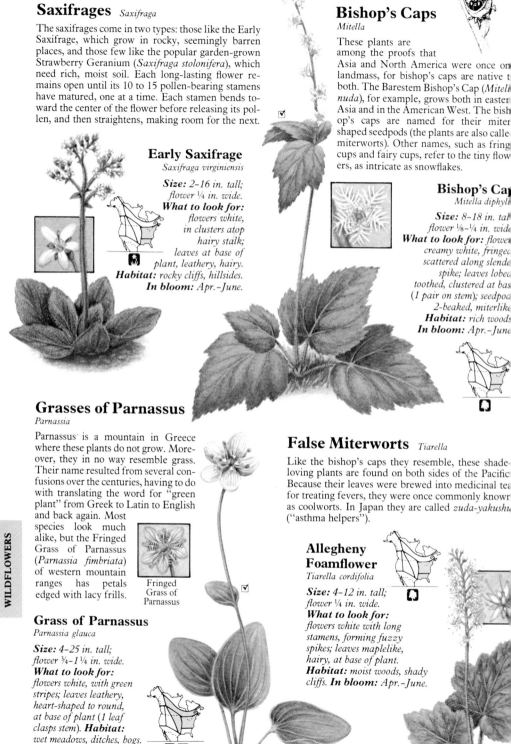

seedpod

Saxifrages *Saxifraga*

The saxifrages come in two types: those like the Early Saxifrage, which grow in rocky, seemingly barren places, and those few like the popular garden-grown Strawberry Geranium (*Saxifraga stolonifera*), which need rich, moist soil. Each long-lasting flower remains open until its 10 to 15 pollen-bearing stamens have matured, one at a time. Each stamen bends toward the center of the flower before releasing its pollen, and then straightens, making room for the next.

Early Saxifrage
Saxifraga virginiensis

Size: 2–16 in. tall; flower ¼ in. wide.
What to look for: flowers white, in clusters atop hairy stalk; leaves at base of plant, leathery, hairy.
Habitat: rocky cliffs, hillsides.
In bloom: Apr.–June.

Bishop's Caps
Mitella

These plants are among the proofs that Asia and North America were once on landmass, for bishop's caps are native t both. The Barestem Bishop's Cap (*Mitell nuda*), for example, grows both in easter Asia and in the American West. The bish op's caps are named for their miter shaped seedpods (the plants are also calle miterworts). Other names, such as fring cups and fairy cups, refer to the tiny flow ers, as intricate as snowflakes.

Bishop's Cap
Mitella diphyll

Size: 8–18 in. tal flower ⅛–¼ in. wide
What to look for: flowe creamy white, fringe scattered along slende spike; leaves lobe toothed, clustered at bas (1 pair on stem); seedpo 2-beaked, miterlik **Habitat:** rich wood **In bloom:** Apr.–June

Grasses of Parnassus
Parnassia

Parnassus is a mountain in Greece where these plants do not grow. Moreover, they in no way resemble grass. Their name resulted from several confusions over the centuries, having to do with translating the word for "green plant" from Greek to Latin to English and back again. Most species look much alike, but the Fringed Grass of Parnassus (*Parnassia fimbriata*) of western mountain ranges has petals edged with lacy frills.

Fringed Grass of Parnassus

Grass of Parnassus
Parnassia glauca

Size: 4–25 in. tall; flower ¾–1¼ in. wide.
What to look for: flowers white, with green stripes; leaves leathery, heart-shaped to round, at base of plant (1 leaf clasps stem). **Habitat:** wet meadows, ditches, bogs.
In bloom: July–Oct.

False Miterworts *Tiarella*

Like the bishop's caps they resemble, these shade loving plants are found on both sides of the Pacific Because their leaves were brewed into medicinal tea for treating fevers, they were once commonly known as coolworts. In Japan they are called *zuda-yakush* ("asthma helpers").

Allegheny Foamflower
Tiarella cordifolia

Size: 4–12 in. tall; flower ¼ in. wide.
What to look for: flowers white with long stamens, forming fuzzy spikes; leaves maplelike, hairy, at base of plant.
Habitat: moist woods, shady cliffs. **In bloom:** Apr.–June.

Gordon's Ivesia

Ivesia gordoni

Size: *2–10 in. tall; flower ⅛–¼ in. wide.*
What to look for: *flowers yellow, starlike, clustered atop wiry stems; leaves fernlike, mostly at base of plant.*
Habitat: *mountain slopes, ridges, riverbanks.*
In bloom: *June–Aug.*

Ivesias *Ivesia*

Most of the 20 species in this group are limited to the Sierra Nevada of California. Gordon's Ivesia is the most striking exception; it grows as far north as Washington's Cascade mountains and eastward into the Rockies of Colorado and Montana.

Wild Strawberry

Fragaria virginiana

Size: *2–10 in. tall; flower ½–¾ in. wide.*
What to look for: *leaflets hairy, in 3's; white flowers and red "berries" clustered among leaves.*
Habitat: *meadows, clearings.* **In bloom:** *Apr.–July.*

Strawberries *Fragaria*

"Doubtless God could have made a better berry," wrote Izaak Walton, "but doubtless God never did." In fact, the juicy strawberry is not a berry at all, but the pulpy center of the flower, and each of its apparent seeds is actually a complete one-seeded fruit.

Queen of the Prairie

Filipendula rubra

Size: *2–6 ft. tall; flower ¼ in. wide.*
What to look for: *flowers pink, in flat-topped clusters on tall stalks; leaves large, toothed, deeply divided.*
Habitat: *moist prairies, meadows, marshes.*
In bloom: *June–Aug.*

Meadowsweets

Filipendula

Only one species of this group, the spectacular Queen of the Prairie, is native to North America. Other species, including the shorter Queen of the Meadow (*Filipendula ulmaria*), were imported from Europe or Asia.

Steeplebush

Spiraea tomentosa

Size: *2–4 ft. tall; flower ⅛–¼ in. wide.*
What to look for: *flowers pink, in dense steeple-shaped clusters at ends of branches; leaves oblong, toothed, with woolly undersides.*
Habitat: *wet fields, meadows.*
In bloom: *July–Sept.*

Spireas *Spiraea*

These shrubby plants are closely related to the meadowsweets, and are often known by the same name. Native wild spireas, such as the Steeplebush, though less showy than the larger garden species from Asia, are often used for landscaping.

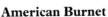

American Burnet

Sanguisorba canadensis

Size: *2–6 ft. tall; flower ⅛–¼ in. wide.*
What to look for: *flowers white with long stamens, in dense, fuzzy spikes; leaves divided into many toothed leaflets.*
Habitat: *moist open ground.* **In bloom:** *June–Oct.*

Burnets *Sanguisorba*

It is a botanical truism that petalless flowers are pollinated by the wind; but as the burnets demonstrate, such truisms are not always true. Bees, butterflies, and other insects are attracted by the colored sepals, the long-stalked stamens, and the fragrance of the flowers. Several Eurasian species now grow in North America.

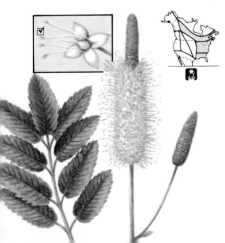

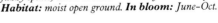

Marsh Cinquefoil
Potentilla palustris

Size: 4–24 in. tall; flower ¾–1 in. wide.
What to look for: flowers crimson, star-shaped, scattered on slender stems; leaflets toothed, in groups of 5–7.
Habitat: wet meadows, swamps, marshes. **In bloom:** June–Aug.

Silverweed
Potentilla anserina

Size: stem to 5 ft. long; flower ½–1 in. wide.
What to look for: flowers yellow with oval petals, borne singly on slender stalks along trailing stems; leaves divided into 7–15 leaflets; leaflets toothed, hairy, silvery underneath. **Habitat:** moist open sand, beaches, salt marshes. **In bloom:** May–Sep.

Fivefingers
Potentilla simplex

Size: stem to 3 ft. long; flower ¼–½ in. wide.
What to look for: flowers yellow with blunt petals, borne singly on slender stalks along trailing stems; leaflets toothed, in groups of 5. **Habitat:** dry open woods, meadows, roadsides. **In bloom:** Apr.–June.

Tall Cinquefoil
Potentilla arguta

Size: 1–3 ft. tall; flower ½–¾ in. wide.
What to look for: flowers creamy white with yellow centers, borne in loose clusters atop branching stems; leaves divided into 7–11 oval, toothed leaflets. **Habitat:** dry open woods, prairies. **In bloom:** June–Aug.

Cinquefoils *Potentilla*

The name cinquefoil means "five-leaf." Indeed, the leaves of many species, such as Fivefingers, are divided into 5 leaflets, but in others the number may vary from 3 to 15 or more. Of the world's more than 300 cinquefoil species, about one-third grow in North America, in habitats ranging from swamplands to dry rocky fields. Like many weeds that invade barren areas where others of their own kind are scarce, most cinquefoils bear flowers that can produce viable seeds with or without fertilization.

Avens *Geum*

When the flowers of avens produce fruit, each tiny, nutlike seed retains the style (the stalklike extension of the seed-producing organ). In some woodland species, such as the eastern Redroot (*Geum canadense*), these styles have hooks and adhere to the fur of animals, who thus help to disperse the seeds. In others, such as the avens known as Prairie Smoke, the styles form feathery sails that are caught and carried by the wind.

Purple Avens
Geum rivale

Size: 1–4 ft. tall; flower ½ in. wide.
What to look for: flowers brownish purple, nodding atop hairy stalks; fruits like soft burrs; leaves hairy, toothed; leaves at base much divided, with large leaflet at tip; leaves on stem 3-fingered. **Habitat:** wet meadows, bogs. **In bloom:** May–Aug.

Prairie Smoke
Geum triflorum

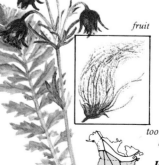

fruit

Size: 4–16 in. tall; flower ¼–½ in. wide.
What to look for: flowers red-purple, urn-shaped, nodding; fruits with long feathery tails; leaves much divided, toothed, lobed. **Habitat:** dry prairies, limestone, gravel, lakeshores. **In bloom:** Apr.–Aug.

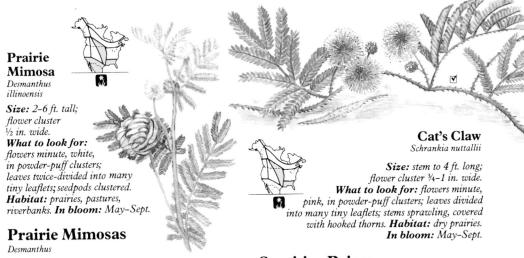

Prairie Mimosa
Desmanthus illinoensis

Size: *2-6 ft. tall; flower cluster ½ in. wide.*
What to look for: *flowers minute, white, in powder-puff clusters; leaves twice-divided into many tiny leaflets; seedpods clustered.*
Habitat: *prairies, pastures, riverbanks.* **In bloom:** *May-Sept.*

Prairie Mimosas
Desmanthus

Like the true mimosas for which they are named, these shrubby plants bear leaves that are twice-divided; each leaf is divided into several long stalks, each of which bears a double row of small leaflets. The fluffy flower clusters are made up of 40 to 50 tiny flowers, each with five long stamens.

Cat's Claw
Schrankia nuttallii

Size: *stem to 4 ft. long; flower cluster ¾-1 in. wide.*
What to look for: *flowers minute, pink, in powder-puff clusters; leaves divided into many tiny leaflets; stems sprawling, covered with hooked thorns.* **Habitat:** *dry prairies.* **In bloom:** *May-Sept.*

Sensitive Briers *Schrankia*

Each of these plants' leaflets is supported by a small, water-filled swelling at the base. When these are jarred, loss of osmotic pressure causes the water to leave the cells, and the leaflets fold up. So sensitive are these organs that they respond to vibrations carried from one interlacing branch to another.

Hog Potato
Hoffmanseggia densiflora

Size: *5-16 in. tall; flower ½ in. wide.*
What to look for: *flowers yellow and orange, in erect spikes; leaves fernlike, mostly at base of plant; seedpods flat, about 1 in. long.*
Habitat· *dry grasslands, scrublands; alkaline deserts.* **In bloom:** *Apr.-Sept.*

Hog Potatoes *Hoffmanseggia*

The tuberlike swellings on the roots are edible and nutritious, though hardly tasty. One species is known in Spanish as *Camote de Raton* ("Mouse's Sweet Potato"). To the Indians of the Southwest, the plants were valuable as emergency rations because they grow where other food is scarce.

Sennas *Cassia*

Sennas have been used medicinally since ancient times. The dried leaves of Wild Senna yield an effective laxative, and in the old days they were often gathered from the wild and sold to apothecaries. Commercial markets, however, prefer the more potent Golden Shower (*Cassia fistula*), imported from India.

seedpod

Wild Senna
Cassia marilandica

Size: *3-6 ft. tall; flower ¾-1 in. wide.*
What to look for: *flowers bright yellow with brown centers; leaflets oval, 4-8 pairs on each stalk; seedpods flat, segmented.*
Habitat: *roadsides, thickets, prairies, wet woods.*
In bloom: *July-Aug.*

Partridge Pea
Cassia fasciculata

Size: *6-30 in. tall; flower ¾-1½ in. wide.*
What to look for: *flowers bright yellow with brown centers; leaflets narrow, 6-18 pairs on each stalk; seedpods small, flat.*
Habitat: *meadows, fields, prairies.* **In bloom:** *July-Sept.*

Vetches
Vicia

Cow Vetch
Vicia cracca

Size: stem to 6 ft. long; flower ¼–½ in. long.
What to look for: stems climbing or sprawling; flowers violet to blue, in dense, one-sided spikes; leaves divided, ending in 2 tendrils.
Habitat: fields, grasslands.
In bloom: May–Aug.

An Old World vetch, the Broad Bean (*Vicia faba*), is one of the earliest plants known to have been cultivated by man and is still grown as a winter vegetable. The Cow Vetch is also widely cultivated, though generally for use as fodder rather than for human consumption. When grown as a cover crop, it is plowed under in the fall to enrich the soil.

Beach Pea
Lathyrus japonicus

Size: stem 2–3 ft. long; flower ¾–1 in. long.
What to look for: plants sprawling; flowers red-purple (maturing to blue and white), in clusters; leaves divided, tendriled.
Habitat: open beaches, dunes.
In bloom: June–Aug.

Pride
Calif

Wild Peas *Lathyrus*

Wild peas, or vetchlings, are closely related to the vetches. (Botanists tell them apart by the placement of small hairs inside the flowers.) Many species are grown as fodder or cover crops or—like the Sweet Pea (*Lathyrus odoratus*)—for floral beauty. The crimson Pride of California (*Lathyrus splendens*) is outstanding among the Pacific Coast's many wild peas.

Fragrant Leadplant
Amorpha nana

Size: 1–3 ft. tall; flower ⅛–¼ in. long.
What to look for: flowers purple with long yellow stamens, in dense slender spikes; leaves divided into small oval leaflets.
Habitat: dry prairies.
In bloom: June–July.

Leadplants *Amorpha*

All plants need nitrogen to grow, but they cannot take it directly from the air. It must be "fixed"—converted to a water-soluble compound—before plant roots can use it. Legumes such as leadplants have special nodules in their roots that house nitrogen-fixing bacteria. It is this trait that makes them important cover crops. When they die back or are plowed under after a season's growth, the nitrogen stored in their tissues enriches the soil.

Yellow Locoweed

Showy Locoweed
Oxytropis splendens

Size: 4–14 in. tall; flower ½ in. long.
What to look for: flowers pink to blue, in dense spikes; plants covered with silky white hairs; leaflets in whorls along stalk.
Habitat: dry prairies, meadows, mountain slopes.
In bloom: June–Aug.

Locoweeds *Oxytropis*

Ranchers may call any of several poisonous plants locoweeds, but the name properly belongs to this group and to various milk vetches that contain the same addictive, slow-acting poison. Animals seldom eat locoweed unless drought or overgrazing forces them to; then they may become habituated and search for more, even when tastier forage is available. Yellow Locoweed (*Oxytropis campestris*) is widespread in Canada and the northern United States.

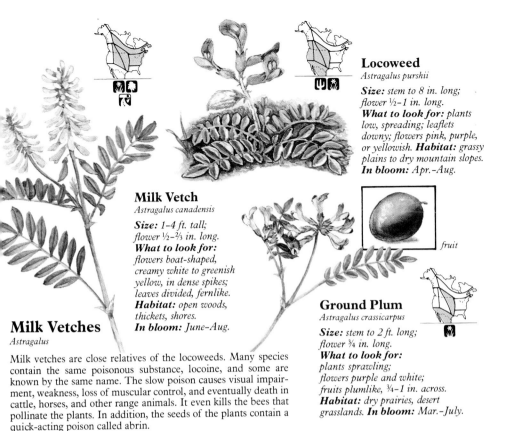

Locoweed
Astragalus purshii

Size: *stem to 8 in. long; flower ½–1 in. long.*
What to look for: *plants low, spreading; leaflets downy; flowers pink, purple, or yellowish.* **Habitat:** *grassy plains to dry mountain slopes.* **In bloom:** *Apr.–Aug.*

fruit

Milk Vetch
Astragalus canadensis

Size: *1–4 ft. tall; flower ½–⅔ in. long.*
What to look for: *flowers boat-shaped, creamy white to greenish yellow, in dense spikes; leaves divided, fernlike.* **Habitat:** *open woods, thickets, shores.* **In bloom:** *June–Aug.*

Ground Plum
Astragalus crassicarpus

Size: *stem to 2 ft. long; flower ¾ in. long.*
What to look for: *plants sprawling; flowers purple and white; fruits plumlike, ¾–1 in. across.* **Habitat:** *dry prairies, desert grasslands.* **In bloom:** *Mar.–July.*

Milk Vetches
Astragalus

Milk vetches are close relatives of the locoweeds. Many species contain the same poisonous substance, locoine, and some are known by the same name. The slow poison causes visual impairment, weakness, loss of muscular control, and eventually death in cattle, horses, and other range animals. It even kills the bees that pollinate the plants. In addition, the seeds of the plants contain a quick-acting poison called abrin.

Hoary Peas *Tephrosia*

These legumes have a variety of names. Toxic to mammals, they are often called goat's rues. Yet many birds eat the seeds; the plants came to be called turkey peas in areas where those wild fowl were once abundant. The tough rootstocks earned the names devil's shoestring and catgut. Used by Indians to poison fish, the roots are a source of the insecticide rotenone.

Licorices *Glycyrrhiza*

The rhizomes, or rootlike underground stems, of these plants yield the popular flavoring for candy and medicines. ("Licorice" is a corruption of the Latin name *Glycyrrhiza*, which means "sweet root.") An Old World species, *Glycyrrhiza glabra*, is the commercial source, but the rhizomes of Wild Licorice were dried and chewed by Indians.

Goat's Rue
Tephrosia virginiana

Size: *6–30 in. tall; flower ½–¾ in. long.*
What to look for: *flowers pink to purple with yellow upper lips, borne in dense clusters; leaves divided into narrow leaflets, covered with silky silver hairs.* **Habitat:** *dry open woods, fields, prairies (often in sand).* **In bloom:** *May–Aug.*

seedpods

Wild Licorice
Glycyrrhiza lepidota

Size: *8–40 in. tall; flower about ½ in. long.*
What to look for: *flowers white to yellow, in dense spikes; leaves divided into lance-shaped leaflets; seedpods prickly, clustered.* **Habitat:** *prairies, meadows, streambanks.* **In bloom:** *May–Aug.*

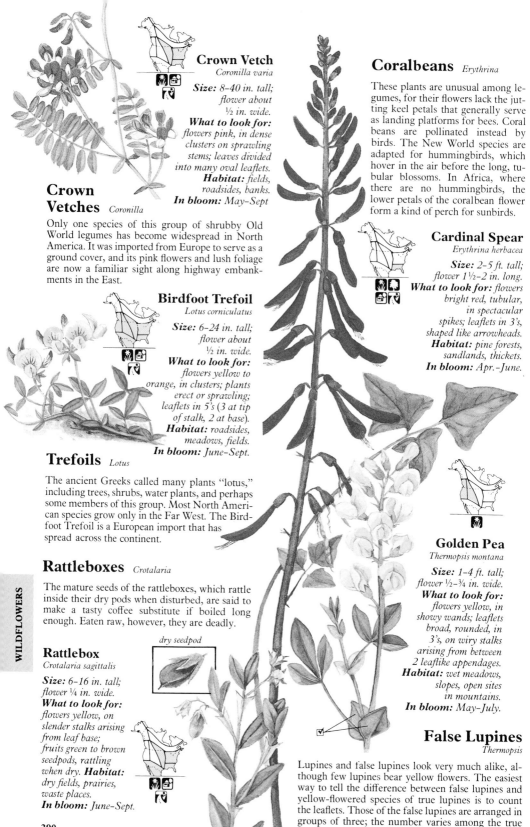

Crown Vetch
Coronilla varia

Size: 8–40 in. tall; flower about ½ in. wide.
What to look for: flowers pink, in dense clusters on sprawling stems; leaves divided into many oval leaflets.
Habitat: fields, roadsides, banks.
In bloom: May–Sept

Crown Vetches *Coronilla*

Only one species of this group of shrubby Old World legumes has become widespread in North America. It was imported from Europe to serve as a ground cover, and its pink flowers and lush foliage are now a familiar sight along highway embankments in the East.

Birdfoot Trefoil
Lotus corniculatus

Size: 6–24 in. tall; flower about ½ in. wide.
What to look for: flowers yellow to orange, in clusters; plants erect or sprawling; leaflets in 5's (3 at tip of stalk, 2 at base).
Habitat: roadsides, meadows, fields.
In bloom: June–Sept.

Trefoils *Lotus*

The ancient Greeks called many plants "lotus," including trees, shrubs, water plants, and perhaps some members of this group. Most North American species grow only in the Far West. The Birdfoot Trefoil is a European import that has spread across the continent.

Rattleboxes *Crotalaria*

The mature seeds of the rattleboxes, which rattle inside their dry pods when disturbed, are said to make a tasty coffee substitute if boiled long enough. Eaten raw, however, they are deadly.

Rattlebox
Crotalaria sagittalis

Size: 6–16 in. tall; flower ¼ in. wide.
What to look for: flowers yellow, on slender stalks arising from leaf base; fruits green to brown seedpods, rattling when dry. **Habitat:** dry fields, prairies, waste places.
In bloom: June–Sept.

dry seedpod

Coralbeans *Erythrina*

These plants are unusual among legumes, for their flowers lack the jutting keel petals that generally serve as landing platforms for bees. Coral beans are pollinated instead by birds. The New World species are adapted for hummingbirds, which hover in the air before the long, tubular blossoms. In Africa, where there are no hummingbirds, the lower petals of the coralbean flower form a kind of perch for sunbirds.

Cardinal Spear
Erythrina herbacea

Size: 2–5 ft. tall; flower 1½–2 in. long.
What to look for: flowers bright red, tubular, in spectacular spikes; leaflets in 3's, shaped like arrowheads.
Habitat: pine forests, sandlands, thickets.
In bloom: Apr.–June.

Golden Pea
Thermopsis montana

Size: 1–4 ft. tall; flower ½–¾ in. wide.
What to look for: flowers yellow, in showy wands; leaflets broad, rounded, in 3's, on wiry stalks arising from between 2 leaflike appendages.
Habitat: wet meadows, slopes, open sites in mountains.
In bloom: May–July.

False Lupines
Thermopsis

Lupines and false lupines look very much alike, although few lupines bear yellow flowers. The easiest way to tell the difference between false lupines and yellow-flowered species of true lupines is to count the leaflets. Those of the false lupines are arranged in groups of three; the number varies among the true lupines, but it is always larger than three.

WILDFLOWERS

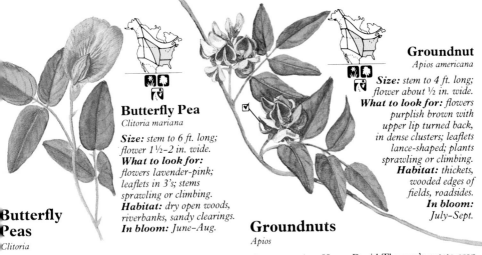

Butterfly Pea
Clitoria mariana

Size: *stem to 6 ft. long; flower 1½-2 in. wide.*
What to look for: *flowers lavender-pink; leaflets in 3's; stems sprawling or climbing.*
Habitat: *dry open woods, riverbanks, sandy clearings.*
In bloom: *June–Aug.*

Groundnut
Apios americana

Size: *stem to 4 ft. long; flower about ½ in. wide.*
What to look for: *flowers purplish brown with upper lip turned back, in dense clusters; leaflets lance-shaped; plants sprawling or climbing.*
Habitat: *thickets, wooded edges of fields, roadsides.*
In bloom: *July-Sept.*

Butterfly Peas
Clitoria

Only one species of this group of tropical legumes is widespread in North America. (Another, *Clitoria fragrans*, grows in the Florida sandlands.) The flowers often turn upside down at maturity, making a landing platform for pollinating insects.

Groundnuts
Apios

One year, when Henry David Thoreau's potato crop failed, he dug groundnuts in the woods and roasted them, as the Pilgrims had learned to do from the Indians long before. He found them nourishing and took pleasure in their nutty flavor.

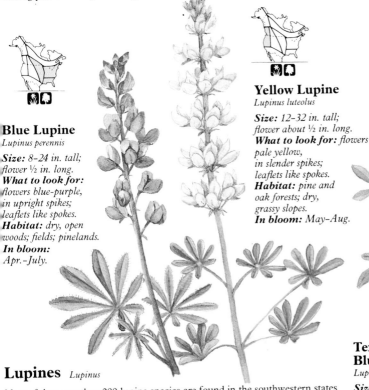

Blue Lupine
Lupinus perennis

Size: *8-24 in. tall; flower ½ in. long.*
What to look for: *flowers blue-purple, in upright spikes; leaflets like spokes.*
Habitat: *dry, open woods; fields; pinelands.*
In bloom: *Apr.-July.*

Yellow Lupine
Lupinus luteolus

Size: *12-32 in. tall; flower about ½ in. long.*
What to look for: *flowers pale yellow, in slender spikes; leaflets like spokes.*
Habitat: *pine and oak forests; dry, grassy slopes.*
In bloom: *May-Aug.*

Texas Bluebonnet
Lupinus subcarnosus

Size: *6-24 in. tall; flower about ½ in. long.*
What to look for: *flowers blue with white centers, in wandlike spikes; leaflets like spokes.*
Habitat: *dry prairies in Texas.*
In bloom: *Apr.-June.*

Lupines *Lupinus*

Most of the more than 200 lupine species are found in the southwestern states and on the Pacific Coast, where their hard, round seeds are valuable food for quail and other game birds. A few grow in the South and Midwest, but only the Blue Lupine is widespread in the Northeast. (These boundaries are becoming less distinct as a result of the cultivation of lupines in gardens.) Several species contain an alkaloid that is toxic to cattle and other grazing animals, but the effects are serious only when the leaves make up a large proportion of the animals' diet or when the extremely poisonous seeds are eaten. The Texas Bluebonnet is the state flower of Texas.

Prairie False Indigo

Baptisia leucantha

Size: 3-6 ft. tall; flower ¾-1 in. long.
What to look for: flowers white, in long wands; leaflets in 3's, gray-green, fleshy.
Habitat: moist prairies; clearings, roadsides.
In bloom: May-July.

False Indigoes *Baptisia*

The colonists found many uses for these bush plants, from brushing away horseflies while plowin (hence the names Horsefly Weed and Shoofly) treating malaria. The commonest use, however, wa as a substitute for the blue dye that has since ancie times been extracted for commercial purposes fro the roots of the Asian Indigo (*Indigofera tinctoria* The false indigoes are members of the legume, pea, family, as are all the plants on the preceding fi pages and the two pages that follow.

Wild Indig

Baptisia tinctor

Size: 1-3 ft. ta
flower about ½ in. lon
What to look for
flowers yellow, in lon
clusters amon
branching stem
leaflets in 3's, blue-gree
Habitat: dr
open wood
clearings, grassland
In bloom: May-Sep

Clovers *Trifolium*

The three-part clover leaf is a recurrent motif in folklore and popular imagery, its use ranging from the Irish Shamrock purportedly chosen by St. Patrick as a symbol of the Trinity to the complex intersections of modern highways. Clover plants are beneficial in many ways: as forage for range animals; as soil-improving cover crops; as a source of honey; and as free food relished by campers and outdoorsmen. Roots, stems, leaves, and flowers are all edible, but should be soaked in salted water or cooked briefly to make them more digestible. Red Clover is the state flower of Vermont.

Crimson Clover

Trifolium incarnatum

Size: 6-34 in. tall; flowerhead 1-2½ in. long.
What to look for: flowers crimson, in dense conical heads; leaflets large, dark green, in 3's.
Habitat: meadows, fields.
In bloom: Apr.-July.

Red Clover

Trifolium pratense

Size: 2-34 in. tall; flowerhead 1 in. long.
What to look for: flowers rose-pink, in dense heads; leaflets pointed, in 3's.
Habitat: meadows, waste places, streets.
In bloom: Mar.-Sept.

White Clover

Trifolium repens

Size: 1-15 in. tall; flowerhead 1 in. long.
What to look for: flowers white with pink bases, in dense heads; leaflets heart-shaped, in 3's.
Habitat: lawns, grasslands, fields.
In bloom: Mar.-Oct.

Rabbit's-foot Clover

Trifolium arvense

Size: 4-18 in. tall; flowerhead ½-1 in. long.
What to look for: flowers white, nearly hidden by pinkish to silvery-tan wool that covers dense heads; leaflets narrow, in 3's.
Habitat: dry fields, grassy banks.
In bloom: May-Oct.

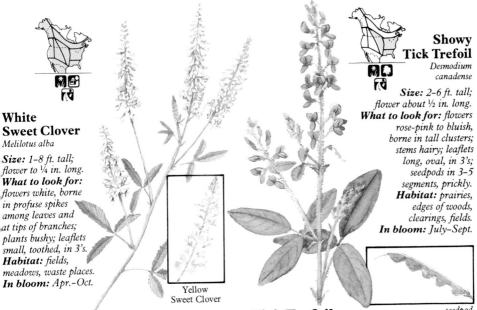

White
Sweet Clover
Melilotus alba

Size: 1-8 ft. tall;
flower to ¼ in. long.
What to look for:
flowers white, borne
in profuse spikes
among leaves and
at tips of branches;
plants bushy; leaflets
small, toothed, in 3's.
Habitat: fields,
meadows, waste places.
In bloom: Apr.-Oct.

Yellow
Sweet Clover

Showy
Tick Trefoil
*Desmodium
canadense*

Size: 2-6 ft. tall;
flower about ½ in. long.
What to look for: flowers
rose-pink to bluish,
borne in tall clusters;
stems hairy; leaflets
long, oval, in 3's;
seedpods in 3-5
segments, prickly.
Habitat: prairies,
edges of woods,
clearings, fields.
In bloom: July-Sept.

seedpod

Sweet Clovers *Melilotus*

Like most of the clovers (*Trifolium*) common in
lawns and meadows, the sweet clovers were originally
imported from the Old World and have long since
spread across North America. White Sweet Clover
and the somewhat shorter Yellow Sweet Clover
(*Melilotus officinalis*) are grown as cover crops, bee
plants, and forage. The fragrance of sweet clover hay
is a cherished memory of many a country childhood.

Tick Trefoils *Desmodium*

These legumes are named for their segmented seedpods, the notorious beggar's ticks. Each detachable
segment contains one seed and is covered with tiny
barbed hairs, which cling tenaciously to clothing,
shoelaces, animal fur, and other textured surfaces.
Thus the seeds are carried away from the parent
plant, lessening the competition between members of
the same species.

Purple
Prairie Clover
*Petalostemum
purpureum*

Size: 8-24 in. tall;
flowerhead ½-2 in. long.
What to look for: flowers
rose-purple, borne
in conical heads (flowering
begins at bottom and
proceeds upward in a ring
around the head); leaflets
narrow, in 3's.
Habitat: prairies.
In bloom: June-Sept.

White
Prairie
Clover

Round-headed
Bush Clover
Lespedeza capitata

Size: 1-4 ft. tall;
flower ¼-½ in. long.
What to look for: plants
silvery, hairy; leaflets in 3's,
densely clustered; flowers
creamy with reddish to brown
markings, in bristly
clusters. **Habitat:** dry open
fields, clearings, prairies.
In bloom: July-Sept.

Prairie Clovers
Petalostemum

Many of the prairie clovers are confined to high
plains in western states and provinces. The Purple
Prairie Clover and the very similar White Prairie
Clover (*Petalostemum candidum*) are more widespread. Like their western cousins, they can survive
periods of drought because their deep root systems
draw in water far below the surface.

Bush Clovers
Lespedeza

About 20 kinds of bush clover grow wild in North
America, including 4 or 5 from abroad (the numbers
are uncertain because the species hybridize quite easily). Important plants for pasturage and hay, they are
among the best crops for improving the nitrogen content of dry soil. The seeds of some species are a primary food for quail.

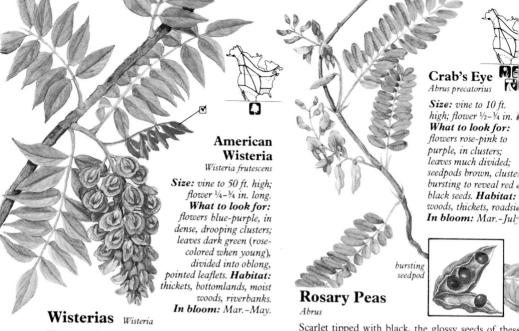

American Wisteria
Wisteria frutescens

Size: *vine to 50 ft. high; flower ¼-¾ in. long.*
What to look for: *flowers blue-purple, in dense, drooping clusters; leaves dark green (rose-colored when young), divided into oblong, pointed leaflets.* **Habitat:** *thickets, bottomlands, moist woods, riverbanks.*
In bloom: *Mar.-May.*

Wisterias   *Wisteria*

This group's two native varieties, American Wisteria and Kentucky Wisteria, are now considered to be one species *(Wisteria frutescens)*. They are not as showy nor as winter-hardy as the garden species imported from Asia. Like the imports, the native wisterias are vigorous twining vines whose woody stems may, over the years, grow to be several inches thick.

Crab's Eye
Abrus precatorius

Size: *vine to 10 ft. high; flower ½-¾ in.*
What to look for: *flowers rose-pink to purple, in clusters; leaves much divided; seedpods brown, cluste bursting to reveal red black seeds.* **Habitat:** *woods, thickets, roadsi*
In bloom: *Mar.-Jul*

bursting seedpod

Rosary Peas
Abrus

Scarlet tipped with black, the glossy seeds of these woody tropical vines have long been used for rosar beads and decorative jewelry. They are, however extremely poisonous; less than one seed, chewed an swallowed, can kill an adult, and toddlers have die merely from sucking on a seed. The single Nort American species grows only in Florida.

Alfalfa
Medicago sativa

Size: *1-3 ft. tall; flower ½ in. long.*
What to look for: *plants erect or sprawling; flowers purple to yellowish, in loose heads; fruits corkscrewlike; leaflets in 3's.* **Habitat:** *fields, waste ground.*
In bloom: *May-Oct.*

Medicks   *Medicago*

Several species in this group of Old World legumes, imported to North America as crop plants, now grow wild all across the continent. Alfalfa was one of the earliest domesticated plants (the name comes from the Arabic for "best fodder"). Flourishing in well-drained nonacidic soils, it is still among the world's most important forage and soil-improving cover crops.

Kudzu
Pueraria lobata

Size: *vine to 75 ft. high; flower ¾-1 in. long.*
What to look for: *plants climbing and sprawling; leaflets oval, pointed, in 3's; flowers red-purple, grape-scented, in long spikes.*
Habitat: *fencerows, woods; overrunning old buildings.*
In bloom: *Aug.-Sept.*

Kudzus
Pueraria

abandoned house overrun by Kudzu

The fast-growing Kudzu was imported from Japan in 1911 to control erosion and restore nitrogen-depleted soil. The edible rootstocks and tough bark fibers were added benefits, and the leaves supplied fodder and chicken feed. But in the warm, wet climate of the Southeast, the Kudzu ran rampant, overgrowing forests, fields, and buildings at the rate of 100 feet a year and more. Today, the kudzu invasion is a serious problem throughout the region.

WILDFLOWERS

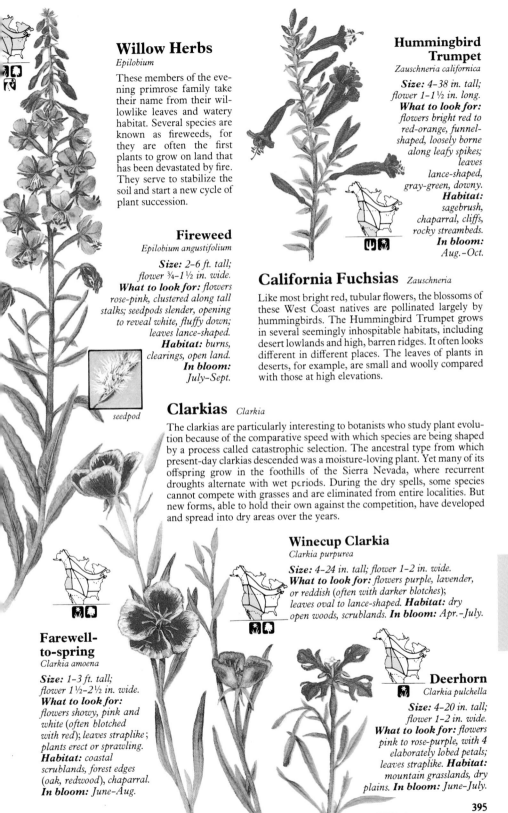

Willow Herbs
Epilobium

These members of the evening primrose family take their name from their willowlike leaves and watery habitat. Several species are known as fireweeds, for they are often the first plants to grow on land that has been devastated by fire. They serve to stabilize the soil and start a new cycle of plant succession.

Fireweed
Epilobium angustifolium

Size: *2–6 ft. tall; flower ¾–1½ in. wide.*
What to look for: *flowers rose-pink, clustered along tall stalks; seedpods slender, opening to reveal white, fluffy down; leaves lance-shaped.*
Habitat: *burns, clearings, open land.*
In bloom: *July–Sept.*

seedpod

Hummingbird Trumpet
Zauschneria californica

Size: *4–38 in. tall; flower 1–1½ in. long.*
What to look for: *flowers bright red to red-orange, funnel-shaped, loosely borne along leafy spikes; leaves lance-shaped, gray-green, downy.*
Habitat: *sagebrush, chaparral, cliffs, rocky streambeds.*
In bloom: *Aug.–Oct.*

California Fuchsias *Zauschneria*

Like most bright red, tubular flowers, the blossoms of these West Coast natives are pollinated largely by hummingbirds. The Hummingbird Trumpet grows in several seemingly inhospitable habitats, including desert lowlands and high, barren ridges. It often looks different in different places. The leaves of plants in deserts, for example, are small and woolly compared with those at high elevations.

Clarkias *Clarkia*

The clarkias are particularly interesting to botanists who study plant evolution because of the comparative speed with which species are being shaped by a process called catastrophic selection. The ancestral type from which present-day clarkias descended was a moisture-loving plant. Yet many of its offspring grow in the foothills of the Sierra Nevada, where recurrent droughts alternate with wet periods. During the dry spells, some species cannot compete with grasses and are eliminated from entire localities. But new forms, able to hold their own against the competition, have developed and spread into dry areas over the years.

Winecup Clarkia
Clarkia purpurea

Size: *4–24 in. tall; flower 1–2 in. wide.*
What to look for: *flowers purple, lavender, or reddish (often with darker blotches); leaves oval to lance-shaped.* **Habitat:** *dry open woods, scrublands.* **In bloom:** *Apr.–July.*

Farewell-to-spring
Clarkia amoena

Size: *1–3 ft. tall; flower 1½–2½ in. wide.*
What to look for: *flowers showy, pink and white (often blotched with red); leaves straplike; plants erect or sprawling.*
Habitat: *coastal scrublands, forest edges (oak, redwood), chaparral.*
In bloom: *June–Aug.*

Deerhorn
Clarkia pulchella

Size: *4–20 in. tall; flower 1–2 in. wide.*
What to look for: *flowers pink to rose-purple, with 4 elaborately lobed petals; leaves straplike.* **Habitat:** *mountain grasslands, dry plains.* **In bloom:** *June–July.*

395

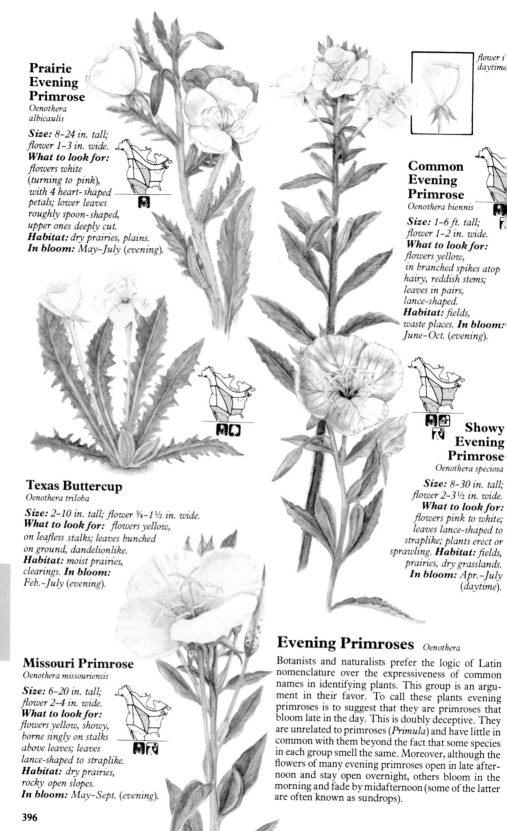

Prairie Evening Primrose
Oenothera albicaulis

Size: 8–24 in. tall; flower 1–3 in. wide.
What to look for: flowers white (turning to pink), with 4 heart-shaped petals; lower leaves roughly spoon-shaped, upper ones deeply cut.
Habitat: dry prairies, plains.
In bloom: May–July (evening).

flower i daytime

Common Evening Primrose
Oenothera biennis

Size: 1–6 ft. tall; flower 1–2 in. wide.
What to look for: flowers yellow, in branched spikes atop hairy, reddish stems; leaves in pairs, lance-shaped.
Habitat: fields, waste places. **In bloom:** June–Oct. (evening).

Texas Buttercup
Oenothera triloba

Size: 2–10 in. tall; flower ¾–1½ in. wide.
What to look for: flowers yellow, on leafless stalks; leaves bunched on ground, dandelionlike.
Habitat: moist prairies, clearings. **In bloom:** Feb.–July (evening).

Showy Evening Primrose
Oenothera speciosa

Size: 8–30 in. tall; flower 2–3½ in. wide.
What to look for: flowers pink to white; leaves lance-shaped to straplike; plants erect or sprawling. **Habitat:** fields, prairies, dry grasslands.
In bloom: Apr.–July (daytime).

Missouri Primrose
Oenothera missouriensis

Size: 6–20 in. tall; flower 2–4 in. wide.
What to look for: flowers yellow, showy, borne singly on stalks above leaves; leaves lance-shaped to straplike.
Habitat: dry prairies, rocky open slopes.
In bloom: May–Sept. (evening).

Evening Primroses *Oenothera*

Botanists and naturalists prefer the logic of Latin nomenclature over the expressiveness of common names in identifying plants. This group is an argument in their favor. To call these plants evening primroses is to suggest that they are primroses that bloom late in the day. This is doubly deceptive. They are unrelated to primroses (*Primula*) and have little in common with them beyond the fact that some species in each group smell the same. Moreover, although the flowers of many evening primroses open in late afternoon and stay open overnight, others bloom in the morning and fade by midafternoon (some of the latter are often known as sundrops).

Spiked Loosestrife
Lythrum salicaria

Size: *2–5 ft. tall; flower ½–¾ in. wide.*
What to look for: *flowers rose to deep magenta, in long, dense wands; leaves lance-shaped, in groups of 2–3 along stout stems.* **Habitat:** *marshes, pond edges, wet meadows, ditches.* **In bloom:** *June–Sept.*

Purple Loosestrifes
Lythrum

North America has several native species of this group, but none is as large, as aggressive, or as spectacular as the imported European species shown here. Dense growths of its waving purple flower spikes have become a familiar sight throughout southeastern Canada, the northeastern states, and into the Midwest.

Mistletoe
Phoradendron leucarpum

Size: *6–30 in. tall; berry ⅛–¼ in. wide; flower minute.*
What to look for: *plants in rounded clumps on tree branches; leaves leathery, spoon-shaped; flowers greenish; berries white.*
Habitat: *tree branches.*
In bloom: *May–July.*

Mistletoes   *Phoradendron*

When Oklahoma chose Mistletoe as its flower in 1893, it was joining in a tradition as old as mythology itself. Since earliest antiquity these parasitic evergreens and their European counterparts (*Viscum*)—the golden bough of lore and legend—have symbolized mankind's shared aspirations and darkest fears.

Bunchberry
Cornus canadensis

Size: *1–12 in. tall; flowerhead ¾–1½ in. wide.*
What to look for: *flowerheads made of tight greenish clusters of flowers and 4 white petallike bracts; whorl of leaves below flowerhead; fruits red, berrylike, clustered.* **Habitat:** *rich woods, thickets, bogs.* **In bloom:** *May–July.*

fruits

Dogwoods   *Cornus*

At first glance, it seems odd that the low-growing Bunchberry is included among this group of upright woody plants (other dogwood species are shown in the tree and shrub sections of this book). But a closer look at the showy, petallike bracts that set off the flower clusters, and at the whorls of lustrous leaves that grow beneath them, reveals the close kinship.

Meadow Beauties   *Rhexia*

These aptly named flowers resemble evening primroses in that they have four large petals surrounding a showy cluster of eight long yellow stamens. However, they lack the evening primroses' characteristic cross-shaped stigma (the tip of the pistil, or female organ). Another way to tell them apart is by the meadow beauties' fruits, described by Thoreau as "perfect little cream pitchers."

Pale Meadow Beauty
Rhexia mariana

Size: *8–25 in. tall; flower ¾–1½ in. wide.*
What to look for: *flowers lavender to white, with sicklelike stamens; plant hairy; fruits urnlike, sticky.* **Habitat:** *fields, meadows, pinelands.* **In bloom:** *June–Sept.*

Deergrass
Rhexia virginica

Size: *4–36 in. tall; flower ¾–1¼ in. wide*
What to look for: *flowers bright pink to maroon, with down-curled stamens; fruits urnlike, sticky; stems square, with 4 long ridges.* **Habitat:** *wet, sandy meadows; bogs; open pinelands.* **In bloom:** *July–Sept.*

fruit

397

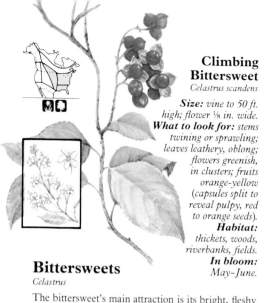

Climbing Bittersweet
Celastrus scandens

Size: vine to 50 ft. high; flower ⅛ in. wide. **What to look for:** stems twining or sprawling; leaves leathery, oblong; flowers greenish, in clusters; fruits orange-yellow (capsules split to reveal pulpy, red to orange seeds). **Habitat:** thickets, woods, riverbanks, fields. **In bloom:** May–June.

Bittersweets
Celastrus

The bittersweet's main attraction is its bright, fleshy fruits. Because these are regularly gathered and sold for decorations, the plants are becoming scarce in many areas. Only one species is native to North America, although the extremely aggressive Oriental Bittersweet (*Celastrus orbiculatus*), imported for gardens, now grows wild in the Northeast.

Allegheny Spurge
Pachysandra procumbens

Size: 6–12 in. tall; flower ¼ in. long. **What to look for:** leaves mottled, in umbrellalike clusters; flowers greenish white, in dense thumb-shaped spikes. **Habitat:** deep woods, clearings. **In bloom:** Mar.–May.

Pachysandras
Pachysandra

The native Allegheny Spurge is evergreen in the Southeast, but in northern areas it dies back each winter. Japanese Spurge (*Pachysandra terminalis*) is a spreading evergreen that was imported as a garden ground cover. Although the leaves of both species resemble those of true spurges (*Euphorbia*), the plants lack the milky sap that marks that group.

"poison oak" form in fall

WILDFLOWERS

Poison Ivy (Poison Oak)
Toxicodendron radicans

Size: vine to 100 ft. high; flower ⅛ in. wide. **What to look for:** vine or shrub; leaflets in 3's (center one long-stalked), glossy green (summer) or bright red (fall), variable in shape (can be toothed, smooth-edged, or deeply lobed); flowers greenish, loosely clustered; berries white, clustered (fall and winter). **Habitat:** woods, fields, thickets, fencerows. **In bloom:** May–July.

Poison Oak
Toxicodendron diversiloba

Size: 1–9 ft. tall; flower ⅛–¼ in. wide. **What to look for:** plants shrubby (occasionally viny); leaflets in 3's (center leaflet long-stalked), reddish green, lobed; flowers greenish white, clustered; berries white, clustered. **Habitat:** woods, thickets, scrub, chaparral. **In bloom:** Apr.–June.

Poison Sumacs
Toxicodendron

These notorious pests are close relatives of true sumacs (*Rhus*), and many botanists include them among that group. True sumacs lack the toxic oil. Until fairly recently, the widespread Poison Ivy was thought to be two distinct species: "Poison Ivy," a vine with pointed leaflets; and "Poison Oak," a shrubby plant with oaklike leaflets. But when cuttings from the same plant were grown in different locations, both forms were produced. Those in moist, shady forests became poison ivy vines; those in dry, sunny places grew into poison oak plants. In the Far West, however, there is a completely different species that is known as the Poison Oak. Usually rather shrubby, it too is variable in leaf shape and growth form. Another poison sumac species is shown in the shrub section of this book.

Tread Softly
Cnidoscolus stimulosus

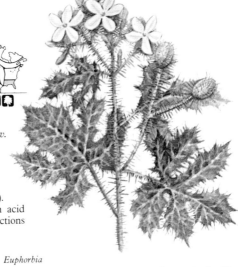

Size: *1-4 ft. tall; flower about 1 in. wide.*
What to look for: *male flowers white to creamy, trumpet-shaped, in clusters with small, greenish female flowers; leaves deeply cut, lobed, mottled; plants covered with stinging hairs.* **Habitat:** *dunes, hammocks, pinelands, coastal plains.* **In bloom:** *Feb.-Nov.*

Spurge Nettles *Cnidoscolus*

The leaves, stems, and even the flowers of these members of the spurge family are covered with stinging hairs similar to those on the true nettles (*Urtica*). Each hair is like a little hypodermic needle, with an acid irritant stored in its swollen base. The combined injections from many hairs can cause painful swelling and rash.

Spurges *Euphorbia*

flowerhead

Included among the world's nearly 1,700 spurge species are the familiar Christmas Poinsettia (*Euphorbia pulcherrima*), from the tropical forests of Mexico and Central America, and the Crown of Thorns (*Euphorbia milii*), from arid Madagascar plateaus. Many spiny succulents native to the deserts of Africa and Asia are also in this group, though they can be hard to tell apart from American cacti. Most spurges contain a bitter, milky sap that is irritating to the skin on contact and poisonous if eaten. Some, including the beautiful Snow-on-the-mountain, are so toxic that bees who visit their flowers often produce poisonous honey.

Cypress Spurge
Euphorbia cyparissias

Size: *8-30 in. tall; flowerhead ¼-½ in. wide.*
What to look for: *flowerheads in flat-topped clusters, showy, made of tiny true flowers between 2 yellow bracts; leaves needlelike.* **Habitat:** *meadows, lawns, fields.* **In bloom:** *Mar.-Sept.*

Milk Purslane
Euphorbia supina

flowerhead

Size: *to 3 ft. long; flowerhead minute.*
What to look for: *stems sprawling, matted; leaves green, with purple mottling; flowerheads clustered at leaf bases.* **Habitat:** *sand, gravel, fields, waste places.* **In bloom:** *May-Sept.*

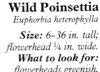

Snow-on-the-mountain
Euphorbia marginata

Size: *6-36 in. tall; flowerheads minute.*
What to look for: *flowerheads greenish, surrounded by white bracts; leaves light green, with white margins.* **Habitat:** *prairies, plains, waste places, fields.* **In bloom:** *June-Oct.*

Wild Poinsettia
Euphorbia heterophylla

Size: *6-36 in. tall; flowerhead ¼ in. wide.*
What to look for: *flowerheads greenish, in flat clusters amid red bracts; leaves marked with red (near flowers).* **Habitat:** *damp sandy clearings.* **In bloom:** *June-Sept.*

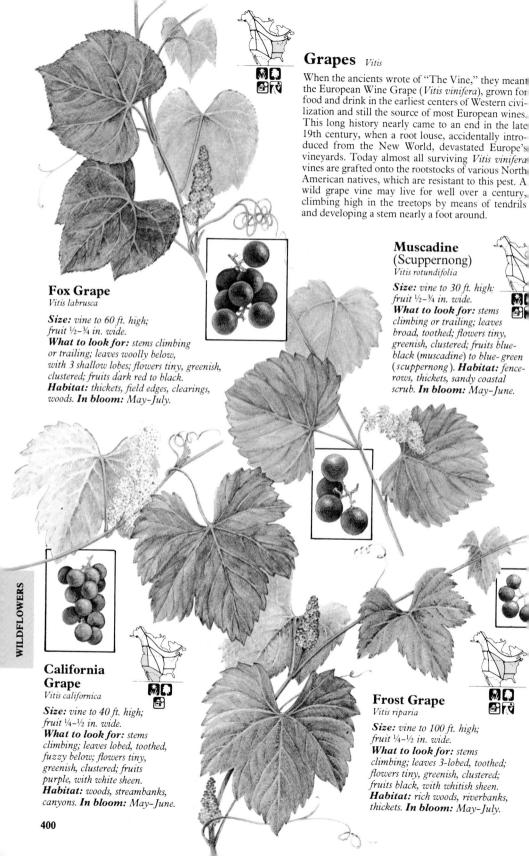

Grapes *Vitis*

When the ancients wrote of "The Vine," they meant the European Wine Grape (*Vitis vinifera*), grown for food and drink in the earliest centers of Western civilization and still the source of most European wines. This long history nearly came to an end in the late 19th century, when a root louse, accidentally introduced from the New World, devastated Europe's vineyards. Today almost all surviving *Vitis vinifera* vines are grafted onto the rootstocks of various North American natives, which are resistant to this pest. A wild grape vine may live for well over a century, climbing high in the treetops by means of tendrils and developing a stem nearly a foot around.

Fox Grape
Vitis labrusca

Size: *vine to 60 ft. high; fruit ½–¾ in. wide.*
What to look for: *stems climbing or trailing; leaves woolly below, with 3 shallow lobes; flowers tiny, greenish, clustered; fruits dark red to black.*
Habitat: *thickets, field edges, clearings, woods.* **In bloom:** *May–July.*

Muscadine (Scuppernong)
Vitis rotundifolia

Size: *vine to 30 ft. high; fruit ½–¾ in. wide.*
What to look for: *stems climbing or trailing; leaves broad, toothed; flowers tiny, greenish, clustered; fruits blue-black (muscadine) to blue-green (scuppernong).* **Habitat:** *fencerows, thickets, sandy coastal scrub.* **In bloom:** *May–June.*

California Grape
Vitis californica

Size: *vine to 40 ft. high; fruit ¼–½ in. wide.*
What to look for: *stems climbing; leaves lobed, toothed, fuzzy below; flowers tiny, greenish, clustered; fruits purple, with white sheen.*
Habitat: *woods, streambanks, canyons.* **In bloom:** *May–June.*

Frost Grape
Vitis riparia

Size: *vine to 100 ft. high; fruit ¼–½ in. wide.*
What to look for: *stems climbing; leaves 3-lobed, toothed; flowers tiny, greenish, clustered; fruits black, with whitish sheen.*
Habitat: *rich woods, riverbanks, thickets.* **In bloom:** *May–July.*

Woodbines *Parthenocissus*

These cousins of the grapes climb in two ways: by twining tendrils, and by modified roots equipped with adhesive pads that cling to walls and other surfaces. Poisonous to humans, the fruits of Virginia Creeper are an important fall and winter food for many songbirds and other wildlife. The group includes Boston Ivy (*Parthenocissus tricuspidata*), which, despite its name, was imported from Asia.

Virginia Creeper
Parthenocissus quinquefolia

Size: *vine to 150 ft. high; fruit ½ in. wide.*
What to look for:
*stems climbing or sprawling;
leaves divided into 3 or 5 stalked leaflets,
green (summer) or red (fall); flowers tiny,
greenish, clustered; fruits dark blue.*
Habitat: *rich woods, riverbanks, thickets,
field edges.* **In bloom:** *June–Aug.*

Geraniums *Geranium*

Several geranium species are also known as cranebills because of the shape of their seedpods. These pods are so constructed that they spread the plant's seeds in a rather violent fashion. As a pod dries, its outer surface contracts, gradually building up tension until it bursts at the seams. Each of its five sections springs upward, and the spoonlike bases catapult seeds as far as 22 feet. The geranium commonly grown in gardens and flowerpots belongs to a closely related group (*Pelargonium*).

Wild Geranium
Geranium maculatum

Size: *1–3 ft. tall;
flower 1–1½ in. wide.*
What to look for: *flowers
5-petaled, purple to rose,
loosely clustered above
paired leaves; leaves
deeply lobed, toothed;
fruits beaklike.* **Habitat:**
clearings, open woods.
In bloom: *Apr.–June.*

Cranesbill
Geranium richardsonii

Size: *1–3 ft. tall;
flower ¾–1 in. wide.*
What to look for: *flowers in
pairs, 5-petaled, white to pink
with purple veins; leaves deeply
lobed, each lobe roughly diamond-
shaped; stems hairy; fruits
beaklike.* **Habitat:** *mountain
meadows, canyons, moist
pinelands.* **In bloom:** *May–Aug.*

Herb Robert
Geranium robertianum

Size: *4–24 in. tall;
flower ¼–½ in. wide.*
What to look for: *flowers
pink to purplish, 5-petaled,
profuse; leaves divided
into lobed leaflets; stems
hairy, sticky; fruits beaklike.*
Habitat: *banks, ditches, woods,
clearings.* **In bloom:** *May–Oct.*

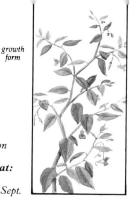

growth form

Jewelweed
Impatiens capensis

Size: *1-8 ft. tall; flower ¾-1 in. long.*
What to look for: *flowers yellow (with red, orange, or brown spots), horn-shaped, on slender stalks; plant bushy, with succulent stems.* **Habitat:** *swampy woods; streambeds; clearings.* **In bloom:** *June-Sept.*

Pale Jewelweed

Touch-me-nots *Impatiens*

This group's hostile-sounding name is not inspired by thorns, spines, stinging hairs, or toxic oils. On the contrary, the juice of Jewelweed—and of the similar Pale Jewelweed (*Impatiens pallida*) found in the East and Midwest—contains a soothing fungicide that makes it an effective treatment for athlete's foot. It also helps ease the burning of nettle stings and inflammation from Poison Ivy. (Happily, Jewelweeds often grow in the same places as these problem plants.) The name touch-me-not comes from the explosive fruits: the swollen capsules burst at a touch to disperse the seeds.

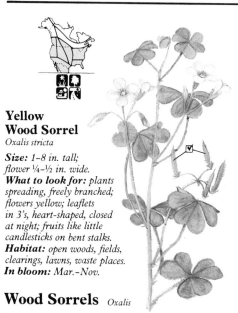

Yellow Wood Sorrel
Oxalis stricta

Size: *1-8 in. tall; flower ¼-½ in. wide.*
What to look for: *plants spreading, freely branched; flowers yellow; leaflets in 3's, heart-shaped, closed at night; fruits like little candlesticks on bent stalks.*
Habitat: *open woods, fields, clearings, lawns, waste places.*
In bloom: *Mar.-Nov.*

Wood Sorrels *Oxalis*

Several plants with pleasantly sour foliage are known as sorrel (from the old German for "sour"), and in fact, the wood sorrels are called sour grasses or sour clovers in many places. Popular salad ingredients for centuries, they were also used by old-time herbalists to treat various stomach ailments and to cure scurvy (they are rich in vitamin C). It is now known, however, that eating too much oxalic acid, the chemical responsible for the sourness, tends to inhibit the body's absorption of calcium. The special flavor of wood sorrel should thus be enjoyed only occasionally.

Violet Wood Sorrel
Oxalis violacea

Size: *1-6 in. tall; flower ½-¾ in. wide.*
What to look for: *flowers purple, on slender stalks; leaflets in 3's, heart-shaped, purplish below.*
Habitat: *open woods, clearings, thickets, prairies.*
In bloom: *Apr.-Oct.*

Common Wood Sorrel
Oxalis montana

Size: *1-6 in. tall; flower ¾ in. wide.*
What to look for: *flowers white with purplish stripes, on slender stalks; leaflets in 3's, heart-shaped, closed at night.*
Habitat: *rich woods; swampy lowlands.*
In bloom: *May-Aug.*

402

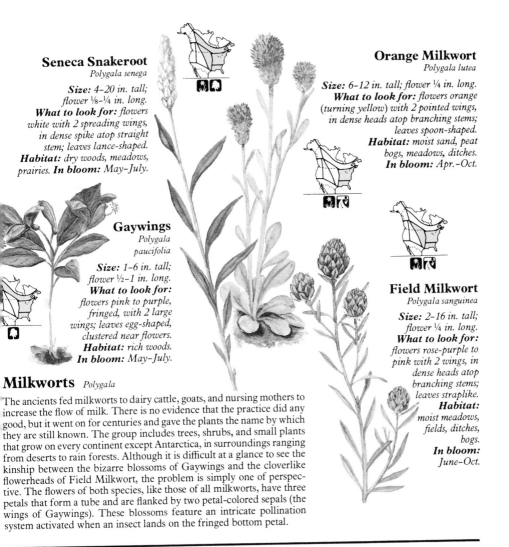

Seneca Snakeroot
Polygala senega

Size: 4–20 in. tall; flower ⅛–¼ in. long. **What to look for:** flowers white with 2 spreading wings, in dense spike atop straight stem; leaves lance-shaped. **Habitat:** dry woods, meadows, prairies. **In bloom:** May–July.

Orange Milkwort
Polygala lutea

Size: 6–12 in. tall; flower ¼ in. long. **What to look for:** flowers orange (turning yellow) with 2 pointed wings, in dense heads atop branching stems; leaves spoon-shaped. **Habitat:** moist sand, peat bogs, meadows, ditches. **In bloom:** Apr.–Oct.

Gaywings
Polygala paucifolia

Size: 1–6 in. tall; flower ½–1 in. long. **What to look for:** flowers pink to purple, fringed, with 2 large wings; leaves egg-shaped, clustered near flowers. **Habitat:** rich woods. **In bloom:** May–July.

Field Milkwort
Polygala sanguinea

Size: 2–16 in. tall; flower ¼ in. long. **What to look for:** flowers rose-purple to pink with 2 wings, in dense heads atop branching stems; leaves straplike. **Habitat:** moist meadows, fields, ditches, bogs. **In bloom:** June–Oct.

Milkworts *Polygala*

The ancients fed milkworts to dairy cattle, goats, and nursing mothers to increase the flow of milk. There is no evidence that the practice did any good, but it went on for centuries and gave the plants the name by which they are still known. The group includes trees, shrubs, and small plants that grow on every continent except Antarctica, in surroundings ranging from deserts to rain forests. Although it is difficult at a glance to see the kinship between the bizarre blossoms of Gaywings and the cloverlike flowerheads of Field Milkwort, the problem is simply one of perspective. The flowers of both species, like those of all milkworts, have three petals that form a tube and are flanked by two petal-colored sepals (the wings of Gaywings). These blossoms feature an intricate pollination system activated when an insect lands on the fringed bottom petal.

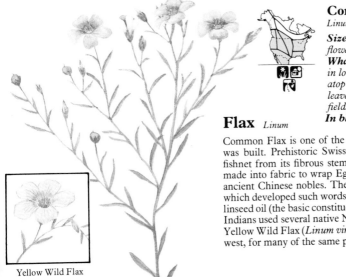

Yellow Wild Flax

Common Flax
Linum usitatissimum

Size: 1–3 ft. tall; flower ¾–1 in. wide. **What to look for:** flowers blue in loose, flat-topped clusters atop slender, branching stems; leaves lance-shaped. **Habitat:** fields, waste places, along railways. **In bloom:** Feb.–Sept.

Flax *Linum*

Common Flax is one of the plants upon which civilization was built. Prehistoric Swiss lake dwellers made rope and fishnet from its fibrous stems and ate its oily seeds. It was made into fabric to wrap Egyptian mummies and to clothe ancient Chinese nobles. The Romans called it *linum,* from which developed such words as line, linen, lingerie, lint, and linseed oil (the basic constituent of linoleum). The American Indians used several native North American species, such as Yellow Wild Flax (*Linum virginianum*) of the East and Midwest, for many of the same purposes.

403

berries

Wild Sarsaparilla
Aralia nudicaulis

Size: 5–16 in. tall; flower ⅛ in. wide.
What to look for: single leaf divided into 3 groups of 5 toothed leaflets; flowers creamy, in 3 spherical clusters on branched, leafless stalk; berries dark purple.
Habitat: woods.
In bloom: May–July.

Aralias *Aralia*

Like many members of the ginseng family, North America's aralias are prized for their aromatic roots. Those of the Wild Sarsaparilla served the Indians as emergency rations and were brewed by settlers into root beer and medicinal tea. The roots of American Spikenard produce a less pungent beverage, but it was even more highly regarded as a treatment for coughs, backaches, and other ailments. California Spikenard (*Aralia californica*), found along the Pacific Coast, is somewhat larger than American Spikenard and bears up to three times as many flowers in each of its spherical clusters.

American Spikenard
Aralia racemosa

Size: 2–10 ft. tall; flower ⅛ in. wide.
What to look for: leaves divided into many oval leaflets; flowers greenish, in round clusters on branched stalks; berries dark red to purple. **Habitat:** rich woods, clearings. **In bloom:** June–Aug.

Carolina Jessamine
Gelsemium sempervirens

Size: to 40 ft. high; flower 1 in. wide.
What to look for: climbing, tangled vine; flowers yellow, trumpetlike, with 5 flaring lobes; leaves in pairs, lance-shaped to oval. **Habitat:** thickets, hammocks, forest edges.
In bloom: Jan.–May.

Yellow Jessamines
Gelsemium

South Carolina's state flower, the Carolina Jessamine, is a common sight along roadsides throughout the southeastern United States. Its vivid yellow flowers, though fragrant and beautiful, are dangerous—children sucking out the nectar have been poisoned. The flowers, and all other parts of the plant, contain a lethal alkaloid similar to strychnine.

Wormroots
Spigelia

The difference between poison and medicine is often a matter of how much is used, and how carefully. Spigeline, the toxic alkaloid extracted from the roots of these plants, is a case in point. The Indians used it in small doses to expel tapeworms and roundworms, and they taught their techniques to colonists. Soon the plants were being shipped in bales to Europe for pharmaceutical processing.

Indian Pink
Spigelia marilandica

Size: 1–2 ft. tall; flower 1–2 in. long.
What to look for: flowers red, tubular, with 5 yellow, pointed lobes, in clusters atop erect stem; leaves in pairs, oval.
Habitat: woods, thickets, clearings.
In bloom: Apr.–June.

WILDFLOWERS

404

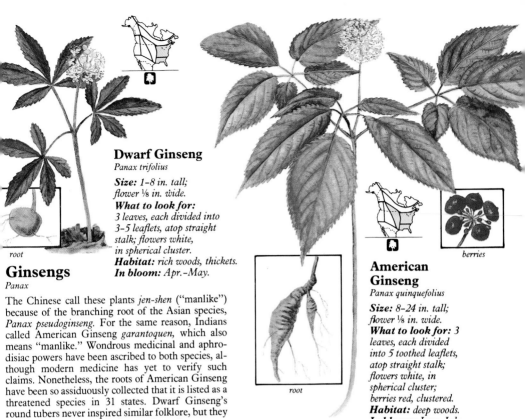

Dwarf Ginseng
Panax trifolius

Size: *1–8 in. tall;
flower ⅛ in. wide.*
What to look for:
*3 leaves, each divided into
3–5 leaflets, atop straight
stalk; flowers white,
in spherical cluster.*
Habitat: *rich woods, thickets.*
In bloom: *Apr.–May.*

root

berries

Ginsengs
Panax

The Chinese call these plants *jen-shen* ("manlike") because of the branching root of the Asian species, *Panax pseudoginseng.* For the same reason, Indians called American Ginseng *garantoquen,* which also means "manlike." Wondrous medicinal and aphrodisiac powers have been ascribed to both species, although modern medicine has yet to verify such claims. Nonetheless, the roots of American Ginseng have been so assiduously collected that it is listed as a threatened species in 31 states. Dwarf Ginseng's round tubers never inspired similar folklore, but they were valued as food by Indians and woodsmen.

American Ginseng
Panax quinquefolius

Size: *8–24 in. tall;
flower ⅛ in. wide.*
What to look for: *3
leaves, each divided
into 5 toothed leaflets,
atop straight stalk;
flowers white, in
spherical cluster;
berries red, clustered.*
Habitat: *deep woods.*
In bloom: *June–July.*

root

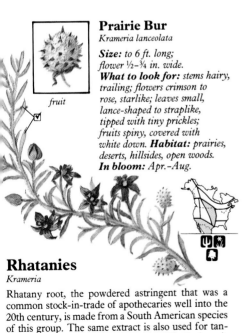

Prairie Bur
Krameria lanceolata

Size: *to 6 ft. long;
flower ½–¾ in. wide.*
What to look for: *stems hairy,
trailing; flowers crimson to
rose, starlike; leaves small,
lance-shaped to straplike,
tipped with tiny prickles;
fruits spiny, covered with
white down.* **Habitat:** *prairies,
deserts, hillsides, open woods.*
In bloom: *Apr.–Aug.*

fruit

Rhatanies
Krameria

Rhatany root, the powdered astringent that was a common stock-in-trade of apothecaries well into the 20th century, is made from a South American species of this group. The same extract is also used for tanning leather and flavoring port wine. North America's species—most of which are known as prairie burs because of their spiny fruits—have also been used medicinally, as well as for tanning and dyeing.

Harbingers of Spring *Erigenia*

On the floor of the eastern deciduous forests where this plant grows (there is only one species), sunshine is a brief phenomenon of spring and must be quickly taken advantage of. Nourished by food energy stored in the bulbous corm, the Harbinger of Spring's flower stalk arises and blossoms long before leaf buds swell on most trees—in fact, its fruit often begins to form before its own leaves have unfurled.

Harbinger of Spring
Erigenia bulbosa

Size: *2–10 in. tall;
flower ¼ in. wide.*
What to look for:
*flowers white, in
loose clusters atop
stalk with 1 small,
divided leaf;
leaves at base
divided into
2–3 leaflets,
usually
developing
after flowers.*
Habitat:
rich woods.
In bloom:
Feb.–May.

Heartleaf Alexanders

central flower

Golden Alexanders
Zizia aurea

Size: *1–3 ft. tall; flower ⅛–¼ in. wide.*
What to look for: *flowers yellow, in flat-topped compound umbels; leaflets in 2's or 3's, toothed.*
Habitat: *moist open woods, meadows, thickets, shores.*
In bloom: *Apr.–June.*

Zizias   *Zizia*

The flowers of zizias, like those of most of the carrot family, are borne in umbels—clusters with branches that radiate from a central point like the ribs of an umbrella. Golden Alexanders is the commonest eastern species. Heartleaf Alexanders (*Zizia aptera*), commoner in the Midwest, can be recognized by the heart-shaped leaves that arise on separate stalks from the base of its stem.

Queen Anne's Lace
Daucus carota

Size: *1–5 ft. tall; flower ⅛ in. wide.*
What to look for: *flowers creamy white, in flat-topped compound umbels with feathery green collars (usually with single dark flower in center); leaves fernlike; stems hairy; fruits spiny, in dried seedheads like birds' nests.*
Habitat: *fields, meadows, roadsides, open woods.*
In bloom: *May–Oct.*

seedhead

Carrots   *Daucus*

The garden carrot is a large-rooted variety (*sativa*) of Queen Anne's Lace. The wild variety's roots are also edible, but there is danger of confusing it with any of several poisonous plants, such as Poison Hemlock and Water Hemlock (*Cicuta maculata*). Look for the dark flower that is usually found in the center of the lacy, white umbel of Queen Anne's Lace.

Cow Parsnip
Heracleum lanatum

Size: *2–10 ft. tall; flower ⅛–¼ in. wide.*
What to look for: *flowers white, in flat-topped compound umbels; leaflets in 3's, large, deeply lobed, toothed; sheaths at leaf bases; plants hairy.*
Habitat: *meadows, pastures, marshe*
In bloom: *Apr.–Sept.*

Cow Parsnips
Heracleum

When the radiating branches of an umbel end in smaller umbels, the cluster is called a compound umbel. It is the commonest flower form among members of the carrot family, and is displayed by cow parsnips and all but two of the plants shown on these two pages. The flowers are usually wide open and shallow, so that the nectar and pollen are easily reached by the short tongues of beetles and flies.

flower close-up

WILDFLOWERS

406

Rattlesnake Master

Eryngium yuccifolium

Size: 2-5 ft. tall; flower ⅛ in. wide.
What to look for: flowers white, in dense bristly heads; leaves long, spiny, strap-shaped. **Habitat:** prairies, thickets, open woods.
In bloom: July-Aug.

Eryngoes *Eryngium*

The eryngoes are exceptional among the carrot family on several counts. They are one of the few groups with spiny leaves. Their flowers are borne in dense heads rather than the usual umbels, and each flower forms a tube whose nectar can be reached only by such long-tongued insects as bees and butterflies. The roots of Rattlesnake Master were once reputed to cure snakebite.

Poison Hemlock

Conium maculatum

Size: 2-9 ft. tall; flower ⅛-¼ in. wide.
What to look for: flowers white, in many flat-topped umbels; leaves parsleylike. **Habitat:** wet fields, meadows, ditches.
In bloom: June-Sept.

Poison Hemlocks
Conium

One poison hemlock species grows in South Africa; the only other is a European weed, which is now found throughout much of North America. All parts of the plant are deadly; it was the source of the poison used to execute Socrates and other Athenian dissidents of the time.

Great Angelica

Angelica atropurpurea

Size: 1-9 ft. tall; flower ¼ in. wide.
What to look for: flowers greenish white, in compound umbels; leaves divided into many toothed leaflets; sheaths at leaf bases; stems purple.
Habitat: thickets, bottomlands, swamps, meadows.
In bloom: June-Oct.

Angelicas
Angelica

This group includes the garden Angelica (*Angelica archangelica*), whose leaves were once believed to be a cure-all for contagious diseases and whose stems are traditionally candied to decorate Christmas cakes in France. The celerylike leafstalks of wild species are also edible. Other members of the carrot family supply such foodstuffs as anise, caraway, celery, dill, fennel, lovage, and parsley.

Water Pennywort

Hydrocotyle umbellata

Size: 1-14 in. tall; flower ⅛ in. wide.
What to look for: plants creeping; leaves round, on stalks attached to center; flowers white, in spherical umbels.
Habitat: wet banks, beaches, marshes, swamps.
In bloom: June-Sept.

Pennyworts *Hydrocotyle*

The pennyworts can be recognized by their small, rounded leaves. There are more than 50 species worldwide, including nearly a dozen in North America. The Water Pennywort grows along both coasts and in swampy areas near Lake Michigan. A similar species, *Hydrocotyle verticillata*, bears several umbels in tiers on each stalk.

WILDFLOWERS

407

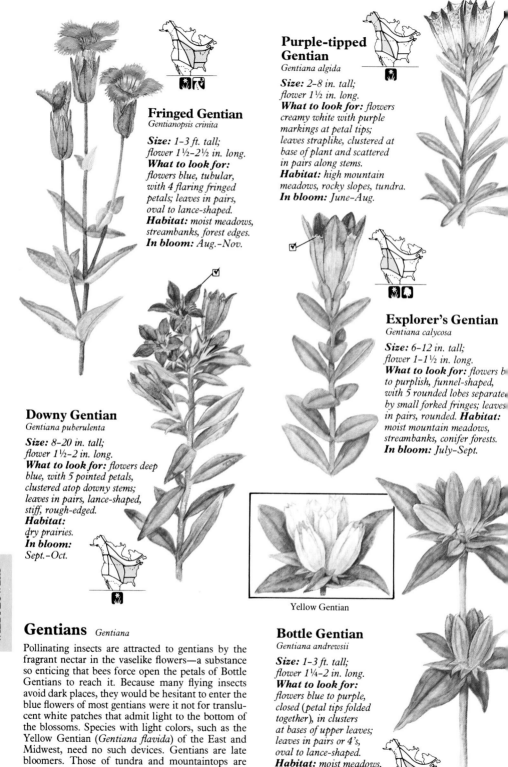

Purple-tipped Gentian
Gentiana algida

Size: 2-8 in. tall; flower 1½ in. long.
What to look for: flowers creamy white with purple markings at petal tips; leaves straplike, clustered at base of plant and scattered in pairs along stems.
Habitat: high mountain meadows, rocky slopes, tundra.
In bloom: June–Aug.

Fringed Gentian
Gentianopsis crinita

Size: 1-3 ft. tall; flower 1½-2½ in. long.
What to look for: flowers blue, tubular, with 4 flaring fringed petals; leaves in pairs, oval to lance-shaped.
Habitat: moist meadows, streambanks, forest edges.
In bloom: Aug.-Nov.

Explorer's Gentian
Gentiana calycosa

Size: 6-12 in. tall; flower 1-1½ in. long.
What to look for: flowers blue to purplish, funnel-shaped, with 5 rounded lobes separated by small forked fringes; leaves in pairs, rounded. **Habitat:** moist mountain meadows, streambanks, conifer forests.
In bloom: July-Sept.

Downy Gentian
Gentiana puberulenta

Size: 8-20 in. tall; flower 1½-2 in. long.
What to look for: flowers deep blue, with 5 pointed petals, clustered atop downy stems; leaves in pairs, lance-shaped, stiff, rough-edged.
Habitat: dry prairies.
In bloom: Sept.-Oct.

Yellow Gentian

Gentians *Gentiana*

Pollinating insects are attracted to gentians by the fragrant nectar in the vaselike flowers—a substance so enticing that bees force open the petals of Bottle Gentians to reach it. Because many flying insects avoid dark places, they would be hesitant to enter the blue flowers of most gentians were it not for translucent white patches that admit light to the bottom of the blossoms. Species with light colors, such as the Yellow Gentian (*Gentiana flavida*) of the East and Midwest, need no such devices. Gentians are late bloomers. Those of tundra and mountaintops are sometimes still in blossom when the snows come, and finish their flowering cycle in the spring.

Bottle Gentian
Gentiana andrewsii

Size: 1-3 ft. tall; flower 1¼-2 in. long.
What to look for: flowers blue to purple, closed (petal tips folded together), in clusters at bases of upper leaves; leaves in pairs or 4's, oval to lance-shaped.
Habitat: moist meadows, fields, thickets, ditches.
In bloom: Aug.-Oct.

Columboes *Frasera*

These plants may be known by several names in the course of their growth cycle. At first, when they produce clusters of long leaves much prized by browsing animals, they are often called elkweeds. When the tall stems arise—often in the following year—they take a pyramidal form that inspires the name monument plants. Deertongue—named for the shape of its leaves—and a similar eastern species, *Frasera caroliniensis*, are also known as Green Gentians.

Deertongue
Frasera speciosa

Size: *2-7 ft. tall; flower 1-1½ in. wide.*
What to look for: *flowers pale green with tiny spots, 4-petaled, borne on long stalks from leaf bases; leaves straplike, clustered at base and along stem.* **Habitat:** *desert scrub, prairies, open pine forests.*
In bloom: *June-Aug.*

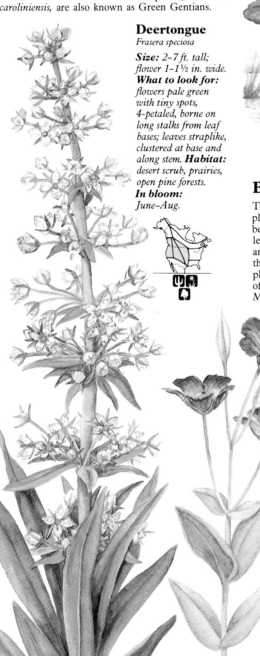

Buckbean
Menyanthes trifoliata

Size: *4-12 in. tall; flower ½-1 in. wide.*
What to look for: *flowers white, starlike, hairy, clustered atop leafless stalks; leaflets in 3's, leathery, oblong.*
Habitat: *swamps, marshes, forest bogs, ditches, shallow water.*
In bloom: *Apr.-Sept.*

Buckbeans *Menyanthes*

The world's only buckbean species is a distinctive plant, easily identified by its clusters of thickly bearded white flowers and its leathery three-part leaves. Both rise on stalks above the surface of bogs and shallow ponds. Although many botanists include the Buckbean in the gentian family, many others place it in a family all its own. It is known by a variety of names, such as Bogbean, Bognut, Marsh Clover, Moorflower, and Water Shamrock.

Bluebells
Eustoma grandiflorum

Size: *8-26 in. tall; flower 1½-3 in. wide.*
What to look for: *flowers blue to purplish (or yellow with purple tinges), cuplike; leaves in pairs, oval, bases clasping stem.* **Habitat:** *moist prairies, fields, pond edges.*
In bloom: *June-Sept.*

Prairie Gentians *Eustoma*

Two of this group's three species grow in warmer parts of North America; the third is native to the tropics of Central and South America. Though Bluebells is mainly a western species, it may occasionally be found along the Gulf Coast. The Catchfly Gentian (*Eustoma exaltatum*), with flowers of rose, purple, or white, ranges from the desert mountains of southern California to the hammocks and coastal sands of Florida. The leaves of both species have a waxy bloom that can be rubbed off with the fingertips.

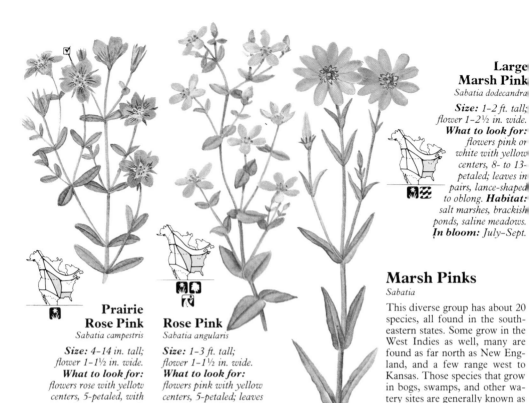

Large Marsh Pink
Sabatia dodecandra

Size: *1-2 ft. tall; flower 1-2½ in. wide.* **What to look for:** *flowers pink or white with yellow centers, 8- to 13-petaled; leaves in pairs, lance-shaped to oblong.* **Habitat:** *salt marshes, brackish ponds, saline meadows.* **In bloom:** *July-Sept.*

Prairie Rose Pink
Sabatia campestris

Size: *4-14 in. tall; flower 1-1½ in. wide.* **What to look for:** *flowers rose with yellow centers, 5-petaled, with pointed green sepals between petals; leaves in pairs, oval.* **Habitat:** *prairies, fields, meadows.* **In bloom:** *July-Sept.*

Rose Pink
Sabatia angularis

Size: *1-3 ft. tall; flower 1-1½ in. wide.* **What to look for:** *flowers pink with yellow centers, 5-petaled; leaves in pairs, egg-shaped, upper ones clasping stems; stems square, with sharp lengthwise ridges.* **Habitat:** *open woods, meadows, fields, prairies.* **In bloom:** *July-Sept.*

Marsh Pinks
Sabatia

This diverse group has about 20 species, all found in the southeastern states. Some grow in the West Indies as well, many are found as far north as New England, and a few range west to Kansas. Those species that grow in bogs, swamps, and other watery sites are generally known as marsh pinks; others are usually called rose pinks. Those that adapt to both wet and dry soils may be known by both names, depending on where they are encountered.

Rosita
Centaurium calycosum

Size: *4-24 in. tall; flower ¼-½ in. wide.* **What to look for:** *flowers funnel-shaped, 5-petaled, pink with white throats; leaves in pairs, lance-shaped to oblong.* **Habitat:** *moist meadows, streambanks, salt marshes.* **In bloom:** *Apr.-June.*

Centauries *Centaurium*

According to Greek myth, Chiron, the wisest and most benevolent of the centaurs, was skilled in the use of medicinal plants and passed on much of his skill to various Greek heroes. He is said to have treated wounds with the bitter, antiseptic juice of these plants, and so they came to be named after him. Most centaury species found in the eastern states are European imports, but several attractive species are native to the Far West.

Rubber Vines
Echites

These tropical lianas (woody vines), with their latexlike sap, belong to the infamous dogbane family. Like most plants in the family, they are poisonous. The Devil's Potato, one of three species that grow along the Florida coast and in the Keys, is named for its large, tuberous, toxic root.

Devil's Potato
Echites umbellata

Size: *to 20 ft. long; flower 2-2½ in. long.* **What to look for:** *stems trailing, intertwined; flowers white to greenish, tubular, with 5 twisted, frilled petals; leaves in pairs, egg-shaped.* **Habitat:** *coastal hammocks, swamps.* **In bloom:** *all year.*

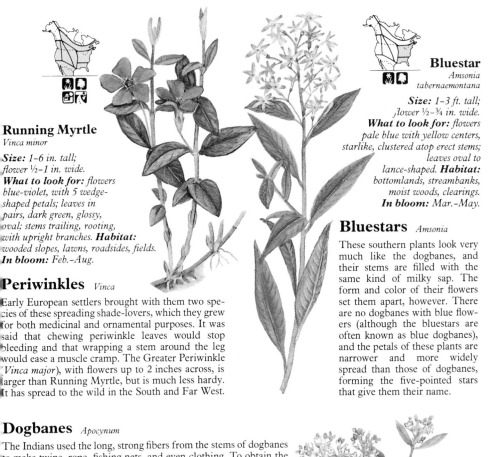

Running Myrtle
Vinca minor

Size: *1-6 in. tall; flower ½-1 in. wide.*
What to look for: *flowers blue-violet, with 5 wedge-shaped petals; leaves in pairs, dark green, glossy, oval; stems trailing, rooting, with upright branches.* **Habitat:** *wooded slopes, lawns, roadsides, fields.*
In bloom: *Feb.-Aug.*

Periwinkles   *Vinca*

Early European settlers brought with them two species of these spreading shade-lovers, which they grew for both medicinal and ornamental purposes. It was said that chewing periwinkle leaves would stop bleeding and that wrapping a stem around the leg would ease a muscle cramp. The Greater Periwinkle (*Vinca major*), with flowers up to 2 inches across, is larger than Running Myrtle, but is much less hardy. It has spread to the wild in the South and Far West.

Bluestar
Amsonia tabernaemontana

Size: *1-3 ft. tall; flower ½-¾ in. wide.*
What to look for: *flowers pale blue with yellow centers, starlike, clustered atop erect stems; leaves oval to lance-shaped.* **Habitat:** *bottomlands, streambanks, moist woods, clearings.*
In bloom: *Mar.-May.*

Bluestars   *Amsonia*

These southern plants look very much like the dogbanes, and their stems are filled with the same kind of milky sap. The form and color of their flowers set them apart, however. There are no dogbanes with blue flowers (although the bluestars are often known as blue dogbanes), and the petals of these plants are narrower and more widely spread than those of dogbanes, forming the five-pointed stars that give them their name.

Dogbanes   *Apocynum*

The Indians used the long, strong fibers from the stems of dogbanes to make twine, rope, fishing nets, and even clothing. To obtain the fibers, they treated the stems in much the same way that flax is treated: first the stems were retted, or allowed to soak in water until the soft tissues rotted; then they were beaten to separate the fibers, which were rinsed and combed clean. Most dogbanes, including the two species shown here, are poisonous to livestock, but because of their latexlike sap, few animals willingly eat them.

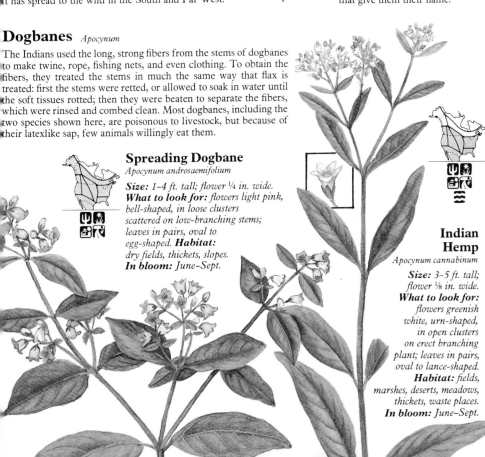

Spreading Dogbane
Apocynum androsaemifolium

Size: *1-4 ft. tall; flower ¼ in. wide.*
What to look for: *flowers light pink, bell-shaped, in loose clusters scattered on low-branching stems; leaves in pairs, oval to egg-shaped.* **Habitat:** *dry fields, thickets, slopes.*
In bloom: *June-Sept.*

Indian Hemp
Apocynum cannabinum

Size: *3-5 ft. tall; flower ⅛ in. wide.*
What to look for: *flowers greenish white, urn-shaped, in open clusters on erect branching plant; leaves in pairs, oval to lance-shaped.* **Habitat:** *fields, marshes, deserts, meadows, thickets, waste places.*
In bloom: *June-Sept.*

Milkweeds *Asclepias*

There is a legend of the Old West about a runty outlaw who drank rattlesnake venom every morning so he could kill a big man by spitting in his eye. Milkweeds furnish similar

milkweed flower

venom for Monarch butterflies. The leaves are poison ous to most animals, but Monarch caterpillars and few others eat nothing else. As a result, they—and th butterflies they become—are themselves toxic to poter tial predators. The crownlike flowers of milkweeds ai cunning traps for insect pollinators, second in their ir tricacy only to the orchids. Each blossom has five nec tar cups with smooth, incurved horns growing fror them. When an insect lands, its foot slips on a horn an goes into a slit between two cups. If the insect is nc strong enough to pull its leg out, it dies there. If it strong enough, it comes away carrying two bags of po' len, called pollinia, like saddlebags. At the next flowe its foot slips again; this time, as it picks up mor pollinia, it deposits the first two beside the cups, wher the pollen develops to fertilize future seeds.

Common Milkweed

Asclepias syriaca

Size: *2-6 ft. tall; flower ½ in. wide.*
What to look for: *flowers pink to lavender, star-shaped, in dense rounded clusters at top of straight stem; leaves in pairs, broad, oval; sap milky; seedpods warty, filled with downy fluff.*
Habitat: *fields, meadows.*
In bloom: *June-Aug.*

seedpod

Swam Milkwee

Asclepi incarna

Size: *1-5 ft. ta flower ¼-½ in. wid*
What to look for *flowers deep pin to rose, star-shapec in dense cluste at top of straigl stem; leaves i pairs, narrow, lance shaped; sap milk*
Habitat: *marshe swamps, wet meadow*
In bloom: *May-Sep*

Butterfly Weed

Asclepias tuberosa

Size: *1-3 ft. tall; flower ¼-½ in. wide.*
What to look for: *flowers bright orange, star-shaped, in dense, flat-topped clusters at top of erect or sprawling stem; leaves alternate; sap not milky.*
Habitat: *sandy fields, prairies, dry pinelands.*
In bloom: *June-Sept.*

Sand Milkweed
Asclepias amplexicaulis

Size: *2–3 ft. tall; flower ½ in. wide.*
What to look for: *flowers purple to greenish, star-shaped, in dense spherical clusters atop straight stem; leaves in pairs, with wavy edges; sap milky.* **Habitat:** *dry fields, sandy prairies.* **In bloom:** *May–Aug.*

Desert Milkweed
Asclepias erosa

Size: *2–4 ft. tall; flower ¼–½ in. wide.*
What to look for: *flowers greenish yellow, star-shaped, in dense rounded clusters at top of erect stem; leaves in pairs; sap milky.* **Habitat:** *deserts, dry scrublands.* **In bloom:** *Apr.–Oct.*

Whorled Milkweed
Asclepias verticillata

Size: *1–3 ft. tall; flower ¼ in. wide.*
What to look for: *flowers white, star-shaped, in dense rounded clusters along slender stem; leaves in whorls, narrow; sap milky.* **Habitat:** *dry slopes, fields, open woods.* **In bloom:** *May–Oct. (north); all year (south).*

Green Milkweed
Asclepias cryptoceras

Size: *stem to 1 ft. long; flower ½–1 in. wide.*
What to look for: *flowers greenish yellow with reddish crownlike centers, star-shaped, hornless, in clusters at ends of sprawling stems; leaves in pairs, rounded, grayish green; sap milky.* **Habitat:** *sandy or gravelly slopes, dry plains, open pinelands, sagebrush scrublands, deserts.* **In bloom:** *Apr.–June.*

413

Nightshades *Solanum*

This contradictory group gives us potatoes and eggplants as well as many poisonous plants. In fact, the contradiction often exists within a single species. Some parts of the Potato (*Solanum tuberosum*), for example, are poisonous; and although the ripe berries of the Black Nightshade are used for pies and jams, the leaves and unripened berries are deadly. The Bittersweet Nightshade—so called because the taste of its root and berries changes in the mouth of one foolish enough to chew them—is sometimes known as the Deadly Nightshade, a name that properly belongs to an even more toxic European relative, *Atropa belladonna*. The Horse Nettle and the Buffalo Bur also contain poisons, but their thorns discourage consumption by livestock and humans.

Buffalo Bur
Solanum rostratum

Size: *8–28 in. tall; flower 1 in. wide.*
What to look for: *flowers yellow, broadly star-shaped; leaves deeply lobed, prickly; fruits spiny.* **Habitat:** *fields, prairies, dry pastures, waste places.*
In bloom: *Apr.–Oct.*

Bittersweet Nightshade
Solanum dulcamara

Size: *1–8 ft. high; flower ½ in. wide.*
What to look for: *stems climbing or sprawling; flowers star-shaped with 5 purple petals backswept from pointed yellow "nose"; leaves spade-shaped, usually with 2 pointed lobes at base; berries green, turning red when ripe.*
Habitat: *open woods, fields, thickets, swamps.*
In bloom: *Apr.–Sep.*

Horse Nettle
Solanum carolinense

Size: *1–3 ft. tall; flower ¾–1 in. wide.*
What to look for: *flowers white to violet, star-shaped; stems and oaklike leaves spiny; berries yellow.*
Habitat: *fields, meadows, waste places.*
In bloom: *May–Oct.*

Black Nightshade
Solanum americanum

Size: *1–3 ft. tall; flower ¼–½ in. wide.*
What to look for: *flowers star-shaped, with 5 white petals backswept from yellow "nose"; leaves oval to lance-shaped; berries green, turning black.*
Habitat: *fields, meadows, waste places.*
In bloom: *Mar.–Nov.*

414

Virginia Ground Cherry
Physalis virginiana

Size: *1–3 ft. tall; flower ¾–1 in. wide.*
What to look for: *flowers yellow with purplish blotches in center; fruits papery, 5-sided, lantern-shaped, containing fleshy berry.*
Habitat: *fields, prairies, open woods, waste places.*
In bloom: *May–Aug.*

White-flowered Ground Cherry
Leucophysalis grandiflora

Size: *1–3 ft. tall; flower 1¼–2 in. wide.*
What to look for: *flowers white, saucerlike, with 5 points; leaves oval to lance-shaped; stems sticky, hairy.*
Habitat: *open woods, sandy clearings.* **In bloom:** *June–Aug.*

fruit

Ground Cherries *Physalis*

Each fleshy fruit of these plants is enclosed in a lanternlike husk. When green, the berries, like the young leaves, are poisonous. But when the berries are fully ripe, they are edible and sweet—a favorite trail snack of many hikers. Some species, known as Strawberry Tomatoes, are grown for food. The ornamental Chinese Lantern Plant (*Physalis alkekengi*) is cultivated for its bright red husks.

Ground Cherries *Leucophysalis*

These ground cherries differ from the *Physalis* ground cherries in that their fruits have no papery husks. Despite the shared name, the berries of both groups are more like little tomatoes than cherries. Tomatoes grown in gardens (*Lycopersicon*) also belong to the nightshade family, as do all the plants shown on these two pages; and their unripe fruits are also poisonous if eaten raw.

Thornapples *Datura*

British troops were sent to Jamestown in 1676 to suppress a rebellion. Short of rations, they cooked the foliage of the plant that has ever after been known familiarly as Jimsonweed. The result was described by Robert Beverley in his *History and Present State of Virginia* (1705). "They turn'd natural fools upon it for several days. One would blow up a feather in the air; another would dart straws at it with much fury; and another stark naked was sitting up in a corner like a monkey, grinning and making mows at them." After 11 days, they "return'd to themselves again, not remembering any thing that had pass'd." Had the British not cooked the leaves, few would have survived, for the potent hallucinogens produced by thornapple plants are extremely toxic. Another species, the Indian Apple, or Sacred Datura (*Datura meteloides*), with flowers up to 10 inches long, was used by Indians of the Southwest for a variety of rituals.

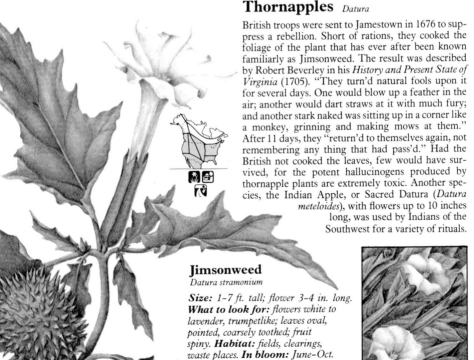

Jimsonweed
Datura stramonium

Size: *1–7 ft. tall; flower 3–4 in. long.*
What to look for: *flowers white to lavender, trumpetlike; leaves oval, pointed, coarsely toothed; fruit spiny.* **Habitat:** *fields, clearings, waste places.* **In bloom:** *June–Oct.*

Indian Apple

Ivyleaf Morning Glory
Ipomoea hederacea

Size: *to 10 ft. high; flower 1–1½ in. wide.*
What to look for: *stems twining; flowers trumpet-shaped with 5 pointed petals, sky-blue (turning rose-purple); leaves hairy, deeply lobed.*
Habitat: *fencerows, fields, waste places.*
In bloom: *June–Nov.*

Common Morning Glory
Ipomoea purpurea

Size: *to 10 ft. high; flower 1½–2 in. wide.*
What to look for: *stems twining; flowers trumpet-shaped, blue, purple, pink, or white; leaves heart-shaped.*
Habitat: *fencerows, fields, waste places.*
In bloom: *June–Oct.*

Bush Morning Glory
Ipomoea leptophylla

Size: *2–4 ft. long; flower 2–2½ in. wide.*
What to look for: *stems sprawling, bushy; flowers trumpet-shaped, rose to purple; leaves straplike.*
Habitat: *dry prairies, sandy fields.*
In bloom: *May–July.*

Morning Glories
Ipomoea

To appreciate the imagery in this group's name, you have only to see the colorful and fragrant blossoms, which open soon after dawn and close a few hours later. Unfortunately, the technical name, from the Greek for "wormlike," is equally apt. The viny stems wind their way up the stalks of other plants, and the large leaves rob them of sunlight. Such crops as corn, cotton, and soybeans may be seriously affected. Several morning glory species are valued for their edible tubers, including the Sweet Potato (*Ipomoea batatas*). The giant tuber of the Wild Potato Vine, also known as Man of the Earth, weighs up to 30 pounds, and was an important food for Indians and settlers.

Wild Potato Vine
Ipomoea pandurata

Size: *to 20 ft. long; flower 2–3 in. wide.*
What to look for: *stems trailing or climbing; flowers trumpet-shaped, white with pink centers; leaves heart- or fiddle-shaped.* **Habitat:** *dry fields, plains, thickets, open woods.*
In bloom: *May–Sept.*

WILDFLOWERS

416

Field Bindweed
Convolvulus arvensis

Size: to 15 ft. high; flower ½–¾ in. wide.
What to look for: flowers trumpet-shaped, white (often with purple to lavender lines on back); leaves arrow-shaped; stems tangled, climbing or sprawling.
Habitat: hedgerows, thickets, fields.
In bloom: May–Oct.

Hedge Bindweed
Calystegia sepium

Size: to 15 ft. high; flower 1½–2 in. wide.
What to look for: flowers trumpet-shaped, white to pinkish; leaves triangular to arrow-shaped; stems creeping or climbing.
Habitat: hedges, thickets, waste places, marshes.
In bloom: Apr.–Sept.

Bindweeds
Convolvulus

Less spectacular but even more troublesome than the morning glories, these pernicious weeds overgrow many crops. The Field Bindweed is particularly difficult to control. Tearing up its roots with a plow or hoe does not kill the plant, but scatters fragments that often grow into many new individuals.

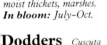

Dodder
Cuscuta cephalanthii

Size: to 10 ft. high; flower ⅛ in. wide.
What to look for: stems creamy-orange, twining on shrubs and other plants; flowers bell-shaped, white, in dense clusters. **Habitat:** moist thickets, marshes.
In bloom: July–Oct.

Dodders   *Cuscuta*

Unlike the rest of the morning glory family, the dodders are true parasites, drawing their sustenance directly from the host plants. The seeds take root in the ground, and the young shoots rotate until they come in contact with something climbable. If it turns out to be a suitable host, the dodder sinks parasitic roots (called haustoria) into its stem and begins drawing nourishment through them. Soon its own connection with the soil withers away.

Cypress Vine
Quamoclit pennata,

Size: to 15 ft. high; flower 1½ in. long.
What to look for: flowers tubular with star-shaped flare, bright red; leaves featherlike; stem slender, twining.
Habitat: fields, waste places.
In bloom: July–Oct.

Starglories   *Quamoclit*

These tropical vines are sold in North America as garden annuals, often under the name Red Morning Glory. They have turned out to be surprisingly hardy and have spread to the wild in many places. One broad-leaved species, *Quamoclit coccinea*, is found as far north as Michigan and New England.

Moonflowers   *Calonyction*

The moonflowers could easily be called evening glories because—although they are members of the morning glory family—their large, extremely fragrant blossoms open only at night. Like most night-bloomers, they are pollinated by moths that are attracted by the glowing whiteness and strong scent of the flowers.

Moonflower
Calonyction aculeatum

Size: to 30 ft. high; flower 4–5 in. wide.
What to look for: flowers saucer-shaped at tip of slender tube, white, fragrant; leaves oval to heart-shaped; vine climbing or trailing. **Habitat:** hammocks, burned fields, waste places, thickets. **In bloom:** all year.

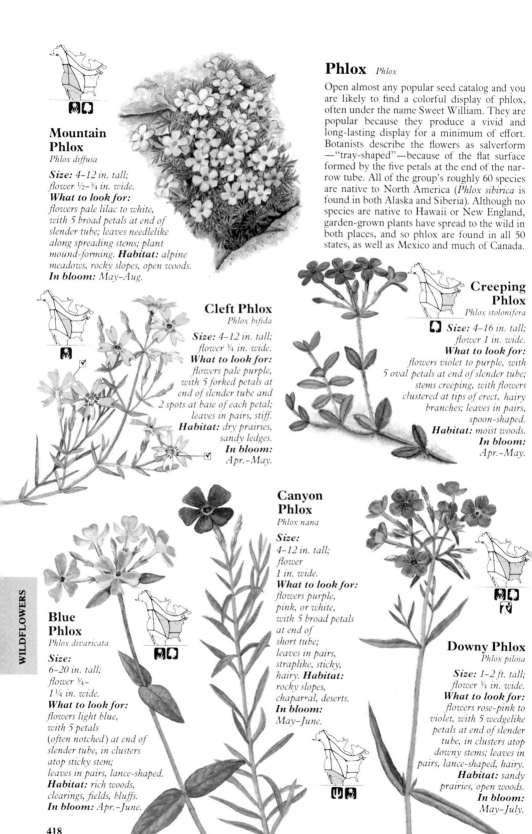

Mountain Phlox
Phlox diffusa

Size: 4-12 in. tall; flower ½-¾ in. wide. **What to look for:** flowers pale lilac to white, with 5 broad petals at end of slender tube; leaves needlelike along spreading stems; plant mound-forming. **Habitat:** alpine meadows, rocky slopes, open woods. **In bloom:** May-Aug.

Phlox *Phlox*

Open almost any popular seed catalog and you are likely to find a colorful display of phlox, often under the name Sweet William. They are popular because they produce a vivid and long-lasting display for a minimum of effort. Botanists describe the flowers as salverform —"tray-shaped"—because of the flat surface formed by the five petals at the end of the narrow tube. All of the group's roughly 60 species are native to North America (*Phlox sibirica* is found in both Alaska and Siberia). Although no species are native to Hawaii or New England, garden-grown plants have spread to the wild in both places, and so phlox are found in all 50 states, as well as Mexico and much of Canada.

Creeping Phlox
Phlox stolonifera

Size: 4-16 in. tall; flower 1 in. wide. **What to look for:** flowers violet to purple, with 5 oval petals at end of slender tube; stems creeping, with flowers clustered at tips of erect, hairy branches; leaves in pairs, spoon-shaped. **Habitat:** moist woods. **In bloom:** Apr.-May.

Cleft Phlox
Phlox bifida

Size: 4-12 in. tall; flower ¾ in. wide. **What to look for:** flowers pale purple, with 5 forked petals at end of slender tube and 2 spots at base of each petal; leaves in pairs, stiff. **Habitat:** dry prairies, sandy ledges. **In bloom:** Apr.-May.

Canyon Phlox
Phlox nana

Size: 4-12 in. tall; flower 1 in. wide. **What to look for:** flowers purple, pink, or white, with 5 broad petals at end of short tube; leaves in pairs, straplike, sticky, hairy. **Habitat:** rocky slopes, chaparral, deserts. **In bloom:** May-June.

Blue Phlox
Phlox divaricata

Size: 6-20 in. tall; flower ¾- 1¼ in. wide. **What to look for:** flowers light blue, with 5 petals (often notched) at end of slender tube, in clusters atop sticky stem; leaves in pairs, lance-shaped. **Habitat:** rich woods, clearings, fields, bluffs. **In bloom:** Apr.-June.

Downy Phlox
Phlox pilosa

Size: 1-2 ft. tall; flower ¾ in. wide. **What to look for:** flowers rose-pink to violet, with 5 wedgelike petals at end of slender tube, in clusters atop downy stems; leaves in pairs, lance-shaped, hairy. **Habitat:** sandy prairies, open woods. **In bloom:** May-July.

Greek Valerian
Polemonium reptans

Size: *6-18 in. tall;*
flower ½-¾ in. wide.
What to look for:
flowers blue, bell-shaped,
in loose clusters;
leaves ladderlike, divided
into 5-15 leaflets.
Habitat: *rich woods.*
In bloom: *Apr.-June.*

Jacob's Ladders *Polemonium*

The long compound leaves with runglike leaflets that give this group its name are most obvious in such large, upright species as Greek Valerian. The small leaflets of the blue-flowered Sky Pilot (*Polemonium viscosum*) are so tightly crowded that they form fuzzy tubes rather than ladders. This is true of several other mat-forming species that grow in tundra areas and on mountain ridges in the West.

Lilac Sunbonnets
Langloisia punctata

Size: *1-6 in. tall; flower ¾-1 in. wide.*
What to look for: *flowers pale lilac*
with purple spots, bowl-shaped;
leaves triangular, with spiny lobes;
plants tuft- or mat-forming.
Habitat: *rocky slopes, open pine scrub*
(Mojave Desert). **In bloom:** *Apr.-June.*

Langloisias *Langloisia*

When the brief rainy season arrives in the deserts of California, these small plants spring suddenly into existence, bearing flowers that seem all out of proportion to the size of the plants. They are gone again with almost as little warning when the rains cease. Some species range southward into Mexico and others grow as far north as Oregon and Idaho, but the range of most is as limited as their lifespan.

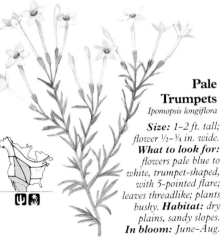

Pale Trumpets
Ipomopsis longiflora

Size: *1-2 ft. tall;*
flower ½-¾ in. wide.
What to look for:
flowers pale blue to
white, trumpet-shaped,
with 5-pointed flare;
leaves threadlike; plants
bushy. **Habitat:** *dry*
plains, sandy slopes.
In bloom: *June-Aug.*

Standing Cypress
Ipomopsis rubra

Size: *2-6 ft. tall;*
flower ½ in. wide.
What to look for:
flowers red, trumpet-
shaped, with 5-pointed
flare, in plumelike
cluster at top of leafy
stem; leaves threadlike.
Habitat: *sandy fields,*
pastures, riverbanks,
waste places.
In bloom: *May-Aug.*

Gilias *Ipomopsis*

The richly varied gilias make up one of those plant groups in which botanists can watch evolution in action. Its many species and subspecies, all native to the New World, produce new varieties and hybrids with notable frequency. The result is a process of trial and error whereby the group as a whole survives in a changing world and—because it adapts more quickly than most plants—continually expands its range into new habitats.

Navarretia
Navarretia breweri

Size: ½–4 in. tall; flower ⅛ in. wide.
What to look for: stems brownish, hairy, much branched, covered with hairlike spiky leaves; flowers yellow, star-shaped, profuse. **Habitat:** deserts to moist valleys, mountain slopes, mesas, pinyon forests.
In bloom: June–Aug.

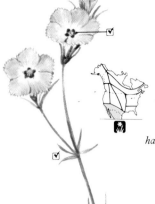

Ground Pink
Linanthus dianthiflorus

Size: 1–8 in. tall; flower ¾–1 in. wide.
What to look for: flowers pink with dark centers, bowl-shaped, with 5 sharply toothed petals; leaves in pairs, hairlike. **Habitat:** sandy grasslands, chaparral, sagebrush areas.
In bloom: Feb.–Apr.

Navarretias *Navarretia*

Early settlers in the western states, like pioneers everywhere, found little need to speak about plants that were neither useful, troublesome, nor spectacular. Botanists of the day, however, were quick to study and to name the members of the new flora. As a result, many such innocuous charmers as the navarretias have only the Latinized names that the botanists gave them. The foul-smelling Skunkweed (*Navarretia squarrosa*) is an exception.

Linanthuses *Linanthus*

Included for many years among the gilias, these plants are now regarded as a separate group, set apart by the odd form of their paired leaves. Each leaf is so deeply divided that a pair of leaves often looks like a grassy tuft sprouting along the stem. Most of the group's nearly 40 species are native to California, several ranging south to Mexico and north into the Cascade mountains. A few are found as far east as Colorado and the Northern Plains.

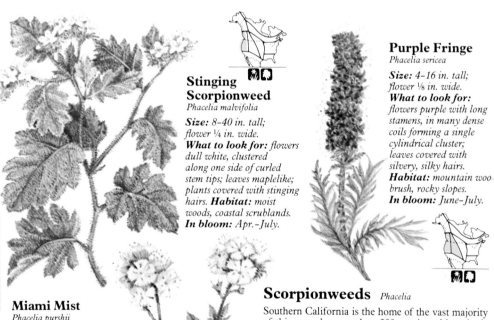

Stinging Scorpionweed
Phacelia malvifolia

Size: 8–40 in. tall; flower ¼ in. wide.
What to look for: flowers dull white, clustered along one side of curled stem tips; leaves maplelike; plants covered with stinging hairs. **Habitat:** moist woods, coastal scrublands.
In bloom: Apr.–July.

Purple Fringe
Phacelia sericea

Size: 4–16 in. tall; flower ⅛ in. wide.
What to look for: flowers purple with long stamens, in many dense coils forming a single cylindrical cluster; leaves covered with silvery, silky hairs. **Habitat:** mountain woo brush, rocky slopes.
In bloom: June–July.

Miami Mist
Phacelia purshii

Size: 6–16 in. tall; flower ½ in. wide.
What to look for: flowers pale blue, with 5 fringed petals, in loose clusters at ends of stems; leaves divided into straplike sections. **Habitat:** moist woods, clearings, fields.
In bloom: Apr.–June.

Scorpionweeds *Phacelia*

Southern California is the home of the vast majority of this group's more than 200 species, although almost every part of North America, from the Yukon to the Florida coast, has at least one native species. The hallmark of the group is a cluster of young flowers, coiled like a scorpion's tail, at the end of a stem. The flowers are all borne on one side of this cluster. In most species the coil straightens somewhat as the blossoms mature; in others, each flower's stalk grows so long that the clustered appearance is all but lost. Nearly all scorpionweeds are valued as bee plants. They tend to blanket areas where few other plants grow, and their flowers yield a flavorsome honey.

WILDFLOWERS

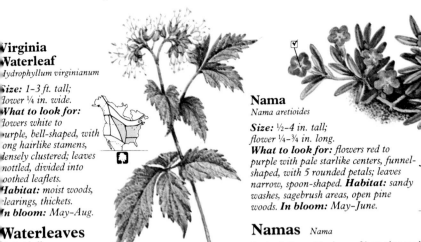

Virginia Waterleaf
Hydrophyllum virginianum

Size: *1-3 ft. tall; flower ¼ in. wide.*
What to look for: *flowers white to purple, bell-shaped, with long hairlike stamens, densely clustered; leaves mottled, divided into toothed leaflets.*
Habitat: *moist woods, clearings, thickets.*
In bloom: *May-Aug.*

Waterleaves
Hydrophyllum

A blotchy, light green pattern gives a look of fine watermarked stationery to the foliage of many waterleaf species. This may be the reason for the group's name, or it may have been inspired by the juicy leaves of several species, including the Virginia Waterleaf. The leaves are edible raw or cooked, giving rise to such additional names as John's Cabbage, Iroquois Greens, and Shawnee Salad.

Nama
Nama aretioides

Size: *½-4 in. tall; flower ¼-¾ in. long.*
What to look for: *flowers red to purple with pale starlike centers, funnel-shaped, with 5 rounded petals; leaves narrow, spoon-shaped.* **Habitat:** *sandy washes, sagebrush areas, open pine woods.* **In bloom:** *May-June.*

Namas   *Nama*

In the informal lexicon of botanists and other nature lovers, a belly plant is one that is so tiny that the best way to find it, and the only way to study it, is from the prone position. In time of drought, these inhabitants of western deserts, plains, and mountain canyons are single-flowered belly plants. But in a rainy year, most species put forth many stems, spreading into luxuriant leafy mats and covering themselves with a profusion of colorful blossoms.

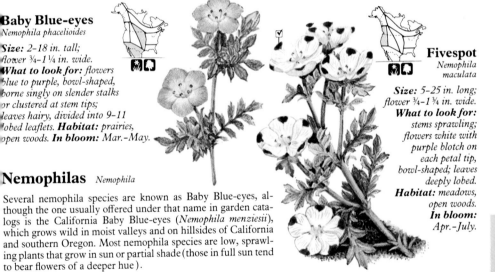

Baby Blue-eyes
Nemophila phacelioides

Size: *2-18 in. tall; flower ¾-1¼ in. wide.*
What to look for: *flowers blue to purple, bowl-shaped, borne singly on slender stalks or clustered at stem tips; leaves hairy, divided into 9-11 lobed leaflets.* **Habitat:** *prairies, open woods.* **In bloom:** *Mar.-May.*

Nemophilas   *Nemophila*

Several nemophila species are known as Baby Blue-eyes, although the one usually offered under that name in garden catalogs is the California Baby Blue-eyes (*Nemophila menziesii*), which grows wild in moist valleys and on hillsides of California and southern Oregon. Most nemophila species are low, sprawling plants that grow in sun or partial shade (those in full sun tend to bear flowers of a deeper hue).

Fivespot
Nemophila maculata

Size: *5-25 in. long; flower ¾-1¾ in. wide.*
What to look for: *stems sprawling; flowers white with purple blotch on each petal tip, bowl-shaped; leaves deeply lobed.* **Habitat:** *meadows, open woods.* **In bloom:** *Apr.-July.*

Sandfoods   *Ammobroma*

The world's only Sandfood species looks like nothing so much as a tennis ball half-buried in the sand, covered with tiny purple flowers. But this fuzzy gray growth, which merely hints at what lies beneath, is the top of a long underground stem that is attached to the deep root of a woody desert plant. Since the Sandfood contains no chlorophyll, it does not manufacture its own food. Instead, it draws sustenance from the root of a host plant through its own parasitic roots. The yam-flavored stems were a dietary staple of the Indians in California's Colorado Desert.

Sandfood
Ammobroma sonorae

Size: *1-2 in. tall; 2-5 in. wide; flower ⅛ in. wide or less.*
What to look for: *flowers purple, in rings on fuzzy gray mound; stem scaly, gray, subterranean, 2-5 ft. long.* **Habitat:** *Colorado Desert.* **In bloom:** *Mar.-Apr.*

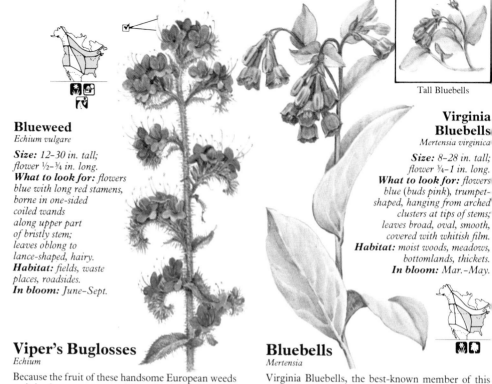

Tall Bluebells

Blueweed
Echium vulgare

Size: *12–30 in. tall; flower ½–¾ in. long.*
What to look for: *flowers blue with long red stamens, borne in one-sided coiled wands along upper part of bristly stem; leaves oblong to lance-shaped, hairy.*
Habitat: *fields, waste places, roadsides.*
In bloom: *June–Sept.*

Virginia Bluebells
Mertensia virginica

Size: *8–28 in. tall; flower ¾–1 in. long.*
What to look for: *flowers blue (buds pink), trumpet-shaped, hanging from arched clusters at tips of stems; leaves broad, oval, smooth, covered with whitish film.*
Habitat: *moist woods, meadows, bottomlands, thickets.*
In bloom: *Mar.–May.*

Viper's Buglosses
Echium

Because the fruit of these handsome European weeds and shrubs seems to resemble a viper's head, the ancients considered the plants a cure—even a preventive—for snakebite. The second part of the name, bugloss, is from the Greek for "ox tongue." Whether it was inspired by the rough-textured leaves or by the open-mouthed flowers with their protruding red stamens is open to conjecture.

Bluebells
Mertensia

Virginia Bluebells, the best-known member of this group, was never as limited in range as its name implies; the English named it at a time when they still referred to Massachusetts as North Virginia. Among the many western species are the Tall Bluebells (*Mertensia paniculata*) of the Northern Plains and Pacific Northwest, and the tiny Alpine Bluebells (*Mertensia alpina*) of the high Rockies.

Forget-me-not
Myosotis scorpioides

Size: *4–24 in. tall; flower ¼ in. wide.*
What to look for: *flowers sky-blue with yellow centers, in flat wands with coiled tips; stems erect or sprawling; leaves oblong, hairy.* **Habitat:** *streambanks, ditches, marshes.*
In bloom: *May–Sept.*

Forget-me-nots
Myosotis

Alaskans chose the forget-me-not as their state flower because it is "emblematic of the quality of constancy, the dominant trait of the intrepid pioneers" who settled the territory. The delicate waterside plants have similar names in many languages (in Japan, for example, they are called *wasurena gusa*, or "do-not-forget herbs"). The name is usually justified by a legend about a lover tragically lost.

Hoary Puccoon
Lithospermum canescens

Size: *4–20 in. tall; flower ½ in. wide.*
What to look for: *flowers orange to yellow, in flat wands with coiled tips; leaves lance-shaped; plant densely covered with gray hairs.* **Habitat:** *sandy prairies, fields; open woods.*
In bloom: *Apr.–June.*

Gromwells
Lithospermum

The roots of the Hoary Puccoon yield a yellow dye. Other gromwell species that give red or purple dyes are also known as puccoons—an Indian word for any herbal source of dye or paint. The name gromwell is from the Old French *gromil*, which referred to the hard white nutlets. Because of these stonelike fruits, the plants were prescribed by many herbalists as a cure for kidney stones.

WILDFLOWERS

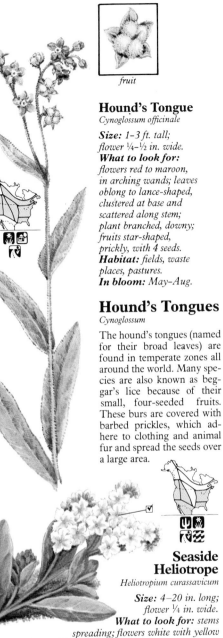

fruit

Hound's Tongue
Cynoglossum officinale

Size: *1–3 ft. tall;
flower ¼–½ in. wide.*
What to look for:
*flowers red to maroon,
in arching wands; leaves
oblong to lance-shaped,
clustered at base and
scattered along stem;
plant branched, downy;
fruits star-shaped,
prickly, with 4 seeds.*
Habitat: *fields, waste
places, pastures.*
In bloom: *May–Aug.*

Hound's Tongues
Cynoglossum

The hound's tongues (named
for their broad leaves) are
found in temperate zones all
around the world. Many species are also known as beggar's lice because of their
small, four-seeded fruits.
These burs are covered with
barbed prickles, which adhere to clothing and animal
fur and spread the seeds over
a large area.

Seaside Heliotrope
Heliotropium curassavicum

Size: *4–20 in. long;
flower ¼ in. wide.*
What to look for: *stems
spreading; flowers white with yellow
in throat (often with purple spots), funnel-shaped,
in curled spikes; leaves spoon-shaped, succulent.*
Habitat: *salty deserts, alkaline
plains, seashores.*
In bloom: *Mar.–Oct.*

Heliotropes
Heliotropium

The vast majority of this group's nearly 250 species
are tropical; the Garden Heliotrope (*Heliotropium
arborescens*), valued for the vanillalike fragrance of its
purple flowers, is native to Peru. The salt-loving Quail
Plant also originated in South America, but has
spread throughout the world. In inland areas it is
named for the birds that feed on its fruits; in coastal
areas it is often known as the Seaside Heliotrope.

Fiddleneck
*Amsinckia
tessellata*

Size: *8–25 in. tall;
flower ½ in. long.*
What to look for: *flowers
orange, tubular, in coiled or
twisted spikes; leaves narrow,
lance-shaped; plants covered
with stiff hairs.*
Habitat: *sandy plains,
desert scrub, open
woods.* **In bloom:**
Mar.–June.

Fiddlenecks
Amsinckia

The tightly coiled flower clusters for which this
group is named are typical of most of the borage family (which includes all the plants on these two pages).
The buds are borne along one side of the coiled stalk,
which unfurls as the flowers open. Fiddlenecks are
native to western deserts and dry plains, where they
are valued for forage (in Arizona they are called
saccato gordo, from the Spanish for "fat grass"). Several species have recently spread to the East.

Sulphur-throated Forget-me-not
Cryptantha flavoculata

Size: *4–14 in. tall;
flower ⅛ in. wide.*
What to look for: *flowers
white with yellow throats,
in dense curling spikes;
leaves narrow, spatula-shaped,
covered with silky hairs.*
Habitat: *deserts, dry open
woods, sagebrush areas.*
In bloom: *May–July.*

White Forget-me-nots
Cryptantha

This group's name is misleading:
some true forget-me-nots (*Myosotis*) bear white flowers, and at
least one of these hairy western
plants, *Cryptantha flava*, has yellow blossoms. Most of the
group's 100-odd species, however, bear small white flowers
and are so alike that botanists
turn to obscure technical differences to tell them apart.

423

Plantains   *Plantago*

These commonplace weeds were prized in years gone by—and are still valued by many—for their tasty and nutritious foliage, richer than spinach in iron and vitamins A and C. The weedy persistence that makes them the despair of gardeners and lawn tenders is a virtue in the eyes of those who cook and eat the very young leaves. A new leafy whorl appears a day or two after the plant is cut to the ground.

Common Plantain
Plantago major

Size: *2-20 in. tall; flower ⅛ in. wide.*
What to look for: *flowers greenish white, in dense spikes arising from center of leafy rosette; leaves broad, oval, with prominent ribs, long stalks.* **Habitat:** *fields, meadows, lawns, sidewalks, roadsides, waste places.*
In bloom: *Apr.-Oct.*

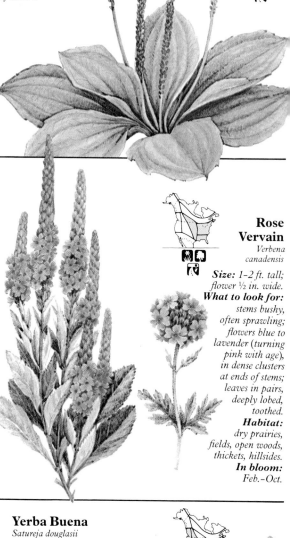

Hoary Vervain
Verbena stricta

Size: *1-4 ft. tall; flower ¼ in. wide.*
What to look for: *flowers lavender to deep blue, in rings around spikes; leaves in pairs, toothed; plants covered with white hairs.* **Habitat:** *prairies, fields, waste places.*
In bloom: *June-Sept.*

Vervains   *Verbena*

Although modern medicine has yet to discover any medicinal use for the vervains, they have had an honored place in folk medicine through the ages. Ancient Greeks, Persians, and Romans, Celtic Druids, and American Indians all revered them as sacred. They were later held to be proof against witchcraft and curses of all kinds, and came to be prescribed by European herbalists and Indian medicine men alike to treat jaundice, dropsy, and various ailments of the stomach, kidneys, and bladder.

Rose Vervain
Verbena canadensis

Size: *1-2 ft. tall; flower ½ in. wide.*
What to look for: *stems bushy, often sprawling; flowers blue to lavender (turning pink with age), in dense clusters at ends of stems; leaves in pairs, deeply lobed, toothed.* **Habitat:** *dry prairies, fields, open woods, thickets, hillsides.*
In bloom: *Feb.-Oct.*

Savories   *Satureja*

"Hot lavender, mints, savory, marjoram:/ . . . these are flowers/Of middle summer, and I think they are given/To men of middle age." The midsummer blossoms listed by Shakespeare in these lines from *The Winter's Tale* belong to the mint family, members of which are shown on the following six pages. Like most of the family, the savories have been used for centuries to season food and to treat such midlife complaints as heartburn and indigestion.

Yerba Buena
Satureja douglasii

Size: *to 2 ft. long; flower ½ in. long.*
What to look for: *flowers white to purplish, borne singly at leaf bases; leaves oval to heart-shaped, in pairs along trailing, square stems.*
Habitat: *shady woods, scrub.*
In bloom: *Apr.-Sept.*

424

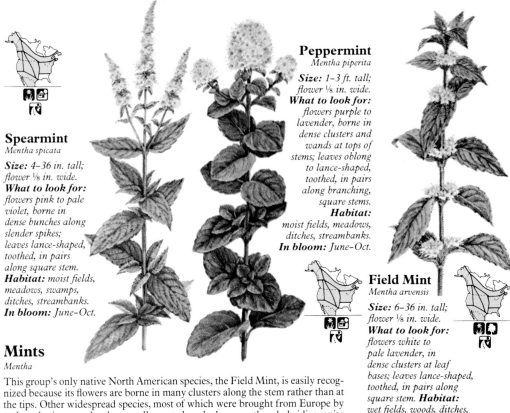

Spearmint
Mentha spicata

Size: 4–36 in. tall;
flower ⅛ in. wide.
What to look for:
flowers pink to pale
violet, borne in
dense bunches along
slender spikes;
leaves lance-shaped,
toothed, in pairs
along square stem.
Habitat: moist fields,
meadows, swamps,
ditches, streambanks.
In bloom: June–Oct.

Peppermint
Mentha piperita

Size: 1–3 ft. tall;
flower ⅛ in. wide.
What to look for:
flowers purple to
lavender, borne in
dense clusters and
wands at tops of
stems; leaves oblong
to lance-shaped,
toothed, in pairs
along branching,
square stems.
Habitat:
moist fields, meadows,
ditches, streambanks.
In bloom: June–Oct.

Field Mint
Mentha arvensis

Size: 6–36 in. tall;
flower ⅛ in. wide.
What to look for:
flowers white to
pale lavender, in
dense clusters at leaf
bases; leaves lance-shaped,
toothed, in pairs along
square stem. **Habitat:**
wet fields, woods, ditches,
shores, streambanks.
In bloom: July–Sept.

Mints
Mentha

This group's only native North American species, the Field Mint, is easily recognized because its flowers are borne in many clusters along the stem rather than at the tips. Other widespread species, most of which were brought from Europe by early colonists, are harder to tell apart, largely because they hybridize quite freely. Peppermint, for example, is believed to be a cross between Spearmint and Water Mint (*Mentha aquatica*). The pungent oils that give mint leaves their distinctive flavors are said to repel several insect pests, including some caterpillars, beetles, ants, and mosquitoes.

Virginia Mountain Mint
Pycnanthemum virginianum

Size: 8–30 in. tall;
flower ⅛ in. wide.
What to look for:
flowers white with purple
spots, in dense heads;
leaves straplike to
lance-shaped, in pairs
along square stems.
Habitat: moist prairies,
meadows, thickets, open
woods, streambanks.
In bloom: July–Sept.

Mountain Mints
Pycnanthemum

Despite the name by which the group is known, only a few species are commonly found in the mountains. The great majority, including the Virginia Mountain Mint, are lowland plants that thrive in woods and prairies.

Heal-all
Prunella vulgaris

Size: 2–28 in. tall;
flower ½ in. long.
What to look for:
plants erect or matted;
flowers violet to pink
or white, in dense
clusters; leaves lance-shaped, in pairs on
square stems. **Habitat:**
fields, woods, waste
places, streambanks.
In bloom: Apr.–Nov.

Selfheals
Prunella

Heal-all has been used by many peoples to clean open sores and fresh wounds, but its ancient reputation as a wonder drug was due to the yawning shape of its flowers. According to the Doctrine of Signatures, believed by many 17th-century physicians, these gullet-like blossoms were a divine sign that the plant was meant to cure diseases of the mouth and throat.

American Germander
Teucrium canadense

Size: 1–4 ft. tall; flower ½–¾ in. long.
What to look for: flowers pink to lavender, with large lower lip, in dense spike atop square stem; leaves in pairs, oblong to lance-shaped, toothed. **Habitat:** moist woods, thickets, streambanks, shores, waste places.
In bloom: June–Sept.

Germanders
Teucrium

The flowers of most members of the mint family—the four-petaled mints (*Mentha*) are themselves exceptions—are like open mouths with two distinct lips. In the germanders, the lower lip is a large landing platform for bees and the upper is small and cleft, so that it resembles two front teeth.

Catnip
Nepeta cataria

Size: 6–36 in. tall; flower ½ in. long.
What to look for: flowers pale violet to white, purple-dotted, in crowded clusters at ends of stem and branches; leaves in pairs, scalloped, heart-shaped; plant velvety, musty-smelling. **Habitat:** waste places, fields.
In bloom: June–Oct.

Catmints *Nepeta*

The catmints' well-known effect on cats seems to be a strange side effect of an oil whose main value is defensive. It is repellent, sometimes even toxic, to many leaf-eating insects. Catnip is a European native that was imported by the colonists, who brewed the leaves into a bracing tea.

Woundwort
Stachys palustris

Size: 1–3 ft. tall; flower ½–¾ in. long.
What to look for: flowers magenta, mottled with purple, tubular with lobed lower lip, in leafy clusters near top of square stem; leaves in pairs, lance-shaped, toothed. **Habitat:** moist meadows, grassy marshes, shores, ditches.
In bloom: June–Sept.

Betonies
Stachys

The betonies are also known as hedge nettles because their hairy leaves are reminiscent of nettles. Unlike nettles, however, betonies have no stinging hairs; in fact, the leaves of the Woundwort were used for centuries to bandage open wounds, staunching the flow of blood and easing the pain.

Carpet Bugleweed
Ajuga reptans

Size: 4–12 in. tall; flower ½–¾ in. long.
What to look for: plants mat-forming; flowers blue, in leafy spikes atop square stems that arise from spreading runners; leaves in pairs, oval. **Habitat:** fields, waste places.
In bloom: May–July.

Bugleweeds
Ajuga

The bugleweeds were brought to North America by the colonists, who grew them for such medicinal uses as the herbalist Nicholas Culpeper described in 1653: "Many times such as give themselves much to drinking are troubled with strange fancies, strange sights in the night time, and some with voices . . . . These I have known cured by taking only two spoonfuls of the syrup of this herb after supper two hours, when you go to bed."

Deadnettles *Lamium*

The deadnettles' hairy leaves may look like nettle leaves, but they lack the sting. Most of the group, including Henbit, are cool-weather weeds; they die back in the heat of summer only to regrow, flower again, and produce a new crop of seedlings. These persist through winter to blossom and set seed the following spring. The seeds of Henbit are eaten by many birds, including hens.

Henbit
Lamium amplexicaule

Size: 4–12 in. tall; flower ½–¾ in. long.
What to look for: flowers pink to purple, in whorls near ends of stems; stems square, upright or sprawling, branched; leaves in pairs, scalloped (upper leaves clasp stem). **Habitat:** fields, waste places.
In bloom: Mar.–Nov.

Mountain Monardella
Monardella odoratissima

Size: *6–14 in. tall;
flower ½ in. wide.*
What to look for: *flowers pale rose
to purple, star-shaped, borne in
dense heads; stem square, branching,
often woody; leaves in pairs, lance-shaped.*
Habitat: *dry slopes.*
In bloom: *May–Sept.*

Monardellas
Monardella

Most species of this group grow
only in California, some in a single
range of mountains or a limited
part of the Mojave Desert. Various
species are occasionally known by
such names as Mountain Pennyroyal, Desert Pennyroyal, and Coyote Mint, but none of these names
seems to have become firmly af-
fixed to any one species.

Gill-over-the-ground
Glechoma hederacea

Size: *to 3 ft. long;
flower ½–¾ in. long.*
What to look for: *flowers blue,
in small clusters at leaf bases;
leaves scalloped, heart-shaped,
in pairs; stems square, creeping.*
Habitat: *fields, moist woods,
waste places.* **In bloom:**
Apr.–June.

Ground Ivies   *Glechoma*

Gill-over-the-ground, the only species of this Eurasian group to become established in the New World,
was once widely used in France to brew beer (the
French word *guiller* means "to ferment beer"). In
England, gill tea was drunk regularly by house paint-
ers to combat "painter's colic," caused by the lead in
their paint—the leaves are rich in vitamin C, which is
used to counteract lead poisoning.

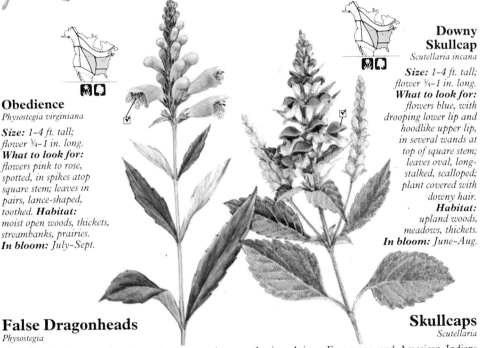

Obedience
Physostegia virginiana

Size: *1–4 ft. tall;
flower ¾–1 in. long.*
What to look for:
*flowers pink to rose,
spotted, in spikes atop
square stem; leaves in
pairs, lance-shaped,
toothed.* **Habitat:**
*moist open woods, thickets,
streambanks, prairies.*
In bloom: *July–Sept.*

Downy Skullcap
Scutellaria incana

Size: *1–4 ft. tall;
flower ¾–1 in. long.*
What to look for:
*flowers blue, with
drooping lower lip and
hoodlike upper lip,
in several wands at
top of square stem;
leaves oval, long-
stalked, scalloped;
plant covered with
downy hair.*
Habitat:
*upland woods,
meadows, thickets.*
In bloom: *June–Aug.*

False Dragonheads
Physostegia

Plant breeders have produced several garden varieties of these showy members of the mint family,
whose snapdragonlike flowers range from white to
pink, red, and many shades of purple. Like many
wild species, they are often known as obedience
or obedient plants because their flowers—whether
moved backward, forward, or sideways—will hold
the position in which they are left.

Skullcaps
Scutellaria

Ancient Asians, Europeans, and American Indians
all believed that these plants could cure hysteria, con-
vulsions, and all manner of nervous disorders. Small
wonder that modern research has found an effective
antispasmodic, scutellaine, in the flower extract. Despite its name and time-honored reputation, however,
the Mad Dog Skullcap (*Scutellaria lateriflora*) does
not cure rabies in man or beast.

427

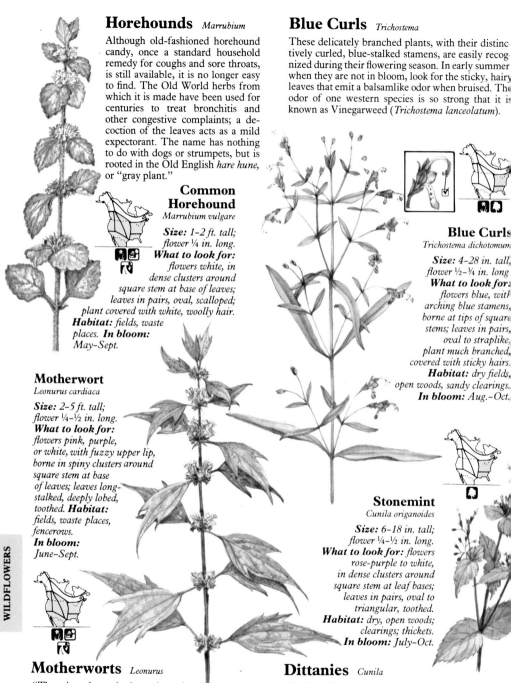

Horehounds *Marrubium*

Although old-fashioned horehound candy, once a standard household remedy for coughs and sore throats, is still available, it is no longer easy to find. The Old World herbs from which it is made have been used for centuries to treat bronchitis and other congestive complaints; a decoction of the leaves acts as a mild expectorant. The name has nothing to do with dogs or strumpets, but is rooted in the Old English *hare hune,* or "gray plant."

Common Horehound
Marrubium vulgare

Size: *1–2 ft. tall; flower ¼ in. long.* **What to look for:** *flowers white, in dense clusters around square stem at base of leaves; leaves in pairs, oval, scalloped; plant covered with white, woolly hair.* **Habitat:** *fields, waste places.* **In bloom:** *May–Sept.*

Motherwort
Leonurus cardiaca

Size: *2–5 ft. tall; flower ¼–½ in. long.* **What to look for:** *flowers pink, purple, or white, with fuzzy upper lip, borne in spiny clusters around square stem at base of leaves; leaves long-stalked, deeply lobed, toothed.* **Habitat:** *fields, waste places, fencerows.* **In bloom:** *June–Sept.*

Motherworts *Leonurus*

"There is no better herb to take melancholy vapours from the heart and to strengthen it," wrote Nicholas Culpeper, the 17th-century herbalist. "It makes mothers joyful and settles the womb, therefore it is called Motherwort." Early colonists brought this highly lauded plant to North America, along with many other members of the mint family, to grow in their herb gardens for medicinal and culinary uses.

Blue Curls *Trichostema*

These delicately branched plants, with their distinctively curled, blue-stalked stamens, are easily recognized during their flowering season. In early summer when they are not in bloom, look for the sticky, hairy leaves that emit a balsamlike odor when bruised. The odor of one western species is so strong that it is known as Vinegarweed (*Trichostema lanceolatum*).

Blue Curls
Trichostema dichotomum

Size: *4–28 in. tall; flower ½–¾ in. long* **What to look for:** *flowers blue, with arching blue stamens, borne at tips of square stems; leaves in pairs, oval to straplike; plant much branched, covered with sticky hairs.* **Habitat:** *dry fields, open woods, sandy clearings.* **In bloom:** *Aug.–Oct.*

Stonemint
Cunila origanoides

Size: *6–18 in. tall; flower ¼–½ in. long.* **What to look for:** *flowers rose-purple to white, in dense clusters around square stem at leaf bases; leaves in pairs, oval to triangular, toothed.* **Habitat:** *dry, open woods; clearings; thickets.* **In bloom:** *July–Oct.*

Dittanies *Cunila*

The New World dittanies were so named because of a superficial resemblance to Europe's Dittany, or Gas Plant (*Dictamnus albus*), a member of the rue family. Most of the group's 16 species are found in Mexico and South America. The leaves of the North American Stonemint were brewed by Indians and settlers into a tea, which they used as a stimulant in treating fevers and the effects of snakebite.

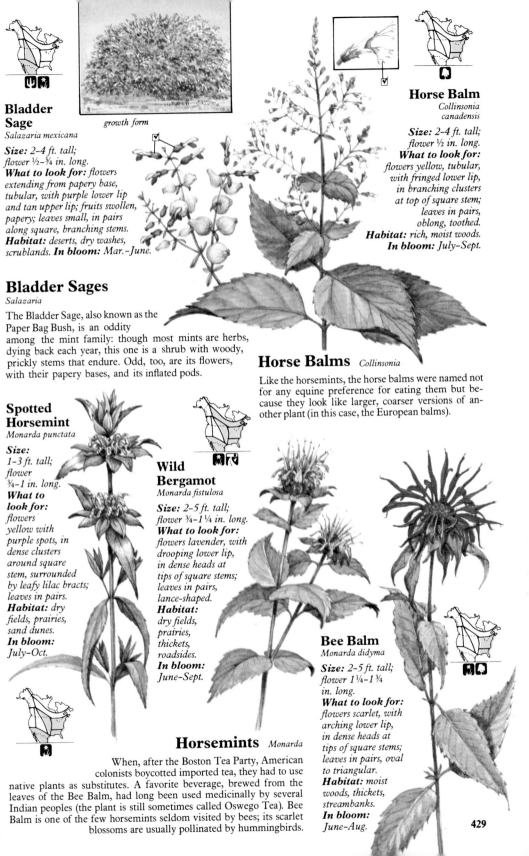

Bladder Sage
Salazaria mexicana

Size: *2-4 ft. tall; flower ½-¾ in. long.*
What to look for: *flowers extending from papery base, tubular, with purple lower lip and tan upper lip; fruits swollen, papery; leaves small, in pairs along square, branching stems.*
Habitat: *deserts, dry washes, scrublands.* **In bloom:** *Mar.-June.*

growth form

Horse Balm
Collinsonia canadensis

Size: *2-4 ft. tall; flower ½ in. long.*
What to look for: *flowers yellow, tubular, with fringed lower lip, in branching clusters at top of square stem; leaves in pairs, oblong, toothed.*
Habitat: *rich, moist woods.*
In bloom: *July-Sept.*

Bladder Sages
Salazaria

The Bladder Sage, also known as the Paper Bag Bush, is an oddity among the mints family: though most mints are herbs, dying back each year, this one is a shrub with woody, prickly stems that endure. Odd, too, are its flowers, with their papery bases, and its inflated pods.

Horse Balms   *Collinsonia*

Like the horsemints, the horse balms were named not for any equine preference for eating them but because they look like larger, coarser versions of another plant (in this case, the European balms).

Spotted Horsemint
Monarda punctata

Size: *1-3 ft. tall; flower ¾-1 in. long.*
What to look for: *flowers yellow with purple spots, in dense clusters around square stem, surrounded by leafy lilac bracts; leaves in pairs.*
Habitat: *dry fields, prairies, sand dunes.*
In bloom: *July-Oct.*

Wild Bergamot
Monarda fistulosa

Size: *2-5 ft. tall; flower ¾-1¼ in. long.*
What to look for: *flowers lavender, with drooping lower lip, in dense heads at tips of square stems; leaves in pairs, lance-shaped.*
Habitat: *dry fields, prairies, thickets, roadsides.*
In bloom: *June-Sept.*

Bee Balm
Monarda didyma

Size: *2-5 ft. tall; flower 1¼-1¾ in. long.*
What to look for: *flowers scarlet, with arching lower lip, in dense heads at tips of square stems; leaves in pairs, oval to triangular.*
Habitat: *moist woods, thickets, streambanks.*
In bloom: *June-Aug.*

Horsemints   *Monarda*

When, after the Boston Tea Party, American colonists boycotted imported tea, they had to use native plants as substitutes. A favorite beverage, brewed from the leaves of the Bee Balm, had long been used medicinally by several Indian peoples (the plant is still sometimes called Oswego Tea). Bee Balm is one of the few horsemints seldom visited by bees; its scarlet blossoms are usually pollinated by hummingbirds.

Tropical Sage
Salvia coccinea

Size: *1-3 ft. tall; flower 1 in. long.*
What to look for: *flowers scarlet, with drooping lower lip, in whorls along square stem; leaves in pairs, triangular to heart-shaped.*
Habitat: *open woods, sandy hammocks, waste places.*
In bloom: *Feb.-Nov.*

Blue Sage
Salvia azure

Size: *2-5 ft. tal flower ½-1 in. long*
What to look for *flowers blue, tubular with drooping lower lip borne in wandlike cluste along square stem leaves in pairs, lance-shaped*
Habitat: *dry plains, prairie sandy pinelands*
In bloom: *May-Oct*

Chia
Salvi columbiaria

Size. *4-25 in. tal flower ½- ¾ in. long*
What to look for: *flowers blue to purple, tubular in dense cluster amid spiny bracts; leaves mostly at base of square stem, crinkly, lobed.*
Habitat: *deserts dry scrublands, chaparral, open woods.*
In bloom: *Mar.-June.*

Cancerweed
Salvia lyrata

Size: *1-2 ft. tall; flower ¾-1¼ in. long.*
What to look for: *flowers blue-purple, tubular, with large lower lip, borne in whorls along square stem; leaves mostly at base of plant, deeply lobed.*
Habitat: *dry, open woods; clearings; sandy meadows; fields.* **In bloom:** *Apr.-July.*

Sages *Salvia*

Most kinds of sage are superb honey plants, well adapted for pollination by bees. When a bee's tongue strikes a small plate within a freshly opened flower, a pair of hinged stamens pivots down to coat the insect's back with pollen. When the bee visits an older flower, some pollen is removed by a precisely placed stigma. (Red-flowered species, such as the Tropical Sage, are similarly adapted to hummingbird pollination.) Like many other members of the mint family, the sages have furnished food and medicine for centuries. The seeds of Cancerweed were made into an ointment for open sores. The Indians ground the seeds of Chia into flour, and the Spaniards used its leaves to poultice gunshot wounds. The familiar Garden Sage (*Salvia officinalis*) was once reputed to restore lost youth.

Purple Gerardia
Agalinis purpurea

Size: *1-4 ft. tall; flower ½-1½ in. wide.*
What to look for: *flowers rose-pink, funnel-shaped, with 5 flaring petals, borne on slender stalks from bases of upper leaves; leaves in pairs, straplike.*
Habitat: *moist fields, thickets, meadows, shores.*
In bloom: *Aug.-Oct.*

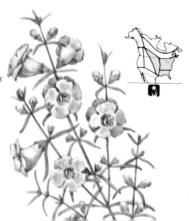

Gerardias *Agalinis*

The gerardias are part-time, or facultative, parasites (as are Indian paintbrushes, yellow rattles, and a few other members of the snapdragon family). Perfectly able to survive on their own, they will take nourishment from the roots of other plants if the opportunity arises. Their pink or crimson flowers open in the morning and last only half a day, falling off by afternoon if brushed too hard by a butterfly's wing.

WILDFLOWERS

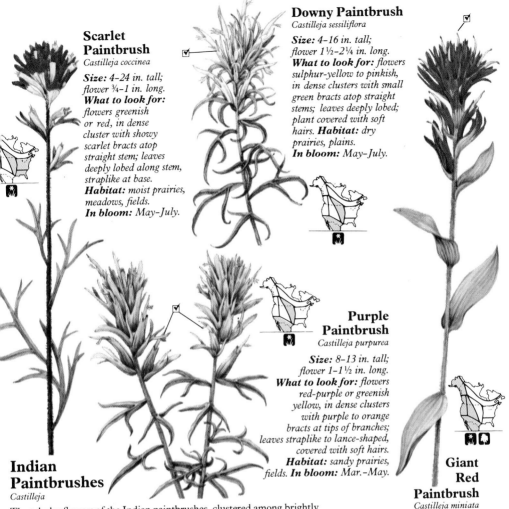

Scarlet Paintbrush
Castilleja coccinea

Size: *4–24 in. tall; flower ¾–1 in. long.* **What to look for:** *flowers greenish or red, in dense cluster with showy scarlet bracts atop straight stem; leaves deeply lobed along stem, straplike at base.* **Habitat:** *moist prairies, meadows, fields.* **In bloom:** *May–July.*

Downy Paintbrush
Castilleja sessiliflora

Size: *4–16 in. tall; flower 1½–2¼ in. long.* **What to look for:** *flowers sulphur-yellow to pinkish, in dense clusters with small green bracts atop straight stems; leaves deeply lobed; plant covered with soft hairs.* **Habitat:** *dry prairies, plains.* **In bloom:** *May–July.*

Purple Paintbrush
Castilleja purpurea

Size: *8–13 in. tall; flower 1–1½ in. long.* **What to look for:** *flowers red-purple or greenish yellow, in dense clusters with purple to orange bracts at tips of branches; leaves straplike to lance-shaped, covered with soft hairs.* **Habitat:** *sandy prairies, fields.* **In bloom:** *Mar.–May.*

Indian Paintbrushes
Castilleja

The tubular flowers of the Indian paintbrushes, clustered among brightly colored bracts (modified leaves), offer no landing place for bees or other pollinators; the plants therefore depend on hovering insects and hummingbirds for cross-fertilization. The pistil and the pollen-bearing stamens arch downward from the tip of the flower's upper lip, or galea, to touch the heads of these nectar-seeking creatures as they thrust their tongues or bills into the blossom. Identification within the group is often difficult; botanists depend largely on technical differences in the shape of the galea to tell similar species apart. The red-flowered Wyoming Paintbrush (*Castilleja linariaefolia*) is that state's flower.

Giant Red Paintbrush
Castilleja miniata

Size: *1–3 ft. tall; flower ¾–1¼ in. long.* **What to look for:** *flowers greenish with red tips, in dense clusters with red bracts atop straight stems; leaves straplike.* **Habitat:** *mountain meadows, coniferous forests, streambanks, ledges.* **In bloom:** *May–Sept.*

Blue-eyed Mary
Collinsia verna

Size: *6–20 in. tall; flower ½–¾ in. wide.* **What to look for:** *flowers white (upper lip) and blue (lower lip), in loose whorls around top of stem; leaves in pairs, oval; stems erect or sprawling.* **Habitat:** *moist woods, thickets, bottomlands.* **In bloom:** *Apr.–June.*

Blue-eyed Marys
Collinsia

Most of this group's 20 species are limited to the Pacific states. Many are known as Chinese houses because their flowers, arranged in a series of tight whorls along the stem, give the impression of a pagoda's ascending roofs. Although the flowers seem to have only four petals, there is actually a fifth in the center of the lower lip, folded lengthwise over the pollen-bearing stamens.

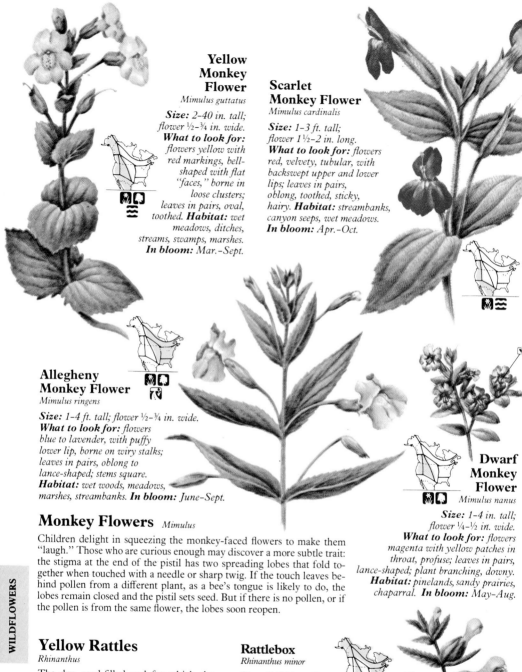

Yellow Monkey Flower
Mimulus guttatus

Size: 2–40 in. tall; flower ½–¾ in. wide. **What to look for:** flowers yellow with red markings, bell-shaped with flat "faces," borne in loose clusters; leaves in pairs, oval, toothed. **Habitat:** wet meadows, ditches, streams, swamps, marshes. **In bloom:** Mar.–Sept.

Scarlet Monkey Flower
Mimulus cardinalis

Size: 1–3 ft. tall; flower 1½–2 in. long. **What to look for:** flowers red, velvety, tubular, with backswept upper and lower lips; leaves in pairs, oblong, toothed, sticky, hairy. **Habitat:** streambanks, canyon seeps, wet meadows. **In bloom:** Apr.–Oct.

Allegheny Monkey Flower
Mimulus ringens

Size: 1–4 ft. tall; flower ½–¾ in. wide. **What to look for:** flowers blue to lavender, with puffy lower lip, borne on wiry stalks; leaves in pairs, oblong to lance-shaped; stems square. **Habitat:** wet woods, meadows, marshes, streambanks. **In bloom:** June–Sept.

Dwarf Monkey Flower
Mimulus nanus

Size: 1–4 in. tall; flower ¼–½ in. wide. **What to look for:** flowers magenta with yellow patches in throat, profuse; leaves in pairs, lance-shaped; plant branching, downy. **Habitat:** pinelands, sandy prairies, chaparral. **In bloom:** May–Aug.

Monkey Flowers *Mimulus*

Children delight in squeezing the monkey-faced flowers to make them "laugh." Those who are curious enough may discover a more subtle trait: the stigma at the end of the pistil has two spreading lobes that fold together when touched with a needle or sharp twig. If the touch leaves behind pollen from a different plant, as a bee's tongue is likely to do, the lobes remain closed and the pistil sets seed. But if there is no pollen, or if the pollen is from the same flower, the lobes soon reopen.

Yellow Rattles
Rhinanthus

The dry, seed-filled pod for which the group is named develops rather quickly from the swollen green base of each flower. It is not unusual to find a single plant with a flattened green bud on top, several flowers in progressive stages of development along the stem, and a puffy brown capsule or two near the bottom. Yellow rattles are northern plants, found in all lands that touch upon the Arctic Circle—a distribution pattern that botanists call circumboreal.

Rattlebox
Rhinanthus minor

Size: 8–24 in. tall; flower ½–¾ in. long. **What to look for:** flowers yellow, tubular, with hoodlike upper lip, protruding from swollen green base, borne along one side of upright stems; leaves in pairs, oblong to triangular, toothed. **Habitat:** fields, thickets, tundra, alpine meadows. **In bloom:** May–Sept.

Beardtongues *Penstemon*

Both the scientific and the common name of this group refer to the prominent fifth stamen, a projection lacking the pollen cases that crown the ends of the other four. In most beardtongue species, this infertile stamen is covered instead with a fuzzy growth of hair, which all but closes the throat of the flower. Because the shape of the opening, as well as the color of the flower, varies from species to species, different kinds of beardtongue attract and admit different kinds of pollinators. In this way, even though several species may grow in the same area, each maintains its individuality.

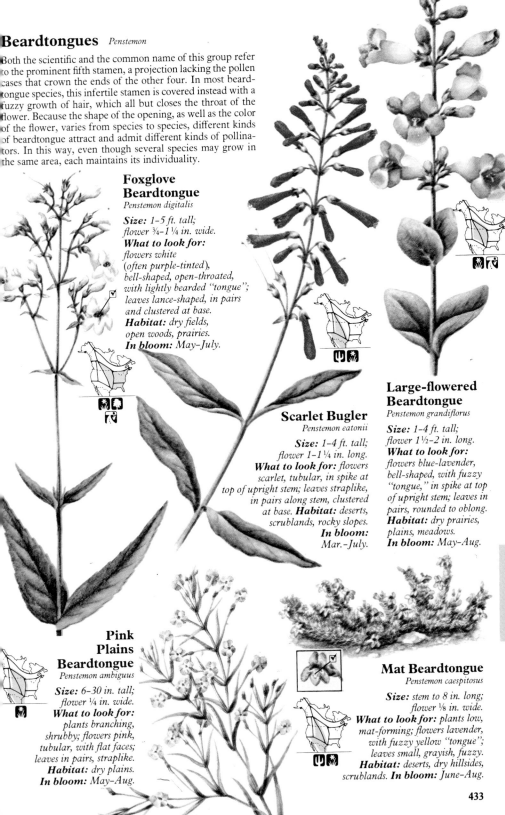

Foxglove Beardtongue
Penstemon digitalis

Size: *1–5 ft. tall; flower ¾–1¼ in. wide.*
What to look for: *flowers white (often purple-tinted), bell-shaped, open-throated, with lightly bearded "tongue"; leaves lance-shaped, in pairs and clustered at base.*
Habitat: *dry fields, open woods, prairies.*
In bloom: *May–July.*

Scarlet Bugler
Penstemon eatonii

Size: *1–4 ft. tall; flower 1–1¼ in. long.*
What to look for: *flowers scarlet, tubular, in spike at top of upright stem; leaves straplike, in pairs along stem, clustered at base.* **Habitat:** *deserts, scrublands, rocky slopes.*
In bloom: *Mar.–July.*

Large-flowered Beardtongue
Penstemon grandiflorus

Size: *1–4 ft. tall; flower 1½–2 in. long.*
What to look for: *flowers blue-lavender, bell-shaped, with fuzzy "tongue," in spike at top of upright stem; leaves in pairs, rounded to oblong.*
Habitat: *dry prairies, plains, meadows.*
In bloom: *May–Aug.*

Pink Plains Beardtongue
Penstemon ambiguus

Size: *6–30 in. tall; flower ¼ in. wide.*
What to look for: *plants branching, shrubby; flowers pink, tubular, with flat faces; leaves in pairs, straplike.*
Habitat: *dry plains.*
In bloom: *May–Aug.*

Mat Beardtongue
Penstemon caespitosus

Size: *stem to 8 in. long; flower ⅛ in. wide.*
What to look for: *plants low, mat-forming; flowers lavender, with fuzzy yellow "tongue"; leaves small, grayish, fuzzy.*
Habitat: *deserts, dry hillsides, scrublands.* **In bloom:** *June–Aug.*

433

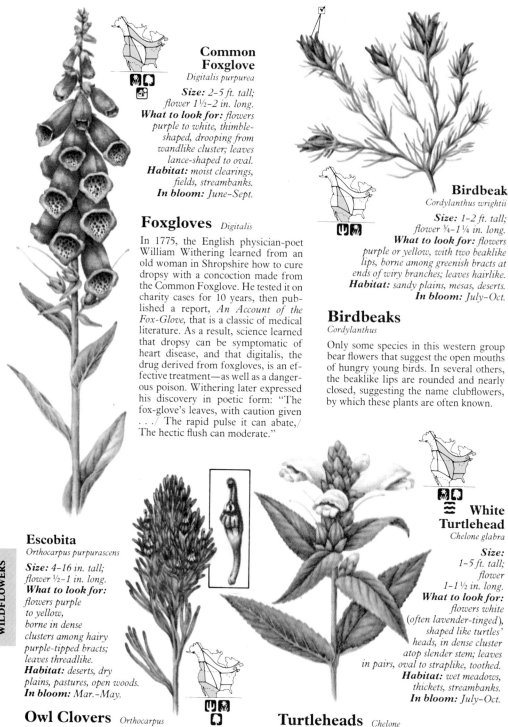

Common Foxglove
Digitalis purpurea

Size: *2–5 ft. tall; flower 1½–2 in. long.*
What to look for: *flowers purple to white, thimble-shaped, drooping from wandlike cluster; leaves lance-shaped to oval.*
Habitat: *moist clearings, fields, streambanks.*
In bloom: *June–Sept.*

Foxgloves *Digitalis*

In 1775, the English physician-poet William Withering learned from an old woman in Shropshire how to cure dropsy with a concoction made from the Common Foxglove. He tested it on charity cases for 10 years, then published a report, *An Account of the Fox-Glove,* that is a classic of medical literature. As a result, science learned that dropsy can be symptomatic of heart disease, and that digitalis, the drug derived from foxgloves, is an effective treatment—as well as a dangerous poison. Withering later expressed his discovery in poetic form: "The fox-glove's leaves, with caution given . . ./ The rapid pulse it can abate,/ The hectic flush can moderate."

Birdbeak
Cordylanthus wrightii

Size: *1–2 ft. tall; flower ¾–1¼ in. long.*
What to look for: *flowers purple or yellow, with two beaklike lips, borne among greenish bracts at ends of wiry branches; leaves hairlike.*
Habitat: *sandy plains, mesas, deserts.*
In bloom: *July–Oct.*

Birdbeaks
Cordylanthus

Only some species in this western group bear flowers that suggest the open mouths of hungry young birds. In several others, the beaklike lips are rounded and nearly closed, suggesting the name clubflowers, by which these plants are often known.

Escobita
Orthocarpus purpurascens

Size: *4–16 in. tall; flower ½–1 in. long.*
What to look for: *flowers purple to yellow, borne in dense clusters among hairy purple-tipped bracts; leaves threadlike.*
Habitat: *deserts, dry plains, pastures, open woods.*
In bloom: *Mar.–May.*

White Turtlehead
Chelone glabra

Size: *1–5 ft. tall; flower 1–1½ in. long.*
What to look for: *flowers white (often lavender-tinged), shaped like turtles' heads, in dense cluster atop slender stem; leaves in pairs, oval to straplike, toothed.*
Habitat: *wet meadows, thickets, streambanks.*
In bloom: *July–Oct.*

Owl Clovers *Orthocarpus*

The owl clovers' flowers, like those of the Indian paintbrushes, are clustered among showy bracts. They are usually more conspicuous, however, and in some species look like little roosting owls. Those of the Escobita, or Little Broom, often blend in with the purplish bracts, but occasionally are bright yellow.

Turtleheads *Chelone*

The two-lipped flowers of many members of the snapdragon family call to mind various animals, such as snakes, monkeys, elephants, birds, and, of course, snapping dragons. But none are more precisely evocative than the flowers of the turtleheads, several kinds of which are popular in garden borders.

WILDFLOWERS

Mountain Kittentails

Synthyris missurica

Size: *4-24 in. tall; flower ½ in. long.*
What to look for: *flowers blue-purple, in dense fuzzy spike; leaves heart- to kidney-shaped, arising from base of plant and in pairs along stem.*
Habitat: *open mountain slopes, pine forests.* **In bloom:** *May-June.*

Kittentails *Synthyris*

Even though their flowers lack the distinctive lower lip that, in most members of the snap-dragon family, serves as a landing platform for bees, the kittentails are generally bee-pollinated. The insects cling to the flower cluster's fuzzy surface, composed of two stamens projecting from each blossom.

Alpine Besseya

Besseya alpina

Size: *2-6 in. tall; flower ¼ in. long.*
What to look for: *flowers pale purple, in dense fuzzy spike; leaves oval to heart-shaped, arising from base of plant and scattered along stem.*
Habitat: *rocky meadows at high elevations.* **In bloom:** *Aug.-Sept.*

Besseyas *Besseya*

To the untrained eye, it is hard to tell the difference between the besseyas (named for the American botanist Charles Bessey) and the kittentails. Some botanists, in fact, have lumped both groups together, usually under the name *Synthyris*.

Ghost Flower

Mohavea confertiflora

Size: *4-16 in. tall; flower 1-1½ in. long.*
What to look for: *flowers pale yellow with purple dots, translucent; leaves narrow, lance-shaped, hairy.*
Habitat: *desert scrublands, sandy washes, dry slopes.*
In bloom: *Mar.-Apr.*

Mohaveas
Mohavea

This group's two species grow in the Mojave Desert and a few surrounding areas. The Ghost Flower is the larger and more widespread of the two; the Lesser Mohavea (*Mohavea breviflora*), with small, bright yellow flowers, is common only from the central Mojave to Death Valley.

Northern False Foxglove

Aureolaria flava

Size: *2-8 ft. tall; flower 1½-2¼ in. long.*
What to look for: *flowers yellow, funnel-shaped, with 5 rounded petals, borne in wandlike cluster; leaves in pairs, deeply cleft; stem often purplish.*
Habitat: *woods, thickets.*
In bloom: *July-Sept.*

False Foxgloves
Aureolaria

The colonists found many plants in the New World that reminded them of familiar European species. Among them were these tall semiparasites (they draw part of their sustenance from the roots of oaks), whose wandlike clusters of yellow flowers are reminiscent of the pink, purple, or white blossoms of the true foxgloves. The American Indians used some species medicinally in much the same way that true foxgloves were used in Europe.

Birdseye Speedwell
Veronica persica

Size: *4–12 in. long; flower ¼–½ in. wide.*
What to look for: *stems spreading, hairy; flowers blue with dark lines and pale centers, borne on slender stalks from leaf bases; leaves oval, toothed, scattered along stems.*
Habitat: *lawns, fields, waste places.*
In bloom: *Apr.–Aug.*

Water Speedwell
Veronica anagallis-aquatica

Size: *1–4 ft. long; flower ¼ in. wide.*
What to look for: *stems creeping, with upright tips; flowers lilac-blue, in wands from bases of leaves near stem tips; leaves in pairs, oval to straplike.*
Habitat: *streams, banks, marshes, ditches, ponds.*
In bloom: *May–Sept.*

Speedwells *Veronica*

No one knows how these plants came to be called speedwells. At least three persuasive theories are current: one, that their bright blue flowers, abundant along roadsides and riverbanks, seem to speed the traveler upon his journey; two, that the weedy species, such as Birdseye Speedwell, proliferate with notable speed; and three, that the English peasants, who brewed the leaves of some species into an expectorant for treating coughs and congestion, may once have known them as "spit-wells." Whatever the origin of the name, it has belonged exclusively to these members of the snapdragon family since the 16th century or earlier.

Common Mullein
Verbascum thapsus

Size: *1–8 ft. tall; flower ¼–1 in. wide.*
What to look for: *flowers yellow, in dense spike at top of stout stem; leaves oblong, velvety, gray-green, clustered at base of plant and along stem.*
Habitat: *fields, old pastures, roadsides.* ***In bloom:*** *June–Sept.*

Mulleins *Verbascum*

Most of these Eurasian weeds are biennial—they require two years to complete their life cycle. In the first summer they form large, ground-hugging rosettes of leaves that last through the winter. (It is for the texture of its leaves that the Common Mullein is also known as Velvet Plant and Flannel Leaf.) The upright flowering stems arise from the centers of these rosettes the following spring and bear their blossoms, a few at a time, all summer long. The Common Mullein's tall, stout stem has inspired such names as Jacob's Staff and Shepherd's Club; the Moth Mullein is named for the flowers themselves, with their spreading petals and antennalike stamens.

white flower

Moth Mullein
Verbascum blattaria

Size: *1–3 ft. tall; flower 1 in. wide.*
What to look for: *flowers yellow or white with widespread petals and fuzzy purplish center, borne in open wand at top of slender stem; leaves lance-shaped to oval, toothed, clustered at base of plant and scattered along stem.* ***Habitat:*** *fields, waste places, roadsides.*
In bloom: *June–Sept.*

436

Towering Lousewort
Pedicularis bracteosa

Size: *1–4 ft. tall; flower ½–1 in. long.* **What to look for:** *flowers yellow, rose, or purple, with beaklike upper lip, in dense spike; leaves divided, scattered along stem.* **Habitat:** *mountain meadows, slopes, open woods.* **In bloom:** *June–Aug.*

Wood Betony
Pedicularis canadensis

Size: *6–16 in. tall; flower ½–1 in. long.* **What to look for:** *flowers brownish red to yellow, with beaklike upper lip, in short, dense spike; leaves deeply lobed.* **Habitat:** *open woods, thickets, prairies.* **In bloom:** *Apr.–June.*

Elephant Heads
Pedicularis groenlandica

Size: *8–24 in. tall; flower ¾–1 in. long.* **What to look for:** *flowers pink to purple, shaped like elephants' heads with upraised trunks, in dense spike; leaves divided or deeply lobed, clustered at base of plant and scattered along stem.* **Habitat:** *wet mountain meadows, open woods.* **In bloom:** *June–Aug.*

Louseworts *Pedicularis*

To reach the nectar within a Wood Betony blossom, a bee lifts the right side of the flower's upper lip (the left side is sealed), causing the pollen-receptive stigma to dip down and touch its body. Inside, the bee receives fresh pollen on the place that will be touched by the next flower's stigma. The Elephant Heads' blossoms contain no nectar, but bumblebees seek the pollen itself. To coat itself with a cloud of pollen, a bee lands on the "trunk" and vibrates its wings; meanwhile the trunk has curled around and touched the front of the bee's abdomen with the stigma, receiving pollen from a flower visited earlier.

Culver's Roots
Veronicastrum

The identity of Dr. Culver is unknown, beyond the belief that a man by that name, sometime before 1716 (when Cotton Mather wrote of the plant), popularized the use of the dried root as a laxative and cathartic. Only two species exist—one in North America, the other in Siberia.

Culver's Root
Veronicastrum virginicum

Size: *2–7 ft. tall; flower ⅛–¼ in. wide.* **What to look for:** *flowers white to purplish, in dense spikes near top of upright stem; leaves lance-shaped, in whorls around stem.* **Habitat:** *open woods, thickets; moist meadows, prairies.* **In bloom:** *June–Sept.*

Butter and Eggs
Linaria vulgaris

Size: *6–36 in. tall; flower 1 in. long.* **What to look for:** *flowers yellow with orange patch in throat, spurred, in spikes at tips of leafy stems; leaves grasslike.* **Habitat:** *fields, waste places, roadsides.* **In bloom:** *May–Sept.*

Toadflax *Linaria*

A patch of color marking the narrow entrance to the nectar supply suggests that these flowers are pollinated during the day; such nectar guides are useless in the dark. The nectar is in a long spur, which tells us that the pollinators are probably hummingbirds and long-tongued insects.

437

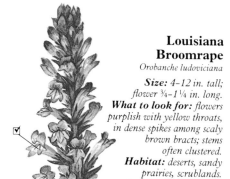

Louisiana Broomrape
Orobanche ludoviciana

Size: *4–12 in. tall; flower ¾–1¼ in. long.*
What to look for: *flowers purplish with yellow throats, in dense spikes among scaly brown bracts; stems often clustered.*
Habitat: *deserts, sandy prairies, scrublands.*
In bloom: *Mar.–Aug.*

Naked Broomrape
Orobanche uniflora

Size: *1–6 in. tall; flower ½–1 in. long.*
What to look for: *flowers creamy white to pale lavender, with yellow throats, borne singly atop pale stalks; leaves scalelike, at base of stalks.*
Habitat: *damp woods, thickets.*
In bloom: *Apr.–June.*

Broomrapes   *Orobanche*

Like all members of the cancerroot family, the broomrapes contain no chlorophyll and cannot manufacture their own food. Instead, they sink parasitic roots into the roots of other plants and draw out nourishment. The broomrape group is named for a European plant that lives on the roots of broom plants. The Louisiana Broomrape—named for the territory, not the state—parasitizes tomato plants as well as several western members of the composite family, particularly the Burrobush (*Franseria dumosa*) and the sagebrushes (*Artemisia*). The Naked Broomrape can choose among many hosts but seems to prefer the stonecrops (*Sedum*); it is occasionally found growing upon garden specimens.

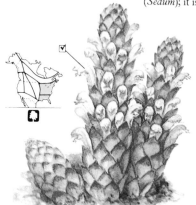

Beechdrops
Epifagus virginiana

Size: *5–16 in. tall; flower ¼–½ in. long.*
What to look for: *stems pale brown, branching; flowers white with brownish purple stripes, tubular (near tips) or budlike (near base).*
Habitat: *beech woods, thickets.*
In bloom: *Aug.–Oct.*

Squawroot
Conopholis americana

Size: *2–10 in. tall; flower ½ in. long.*
What to look for: *stems covered with overlapping, tawny yellow scales (turning brown); flowers yellow with hooded upper lip, borne between scales on upper part of stem.* **Habitat:** *rich woods (often oak).* **In bloom:** *Apr.–July.*

Squawroots   *Conopholis*

The scaly stems of these members of the cancerroot family look somewhat like clusters of pine cones standing on end. There is little chance of confusing them with real pine cones, however, since they are parasites on the roots of deciduous trees—chiefly oaks. The soft, yellow scales (actually modified leaves) turn hard and brown after the flowers have faded.

Beechdrops
Epifagus

Although Beechdrops is a parasite of beech trees, it does little or no harm to its host. Instead of penetrating the tree's roots with its own, as other members of the cancerroot family do, it gets its nutrients with the help of an intermediate fungus in the soil. The upper flowers of Beechdrops are often visited by bees, but these blossoms are usually sterile; the lower, unopened flowers produce abundant seed by self-pollination.

Cross Vine
Bignonia capreolata

Size: *to 75 ft. high;
flower 2 in. long.*
What to look for: *stems thick, climbing;
flowers red and orange, bell-shaped, in showy
clusters; leaves divided into two leaflets,
with a climbing tendril between each pair.*
Habitat: *rich woods, swamps, bottomlands.*
In bloom: *Apr.–June.*

Trumpet Creeper
Campsis radicans

Size: *to 50 ft. high;
flower 2½–3 in. long.*
What to look for: *stems climbing or
sprawling; flowers orange to scarlet,
trumpet-shaped, in showy clusters;
leaves divided into 7–11 leaflets.*
Habitat: *moist woods,
thickets, streambanks.*
In bloom: *July–Sept.*

Cross Vines *Bignonia*

If you cut through the stem of a Cross Vine you
will see the pattern of a cross on the face of the
cut—a key symbol in the eyes of the priests and
missionaries who accompanied many of the early
explorers to the Southeast. The group has only
one species.

Trumpet Creepers *Campsis*

One species of this group is native to North
America; the only other, *Campsis grandiflora*, is
Asian in origin. Both species are cultivated for
the sake of their colorful flowers, but the rampant habit of our native species has made it a
troublesome weed in many places.

Ruellia
Ruellia strepens

Size: *1–4 ft. tall;
flower 1 in. wide.*
What to look for: *flowers
blue-violet, tubular, with 5
spreading petals, on short
leafy stalks along stem;
leaves in pairs, oblong.*
Habitat: *open woods, thickets.*
In bloom:
May–July.

Ruellias
Ruellia

It seems odd that a group
of plants as showy and distinctive as these has never
acquired a common name.
(Some low-growing species
resemble petunias and are
occasionally called wild
petunias, but the name has
never gained currency.)
About 20 of the group's 250
species grow in temperate
and subtropical North
America; the rest are limited to the tropics.

Water Willow
Justicia americana

Size: *1–3 ft. tall;
flower ½ in. wide.*
What to look for:
*stems erect, rising
in colonies from water;
leaves lance-shaped, in
pairs; flowers white with
violet markings,
on long stalks
arising at leaf bases.*
Habitat: *streams, ponds,
lakeshores, swamps.*
In bloom: *June–Oct.*

Water Willows *Justicia*

Although these water-loving plants are unrelated to
the willows (*Salix*), their name is not inappropriate.
Colonies of their supple stems arising from streams,
ponds, and the edges of lakes are often mistaken for
low-growing willows, because of both the shape of
their leaves and their watery habitat.

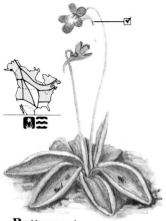

Butterwort
Pinguicula vulgaris

Size: 2–6 in. tall;
flower ¼–½ in. wide.
What to look for:
flowers violet, with spurs;
leaves greenish yellow, buttery,
sticky, clustered at base of stalks.
Habitat: wet rocks,
meadows, boggy areas.
In bloom: June–Aug.

Butterworts   *Pinguicula*

Small insects alighting on a butterwort leaf are trapped by its sticky
yellowish surface. After a time, the
leaf edges curl over, and the plant
secretes enzymes that extract nitrogen and other vital elements
from the accumulated victims.
Then the leaf reopens.

Swollen Bladderwort
Utricularia inflata

Size: to 10 ft. across;
stalk 5–12 in. tall; flower ½–¾ in. wide.
What to look for: flowers yellow, shieldlike,
clustered atop leafless stalk; stems swollen,
floating beneath surface; leaves feathery,
bearing many small bladders.
Habitat: ponds, ditches. **In bloom:** May–Aug.

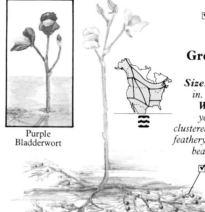

Purple
Bladderwort

Greater Bladderwort
Utricularia vulgaris

Size: to 7 ft. across; stalk 4–24
in. tall; flower ½–¾ in. wide.
What to look for: flowers
yellow, snapdragon-shaped,
clustered atop leafless stalk; leaves
feathery, floating beneath surface,
bearing many small bladders.
Habitat: ponds,
bays, marshes.
In bloom: May–Sept.

Bladderworts
Utricularia

Each little bladder among the plumelike
underwater leaves of these carnivorous plants
has a trapdoor triggered by sensitive hairs. When tiny water animals
touch the hairs, the door opens and the creatures are sucked in, to be
digested for the nutrients in their bodies. The Purple Bladderwort
(*Utricularia purpurea*), with its whorled leaves, is one of the few native
species in this group whose flowers are not yellow.

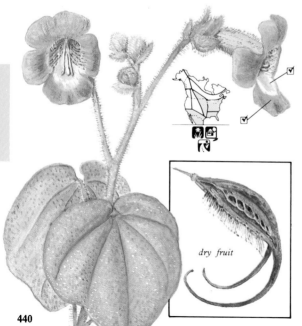

dry fruit

Unicorn Plant
Proboscidea louisianica

Size: 1–3 ft. tall; flower 1½ in. wide.
What to look for: flowers pink with
yellow throats, bell-shaped, with large
lower lip; leaves heart-shaped, sticky,
downy; stems downy; fruits fleshy, green,
with single horn on end (becoming hard,
brown, with 2 claws). **Habitat:** fields,
streambanks, waste places, roadsides.
In bloom: June–Sept.

Unicorn Plants   *Proboscidea*

This group of nine species may be known by
either of two names, depending on one's atti-
tude toward their fruits. Early in their development, the fruits are green and fleshy,
with a single unicornlike "horn" at the end.
They are edible and may be pickled like
cucumbers. As the fruits dry, however, they
grow hard and brown and finally split open,
the horn forming two hooks that can catch
in the fur—and even in the ears and nostrils—of livestock. Ranchers and sheepherders therefore call them devil's claws.

Venus' Looking Glass
Triodanis perfoliata

Size: *4–30 in. tall;
flower ½–¾ in. wide.*
What to look for:
*flowers blue or violet,
bowl-shaped, borne at bases of leaves
(those at top of stem budlike);
leaves shell-like, clasping stem.*
Habitat: *open woods, fields,
waste places.* **In bloom:** *May–June.*

Venus' Looking Glasses
Triodanis

This group's name is borrowed
from a European cousin, whose
seeds are round, flat, and nearly
mirror-bright. The seeds of the
North American plants are not so
precisely shaped, but they are
hard and shiny enough to warrant the looking-glass name. Unlike the original Venus' Looking
Glass, these plants produce self-
pollinating flowers that remain
closed, as well as open blossoms
lower on the stem.

Harebell
Campanula rotundifolia

Size: *4–20 in. tall;
flower ¾ in. wide.*
What to look for: *flowers blue to
lavender, bell-shaped, on hairlike
stalks from tops of stems; leaves
slender, scattered along stems
(round, long-stalked leaves at base
of stems are gone by flowering time).*
Habitat: *fields, prairies, cliffs,
rocky banks, dry open woods.*
In bloom: *June–Oct.*

Southern Harebell
Campanula divaricata

Size: *1–3 ft. tall;
flower ¼ in. wide.*
What to look for:
*flowers blue, bell-shaped,
with 5 upturned petals,
and long, protruding pistil,
hanging from slender stalks;
leaves lance-shaped to oval,
toothed; stems slender,
branching.* **Habitat:**
dry woods, rocky hillsides.
In bloom: *July–Sept.*

Tall Bellflower
Campanula americana

Size: *2–7 ft. tall;
flower 1 in. wide.*
What to look for:
*flowers blue, star-shaped, borne
at bases of upper leaves and clustered
at top of wandlike, hairy stem; leaves lance-
shaped to oval, toothed.* **Habitat:** *moist woods,
thickets, shady roadsides.* **In bloom:** *June–Sept.*

Bellflowers *Campanula*

In some plants, cross-pollination occurs because the pollen-producing
stamens and seed-producing pistil develop in different flowers; sometimes they are even borne on different plants. In others, the two organs are
in separate parts of the same flower. In the bellflowers, however, each
blossom has two distinct stages of development. First the stamens produce pollen, and the stigmas at the tip of the pistil remain closed. The
pollen falls and collects inside the flower, to be picked up on the bodies of
bees and carried to older blossoms, where the stigmas have opened. As a
last resort, if the pistil remains unfertilized, its tip curls around to pick up
a little loose pollen from inside its own flower.

441

Horned Downingia
Downingia bicornuta

Size: *3-10 in. tall; flower ¼-½ in. wide.*
What to look for: *flowers blue, with pale centers and 2 yellow horns on lower lip; leaves small, straplike.*
Habitat: *muddy places, ditches, moist open woods.*
In bloom: *Apr.-July.*

Calico Flower
Downingia elegans

Size: *4-16 in. tall; flower ¼-½ in. wide.*
What to look for: *flowers blue, with white spot and 2 yellow ridges on lower lip, long stamen column protruding from center; leaves straplike.*
Habitat: *wet ditches, woods; muddy places.*
In bloom: *June-Sept.*

Downingias *Downingia*

At first glance, these low-growing plants of the western states might be taken for violets, blanketing muddy wetlands with their blue to purple blossoms. A closer look, however, shows them to be members of the lobelia family. The flowers have two lobed lips, rather than the violets' five separate petals, and the stamens are fused into a central column.

Cardinal Flower
Lobelia cardinalis

Size: *1-5 ft. tall; flower 1½-1¾ in. long.*
What to look for: *flowers bright red, tubular, with red stamen tube projecting between lobes of upper lip, borne in spike at top of erect stem; leaves lance-shaped, toothed.*
Habitat: *marshes, meadows, lakeshores, streambanks, low open woods.*
In bloom: *July-Sept.*

Great Blue Lobelia
Lobelia siphilitica

Size: *1-4 ft. tall; flower ¾-1¼ in. long.*
What to look for: *flowers blue, tubular, with stamen tube above upper lip; leaves lance-shaped to oval, toothed.*
Habitat: *marshes, meadows, lakeshores, streambanks, open woods.*
In bloom: *Aug.-Sept.*

Indian Tobacco
Lobelia inflata

Size: *4-36 in. tall; flower ¼ in. long.*
What to look for: *flowers blue to white, bell-shaped, protruding from inflated green cup, borne in open wands; leaves oblong.*
Habitat: *fields, open woods, waste places.*
In bloom: *June-Oct.*

Lobelias *Lobelia*

Among this group's more than 375 species are plants contrasting sharply in size: there are treelike African giants with stems nearly 30 feet tall as well as 2- to 6-inch dwarfs, used by gardeners for edging. All bear tubular flowers that are divided into two lips, the upper one with two lobes and the lower with three, and all have five stamens united into a tube. Pollen at the end of this tube is deposited onto pollinating animals—hummingbirds in the case of the odorless red Cardinal Flower, bees or butterflies for the other two species shown on this page.

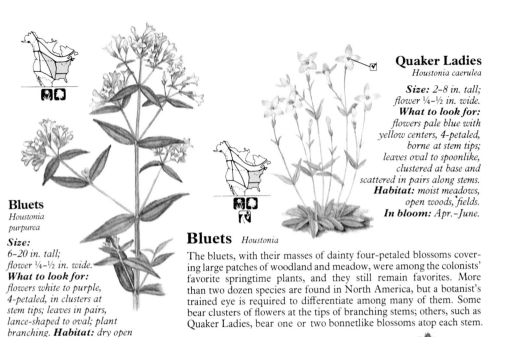

Quaker Ladies
Houstonia caerulea

Size: *2–8 in. tall;*
flower ¼–½ in. wide.
What to look for:
flowers pale blue with
yellow centers, 4-petaled,
borne at stem tips;
leaves oval to spoonlike,
clustered at base and
scattered in pairs along stems.
Habitat: *moist meadows,*
open woods, fields.
In bloom: *Apr.–June.*

Bluets
Houstonia
purpurea

Size:
6–20 in. tall;
flower ¼–½ in. wide.
What to look for:
flowers white to purple,
4-petaled, in clusters at
stem tips; leaves in pairs,
lance-shaped to oval; plant
branching. **Habitat:** *dry open*
woods, pine barrens, prairies.
In bloom: *May–July.*

Bluets *Houstonia*

The bluets, with their masses of dainty four-petaled blossoms covering large patches of woodland and meadow, were among the colonists' favorite springtime plants, and they still remain favorites. More than two dozen species are found in North America, but a botanist's trained eye is required to differentiate among many of them. Some bear clusters of flowers at the tips of branching stems; others, such as Quaker Ladies, bear one or two bonnetlike blossoms atop each stem.

Twinberries *Mitchella*

North America has one of the world's two twinberry species. (The other grows in Japan.) The paired flowers at the stem tips are joined at the base like Siamese twins; as they mature, their ovaries fuse, finally forming the edible, two-part fruits for which the group is named.

Partridgeberry
Mitchella repens

Size: *to 3 ft. long; flower ¼ in. wide.*
What to look for: *stems creeping,*
matted; flowers white to purplish, fuzzy,
4-petaled, borne in pairs; leaves in
pairs, round, evergreen with white
markings; berries red, double.
Habitat: *woods.* **In bloom:**
May–July.

Trompetilla
Bouvardia ternifolia

Size: *1–3 ft. tall;*
flower ¾–1¼ in. long.
What to look for: *flowers*
scarlet, trumpetlike, with
4 flaring petals, fuzzy,
in clusters at stem tips;
plant shrubby; leaves
oval to lance-shaped,
in clusters of 3–4.
Habitat: *deserts,*
rocky slopes, plains.
In bloom: *May–Nov.*

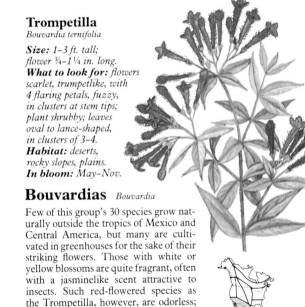

Bouvardias *Bouvardia*

Few of this group's 30 species grow naturally outside the tropics of Mexico and Central America, but many are cultivated in greenhouses for the sake of their striking flowers. Those with white or yellow blossoms are quite fragrant, often with a jasminelike scent attractive to insects. Such red-flowered species as the Trompetilla, however, are odorless; they attract hummingbird pollinators entirely by their color.

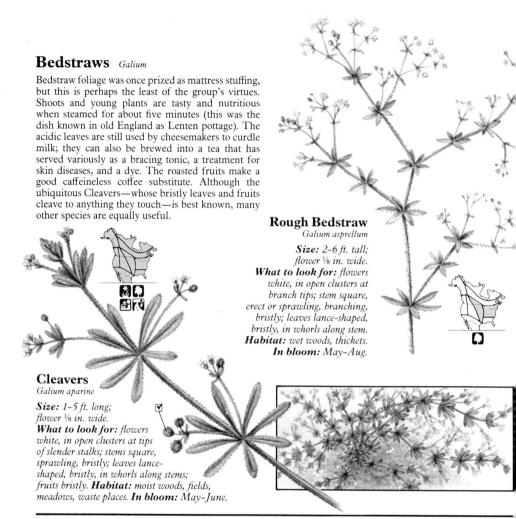

Bedstraws *Galium*

Bedstraw foliage was once prized as mattress stuffing, but this is perhaps the least of the group's virtues. Shoots and young plants are tasty and nutritious when steamed for about five minutes (this was the dish known in old England as Lenten pottage). The acidic leaves are still used by cheesemakers to curdle milk; they can also be brewed into a tea that has served variously as a bracing tonic, a treatment for skin diseases, and a dye. The roasted fruits make a good caffeineless coffee substitute. Although the ubiquitous Cleavers—whose bristly leaves and fruits cleave to anything they touch—is best known, many other species are equally useful.

Rough Bedstraw
Galium asprellum

Size: *2-6 ft. tall; flower ⅛ in. wide.*
What to look for: *flowers white, in open clusters at branch tips; stem square, erect or sprawling, branching, bristly; leaves lance-shaped, bristly, in whorls along stem.*
Habitat: *wet woods, thickets.*
In bloom: *May–Aug.*

Cleavers
Galium aparine

Size: *1-5 ft. long; flower ⅛ in. wide.*
What to look for: *flowers white, in open clusters at tips of slender stalks; stems square, sprawling, bristly; leaves lance-shaped, bristly, in whorls along stems; fruits bristly.* **Habitat:** *moist woods, fields, meadows, waste places.* **In bloom:** *May–June.*

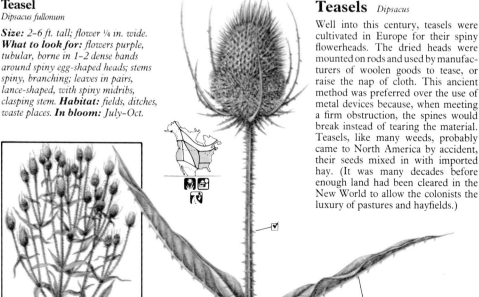

Teasel
Dipsacus fullonum

Size: *2-6 ft. tall; flower ¼ in. wide.*
What to look for: *flowers purple, tubular, borne in 1-2 dense bands around spiny egg-shaped heads; stems spiny, branching; leaves in pairs, lance-shaped, with spiny midribs, clasping stem.* **Habitat:** *fields, ditches, waste places.* **In bloom:** *July–Oct.*

Teasels *Dipsacus*

Well into this century, teasels were cultivated in Europe for their spiny flowerheads. The dried heads were mounted on rods and used by manufacturers of woolen goods to tease, or raise the nap of cloth. This ancient method was preferred over the use of metal devices because, when meeting a firm obstruction, the spines would break instead of tearing the material. Teasels, like many weeds, probably came to North America by accident, their seeds mixed in with imported hay. (It was many decades before enough land had been cleared in the New World to allow the colonists the luxury of pastures and hayfields.)

Trumpet Honeysuckle
Lonicera sempervirens

Size: *to 10 ft. high; flower 1–2¼ in. long.*
What to look for: *vine climbing or trailing; flowers trumpetlike, red with yellow throats, borne in whorled clusters; leaves oblong, in pairs, upper pairs often joined around stem.*
Habitat: *woods, thickets.*
In bloom: *Mar.–Sept.*

Japanese Honeysuckle
Lonicera japonica

Size: *to 60 ft. high; flower 1–1½ in. long.*
What to look for: *vine climbing or trailing; flowers white (turning yellow), very fragrant, tubular, with backswept petals and showy stamens; leaves in pairs, oval to oblong.* **Habitat:** *fields, forests, thickets, waste places, fencerows.*
In bloom: *Apr.–Nov.*

Honeysuckles
Lonicera

Any child who has picked a honeysuckle blossom to taste the sweet nectar from its nipplelike base can appreciate the group's evocative name. There are many native North American species, but none is so widespread or pervasive as the imported Japanese Honeysuckle. Introduced as a fragrant ornamental for screenings and trellises and used as a ground cover for road banks and other easily eroded sites, it soon outgrew its assigned roles. With the help of birds that relish the small black fruits, the seeds have spread far and wide, producing tangled vines that have overgrown and now threaten to strangle whole forests in the East.

Twinflowers *Linnaea*

It is unheard-of for a botanist to name a plant after himself, and so Carolus Linnaeus asked a friend to give his name to this smallest member of the honeysuckle family. The creator of the system of biological classification later described his favorite plant as ". . . a plant of Lappland, lowly, insignificant, flowering for but a brief space—from Linnaeus, who resembles it." In his best-known portrait, he holds a sprig of Twinflower in his hand. There is only one species, which is common in northern regions of Eurasia and North America.

Twinflower
Linnaea borealis

Size: *to 3 ft. long; flower ½ in. long.*
What to look for: *vine slender, trailing; flowers pink, bell-shaped, nodding in pairs atop slender, downy stalks; leaves in pairs, round to oval, thick.* **Habitat:** *cool moist woods, peat bogs.*
In bloom: *June–Aug.*

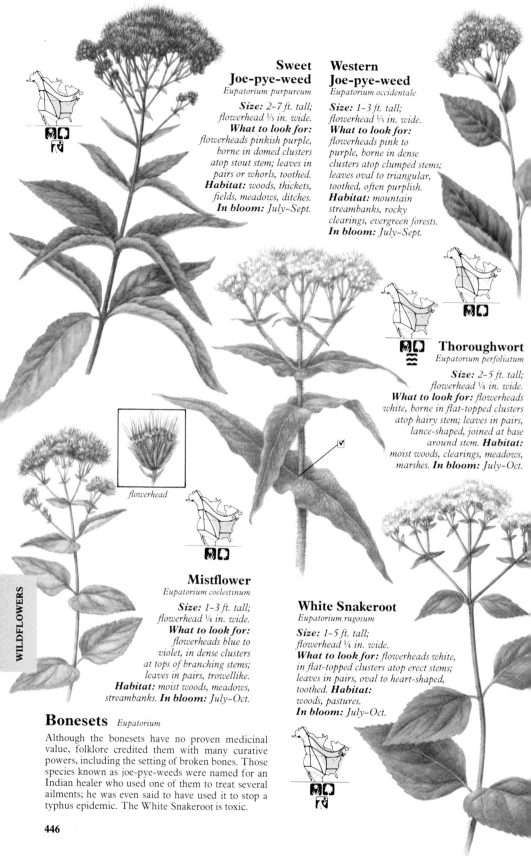

Sweet Joe-pye-weed
Eupatorium purpureum

Size: 2-7 ft. tall; flowerhead ⅓ in. wide. **What to look for:** flowerheads pinkish purple, borne in domed clusters atop stout stem; leaves in pairs or whorls, toothed. **Habitat:** woods, thickets, fields, meadows, ditches. **In bloom:** July–Sept.

Western Joe-pye-weed
Eupatorium occidentale

Size: 1-3 ft. tall; flowerhead ⅓ in. wide. **What to look for:** flowerheads pink to purple, borne in dense clusters atop clumped stems; leaves oval to triangular, toothed, often purplish. **Habitat:** mountain streambanks, rocky clearings, evergreen forests. **In bloom:** July–Sept.

Thoroughwort
Eupatorium perfoliatum

Size: 2-5 ft. tall; flowerhead ¼ in. wide. **What to look for:** flowerheads white, borne in flat-topped clusters atop hairy stem; leaves in pairs, lance-shaped, joined at base around stem. **Habitat:** moist woods, clearings, meadows, marshes. **In bloom:** July–Oct.

flowerhead

Mistflower
Eupatorium coelestinum

Size: 1-3 ft. tall; flowerhead ¼ in. wide. **What to look for:** flowerheads blue to violet, in dense clusters at tops of branching stems; leaves in pairs, trowellike. **Habitat:** moist woods, meadows, streambanks. **In bloom:** July–Oct.

White Snakeroot
Eupatorium rugosum

Size: 1-5 ft. tall; flowerhead ¼ in. wide. **What to look for:** flowerheads white, in flat-topped clusters atop erect stems; leaves in pairs, oval to heart-shaped, toothed. **Habitat:** woods, pastures. **In bloom:** July–Oct.

Bonesets *Eupatorium*

Although the bonesets have no proven medicinal value, folklore credited them with many curative powers, including the setting of broken bones. Those species known as joe-pye-weeds were named for an Indian healer who used one of them to treat several ailments; he was even said to have used it to stop a typhus epidemic. The White Snakeroot is toxic.

446

Ironweeds *Vernonia*

The huge composite family, which includes all the plants shown on these and the next 10 pages, is marked by dense flowerheads, so tightly packed that each head looks like a single blossom. The individual flowers (florets) that make up the flowerheads of an ironweed or a boneset are all tubular and contain a rich nectar. Beekeepers value ironweeds for honey; farmers named them for their tough stems that stand upright through the winter.

Golden Aster
Chrysopsis villosa

Size: *4-20 in. tall; flowerhead 1-1½ in. wide.*
What to look for: *flowerheads yellow, with central disk surrounded by oblong ray flowers, borne in loose clusters at tops of hairy, branching stems; leaves spatula- to lance-shaped, hairy.*
Habitat: *dry prairies, hillsides, chaparral, desert scrublands.*
In bloom: *June-Oct.*

Golden Asters *Chrysopsis*

The flowerheads of golden asters, like those of asters, sunflowers, and many other members of the composite family, are composed of two kinds of florets. Those in the center, called disk flowers, are like the tubular florets found on the other plants on this page. Those around the outside, called ray flowers, look more like petals than blossoms, but each is a separate floret with five petals of its own, fused into a flat surface.

Climbing Hempweeds *Mikania*

Members of this largely tropical group are among the few vines in the composite family. Three of the group's 150 species are found in North America, but only the Climbing Boneset is widespread (the others are confined to Florida). Like the bonesets, the climbing hempweeds bear flowerheads that are made up entirely of five-petaled, tubular florets.

Climbing Boneset
Mikania scandens

Size: *to 20 ft. high; flowerhead ¼ in. wide.*
What to look for: *flowerheads white to pinkish, borne in dense clusters on short stalks along twining stem; leaves in pairs, heart-shaped, long-stalked.*
Habitat: *swamps, wet thickets, hammocks.*
In bloom: *June-Oct.*

Tall Ironweed
Vernonia altissima

Size: *2-10 ft. tall; flowerhead ⅓ in. wide.*
What to look for: *flowerheads red-purple, bristly, borne in open clusters at top of tough stem; leaves lance-shaped, toothed, with downy undersides.* **Habitat:** *rich woods, bottomlands, moist meadows, clearings.*
In bloom: *Aug.-Oct.*

Rough Blazing Star
Liatris aspera

Size: *1-4 ft. tall; flowerhead ¾-1¼ in. wide.*
What to look for: *flowerheads purple, with tubular disk flowers and bristly pappus emerging from cuplike base of rounded pinkish bracts, borne in leafy spike at top of wandlike stem; leaves narrow, straplike, rough-textured.* **Habitat:** *dry fields, prairies, roadsides.*
In bloom: *Aug.–Oct.*

Gayfeather
Liatris spicata

Size: *1-5 ft. tall; flowerhead ¼ in. wide.*
What to look for: *flowerheads rose-purple, with tubular disk flowers and feathery pappus emerging from cuplike base of wedge-shaped purplish bracts, borne in dense spike at top of wandlike stem; leaves narrow, straplike.* **Habitat:** *meadows, moist prairies, edges of marshes.*
In bloom: *July–Sept.*

Blazing Stars   *Liatris*

The pioneers who crossed the tallgrass prairies of the Midwest in late summer and fall made their way through unbroken miles of purple blazing stars intermixed with golden-rods in bloom—an awesome vista that has now all but vanished. Like the goldenrods, the blazing stars constitute a most distinctive group in which the species are variable and hybridize quite freely, so that precise identification is often difficult. The flowerheads of a blazing star are thistlelike, each composed of many tubular disk flowers emerging from a base of overlapping bracts. (The shape of these bracts is a help in identifying species.) The group is unusual in that flowering begins at the top of a stem and proceeds down-ward; as the flowerheads develop into fruiting heads, they put forth a growth called the pappus, made up of long, feathery bristles atop the one-seeded fruits.

Gumweeds   *Grindelia*

The Indians boiled the roots and flower-heads of these plants to extract the gummy resin, which they used to treat such respi-ratory ailments as asthma, bronchitis, and whooping cough. Today, several gum-weed species are commercially grown for this extract, which is used in cough drops and soothing syrups. The Common Gum-weed, like most of the group, is native to the West, but its seeds were carried over much of the continent in cattle cars filled with animals that had eaten the plant. Its flowerheads usually contain both tubular disk flowers and petallike ray flowers; the heads emerge from a cuplike structure of green bracts—their pointed tips curled out and downward. Some individuals, however, like some other gumweed spe-cies, lack ray flowers altogether.

Common Gumweed
Grindelia squarrosa

Size: *6-30 in. tall; flowerhead 1-1½ in. wide.*
What to look for: *flowerheads yellow, with disk and ray flowers emerging from gummy, cuplike base of pointed green bracts; leaves oblong, toothed, covered with translucent dots.* **Habitat:** *dry fields, mountain meadows, prairies, waste places, railroad sidings.*
In bloom: *July–Sept.*

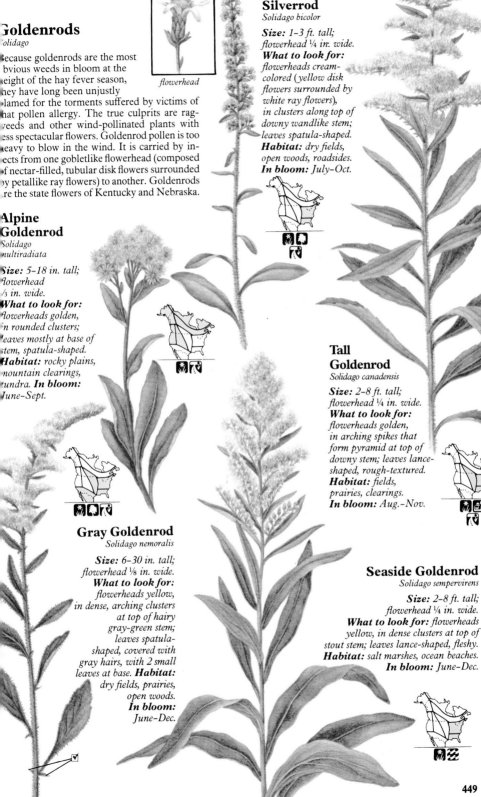

Goldenrods
Solidago

Because goldenrods are the most obvious weeds in bloom at the height of the hay fever season, they have long been unjustly blamed for the torments suffered by victims of that pollen allergy. The true culprits are ragweeds and other wind-pollinated plants with less spectacular flowers. Goldenrod pollen is too heavy to blow in the wind. It is carried by insects from one gobletlike flowerhead (composed of nectar-filled, tubular disk flowers surrounded by petallike ray flowers) to another. Goldenrods are the state flowers of Kentucky and Nebraska.

flowerhead

Silverrod
Solidago bicolor

Size: *1–3 ft. tall; flowerhead ¼ in. wide.*
What to look for: *flowerheads cream-colored (yellow disk flowers surrounded by white ray flowers), in clusters along top of downy wandlike stem; leaves spatula-shaped.*
Habitat: *dry fields, open woods, roadsides.*
In bloom: *July-Oct.*

Alpine Goldenrod
Solidago multiradiata

Size: *5–18 in. tall; flowerhead ⅓ in. wide.*
What to look for: *flowerheads golden, in rounded clusters; leaves mostly at base of stem, spatula-shaped.*
Habitat: *rocky plains, mountain clearings, tundra.* **In bloom:** *June-Sept.*

Tall Goldenrod
Solidago canadensis

Size: *2–8 ft. tall; flowerhead ¼ in. wide.*
What to look for: *flowerheads golden, in arching spikes that form pyramid at top of downy stem; leaves lance-shaped, rough-textured.*
Habitat: *fields, prairies, clearings.*
In bloom: *Aug.-Nov.*

Gray Goldenrod
Solidago nemoralis

Size: *6–30 in. tall; flowerhead ⅛ in. wide.*
What to look for: *flowerheads yellow, in dense, arching clusters at top of hairy gray-green stem; leaves spatula-shaped, covered with gray hairs, with 2 small leaves at base.* **Habitat:** *dry fields, prairies, open woods.*
In bloom: *June-Dec.*

Seaside Goldenrod
Solidago sempervirens

Size: *2–8 ft. tall; flowerhead ¼ in. wide.*
What to look for: *flowerheads yellow, in dense clusters at top of stout stem; leaves lance-shaped, fleshy.*
Habitat: *salt marshes, ocean beaches.*
In bloom: *June–Dec.*

WILDFLOWERS

449

Yellow Fleabane
Erigeron linearis

Size: *2–12 in. tall; flowerhead ½–1 in. wide.*
What to look for: *flowerheads yellow, borne singly atop upright, often branching stems; leaves grasslike, clustered at base of plant and scattered along stems.*
Habitat: *dry mountain slopes, scrublands, open woods.*
In bloom: *May–Aug.*

Fleabanes *Erigeron*

Fleabanes are often confused with asters, but they tend to be smaller and weedier and usually bloom earlier in the year. The ray flowers that fringe their flowerheads are narrower and more numerous than those of asters, and at the base of each flowerhead is a single circle of small green bracts, rather than several overlapping circles as in most asters. It was once common practice to hang fleabane in houses in order to rid them of fleas.

Daisy Fleabane
Erigeron philadelphicus

Size: *8–28 in. tall; flowerhead ½–1 in. wide.*
What to look for: *flowerheads with many white or pink ray flowers around yellow central disk, borne in loose clusters; leaves spatula-shaped, clustered at base and scattered along hairy stem.* **Habitat:** *moist meadows, woods, streambanks.*
In bloom: *Apr.–Aug.*

Marsh Fleabanes *Pluchea*

These foul-smelling marsh plants seem to have little in common with the fleabanes, beyond the facts that both groups are members of the composite family and that both have been used to drive away fleas. The flowerheads of the marsh fleabanes are composed entirely of tubular disk flowers, quite unlike the fringed fleabane blossoms. The leaves of most species emit a fetid odor when bruised, strongest and most repulsive in the Stinking Fleabane.

Stinking Fleabane
Pluchea foetida

Size: *20–36 in. tall; flowerhead ⅓ in. wide.*
What to look for: *flowerheads creamy white, borne in rounded clusters at branch tips; leaves oval, toothed, clasping downy stem.*
Habitat: *swamps, marshes, ditches, coastal savannas.*
In bloom: *July–Oct.*

Easter Daisy
Townsendi exscap

Size: *1–4 in. tall flowerhea 1–2¼ in. wide*
What to look for: *flowerhead with white to purplish ray flower around yellow, often bristly, central disk on short stems; leaves grasslike or spatula-shaped clustered at base.* **Habitat:** *dry hillside grassy plains.* **In bloom:** *Mar.–June*

Stemless Daisies *Townsendi*

Not truly stemless, these low-growing plants of th western mountains bear a profusion of such dispro portionately large, daisylike flowerheads that th stems seem to disappear beneath a cushion of bloom

White Heath Aster
Aster ericoides

Size: *1–3 ft. tall; flowerhead ½ in. wide.*
What to look for: *plant bushy; flowerheads profuse, with white ray flowers around small yellow central disk; leaves narrow, straplike.* **Habitat:** *dry prairies, fields, roadsides.*
In bloom: *July–Dec.*

Blue Wood Aster
Aster cordifolius

Size: *1–4 ft. tall; flowerhead ½–1 in. wide.*
What to look for: *flowerheads with short blue or violet ray flowers around yellow central stems; leaves heart-shaped, toothed, hairy.* **Habitat:** *open woods, thickets, clearings.* **In bloom:** *Aug.–Oct.*

Stiff Aster
Aster linariifolius

Size: *4–24 in. tall; flowerhead ¾–1¼ in. wide.*
What to look for: *flowerheads with blue to pink ray flowers around yellow central disk, borne at tips of wiry stems; leaves needlelike.* **Habitat:** *dry prairies, meadows, open woods.* **In bloom:** *July–Oct.*

Leafy Aster
Aster foliaceus

Size: *4–36 in. tall; flowerhead 1–2 in. wide.*
What to look for: *flowerheads with narrow blue to rose-purple ray flowers around yellow central disk, borne at top of leafy stem; leaves oval to lance-shaped, upper leaves clasping stem.* **Habitat:** *mountain ridges, meadows, open slopes; moist woods.* **In bloom:** *July–Sept.*

New England Aster
Aster novae-angliae

Size: *2–7 ft. tall; flowerhead 1–2 in. wide.*
What to look for: *flowerheads with pink to purple ray flowers around yellow central disk, clustered at top of hairy, sticky stems; leaves lance-shaped, clasping stem.* **Habitat:** *moist fields, meadows, roadsides.* **In bloom:** *July–Oct.*

Asters *Aster*

The starburst flowerheads of wild asters are among the familiar pleasures of late summer and autumn. (The name aster is from the Greek for "star," and the plants were once commonly known in England as starworts.) Some of the group's nearly 600 species are popular garden flowers. Others, such as the coarse White Heath Aster, are troublesome weeds; because masses of its tough stems have been known to break mowing blades, it has also been called Steelweed.

Elecampane
Inula helenium

Size: *2-6 ft. tall;*
flowerhead 2-4 in. wide.
What to look for:
flowerheads yellow, with
long scraggly ray flowers
around darker central disk;
leaves clasping stem,
large, toothed, rough-
textured above, woolly
below. **Habitat:** *fields,*
waste places, roadsides.
In bloom: *May–Sept.*

Inulas *Inula*

About 2,400 years ago Hippocrates prescribed the root of Elecampane for lung disorders. It continued to be used medicinally through the centuries, known sometimes as Elfwort (when the ailment was called "elf sickness") and sometimes as Horseheal (when the patients were draft animals). It is the only member of this Eurasian group found in the New World, to which it was brought by the colonists.

Cocklebur
Xanthium strumarium

Size: *1-6 ft. tall; flowerhead minute.*
What to look for: *plant bushy; leaves oval*
to wedge-shaped, toothed; flowerheads
greenish, borne in short-lived spikes
(male) and clusters at leaf bases (female);
fruits egg-shaped, prickly. **Habitat:** *fields,*
waste places. **In bloom:** *Aug.–Oct.*

Cockleburs *Xanthium*

The two seeds in a cocklebur's spiny fruit are covered by airtight coats. Because the seeds need oxygen to germinate, they remain dormant until these coats begin to wear away. One seed invariably requires much more oxygen than the other, and so remains dormant a year longer. Thus each bur produces two generations of offspring—one reason these weeds are notoriously difficult to eradicate.

Pearly Everlasting
Anaphalis
margaritacea

Size: *1-3 ft. tall;*
flowerhead ¼-½ in. wide.
What to look for:
flowerheads of yellowish
disk flowers surrounded
by pearly white bracts,
borne in flat-topped
clusters atop woolly
stem; leaves straplike
to lance-shaped,
woolly below.
Habitat: *dry plains, fields,*
mountain slopes, roadsides.
In bloom: *July–Sept.*

Everlastings *Anaphalis*

Several other members of the composite family are also known as everlastings, including the cudweeds and the pussytoes. All bear long-lasting flowerheads that are popular in dried arrangements. Of this group's nearly three dozen species, only the Pearly Everlasting is native to North America. The flowerheads are composed entirely of disk flowers; the pearly white fringe around the outside is made up of bracts rather than the more familiar ray flowers.

452

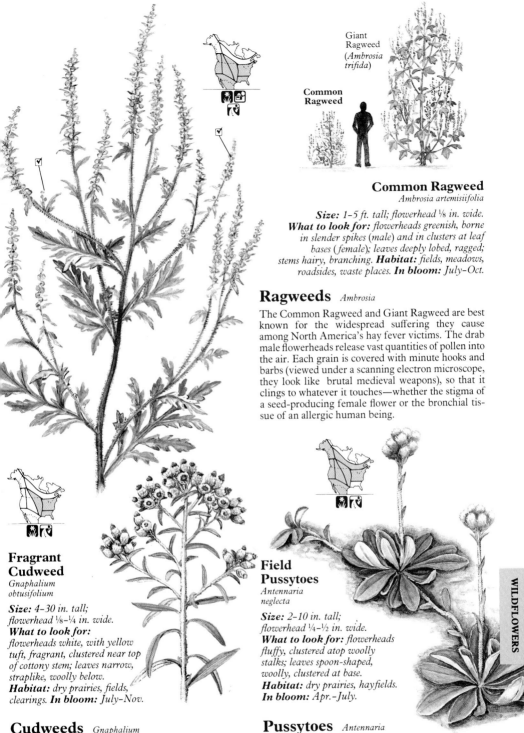

Common Ragweed
Ambrosia artemisiifolia

Size: *1-5 ft. tall; flowerhead ⅛ in. wide.*
What to look for: *flowerheads greenish, borne in slender spikes (male) and in clusters at leaf bases (female); leaves deeply lobed, ragged; stems hairy, branching.* **Habitat:** *fields, meadows, roadsides, waste places.* **In bloom:** *July-Oct.*

Ragweeds *Ambrosia*

The Common Ragweed and Giant Ragweed are best known for the widespread suffering they cause among North America's hay fever victims. The drab male flowerheads release vast quantities of pollen into the air. Each grain is covered with minute hooks and barbs (viewed under a scanning electron microscope, they look like brutal medieval weapons), so that it clings to whatever it touches—whether the stigma of a seed-producing female flower or the bronchial tissue of an allergic human being.

Fragrant Cudweed
Gnaphalium obtusifolium

Size: *4-30 in. tall; flowerhead ⅛-¼ in. wide.*
What to look for: *flowerheads white, with yellow tuft, fragrant, clustered near top of cottony stem; leaves narrow, straplike, woolly below.* **Habitat:** *dry prairies, fields, clearings.* **In bloom:** *July-Nov.*

Field Pussytoes
Antennaria neglecta

Size: *2-10 in. tall; flowerhead ¼-½ in. wide.*
What to look for: *flowerheads fluffy, clustered atop woolly stalks; leaves spoon-shaped, woolly, clustered at base.* **Habitat:** *dry prairies, hayfields.* **In bloom:** *Apr.-July.*

Cudweeds *Gnaphalium*

When a cow loses its cud, the cause is usually a stomach inflammation. Though old-time dairy farmers did not know that the cudweeds, like the closely related everlastings and pussytoes, contain a soothing antibiotic, they were well aware that feeding cudweed to afflicted cattle helped to restore digestion.

Pussytoes *Antennaria*

The tubular disk flowers that make up the pussytoes' fluffy flowerheads can produce seed with or without fertilization (the latter case is called apomixis). Thus, individual variations that arise from cross-pollination are later preserved in clonelike offspring. The result is a confusing array of species and varieties.

WILDFLOWERS

453

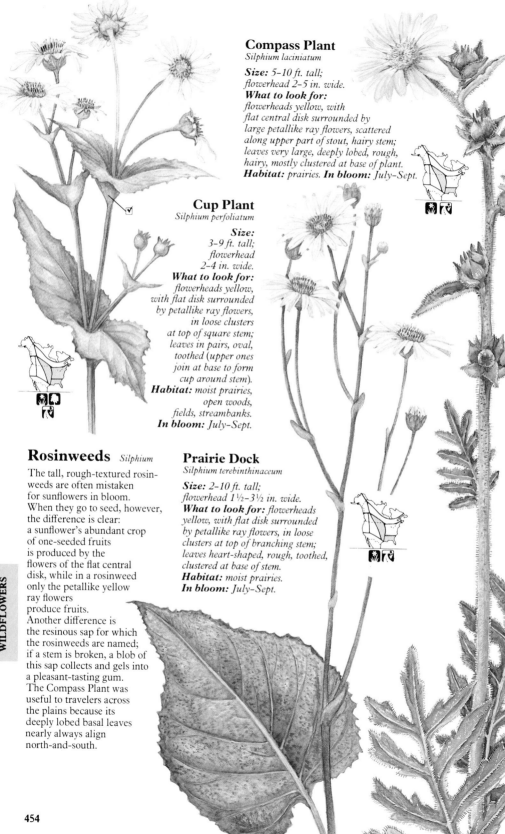

Compass Plant
Silphium laciniatum

Size: *5–10 ft. tall; flowerhead 2–5 in. wide.*
What to look for: *flowerheads yellow, with flat central disk surrounded by large petallike ray flowers, scattered along upper part of stout, hairy stem; leaves very large, deeply lobed, rough, hairy, mostly clustered at base of plant.*
Habitat: *prairies.* **In bloom:** *July–Sept.*

Cup Plant
Silphium perfoliatum

Size: *3–9 ft. tall; flowerhead 2–4 in. wide.*
What to look for: *flowerheads yellow, with flat disk surrounded by petallike ray flowers, in loose clusters at top of square stem; leaves in pairs, oval, toothed (upper ones join at base to form cup around stem).*
Habitat: *moist prairies, open woods, fields, streambanks.*
In bloom: *July–Sept.*

Rosinweeds *Silphium*

The tall, rough-textured rosinweeds are often mistaken for sunflowers in bloom. When they go to seed, however, the difference is clear: a sunflower's abundant crop of one-seeded fruits is produced by the flowers of the flat central disk, while in a rosinweed only the petallike yellow ray flowers produce fruits. Another difference is the resinous sap for which the rosinweeds are named; if a stem is broken, a blob of this sap collects and gels into a pleasant-tasting gum. The Compass Plant was useful to travelers across the plains because its deeply lobed basal leaves nearly always align north-and-south.

Prairie Dock
Silphium terebinthinaceum

Size: *2–10 ft. tall; flowerhead 1½–3½ in. wide.*
What to look for: *flowerheads yellow, with flat disk surrounded by petallike ray flowers, in loose clusters at top of branching stem; leaves heart-shaped, rough, toothed, clustered at base of stem.*
Habitat: *moist prairies.*
In bloom: *July–Sept.*

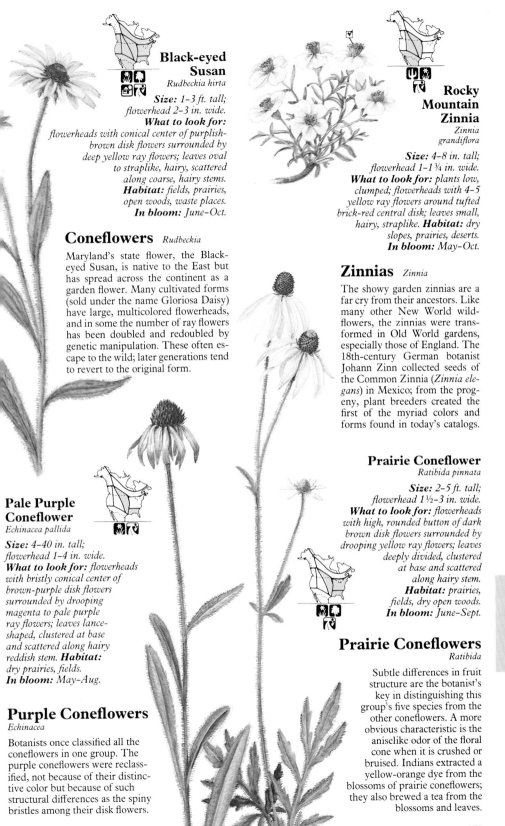

Black-eyed Susan
Rudbeckia hirta

Size: *1–3 ft. tall; flowerhead 2–3 in. wide.*
What to look for: *flowerheads with conical center of purplish-brown disk flowers surrounded by deep yellow ray flowers; leaves oval to straplike, hairy, scattered along coarse, hairy stems.*
Habitat: *fields, prairies, open woods, waste places.*
In bloom: *June–Oct.*

Coneflowers *Rudbeckia*

Maryland's state flower, the Black-eyed Susan, is native to the East but has spread across the continent as a garden flower. Many cultivated forms (sold under the name Gloriosa Daisy) have large, multicolored flowerheads, and in some the number of ray flowers has been doubled and redoubled by genetic manipulation. These often escape to the wild; later generations tend to revert to the original form.

Pale Purple Coneflower
Echinacea pallida

Size: *4–40 in. tall; flowerhead 1–4 in. wide.*
What to look for: *flowerheads with bristly conical center of brown-purple disk flowers surrounded by drooping magenta to pale purple ray flowers; leaves lance-shaped, clustered at base and scattered along hairy reddish stem.* **Habitat:** *dry prairies, fields.*
In bloom: *May–Aug.*

Purple Coneflowers
Echinacea

Botanists once classified all the coneflowers in one group. The purple coneflowers were reclassified, not because of their distinctive color but because of such structural differences as the spiny bristles among their disk flowers.

Rocky Mountain Zinnia
Zinnia grandiflora

Size: *4–8 in. tall; flowerhead 1–1¾ in. wide.*
What to look for: *plants low, clumped; flowerheads with 4–5 yellow ray flowers around tufted brick-red central disk; leaves small, hairy, straplike.* **Habitat:** *dry slopes, prairies, deserts.*
In bloom: *May–Oct.*

Zinnias *Zinnia*

The showy garden zinnias are a far cry from their ancestors. Like many other New World wildflowers, the zinnias were transformed in Old World gardens, especially those of England. The 18th-century German botanist Johann Zinn collected seeds of the Common Zinnia (*Zinnia elegans*) in Mexico; from the progeny, plant breeders created the first of the myriad colors and forms found in today's catalogs.

Prairie Coneflower
Ratibida pinnata

Size: *2–5 ft. tall; flowerhead 1½–3 in. wide.*
What to look for: *flowerheads with high, rounded button of dark brown disk flowers surrounded by drooping yellow ray flowers; leaves deeply divided, clustered at base and scattered along hairy stem.*
Habitat: *prairies, fields, dry open woods.*
In bloom: *June–Sept.*

Prairie Coneflowers
Ratibida

Subtle differences in fruit structure are the botanist's key in distinguishing this group's five species from the other coneflowers. A more obvious characteristic is the aniselike odor of the floral cone when it is crushed or bruised. Indians extracted a yellow-orange dye from the blossoms of prairie coneflowers; they also brewed a tea from the blossoms and leaves.

Common Sunflower
Helianthus annuus

Size: *2–12 ft. tall; flowerhead 3–10 in. wide.*
What to look for: *flowerheads with petallike yellow ray flowers around flat brownish central disk, nodding sunward atop stout, hairy stem; leaves oval to heart-shaped, toothed, rough.*
Habitat: *fields, prairies, waste places.*
In bloom: *June–Oct.*

Jerusalem Artichoke
Helianthus tuberosus

Size: *3–10 ft. tall; flowerhead 2–4 in. wide.*
What to look for: *flowerheads yellow, with long ray flowers around flat central disk, loosely clustered at top of hairy, branching stem; leaves in pairs, oval to lance-shaped, toothed.*
Habitat: *moist fields, open woods, thickets, waste places, bottomlands.*
In bloom: *Aug.–Oct.*

Sunflowers
Helianthus

The reason sunflowers face the sun is, paradoxically, that light inhibits growth in the stem; hence the shaded side of the stem grows faster, tipping the flowerhead toward the sun. The Common Sunflower, grown worldwide for its oil-rich seeds, is both the state flower of Kansas and the floral emblem of the Soviet Union. The Jerusalem Artichoke, whose name is a corruption of the Italian *girasole* ("turns to the sun"), is widely cultivated for its edible tubers—the so-called artichokes.

Bur Marigold
Bidens cernua

Size: *6–36 in. tall; flowerhead ¾–2 in. wide.*
What to look for: *flowerheads yellow, with broad ray flowers around slightly darker, buttonlike central disk, profuse, nodding; leaves in pairs, lance-shaped to oblong, toothed.*
Habitat: *wet meadows, marshes, lakeshores, streambanks.*
In bloom: *Aug.–Oct.*

fruit

Sticktights
Bidens

Beggar's ticks, stickseeds, devil's pitchforks, harvest lice, cow lice, Spanish needles— most of the names by which these widespread weeds are none-too-fondly known refer to their small, one-seeded fruits. These cling to fur, feathers, and clothing by means of barbed prongs. The flowerheads of most species have only tubular disk flowers; those with yellow ray flowers are often called bur marigolds.

WILDFLOWERS

Golden Tickseed
Coreopsis tinctoria

Size: *1–4 ft. tall;
flowerhead 1–1¾ in. wide.*
What to look for:
*flowerheads with notched,
two-tone ray flowers
around reddish central disk,
clustered at top of
branching stem; leaves
deeply divided.*
Habitat: *dry fields,
prairies, scrublands.*
In bloom: *June–Aug.*

Tickseed
Coreopsis lanceolata

Size: *8–30 in. tall;
flowerhead 1½–3 in. wide.*
What to look for:
*flowerheads yellow, with
notched ray flowers
around buttonlike
central disk, borne
singly atop long stalks;
leaves lance-shaped,
mostly clustered at
base of plant.*
Habitat: *dry fields, prairies.*
In bloom: *May–Aug.*

Navajo Tea
*Thelesperma
subnudum*

Size: *4–15 in. tall;
flowerhead
1½–2½ in. wide.*
What to look for:
*flowerheads with
yellow ray flowers
around brownish
central disk;
leaves divided into threadlike
leaflets, mostly clustered at
base of plant.* **Habitat:** *dry
plains, open hillsides, deserts.*
In bloom: *May–July.*

Greenthreads
Thelesperma

The finely divided leaves for
which this group is named were
brewed into tea by various Indian peoples of the Southwest.

Tickseeds   *Coreopsis*

One must look carefully at the petallike ray flowers of most members of the
composite family in order to realize that each is actually a separate blossom
with five fused petals. The notched and grooved ray flowers of a tickseed,
however, illustrate this at a glance. The group is named for the appearance
of its hard, flat, one-seeded fruits.

Mule Ears
*Wyethia
arizonica*

Size: *1–2 ft. tall;
flowerhead
1½–2½ in. wide.*
What to look for:
*flowerheads yellow,
with long ray flowers
around flat central
disk; leaves large,
hairy, mostly clustered
at base of plant.*
Habitat: *mountain
pinelands, clearings,
streambanks, thickets.*
In bloom: *May–Aug.*

Wingstem
Verbesina alterniflora

Size: *2–6 ft. tall;
flowerhead 1–2 in. wide.*
What to look for:
*flowerheads yellow,
with rounded central disk
surrounded by a few drooping
ray flowers; leaves lance-shaped,
the edges joining ridges along stem.*
Habitat: *moist woods,
thickets, clearings.*
In bloom:
Aug.–Oct.

Mule Ears   *Wyethia*

These are long-lived plants of mountain slopes and
mesas, with heavy taproots that put forth aromatic
leaves each spring. They are named for these large,
hairy leaves, although a few species growing in exceptionally dry places produce narrow, water-conserving
foliage instead.

Wingstems
Verbesina

This group's single species is also
known as the Golden Ironweed because of its tough stem. The edges of
the leaves seem to run down into narrow ridges, or wings, along the stem.

WILDFLOWERS

457

Tidy Tips
Layia
chrysanthemoides

Size: *4–20 in. tall;*
flowerhead
1–1¾ in. wide.
What to look for:
flowerheads mostly yellow,
with notched, white-tipped
ray flowers around
brown-specked central disk;
leaves deeply lobed.
Habitat: *oak woods, meadows*
(California's Coast Ranges).
In bloom: *Mar.–June.*

Layias *Layia*

"Tidy tips" is a name shared by many of this group's 15 species that have yellow ray flowers neatly tipped with white. Several species have solid yellow flowerheads, and a few, such as the White Daisy (*Layia glandulosa*) of the Pacific Coast, have pure white ray flowers.

Alpine Gold
Hulsea
algida

Size:
5–18 in. tall;
flowerhead
1½–2 in. wide.
What to look for:
flowerheads yellow,
with bristly central disk
fringed by many narrow ray
flowers; leaves oblong
to spatula-shaped,
densely hairy,
clustered at base
of plant. **Habitat:**
high mountain slopes.
In bloom:
July–Aug.

Hulseas
Hulsea

Like many other western mountain plants, the hulseas bear most of their succulent, aromatic leaves clustered close to the ground. This huddled posture, along with the woolly gray fuzz that often covers the foliage, helps the plants survive the drying winds that sweep their rigorous habitat.

Mountain Sunflower
Hymenoxys acaulis

Size: *4–12 in. tall;*
flowerhead 1–2 in. wide.
What to look for: *flowerheads*
yellow, with domelike central disk
surrounded by notched ray flowers;
leaves straplike, silky, clustered at base of plant.
Habitat: *dry hillsides, plains, open pine woods.*
In bloom: *Apr.–July.*

Mountain Sunflowers *Hymenoxys*

Western stockmen watch for these toxic plants on their rangeland, for they are a clear sign of overgrazing. Sheepherders dread their appearance on another count as well: at least two species are especially poisonous to their woolly charges.

Desert Marigold
Baileya pleniradiata

Size: *6–25 in. tall;*
flowerhead 1–1½ in. wide.
What to look for:
flowerheads golden to
pale yellow, with many
ray flowers that dry and
droop with age; leaves
narrow, deeply lobed,
covered with woolly hair.
Habitat: *deserts, dry*
scrublands. **In bloom:**
Mar.–June; Sept.–Nov.

Desert Marigolds
Baileya

When water is available, the stems and leaves of these desert dwellers grow firm and juicy; as the water disappears during dry spells, the plants become thin and spindly. The dense woolly coat that shades their leaves helps retain moisture, and each soft hair collects a drop of morning dew. The ray flowers become dry and papery as they age, so that water loss from them is kept to a minimum.

Goldfields
Lasthenia chrysostoma

Size: *1–16 in. tall;*
flowerhead ¾–1½ in. wide.
What to look for:
flowerheads yellow,
with domelike central
disk surrounded by ray
flowers; leaves narrow,
in pairs along hairy stems.
Habitat: *meadows,*
open woods, plains, deserts.
In bloom: *Mar.–May.*

Lasthenias   *Lasthenia*

At the height of its blooming period,
Goldfields blankets thousands of acres
—from Oregon's mountain woodlands
to the dry islands of Baja California—
with rich golden yellow.

growth form

Dusty Maiden
Chaenactis douglasii

Size: *4–18 in. tall;*
flowerhead ¾–1 in. wide.
What to look for: *flowerheads white, pinkish,*
or lavender, tufted, with many tubular disk
flowers, numerous at tips of branching stem;
leaves lacily divided. **Habitat:** *dry mountain*
slopes, deserts, open woods, chaparral.
In bloom: *June–Aug.*

Pincushions   *Chaenactis*

The pincushions are also called false
yarrows. Unlike true yarrows, they have
only tubular disk flowers in their "cushions," although the outer flowers are often
large enough to look somewhat like the
yarrows' ray flowers.

Bitterweed
Helenium amarum

Size: *6–30 in. tall;*
flowerhead 1 in. wide.
What to look for: *stem*
branching, shrubby, covered with
narrow leaves; flowerheads yellow,
with domelike central disk surrounded
by ragged ray flowers. **Habitat:** *dry*
fields, prairies. **In bloom:** *July–Oct.*

Sneezeweeds   *Helenium*

Indians used the powdered flowerheads of sneezeweeds as snuff to
provoke violent sneezing and rid the
body of evil spirits. Several species
are toxic to sheep; cattle that eat
Bitterweed give bitter milk.

Firewheel
Gaillardia pulchella

Size: *4–25 in. tall;*
flowerhead 1–3 in. wide.
What to look for:
flowerheads showy, with
reddish disk surrounded
by ray flowers of red,
orange, and yellow; leaves
usually toothed or lobed, hairy.
Habitat: *dry plains,*
sandy fields, prairies.
In bloom: *May–Aug.*

Blanketflowers
Gaillardia

One reason for the blanketflowers'
popularity among gardeners is that
their spectacular flowerheads—like
those of most members of the composite family—last for a long while.
The tubular disk flowers open one at
a time, beginning at the outer edge of
the disk and proceeding in a spiral,
and the petallike ray flowers remain
showy throughout the process.

Oxeye Daisy
Leucanthemum vulgare

Size: *8–30 in. tall;*
flowerhead 1¼–2½ in. wide.
What to look for: *flowerheads with*
"dented" yellow disk surrounded by
white petallike ray flowers;
leaves lobed, toothed.
Habitat: *prairies, fields.*
In bloom: *May–Oct.*

Chrysanthemums *Leucanthemum*

Garden mums are hybrids of several Oriental species belonging to this group. The Oxeye Daisy, which is actually a chrysanthemum, is one of many similar-looking plants called daisies. Chaucer's "dayeseye, or . . . eye of day" and Shakespeare's "daisies pied" refer to the English Daisy (*Bellis perennis*).

Brass Buttons
Cotula coronopifolia

Size:
6–16 in. long;
flowerhead
¼–½ in. wide.
What to look for:
stems sprawling; flowerheads
yellow, buttonlike, borne singly
on upright stalks; leaves
straplike to lance-shaped, lobed.
Habitat: *tidal flats, wet meadows,*
ditches. **In bloom:** *Mar.–Dec.*

Brass Buttons *Cotula*

The little yellow flowerheads for which these plants are named seem to contain only tubular disk flowers, but a close look at the edges reveals a fringe of tiny ray flowers.

Common Tansy
Tanacetum vulgare

Size: *1–5 ft. tall;*
flowerhead ¼–½ in. wide.
What to look for:
flowerheads yellow,
buttonlike, borne in dense,
flat-topped clusters at
top of upright stem;
leaves divided, toothed.
Habitat: *fields, waste places,*
roadsides. **In bloom:** *July–Oct.*

Pineapple Weed
Matricaria matricarioides

Size: *4–16 in. tall;*
flowerhead ¼ in. wide.
What to look for:
flowerheads yellow,
spherical, borne at
tips of leafy branches;
leaves finely divided,
pineapple-scented.
Habitat: *fields,*
waste places, roadsides,
railroad embankments.
In bloom: *May–Sept.*

Tansies *Tanacetum*

Tansy leaves and flowerheads have been used medicinally since ancient times, but always with great care, for an overdose can be fatal. The leaves contain an effective insect repellent; it was once common practice to rub raw meat with them in order to ward off flies. They were also used in burial rites.

Wild Chamomiles *Matricaria*

The fernlike leaves of several species in this group give off the odor of fresh pineapple when bruised. Most members of the group bear daisylike flowerheads, with the yellow center disk surrounded by white ray flowers. The Pineapple Weed's spherical flowerheads, however, have only tubular disk flowers.

WILDFLOWERS

460

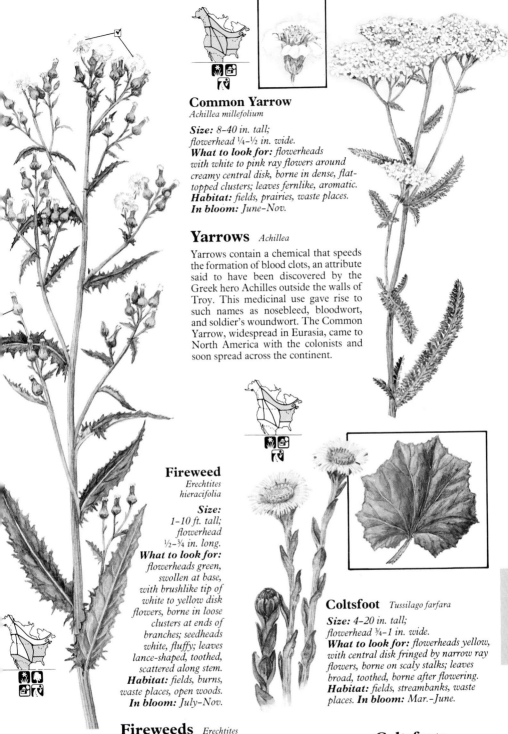

Common Yarrow
Achillea millefolium

Size: *8–40 in. tall;*
flowerhead ¼–½ in. wide.
What to look for: *flowerheads*
with white to pink ray flowers around
creamy central disk, borne in dense, flat-
topped clusters; leaves fernlike, aromatic.
Habitat: *fields, prairies, waste places.*
In bloom: *June–Nov.*

Yarrows   *Achillea*

Yarrows contain a chemical that speeds the formation of blood clots, an attribute said to have been discovered by the Greek hero Achilles outside the walls of Troy. This medicinal use gave rise to such names as nosebleed, bloodwort, and soldier's woundwort. The Common Yarrow, widespread in Eurasia, came to North America with the colonists and soon spread across the continent.

Fireweed
Erechtites
hieracifolia

Size:
1–10 ft. tall;
flowerhead
½–¾ in. long.
What to look for:
flowerheads green,
swollen at base,
with brushlike tip of
white to yellow disk
flowers, borne in loose
clusters at ends of
branches; seedheads
white, fluffy; leaves
lance-shaped, toothed,
scattered along stem.
Habitat: *fields, burns,*
waste places, open woods.
In bloom: *July–Nov.*

Coltsfoot   *Tussilago farfara*

Size: *4–20 in. tall;*
flowerhead ¾–1 in. wide.
What to look for: *flowerheads yellow,*
with central disk fringed by narrow ray
flowers, borne on scaly stalks; leaves
broad, toothed, borne after flowering.
Habitat: *fields, streambanks, waste*
places. **In bloom:** *Mar.–June.*

Fireweeds   *Erechtites*

These tall, weedy plants, their light seeds carried far in parachutelike fruits, are often among the first plants to become established in the open, nutrient-rich soil left by a fire. Other plants known as fireweeds for the same reason include species of willow herbs, plantains, ragworts, and thornapples.

Coltsfoots   *Tussilago*

The distinctive leaves for which the Coltsfoot is named appear in summer after the flowers have died back. The single species has been so highly regarded as a medicinal plant that the outline of its leaf was used as a symbol for apothecary shops in Europe.

Spotted Knapweed
Centaurea maculosa

Size: *1-4 ft. tall;*
flowerhead ¾-1 in. wide.
What to look for:
*flowerheads rose-pink, with long, tubular
disk flowers spreading from urn-shaped base;
leaves divided into narrow sections, scattered
along wiry, branching stem.* **Habitat:** *fields,
dry pastures, roadsides.* **In bloom:** *June-Oct.*

Knapweeds   *Centaurea*

The knapweeds are named for their thistlelike
flowerheads, in which tubular disk flowers
emerge from a knobby cup of bracts. (*Knap* is
from the Old English for "knob.") Germany's
national flower, the Cornflower, or Bachelor's
Button (*Centaurea cyanus*), is the group's most
popular garden plant.

Nodding Thistle
Carduus nutans

Size: *2-7 ft. tall;*
*flowerhead
1½-2½ in. wide.*
What to look for:
*flowerheads rose-purple,
with disk flowers and
soft hairs emerging from
a purplish base of spiny
bracts, nodding at ends
of branches; leaves
divided into spine-tipped
lobes, scattered along
spiny, branching stem.*
Habitat: *fields,
pastures, waste places.*
In bloom: *June-Oct.*

Plumeless Thistles
Carduus

In the flowerheads of this group,
each flower is surrounded by
long pappus hairs that are simple
and unbranched. The plants are
therefore called plumeless, setting them apart from other thistles, whose ornate blossoms
have finely divided
pappus hairs.

Golden Ragwort
Senecio aureus

Size: *1-3 ft. tall; flowerhead ½-¾ in. wide.*
What to look for: *flowerheads golden yellow,
loosely clustered atop upright stem; leaves
lance-shaped and lobed (along stem) or heart-shaped
and long-stalked (at base of plant), often reddish below.*
Habitat: *moist woods, meadows, swamps.*
In bloom: *Apr.-July.*

Groundsels   *Senecio*

Groundsels have a long history of medicinal use.
Golden Ragwort, for example, is also known as
Squaw Weed because it was used to ease the pain of
childbirth. Among the group's nearly 3,000 species is
the popular Florist's Cineraria (*Senecio hybridus*).

Burdocks *Arctium*

Nearly every part of a burdock is edible. The Great Burdock (*Arctium lappa*) is cultivated in parts of Europe and Asia for its large tap-root. Although the Common Burdock's root is smaller, it is no less tasty when peeled and boiled. The young leaves make a good potherb. The pithy cores of the flowering stem and of the large basal leaf-stalks may be eaten raw or cooked like asparagus after the bitter green rind has been stripped away.

Common Burdock
Arctium minus

Size: *1–5 ft. tall; flowerhead ½–1 in. wide.*
What to look for: *flowerheads purple to whitish, with disk flowers emerging from end of spiny ball of bracts, borne in clusters along upper part of stem; leaves heart-shaped, large, mostly clustered at base of plant.*
Habitat: *fields, pastures, waste places.*
In bloom: *July–Oct.*

growth form

Bull Thistle
Cirsium vulgare

Size: *2–6 ft. tall; flowerhead 1½–3 in. wide.*
What to look for: *flowerheads rose-purple, with slender disk flowers and feathery pappus hairs emerging from cuplike base of spiny green bracts; leaves spiny, divided into spine-tipped lobes, scattered along stout, spiny stem.* **Habitat:** *fields, pastures, waste places, meadows.*
In bloom: *June–Oct.*

Canada Thistle
Cirsium arvense

Size: *1–4 ft. tall; flowerhead ½–1 in. wide.*
What to look for: *flowerheads pink to purple, with slender disk flowers and feathery pappus hairs emerging from cuplike base of prickly green bracts; leaves spiny, divided into spine-tipped lobes, scattered along slender, branching stem.* **Habitat:** *fields, pastures, waste places.*
In bloom: *June–Aug.*

Thistles *Cirsium*

It is against the law in 37 states to allow the Canada Thistle to grow on one's land. Despite its outlaw status, the spiny fugitive flourishes, spreading by means of tufted airborne fruits and fast-creeping roots. A related thistle was the emblem of the Scottish Stuart clan, and when the Stuarts became the royal house of Scotland, their thistle became the national flower.

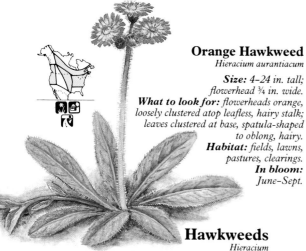

Orange Hawkweed
Hieracium aurantiacum

Size: *4–24 in. tall;*
flowerhead ¾ in. wide.
What to look for: *flowerheads orange,*
loosely clustered atop leafless, hairy stalk;
leaves clustered at base, spatula-shaped
to oblong, hairy.
Habitat: *fields, lawns,*
pastures, clearings.
In bloom:
June–Sept.

Rattlesnake Weed
Hieracium venosum

Size: *8–30 in. tall;*
flowerhead ½–1 in. wide.
What to look for:
flowerheads yellow,
loosely clustered at
top of slender stalk;
leaves clustered at base,
spatula-shaped,
with purple veins.
Habitat: *dry open*
woods, clearings.
In bloom: *May–Oct.*

Hawkweeds
Hieracium

Hawkweeds, like the other members of the composite family shown on this and the next three pages, bear flowerheads with no tubular disk flowers, but only flat ray flowers like the "petals" of a daisy. Although insects are drawn to their nectar, some of these plants—including hawkweeds and dandelions—produce seed without pollination. Hence, their genes are unmixed, and each offspring is a clonelike duplicate of the seed-producing parent.

seedhead

Dandelion
Taraxacum officinale

Size: *1–20 in. tall;*
flowerhead ¾–2 in. wide.
What to look for: *flowerheads yellow, atop hollow*
stalks; seedheads white, fluffy; leaves clustered
at base, deeply toothed. **Habitat:** *fields, lawns,*
woods, swamps, prairies. **In bloom:** *all year.*

Dandelions *Taraxacum*

No weed is more successful than the dandelion. Its leaves exude an ethylene gas that discourages competition. A small fragment of its gluttonous taproot will grow into a new plant. Its parachute-borne fruits can stay aloft almost indefinitely as long as the relative humidity is less than 70 percent—which means that when the humidity rises (often just before a life-giving rain), dandelion seeds come to earth.

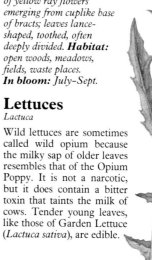

Wild Lettuce
Lactuca canadensis

Size: *1–10 ft. tall;*
flowerhead ½–¾ in. wide.
What to look for: *flowerheads*
of yellow ray flowers
emerging from cuplike base
of bracts; leaves lance-
shaped, toothed, often
deeply divided. **Habitat:**
open woods, meadows,
fields, waste places.
In bloom: *July–Sept.*

Lettuces
Lactuca

Wild lettuces are sometimes called wild opium because the milky sap of older leaves resembles that of the Opium Poppy. It is not a narcotic, but it does contain a bitter toxin that taints the milk of cows. Tender young leaves, like those of Garden Lettuce (*Lactuca sativa*), are edible.

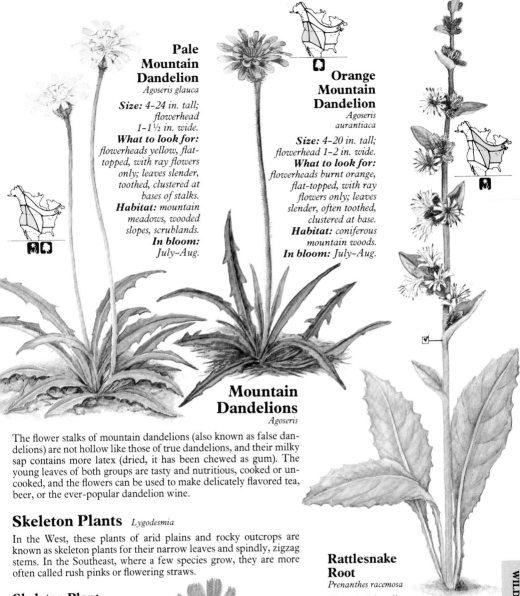

Pale Mountain Dandelion
Agoseris glauca

Size: 4-24 in. tall; flowerhead 1-1½ in. wide.
What to look for: flowerheads yellow, flat-topped, with ray flowers only; leaves slender, toothed, clustered at bases of stalks.
Habitat: mountain meadows, wooded slopes, scrublands.
In bloom: July-Aug.

Orange Mountain Dandelion
Agoseris aurantiaca

Size: 4-20 in. tall; flowerhead 1-2 in. wide.
What to look for: flowerheads burnt orange, flat-topped, with ray flowers only; leaves slender, often toothed, clustered at base.
Habitat: coniferous mountain woods.
In bloom: July-Aug.

Mountain Dandelions
Agoseris

The flower stalks of mountain dandelions (also known as false dandelions) are not hollow like those of true dandelions, and their milky sap contains more latex (dried, it has been chewed as gum). The young leaves of both groups are tasty and nutritious, cooked or uncooked, and the flowers can be used to make delicately flavored tea, beer, or the ever-popular dandelion wine.

Skeleton Plants *Lygodesmia*

In the West, these plants of arid plains and rocky outcrops are known as skeleton plants for their narrow leaves and spindly, zigzag stems. In the Southeast, where a few species grow, they are more often called rush pinks or flowering straws.

Skeleton Plant
Lygodesmia grandiflora

Size: 4-12 in. tall; flowerhead 1½-2 in. wide.
What to look for: flowerheads pink, with single row of petallike, notched ray flowers; leaves grasslike, mostly clustered at base of slender, branching stem. **Habitat:** sandy plains, gravelly slopes.
In bloom: May-July.

Rattlesnake Root
Prenanthes racemosa

Size: 1-5 ft. tall; flowerhead ½ in. wide.
What to look for: flowerheads pinkish or purplish white, with ray flowers only, borne in clusters at leaf bases along stout stem; leaves spatula-shaped and toothed (base of stem) or oval (clasping stem). **Habitat:** moist plains, meadows, streambanks.
In bloom: Aug.-Sept.

Rattlesnake Roots
Prenanthes

Snakebite victims were once treated by applying poultices soaked in the bitter, milky juice of these plants—said to taste like rattlesnake venom.

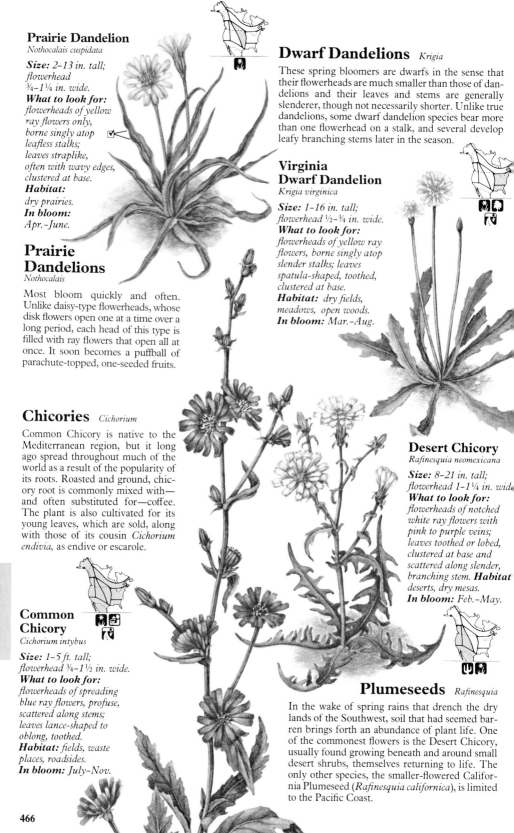

Prairie Dandelion
Nothocalais cuspidata

Size: *2–13 in. tall; flowerhead ¾–1¼ in. wide.*
What to look for: *flowerheads of yellow ray flowers only, borne singly atop leafless stalks; leaves straplike, often with wavy edges, clustered at base.*
Habitat: *dry prairies.*
In bloom: *Apr.–June.*

Prairie Dandelions
Nothocalais

Most bloom quickly and often. Unlike daisy-type flowerheads, whose disk flowers open one at a time over a long period, each head of this type is filled with ray flowers that open all at once. It soon becomes a puffball of parachute-topped, one-seeded fruits.

Chicories *Cichorium*

Common Chicory is native to the Mediterranean region, but it long ago spread throughout much of the world as a result of the popularity of its roots. Roasted and ground, chicory root is commonly mixed with—and often substituted for—coffee. The plant is also cultivated for its young leaves, which are sold, along with those of its cousin *Cichorium endivia*, as endive or escarole.

Common Chicory
Cichorium intybus

Size: *1–5 ft. tall; flowerhead ¾–1½ in. wide.*
What to look for: *flowerheads of spreading blue ray flowers, profuse, scattered along stems; leaves lance-shaped to oblong, toothed.*
Habitat: *fields, waste places, roadsides.*
In bloom: *July–Nov.*

Dwarf Dandelions *Krigia*

These spring bloomers are dwarfs in the sense that their flowerheads are much smaller than those of dandelions and their leaves and stems are generally slenderer, though not necessarily shorter. Unlike true dandelions, some dwarf dandelion species bear more than one flowerhead on a stalk, and several develop leafy branching stems later in the season.

Virginia Dwarf Dandelion
Krigia virginica

Size: *1–16 in. tall; flowerhead ½–¾ in. wide.*
What to look for: *flowerheads of yellow ray flowers, borne singly atop slender stalks; leaves spatula-shaped, toothed, clustered at base.*
Habitat: *dry fields, meadows, open woods.*
In bloom: *Mar.–Aug.*

Desert Chicory
Rafinesquia neomexicana

Size: *8–21 in. tall; flowerhead 1–1¼ in. wide.*
What to look for: *flowerheads of notched white ray flowers with pink to purple veins; leaves toothed or lobed, clustered at base and scattered along slender, branching stem.* **Habitat** *deserts, dry mesas.*
In bloom: *Feb.–May.*

Plumeseeds *Rafinesquia*

In the wake of spring rains that drench the dry lands of the Southwest, soil that had seemed barren brings forth an abundance of plant life. One of the commonest flowers is the Desert Chicory, usually found growing beneath and around small desert shrubs, themselves returning to life. The only other species, the smaller-flowered California Plumeseed (*Rafinesquia californica*), is limited to the Pacific Coast.

WILDFLOWERS

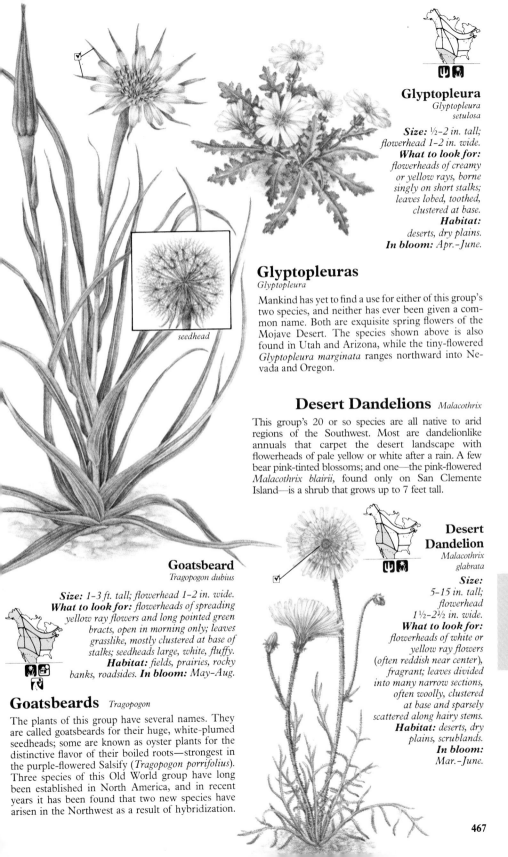

Glyptopleura
*Glyptopleura
setulosa*

Size: *½-2 in. tall;
flowerhead 1-2 in. wide.*
What to look for:
*flowerheads of creamy
or yellow rays, borne
singly on short stalks;
leaves lobed, toothed,
clustered at base.*
Habitat:
deserts, dry plains.
In bloom: *Apr.-June.*

seedhead

Glyptopleuras
Glyptopleura

Mankind has yet to find a use for either of this group's two species, and neither has ever been given a common name. Both are exquisite spring flowers of the Mojave Desert. The species shown above is also found in Utah and Arizona, while the tiny-flowered *Glyptopleura marginata* ranges northward into Nevada and Oregon.

Desert Dandelions *Malacothrix*

This group's 20 or so species are all native to arid regions of the Southwest. Most are dandelionlike annuals that carpet the desert landscape with flowerheads of pale yellow or white after a rain. A few bear pink-tinted blossoms; and one—the pink-flowered *Malacothrix blairii*, found only on San Clemente Island—is a shrub that grows up to 7 feet tall.

Desert Dandelion
*Malacothrix
glabrata*

Size:
*5-15 in. tall;
flowerhead
1½-2½ in. wide.*
What to look for:
*flowerheads of white or
yellow ray flowers
(often reddish near center),
fragrant; leaves divided
into many narrow sections,
often woolly, clustered
at base and sparsely
scattered along hairy stems.*
Habitat: *deserts, dry
plains, scrublands.*
In bloom:
Mar.-June.

Goatsbeard
Tragopogon dubius

Size: *1-3 ft. tall; flowerhead 1-2 in. wide.*
What to look for: *flowerheads of spreading
yellow ray flowers and long pointed green
bracts, open in morning only; leaves
grasslike, mostly clustered at base of
stalks; seedheads large, white, fluffy.*
Habitat: *fields, prairies, rocky
banks, roadsides.* **In bloom:** *May-Aug.*

Goatsbeards *Tragopogon*

The plants of this group have several names. They are called goatsbeards for their huge, white-plumed seedheads; some are known as oyster plants for the distinctive flavor of their boiled roots—strongest in the purple-flowered Salsify (*Tragopogon porrifolius*). Three species of this Old World group have long been established in North America, and in recent years it has been found that two new species have arisen in the Northwest as a result of hybridization.

467

Water Plantain
Alisma subcordatum

Size: *4–36 in. tall, flower ¼ in. wide.*
What to look for: *leaves oval to heart-shaped, on long stalks; flowers white, 3-petaled, profusely borne at tips of branching stalk.*
Habitat: *rivers, lakes, ditches, muddy shores.*
In bloom: *June–Sept.*

Water Plantains
Alisma

Throughout the Northern Hemisphere, members of this group can be found growing in shallow water and wet ground. They are unrelated to plantains, but owe their name to the similar shape of their long-stalked leaves. In deep enough water they often bear ribbonlike underwater leaves as well.

Wapato
Sagittaria latifolia

Size: *1–5 ft. tall; flower ¾–1½ in. wide.*
What to look for: *leaves arrowhead-shaped, on long stalks; flowers white, 3-petaled, with fuzzy yellow centers (male) or green mounds (female), in whorls of 3; fruits in dense round heads.* **Habitat:** *rivers, lakes, ponds, marshes.*
In bloom: *July–Sept.*

Arrowheads
Sagittaria

The starchy, new-potato–like tubers of arrowheads were a dietary staple of many Indian peoples; Lewis and Clark learned the name Wapato from the Chinooks of the Pacific Northwest. The tubers form along the roots within 5 feet of the parent plant. Because they float when broken loose from the root, barefoot waders could easily gather them from the muddy bottoms of rivers and lakes.

Burheads *Echinodorus*

Despite their spiny fruits, these members of the water plantain family are often mistaken for arrowheads (not all arrowhead species bear arrowhead-shaped leaves). Burhead flowers are bisexual, while arrowheads bear separate male and female flowers in two tiers on the same stalk.

Texas Mudbaby
Echinodorus cordifolius

Size: *5–16 in. tall; flower ½–1 in. wide.*
What to look for: *leaves heart-shaped to oval, on long stalks; flowers white, 3-petaled, borne in whorls on upright stalks and along arched rooting stems; fruits in bristly round heads.* **Habitat:** *muddy banks, shallow water.* **In bloom:** *July–Oct.*

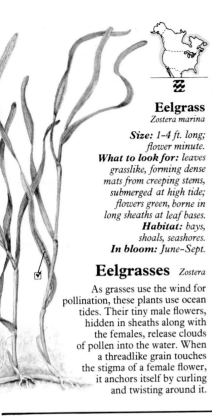

Eelgrass
Zostera marina

Size: *1–4 ft. long; flower minute.*
What to look for: *leaves grasslike, forming dense mats from creeping stems, submerged at high tide; flowers green, borne in long sheaths at leaf bases.*
Habitat: *bays, shoals, seashores.*
In bloom: *June–Sept.*

Eelgrasses *Zostera*

As grasses use the wind for pollination, these plants use ocean tides. Their tiny male flowers, hidden in sheaths along with the females, release clouds of pollen into the water. When a threadlike grain touches the stigma of a female flower, it anchors itself by curling and twisting around it.

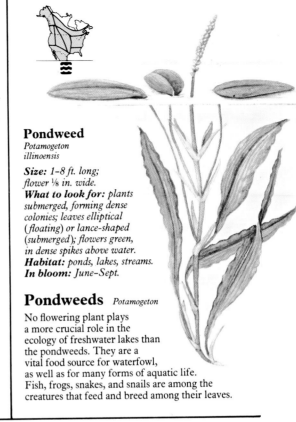

Pondweed
Potamogeton illinoensis

Size: *1–8 ft. long; flower ⅛ in. wide.*
What to look for: *plants submerged, forming dense colonies; leaves elliptical (floating) or lance-shaped (submerged); flowers green, in dense spikes above water.*
Habitat: *ponds, lakes, streams.*
In bloom: *June–Sept.*

Pondweeds *Potamogeton*

No flowering plant plays a more crucial role in the ecology of freshwater lakes than the pondweeds. They are a vital food source for waterfowl, as well as for many forms of aquatic life. Fish, frogs, snakes, and snails are among the creatures that feed and breed among their leaves.

female flowers   male flower (enlarged)

Water Celery
Vallisneria americana

Size: *2–8 ft. long; flower minute (male) or ¼ in. wide (female).*
What to look for: *leaves long, slender, submerged; flowers greenish, at tips of coiled stalks (female) or tiny, free-floating (male).*
Habitat: *quiet freshwater.*
In bloom: *July–Oct.*

Tapegrasses *Vallisneria*

This group's female flowers are borne at the ends of spiraling stalks that maintain just enough tension to form dimples on the water surface. The tiny male flowers are released to float free. They are drawn into the dimples and pollination occurs, after which the stalks coil tighter and the developing fruits are pulled underwater.

Waterweed
Elodea canadensis

Size: *1–10 ft. long; flower ⅛–½ in. wide.*
What to look for: *stems submerged or floating; leaves oval, densely borne in whorls of 3; flowers white, 3-petaled, with yellow centers (male) or 3 purple pistils (female), borne atop slender stalks above water surface.* **Habitat:** *lakes, ponds, springs, quiet streams.*
In bloom: *July–Sept.*

Elodeas *Elodea*

When you buy a handful of greenery for your aquarium, it is probably a member of this group. Although elodea flowers are pollinated on the surface of the water, the plants are propagated chiefly by means of broken fragments of the weak, buoyant stems.

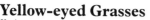

Yellow-eyed Grasses
Xyris

Despite their grasslike leaves, the yellow-eyed grasses are more closely related to the pineapple family than they are to the grass family—a kinship that is revealed by a close look at the knobby head from which the small yellow flowers emerge, one or two at a time. Most North American species are confined to the coastal bogs and marshes of the Southeast; Twisted Yellow-eyed Grass spreads much farther north and west.

Twisted Yellow-eyed Grass
Xyris torta

Size: *6–36 in. tall; flower ⅛–¼ in. wide.*
What to look for: *flowers yellow, 3-petaled, borne from conelike head atop leafless, wiry stalk; leaves clustered at base, stiff, grasslike, often twisted.* ***Habitat:*** *bogs, meadows, shores.*
In bloom: *July–Sept.*

Pipeworts *Eriocaulon*

Most of this group's nearly 400 species are tropical and subtropical. However, several are abundant along lakeshores and riverbanks throughout the Southeast and the Middle Atlantic states. The Northern Pipewort (*Eriocaulon aquaticum*) is found as far north as Newfoundland. The species all look much alike; several are called Hatpins.

Hatpins
Eriocaulon compressum

Size: *8–30 in. tall; flowerhead ¼–½ in. wide.*
What to look for: *flowers white, minute, borne in dense buttonlike head atop wiry, leafless stalk; leaves clustered at base, grasslike, soft.* ***Habitat:*** *bogs, pond edges.*
In bloom: *May–July.*

Asiatic Dayflower
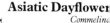
Commelina communis

Size: *6–30 in. long; flower ¾–1 in. wide.*
What to look for: *stems fleshy, sprawling; flowers blue, with 2 large round petals above a single inconspicuous white petal, borne one at a time from small green cups; leaves lance-shaped.*
Habitat: *yards, fields, open woods, waste places.*
In bloom: *June–Oct.*

Dayflowers *Commelina*

Each of a dayflower's many short-lived blossoms (they last but a single morning) has two large, showy blue petals and one insignificant white petal. This characteristic prompted Linnaeus to name the group after the three Commelin brothers: two were notable Dutch botanists of the 17th century, and the third died young ". . . before accomplishing anything in botany."

Spiderwort
Tradescantia ohiensis

Size: *8–36 in. tall; flower 1–1½ in. wide.*
What to look for: *flowers blue to purple (occasionally white), 3-petaled, borne in loose clusters at base of a pair of leaves at stem tip; leaves long, narrow, with large sheaths at base.*
Habitat: *prairies, open woods, thickets, meadows.*
In bloom: *Apr.–July.*

white flower

Spiderworts
Tradescantia

Spiderworts are among the world's most sensitive—and certainly the most attractive—devices for detecting nuclear radiation. The stamen hairs on a plant that has been exposed to low-level radiation change from blue to pink in proportion to the dose received. By counting, under a microscope, the number of cells in a hair that have so changed, a scientist can index the severity of radiation.

WILDFLOWERS

growth form

growth form

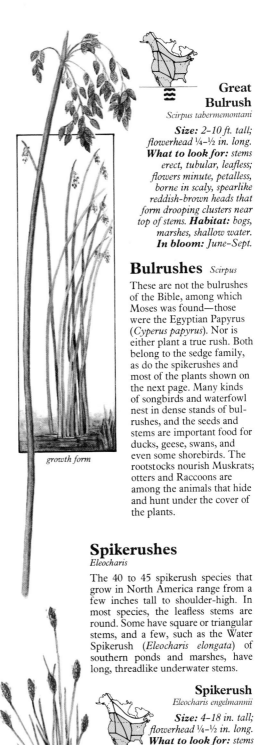

Great Bulrush
Scirpus tabermemontani

Size: *2–10 ft. tall; flowerhead ¼–½ in. long.*
What to look for: *stems erect, tubular, leafless; flowers minute, petalless, borne in scaly, spearlike reddish-brown heads that form drooping clusters near top of stems.* **Habitat:** *bogs, marshes, shallow water.*
In bloom: *June–Sept.*

Bulrushes *Scirpus*

These are not the bulrushes of the Bible, among which Moses was found—those were the Egyptian Papyrus (*Cyperus papyrus*). Nor is either plant a true rush. Both belong to the sedge family, as do the spikerushes and most of the plants shown on the next page. Many kinds of songbirds and waterfowl nest in dense stands of bulrushes, and the seeds and stems are important food for ducks, geese, swans, and even some shorebirds. The rootstocks nourish Muskrats; otters and Raccoons are among the animals that hide and hunt under the cover of the plants.

Spikerushes
Eleocharis

The 40 to 45 spikerush species that grow in North America range from a few inches tall to shoulder-high. In most species, the leafless stems are round. Some have square or triangular stems, and a few, such as the Water Spikerush (*Eleocharis elongata*) of southern ponds and marshes, have long, threadlike underwater stems.

Spikerush
Eleocharis engelmannii

Size: *4–18 in. tall; flowerhead ¼–½ in. long.*
What to look for: *stems erect, wiry, leafless; flowers minute, petalless, in scaly, spearlike brown heads atop stems.* **Habitat:** *marshes, swamps, wet meadows, shores.* **In bloom:** *May–Oct.*

Soft Rush
Juncus effusus

Size: *1–6 ft. tall; flower ⅛ in. wide.*
What to look for: *stems erect, grasslike, each ending in a tubular, sharp-pointed leaf; leaves at base of stems small, spearlike; flowers straw-colored to brown, borne in dense clusters near tops of stems.*
Habitat: *marshes, bogs, riverbanks, lakeshores, ditches, wet thickets.*
In bloom: *June–Sept.*

Rushes *Juncus*

Prehistoric peoples used rush stems for binding and basketmaking. The resilient stems still serve these purposes and are woven into mats, hats, chair seats, boats, and other items as well. Although the papery leaves and small flower clusters resemble those of sedges and grasses, the group is more closely related to the lily family. Its three-petaled flowers—though wind-pollinated and much less showy than those of most lilies—have the same basic structure; its fruits are lilylike seed-filled capsules rather than the grains of grasses and sedges.

Chufa
Cyperus esculentus

Size: *6-30 in. tall; flowerhead ¼-1 in. long.*
What to look for: *flowers minute, borne in scaly heads that form loose clusters atop triangular stem; leaves grasslike, stiff, clustered at base and in umbrellalike whorl at top of stem.* **Habitat:** *wet fields, meadows, pastures.*
In bloom: *Aug.-Oct.*

Umbrella Sedges
Cyperus

The umbrella sedges are typical of the sedge family—wetland plants whose triangular stems are topped by clusters of compact flowerheads. In this group, the clusters splay from an umbrellalike whorl of leaves. Chufa is also known as Yellow Nutgrass for its edible tubers.

Cottongrass
Eriophorum angustifolium

Size: *1-2 ft. tall; flowerhead 1-2 in. wide.*
What to look for: *flowers with silky white hairs, forming cottony tufts atop triangular stems; leaves grasslike, sparsely scattered along stem.* **Habitat:** *tundra, bogs, moist prairies, meadows.*
In bloom: *May-Aug.*

Cottongrasses
Eriophorum

Like a snowfall out of season, compact stands of cottongrass clothe northern bogs and meadows with a soft blanket of white in summer and fall. North America's 10 species are largely circumboreal—that is, they are found growing in all lands that touch upon the Arctic Circle.

Porcupine Sedge
Carex hystericina

Size: *1-3 ft. tall; flowerhead 1-2½ in. long.*
What to look for: *leaves long, rough-textured, clustered at base and scattered along triangular stems; flowers greenish, in narrow spike atop stem (male) and drooping, bristly spikes near top of stem (female).* **Habitat:** *marshes, swamps, ditches, shores.*
In bloom: *June-Oct.*

Sedges *Carex*

Most of the world's nearly 2,000 species of sedge grow in wet ground, but at least a few are common in nearly every habitat, from arid plains to high mountain slopes. Such northern species as the Bear Sedge (*Carex ursina*) and the Russet Sedge (*Carex saxatilis*) dominate large stretches of the Arctic tundra.

Giant Cane
Arundinaria gigantea

Size: *5-30 ft. tall; spikelet 1½-2½ in. long.*
What to look for: *stems tough, woody, forming dense thickets, or canebrakes; leaves elliptical to lance-shaped; spikelets scaly, in branching clusters.* **Habitat:** *swamps, wet woods, streambanks, bottomlands.*
In bloom: *Apr.-May (infrequently).*

Bamboos
Arundinaria

Among the grass family's bamboo tribe (comprising about 60 groups with more than 700 species), only the Giant Cane is native to North America. Like many other bamboos, it flowers only once every 40 to 50 years, spreading in the meantime by underground stems, or rhizomes. All the plants in a given area blossom at once; then the stems die back, no matter how young each may actually be. Within a period of four to five years, all the individuals of a species anywhere in the world flower, set seed, and die.

Spikegrasses _Uniola_

To appreciate the diverse beauty of the huge grass family—shown here and on the next four pages—it helps to view its members as a field mouse might. Note the form and texture of the narrow leaf blades. Then study how the intricately structured flowerheads (called spikelets) are clustered high atop the hollow stems. In Sea Oats (an endangered species), they form many elegantly drooping spikes that sway in the coastal breezes.

Sea Oats
Uniola paniculata

Size: _3–6 ft. tall; spikelet ½–1 in. long._
What to look for: _spikelets straw-colored to violet, in flat spikes that form flaglike clusters at top of stout stem; leaves ribbonlike, curling._ **Habitat:** _coastal dunes._
In bloom: _June–Nov._

Kentucky Bluegrass
Poa pratensis

Size: _2–36 in. tall; spikelet ⅛–¼ in. long._
What to look for: _leaves ribbonlike, in tufts and scattered on stem; spikelets in open branching clusters atop wiry stems; plants sod-forming._
Habitat: _lawns, fields, prairies, meadows, open woods._
In bloom: _May–Aug._

Bluegrasses _Poa_

No grass is more highly prized for pasturage than the bluegrasses, and among the group of about 250 species, none ranks higher than Kentucky Bluegrass. Like the similar Canada Bluegrass (_Poa compressa_), it originated in the Old World but has spread across North America.

Reedgrasses
Phragmites

Second in height only to the Giant Cane among native grasses, reedgrasses form dense and enormous stands in ponds, marshes, and streams throughout much of the world. The plumelike clusters of silky-haired spikelets are attractive but unproductive; the plants seldom produce seed but spread by means of rootstocks that may be 30 feet long.

Reedgrass
Phragmites australis

Size: _4–15 ft. tall; spikelet ½ in. long._
What to look for: _spikelets tawny to purplish, with many soft hairs, borne in long spikes that form plumelike cluster atop stout stem; leaves straplike to lance-shaped, stiff, scattered along stem._ **Habitat:** _marshes, shores, streambanks, ditches._
In bloom: _July–Sept._

Common Rye
Secale cereale

Size: _18–36 in. tall; spikelet ½ in. long._
What to look for: _spikelets with stiff awns, in dense spike atop erect stem; leaves soft, ribbonlike, scattered along stem._ **Habitat:** _fields, waste places, roadsides._
In bloom: _June–Aug._

Ryes _Secale_

Like many cereal grasses, the ryes bear compact spikelets that usually contain only two seed-producing flowers and are tightly clustered in a single spike. Common Rye originated in Eurasia and is cultivated in many parts of the world. In North America, it is often planted along roadsides to control erosion.

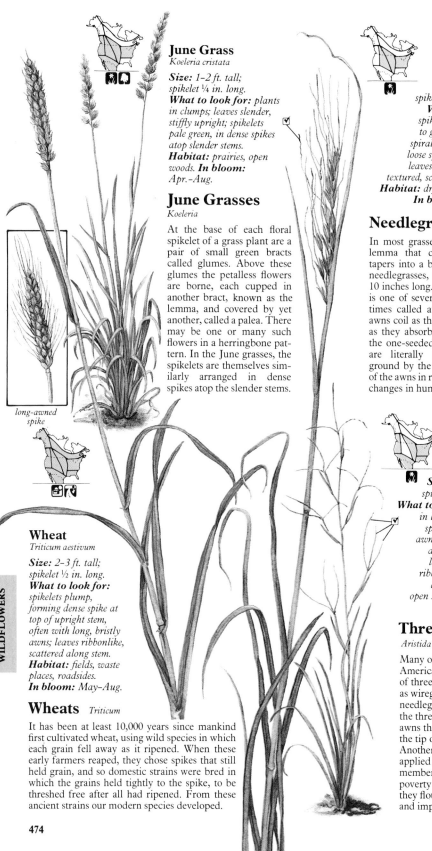

June Grass
Koeleria cristata

Size: *1-2 ft. tall; spikelet ¼ in. long.*
What to look for: *plants in clumps; leaves slender, stiffly upright; spikelets pale green, in dense spikes atop slender stems.*
Habitat: *prairies, open woods.* **In bloom:** *Apr.-Aug.*

June Grasses
Koeleria

At the base of each floral spikelet of a grass plant are a pair of small green bracts called glumes. Above these glumes the petalless flowers are borne, each cupped in another bract, known as the lemma, and covered by yet another, called a palea. There may be one or many such flowers in a herringbone pattern. In the June grasses, the spikelets are themselves similarly arranged in dense spikes atop the slender stems.

long-awned spike

Wheat
Triticum aestivum

Size: *2-3 ft. tall; spikelet ½ in. long.*
What to look for: *spikelets plump, forming dense spike at top of upright stem, often with long, bristly awns; leaves ribbonlike, scattered along stem.* **Habitat:** *fields, waste places, roadsides.* **In bloom:** *May-Aug.*

Wheats   *Triticum*

It has been at least 10,000 years since mankind first cultivated wheat, using wild species in which each grain fell away as it ripened. When these early farmers reaped, they chose spikes that still held grain, and so domestic strains were bred in which the grains held tightly to the spike, to be threshed free after all had ripened. From these ancient strains our modern species developed.

Porcupine Grass
Stipa spartea

Size: *2-5 ft. tall; spikelet 1-1½ in. long.*
What to look for: *spikelets straw-colored to greenish, with long, spirally twisted awns, in loose spike atop tall stem; leaves ribbonlike, rough-textured, scattered along stem.*
Habitat: *dry prairies, barrens.* **In bloom:** *May-July.*

Needlegrasses   *Stipa*

In most grasses, the tiny green lemma that cups each flower tapers into a bristlelike awn. In needlegrasses, this awn may be 10 inches long. Porcupine Grass is one of several species (sometimes called augerseeds) whose awns coil as they dry and uncoil as they absorb moisture. When the one-seeded grains fall, they are literally drilled into the ground by the corkscrew action of the awns in response to nightly changes in humidity.

Prairie Three-awn
Aristida oligantha

Size: *6-20 in. tall; spikelet ¾-1 in. long.*
What to look for: *plants in low, bushy clumps; spikelets with 3 long awns, loosely clustered along upright stem; leaves threadlike to ribbonlike.* **Habitat:** *dry prairies, fields, open slopes.* **In bloom:** *July-Oct.*

Three-awns
Aristida

Many of North America's 40 species of three-awn are known as wiregrasses or needlegrasses because of the three sharp-pointed awns that project from the tip of each lemma. Another name often applied to various members of the group is poverty grass because they flourish in arid and impoverished soil.

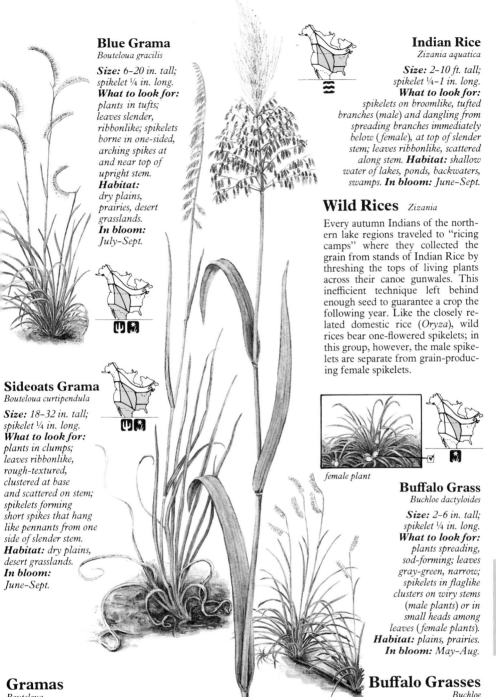

Blue Grama
Bouteloua gracilis

Size: 6–20 in. tall; spikelet ¼ in. long. **What to look for:** plants in tufts; leaves slender, ribbonlike; spikelets borne in one-sided, arching spikes at and near top of upright stem. **Habitat:** dry plains, prairies, desert grasslands. **In bloom:** July–Sept.

Sideoats Grama
Bouteloua curtipendula

Size: 18–32 in. tall; spikelet ¼ in. long. **What to look for:** plants in clumps; leaves ribbonlike, rough-textured, clustered at base and scattered on stem; spikelets forming short spikes that hang like pennants from one side of slender stem. **Habitat:** dry plains, desert grasslands. **In bloom:** June–Sept.

Gramas
Bouteloua

In the days when vast herds of Bison roamed the western prairies, the gramas made up a large part of their diet. Today, these grasses serve as forage for many other wild and domesticated grazers. They are especially well adapted to the northern High Plains and to the arid Southwest, where they grow rapidly during the short rainy season and are cured by the dry winds that follow into a high-protein standing hay.

Indian Rice
Zizania aquatica

Size: 2–10 ft. tall; spikelet ¼–1 in. long. **What to look for:** spikelets on broomlike, tufted branches (*male*) and dangling from spreading branches immediately below (*female*), at top of slender stem; leaves ribbonlike, scattered along stem. **Habitat:** shallow water of lakes, ponds, backwaters, swamps. **In bloom:** June–Sept.

Wild Rices   *Zizania*

Every autumn Indians of the northern lake regions traveled to "ricing camps" where they collected the grain from stands of Indian Rice by threshing the tops of living plants across their canoe gunwales. This inefficient technique left behind enough seed to guarantee a crop the following year. Like the closely related domestic rice (*Oryza*), wild rices bear one-flowered spikelets; in this group, however, the male spikelets are separate from grain-producing female spikelets.

female plant

Buffalo Grass
Buchloe dactyloides

Size: 2–6 in. tall; spikelet ¼ in. long. **What to look for:** plants spreading, sod-forming; leaves gray-green, narrow; spikelets in flaglike clusters on wiry stems (*male plants*) or in small heads among leaves (*female plants*). **Habitat:** plains, prairies. **In bloom:** May–Aug.

Buffalo Grasses
Buchloe

This group's only species is the most important short forage grass of the central Great Plains. Because of its creeping underground runners, or stolons, it is one of the few western grasses capable of forming soil-binding sod; most others grow in bunches. Early settlers on the Great Plains stacked slabs of this sod to make their houses, which they called soddies.

WILDFLOWERS

475

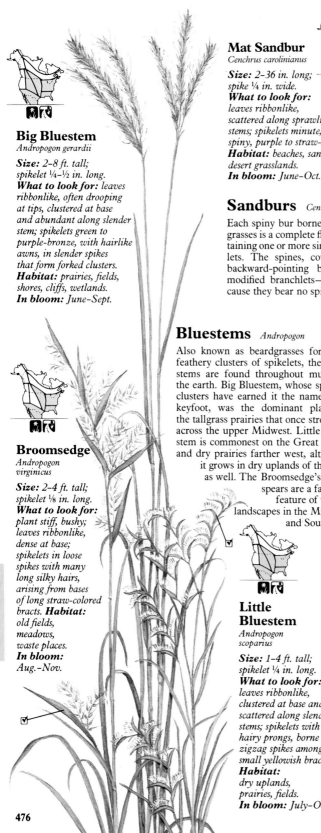

Mat Sandbur

Cenchrus carolinianus

Size: *2–36 in. long; spike ¼ in. wide.*
What to look for: *leaves ribbonlike, scattered along sprawling stems; spikelets minute, enclosed in spiny, purple to straw-colored burs.*
Habitat: *beaches, sandy fields, desert grasslands.*
In bloom: *June–Oct.*

Sandburs   *Cenchrus*

Each spiny bur borne by these spreading grasses is a complete flowering spike, containing one or more single-flowered spikelets. The spines, covered with minute backward-pointing barbs, are actually modified branchlets—termed sterile because they bear no spikelets of their own.

Big Bluestem

Andropogon gerardii

Size: *2–8 ft. tall; spikelet ¼–½ in. long.*
What to look for: *leaves ribbonlike, often drooping at tips, clustered at base and abundant along slender stem; spikelets green to purple-bronze, with hairlike awns, in slender spikes that form forked clusters.*
Habitat: *prairies, fields, shores, cliffs, wetlands.*
In bloom: *June–Sept.*

Bluestems   *Andropogon*

Also known as beardgrasses for their feathery clusters of spikelets, the bluestems are found throughout much of the earth. Big Bluestem, whose splayed clusters have earned it the name Turkeyfoot, was the dominant plant of the tallgrass prairies that once stretched across the upper Midwest. Little Bluestem is commonest on the Great Plains and dry prairies farther west, although it grows in dry uplands of the East as well. The Broomsedge's russet spears are a familiar feature of winter landscapes in the Midwest and Southeast.

Broomsedge

Andropogon virginicus

Size: *2–4 ft. tall; spikelet ⅛ in. long.*
What to look for: *plant stiff, bushy; leaves ribbonlike, dense at base; spikelets in loose spikes with many long silky hairs, arising from bases of long straw-colored bracts.* **Habitat:** *old fields, meadows, waste places.*
In bloom: *Aug.–Nov.*

Little Bluestem

Andropogon scoparius

Size: *1–4 ft. tall; spikelet ¼ in. long.*
What to look for: *leaves ribbonlike, clustered at base and scattered along slender stems; spikelets with hairy prongs, borne in zigzag spikes among small yellowish bracts.*
Habitat: *dry uplands, prairies, fields.*
In bloom: *July–Oct.*

Yellow Indian Grass

Sorghastrum nutans

Size: *3–10 ft. tall; spikelet ¼–½ in. long.*
What to look for: *leaves ribbonlike, rough-textured, clustered at base and scattered along slender stem; spikelets golden-brown, hairy, with long awns, borne in 2's or 3's, forming plumelike cluster.*
Habitat: *moist prairies, fields, barrens.*
In bloom: *Aug.–Sept.*

Indian Grasses

Sorghastrum

The deep, black topsoil that nourished vast sweeps of such plants as Yellow Indian Grass and Big Bluestem proved ideal for growing another kind of tall American grass. And so, behind the plows of settlers, the tallgrass prairies were transformed in the course of a few decades into today's productive corn belt.

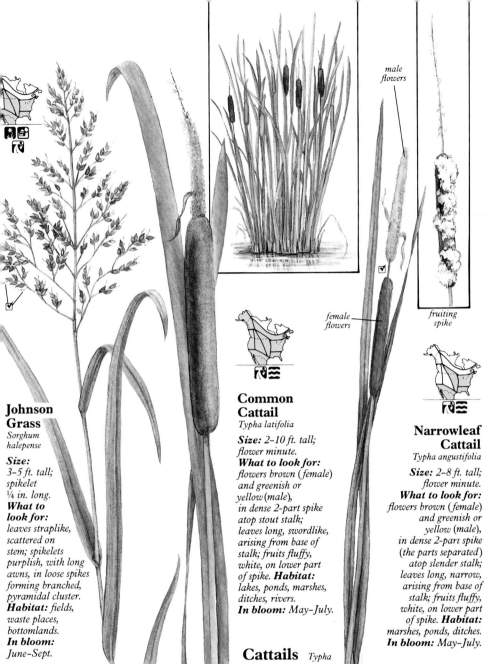

male
flowers

female
flowers

fruiting
spike

Johnson Grass

Sorghum halepense

Size: 3–5 ft. tall; spikelet ¼ in. long.
What to look for: leaves straplike, scattered on stem; spikelets purplish, with long awns, in loose spikes forming branched, pyramidal cluster. **Habitat:** fields, waste places, bottomlands. **In bloom:** June–Sept.

Sorghums

Sorghum

These grasses were prized in ancient Africa and Asia as a source of grain, forage, and syrup. Many kinds are now grown in North America for the same purposes. Johnson Grass is said to have been imported from Turkey in the 1830's, by William Johnson of Alabama, for testing as a hay crop. It soon escaped cultivation and has become a troublesome weed.

Common Cattail

Typha latifolia

Size: 2–10 ft. tall; flower minute.
What to look for: flowers brown (*female*) and greenish or yellow (*male*), in dense 2-part spike atop stout stalk; leaves long, swordlike, arising from base of stalk; fruits fluffy, white, on lower part of spike. **Habitat:** lakes, ponds, marshes, ditches, rivers.
In bloom: May–July.

Cattails *Typha*

One need never starve where cattails grow. In fall and winter, the starchy rhizomes can be peeled and cooked like potatoes or dried and pounded into flour. The dormant sprouts that grow from them are tastiest steamed, a dish known as Russian asparagus. In spring and early summer, the young shoots can be eaten raw or cooked, and the immature flower spikes can be boiled and eaten like miniature ears of corn. Later on, the abundant pollen produced by the male flowers that make up the top half of the flowering spike can be used without grinding as a fine-textured flour. The leaves are not edible, but they have been woven into mats, chair seats, baskets, and even roofs. The fluffy white fruits have been used to stuff pillows, and campers have found them a good emergency replacement for down in sleeping bags and jackets.

Narrowleaf Cattail

Typha angustifolia

Size: 2–8 ft. tall; flower minute.
What to look for: flowers brown (*female*) and greenish or yellow (*male*), in dense 2-part spike (the parts separated) atop slender stalk; leaves long, narrow, arising from base of stalk; fruits fluffy, white, on lower part of spike. **Habitat:** marshes, ponds, ditches.
In bloom: May–July.

WILDFLOWERS

477

tree with Spanish Moss

Spanish Moss
Tillandsia usneoides

Size: *to 25 ft. long; flower ¼ in. wide.* **What to look for:** *stems gray, covered with scalelike gray-green leaves, hanging in mosslike swags; flowers green, small, rarely seen.* **Habitat:** *tree limbs, wires, poles.* **In bloom:** *Apr.–July.*

Bunchmoss
Tillandsia recurvata

Size: *2-6 in. tall; flower ½ in. long.* **What to look for:** *leaves gray, fuzzy, hairlike, forming rounded clumps; flowers blue to violet, borne in slender spikes at tips of wiry stems.* **Habitat:** *trees, wires, poles, gutters, fences.* **In bloom:** *all year.*

Tree Mosses   *Tillandsia*

Despite their evil reputation, neither Spanish Moss nor Bunchmoss is parasitic. Like most members of the pineapple (or bromeliad) family, they are epiphytes: they attach themselves to trees for support but take no direct nourishment from their hosts. (The worst damage they are likely to cause is the loss of a weak branch, weighed down during a tropical storm by the additional wet foliage.) They live on nutrients leached from leaves and dead bark by the rain. They even make use of dust particles trapped by the silvery scales covering their branches and leaves, and so can flourish on fence posts and phone wires.

Strap-leaved Air Plant
Guzmania monostachia

Size: *1-2 ft. tall; flower ¼–½ in. long.* **What to look for:** *leaves straplike, in rosette with cuplike base; flowers white, borne among green to vermilion bracts at top of erect stalk.* **Habitat:** *hammocks, subtropical forests.* **In bloom:** *all year.*

Air Plants   *Guzmania*

This group is one of several in the pineapple family whose epiphytic members are known as air plants. Like many others in the family, they collect water in the cups formed by the bases of their leaves and, through the leaves, absorb nutrients dissolved in the water. Only one of the group's 126 species is native to North America; most come from the forests of tropical America.

Skunk Cabbages   *Symplocarpus*

So intense is the heat generated within the developing floral sheath (called a spathe) of the Skunk Cabbage in late winter that it thaws the frozen earth and melts a circle in the snow. Flies and gnats, attracted by the plant's fetid odor, pollinate the tiny flowers on its knoblike spike (spadix). In Sumatra there grows a giant, foul-smelling distant relative with a 15-foot spadix, which is occasionally pollinated by elephants drinking water from its spathe.

Skunk Cabbage
Symplocarpus foetidus

Size: *6-40 in. tall; flower ¼ in. wide.* **What to look for:** *spathe purple and green, enclosing knoblike flower-covered spadix; leaves large, appearing after plant has flowered.* **Habitat:** *swamps; wet woods, meadows.* **In bloom:** *Feb.–Apr.*

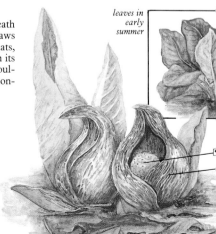

leaves in early summer

Jack-in-the-pulpit
Arisaema triphyllum

Size: *1-3 ft. tall; flower ⅛ in. wide.*
What to look for: *spathe with purple and green stripes, hooded, enclosing clublike spadix (flowers clustered at base); leaves divided into 3 oval leaflets; berries red, clustered.*
Habitat: *moist woods.*
In bloom: *Apr.-July.*

Green Dragon
Arisaema dracontium

Size: *1-4 ft. tall; flower ⅛ in. wide.*
What to look for: *spadix long, slender (flowers clustered at base), emerging from green spathe; single leaf divided into many leaflets.* **Habitat:** *moist woods, streambanks.*
In bloom: *Apr.-June.*

Dragon Arums *Arisaema*

Members of the largely tropical arum family—which includes such popular houseplants as philodendrons and caladiums—bear their small flowers on the surface of a fleshy spike, called a spadix ("Jack" in Jack-in-the-pulpit), which is usually surrounded by a large bract, called a spathe. In the dragon arums the flowers occur near the base of the spathe and are pollinated by insects drawn to odors from within. Jack-in-the-pulpit attracts mosquitoes with its smell of a stagnant pool.

berries

Sweet Flags *Acorus*

The spadix of a sweet flag seems to jut from halfway up one of the plant's upright leaves. A closer look shows that it grows atop a flattened stalk, with a leaflike spathe rising above it. The underground stems, or rhizomes, were once used to make a popular gingery candy, and the leaves have been used since ancient times as a sweet-smelling floor covering.

Calamus
Acorus calamus

Size: *1-6 ft. tall; flower ⅛ in. wide.*
What to look for: *leaves slender, swordlike, light green, forming dense stands; flower-covered spadix cylindrical, yellowish, jutting from edge of leaflike stem and spathe.* **Habitat:** *bogs, marshes, streams, lakes, ponds.*
In bloom: *Apr.-Aug.*

Water Arum
Calla palustris

Size: *4-10 in. tall; flower ⅛-¼ in. wide.*
What to look for: *flower-covered spadix knobby, yellow, at base of open white spathe; leaves heart-shaped, leathery.* **Habitat:** *bogs, swamps, ponds.*
In bloom: *Apr.-Aug.*

Water Arums *Calla*

Water Dragon, Wild Calla, Swamp Robin—all are names for this group's single species, found growing in cold, shady bogs and swamps all around the Northern Hemisphere. The plant's white floral spathe resembles that of the popular calla lilies (*Zantedeschia*) of southern Africa—distant relatives within the arum family. Although insects are the Water Arum's major pollinators, water snails may also play a role in pollination.

Golden Club
Orontium aquaticum

Size: *1–2 ft. tall; flower ⅛–¼ in. wide.*
What to look for: *flower-covered spadix golden yellow, at tip of long white and red stalk with small spathe at base; leaves long-stalked, oblong, pointed.*
Habitat: *swamps, ponds, streams.*
In bloom: *Apr.–June.*

Golden Clubs *Orontium*

Unlike most of the arum family, the Golden Club appears to have no spathe, but only a yellow spadix at the tip of a clublike stalk. The spathe exists, however, in the form of a leaflike collar at the base of the stalk. The single species is also called Neverwet because its waxy leaves repel water.

Pickerelweed
Pontederia cordata

Size: *1–4 ft. tall; flower ¼–½ in. wide.*
What to look for: *flowers blue with 2 yellow spots on upper center petal, in dense spike atop stalk bearing one leaf; leaves on long stalks, heart- to lance-shaped.*
Habitat: *ponds, lakeshores, swamps, streams, marshes.*
In bloom: *June–Nov.*

Pickerelweeds
Pontederia

Botanists disagree about whether North America has one or two native pickerelweed species. Some consider the narrow-leaved plant of the Southeast to be only a variety of the species shown here. In the opinion of others, it is a distinct species.

Green Arrow
Peltandra virginica

Size: *1–3 ft. tall; flower ⅛–¼ in. wide.*
What to look for: *leaves arrow-shaped, long-stalked, leathery; flower-covered spadix hidden within long green spathe.* **Habitat:** *swamps, bogs, ponds, streams, lakeshores.*
In bloom: *Apr.–June.*

Arrow Arums
Peltandra

Arrow arums are easily confused with arrowheads (*Sagittaria*) when neither plant is in bloom. To tell the leaves apart, look at the veins: in this group, they run diagonally outward from the midrib, while those of the arrowheads run parallel to it. Indians pounded the roots of both the Green Arrow and the Golden Club into flour.

Water Hyacinths *Eichhornia*

Once sold as an ornamental, the tropical Water Hyacinth is now the world's worst aquatic weed. It increases a thousandfold in two months, and is eaten by so few animals (in North America, only the rare Manatee) that it quickly chokes warm waterways.

Water Hyacinth
Eichhornia crassipes

Size: *2–37 in. tall; flower 1½–2½ in. wide.*
What to look for: *plants floating on inflated leafstalks; leaves round to kidney-shaped, fleshy; flowers purple with yellow "eye" on upper center petal, borne in showy spike.*
Habitat: *rivers, lakes, bayous.*
In bloom: *Apr.–Oct.*

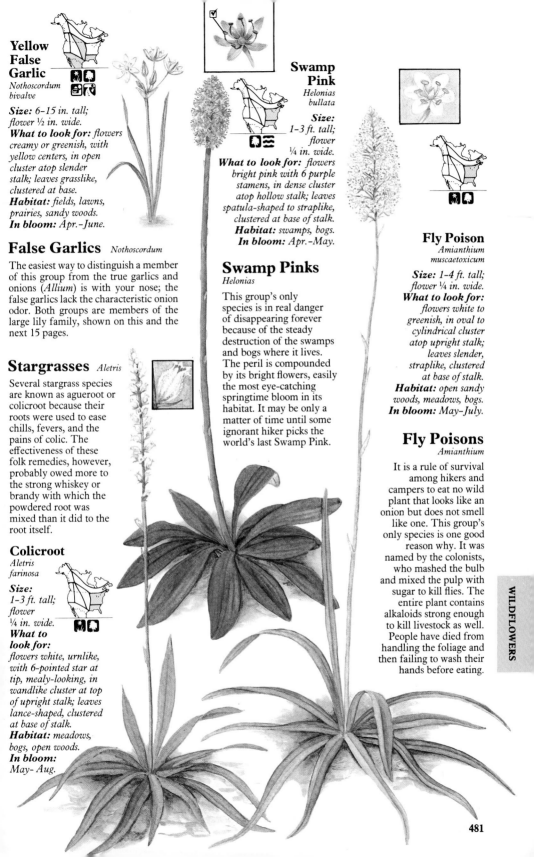

Yellow False Garlic

Nothoscordum bivalve

Size: *6–15 in. tall; flower ½ in. wide.*
What to look for: *flowers creamy or greenish, with yellow centers, in open cluster atop slender stalk; leaves grasslike, clustered at base.*
Habitat: *fields, lawns, prairies, sandy woods.*
In bloom: *Apr.–June.*

False Garlics   *Nothoscordum*

The easiest way to distinguish a member of this group from the true garlics and onions (*Allium*) is with your nose; the false garlics lack the characteristic onion odor. Both groups are members of the large lily family, shown on this and the next 15 pages.

Stargrasses   *Aletris*

Several stargrass species are known as agueroot or colicroot because their roots were used to ease chills, fevers, and the pains of colic. The effectiveness of these folk remedies, however, probably owed more to the strong whiskey or brandy with which the powdered root was mixed than it did to the root itself.

Colicroot

Aletris farinosa

Size: *1–3 ft. tall; flower ¼ in. wide.*
What to look for: *flowers white, urnlike, with 6-pointed star at tip, mealy-looking, in wandlike cluster at top of upright stalk; leaves lance-shaped, clustered at base of stalk.*
Habitat: *meadows, bogs, open woods.*
In bloom: *May–Aug.*

Swamp Pink

Helonias bullata

Size: *1–3 ft. tall; flower ¼ in. wide.*
What to look for: *flowers bright pink with 6 purple stamens, in dense cluster atop hollow stalk; leaves spatula-shaped to straplike, clustered at base of stalk.*
Habitat: *swamps, bogs.*
In bloom: *Apr.–May.*

Swamp Pinks
Helonias

This group's only species is in real danger of disappearing forever because of the steady destruction of the swamps and bogs where it lives. The peril is compounded by its bright flowers, easily the most eye-catching springtime bloom in its habitat. It may be only a matter of time until some ignorant hiker picks the world's last Swamp Pink.

Fly Poison

Amianthium muscaetoxicum

Size: *1–4 ft. tall; flower ¼ in. wide.*
What to look for: *flowers white to greenish, in oval to cylindrical cluster atop upright stalk; leaves slender, straplike, clustered at base of stalk.*
Habitat: *open sandy woods, meadows, bogs.*
In bloom: *May–July.*

Fly Poisons
Amianthium

It is a rule of survival among hikers and campers to eat no wild plant that looks like an onion but does not smell like one. This group's only species is one good reason why. It was named by the colonists, who mashed the bulb and mixed the pulp with sugar to kill flies. The entire plant contains alkaloids strong enough to kill livestock as well. People have died from handling the foliage and then failing to wash their hands before eating.

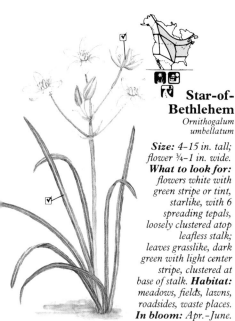

Star-of-Bethlehem

Ornithogalum umbellatum

Size: 4–15 in. tall; flower ¾–1 in. wide.
What to look for: flowers white with green stripe or tint, starlike, with 6 spreading tepals, loosely clustered atop leafless stalk; leaves grasslike, dark green with light center stripe, clustered at base of stalk. **Habitat:** meadows, fields, lawns, roadsides, waste places. **In bloom:** Apr.–June.

Stars-of-Bethlehem
Ornithogalum

Flowers of the lily family have three petals and three sepals. In the stars-of-Bethlehem, as in most members of the family, the petals and sepals are so much alike that botanists coined the term "tepals" to describe them. These poisonous plants originated in Africa and Eurasia, but a few species, imported as early-flowering garden plants, have spread to the wild in North America.

Alp Lily
Lloydia serotina

Size: 2–6 in. tall; flower ¼–½ in. wide.
What to look for: flowers white with purple veins, borne singly on slender stalks; leaves in clumps, grasslike to hairlike. **Habitat:** tundra, high mountain peaks. **In bloom:** July–Aug.

Alp Lilies   *Lloydia*

Most members of the lily family grow either from fleshy bulbs, which help them survive arid conditions, or from rhizomes or tubers, which help them survive long winters. The alp lilies are unusual in that they have both bulbs and rhizomes. About a dozen species of these delicate-looking but stalwart little plants grow high in the mountains of Europe and Asia; only one is also found in North America's Rockies and Arctic tundra.

Brodiaea Lilies   *Brodiaea*

Surely no plant bears a common name so impressively literary as Ithuriel's Spear (Ithuriel was the angel in *Paradise Lost* who, with a touch of his spear, transformed Satan from a toad to his true image). The species is also known as Grassnut for its flavorsome bulblike corms, and is sometimes listed in catalogs as Triplet Lily. Others of the group familiar to gardeners include the Harvest Lily, Blue-dicks, and Pretty Face. The Snake Lily is unique in the lily family because of its twining, vinelike stalk, which will continue to climb and flower even after it has been severed from the ground.

Ithuriel's Spear
Triteleia laxa

Size: 5–30 in. tall; flower ¾–1¾ in. long.
What to look for: flowers purple to blue or white, funnel-shaped, loosely clustered atop leafless stalk; leaves long, slender, arising from base of stalk. **Habitat:** fields, grassy hillsides, coastal sagebrush areas, open woods. **In bloom:** Apr.–Aug.

Harvest Lily
Brodiaea elegans

Size: 4–18 in. tall; flower 1–1½ in. wide.
What to look for: flowers violet to deep purple, funnel-shaped, with 6 spreading tepals, loosely clustered atop leafless stalk; leaves long, grasslike, arising from base of stalk (often withered by flowering time). **Habitat:** dry plains, grassy hillsides, pine forests. **In bloom:** Apr.–July.

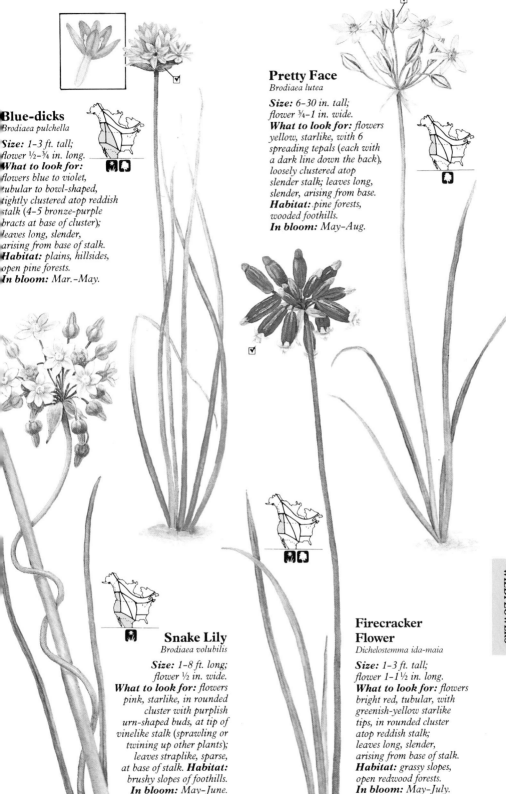

Blue-dicks
Brodiaea pulchella

Size: 1-3 ft. tall;
flower ½-¾ in. long.
What to look for:
flowers blue to violet,
tubular to bowl-shaped,
tightly clustered atop reddish
stalk (4-5 bronze-purple
bracts at base of cluster);
leaves long, slender,
arising from base of stalk.
Habitat: plains, hillsides,
open pine forests.
In bloom: Mar.-May.

Pretty Face
Brodiaea lutea

Size: 6-30 in. tall;
flower ¾-1 in. wide.
What to look for: flowers
yellow, starlike, with 6
spreading tepals (each with
a dark line down the back),
loosely clustered atop
slender stalk; leaves long,
slender, arising from base.
Habitat: pine forests,
wooded foothills.
In bloom: May-Aug.

Snake Lily
Brodiaea volubilis

Size: 1-8 ft. long;
flower ½ in. wide.
What to look for: flowers
pink, starlike, in rounded
cluster with purplish
urn-shaped buds, at tip of
vinelike stalk (sprawling or
twining up other plants);
leaves straplike, sparse,
at base of stalk. **Habitat:**
brushy slopes of foothills.
In bloom: May-June.

Firecracker Flower
Dichelostemma ida-maia

Size: 1-3 ft. tall;
flower 1-1½ in. long.
What to look for: flowers
bright red, tubular, with
greenish-yellow starlike
tips, in rounded cluster
atop reddish stalk;
leaves long, slender,
arising from base of stalk.
Habitat: grassy slopes,
open redwood forests.
In bloom: May-July.

483

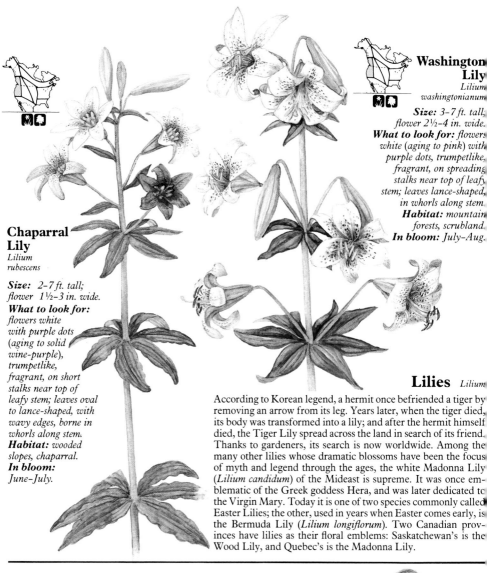

Size: *3–7 ft. tall; flower 2½–4 in. wide.*
What to look for: *flowers white (aging to pink) with purple dots, trumpetlike, fragrant, on spreading stalks near top of leafy stem; leaves lance-shaped, in whorls along stem.*
Habitat: *mountain forests, scrubland.*
In bloom: *July–Aug.*

Chaparral Lily
Lilium rubescens

Size: *2–7 ft. tall; flower 1½–3 in. wide.*
What to look for: *flowers white with purple dots (aging to solid wine-purple), trumpetlike, fragrant, on short stalks near top of leafy stem; leaves oval to lance-shaped, with wavy edges, borne in whorls along stem.*
Habitat: *wooded slopes, chaparral.*
In bloom: *June–July.*

Lilies *Lilium*

According to Korean legend, a hermit once befriended a tiger by removing an arrow from its leg. Years later, when the tiger died, its body was transformed into a lily; and after the hermit himself died, the Tiger Lily spread across the land in search of its friend. Thanks to gardeners, its search is now worldwide. Among the many other lilies whose dramatic blossoms have been the focus of myth and legend through the ages, the white Madonna Lily (*Lilium candidum*) of the Mideast is supreme. It was once emblematic of the Greek goddess Hera, and was later dedicated to the Virgin Mary. Today it is one of two species commonly called Easter Lilies; the other, used in years when Easter comes early, is the Bermuda Lily (*Lilium longiflorum*). Two Canadian provinces have lilies as their floral emblems: Saskatchewan's is the Wood Lily, and Quebec's is the Madonna Lily.

Orange Daylily
Hemerocallis fulva

Size: *2–6 ft. tall; flower 3–5 in. wide.*
What to look for: *flowers tawny orange, trumpet-shaped, borne one or two at a time at top of leafless stalk; leaves long, swordlike, arising from base of stalk.*
Habitat: *fields, meadows, waste places.*
In bloom: *May–July.*

growth form

Daylilies *Hemerocallis*

North America's two daylily species—the lemon-scented Yellow Daylily (*Hemerocallis flava*) is not shown here—are hybrids from Eurasian species, and neither produces viable seeds. Instead, they spread by fibrous rootstocks, quite unlike the bulbs or corms of most true lilies. Another difference is that a daylily's short-lived flowers are borne in irregular bunches on a leafless stalk.

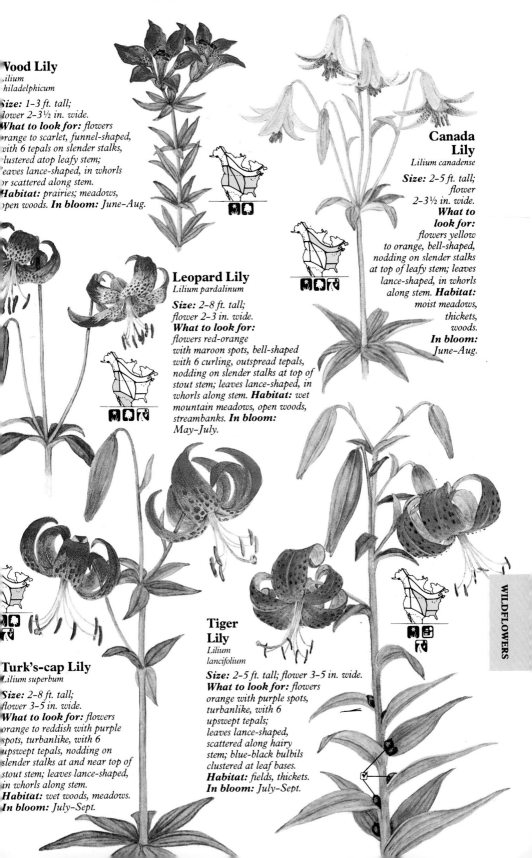

Wood Lily
Lilium
philadelphicum

Size: *1–3 ft. tall;*
flower 2–3½ in. wide.
What to look for: *flowers*
orange to scarlet, funnel-shaped,
with 6 tepals on slender stalks,
clustered atop leafy stem;
leaves lance-shaped, in whorls
or scattered along stem.
Habitat: *prairies; meadows,*
open woods. **In bloom:** *June–Aug.*

Canada Lily
Lilium canadense

Size: *2–5 ft. tall;*
flower
2–3½ in. wide.
What to
look for:
flowers yellow
to orange, bell-shaped,
nodding on slender stalks
at top of leafy stem; leaves
lance-shaped, in whorls
along stem. **Habitat:**
moist meadows,
thickets,
woods.
In bloom:
June–Aug.

Leopard Lily
Lilium pardalinum

Size: *2–8 ft. tall;*
flower 2–3 in. wide.
What to look for:
flowers red-orange
with maroon spots, bell-shaped
with 6 curling, outspread tepals,
nodding on slender stalks at top of
stout stem; leaves lance-shaped, in
whorls along stem. **Habitat:** *wet*
mountain meadows, open woods,
streambanks. **In bloom:**
May–July.

Turk's-cap Lily
Lilium superbum

Size: *2–8 ft. tall;*
flower 3–5 in. wide.
What to look for: *flowers*
orange to reddish with purple
spots, turbanlike, with 6
upswept tepals, nodding on
slender stalks at and near top of
stout stem; leaves lance-shaped,
in whorls along stem.
Habitat: *wet woods, meadows.*
In bloom: *July–Sept.*

Tiger Lily
Lilium
lancifolium

Size: *2–5 ft. tall; flower 3–5 in. wide.*
What to look for: *flowers*
orange with purple spots,
turbanlike, with 6
upswept tepals;
leaves lance-shaped,
scattered along hairy
stem; blue-black bulbils
clustered at leaf bases.
Habitat: *fields, thickets.*
In bloom: *July–Sept.*

Desert Mariposa
Calochortus kennedyi

Size: 4–15 in. tall; flower 2–3½ in. wide. **What to look for:** *flowers bowl-shaped, yellow to vermilion, with brown-purple spots at petal bases; leaves straplike, mostly at base of stem.* **Habitat:** *deserts, dry slopes, pinyon forests.* **In bloom:** *Apr.–June.*

Sego Lily
Calochortus nuttallii

Size: 6–20 in. tall; flower 2–2½ in. wide. **What to look for:** *flowers bowl-shaped, usually white with yellow and purple spots; leaves slender, with rolled edges, mostly at base of stem.* **Habitat:** *dry plains, slopes, pinelands.* **In bloom:** *May–Aug.*

yellow form

Cat's Ear
Calochortus coeruleus

Size: 1–6 in. tall; flower ½–¾ in. wide. **What to look for:** *flowers pale blue to white, fringed, fuzzy; leaves straplike, mostly at base of stem.* **Habitat:** *open woods, rocky slopes.* **In bloom:** *May–July.*

White Mariposa
Calochortus venustus

Size: 8–24 in. tall; flower 2–3 in. wide. **What to look for:** *flowers bowl-shaped, white, yellow, red, or purple (usually with 2–3 dark blotches on each petal); leaves grasslike, mostly at base of stem.* **Habitat:** *dry meadows, slopes, open woods.* **In bloom:** *May–July.*

purple

Mariposa Lilies   *Calochortus*

Before the Mormon pioneers succeeded in making the desert around the Great Salt Lake productive, they lived in part on the bulbs of mariposa lilies, as the Utes and Paiutes and other Indians of the area had been doing for centuries. And when the Mormons' first crops were destroyed by insect swarms, mariposa bulbs were all that kept them from starving. To commemorate the ordeal, Utah chose the Sego Lily as its state flower (*sego* is the Shoshone word for any edible bulb). The bulbs have a nutty flavor when eaten raw; cooked, they resemble potatoes. The tuliplike flowers of most species are extremely variable in color.

Yellow Mandarin
Disporum lanuginosum

Size: 15–30 in. tall; flower ¾–1 in. wide. **What to look for:** *flowers greenish yellow, bell-shaped, dangling at tips of leafy branches; leaves oval with pointed tips, downy.* **Habitat:** *rich woods, thickets.* **In bloom:** *May–June.*

Fairybells   *Disporum*

These woodland members of the lily family have two names, both descriptive of their delicate hanging flowers. In the western states they are usually called fairybells. Easterners are more likely to know their local species as mandarins or mandarin lanterns.

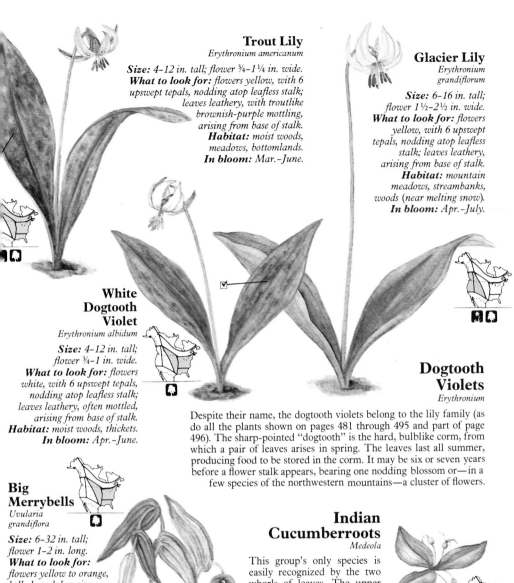

Trout Lily
Erythronium americanum

Size: *4–12 in. tall; flower ¾–1¼ in. wide.*
What to look for: *flowers yellow, with 6 upswept tepals, nodding atop leafless stalk; leaves leathery, with troutlike brownish-purple mottling, arising from base of stalk.*
Habitat: *moist woods, meadows, bottomlands.*
In bloom: *Mar.–June.*

Glacier Lily
Erythronium grandiflorum

Size: *6–16 in. tall; flower 1½–2½ in. wide.*
What to look for: *flowers yellow, with 6 upswept tepals, nodding atop leafless stalk; leaves leathery, arising from base of stalk.*
Habitat: *mountain meadows, streambanks, woods (near melting snow).*
In bloom: *Apr.–July.*

White Dogtooth Violet
Erythronium albidum

Size: *4–12 in. tall; flower ¾–1 in. wide.*
What to look for: *flowers white, with 6 upswept tepals, nodding atop leafless stalk; leaves leathery, often mottled, arising from base of stalk.*
Habitat: *moist woods, thickets.*
In bloom: *Apr.–June.*

Dogtooth Violets
Erythronium

Despite their name, the dogtooth violets belong to the lily family (as do all the plants shown on pages 481 through 495 and part of page 496). The sharp-pointed "dogtooth" is the hard, bulblike corm, from which a pair of leaves arises in spring. The leaves last all summer, producing food to be stored in the corm. It may be six or seven years before a flower stalk appears, bearing one nodding blossom or—in a few species of the northwestern mountains—a cluster of flowers.

Big Merrybells
Uvularia grandiflora

Size: *6–32 in. tall; flower 1–2 in. long.*
What to look for: *flowers yellow to orange, bell-shaped, hanging from tips of leafy branches; leaves oval with pointed tips, their bases clasping stem.*
Habitat: *rich woods.*
In bloom: *Apr.–June.*

Merrybells
Uvularia

Hikers along the Appalachian Trail are charmed in spring and early summer by dainty merrybell blossoms. The asparaguslike shoots, arising from spreading rootstocks, were once eaten, but such exploitation today threatens the group's survival.

Indian Cucumberroots
Medeola

This group's only species is easily recognized by the two whorls of leaves. The upper whorl usually has three leaves, and from its center droop the distinctive flowers or the dark purple berries. The cucumber-like "root" is actually an underground stem, or rhizome.

Indian Cucumberroot
Medeola virginiana

Size: *1–3 ft. tall; flower ½–¾ in. wide.*
What to look for: *flowers greenish yellow, with 6 tepals upswept from reddish stamens and 3 fuzzy brown stigmas; leaves borne in 2 whorls along stem.*
Habitat: *rich woods, bottomlands.*
In bloom: *May–June.*

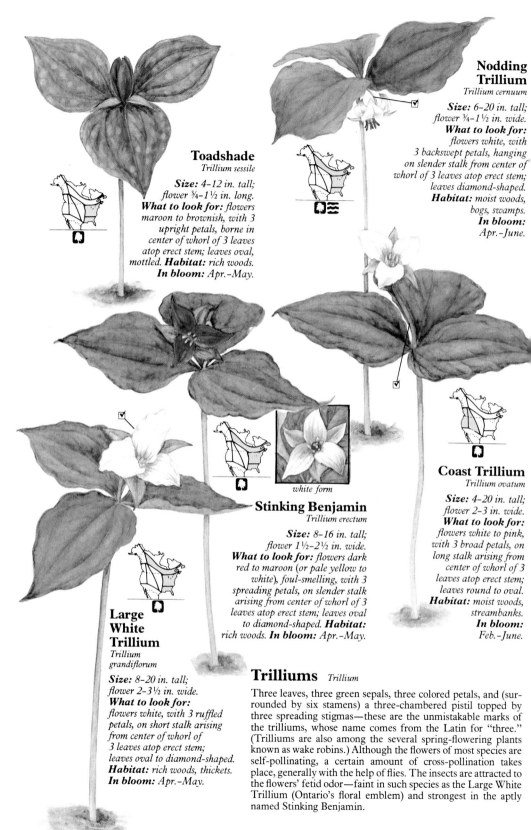

Nodding Trillium
Trillium cernuum

Size: *6–20 in. tall; flower ¾–1½ in. wide.*
What to look for: *flowers white, with 3 backswept petals, hanging on slender stalk from center of whorl of 3 leaves atop erect stem; leaves diamond-shaped.*
Habitat: *moist woods, bogs, swamps.*
In bloom: *Apr.–June.*

Toadshade
Trillium sessile

Size: *4–12 in. tall; flower ¾–1½ in. long.*
What to look for: *flowers maroon to brownish, with 3 upright petals, borne in center of whorl of 3 leaves atop erect stem; leaves oval, mottled.* **Habitat:** *rich woods.*
In bloom: *Apr.–May.*

white form

Stinking Benjamin
Trillium erectum

Size: *8–16 in. tall; flower 1½–2½ in. wide.*
What to look for: *flowers dark red to maroon (or pale yellow to white), foul-smelling, with 3 spreading petals, on slender stalk arising from center of whorl of 3 leaves atop erect stem; leaves oval to diamond-shaped.* **Habitat:** *rich woods.* **In bloom:** *Apr.–May.*

Coast Trillium
Trillium ovatum

Size: *4–20 in. tall; flower 2–3 in. wide.*
What to look for: *flowers white to pink, with 3 broad petals, on long stalk arising from center of whorl of 3 leaves atop erect stem; leaves round to oval.* **Habitat:** *moist woods, streambanks.*
In bloom: *Feb.–June.*

Large White Trillium
Trillium grandiflorum

Size: *8–20 in. tall; flower 2–3½ in. wide.*
What to look for: *flowers white, with 3 ruffled petals, on short stalk arising from center of whorl of 3 leaves atop erect stem; leaves oval to diamond-shaped.* **Habitat:** *rich woods, thickets.* **In bloom:** *Apr.–May.*

Trilliums   *Trillium*

Three leaves, three green sepals, three colored petals, and (surrounded by six stamens) a three-chambered pistil topped by three spreading stigmas—these are the unmistakable marks of the trilliums, whose name comes from the Latin for "three." (Trilliums are also among the several spring-flowering plants known as wake robins.) Although the flowers of most species are self-pollinating, a certain amount of cross-pollination takes place, generally with the help of flies. The insects are attracted to the flowers' fetid odor—faint in such species as the Large White Trillium (Ontario's floral emblem) and strongest in the aptly named Stinking Benjamin.

Asparagus
Asparagus officinalis

Size: *1–7 ft. tall; flower ⅛–¼ in. wide.*
What to look for: *plants erect, branching, with clusters of needlelike green branchlets; flowers greenish white, bell-shaped, hanging on slender stalks; berries red.*
Habitat: *fields, meadows, roadsides, railway embankments.* **In bloom:** *May–June.*

edible spears

Asparagus   *Asparagus*

Each spring, tender asparagus spears sprout from long, cordlike roots and, if not harvested, grow into tall stalks with fernlike "foliage." (To locate a productive bed, look in winter for a stand of dry stalks.) The apparent leaves are actually clusters of slender branchlets; the true leaf is a brownish scale at the base of a cluster. The popular Asparagus Fern (*Asparagus setaceus*) is among the group's tropical species often sold as houseplants.

Wild Garlic
Allium canadense

Size: *8–24 in. tall; flower ¼–½ in. wide.*
What to look for: *flowers pink to white, starlike, in loose cluster with many green-brown bulblets atop leafless stem; leaves grasslike, arising from base of stem.* **Habitat:** *moist meadows, prairies, open woods.* **In bloom:** *May–June.*

Wild Leek
Allium tricoccum

Size: *6–18 in. tall; flower ¼–½ in. wide.*
What to look for: *flowers white, starlike, in rounded cluster atop leafless stem; leaves elliptical, clustered at base of stem (withered by flowering time).* **Habitat:** *rich woods.* **In bloom:** *June–July.*

Onions
Allium

The Ojibwa Indians knew the prairies at the southern end of Lake Michigan as *she-kag-ong*, or "place of the wild onion." Today, we call the place Chicago. Onions grow throughout the Northern Hemisphere, and have been used for food and seasoning everywhere. They are a problem for dairy farmers because a cow that eats the leaves—or even breathes much of the vapor from trampled plants—gives evil-tasting milk.

Prairie Onion
Allium stellatum

Size: *8–30 in. tall; flower ¼–½ in. wide.*
What to look for: *flowers pink to lavender, starlike, in rounded cluster atop leafless stem; leaves grasslike, fleshy, arising from base of stem.* **Habitat:** *prairies, rocky slopes.* **In bloom:** *July–Sept.*

Wild Onion
Allium drummondii

Size: *4–12 in. tall; flower ¼–½ in. wide.*
What to look for: *flowers rose-purple to white, in loose cluster atop leafless stem; leaves grasslike, arising from base of stem.* **Habitat:** *dry prairies, plains.* **In bloom:** *Mar.–June.*

leaves in spring

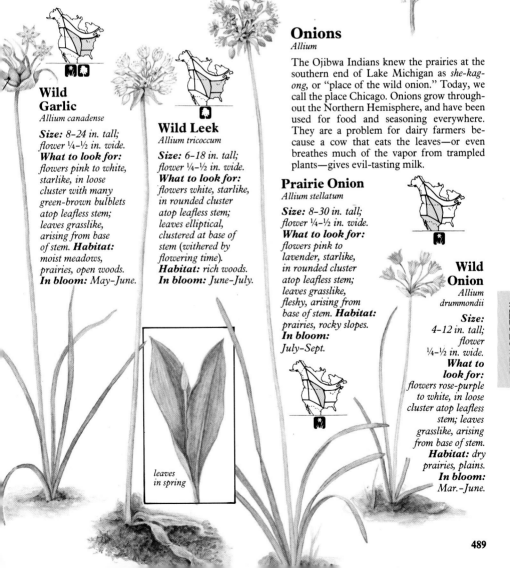

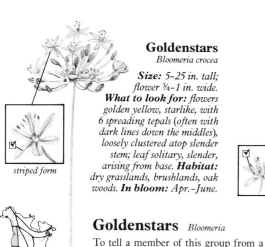

Goldenstars
Bloomeria crocea

Size: 5-25 in. tall; flower ¾-1 in. wide. **What to look for:** flowers golden yellow, starlike, with 6 spreading tepals (often with dark lines down the middles), loosely clustered atop slender stem; leaf solitary, slender, arising from base. **Habitat:** dry grasslands, brushlands, oak woods. **In bloom:** Apr.-June.

striped form

California Bog Asphodel
Narthecium californicum

Size: 1-2 ft. tall; flower ½-¾ in. wide. **What to look for:** flowers greenish yellow, starlike, with red-tipped stamens, in slender cluster near top of stem; leaves grasslike, in dense tuft at base. **Habitat:** wet meadows, marshy woods, bogs. **In bloom:** July-Aug.

Goldenstars *Bloomeria*

To tell a member of this group from a brodiaea lily, look closely at a single flower. In goldenstars, the six tepals (identical petals and sepals) are separated and the six stamens arise on slender filaments from small nectar cups. The tepals of a brodiaea lily spread from a tubelike base, and the stamens form a crownlike central cluster.

Bog Asphodels *Narthecium*

These are cousins of the Mediterranean asphodels (*Asphodeline lutea*) of classical mythology, with which the Elysian meadows were said to be strewed. The rare New Jersey Bog Asphodel (*Narthecium americanum*) of eastern pine barrens and coastal plains is smaller than its California counterpart.

Yellow Stargrass
Hypoxis hirsuta

Size: 2-12 in. tall; flower ½-¾ in. wide. **What to look for:** flowers yellow, starlike, in open cluster atop leafless stem; leaves long, grasslike, in tufts. **Habitat:** meadows, prairies, fields, open woods, thickets. **In bloom:** Apr.-Sept.

Soap Plant
Chlorogalum pomeridianum

Size: 2-10 ft. tall; flower 1-2 in. wide. **What to look for:** flowers white with purple or green midveins, in branching clusters at top of stout stem; leaves straplike with wavy edges, clustered at base of stem. **Habitat:** dry plains, scrublands, open woods. **In bloom:** May-Aug. (evening).

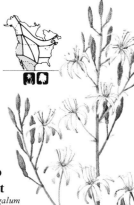

leaves (at base)

Stargrasses *Hypoxis*

Like the stargrasses shown on page 481, plants in this group are not grasses at all, but members of the lily family. These stargrasses seem more deserving of the name, with their small clusters of bright white or yellow six-pointed blossoms twinkling among the tufts of slender green leaves.

Soap Plants *Chlorogalum*

Western Indians made mats and brushes from the coarse fibers covering soap plant bulbs. The bulbs themselves were used for soap or thrown into ponds to suffocate fish. They were also roasted and eaten, and the juice was salvaged to make glue for feathering arrows and a paste for treating poison oak rashes.

Atamasco Lily
Zephyranthes atamasco

Size: *4–12 in. tall; flower 2–3½ in. wide.*
What to look for: *flowers white with reddish tints, funnel-shaped, atop leafless stalk; leaves grasslike, arising from base of stalk.* **Habitat:** *wet woods, clearings, bottomlands.* **In bloom:** *Mar.–May.*

Goldencrest
Lophiola americana

Size: *1–3 ft. tall; flower ¼ in. wide.*
What to look for: *flowers woolly outside with tufts of bright yellow hair inside, in dense clusters at top of white woolly stem; leaves long, grasslike, arising from base of stem.* **Habitat:** *bogs, wet pinelands, moist savannas.* **In bloom:** *May–Sept.*

Zephyr Lilies *Zephyranthes*

The soft west wind that often follows spring rains brings with it, in the Southeast and along the Gulf Coast, the fragrant blossoms of several species of zephyr lilies, also known as rain lilies. The red-tinged Atamasco Lily (from an Algonquian word for "it is red") is one of two species sometimes used as substitutes for Easter Lilies.

Goldencrests *Lophiola*

The Goldencrest in bloom is not likely to be mistaken for any other plant. A close look at one of the small woolly flowers underlines the plant's singularity: the six tepals are maroon inside, but their color is obscured by the bright tufts of yellow hair that cover them. There is only one species.

Swamp Lily
Crinum americanum

Size: *1–3 ft. tall; flower 3½–5½ in. wide.*
What to look for: *flowers white with pink markings, starlike, clustered atop stout stalk; leaves straplike, slightly toothed.* **Habitat:** *marshes, cypress swamps, wet forests, streambanks.* **In bloom:** *May–Nov.*

Yellow Bell
Fritillaria pudica

Size: *3–12 in. tall; flower ½–¾ in. wide.*
What to look for: *flowers yellow, 1–3 borne nodding atop leafless stalks; leaves sparse, straplike, mostly at base of stem.* **Habitat:** *desert grasslands, hillsides, open woods, scrublands.* **In bloom:** *Mar.–June.*

Crinum Lilies *Crinum*

Greenhouse enthusiasts and southern gardeners probably know several of this group's many tropical species and even more hybrids. A few kinds, such as the Milk-and-wine Lily (*Crinum latifolium zeylanicum*), are hardy in gardens as far north as New York. The Swamp Lily is the only species native to the continental United States.

Fritillaries *Fritillaria*

The bulblike corm from which a fritillary sprouts is surrounded by a peculiar mass of bulblets that look like grains of rice. Bears and rodents seek out the corms, and various browsing animals feed on the green parts. The starchy corms and green pods are tasty and nutritious raw or cooked, and were often eaten by Indians and Eskimos.

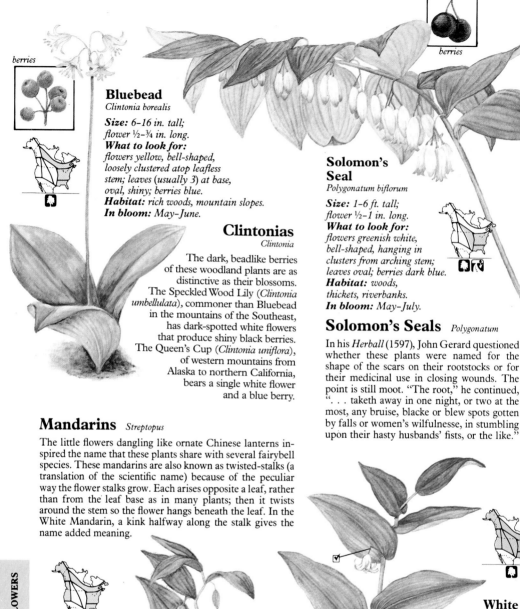

berries

Bluebead
Clintonia borealis

*Size: 6–16 in. tall;
flower ½–¾ in. long.*
What to look for:
*flowers yellow, bell-shaped,
loosely clustered atop leafless
stem; leaves (usually 3) at base,
oval, shiny; berries blue.*
Habitat: rich woods, mountain slopes.
In bloom: May–June.

Clintonias
Clintonia

The dark, beadlike berries
of these woodland plants are as
distinctive as their blossoms.
The Speckled Wood Lily (*Clintonia
umbellulata*), commoner than Bluebead
in the mountains of the Southeast,
has dark-spotted white flowers
that produce shiny black berries.
The Queen's Cup (*Clintonia uniflora*),
of western mountains from
Alaska to northern California,
bears a single white flower
and a blue berry.

berries

Solomon's Seal
Polygonatum biflorum

*Size: 1–6 ft. tall;
flower ½–1 in. long.*
What to look for:
*flowers greenish white,
bell-shaped, hanging in
clusters from arching stem;
leaves oval; berries dark blue.*
*Habitat: woods,
thickets, riverbanks.*
In bloom: May–July.

Solomon's Seals *Polygonatum*

In his *Herball* (1597), John Gerard questioned
whether these plants were named for the
shape of the scars on their rootstocks or for
their medicinal use in closing wounds. The
point is still moot. "The root," he continued,
". . . taketh away in one night, or two at the
most, any bruise, blacke or blew spots gotten
by falls or women's wilfulnesse, in stumbling
upon their hasty husbands' fists, or the like."

Mandarins *Streptopus*

The little flowers dangling like ornate Chinese lanterns inspired the name that these plants share with several fairybell
species. These mandarins are also known as twisted-stalks (a
translation of the scientific name) because of the peculiar
way the flower stalks grow. Each arises opposite a leaf, rather
than from the leaf base as in many plants; then it twists
around the stem so the flower hangs beneath the leaf. In the
White Mandarin, a kink halfway along the stalk gives the
name added meaning.

White Mandarin
*Streptopus
amplexifolius*

*Size:
1–4 ft. tall;
flower ½ in. long.*
What to look for:
*flowers creamy white, bell-shaped,
with 6 up-curled tepals, hanging
singly beneath leaves on sharply
twisted threadlike stalks; leaves oval,
their bases embracing zigzag stem.*
Habitat: rich woods, thickets.
In bloom: May–July.

Rose Mandarin
Streptopus roseus

*Size: 6–30 in. tall;
flower ¼–½ in. long.*
What to look for:
*flowers pink to purple,
bell-shaped, hanging
singly beneath leaves
on threadlike twisted
stalks; leaves oval,
scattered along zigzag
stem. Habitat: rich woods,
thickets. In bloom: May–July.*

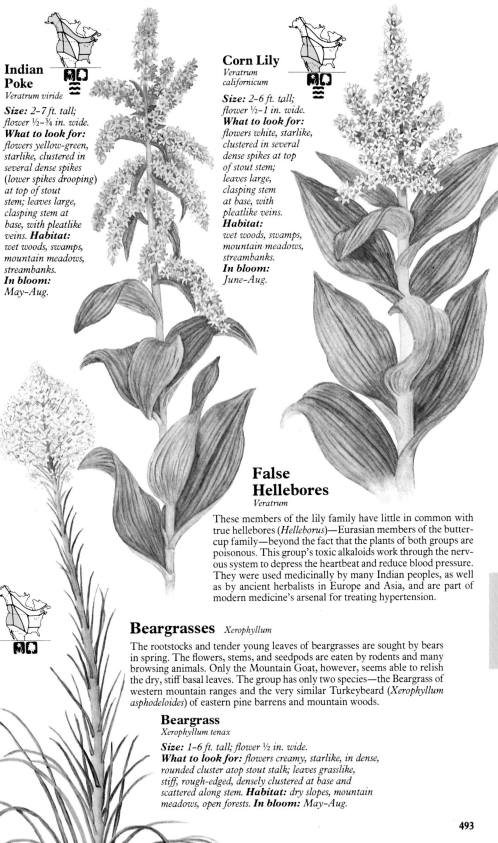

Indian Poke
Veratrum viride

Size: *2–7 ft. tall; flower ½–¾ in. wide.*
What to look for: *flowers yellow-green, starlike, clustered in several dense spikes (lower spikes drooping) at top of stout stem; leaves large, clasping stem at base, with pleatlike veins.* **Habitat:** *wet woods, swamps, mountain meadows, streambanks.* **In bloom:** *May–Aug.*

Corn Lily
Veratrum californicum

Size: *2–6 ft. tall; flower ½–1 in. wide.*
What to look for: *flowers white, starlike, clustered in several dense spikes at top of stout stem; leaves large, clasping stem at base, with pleatlike veins.* **Habitat:** *wet woods, swamps, mountain meadows, streambanks.* **In bloom:** *June–Aug.*

False Hellebores
Veratrum

These members of the lily family have little in common with true hellebores (*Helleborus*)—Eurasian members of the buttercup family—beyond the fact that the plants of both groups are poisonous. This group's toxic alkaloids work through the nervous system to depress the heartbeat and reduce blood pressure. They were used medicinally by many Indian peoples, as well as by ancient herbalists in Europe and Asia, and are part of modern medicine's arsenal for treating hypertension.

Beargrasses   *Xerophyllum*

The rootstocks and tender young leaves of beargrasses are sought by bears in spring. The flowers, stems, and seedpods are eaten by rodents and many browsing animals. Only the Mountain Goat, however, seems able to relish the dry, stiff basal leaves. The group has only two species—the Beargrass of western mountain ranges and the very similar Turkeybeard (*Xerophyllum asphodeloides*) of eastern pine barrens and mountain woods.

Beargrass
Xerophyllum tenax

Size: *1–6 ft. tall; flower ½ in. wide.*
What to look for: *flowers creamy, starlike, in dense, rounded cluster atop stout stalk; leaves grasslike, stiff, rough-edged, densely clustered at base and scattered along stem.* **Habitat:** *dry slopes, mountain meadows, open forests.* **In bloom:** *May–Aug.*

Sand Lily
Leucocrinum montanum

Size: *2-6 in. tall;*
flower 1-1½ in. wide.
What to look for: *flowers white,*
tubular, with star-shaped
flare, clustered among a clump
of grasslike leaves. **Habitat:**
mountain meadows, scrublands.
In bloom: *Apr.-June.*

single
male
flower

Fairy Wands
Chamaelirium

This group's single
species is also
called Devil's Bit
and Blazing Star.
Its male and female
flowers are borne
on separate plants.
The long flower
cluster on a male
plant (shown here)
tapers to a graceful,
drooping tip. On a
female plant, the
flower cluster is
shorter, and it
stands upright.

Fairy Wand
Chamaelirium
luteum

Size: *1-4 ft. tall;*
flower ¼ in. wide.
What to look for:
flowers white, in
dense wand atop stem;
leaves spatula-shaped,
densely clustered at
base and scattered
along stem. **Habitat:**
wet woods, meadows,
bogs. **In bloom:**
May-July.

Sand Lilies *Leucocrinum*

The fragrant flowers of the Sand Lily nestle at ground level, amid a rosette
of grasslike leaves. The stalks are underground, springing directly from the
fleshy rootstock. The group's only species is also called the Mountain Lily,
Star Lily, and Star-of-Bethlehem.

Camases *Camassia*

Baked in an oven of hot stones, the quamash bulb was the most important
plant food of the Indian peoples of the Northwest. When the government
forced those peaceful tribes to abandon lands where the Quamash grew, the
bloody Plateau Wars began, ending with the bitter defeat of Chief Joseph's
Nez Percé in 1877. The bulbs of all five camas species are nutritious, but the
plants can all too easily be confused with poisonous relatives.

Quamash
Camassia quamash

Size: *8-30 in. tall;*
flower 1-2½ in. wide.
What to look for:
flowers blue, starlike,
in dense wandlike
cluster atop leafless
stem; leaves grasslike,
clustered at base of stem.
Habitat: *moist meadows.*
In bloom: *Apr.-July.*

Wild Hyacinth
Camassia scilloides

Size: *8-24 in. tall;*
flower ½-1 in. wide.
What to look for:
flowers pale blue,
starlike, in dense
wandlike cluster
atop leafless stem;
leaves grasslike,
clustered at base of stem.
Habitat: *moist meadows,*
prairies, open woods.
In bloom:
Apr.-June.

WILDFLOWERS

Alkali Grass
Zigadenus elegans

Size: *1-3 ft. tall; flower ½-1 in. wide.*
What to look for: *flowers white with green centers, starlike, in wandlike cluster at top of erect stem; leaves grasslike, mostly clustered at base of stem.* **Habitat:** *mountain meadows, prairies, open woods.*
In bloom: *June–Aug.*

Death Camases
Zigadenus

The most notable difference between a camas and a death camas is that, if you eat the bulb of a death camas, you will probably die. Because camas bulbs are not at their best during flowering season, when their blue blossoms set them apart, it was important for Indian food gatherers to recognize subtle differences between the bulbs.

Canada Mayflower
Maianthemum canadense

berries

Size: *2-6 in. tall; flower ⅛-¼ in. wide.*
What to look for: *flowers white, with 4 tepals, in dense spike atop stem with 2-3 leaves; leaves oval or heart-shaped; berries red, speckled.*
Habitat: *moist woods, thickets, clearings.*
In bloom: *May-July.*

False Lilies of the Valley *Maianthemum*

These woodland plants differ from all other members of the lily family—including the true lilies of the valley (*Convallaria*)—in that the flower parts are in twos and fours rather than threes and sixes. In addition to the leaves borne on each flowering stem, many leaves arise singly from the rootstock, but these usually wither before flowering time.

berries

Solomon's Zigzag
Smilacina racemosa

Size: *1-3 ft. tall; flower ⅛-¼ in. wide.*
What to look for: *flowers white, starlike, in dense, branching cluster at top of zigzag stem; leaves oval, alternating along stem; berries red.*
Habitat: *rich woods.*
In bloom: *Mar.-July.*

Bunchflower
Melanthium virginicum

Size: *2-5 ft. tall; flower ½-1 in. wide.*
What to look for: *flowers greenish white (turning purple), starlike, in dense spikes at top of erect stem; leaves grasslike, mostly clustered at base of stem.*
Habitat: *moist meadows, woods, prairies.*
In bloom: *June–Aug.*

Bunchflowers
Melanthium

As a bunchflower ages, the blossom turns from greenish white to purple, finally becoming almost black (the scientific name means "black flower"). This characteristic, along with the narrower leaves borne mostly at the base of the stem, is the easiest way to differentiate members of this North American group from the similar-looking false hellebores.

False Solomon's Seals
Smilacina

When not in flower or fruit, a false Solomon's seal can be hard to tell from the genuine article, but when the flowers or berries are seen clustered at the stem's tip rather than dangling along its length, identification is simple. Because of this cluster, members of the group are also known as Solomon's plumes.

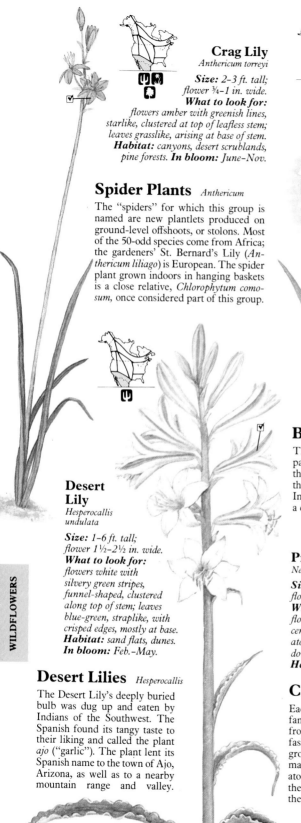

Crag Lily
Anthericum torreyi

Size: 2–3 ft. tall; flower ¾–1 in. wide.
What to look for: flowers amber with greenish lines, starlike, clustered at top of leafless stem; leaves grasslike, arising at base of stem. **Habitat:** canyons, desert scrublands, pine forests. **In bloom:** June–Nov.

Spider Plants   *Anthericum*

The "spiders" for which this group is named are new plantlets produced on ground-level offshoots, or stolons. Most of the 50-odd species come from Africa; the gardeners' St. Bernard's Lily (*Anthericum liliago*) is European. The spider plant grown indoors in hanging baskets is a close relative, *Chlorophytum comosum*, once considered part of this group.

Desert Lily
Hesperocallis undulata

Size: 1–6 ft. tall; flower 1½–2½ in. wide.
What to look for: flowers white with silvery green stripes, funnel-shaped, clustered along top of stem; leaves blue-green, straplike, with crisped edges, mostly at base. **Habitat:** sand flats, dunes. **In bloom:** Feb.–May.

Desert Lilies   *Hesperocallis*

The Desert Lily's deeply buried bulb was dug up and eaten by Indians of the Southwest. The Spanish found its tangy taste to their liking and called the plant *ajo* ("garlic"). The plant lent its Spanish name to the town of Ajo, Arizona, as well as to a nearby mountain range and valley.

White Blue-eyed Grass
Sisyrinchium albidum

Size: 4–16 in. tall; flower ½ in. wide.
What to look for: flowers white to pale blue, starlike, borne on wiry stalks atop flat stem; leaves grasslike, stiff, mostly at base. **Habitat:** dry fields, meadows. **In bloom:** Apr.–June.

Blue-eyed Grass
Sisyrinchium angustifolium

Size: 6–24 in. tall; flower ¾–1 in. wide.
What to look for: flowers blue to violet, starlike, borne on wiry stalks atop flat stems; leaves grasslike, stiff, mostly at base. **Habitat:** wet meadows, fields, woods. **In bloom:** May–July.

Blue-eyed Grasses   *Sisyrinchium*

The blue-eyed grasses are identifiable as part of the iris family by the way in which their leaves overlap at the base and by the three stamens in the center of each flower. In this group, the stamens are joined to form a central column around the pistil.

Prairie Iris
Nemastylis geminiflora

Size: 5–24 in. tall; flower 1¾–2½ in. wide.
What to look for: flowers blue with white centers, borne singly or in pairs atop stem; leaves swordlike, with crease down center, mostly at base of stem. **Habitat:** prairies. **In bloom:** Mar.–June.

Celestial Lilies   *Nemastylis*

Each year, these members of the iris family produce new bulbs. They differ from most plants that reproduce in this fashion, however, in that the new bulb grows directly beneath the old one. As many as six bulbs may accumulate, one atop another, with the stem and leaves of the bottom one pushing up through all the others. They also reproduce by seed.

Irises *Iris*

Iris was the Greek goddess of the rainbow, whose role was often to bring peace after one of the gods' stormy confrontations. The plants of this bright, colorful group well deserve her name. An iris blossom seems to have nine petals; the outer three (called falls) are really sepals, the next three (the standards) are true petals, and the center three are crestlike branches of the pistil. The base of each fall combines with one of the crests to form a tube, its entrance marked by lines, a splotch of color, or a fuzzy beard. When a pollinating insect or bird seeks the nectar at the base of the tube, the stigma at the top of the crest dips down to receive pollen from its body. Inside the tube, the stamen waits to dust the creature with more pollen. The iris is Tennessee's state flower.

Dwarf Blue Flag
Iris verna

Size: *5–12 in. tall; flower 1½–2 in. wide.*
What to look for: *flowers violet (yellow blotches on falls), with upright standards; leaves stiff, mostly clustered at base of stalk.*
Habitat: *pine barrens, sandy woods, peaty soil.*
In bloom: *Mar.–May.*

Rocky Mountain Iris
Iris missouriensis

Size: *1–3 ft. tall; flower 2½–3 in. wide.*
What to look for: *flowers blue to lilac (yellow, white, and purple markings on falls), with upright standards; leaves swordlike, pale green, densely clustered at base of stout stalk.* **Habitat:** *moist meadows, flatlands.*
In bloom: *May–July.*

Southern Blue Flag
Iris virginica

Size: *18–30 in. tall; flower 2½–3½ in. wide.*
What to look for: *flowers pale lavender to violet (downy yellow blotches on falls), with spreading standards; leaves swordlike, arching, mostly clustered at base of lax, arching stalk.* **Habitat:** *marshes, swamps, lakeshores.*
In bloom: *Apr.–July.*

Red Flag
Iris fulva

Size: *2–5 ft. tall; flower 3–4 in. wide.*
What to look for: *flowers reddish brown to bronze, with dark veins on spreading falls and standards; leaves swordlike, densely clustered at base and scattered along branching stalk.* **Habitat:** *wet meadows, marshes, streambanks.*
In bloom: *Apr.–June.*

Yellow Flag
Iris pseudacorus

Size: *2–3 ft. tall; flower 3–4 in. wide.*
What to look for: *flowers yellow (dark lines on broad falls), with small upright standards; leaves stiff, swordlike, mostly at base of stalk.* **Habitat:** *wet meadows, marshes, swamps, streambanks, lakeshores.*
In bloom: *Apr.–Aug.*

497

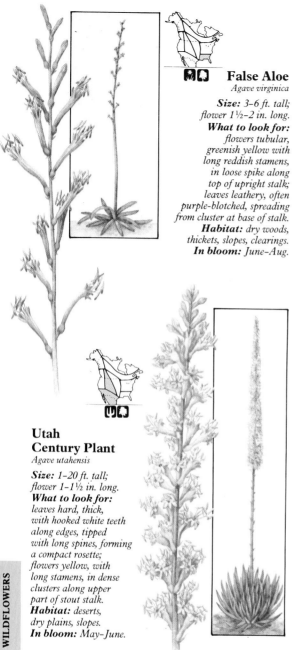

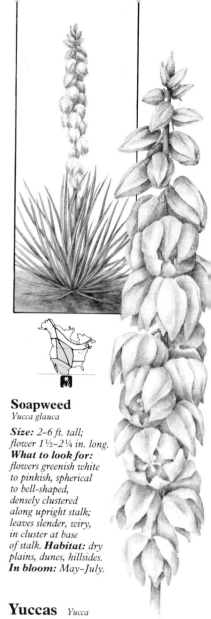

False Aloe
Agave virginica

Size: *3–6 ft. tall;*
flower 1½–2 in. long.
What to look for:
flowers tubular,
greenish yellow with
long reddish stamens,
in loose spike along
top of upright stalk;
leaves leathery, often
purple-blotched, spreading
from cluster at base of stalk.
Habitat: *dry woods,*
thickets, slopes, clearings.
In bloom: *June–Aug.*

Utah
Century Plant
Agave utahensis

Size: *1–20 ft. tall;*
flower 1–1½ in. long.
What to look for:
leaves hard, thick,
with hooked white teeth
along edges, tipped
with long spines, forming
a compact rosette;
flowers yellow, with
long stamens, in dense
clusters along upper
part of stout stalk.
Habitat: *deserts,*
dry plains, slopes.
In bloom: *May–June.*

Soapweed
Yucca glauca

Size: *2–6 ft. tall;*
flower 1½–2¼ in. long.
What to look for:
flowers greenish white
to pinkish, spherical
to bell-shaped,
densely clustered
along upright stalk;
leaves slender, wiry,
in cluster at base
of stalk. **Habitat:** *dry*
plains, dunes, hillsides.
In bloom: *May–July.*

Century Plants *Agave*

This group's name is an exaggeration at best: no century plant has been known to reach the age of 100 years, although many species live several decades before putting forth their treelike flower stalks. The tubular flowers are pollinated by long-tongued bats, which crawl down the spikes or hover in midair while lapping the sweet nectar. (Some bats migrate northward from Mexico every year, following the flowering season.) Although many agave species, including the Utah Century Plant, die after flowering, the False Aloe and some other bulbous species produce a new cluster of spine-tipped leaves and a new flowering stalk each summer.

Yuccas *Yucca*

The pollination of a yucca is a task that can be performed by only one group of moths. Conversely, the continued existence of yucca moths depends on their ability to pollinate yuccas. An adult yucca moth never eats. Its mouthparts have but one function: to gather grains of yucca pollen and knead them into a ball. After mating, a female moth makes such a ball and flies with it to a different flower. There she injects her eggs into the embryonic seedpod at the base of the pistil, then climbs to the top of the pistil and stuffs the ball of pollen down inside. Caterpillars hatching from the eggs live on some of the developing seeds until they pupate. New Mexico's state flower is a yucca, and so is the Joshua-tree, shown in the tree section of this book.

WILDFLOWERS

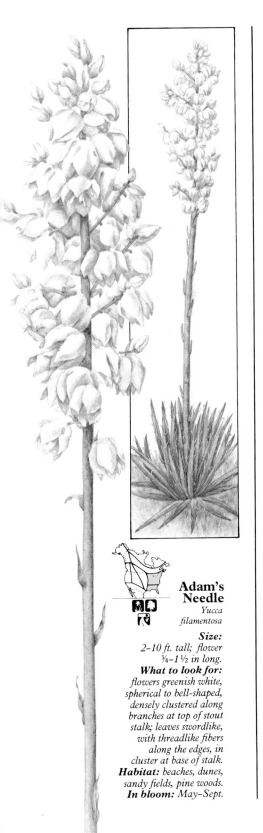

Greenbriers *Smilax*

Most greenbrier species are woody vines whose thorny stems can form nearly impenetrable tangles in eastern forests. The rootstocks of several tropical kinds yield the drug sarsaparilla, used as a tonic and an aphrodisiac (not to be confused with the beverage that was once flavored with birch oil and sassafras bark). The Carrion Flower, named for the fly-attracting odor of its greenish-white flowers, is among the few herbaceous greenbriers, whose thornless stems die back to the ground each winter.

Carrion Flower
Smilax herbacea

Size: *2-9 ft. high; flower ⅛-¼ in. wide.*
What to look for: *flowers greenish white, in round clusters along climbing stems; leaves oval to heart-shaped, with long tendrils at base; berries blue to purple.* **Habitat:** *woods, thickets, fencerows.*
In bloom: *May-June.*

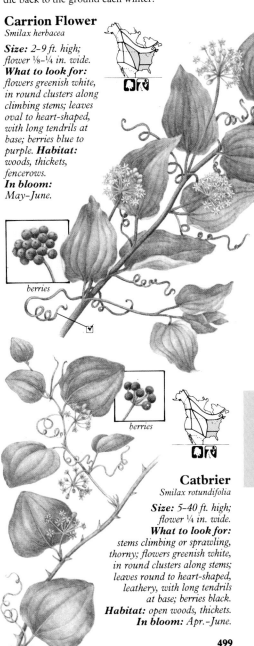

berries

Catbrier
Smilax rotundifolia

Size: *5-40 ft. high; flower ¼ in. wide.*
What to look for: *stems climbing or sprawling, thorny; flowers greenish white, in round clusters along stems; leaves round to heart-shaped, leathery, with long tendrils at base; berries black.*
Habitat: *open woods, thickets.*
In bloom: *Apr.-June.*

berries

Adam's Needle
Yucca filamentosa

Size: *2-10 ft. tall; flower ¾-1½ in. long.*
What to look for: *flowers greenish white, spherical to bell-shaped, densely clustered along branches at top of stout stalk; leaves swordlike, with threadlike fibers along the edges, in cluster at base of stalk.*
Habitat: *beaches, dunes, sandy fields, pine woods.*
In bloom: *May-Sept.*

WILDFLOWERS

499

Moccasin Flower
Cypripedium acaule

Size: *6–16 in. tall; flower 2–5 in. wide.*
What to look for: *flowers magenta to white, with veined slipperlike lip and purplish-brown twisted side petals; leaves oval, paired, at base of stem.* **Habitat:** *woods, thickets, pine barrens, bogs.*
In bloom: *Apr.–July.*

Showy Lady's Slipper
Cypripedium reginae

Size: *1–3 ft. tall; flower 2–4 in. wide.*
What to look for: *flowers with rose-pink slipperlike lip and white tepals, borne singly or in pairs; leaves clasping stem.* **Habitat:** *woods, bogs.*
In bloom: *May–Aug.*

Yellow Lady's Slipper
Cypripedium calceolus

Size: *4–24 in. tall; flower 2–6 in. wide.*
What to look for: *flowers yellow, with slipperlike lip and brown to greenish spiral side petals, borne singly or in pairs; leaves oval, clasping stem.* **Habitat:** *rich woods, swamps, bogs.*
In bloom: *Apr.–Aug.*

Mountain Lady's Slipper
Cypripedium montanum

Size: *10–28 in. tall; flower 2–4 in. wide.*
What to look for: *flowers with white slipperlike lip and purplish spiral side petals, 1–3 borne near top of stem; leaves clasping stem.* **Habitat:** *open woods, slopes.*
In bloom: *May–July.*

White Lady's Slipper
Cypripedium candidum

Size: *6–14 in. tall; flower 1–2 in. wide.*
What to look for: *flowers with white slipperlike lip and greenish spiral side petals; leaves oblong, sheathing stem.* **Habitat:** *moist meadows, prairies, bogs.*
In bloom: *Apr.–June.*

Lady's Slippers *Cypripedium*

The Showy Lady's Slipper is the provincial emblem of Prince Edward Island and the state flower of Minnesota. Like the rest of this group, it depends for pollination on the gullibility of insects. Although no nectar is contained in the slipperlike pouch formed by the lower petal, or lip, bees are attracted by a nectarlike scent from within. Once inside, the unsatisfied insect can escape only by squeezing through one of two small channels at the rear of the pouch, where its back is coated with pollen. Undaunted, it proceeds to another blossom and repeats the process, still getting no nectar but leaving some pollen on the female stigma as it pushes toward an exit channel.

Three Birds
Triphora trianthophora

Size: *3–12 in. tall;*
flower ½–¾ in. wide.
What to look for:
flowers pale pink to white, with
greenish markings on ruffled lip,
usually borne in 3's, nodding,
at top of leafy stem; leaves oval,
fleshy, clasping stem. **Habitat:**
rich woods. **In bloom:** *July–Oct.*

Nodding Pogonias   *Triphora*

Flowers of the orchid family (shown on these two and the next six pages) have three sepals and three petals arranged around a central column, or gynostemium, which contains both the pollen-producing stamens and the pollen-receptive stigma of the pistil. The lowermost petal is enlarged to form a lip, which in this group serves as a landing strip for insects.

Calypso
Calypso bulbosa

Size: *2–8 in. tall; flower 1–2 in. wide.*
What to look for: *flowers rose-pink,*
with yellow and purplish markings on
pouchlike lip; leaf oval, solitary,
at base of stem. **Habitat:** *cool mossy*
woods, bogs. **In bloom:** *Apr.–July.*

Calypsos   *Calypso*

At first glance, this group's only species might be taken for one of the lady's slippers (it is often called Fairy Slipper). The only resemblance, however, is the shape of the lip petal. Odorless and nectarless, the Calypso attracts insects with the tuft of yellow hairs on its lip, which look like the stamens of some nectar-rich flowers.

Dragon's Mouth
Arethusa bulbosa

Size: *2–10 in. tall;*
flower 1–1½ in. wide.
What to look for:
flowers magenta-pink,
with purplish markings
and yellow bristles
on broad lip; leaf solitary, grasslike,
borne after flower fades. **Habitat:** *bogs.*
In bloom: *May–Aug.*

Dragon's Mouths   *Arethusa*

This group once included all the plants shown on this page except the Calypso. One by one, the other pogonias were reclassified, and now the group has only one species. It is a rare bog orchid, which blooms briefly before producing its grasslike leaf. Pollinating insects (usually bumblebees), attracted by the flower's sweet scent, land on the lip and are guided by three yellow-crested ridges to the nectar in the throat.

Rosebud Orchid
Cleistes divaricata

Size: *6–28 in. tall;*
flower 1–2 in. long.
What to look for: *flowers*
pink to white, tubular,
with 3 spreading brownish sepals
and a leaflike green bract;
leaf oval to lance-shaped,
solitary, partway up slender stem.
Habitat: *moist pine barrens,*
bogs, sandy meadows.
In bloom: *Apr.–July.*

Spreading Pogonias
Cleistes

In these orchids, the three spreading sepals are clearly different from the petals, which form a tube around the central column. (In the Calypso and many other orchids, only the lip petal is markedly different; the other five nearly identical parts are often called tepals, as are the petals and sepals found in much of the lily family.) The Rosebud Orchid is North America's only representative of this largely tropical group.

Rose Pogonia
Pogonia ophioglossoides

Size: *3–24 in. tall;*
flower ½–1 in. wide.
What to look for:
flowers rose-pink to
white, with yellow
bristles in center of fringed lip;
leaf oval to elliptical, solitary,
partway up slender stem.
Habitat: *wet meadows,*
bogs, swamps, ditches.
In bloom: *May–Aug.*

Pogonias   *Pogonia*

At the tip of the column overhanging the fringed lip of a pogonia blossom are paired bags of pollen (pollinia), and beyond them is the pollen-receptive stigma. As an insect enters the fragrant flower, a flap covers the pollinia, so that the insect's back touches only the stigma. Withdrawing, the insect uncovers the pollinia, and bits of pollen adhere to its back, to be carried to the stigma of another pogonia flower.

Heartleaf Twayblade

Listera cordata

Size: *3–11 in. tall; flower ⅛–¼ in. wide.*
What to look for: *flowers green to purplish, with 2 small prongs at base of cleft lip, in wandlike cluster; leaves heart-shaped, paired on stem.*
Habitat: *rich woods.*
In bloom: *May–Aug.*

Twayblades *Listera*

green flower

When an insect, following a trail of nectar up the split lip of a twayblade blossom, touches a sensitive trigger at the tip of the column, a squirt of quick-drying glue shoots out, and with it two pollinia. The startled insect flies away, carrying the pollinia on its back. The trigger mechanism then rises, exposing the stigma to receive pollen from the back of the next insect.

Large Twayblade

Liparis lilifolia

Size: *4–12 in. tall; flower ½–¾ in. wide.*
What to look for: *flowers with purplish lip, threadlike side petals, and greenish rolled sepals, borne on long stalks along stem; leaves shiny, paired at base of stem.* **Habitat:** *rich woods.* **In bloom:** *May–July.*

Twayblades *Liparis*

These twayblades have little in common with the twayblades shown at the top of this page, beyond the fact that the plants of both groups are wild orchids with only two leaves. (*Tway* is from the Old English for "two.") The large leaves of this group spring from the base of the plant, whereas the *Listera* twayblades bear a pair of small leaves midway up the stem.

Spotted Coralroot

Corallorhiza maculata

Size: *8–30 in. tall; flower ½ in. wide.*
What to look for: *flowers purplish, with purple spots on ruffled white lip, in wandlike cluster at top of purple to yellowish leafless stalk.*
Habitat: *rich woods.*
In bloom: *Apr.–Sept.*

Striped Coralroot

Corallorhiza striata

Size: *9–20 in. tall; flower ¾–1 in. wide.*
What to look for: *flowers yellowish with pink to purple stripes, in wandlike cluster at top of magenta to yellowish leafless stalk.*
Habitat: *rich woods.*
In bloom: *May–Aug.*

Coralroots *Corallorhiza*

An orchid seed contains no stored nutrients. Before it can develop, it must be "infected" by a specialized fungus that establishes a symbiotic relationship, sharing food and enzymes until the young plant can survive on its own. Coralroots, however, never become self-sufficient. Despite the name, they have no roots but only hard, branching rhizomes, which continue to derive nourishment from fungi in the soil. After several years, the leafless flower stalk sprouts, containing little or no food-producing chlorophyll. Its only function is to develop seeds.

Showy Orchis
Galearis spectabilis

Size: *5–12 in. tall; flower ½–¾ in. wide.*
What to look for: *flowers purple to pink, helmetlike, with white lip and spur, clustered among leaflike bracts; leaves shiny, paired at base of stem.*
Habitat: *rich woods.*
In bloom: *Apr.–June.*

Orchises *Galearis*

No one knows why bees or dragonflies thrust their tongues into the spur at the rear of an orchis blossom— the flower is odorless, the spur nectarless—but they do so regularly, coming away with one or two stalked clumps of pollen (pollinia) glued to their heads like horns. The stalks dry within 30 seconds, arching forward so the pollen will touch the stigma of the next blossom.

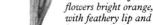

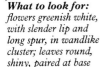

Round-leaved Rein Orchid
Platanthera orbiculata

Size: *6–24 in. tall; flower ¾–1½ in. wide.*
What to look for: *flowers greenish white, with slender lip and long spur, in wandlike cluster; leaves round, shiny, paired at base of stem.* **Habitat:** *rich, moist woods.*
In bloom: *June–Sept.*

Prairie Fringed Orchid
Platanthera leucophaea

Size: *1–4 ft. tall; flower ¾–1½ in. wide.*
What to look for: *flowers white, with 3-part fringed lip and long spur, in open spike at top of stout leafy stem; leaves lance-shaped, their bases sheathing stem.* **Habitat:** *wet prairies, meadows, bogs.* **In bloom:** *May–Aug.*

Purple Fringed Orchid
Platanthera psycodes

Size: *1–3 ft. tall; flower ½–¾ in. wide.*
What to look for: *flowers lavender to purple, with 3-part fringed lip and long spur, in dense spike at top of leafy stem.*
Habitat: *wet woods, meadows, ditches, swamps, bogs.*
In bloom: *June–Aug.*

Orange Fringed Orchid
Platanthera ciliaris

Size: *1–3 ft. tall; flower ½–¾ in. wide.*
What to look for: *flowers bright orange, with feathery lip and long spur, in dense spike at top of leafy stem.* **Habitat:** *moist woods, meadows, bogs.*
In bloom: *June–Sept.*

Rein Orchids *Platanthera*

"If insects had not been developed on the face of the Earth," wrote Charles Darwin, "our plants would not have been decked with beautiful flowers, but only such poor flowers as we see . . . on grasses, spinach, docks, and nettles, which are all pollinated by the agency of the wind." The flowers of the orchid family, more clearly than any others, illustrate the great naturalist's thesis. Many seem to have been designed by a humorous and infinitely clever mind to attract and exploit specific insects. When a long-tongued moth or butterfly sips nectar from the deep spur of a rein orchid blossom, a stalked pollinium or two becomes glued to its head in such a way that the pollen must touch the stigma of the next blossom visited. Some tiny orchids of the Far North use nectar-drinking mosquitoes in the same way.

Puttyroot
Aplectrum hyemale

Size: 1–2 ft. tall; flower ½–¾ in. wide.
What to look for: flowers yellowish to dull purple with purple-spotted white lip, in loose spike at top of leafless stalk; leaf solitary, withered before flower stalk arises.
Habitat: moist, rich woods.
In bloom: May–June.

Puttyroots *Aplectrum*

This group's single species is often called Adam-and-Eve because of the way one bulblike corm develops from another. The corm from which the leaf arises in summer also produces a second corm, at the end of a short underground branch. The leaf lasts through the winter, fading before the flower stalk sprouts from the offshoot corm. The original corm withers as the cycle is repeated. Settlers made glue from crushed puttyroot corms.

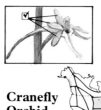

Cranefly Orchid
Tipularia discolor

Size: 4–24 in. tall; flower ¼–½ in. wide.
What to look for: flowers pale greenish purple, with slender lip and long spur, lopsided (3 tepals on one side); leaf solitary, withering before stalk arises.
Habitat: rich woods.
In bloom: June–Sept.

Cranefly Orchids *Tipularia*

Like a swarm of crippled craneflies clinging to a straw, the delicate flower stalk of a Cranefly Orchid presents a bizarre image to sharp-eyed observers. Each year a new corm forms at the tip of a row of old corms. In most years, the lead corm produces only a single overwintering leaf. Occasionally, a flower stalk arises instead.

Rattlesnake Plantains
Goodyera

It is easy to see why these orchids are called plantains, with their slender flower stalks arising from plantainlike rosettes of broad leaves. The other part of their name refers to the evergreen leaves, usually marked with a white pattern reminiscent of snakeskin. The flowers, like those of the related ladies' tresses, are mostly pollinated by bumblebees seeking nectar from the pouchy lip.

Menzies' Rattlesnake Plantain
Goodyera oblongifolia

Size: 12–18 in. tall; flower ¼–½ in. wide.
What to look for: flowers greenish white, in spiral or one-sided spike at top of hairy stalk; leaves clustered at base, usually with faint white mottling.
Habitat: woods.
In bloom: June–Sept.

Downy Rattlesnake Plantain
Goodyera repens

Size: 7–18 in. tall; flower ¼–½ in. wide.
What to look for: flowers greenish white, in dense spike at top of downy stalk; leaves clustered at base, hairy, with white markings.
Habitat: woods, thickets.
In bloom: July–Aug.

Nodding Ladies' Tresses
Spiranthes cernua

Size: *3–20 in. tall; flower ⅛–½ in. wide.*
What to look for: *flowers white, nodding, in dense spirals at top of leafless stalk; leaves grasslike, arising from base of stalk.*
Habitat: *moist meadows, bogs; fields, prairies.*
In bloom: *Aug.–Nov.*

Slender Ladies' Tresses
Spiranthes lacera

Size: *8–30 in. tall; flower ⅛–¼ in. wide.*
What to look for: *flowers greenish white, in long spiral at top of slender stalk; leaves oval, clustered at base, often withered by flowering time.*
Habitat: *dry meadows, fields, prairies, open woods.*
In bloom: *June–Oct.*

Leafless Beaked Orchid
Spiranthes lanceolata

Size: *12–30 in. tall; flower ¼–½ in. wide.*
What to look for: *flowers red, in dense spike at top of stout, reddish stalk; leaves large, elliptical, clustered at base, usually withered by flowering time.*
Habitat: *meadows, fields, open woods.*
In bloom: *Apr.–July.*

Grass Pink
Calopogon tuberosus

Size: *1–3 ft. tall; flower ¾–1½ in. wide.*
What to look for: *flowers purplish pink with yellow tuft near top of upright lip, in loose cluster at top of slender stalk; leaf solitary, long, grasslike, arising from base of stalk.* **Habitat:** *bogs, swamps, wet meadows, streambanks.*
In bloom: *May–Aug.*

Grass Pinks
Calopogon

These are among the few orchids whose flowers are right-side-up. (Most orchid blossoms rotate as they develop, so the lip is on the bottom.) The flowers have no nectar, but the stamenlike fringe on the lip makes them resemble flowers that do, and they often grow among such plants. When an insect in search of nectar lands on these false stamens, the lip dips forward and drops the creature indecorously on the column beneath. Scrambling to right itself, the insect either picks up or leaves behind a load of pollen.

Ladies' Tresses
Spiranthes

A bumblebee sipping nectar invariably starts at the bottom of a floral spike and works its way up. The ladies' tresses, like the rattlesnake plantains, take advantage of this habit to ensure cross-pollination. When a flower first opens, the lip and the overhanging column are so close together that a bee cannot reach the nectar inside. As it tries, however, a pair of pollinia from the tip of the column become glued to its head or back. Later, the lip drops a little, and a bee can then crawl inside, brushing against the sticky stigma on the underside of the column. Because the flowers at the bottom of the braidlike spike open first, a bumblebee carries pollen from the young flowers at the top of one spike to the older flowers at the bottom of another.

Dingy Dancing Lady
Oncidium undulatum

Size: *1–6 ft. long; flower 1–1½ in. wide.*
What to look for: *flowers yellow with reddish mottling and white center, in large spray on arching, leafless stalk; leaf solitary, elliptical, often tinged with red; plants forming clumps on tree branches.*
Habitat: *swamps, hammocks, forests.*
In bloom: *Dec.–June.*

Dancing Ladies   *Oncidium*

The nectarless flowers of this group's more than 500 species deceive potential pollinators in various ways. Some look like the males of a kind of territorial bee and buzz threateningly at the breath of a breeze—provoking an attack from a real male bee, during which pollen is transferred. The Dingy Dancing Lady seems to mimic other flowers that offer nectar.

Butterfly Orchid
Epidendrum tampense

Size: *3–30 in. tall; flower 1–1½ in. wide.*
What to look for: *flowers dull green, with scoop-shaped white lip marked with purple, fragrant, in large spray at tip of leafless stalk; leaves straplike, arising from cluster of gray-green pseudobulbs.* **Habitat:** *tree trunks, branches, rocky outcrops in southern Florida.*
In bloom: *all year.*

Crested Coralroot
Hexalectris spicata

Size: *1–2 ft. tall; flower ¾–1 in. wide.*
What to look for: *flowers with dark purple stripes on yellowish tepals and scoop-shaped lavender lip, with white column in center, in wandlike cluster at top of purple to yellowish leafless stalk.*
Habitat: *rich woods.*
In bloom: *Apr.–Aug.*

Epidendrums
Epidendrum

There are no parasitic orchids. Although the family's many epiphytes, or tree dwellers, were once thought to be parasitic, they take no nourishment from the trees (and occasional rocks) upon which they grow. The nutrients that their clinging roots gather with great efficiency from surface moisture are often stored in fleshy pseudobulbs—the swellings at the base of the stem. Most epidendrums are epiphytes.

Cockscomb Orchids
Hexalectris

The cockscomb orchids (named for the fleshy crests along the rear of the lip) are close cousins of the coralroots. They, too, have no roots and precious little chlorophyll, deriving nourishment from symbiotic fungi. The flowers of both groups are mostly pollinated by bees. As a bee withdraws from the nectary behind the lip, four bags of pollen (pollinia) become glued to its back.

Palm Polly
Polyrrhiza lindenii

Size: *6–13 in. long;
flower 2½–3 in. wide.*
What to look for:
*flowers greenish white, with white
lip divided into 2 twisted lobes and long
slender spur, at tip of leafless arching stalk;
roots green, spreading on tree trunks.*
Habitat: *swamps, hammocks, forests in
southern Florida.* **In bloom:** *Apr.–Aug.*

Polyrrhizas   *Polyrrhiza*

Only one member of this small group of leafless West
Indian orchids is also found in Florida, where it
clings to the trunks of Live Oaks, Royalpalms, and
other trees. The green roots contain chlorophyll and
manufacture food—a function that is usually performed by foliage. The flowers are pollinated by an
exceptionally long-tongued hawk moth, which sips
nectar from the monkey-tail spur.

Vanilla Orchid
Vanilla planifolia

Size: *2–20 ft. high;
flower 3–4½ in. wide.*
What to look for:
*flowers creamy green,
with fringed tubular
greenish-yellow lip,
in clusters along
climbing stem; leaves oblong, fleshy;
seedpods long, green to brown.*
Habitat: *forests.*
In bloom: *all year.*

Vanilla Orchids
Vanilla

Vanilla orchids are pollinated infrequently in nature—and by only a few insects and hummingbirds
of the American semitropics. Commercial growers
raise the vines for the popular flavoring extracted
from the seedpods; and because an unpollinated
flower produces no pod, they must pollinate the flowers by hand, lifting the tiny flap that separates the
pollinia at the tip of the column from the stigma farther back and squeezing the two parts together.

Phantom Orchid
Eburophyton austinae

Size: *4–26 in. tall;
flower ¾–1¼ in. wide.*
What to look for:
*flowers white with
yellow spot on lip, in
wandlike cluster at top
of white stem; leaves
scalelike, white.* **Habitat:**
rich mountain woods.
In bloom: *June–Sept.*

Phantom Orchids
Eburophyton

Except for a yellow spot on the
lip of each flower, this group's
one species is ghostly white—the
only North American orchid that
is completely devoid of chlorophyll. Its food is drawn from the
rotting humus of the forest floor,
with the help of symbiotic fungi
that "infect" the plant's fibrous
roots, sharing nutrients with it.

Stream Orchid
Epipactis gigantea

Size: *1–4 ft. tall;
flower 1½–2½ in. wide.*
What to look for:
*flowers greenish to rose,
with maroon veins on
2-part lip (shaped like an
open mouth with outthrust
tongue), borne among leaflike
bracts near top of stem;
leaves lance-shaped, clasping
stem.* **Habitat:** *streambanks,
springs, shores, meadows.*
In bloom: *Mar.–Aug.*

Helleborines   *Epipactis*

The Stream Orchid is pollinated
by flower flies, which land on the
front half of the lip to sip nectar
from the rear half. As they leave,
they brush first against the
stigma on the underside of the
column, then against a gummy
flap, and finally against the
crumbly pollinia—picking up
grains of pollen to carry to the
stigma of the next flower.

WILDFLOWERS

507

Nonflowering Plants

*Ferns, mosses, seaweeds, liverworts, lichens—these are the
lowly plants, in terms of human perception as well as actual height.
Their physical dimensions cannot change, but your opinion
of them can. Open your eyes to their intricate nature;
take delight in the incredible diversity of the natural world.*

"**B**ut there's nothing there!" some children complained as they peered into a terrarium alive with ferns, mosses, and other small plants. They were looking, of course, for animal life, and to them all the greenery was background, not substance.

Out in the wild, people often have much the same response. Trees, wildflowers, mammals, birds—these are the attention grabbers, not the humble mosses and ferns. Nonflowering plants have neither size nor coloration to demand your attention. They tend to be small. (Except for ferns and close relatives of ferns, they lack an internal system for transporting water, and so can't grow very high above the ground.) No colorful flowers or fruits add sparkle to their greenish or brownish foliage. (Tiny spores are their means of reproduction, not flowers and fruits.)

But any feeling of sameness dissolves as you begin to investigate this lilliputian world, to consider the plants as individual entities rather than as a backdrop to animal life. For one thing, in just a single small area you may discover a multitude of species—starlike mosses, strange-looking lichens, ferns with a diversity of texture, color, and form. Just a few feet away, in a spot with different moisture conditions, the species may be completely different. Nor will a particular plant always look the same. As the year progresses, fiddleheads unfurl into fronds; spore stalks develop; leaves become burnished by the touch of fall.

Where to Find Nonflowering Plants

Nonflowering plants generally go hand in hand with moisture, for their complex life cycle cannot be completed without water. But certain species can survive extreme exposure to sun, wind, and drought. For example, drought causes many mosses and lichens (and a few ferns too) to become brown and shriveled, but eventually they will be "resurrected" by rain.

In North America swampy forests have the greatest variety of nonflowering plants and the most luxuriant growth. Royal Ferns unfurl their arching fronds; mosses of many types festoon the fallen logs. In other moist areas, different plants predominate—sphagnum mosses in bogs, Bracken fern in fields, quillworts along the shores of quiet lakes and ponds.

Rocky places furnish good hunting, especially where a crevice or ledge means greater moisture and shade. Even in prairies, where grasses and other flowering plants have the upper hand, boulders create isolated microenvironments where mosses and lichens come into their own.

Though nonflowering plants tend to hug the ground, sometimes you'll find them by looking up, not down. Representatives of a number of groups—lichens, liverworts, freshwater algae, mosses—live on tree bark (and not just on the north side, as legend would have it); and especially in warm, moist places, ferns may be found out on a limb.

How to Use This Section

Of all the nonflowering plants, ferns are the most likely to catch your eye, and so ferns receive the most extensive coverage in this section. Generally more massive and obvious than other nonflowering plants, ferns and fern allies (that is, close relatives of ferns) are more complex in organization, as you can see if you look closely at a leaf or a cross section of stem.

• Ferns are shown on pages 510 through 522, with features important for identification pointed out in the blue-type feature on the first page. Fern allies are on pages 522 through 524. These include clubmosses, spikemosses, quillworts, and horsetails—plants that look very different from ferns but share certain characteristics of structure and reproduction.

• Mosses, liverworts, and hornworts—plants that are usually less than an inch tall and often

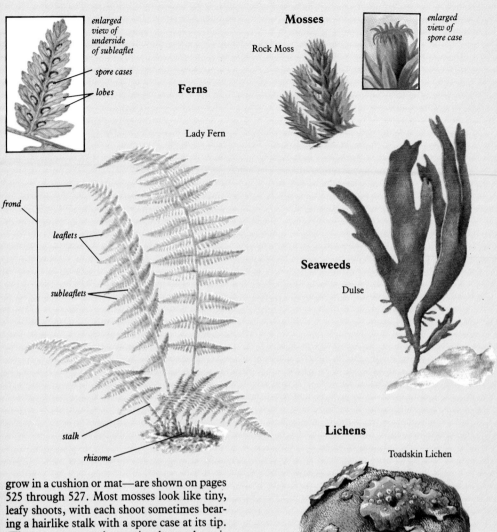

enlarged
view of
underside
of subleaflet

spore cases

lobes

Ferns

Lady Fern

Mosses

Rock Moss

enlarged
view of
spore case

frond

leaflets

subleaflets

Seaweeds

Dulse

stalk

rhizome

Lichens

Toadskin Lichen

grow in a cushion or mat—are shown on pages 525 through 527. Most mosses look like tiny, leafy shoots, with each shoot sometimes bearing a hairlike stalk with a spore case at its tip. (The spore case on the species shown above is of a different type, nearly hidden by the leaves.) Important in the identification of mosses, spore cases are also a source of entertainment: if you pinch them open at the appropriate stage of ripeness, a dust cloud of spores will waft away.

• Seaweeds (marine algae) are covered on pages 528 through 531. The species shown here, Dulse, is classified as a red seaweed; the other categories are green and brown.

• On pages 532 and 533 are the lichens, peculiar combinations of algae and fungi living together in a relationship that benefits them both. There are three types: the crustose lichens (which form thin crusts), the foliose lichens (these are flat and leaflike), and the fruticose lichens (branching like miniature

shrubs). Many lichens, such as the one shown on this page, are a distinctive grayish or brownish green, their green color modified by the strands of fungus mingling with the algae. British Soldiers, one of the fruticose species, has scarlet tips; certain other species are also red or orange, in part or in their entirety.

• Mushrooms and other fungi, sometimes grouped with the nonflowering plants (they too reproduce by spores), are covered in a separate section that begins on page 534.

Ferns. Graceful, airy, and delicate in appearance, ferns have a more subtle beauty than wildflowers, and appreciating them—like identifying them—may require a closer look. Though the typical fern is rather lacy, some species are less finely cut; the leafy fronds may be undivided or divided once (into leaflets), twice (into leaflets and subleaflets), or three times (into leaflets, subleaflets, and lobes). Ferns reproduce by spores, which commonly occur on the underside of the frond but in some species are borne on separate stalks. Fronds (or parts of fronds) with spores are called fertile; those without, sterile. A fern's rhizomes—the rootlike stems that creep on or just below the surface—may also be useful in identification. For a detailed discussion of ferns and other nonflowering plants, consult the preceding two pages.

Cinnamon Fern
Osmunda cinnamomea

Size: *2-3 ft. tall.*
What to look for: *large clumps of fronds; fertile fronds with masses of spore cases (fronds and cases green, turning brown); leaflets on sterile fronds not cut to vein, with brown woolly tuft below base.*
Habitat: *swamps, marshes, wet woods.* **Spores:** *Apr.-June.*

sterile subleaflets

Royal Fern
Osmunda regalis

Size: *2-4 ft. tall.*
What to look for: *large clumps growing from conspicuous root ball; subleaflets large; spore cases in dense clusters at top of fronds; stalks reddish on shaded individuals.*
Habitat: *swamps, marshes.* **Spores:** *Apr.-June.*

Royal Ferns Osmundaceae

These regal ferns are common and conspicuous in eastern wetlands (there are none in the West). The fronds arch out for more than 2 feet; the stalks and roots form large mounds. Plant nurseries use the root masses, popularly known as osmunda, for growing orchids and other plants that do not require soil. Ferns in this family produce short-lived spores—the spores die unless they germinate in a week or two—in brown or blackish clusters.

Interrupted Fern
Osmunda claytoniana

Size: *2-3 ft. tall.*
What to look for: *fertile fronds interrupted by spore-bearing leaflets (or bare near center); other fronds arching outward; leaflets not cut to vein, slightly longer at center of stalk.*
Habitat: *moist woods, roadsides.*
Spores: *May-June.*

FERNS

510

subleaflets

Rattlesnake Fern
Botrychium virginianum

Size: *2-18 in. tall.*
What to look for: *single stalk
with triangular, almost horizontal frond
divided into lacy leaflets; grapelike clusters
of spore cases at top of upright spike.*
Habitat: *rich woods.* **Spores:** *May-July.*

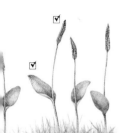

tip of
fertile spike

Adder's Tongue
Ophioglossum vulgatum

Size: *6-10 in. tall.*
What to look for: *single
unfernlike leaf with blunt tip;
spore cases in 2 rows at swollen tip
of upright spike.* **Habitat:** *woods;
meadows; marsh edges; damp grassy ditches.*
Spores: *June-Aug.*

Grape Ferns
and Adder's Tongues
Ophioglossaceae

Although these peculiar ferns baffle botanists
(their relationship to other ferns is unclear), they
are easy to separate from other families: nearly all
species in this group have a single stalk with a
leafy branch at the side and an upright spore-
producing spike. Once thought to be rare, these
leaves are often overlooked because they resemble
other plants or because they are hidden by other
vegetation. Prime sites for finding them include
moist grassy areas, fields, open woods, and, in the
Southeast, cemeteries.

sterile
subleaflet

fertile
subleaflet

Japanese
Climbing Fern
Lygodium japonicum

Size: *5-15 ft. long.*
What to look for:
*frond vinelike, sprawling
over other plants;
sterile leaflets twice divided,
long, triangular, with pointed tip;
small fertile leaflets with spore cases
on narrow projections.*
Habitat: *open woods, brushy areas,
streambanks, roadsides.*
Spores: *Aug.-Sept.*

Curly Grass Ferns
and Climbing Ferns
Schizaeaceae

These plants look like anything but
ferns. Some—the climbing ferns—
resemble ivy; others, such as the
Curly Grass Fern (*Schizaea pusilla*)
of northeastern bogs, look remarkably like grass (a small spore-bearing
cluster at the top of the fertile stalk
unmasks them as ferns).

American
Climbing Fern
Lygodium palmatum

Size: *3-4 ft. tall.*
What to look for:
*frond vinelike, twining
around shrubs or saplings;
leaflets lobed like maple
leaves, paired;
spore cases in pockets
on small leaflets at tip.*
Habitat: *bogs, wet woods.*
Spores: *Aug.-Sept.*

511

Maidenhair Ferns and Relatives

Adiantaceae

Of all ferns, this group is the most xerophytic—that is, adapted to life in dry places. Although the Northern Maidenhair and several other species live in forests, most grow in rocky places. The Southern Maidenhair *(Adiantum capillusveneris)*, for example, flourishes on limestone dampened by waterfall spray—and not just in southern states, but also northward through the Rockies into Canada. This species, along with several close relatives, does well as a house plant, provided it is kept cool.

Maidenhair ferns tend to be small. Although some species, such as the lip ferns, spread out linearly along the underground rootstock, most have clusters (tufts) of fronds. In the clustering species the stalks—often as black, fine, and shiny as a maiden's hair—form small, tight masses.

The spores of these ferns develop not on special stalks but on the leaflets themselves, generally along the veins. In some species the leaf edges roll over the spores, protecting them as they develop. Such rolled-over edges are called false indusia. True indusia (the word *indusium* is Latin for "tunic") are thin protective covers that grow over the spores in the tree fern family and in the spleenworts.

fertile subleaflet

sterile subleaflet

Parsley Fern
(American Rock Brake)
Cryptogramma acrostichoides

Size: *5-10 in. tall.*
What to look for: *fronds smooth, leathery, shiny; sterile fronds with short, wide, toothed subleaflets; fertile fronds tall, upright with narrow subleaflets; edge of fertile subleaflet rolled over spore cases.*
Habitat: *cliffs, talus slopes.* **Spores:** *July–Sept.*

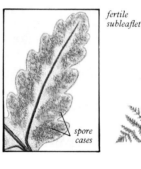

fertile subleaflet

spore cases

Northern Maidenhair
Adiantum pedatum

Size: *12-24 in. tall.*
What to look for: *fan-shaped whorls of leaflets held horizontally; subleaflets oblong, toothed on one edge, with spore cases along toothed edge; black, wiry stalks.*
Habitat: *rich woods.*
Spores: *Aug.-Oct.*

Goldback Fern
Pityrogramma triangularis

Size: *5-15 in. tall.*
What to look for: *fronds triangular, twice divided, green on top, bright yellow to white below; spore cases on underside, scattered along veins.* **Habitat:** *shaded, damp crevices on rocky slopes and streambanks.* **Spores:** *May-July.*

California Maidenhair
Adiantum jordanii

Size: *6-12 in. tall.*
What to look for: *fronds wide, spreading, not horizontal; subleaflets semicircular, with veins in fan shape, on stems; spore cases on rounded edge of subleaflet.*
Habitat: *shaded, moist slopes; streambanks.*
Spores: *June–July.*

fertile subleaflet

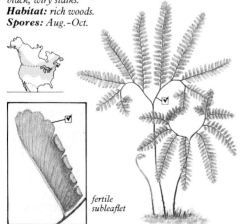

fertile subleaflet

fertile subleaflet

fertile segments

fertile leaflet

Slender Lip Fern
Cheilanthes feei

Size: *4–10 in. tall.*
What to look for: *very finely divided into tiny round segments; fine white hairs above, dense rusty hairs below; stalks hairy; edge of fertile segment rolled over spore cases.* **Habitat:** *dry, shaded rock crevices; cliffs.* **Spores:** *July–Sept.*

Purple Cliff Brake
Pellaea atropurpurea

Size: *10–20 in. tall.*
What to look for: *stalks purple-brown to black, slightly hairy; leaflets and subleaflets large and lance-shaped, triangular, or heart-shaped; fertile fronds taller than sterile; spore cases covered by rolled edge of leaflet.* **Habitat:** *crevices in limestone.* **Spores:** *July–Oct.*

fertile subleaflet

fertile subleaflet

Lace Fern
Cheilanthes gracillima

Size: *4–10 in. tall.*
What to look for: *stalks in clumps; subleaflets elliptical, smooth and dark green above, densely hairy and white to rusty below; spore cases partly covered by rolled edge of subleaflet.* **Habitat:** *rock crevices in mountains.* **Spores:** *July–Sept.*

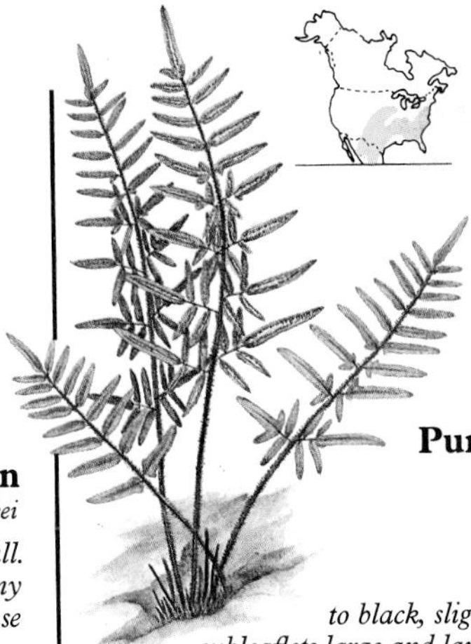

Smooth Cliff Brake
Pellaea glabella

Size: *5–15 in. tall.*
What to look for: *similar to but smaller than Purple Cliff Brake, with shinier, redder, hairless stalks; fertile and sterile fronds alike; spore cases covered by rolled edge.* **Habitat:** *crevices in limestone.* **Spores:** *July–Sept.*

fertile subleaflets

fertile subleaflets

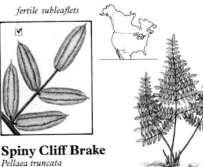

Hairy Lip Fern
Cheilanthes lanosa

Size: *10–18 in. tall.*
What to look for: *stalks scattered (not in clumps); leafy part narrow, longer than lower part of stalk, with rusty hairs (denser below); spore cases partly covered by rolled edge of subleaflet.* **Habitat:** *rocks, cliffs.* **Spores:** *July–Sept.*

Spiny Cliff Brake
Pellaea truncata

Size: *5–15 in. tall.*
What to look for: *very stiff fronds; leaflets at right angle to stalk, divided into small boat-shaped subleaflets with sharp tips; spore cases covered by rolled edge.* **Habitat:** *dry, exposed rock (not limestone).* **Spores:** *June–Sept.*

FERNS

513

spore cases

Filmy Ferns
Hymenophyllaceae

These tiniest of ferns, nearly all tropical, include species with fronds only half an inch long. With translucent leaves just one cell thick and lacking a protective epidermis, they require constant moisture and the deep shade of a rocky grotto.

Appalachian Bristle Fern
Trichomanes boschianum

Size: *2–6 in. long.*
What to look for: *fronds lacy, thin, translucent, on creeping hairy rootstock; spore cases in cuplike structure with bristle.*
Habitat: *deeply shaded recesses in moist sandstone cliffs; caves.* **Spores:** *Aug.–Oct.*

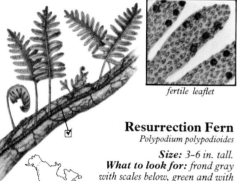
fertile leaflet

Common Polypody
Polypodium virginianum

Size: *4–10 in. tall.*
What to look for: *fronds evergreen, leathery, smooth; leaflets cut almost to stalk; rootstocks intertwined.* **Habitat:** *shaded rocks in woods.* **Spores:** *July–Sept.*

Resurrection Fern
Polypodium polypodioides

Size: *3–6 in. tall.*
What to look for: *frond gray with scales below, green and with sunken midrib and raised dots above (from spore cases on underside); rolls up when dry, revives when wet; rootstock creeping, exposed.* **Habitat:** *rocks (northern part of range); tree trunks, branches (South).* **Spores:** *July–Sept.*

Polypody Ferns   Polypodiaceae

The leaves of these ferns are leathery and evergreen, a character istic of plants growing where moisture is inconstant because o drought, winter winds, or local conditions. Most species in ou area live on rocks thinly covered with soil. Tropical members o this family usually grow on tree branches; the staghorn fern (*Platycerium*) are often grown indoors on slabs of bark. Larg round clusters of spore cases are typical of the group.

Tree Ferns   Cyatheaceae

These ferns of field and woodland are mostly medium to large, with spreading fronds much divided into leaflets and subleaflets. They include Bracken, one of the few ferns with worldwide distribution, and the tall tropical tree ferns (*Cyathea* and *Dicksonia*) cultivated in greenhouses and also outdoors along the California coast and in other warm places. Native species are not commonly grown in gardens (they tend to spread and crowd out the other plants).

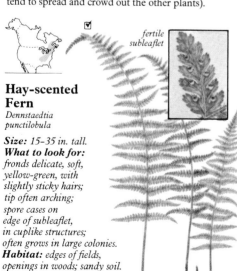
fertile subleaflet

Hay-scented Fern
Dennstaedtia punctilobula

Size: *15–35 in. tall.*
What to look for: *fronds delicate, soft, yellow-green, with slightly sticky hairs; tip often arching; spore cases on edge of subleaflet, in cuplike structures; often grows in large colonies.* **Habitat:** *edges of fields, openings in woods; sandy soil.* **Spores:** *July-Oct.*

Bracken
Pteridium aquilinum

Size: *2-3 ft. tall.*
What to look for: *fronds broad, coarse, horizontal, triangular, usually divided into 3 large triangular leaflets; usually forms large colonies.* **Habitat:** *fields, brushy or burned-over areas, openings in woods; poor soils.* **Spores:** *July–Aug. (often not formed).*

FERNS

Spleenworts Aspleniaceae

This is the most diverse fern family (some 3,000 species worldwide), and any generalization about habitat or appearance will have many exceptions. Spleenworts occur from the tropics to the Arctic; they range in size from the very large to the very small; their fronds may be undivided, finely divided, or somewhere in between. Closely related species within the family show a strong tendency to hybridize, sometimes producing intermediate forms that have their own names and reproduce like normal species. (The Lobed Spleenwort is one example.) The spleenwort family, so called because certain species could supposedly cure diseases of the spleen, includes all the ferns shown on this and the next six pages.

spore cases

Hammock Fern
Thelypteris kunthii

Size: *2-5 ft. tall.*
What to look for: *fronds broad, with dense white hairs; lowest leaflets not reduced in size; edges not rolled over spore cases; veins unbranched.*
Habitat: *hammocks, low woods, rocky slopes.*
Spores: *May-Nov.*

lowest pair of leaflets

Long Beech Fern
Thelypteris phegopteris

Size: *10-20 in. tall.*
What to look for: *fronds arched, triangular, narrow, with "wings" connecting all but the lowest 2 pairs of leaflets; lowest leaflets drooping; stalks and undersides of leaflets hairy.*
Habitat: *damp rocky hillsides, cliffs, woods; often near streams.*
Spores: *July-Sept.*

Broad Beech Fern
Thelypteris hexagonoptera

Size: *15-30 in. tall.*
What to look for: *fronds triangular, broad, with "wings" connecting all leaflets; leaflets with fine hairs on both surfaces.*
Habitat: *rich shaded woods.* **Spores:** *July-Sept.*

lowest pair

sterile leaflet

fertile leaflet

New York Fern
Thelypteris noveboracensis

Size: *15-25 in. tall.*
What to look for: *leaflets longest at center of frond; lowest leaflets tiny, triangular; spore cases near edge of subleaflet (edge not rolled over).* **Habitat:** *moist woods, thickets; in sunny openings.* **Spores:** *June-Sept.*

Marsh Fern
Thelypteris palustris

Size: *15-30 in. tall.*
What to look for: *lowest pair of leaflets as long as, or slightly shorter than, next pair; fertile leaflets on taller fronds, with branched veins, rolled-over edges, and rows of spore cases not near edge.*
Habitat: *marshes, swamps, wet woods, wet meadows.* **Spores:** *July-Sept.*

FERNS

515

fertile
subleaflet

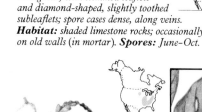

Wall Rue
Asplenium ruta-muraria

Size: 1½–6½ in. long.
What to look for: *fronds dainty,
triangular, with stemmed leaflets
and diamond-shaped, slightly toothed
subleaflets; spore cases dense, along veins.*
Habitat: *shaded limestone rocks; occasionally
on old walls (in mortar).* **Spores:** *June–Oct.*

fertile
leaflet

Maidenhair
Spleenwort
*Asplenium
trichomanes*

Size: 3–8 in. long.
What to look for: *sterile fronds flat, spreading
from center; fertile fronds tall, with spore case
clusters in crescents; stalks stiff, purple-brown,
shiny, persisting after leaflets drop; leaflets oval,
opposite, vaguely toothed.* **Habitat:** *shaded rock
crevices; usually in limestone.* **Spores:** *June–Oct.*

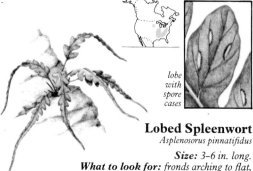

lobe
with
spore
cases

Lobed Spleenwort
Asplenosorus pinnatifidus

Size: 3–6 in. long.
What to look for: *fronds arching to flat,
spreading from center, leathery, with long narrow
tip; lower half or more of frond lobed; spore case
clusters in crescents along veins; hybrid of Mountain
Spleenwort and Walking Fern.* **Habitat:** *sandstone
and other acidic rock cliffs.* **Spores:** *June–Oct.*

fertile
leaflet

Ebony
Spleenwort
Asplenium platyneuron

Size: 6–18 in. tall.
What to look for: *fertile fronds erect;
sterile fronds short, spreading; stalks
shiny, dark brown; leaflets almost oblong,
overlapping stalk at base, with "ear" on
upper edge; spore cases along veins, sometimes
meeting at central vein.* **Habitat:** *old fields,
woods, roadsides.* **Spores:** *May–Nov.*

fertile
subleaflet

Mountain Spleenwort
Asplenium montanum

Size: 3–7 in. long.
What to look for: *fronds thick-textured, shiny green,
twice divided, usually drooping; subleaflets with irregular
edge; spore cases along veins.* **Habitat:** *crevices in
sandstone, quartzite, granite, or schist.* **Spores:** *June–Oct.*

Walking Fern
Camptosorus rhizophyllus

Size: 4–12 in. long.
What to look for: *fronds arrow-shaped, undivided,
arching (eventually flattening), with new plants
at threadlike tips; spore cases scattered, along
network of veins.* **Habitat:** *mossy rocks and cliffs,
especially of limestone.* **Spores:** *July–Oct.*

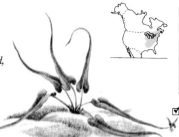

fertile
frond

FERNS

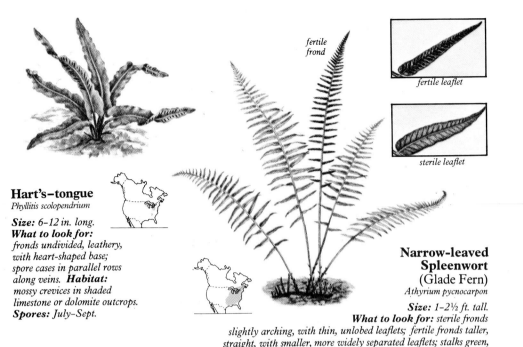

fertile frond

fertile leaflet

sterile leaflet

Hart's–tongue
Phyllitis scolopendrium

Size: *6–12 in. long.*
What to look for:
*fronds undivided, leathery,
with heart-shaped base;
spore cases in parallel rows
along veins.* **Habitat:**
*mossy crevices in shaded
limestone or dolomite outcrops.*
Spores: *July–Sept.*

Narrow-leaved Spleenwort
(Glade Fern)
Athyrium pycnocarpon

Size: *1–2½ ft. tall.*
What to look for: *sterile fronds
slightly arching, with thin, unlobed leaflets; fertile fronds taller,
straight, with smaller, more widely separated leaflets; stalks green,
without long hairs; spore cases in closely spaced lines along veins.*
Habitat: *rich woods, rocky hillsides, ravines.* **Spores:** *Aug.–Oct.*

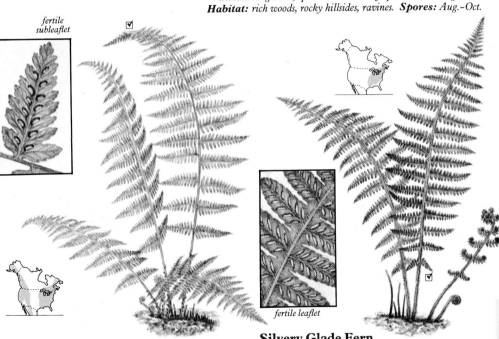

fertile subleaflet

fertile leaflet

Lady Fern
Athyrium filix-femina

Size: *1–3 ft. tall.*
What to look for: *fronds delicate, finely cut,
with drooping tip and minutely toothed subleaflets;
stalk smooth, easily broken, with 2 strands inside;
spore cases short, tightly curved.* **Habitat:** *rich
woods, swamps.* **Spores:** *July–Aug.*

Silvery Glade Fern
Athyrium thelypterioides

Size: *1½–3 ft. tall.*
What to look for: *leaflets firm-textured,
shorter near base, deeply cut (but not to midvein);
lowest pair hangs down; long pale hairs on
undersides, stalks, and midribs; spore case clusters
mostly long, straight, silvery when young.*
Habitat: *rich, damp woods.* **Spores:** *July–Sept.*

FERNS

517

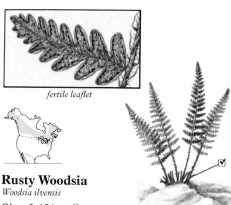

fertile leaflet

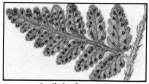

fertile leaflet

Rusty Woodsia
Woodsia ilvensis

Size: *5–15 in. tall.*
What to look for: *stalk with 1 joint, hairy, scaly; stubble of uniform height (stalk breaks at joint); leaflets hairy and white (turning rusty) below; spore cases hairy, near edge.* **Habitat:** *rocky slopes, ledges.*
Spores: *July–Oct.*

Blunt-lobed Woodsia
Woodsia obtusa

Size: *10–20 in. tall.*
What to look for: *stalks not jointed; leaflets widely spaced; stalk and underside of frond with a few delicate, pale tan scales; spore cases scaly.*
Habitat: *boulders; rocky slopes and woods.*
Spores: *July–Oct.*

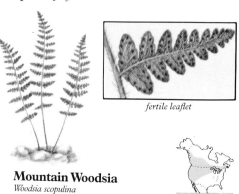

fertile leaflet

fertile leaflet

Mountain Woodsia
Woodsia scopulina

Size: *5–15 in. tall.*
What to look for: *stalks not jointed; no stubble; stalks and undersides of fronds scaleless, with scattered white hairs; spore cases hairy.*
Habitat: *cliffs, talus slopes.* **Spores:** *July–Oct.*

Western Woodsia
Woodsia oregana

Size: *5–15 in. tall.*
What to look for: *stalks not jointed, brown near base and yellow above; no stubble; stalks and undersides of fronds scaleless, without white hairs; spore cases hairy.*
Habitat: *cliffs, talus slopes.* **Spores:** *July–Oct.*

leaflet with spores and bulb

Bulblet Fern
Cystopteris bulbifera

Size: *10–20 in. long.*
What to look for: *fronds widest at base, drooping at tip; leaflets widely spaced, with 1 or more round bulbs (bulbs fall off and grow); stalk and midribs green-pink; spore cases sparse.*
Habitat: *shaded limestone cliffs; white-cedar or hardwood swamps.*
Spores: *June–Aug.*

fertile leaflet

Fragile Fern
(Brittle Fern)
Cystopteris fragilis

Size: *6–12 in. tall.*
What to look for: *fronds erect, widest at center, often dying in summer and then growing back; leaflets thin, widely spaced, once or twice divided; stalks hairless, dark near base, green above, easily broken; spore cases sparse.*
Habitat: *rocks; occasionally in woodland soil.*
Spores: *May–Aug.*

FERNS

518

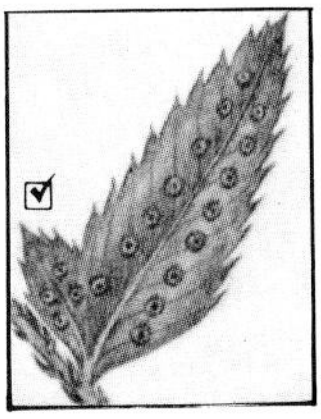

Northern Holly Fern

Polystichum lonchitis

Size: 6-18 in. tall.
What to look for: fronds shiny, dark green, tapering at tip and base; leaflets pointed, bristle-toothed, with "ear"; stalks scaly; spore cases usually in 2 rows. **Habitat:** rocky forests, especially in mountains. **Spores:** July-Sept.

fertile leaflet

Christmas Fern

Polystichum acrostichoides

sterile leaflet

Size: 12-30 in. tall.
What to look for: fronds evergreen, thick; leaflets pointed, minutely toothed, with "ear"; stalks scaly; fertile leaflets smaller, near tip, with 2 rows of spore cases. **Habitat:** woods, streambanks. **Spores:** June-Oct.

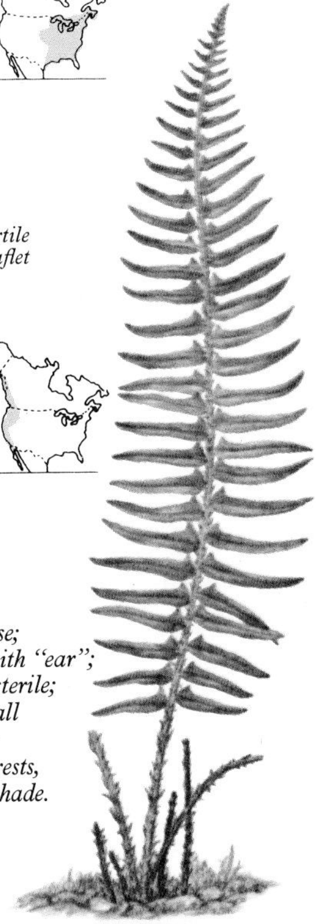

Sensitive Fern

Onoclea sensibilis

Size: 15-30 in. tall.
What to look for: sterile fronds finely veined, divided on lower portion and lobed toward tip; fertile fronds brown, beaded, conspicuous in winter. **Habitat:** wet ground, marshes, swamps. **Spores:** Mar.-May.

Western Sword Fern

fertile leaflet

Polystichum munitum

Size: 20-50 in. tall.
What to look for: fronds erect, evergreen, tapering slightly near base; leaflets bristle-toothed, with "ear"; fertile leaflets similar to sterile; stalks with large and small scales; spore cases in 2 or more rows. **Habitat:** forests, rocky slopes; usually in shade. **Spores:** May-Aug.

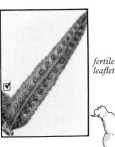

Ostrich Fern

Matteuccia struthiopteris

Size: 2-6 ft. tall.
What to look for: vase-shaped clump; sterile fronds plumelike, widest above midpoint, with deeply lobed leaflets; fertile fronds shorter, hard, brown and erect in winter. **Habitat:** damp woods, swamps, streambanks. **Spores:** Apr.-June.

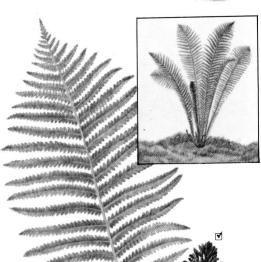

519

Male Fern
Dryopteris filix-mas

Size: *15–30 in. tall.*
What to look for: *fronds lance-shaped, tapering toward base; stalks densely scaled; leaflets thin; spore case clusters kidney-shaped, between center vein and edge.*
Habitat: *rocky slopes, rich forests.* **Spores:** *July–Sept.*

fertile subleaflet

Marginal Wood Fern
Dryopteris marginalis

Size: *15–40 in. tall.*
What to look for: *fronds lance-shaped, evergreen, not tapering toward base; stalks scaly, especially at base; leaflets thick, dark blue-green, curving up at tip; spore case clusters kidney-shaped, at edges.*
Habitat: *forests, rocky slopes, swamps.*
Spores: *June–Oct.*

fertile subleaflet

fertile frond

fertile subleaflet

Crested Wood Fern
Dryopteris cristata

Size: *1½–3 ft. tall.*
What to look for: *fronds narrow; fertile fronds erect, with horizontal leaflets; sterile fronds shorter, spreading, evergreen; lower leaflets smaller, more triangular; spore case clusters kidney-shaped, crowded.* **Habitat:** *swamps, marshes, damp woods.* **Spores:** *June–Sept.*

base of fertile leaflets

Goldie's Wood Fern
Dryopteris goldiana

Size: *2–4 ft. tall.*
What to look for: *fronds very broad, narrowing abruptly at tip; stalks scaly, especially at base; leaflets deeply cut, widest at midpoint; spore case clusters kidney-shaped, not crowded.* **Habitat:** *rich, damp woods.* **Spores:** *July–Oct.*

fertile subleaflet

Toothed Wood Fern
Dryopteris carthusiana

Size: *1½–3 ft. tall.*
What to look for: *fronds very lacy, arching; leaflets triangular; stalks scaly; first downward-pointing subleaflet on lowest leaflets usually longer than its opposite; spore case clusters kidney-shaped.*
Habitat: *swamps, marshes, damp woods.* **Spores:** *July–Oct.*

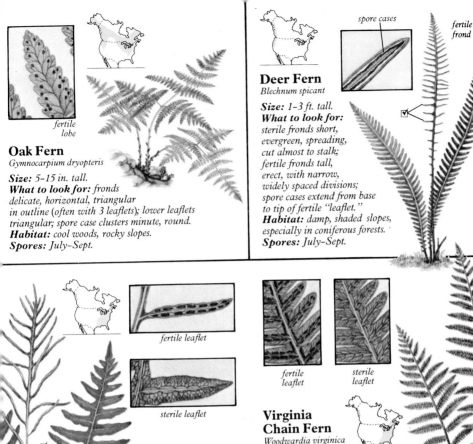

Oak Fern
Gymnocarpium dryopteris

Size: *5-15 in. tall.*
What to look for: *fronds delicate, horizontal, triangular in outline (often with 3 leaflets); lower leaflets triangular; spore case clusters minute, round.*
Habitat: *cool woods, rocky slopes.*
Spores: *July-Sept.*

fertile lobe

Deer Fern
Blechnum spicant

spore cases

fertile frond

Size: *1-3 ft. tall.*
What to look for: *sterile fronds short, evergreen, spreading, cut almost to stalk; fertile fronds tall, erect, with narrow, widely spaced divisions; spore cases extend from base to tip of fertile "leaflet."*
Habitat: *damp, shaded slopes, especially in coniferous forests.*
Spores: *July-Sept.*

fertile leaflet

sterile leaflet

fertile leaflet

sterile leaflet

Virginia Chain Fern
Woodwardia virginica

Size: *2-4 ft. tall.*
What to look for: *fronds resembling Cinnamon Fern's but not clumped; row of netted veins; spore cases beside veins, forming chains; stalks shiny, dark purple-brown.* **Habitat:** *swamps, bogs, wet spots in woods.*
Spores: *July-Sept.*

Netted Chain Fern
Woodwardia areolata

Size: *1½-3½ ft. tall.*
What to look for: *fronds with unpaired leaflets, mostly not cut to stalk; leaflets with netlike veins; sterile fronds dark green; fertile fronds more erect, with narrow leaflets and 2 chainlike rows of spore cases.*
Habitat: *bogs, swamps.*
Spores: *July-Oct.*

part of fertile leaflet

Giant Chain Fern
Woodwardia fimbriata

Size: *4-6 ft. tall.*
What to look for: *fronds huge, oblong, clustered; leaflets deeply cut; spore case clusters long, close to midvein.* **Habitat:** *seepage areas in foothills, mountains.*
Spores: *May-Aug.*

Water Spangles
Salvinia minima

Size: *leaves ¾–1 in. long.*
What to look for: *floating leaves nearly round, hairy above, usually reddish below; spores under leaves, in globular sacs, hanging in water.*
Habitat: *ponds, reservoirs, other still-water areas.* **Spores:** *July–Oct.*

leaves and spore sacs

Water Spangles   Salviniaceae

These peculiar floating ferns, seemingly so tender, become menacing pests when they invade and choke reservoirs. The rootlike masses that hang down in the water are really leaves of a special kind, with round, spore-containing sacs.

leaves

Mosquito Fern
Azolla caroliniana

Size: *leaves to ¹⁄₁₀ in. long.*
What to look for: *masses of floating plants; leaves gray-green (in shade) or reddish (sun), with upper and lower lobes, in 2 overlapping rows.* **Habitat:** *ponds, slow streams, bayous.* **Spores:** *June–Sept.*

Mosquito Ferns   Azollaceae

The connection between mosquito ferns and mosquitoes, some say, is that these aquatic plants stifle mosquito growth. In Asian rice paddies, nitrogen-fixing algae living in their leaves serve to maintain the fertility of the soil. Species microscopically different from the one shown grow in parts of the American West and Midwest.

Hairy Water Clover
Marsilea vestita

Size: *3–6 in. tall.*
What to look for: *floating fronds resembling 4-leaved clovers; spore cases hard, nutlike, at base of stalk.* **Habitat:** *ditches, meadows, shores of rivers and ponds.* **Spores:** *May–Sept.*

Water Clovers
Marsileaceae

Adapted to dry prairies, these unfernlike ferns appear in ponds after spring rains. They go through their life cycle in just a few weeks, starting out as fiddleheads and unrolling like a typical fern. Generally, their cordlike stems are anchored in the mud.

OTHER NONFLOWERING PLANTS

Club-mosses   Lycopodiaceae

Their names belying their position in the plant world, the Ground Pine and other clubmosses are neither low-growing conifers nor types of moss. These delightful evergreens, with their dense, narrow, single-veined leaves, are most closely related to horsetails and ferns. Clubmosses propagate mainly by creeping along the ground, for their spores, usually produced in distinct "cones" (the "clubs"), germinate rarely or not at all. Some species also produce new plants—"plantlets"—on their leaves.

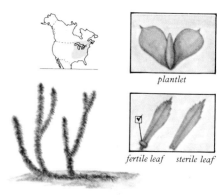

plantlet

fertile leaf   sterile leaf

Shining Club-moss
Lycopodium lucidulum

Size: *3–6 in. tall.*
What to look for: *upright, branching stems; shiny, dark green, delicately toothed leaves; spore cases orange-yellow, at bases of upper leaves; flat, green plantlets on upper leaves.*
Habitat: *moist woods.* **Spores:** *Sept.–Oct.*

fertile branch tip with "cone"

Meadow Spike-moss
Selaginella apoda

Size: *1 in. tall.*
What to look for: *pale green creeping plant with 2 types of leaves (tiny ones in 2 rows along top of stem, larger flat ones on each side); spores in 4-sided "cones" at tips of branches.* **Habitat:** *wet rock seeps, damp meadows; marshes (in tufts of sedges).* **Spores:** *July–Sept.*

522

leaf

branchlet

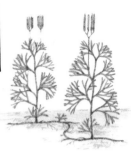

Running Cedar
Lycopodium clavatum

Size: *4–10 in. tall.*
What to look for: *creeping horizontal stems and branching upright stems; narrow leaves tapering to single hair at tip; fertile shoots taller, with spores in clusters of "cones."*
Habitat: *woods, brushy areas; in sandy soils.*
Spores: *Sept.–Oct.*

Running Pine
Lycopodium digitatum

Size: *5–10 in. tall.*
What to look for: *upright stems with flat, fanlike branchlets; long horizontal stems on ground or below leaf litter; leaves small, leathery, flat, with pointed tip, in 4 rows; spores in "cones" at top of taller branched stems.*
Habitat: *dry, upland second-growth woods; in acid soils.*
Spores: *Sept.–Oct.*

leaf

branchlet

Bog Club–moss
Lycopodium inundatum

Size: *3–4 in. tall.*
What to look for: *creeping horizontal stems and unbranched upright stems; narrow, soft, pale green leaves (not evergreen); spores in bushy "cones."*
Habitat: *bogs, sandy marshes, ditches, pine barrens, pond edges.* **Spores:** *Sept.–Oct.*

Tree Club–moss
Lycopodium obscurum

Size: *4–7 in. tall.*
What to look for: *treelike form, branching several times; branches slightly flattened, with very narrow leaves; fertile shoots at top of plant, with spores in clusters of "cones."*
Habitat: *woods, bogs.* **Spores:** *Aug.–Oct.*

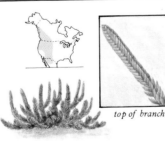

sterile
leaf

top of branch

Rock Spike–moss
Selaginella rupestris

Size: *1–3 in. tall.*
What to look for: *horizontal and upright stems with rather widely spaced branches; sterile leaves narrow, with hairy edges and pointed tip; fertile branches 4-sided, with wider leaves.* **Habitat:** *rocks; soil in dry, sandy woods.* **Spores:** *Aug.–Sept. (often at other times).*

Sagebrush Spike–moss
Selaginella densa

Size: *½–1½ in. tall.*
What to look for: *tight masses of compact, dense branches; leaves narrow, with tiny hairs on edges and a pointed tip.*
Habitat: *sagebrush flats, deserts; dry, rocky slopes; alpine meadows.*
Spores: *Aug.–Sept. (often at other times).*

Spike–mosses
Selaginellaceae

Small and delicate, these plants are easily mistaken for mosses or clubmosses. They form mats or tufts with upright branches rising from creeping, threadlike stems. Minute overlapping leaflets clothe the stems. Some of the branch tips are sterile, others fertile, the latter generally bearing four-sided "cones." One of the strangest spikemosses is the Resurrection Plant (*Selaginella lepidophylla*) of southern Texas and Mexico, often sold as a novelty. When dry, it curls into a tight ball; watered, it opens out flat.

Quillworts Isoetaceae

Though quillworts look remarkably like grass (they are sometimes called Merlin's grass), they have spores rather than seeds and are close allies of ferns. Spanning the continent, the group is generally associated with water; quillworts grow in northern and alpine lakes and in temporary ponds on prairies and among rocks. Most have "bulbs" at the base.

Spiny-spored Quillwort
Isoetes echinospora

Size: *3-15 in. tall.*
What to look for: *bulblike base; leaves resembling grass or Chives, appearing jointed; leaf base wide, rounded, with sac holding spores; spores look like sugar granules.* **Habitat:** *in ponds or lakes or on shore.*
Spores: *June-Oct.*

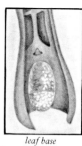

leaf base with spore sac

---

cross section of stem

Field Horsetail
Equisetum arvense

Size: *1-2½ ft. tall.*
What to look for: *coarse plants; whorls of branches at joints; relatively small central canal; spores in "cone" on separate, short-lived, pink-brown stalk.* **Habitat:** *woods, fields, swamps, railroad embankments, roadsides, waste places.*
Spores: *Mar.-May.*

fertile stalk

Smooth Scouring-rush
Equisetum laevigatum

conelike tip

Size: *1-2 ft. tall.*
What to look for: *smooth, stiff stem (dies in winter); large central canal; spore "cone" usually rounded at top.* **Habitat:** *dry fields, prairies, edges of ditches and marshes.*
Spores: *July-Aug.*

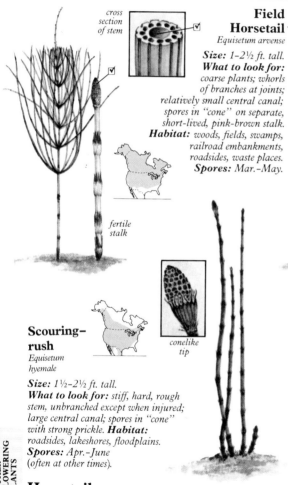

Scouring-rush
Equisetum hyemale

Size: *1½-2½ ft. tall.*
What to look for: *stiff, hard, rough stem, unbranched except when injured; large central canal; spores in "cone" with strong prickle.* **Habitat:** *roadsides, lakeshores, floodplains.*
Spores: *Apr.-June (often at other times).*

conelike tip

Water Horsetail
(Pipes)
Equisetum fluviatile

Size: *2-3 ft. tall.*
What to look for: *delicate, thin, soft stem, usually with branches; very large central canal; spores in "cone."*
Habitat: *swamps, marshes, ponds, ditches.*
Spores: *June-Aug.*

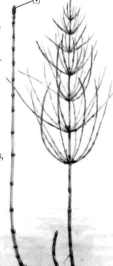

Horsetails Equisetaceae

Hundreds of millions of years ago the spore-bearing horsetails dominated much of the earth, but over the ages, seed-producing plants have usurped their position. Horsetails are easy to recognize: their stems are jointed and ridged, and portions may feel gritty to the touch. The stems of most species have a hollow central canal surrounded by smaller cavities. Horsetails thrive in damp places. The unbranched types, commonly called scouring rushes, were once used for cleaning pots and pans.

Mosses Musci

Plants popularly known as mosses run the gamut from such flowering species as Spanish Moss to algae (Sea Moss) and lichens (Reindeer Moss). In the scientific sense, however, mosses include only certain "lower" plants—lower not because they grow close to the ground (though indeed they do) but because they lack the water-carrying pipelines of ferns and flowering plants. True mosses have a complex life cycle that includes spores rather than seeds. The spores are generally produced at the end of a long stalk, in a covered case whose lid falls off when the spores are mature. Many species can be distinguished from closely related look-alikes only by microscopic examination of their spore cases or leaves.

plants growing in stream

Water Fern Moss
Fissidens grandifrons

Size: 2-4 in. tall.
What to look for: coarse, rigid, dark blue-green plants; leaves in 2 rows, clasping stem, with midrib; leaf base clasps leaf above; spore cases rare.
Habitat: running water; on limestone.

growth form

White Cushion Moss
Leucobryum glaucum

Size: 2-4 in. tall.
What to look for: dense white cushion (blue-green when wet); leaves thick, very narrow, crowded on stem; spore cases rare.
Habitat: moist woods; on soil or very decayed wood.

Cord Moss
Funaria hygrometrica

Size: ½ in. tall.
What to look for: loose, pale yellow-green mat; spore cases numerous, large, asymmetrical, held horizontal or hanging from long, twisted, curled stalk.
Habitat: disturbed places, especially on bare soil and burns; greenhouse pots.

plant with spore case

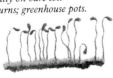

Red Spoonleaf Peat Moss
Sphagnum magellanicum

Size: 6-8 in. tall.
What to look for: spongy, shiny red cushion (pink-green in shade); branches fat, bunched, spreading or drooping, forming rosette at top; leaves round-tipped, overlapping, very concave; spore cases rare.
Habitat: bogs; usually in sun.

plant with spore case

Burned Ground Moss (Purple Moss)
Ceratodon purpureus

Size: to 1 in. tall.
What to look for: dense velvety green tuft (brown when dry); leaves narrow, with edges rolled under the midrib that ends with short red bristle; stems and spore cases purple-red; spore case horizontal, furrowed, with cone-shaped lid.
Habitat: dry, disturbed places; roadsides, fields, roofs.

Broom Moss
Dicranum scoparium

Size: 2-4 in. tall.
What to look for: stems upright, with leaves turned in one direction (looks windswept); leaves narrow, with midrib extending to tip; spore case curved, with beaked lid, at about right angle to stem. **Habitat:** woods; on soil or leaf litter.

OTHER NONFLOWERING PLANTS

525

spore case

spore case

Rock Moss
Grimmia alpicola

Size: 1 in. tall.
What to look for: *rigid plants in small cushion or tuft, green (wet) or blackish (dry); upper leaves erect, nearly hiding spore case; spore case with fringe of red teeth at mouth.* **Habitat:** *exposed places, mountains; on dry limestone rocks.*

Silver Moss
Bryum argenteum

Size: ½ in. tall.
What to look for: *dense, shiny, silver-green cushion of branching plants; leaves broadly oval, tapering abruptly, overlapping, pressed close to stem, with midrib ending before tip; spore case red, hanging, with short-pointed lid.* **Habitat:** *roadsides, sidewalks, roofs, fields, other waste places.*

Delicate Fern Moss
Thuidium delicatulum

Size: 2-4 in. long.
What to look for:
feathery, much-branching mat; leaves on main stem tapered from oval base, pressed close to stem, larger than branch leaves; spore cases not abundant.
Habitat: *woods; on moist or wet soil, leaf litter, decaying wood.*

Tree Moss
Climacium dendroides

Size: 2-4 in. tall.
What to look for:
erect, much-branching stems (resemble little trees), yellow- to dark green; leaves broad, pressed close on stem, narrower and spreading on branches; creeping underground stem; spore cases rare.
Habitat: *swampy areas; on wet humus, decaying wood.*

Woodsy Mnium
(Star Moss)
Mnium cuspidatum

Size: 1-1½ in. tall.
What to look for: *erect stems with oval leaves crowded at top, (smaller at base); creeping stems (not shown) with leaves in 2 rows; spore case nodding, with short-pointed lid, on erect stem.*
Habitat: *woods, fields, lawns, roadsides; in shade.*

Haircap Moss
(Goldilocks)
Polytrichum commune

Size: 6-12 in. tall.
What to look for: *tall, wiry plants; leaves slender, toothed, held straight out (pressed to stem when dry), with long green ridges on upper surface; 4-sided spore case (covered by hairy hood until mature), at top of long stalk; plants without spore cases may have yellow "flower buds."*
Habitat: *woods, edges of bogs.*

Feather Moss
Hypnum imponens

Size: 2-4 in. long.
What to look for: *soft, featherlike, branching, prostrate plants; leaves curled downward; spore case almost upright, on long stalk.* **Habitat:** *swamps, coniferous woods; on decaying logs, on humus, at base of trees.*

Spineleaf Moss
Atrichum undulatum

Size: 1–2½ in. tall.
What to look for: leaves narrow, wavy, with narrow midrib covered by several green ridges; green (brown and very curled when dry), spore case curved, slightly tilted, long-stalked, with beaked lid until mature. **Habitat:** moist woods; on disturbed soil, especially streambanks and uprooted trees.

mature spore case

Four–tooth Moss
Tetraphis pellucida

Size: ½ in. tall.
What to look for: dense tuft of upright stems; leaves elliptical, with midrib to tip; plants without spore cases topped by leafy cup; spore case erect, on long stalk, with 4 narrow triangular teeth at open end. **Habitat:** swamps, woods; on decaying wood, in soil.

sterile plant   *mature spore case*

Liverworts and Hornworts
Hepaticae and Anthocerotae

Liverworts and hornworts lead mosslike lives, and in many species the spore-producing capsule looks much like that of a moss without the lid. Liverworts often reproduce by means of little green buds, called gemmae. The plants take their name—and their reputation as a cure for liver disease—from the flat, liverlike shape of certain species.

Common Hornwort
Anthoceros laevis

Size: ½ in. wide.
What to look for: flat, dark green disk with scalloped edge; spores produced in erect, yellow-green "horn" that splits at tip, exposing slim central column. **Habitat:** disturbed places; bare, moist clay; roadsides, fallow fields.

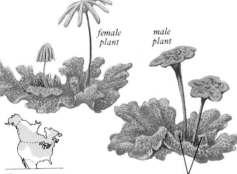

female plant   *male plant*

gemmae cups

Common Liverwort
Marchantia polymorpha

Size: 2–3 in. wide.
What to look for: leathery, dark green, branching ribbons; upper surface with diamond-shaped marks and small cuplike structures containing minute buds (gemmae); umbrella-shaped branches. **Habitat:** moist, bare ground; wet woods, campfire sites, greenhouses, gardens.

Fringed Waterwort
Ricciocarpus natans

Size: ½ in. wide.
What to look for: floating green plants; flat, fan- or heart-shaped; edges shallowly lobed, with dark purple hairlike scales; forked channels corresponding to lobed sections; reproductive structures buried. **Habitat:** marshes, stream backwaters, puddles; stranded on mud.

Braided Liverwort   *Bazzania trilobata*

Size: 4–6 in. long.
What to look for: stem prostrate, forked into equal branches (a series of Y's); leaves in 2 rows, overlapping, dark green, 3-toothed at rounded tip; underside with small, toothed leaves and (occasionally) rootlets; rarely fruiting. **Habitat:** moist coniferous forests; old stumps, peaty banks, rocks.

underside of stem

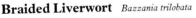

Sea Moss
Bryopsis corticulans

Size: *3–8 in. tall.*
What to look for: *clumps of fernlike seaweed; glossy, dark green; branches usually opposite.*
Habitat: *rocks swept by heavy surf.*

Tube Algae Siphonales

Most of these green algae (and related forms, too) grow in warm waters, where they gradually develop a crust of lime. Such is the case with the Mermaid's Wineglass (*Acetabularia crenulata*) and the Merman's Shaving Brush (*Penicillus capitatus*), whose names describe their appearance with accuracy as well as fantasy. Both species occur in calm seas off Florida; the Wineglass ranges west to Texas.

Irish Moss
Chondrus crispus

Size: *2-6 in. tall.*
What to look for: *clumps of multibranched seaweed; dark purple-green, red-purple, or yellow; tough, leathery.*
Habitat: *tide pools, rock ledges, deeper waters.*

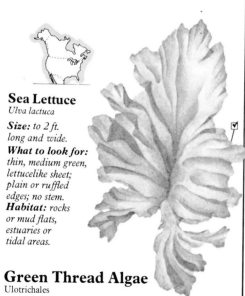

Sea Lettuce
Ulva lactuca

Size: *to 2 ft. long and wide.*
What to look for: *thin, medium green, lettucelike sheet; plain or ruffled edges; no stem.*
Habitat: *rocks or mud flats, estuaries or tidal areas.*

Green Thread Algae
Ulotrichales

Sea Lettuce and seaweeds similar to it grow from the tropics to the Arctic, but most of the other species in this group are inconspicuous freshwater plants. Each plant is divided into individual cells, each surrounded by a wall of cellulose. (Plants in the tube algae group have no cell walls.) The cell wall and other characteristics suggest that plants more complex than algae may have developed from ancestors such as these.

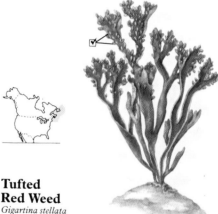

Tufted Red Weed
Gigartina stellata

Size: *2-6 in. tall.*
What to look for: *dark red-purple or brownish clump, with few branches; knobby growths on broad surfaces.* **Habitat:** *lower tide pools, surf-swept rocks.*

Cartilaginous Red Algae Gigartinales

This large group of red seaweeds contains a number of conspicuous and commercially valuable species. Irish Moss, native to both sides of the Atlantic, is the source of carrageenan (carrageen), used in ice cream, yogurt, and certain other foods as a stabilizer and emulsifier; extracts of the plant can be used in milk puddings and fruit jellies. Irish Moss, Tufted Red Weed, and their West Coast relatives often grow abundantly on rocks exposed at low tide.

SEAWEEDS

Laver
*Porphyra
perforata*

Size: *6–12 in. long.*
What to look for: *soft,
slippery, tissue-thin sheet,
variable in color
(gray-pink to purple-red
or gray-green); ruffled edges.*
Habitat: *rocks or
other algae; upper or
middle tidal zone.*

Bang's Primitive Red Algae
Bangiales

The several species called laver look fragile and
shrink markedly when they dry out between tides,
but they are surprisingly strong and resistant to tearing. High in protein and iodine, they can be eaten raw
or cooked and are used as a food or condiment in the
Orient and other places. A Japanese species is one of
the few seaweeds that have been cultivated.

Dulse
(Neptune's Girdle)
Rhodymenia palmata

Size: *12–20 in. tall.*
What to look for: *broad-
bladed plant, with one
blade or several (may have
tiny blades along edges);
red-purple, leathery.*
Habitat: *rocks, shells,
larger algae; tidal areas.*

Rosy-bladed
Red Algae
Rhodymeniales

Munching on Dulse is a custom—and an acquired taste—dating from the Middle Ages in
northern Europe. Closely related species on the
West Coast look much like Dulse; other members
of the group are inflated and resemble bunches of
grapes or fingers on a glove.

Agar Weed
Gelidium robustum

Size: *4–16 in. tall.*
What to look for:
*bushy, erect,
deep red plant;
stem and branches
somewhat flattened;
tough but pliable.*
Habitat: *rocks;
lower tidal zone
and deeper.*

Wormlike Red Algae   Nemalionales

Though seaweed botany may seem esoteric, its importance should not be underrated. Consider the cell
walls of these and other red algae, which contain gelatinous substances extremely resistant to digestion.
Since they are indigestible by man (and therefore
noncaloric), manufacturers use them in diet foods.
Indigestible by nearly all bacteria too, they furnish an
excellent medium, called agar, for growing bacteria
in the laboratory.

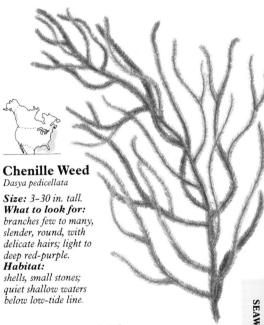

Chenille Weed
Dasya pedicellata

Size: *3–30 in. tall.*
What to look for:
*branches few to many,
slender, round, with
delicate hairs; light to
deep red-purple.*
Habitat:
*shells, small stones;
quiet shallow waters
below low-tide line.*

Vesselled Red Algae   Ceramiales

Chenille Weed is an oddity in this group, whose
members are mainly small and inconspicuous. Large,
feathery, and dramatically colored, it is a favorite for
gluing onto paper and making seaweed pictures.
Many vesselled red algae have a regular and delicate
structure, noticeable when their branches are viewed
through a hand lens or microscope.

SEAWEEDS

529

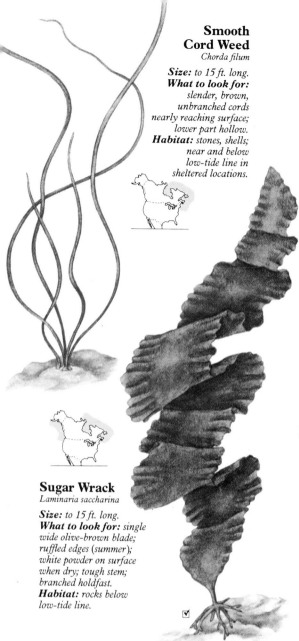

Smooth Cord Weed
Chorda filum

Size: *to 15 ft. long.*
What to look for:
slender, brown, unbranched cords nearly reaching surface; lower part hollow.
Habitat: *stones, shells; near and below low-tide line in sheltered locations.*

Sugar Wrack
Laminaria saccharina

Size: *to 15 ft. long.*
What to look for: *single wide olive-brown blade; ruffled edges (summer); white powder on surface when dry; tough stem; branched holdfast.*
Habitat: *rocks below low-tide line.*

Kelps Laminariales

The most conspicuous brown seaweeds on either coast are the kelps, a group that includes some of the world's largest plants. They have a rather elaborate structure for seaweeds: all but the Smooth Cord Weed have a cylindrical stem, one or more flattened blades, and a specialized holdfast attached to rocks or other solid objects. Kelps reproduce by shedding millions of microscopic spores, which develop into microscopic plantlets. From these plantlets come free-floating gametes, which once united (no mean feat in the open ocean), grow rapidly into mature plants. Some of the largest species, such as the Bull Kelp, attain full size, reproduce, and die within a year.

Rockweeds
Fucales

These are the most advanced brown seaweeds in terms of reproduction. Instead of shedding free-floating spores, as the kelps do, they produce their reproductive cells (gametes) in special, usually swollen, branch tips. As the tide goes out and the tips shrink, the ripe gametes are squeezed out in drops of mucilage. The returning tide sweeps up the gametes, concentrating them and enhancing the chances for successful union. Seaweeds in this group typically live for more than a year; Rockweed and close relatives have a life span of about three years. The group has a wide range on both coasts.

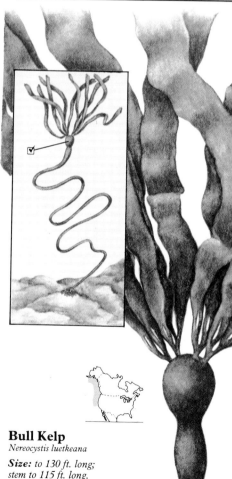

Bull Kelp
Nereocystis luetkeana

Size: *to 130 ft. long; stem to 115 ft. long.*
What to look for: *many floating brown blades coming from stem; bulblike bladder where blades join stem.*
Habitat: *rocks; deep water.*

Rockweed
Fucus vesiculosus

Size: *4–36 in. tall.*
What to look for:
*olive-brown,
mucilaginous seaweed;
stems flattened
with raised midrib,
branching repeatedly
in Y shape; may have
paired oval bladders
on sides of midrib.*
Habitat: *boulders,
ledges; tidal areas.*

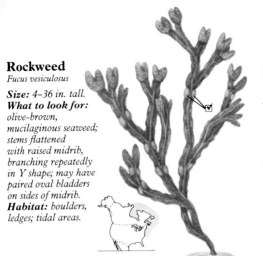

Attached Gulfweed
*Sargassum
filipendula*

Size: *6–36 in. tall.*
What to look for:
*light or yellowish-
brown seaweed with
few to many branches;
leafy blades with toothed
edges; berrylike bladders
on short stems.* **Habitat:**
*rocks, shells; at or
below low-tide line.*

Giant Kelp
*Macrocystis
pyrifera*

Size: *to 230 ft. long;
blades 10–30 in. long.*
What to look for:
*brown seaweed with
long main stem and
leaf-shaped blades
on side stems;
hollow bladder
at base of blade;
leaf-shaped blades
split off from
semicircular
blade at tip.*
Habitat: *rocks,
coarse sand;
deep water.*

Sea Palm
Postelsia palmaeformis

Size: *1–2 ft. tall;
blades 6–10 in. long.*
What to look for: *olive-brown
seaweed resembling miniature
palm tree; stem hollow, flexible,
remaining upright when water
recedes; in large stands.*
Habitat: *surf-swept rocks.*

SEAWEEDS

Lichens Lichenes

Thriving under such stressful conditions as extreme cold and drought, lichens have the remarkable ability to grow where few other plants can—on rocks and tombstones, in deserts and in the Far North. Even more amazing is just what they are: unique combinations of two distinct species, an alga (a primitive aquatic plant) and a fungus. The algae, which can photosynthesize, contribute food; the fungi, it is believed, furnish water and shade.

Reproduction might seem a problem for such partnership plants. In many cases small bits break off and grow into new lichens. Sometimes the fungus produces spores that are released along with a few algal cells. Or wind-blown spores from the fungus may come into contact with free-living algae and develop with them into lichen.

People living in places where lichens are common have found many a use for these curious plants. Boiled in water, they yield fabric dyes used most notably by Scots in coloring Harris tweeds. Some furnish smoking materials, some medicine. Though the Wolf Lichen was reputedly used as an Old World wolf-killer, few species are poisonous to man or beast. Indeed, many can be used as emergency rations, and foraging Reindeer and Caribou depend to an enormous extent on these lowly plants.

Dog Lichen
Peltigera canina

Size: *2½–8 in. long.*
What to look for: *leathery sheet with scalloped edges; upper surface downy, blue-gray or pale brown (dry) to dark brown (moist); underside woolly, white to tan, with pale brown veins; fruiting bodies at edges, erect, rolled, resembling dog's teeth.* **Habitat:** *moist woods, shaded road banks.*

Lung Lichen
Lobaria pulmonaria

Size: *2–10 in. wide.*
What to look for: *irregularly lobed sheet with wrinkled surface; upper surface olive-brown (dry) to bright green (moist); underside mottled tan and white; loosely attached to tree.* **Habitat:** *on tree trunks; hardwood swamps, moist forests.*

Orange Star Lichen
Xanthoria elegans

Size: *1–2 in. wide.*
What to look for: *bright orange rosette; fruiting bodies saucer-shaped, abundant, in center; closely attached to rock.* **Habitat:** *on exposed rocks, especially where birds perch; often on tombstones, lakeside boulders, and mountain cliffs.*

Map Lichen
Rhizocarpon geographicum

Size: *½–4 in. wide.*
What to look for: *bright yellow to green-yellow crust with black outline and fine black cracks; fruiting bodies tiny, black, sunken in upper surface.* **Habitat:** *on exposed rocks; uplands, mountains.*

Toadskin Lichen (Rock Tripe)
Umbilicaria papulosa

Size: *1–4 in. wide.*
What to look for: *flat sheet with torn edges; blistered, light brown, brittle (dry) or leathery (moist) surface; fruiting bodies round, smooth, black; attached to rock by holdfast in center.* **Habitat:** *exposed cliffs, ledges, boulders.*

Cracked Shield Lichen

Parmelia sulcata

Size: 1–4 in. wide.
What to look for: flat leaflike plant with network of cracks and ridges; green-gray above, black below, with many short rootlike attachments.
Habitat: on tree trunks; woods, roadsides.

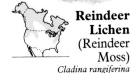

Reindeer Lichen (Reindeer Moss)

Cladina rangiferina

Size: 2½–4 in. tall.
What to look for: large round gray clump; stems branched like antlers, with woolly surface and fingerlike tips; branches often perforated at base.
Habitat: on barren tundra soil; elsewhere in North, on sandy soil.

Beard Lichen

Usnea cavernosa

Size: 6–10 in. long.
What to look for: hanging tufts; pale green-gray, yellow-tinged threads attached to tree by central stem; stem often cracked, with white rubbery core exposed; branches vary in length.
Habitat: on trunks and limbs of conifers.

Flabby Lichen

Evernia mesomorpha

Size: 2–4 in. long.
What to look for: drooping tufts; flabby, pale yellow-green, irregularly angled branches; greenish powder on surface; attached to tree at single point.
Habitat: on trunks of conifers; occasionally on broad-leaved trees.

Wolf Lichen

Letharia vulpina

Size: 1–4 in. long.
What to look for: hanging tufts; irregular yellow to chartreuse branches; powdery surface.
Habitat: on trunks and branches of conifers.

Ladder Lichen

Cladonia verticillata

Size: 1–3 in. tall.
What to look for: tiers of gray-green goblet-shaped cups (each rising from center of one below); flat scales at base, disappearing with age.
Habitat: in sandy soil and on old wood; fields, roadsides; in sun.

Pyxie Cups

Cladonia pyxidata

Size: ½ in. tall.
What to look for: gray stalked goblets, scaly inside and out; large lumpy scales around base of upright portion.
Habitat: in sand, on old wood, on soil-covered rocks; dry, sunny places.

British Soldiers

Cladonia cristatella

Size: 1–1½ in. tall.
What to look for: scarlet tips; stalks lumpy, scaly, gray (dry) or green-gray (moist); inconspicuous scales around base of upright portion.
Habitat: in sandy soil, on old wood; dry, sunny places.

LICHENS

Mushrooms

Whether or not you are already enthusiastic about these lowly plants, read on. The beauty of mushrooms, their diversity, and their intricate lives are sure to intrigue.

The mushroom world is full of surprises. There are green ones, purple ones, ones shaped like birds' nests complete with eggs. Some "blush" when bruised; some glow in the dark; some shoot up before your very eyes.

A Warning Against Eating Wild Mushrooms

Exploring for mushrooms, identifying them, and learning about how they live and grow give a great deal of pleasure to many people, but others are attracted to mushrooms because they are free and exotic items of food. Eating wild mushrooms is extremely risky. Fatally poisonous species as well as ones that will make you unpleasantly ill grow throughout North America, and no general rule allows discrimination between those that are edible and those that are inedible or worse. No wild mushroom should be eaten in any amount or in any form unless it has been identified by an expert and declared safe.

Chanterelle

Jack-o'-lantern

One danger in eating wild mushrooms is that poisonous species can be confused with edible ones. Although the Chanterelle is often considered a "safe" species, it resembles the poisonous Jack-o'-lantern in shape, overall color, and spore color. While the differences may seem obvious, it is rare to have them both at hand for comparison.

Mushrooms form part of the enormous group of organisms called fungi—organisms defined by their habits of growth and their inability to make their own food. Like mosses and ferns, fungi reproduce by tiny spores rather than flowers and seeds. In many species, such as the amanitas, spores develop only on the underside of the cap; in others, they are produced all over the surface (coral fungi) or on the inside (puffballs).

Once released, the spores become dispersed from the parent plant. (The word "plant" is broadly used here, for many scientists put fungi into a separate kingdom.) Air currents blow them away; raindrops wash them away; flying insects transport them to distant places. When the spores land in a favorable location (say, moist soil), an underground network of threads, called a mycelium, develops. The mycelium is often white, and frequently you can find it by poking about in the soil, wood, or other material in which a mushroom or other fungus is growing.

The mycelium produces swellings that enlarge and eventually push above the surface, forming the fleshy structure — the mushroom — that produces spores. A few species, such as the highly prized truffles, never grow above the surface; they are strictly subterranean.

Although the mushroom itself (the part above ground) is generally short-lived, the mycelium may live for decades, even centuries. Its longevity depends on the food supply, for unlike green plants, fungi lack chlorophyll and are unable to make their own food. Where they get their food varies from species to species. Some, such as the Oyster Mushroom, use decaying wood or other dead plant material. Others nourish themselves on living plants (sometimes even other mushrooms) or animals, causing disease or death. One such species pictured in this book is the Orange-colored Cordyceps, which grows on insects.

Still other species—a great many, scientists have discovered—obtain their food from living trees in a way that benefits them both. The mycelium of the mushroom intertwines and fuses with the rootlets of the tree; the mushroom gets the food it needs, and the tree essential nutrients. Sometimes the relationship between mushroom and tree is extraordinarily specific: a particular kind of mushroom will grow under or near only one kind of tree. So if you're "up" on tree identification, you'll have a headstart on identifying mushrooms.

Mushroom hunting is an activity for all seasons, and there are even a few species, such as the Winter Mushroom, that "sprout" only when the weather is cold. But fall, especially after rain, is a prime time for finding mushrooms; wet springs are second-best. Like the famed swallows of Capistrano, mushrooms of a given species will often "return" to the same place at about the same time of year—though in reality, of course, they are there all along, their threads waiting beneath the surface.

How to Use This Section
Different kinds of mushrooms are grouped together according to the location and nature of the structures that bear their spores.

- The most prominent group, the gilled mushrooms and the closely related chanterelles, are shown on pages 536 through 548.
- The tube mushrooms, whose spongy undersides are perforated with small spore-producing openings, are shown at the top of pages 550 and 551.
- The pore (or bracket) fungi, which are hard or firm and often grow like shelves on a stump or tree, have pores that open on the underside and produce the spores. This group begins at the bottom of page 550.
- The teeth fungi, shown at the bottom of pages 552 and 553, produce spores on hanging "teeth." The teeth may be on the underside only, or all over the surface.
- Puffballs and their relatives, which open up to release their spores (the spores develop on the inside), are shown on pages 554 and 555.
- Other groups shown in this book include the coral fungi (page 549), the jelly fungi (page 556), the flask fungi (page 557), and the cup fungi (pages 558 and 559).

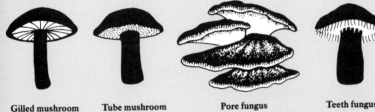

| Gilled mushroom | Tube mushroom | Pore fungus | Teeth fungus | Puffball |

Tips on Identifying Mushrooms

Overall color. To identify mushrooms shown in this section, don't look only at the color of the painting; read the description too. Often a given species will occur in a variety of hues; location is important (mushrooms growing in sunshine tend to be paler than their shaded cousins), and so is age (an old Vermilion Hygrophorus will be yellow rather than vermilion). Of greater significance in identifying a mushroom is whether it shows stains (streaks or blotches of a different color) and whether it changes color when bruised (slice a mushroom lengthwise and give it a pinch).

 gills not attached to stem

gills attached directly to stem

Spore color. Although single spores are invisible to the naked eye, spores en masse have a color, and that color is important in the identification of gilled mushrooms. To collect enough spores to observe their color, place the cap of the mushroom, rounded end up, on some white paper. Cover it with a bowl or drinking glass. Within a few hours, a dusting of spores should appear on the paper beneath the cap. If you don't see any, rub your finger along the paper; white spores will show up against your skin.

Attachment of gills. If the underside of the mushroom has thin plates, or gills, cut it lengthwise to see how the gills are connected with the stem. They may be free (that is, not attached to the stem); or they may be attached in one of several ways, as shown at right.

 gills attached to stem and notched

 gills attached to and running down stem

535

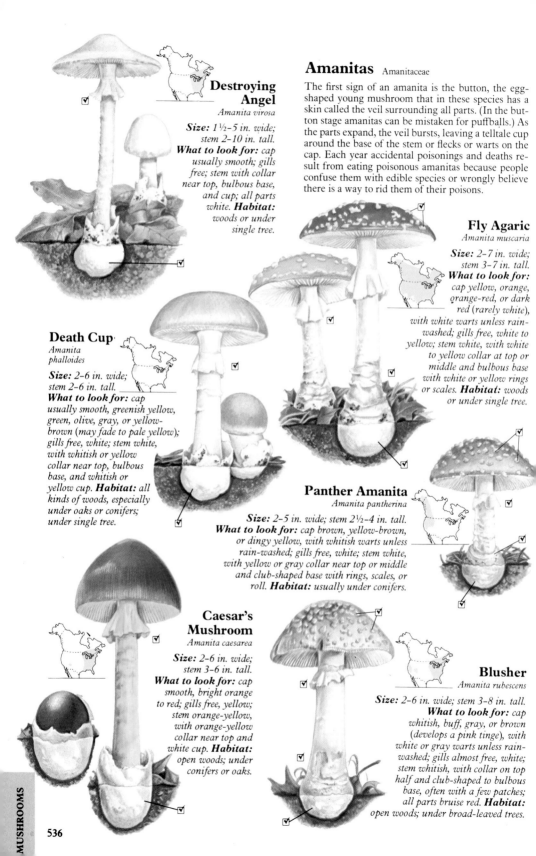

Destroying Angel
Amanita virosa

Size: *1½–5 in. wide; stem 2–10 in. tall.*
What to look for: *cap usually smooth; gills free; stem with collar near top, bulbous base, and cup; all parts white.* **Habitat:** *woods or under single tree.*

Amanitas Amanitaceae

The first sign of an amanita is the button, the egg-shaped young mushroom that in these species has a skin called the veil surrounding all parts. (In the button stage amanitas can be mistaken for puffballs.) As the parts expand, the veil bursts, leaving a telltale cup around the base of the stem or flecks or warts on the cap. Each year accidental poisonings and deaths result from eating poisonous amanitas because people confuse them with edible species or wrongly believe there is a way to rid them of their poisons.

Fly Agaric
Amanita muscaria

Size: *2–7 in. wide; stem 3–7 in. tall.*
What to look for: *cap yellow, orange, orange-red, or dark red (rarely white), with white warts unless rain-washed; gills free, white to yellow; stem white, with white to yellow collar at top or middle and bulbous base with white or yellow rings or scales.* **Habitat:** *woods or under single tree.*

Death Cup
Amanita phalloides

Size: *2–6 in. wide; stem 2–6 in. tall.*
What to look for: *cap usually smooth, greenish yellow, green, olive, gray, or yellow-brown (may fade to pale yellow); gills free, white; stem white, with whitish or yellow collar near top, bulbous base, and whitish or yellow cup.* **Habitat:** *all kinds of woods, especially under oaks or conifers; under single tree.*

Panther Amanita
Amanita pantherina

Size: *2–5 in. wide; stem 2½–4 in. tall.*
What to look for: *cap brown, yellow-brown, or dingy yellow, with whitish warts unless rain-washed; gills free, white; stem white, with yellow or gray collar near top or middle and club-shaped base with rings, scales, or roll.* **Habitat:** *usually under conifers.*

Caesar's Mushroom
Amanita caesarea

Size: *2–6 in. wide; stem 3–6 in. tall.*
What to look for: *cap smooth, bright orange to red; gills free, yellow; stem orange-yellow, with orange-yellow collar near top and white cup.* **Habitat:** *open woods; under conifers or oaks.*

Blusher
Amanita rubescens

Size: *2–6 in. wide; stem 3–8 in. tall.*
What to look for: *cap whitish, buff, gray, or brown (develops a pink tinge), with white or gray warts unless rain-washed; gills almost free, white; stem whitish, with collar on top half and club-shaped to bulbous base, often with a few patches; all parts bruise red.* **Habitat:** *open woods; under broad-leaved trees.*

Napkin Amanita
Amanita citrina

Size: *1–5 in. wide; stem 2½–5 in. tall.*
What to look for: *cap pale greenish yellow, smooth or with flat patches of gray or gray-pink; gills free, whitish or yellow; stem white, with white or yellow collar near top, soft bulbous base, and often with an ill-defined cup.*
Habitat: *under broad-leaved trees or in mixed woods.*

Grisette
Amanita vaginata

Size: *1½–3 in. wide; stem 3–5 in. tall.*
What to look for: *cap smooth, smoky gray; gills free, white; stem whitish or gray, sometimes with rings of flat hairs; no collar; slightly bulbous base with white cup.* **Habitat:** *all kinds of woods.*

Lepiotas Lepiotaceae

Like many amanitas, lepiotas often have a collar on the stem; however, they never have a cup at the stem's base. A number of them thrive under man-made conditions. The Yellow Lepiota (*Lepiota lutea*) grows in greenhouses and in the soil of potted plants. The Blushing Lepiota (*Lepiota americana*), which "blushes" red when it is bruised, prefers the stumps of street and lawn trees, particularly maples.

Smooth Lepiota
Leucoagaricus naucinus

Size: *1½–4 in. wide; stem 2½–5 in. tall.*
What to look for:
cap smooth, white (may be gray near center); gills free, white (grayish pink with age); stem white, with collar near top, club-shaped base, and no cup; cap and stem bruise slowly yellow; spores white to creamy. **Habitat:** *grassy areas.*

Parasol Mushroom
Lepiota procera

Size: *2½–6 in. wide; stem 6–10 in. tall.*
What to look for: *cap surface broken into red-brown scales (except in center), with whitish to pale tan between scales; gills free, white (pink, then brown, with age); stem whitish, with brown scales, movable fringed collar near top, and no cup; spores white.* **Habitat:** *fields, lawns, woodland openings.*

Green Gill Mushroom
Chlorophyllum molybdites

Size: *3–12 in. wide; stem 3–10 in. tall.*
What to look for:
cap white to buff, with buff to brown scales; gills free, whitish (yellowish, then olive, with age); stem smooth, white (dingy brown when old or bruised), with movable collar near top and no cup; spores dull green; often grows in rings. **Habitat:** *grassy areas.*

Shaggy Lepiota
Lepiota rachodes

Size: *3–8 in. wide; stem 4–8 in. tall.*
What to look for: *cap surface broken into pink-gray to dark brown scales, with whitish between scales; gills free, white (brown blotches with age); stem white (bruises yellow or red-brown), with fringed collar and no cup; spores white.* **Habitat:** *woodlands, grassy areas, compost heaps, wood-chip mulch, woodsheds, greenhouses.*

Cone-shaped Hygrophorus
Hygrophorus conicus

Size: 1–2½ in. wide; stem 2–4 in. tall.
What to look for: cap red to yellow-orange, often with olive tints; gills free or partially attached, white (olive, orange, or yellow with age); stem often colored like cap; all parts black when old or bruised; spores white.
Habitat: under conifers.

Russula Hygrophorus
Hygrophorus russula

Size: 2–4½ in. wide; stem 1–3 in. tall.
What to look for: cap slimy when wet, pink or pink-brown, often with dark red streaks; gills attached or running down stem, white (turning pink with dark red spots); stem white (turning pink or red-brown); spores white.
Habitat: under oaks or in oak-pine woods.

Vermilion Hygrophorus
Hygrophorus miniatus

Size: ½–1½ in. wide; stem 1–2 in. tall.
What to look for: cap red (fading to orange or yellow); gills fully or partially attached; gills and stem same color as cap or paler; spores white.
Habitat: in soil or moss under broad-leaved trees or in mixed woods.

Hygrophori Hygrophoraceae

Red, orange, yellow, or shining white—these mushrooms' eye-catching colors add a glimmer of brightness to dimly lighted woods. The Parrot Hygrophorus (*Hygrophorus psittacinus*), widely distributed in North America, is a rich dark green, a most unusual color for a mushroom. One characteristic of this family is tactile: the gills feel waxy when rubbed hard between the fingers.

milk oozes from cut in gills

Orange-brown Lactarius
Lactarius volemus

Size: 2–3 in. wide; stem 2–3 in. tall.
What to look for: cap and stem brown to orange-buff, malodorous; gills attached or partially running down stem, cream colored (slowly bruise brown); milk white, sticky, abundant; spores white.
Habitat: under broad-leaved trees or in mixed woods.

Cottony-margined Milky Cap
Lactarius deceptivus

Size: 2–9 in. wide; stem 1½–4 in. tall.
What to look for: young cap with cottony, rolled-under edge; gills running down stem; stem velvety; all parts white (tan or brown with age); milk white, slowly stains tissue brown; spores white. **Habitat:** under conifers, especially hemlocks, or in mixed woods.

Russulas and Lactarii Russulaceae

Named from the Latin *lactare* ("to secrete milk"), the lactarii ooze a milklike liquid when cut or broken. The milk can be white, carrot-orange, deep blood-red, or even blue, as in the southeastern Blue Lactarius (*Lactarius indigo*). The russulas (from the Latin for "reddish") lack milk and do not always come in the color their name suggests: they can be purple, yellow, orange, green, or even black. Both groups are common woodland mushrooms in summer and fall. Sometimes their caps are scored with teeth marks—a sign that a small mammal has come and gone.

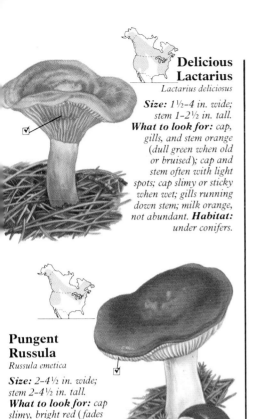

Delicious Lactarius
Lactarius deliciosus

Size: *1½–4 in. wide; stem 1–2½ in. tall.*
What to look for: *cap, gills, and stem orange (dull green when old or bruised); cap and stem often with light spots; cap slimy or sticky when wet; gills running down stem; milk orange, not abundant.* **Habitat:** *under conifers.*

Pungent Russula
Russula emetica

Size: *2–4½ in. wide; stem 2–4½ in. tall.*
What to look for: *cap slimy, bright red (fades with age), with ridges on edge; gills attached, white; stem white; spores white.*
Habitat: *bogs; under conifers in moss.*

Short-stemmed Russula
Russula brevipes

Size: *3–8 in. wide; stem 1–2 in. tall.*
What to look for: *cap depressed in center, white to pale buff (brown with age); gills partially running down stem, white or tinged green, often with brown spots; stem white (bruises brown).* **Habitat:** *under conifers.*

Scaly Lentinus
Lentinus lepideus

Size: *2–8 in. wide; stem 1½–6 in. tall.*
What to look for: *cap whitish to buff, developing small brown scales; gills running down stem, rather far apart, toothed at edges, whitish to buff; stem whitish, with collar near top (often scaly below collar); with age stem turns yellow, base brown to wine-red; spores white to buff.*
Habitat: *on conifer wood.*

Tricholomas and Relatives
Tricholomataceae

A large and diverse family of 1,000 or more species, these mushrooms have little in common except white or lightly colored spores. All of the species on the next 3½ pages belong to this group. Some grow on wood, others in soil, but like all mushrooms, they spring from rootlike filaments called mycelia. The mycelium of the Honey Mushroom can spread underground from the roots of one living tree to another and, unlike most mushrooms, can kill its host. This mycelium is luminescent, causing a glow known as fox fire. The mycelium of the Fairy Ring spreads under lawns in ever-expanding circles, creating dark green rings as it stimulates the growth of grass.

Split-gilled Mushroom
Schizophyllum commune

Size: *½–1 in. wide.*
What to look for: *cap hairy, tough, fan-shaped, white to gray (brownish gray when wet); gills gray, radiating from point of attachment, with edges split or grooved; no stem; spores pinkish.* **Habitat:** *usually in clusters on logs, sticks, stumps of broad-leaved trees.*

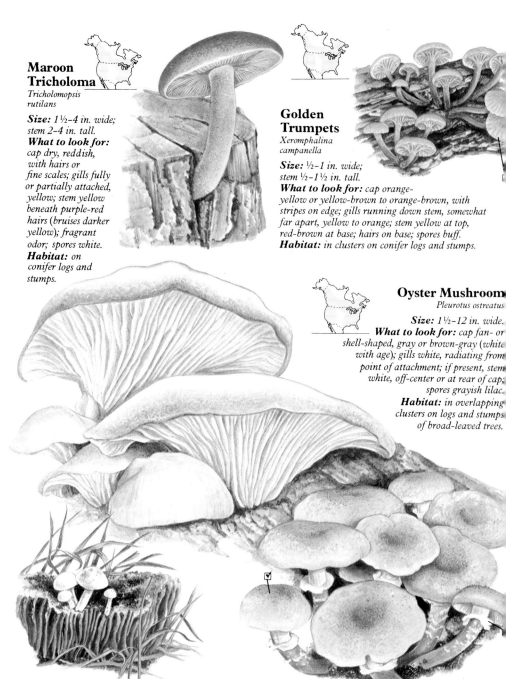

Maroon Tricholoma
Tricholomopsis rutilans

Size: 1½–4 in. wide; stem 2–4 in. tall.
What to look for: cap dry, reddish, with hairs or fine scales; gills fully or partially attached, yellow; stem yellow beneath purple-red hairs (bruises darker yellow); fragrant odor; spores white.
Habitat: on conifer logs and stumps.

Golden Trumpets
Xeromphalina campanella

Size: ½–1 in. wide; stem ½–1½ in. tall.
What to look for: cap orange-yellow or yellow-brown to orange-brown, with stripes on edge; gills running down stem, somewhat far apart, yellow to orange; stem yellow at top, red-brown at base; hairs on base; spores buff.
Habitat: in clusters on conifer logs and stumps.

Oyster Mushroom
Pleurotus ostreatus

Size: 1½–12 in. wide.
What to look for: cap fan- or shell-shaped, gray or brown-gray (white with age); gills white, radiating from point of attachment; if present, stem white, off-center or at rear of cap; spores grayish lilac.
Habitat: in overlapping clusters on logs and stumps of broad-leaved trees.

Parasitic Asterophora
Asterophora lycoperdoides

Size: ½–1 in. wide; stem about 1 in. tall.
What to look for: cap smooth and whitish (powdery and brown when mature); gills attached, whitish, far apart, sometimes narrow and nearly invisible; stem whitish (brown with age); spores brown. **Habitat:** on rotting mushrooms, especially russulas and lactarii.

Honey Mushroom
Armillariella mellea

Size: 1–5 in. wide; stem 1½–6 in. tall.
What to look for: cap slimy when wet, and light to dark yellow, honey-colored, or brown, with fine hairs or scales over center; gills attached or running down stem, white or cream (spotted brown with age); stem white to buff or brown, with collar near top; black stringlike growths in nearby wood and soil; spores white or pale cream. **Habitat:** in clusters on logs and stumps; sometimes at base of tree.

Fairy Ring
Marasmius oreades

Size: ¾–2 in. wide; stem 1–3 in. tall.
What to look for: cap often humped in center, light tan, cream, brown, or red-brown; gills partially attached or free, white to pale buff; stem white to buff at top, buff to brown and often hairy at base; spores white to buff.
Habitat: in groups, arcs, or rings in grassy areas.

Little Wheel Mushroom
Marasmius rotula

Size: ¼–¾ in. wide; stem ½–3 in. tall.
What to look for: cap white, with dark center and ribbed edge; gills white, far apart, joined to collar near top of stem; stem mostly black, shiny, wirelike; spores white.
Habitat: in clusters on decaying leaves or wood under broad-leaved trees.

Pine Mushroom
Armillaria ponderosa

Size: 2½–8 in. wide; stem 1¾–7 in. tall.
What to look for: cap white when young (center turning brown and scaly, edge becoming streaked with flat brown hairs); gills partially attached, white (bruise brown); rufflelike collar; stem white above collar, red-brown and scaly or hairy below; spores white. **Habitat:** under conifers.

Club-footed Clitocybe
Clitocybe clavipes

Size: 1–4 in. wide; stem 1½–3 in. tall.
What to look for: cap brown or gray-brown, often with paler margin; gills running down stem, white to cream; stem brown or dingy buff, with bulbous base; spores white.
Habitat: under conifers; sometimes in mixed woods.

Wood Blewit
Clitocybe nuda

Size: 1½–6 in. wide; stem 1¼–4 in. tall.
What to look for: cap violet (fading to violet-gray or buff, then brown); gills partially attached, pale violet (buff to brown with age); stem pale violet (base turning brown), often with fine white hairs; spores flesh color.
Habitat: woods; occasionally in compost piles.

Jack-o'-lantern
Omphalotus olearius

Size: 2–5 in. wide; stem 2–8 in. tall.
What to look for: cap, gills, and stem orange to orange-yellow, malodorous; gills running down stem, luminescent in the dark; spores white or cream.
Habitat: in large clusters on stumps, buried roots (often of oaks).

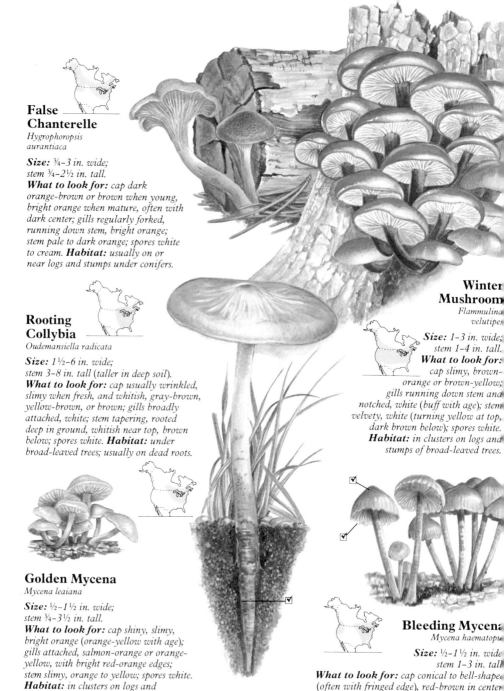

False Chanterelle
Hygrophoropsis aurantiaca

Size: ¾–3 in. wide; stem ¾–2½ in. tall.
What to look for: cap dark orange-brown or brown when young, bright orange when mature, often with dark center; gills regularly forked, running down stem, bright orange; stem pale to dark orange; spores white to cream. **Habitat:** usually on or near logs and stumps under conifers.

Rooting Collybia
Oudemansiella radicata

Size: 1½–6 in. wide; stem 3–8 in. tall (taller in deep soil).
What to look for: cap usually wrinkled, slimy when fresh, and whitish, gray-brown, yellow-brown, or brown; gills broadly attached, white; stem tapering, rooted deep in ground, whitish near top, brown below; spores white. **Habitat:** under broad-leaved trees; usually on dead roots.

Golden Mycena
Mycena leaiana

Size: ½–1½ in. wide; stem ¾–3½ in. tall.
What to look for: cap shiny, slimy, bright orange (orange-yellow with age); gills attached, salmon-orange or orange-yellow, with bright red-orange edges; stem slimy, orange to yellow; spores white. **Habitat:** in clusters on logs and stumps of broad-leaved trees.

Winter Mushroom
Flammulina velutipes

Size: 1–3 in. wide; stem 1–4 in. tall.
What to look for: cap slimy, brown-orange or brown-yellow; gills running down stem and notched, white (buff with age); stem velvety, white (turning yellow at top, dark brown below); spores white. **Habitat:** in clusters on logs and stumps of broad-leaved trees.

Bleeding Mycena
Mycena haematopus

Size: ½–1½ in. wide; stem 1–3 in. tall.
What to look for: cap conical to bell-shaped (often with fringed edge), red-brown in center, red-gray at edge; gills white or gray-red (spotted red-brown with age); stem brown (bleeds red when cut); spores white. **Habitat:** on decaying logs.

Clean Mycena
Mycena pura

Size: ½–1½ in. wide; stem 1–4 in. tall.
What to look for: cap lilac, purple, or dull rose (sometimes tinted gray or brown), with radishlike odor; gills fully or partially attached, white (turning color of cap with age); stem white or color of cap; spores white. **Habitat:** woods.

Waxy Laccaria
Laccaria laccata

Size: ½–2 in. wide;
stem 1–4 in. tall.
What to look for: cap
smooth to rough and brown,
pink-brown, or dull flesh
color (paler with age);
gills attached or partially
running down stem, somewhat
far apart, pink; stem colored
like cap; spores white. **Habitat:**
on moss, humus, or wet soil
in woods; sometimes in open areas.

Russet-scaly Tricholoma
Tricholoma vaccinum

Size: 1½–3 in. wide;
stem 2–3 in. tall.
What to look for:
cap with fine flat hairs
or scales (woolly edge
when young), dry, red-
brown; gills attached
or notched, white,
with red-brown streaks
or spots; stem with
fine flat hairs,
red-brown; spores white.
Habitat: under conifers.

Greenish-yellow Tricholoma
*Tricholoma
flavovirens*

Size: 2–5 in. wide;
stem 1–4 in. tall.
What to look for:
cap green-yellow,
with center often brown;
gills partially attached,
yellow; stem yellow-tinged,
white at top; spores
white. **Habitat:** woods;
especially under pines,
hemlocks, or aspens.

Dingy Tricholoma
Tricholoma portentosum

Size: 1½–4 in. wide;
stem 2–5 in. tall.
What to look for:
cap with flattened
fine dark hairs,
gray or gray-brown,
sometimes violet-tinted;
gills attached or notched,
pale yellow; stem white
or yellowish;
spores white.
Habitat: under conifers.

Volvarias Pluteaceae

Most of the mushrooms in this book are encountered fairly
frequently. The Silky Volvaria is an exception. It is rare, as
are the half dozen or so other native volvarias, and its striking
beauty makes it a choice find. All the members of this small
family have dull pink or rose spores. (The only other mushrooms with pink spores are the rhodophylls and some trich-
olomas.) The cup at the base of the stem further distinguishes some volvarias, but this feature is lacking in the
plutei, the more common group in the family.

Silky Volvaria
Volvariella bombycina

Size: 2–8 in. wide; stem 2–8 in. tall.
What to look for: cap silky, often with
fringed edge, white (slightly yellow with age);
gills free, white (pink, then dull rose, with age);
stem often curved, white, with deep cup at base,
no ring; spores dull pink, rose, or brown-pink.
Habitat: on logs and stumps of broad-leaved
trees and wounds in living trees.

Rhodophylls Entolomataceae

Although the mushrooms in this group are difficult to tell apart, they are easily distinguished from other families. The rhodophylls ("rosy-leaved") have at least one characteristic—rose-colored spores—in common with the volvarias, but their gills are attached to the top of the stem and they have no cup at the base. The fleshy white masses that immediately identify the Abortive Entoloma are malformations: the mycelium of the Honey Mushroom has penetrated the entoloma and caused the entoloma to become deformed.

malformed
(aborted)
entoloma

Abortive Entoloma
Entoloma abortivum

Size: 1½–4 in. wide; stem 1½–4 in. tall.
What to look for: cap gray or brown-gray, sometimes with watery spots; gills attached or running down stem, gray (dingy rose with age); stem gray-white; fleshy white masses often appear nearby. **Habitat:** on decaying wood and humus.

Livid Entoloma
Entoloma sinuatum

Size: 2½–6 in. wide; stem 1½–6 in. tall.
What to look for: cap pale dingy tan or gray-tan; gills notched at stem, whitish to yellow (dingy pink with age); stem thick, solid, white; spores dingy pink. **Habitat:** in mixed woods or under conifers.

Salmon Entoloma
Entoloma salmoneum

Size: ¾–2 in. wide; stem 1½–4½ in. tall.
What to look for: cap conical to bell-shaped, salmon-colored; gills fully or partially attached, orange-salmon; stem colored like cap; spores brown-pink. **Habitat:** woods, bogs.

Slimy Gomphidius
Gomphidius glutinosus

Size: 1–4 in. wide; stem 1½–4 in. tall.
What to look for: cap slimy and gray-brown, red-brown, or purple-gray (blotched black with age); gills running down stem, white (gray with age); stem yellow below slimy collar, white above; spores gray to black. **Habitat:** under conifers.

Gomphidii Gomphidiaceae

The Greek word *gomphos* means "nail" or "peg," a possible allusion to the shape of young mushrooms belonging to this group. When mature, the gills are dark brown or black; they are thick, extend far down the stem, and look somewhat waxy. All 25 species grow under conifers.

Inky Caps and Relatives
Coprinaceae

The caps and gills of the fungi in this family—many of them known as inky caps—blacken with age and melt into an inklike liquid. As the spore-containing liquid drips to the ground, the species renews itself. Fresh Shaggy Manes and some other inky caps are eaten, but once they have started to melt, they should be left alone. Some species are poisonous, and at least one, the Inky Cap, causes nausea if consumed with alcohol.

Shaggy Mane
Coprinus comatus

Size: ¾–2½ in. wide; stem 3–8 in. tall.
What to look for: cap columnar, white with brown top and scales (edges flaring out, cap turning inky, with age); gills white (pink, then inky, with age); stem white, with collar and bulbous base; spores black. **Habitat:** lawns, pastures, roadsides.

melt
ca

544

MUSHROOMS

Smoky-gilled Woodlover
Naematoloma capnoides

Size: ¾–3 in. wide; stem 2–4 in. tall.
What to look for: cap rounded (becoming flattened) and orange, rust, or yellow-brown, with yellow edge; gills attached (becoming free), white (gray, then purple-brown, with age); stem yellow on top with slight hairy ring, brown to rusty below; spores purple-brown. **Habitat:** in clusters on or near conifer wood.

Stropharias and Relatives
Strophariaceae

Many, but not all, of the hallucinogenic mushrooms belong to this colorful family. Certain of the small, rare psilocybes have long been used by Mexican Indians in religious ceremonies; possession of the Cuban Psilocybe (*Psilocybe cubensis*), which grows in Florida and along the Gulf Coast, is illegal in most states.

Brick Top
Naematoloma sublateritium

Size: ¾–4 in. wide; stem 2–4 in. tall.
What to look for: cap brick-red at center, buff and often fringed with hairs (at edge); gills attached, dingy white (purple-gray with age); stem white, often with thin hairy collar near top; spores purple-brown. **Habitat:** in clusters on logs and stumps of broad-leaved trees.

Sulphur Top
Naematoloma fasciculare

Size: ½–3 in. wide; stem 2–5 in. tall.
What to look for: cap green-yellow or yellow (center may be orange or brown); gills attached (becoming free), sulphur- or green-yellow; stem white at top with slight hairy ring, brown below; spores purple-brown. **Habitat:** in clusters on logs and stumps of conifers or broad-leaved trees.

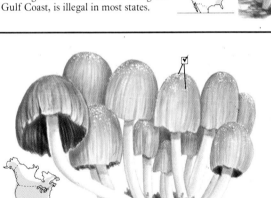

Glistening Inky Cap
Coprinus micaceus

Size: ¾–2½ in. wide; stem 1–3 in. tall.
What to look for: cap conical to bell-shaped, brown or tan, with shiny grains when young (smooth, turning inky with age); gills white (turning inky); stem white; spores black.
Habitat: in clusters on decaying logs, stumps, buried wood.

Inky Cap
Coprinus atramentarius

Size: ¾–3 in. wide; stem 1½–6 in. tall.
What to look for: cap conical to bell-shaped, light brown to gray (inky with age); gills white (gray, then black, with age); stem white, with flattened collar; spores black.
Habitat: on decaying logs, stumps, buried wood.

Haymaker's Mushroom
Panaeolus foenisecii

Size: ½–1½ in. wide; stem 1–3 in. tall.
What to look for: cap dark brown, red-brown, or gray-brown (pale tan with age); gills attached, brown or purple-brown; stem brittle, tan or dingy white; spores dark purple-brown. **Habitat:** grassy areas.

Meadow Mushroom
Agaricus campestris

Size: *¾-4 in. wide; stem 1-3 in. tall.*
What to look for: *cap white or off-white, sometimes with brown streaks or scales and fringed edge; gills free, pink (purple-brown, then black, with age); stem white, with thin collar near top that soon disappears; spores dark purple-brown.* **Habitat:** *open grassy areas.*

Flat-topped Mushroom
Agaricus placomyces

Size: *1½-4 in. wide; stem 3-6 in. tall.*
What to look for: *cap white, with gray- or black-brown scales (especially at center), malodorous; gills free, white (pink, then purple-brown, with age); stem with collar near top, whitish (turning brown near base); spores brown.* **Habitat:** *woods; usually under broad-leaved trees.*

Horse Mushroom
Agaricus arvensis

Size: *2½-8 in. wide; stem 2½-8 in. tall.*
What to look for: *cap white or cream (bruises yellow), sometimes with yellow center or fringed edge; gills free, white (gray-pink, then black-brown, with age); stem white (bruises yellow), with collar (has cottony patches on underside); spores brown.* **Habitat:** *grassy areas.*

Meadow Mushrooms and Relatives   Agaricaceae

Although the mushrooms generally sold in stores are meadow mushrooms (they belong to a species native to Europe), wild meadow mushrooms—or any others, for that matter—should not be eaten unless their identity has been verified by an expert. Young mushrooms in this family are easy to confuse with the deadly amanitas.

Paxilli   Paxillaceae

The soft gills of the mushrooms in this small family (four or five species) separate cleanly from the underside of the cap when you press on them with a finger. The Black-footed Paxillus (*Paxillus atrotomentosus*), with rolled-under edge and hairy stem, is common under conifers.

Involute Paxillus
Paxillus involutus

Size: *1½-6 in. wide; stem 1½-4 in. tall.*
What to look for: *cap light yellow-brown (brown or red-brown with age), with edge rolled under and ribbed until old; gills running down stem, yellow-olive (bruise brown); stem yellow-brown, often with brown streaks or blotches; spores brown.* **Habitat:** *under conifers or in mixed woods.*

Brownie Cap
Conocybe tenera

Size: *½-1 in. wide; stem 1½-3 in. tall.*
What to look for: *cap conical or bell-shaped, brown (tan with age); gills partially attached or free, brown; stem thin, fragile, brown; spores red-brown.* **Habitat:** *grassy areas; sometimes in open woods.*

Bolbitii and Relatives   Bolbitiaceae

The Brownie Cap, a common inhabitant of lawns, is so fragile that it often lasts less than a day—a characteristic shared by many other species in this family. The name of the group comes from the Greek *bolbiton*, "cow dung," on which some of the species grow. The spores of all are brownish, ranging from rusty to earth tones.

Cortinarii and Relatives

Cortinariaceae

A cobweblike veil called the cortina (Latin for "curtain") hangs from the edge of young cortinarius caps. As in all mushroom families, some species in this large, diverse group are poisonous—notably some galerinas, the only mushrooms besides the amanitas to contain amatoxins, deadly poisons that attack the liver and kidneys and have no known antidote. Other mushroom poisons produce severe reactions but are not usually fatal.

Autumn Galerina

Galerina autumnalis

Size: *1–2½ in. wide; stem 1–3 in. tall.*
What to look for: *cap slimy, yellow-brown to brown; gills attached or running down stem, rusty brown; stem brown, with white streaks, thin collar when young; spores rusty brown.* **Habitat:** *on logs.*

Clustered Inocybe

Inocybe fastigiata

Size: *¾–2 in. wide; stem 1½–3 in. tall.*
What to look for: *cap conical or bell-shaped (edge may be split), tan or yellow-brown, with flat radiating hairs, fishy-smelling; gills partially attached or notched, white (gray or olive, then brown, with age); stem white to brown; spores brown.* **Habitat:** *woods.*

Scaly Pholiota

Pholiota squarrosoides

Size: *1–4 in. wide; stem 1½–4 in. tall.*
What to look for: *cap white to buff, slimy beneath pointed brown scales; gills attached or notched, white (brown with age); stem white with buff to brown scales, smooth at top, with hairy ring when young; spores brown.* **Habitat:** *in clusters on logs and stumps of broad-leaved trees.*

Red-zoned Cortinarius

Cortinarius armillatus

Size: *2–5 in. wide; stem 2½–6 in. tall.*
What to look for: *cap red-brown; gills fully or partially attached, rusty brown; stem brown, with red bands; spores rusty brown.* **Habitat:** *under birches or in mixed woods.*

Violet Cortinarius

Cortinarius violaceus

Size: *2–4 in. wide; stem 2½–5 in. tall.*
What to look for: *cap, gills, and stem dark violet; gills fully or partially attached; spores rusty brown.* **Habitat:** *conifer woods.*

Cinnamon Cortinarius

Cortinarius cinnamomeus

Size: *1–2 in. wide; stem 1–3 in. tall.*
What to look for: *cap brown or yellow-brown; gills attached, yellow (brown with age); stem yellow or brown; spores rusty brown.* **Habitat:** *under conifers.*

Red-gilled Cortinarius

Cortinarius semisanguineus

Size: *¾–3 in. wide; stem 1–3 in. tall.*
What to look for: *gills dark blood-red, attached; cap brown-yellow; stem dull yellow; spores rusty brown.* **Habitat:** *in moss under conifers.*

MUSHROOMS

Chanterelles and Relatives

Cantharellaceae

Frilly-edged and frequently trumpet-shaped, the top of a chanterelle looks like that of a typical mushroom. The underside, however, is different: the gills, if present, are widely spaced, have blunt edges, and are often forked or connected by ridges. These culinary delights of summer and early fall can, in some cases, unfortunately be confused with such inedible species as the Jack-o'-lantern and False Chanterelle.

Chanterelle
Cantharellus cibarius

Size: ¾–6 in. wide; stem 1–3 in. tall.
What to look for: cap yellow to orange; gills orange-buff, rather far apart, forked, blunt-edged; stem colored like cap or gills, or paler (bruises dark); spores whitish or pale buff. **Habitat:** woods, roadsides.

Deceptive Craterellus
Craterellus fallax

Size: 1–3 in. wide; 1–5 in. tall.
What to look for: cap funnel-shaped, dark brown (blackish, then gray-brown, with age); underside smooth or slightly wrinkled (no gills), brown (bruises black; turns gray or yellow-gray with age); stem continuous with cap, hollow; spores orange-buff. **Habitat:** woods.

Gill-less Chanterelle
Cantharellus lateritius

Size: 1–3½ in. wide; stem 1–2 in. tall.
What to look for: cap orange (pale yellow-orange with age); underside pale buff, smooth or slightly ridged (no gills); stem colored like cap or paler; spores pale pink-orange. **Habitat:** open broad-leaved woods.

Shaggy Chanterelle
Gomphus floccosus

Size: 1½–6½ in. wide; 3½–8 in. tall.
What to look for: cap funnel-shaped, scaly, sometimes slimy, and yellow-orange, orange, or red-orange (paler with age); gills in form of blunt, shallow ridges and wrinkles; gills and stem cream; spores brown-yellow. **Habitat:** coniferous or mixed woods.

Tubed Cantharellus
Cantharellus tubaeformis

Size: ½–2½ in. wide; stem 1–2 in. tall.
What to look for: cap dark yellow-brown to brown (paler and gray with age); gills far apart, yellow (gray or violet with age), forked, blunt-edged; stem yellow to orange; spores white or yellow. **Habitat:** wet woods, mossy logs.

Pig's Ears
Gomphus clavatus

Size: 1–4 in. wide; 2–5 in. tall.
What to look for: cap flat (depressed with age), pale purple (dingy pale yellow or buff with age); gills in form of shallow veins and ridges, often wrinkled, buff or purple (brownish with age); stem continuous with cap, dingy buff or pale lilac; spores orange-brown. **Habitat:** coniferous woods.

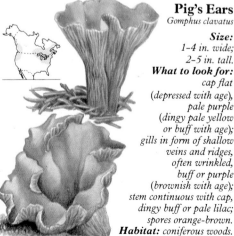

Coral Fungi Clavariaceae

Most of these colorful, fleshy fungi are saprophytes, taking their nutrients from decaying material. A few species are believed to obtain nutrients from living trees, for their "roots" (mycelia) are connected with the roots of the trees. Coral fungi are gill-less, producing spores on the surface of their branches or, in unbranched species, on most of the outside surface.

Spindle Coral
Clavulinopsis fusiformis

Size: ⅛–½ in. wide; ½–6 in. tall.
What to look for: tall, thin, bright yellow spindle, often with pointed tip; large ones often flattened. **Habitat:** in clusters in open woods.

Club Mushroom
Clavariadelphus truncatus

Size: 1–2½ in. wide at top; 3–6 in. tall.
What to look for: clublike shape; top flattened, wrinkled, yellow (gold, then pink-brown, with age); base white. **Habitat:** under conifers.

Golden Clavaria
Ramaria aurea

Size: clump 2–6 in. wide, 2–5 in. tall; stem 1–2 in. tall.
What to look for: branches golden, pale orange, or orange-buff, with yellow tips; stem white; does not change color when injured. **Habitat:** under broad-leaved trees.

Gray Coral
Clavulina cinerea

Size: clump ¾–2½ in. wide, 1–4 in. tall.
What to look for: many gray branches; base often white; branches become narrower toward top. **Habitat:** in clumps on moss and needles under conifers.

Crowned Clavaria
Clavicorona pyxidata

Size: clump 1–3½ in. wide, 2–4 in. tall.
What to look for: slender branches with crownlike tips, white or yellow (pale tan or pink-tan with age, finally brown on lower branches). **Habitat:** in clumps on logs and stumps of broad-leaved trees.

Cauliflower Mushroom
Sparassis radicata

Size: 6–14 in. wide; 6–12 in. tall.
What to look for: cauliflowerlike shape; flattened, leaflike white to yellow "branches"; stem rooted below ground. **Habitat:** under conifers.

American Yellow Bolete

Suillus americanus

Size: *1–4 in. wide; stem 1–3½ in. tall.*
What to look for: *cap bright yellow, with patches of buff to brown (young with fringed edge); underside dull yellow (bruises brown), with tube openings; stem bright yellow, with red or red-brown dots; spores dull red-brown.*
Habitat: *under Eastern White Pine.*

Tube Mushrooms

Boletaceae and Strobilomycetaceae

Instead of gills, tube mushrooms have tubes that open on the underside of the cap and give it a spongelike appearance. Some species retain remnants of the veil (the skin surrounding the young mushroom) as a collar or ring on the stem. The fungi in this group associate with trees; that is, the underground portion of the mushroom is connected with tree rootlets. The relationship may be so rigid that a particular species can grow only under one kind of tree.

Slippery Jack

Suillus luteus

Size: *1½–6 in. wide; stem 1½–4 in. tall.*
What to look for: *cap slimy, brown, yellow-brown, or red-brown; underside white or yellow, with tube openings; stem dotted, pale yellow, with collar; spores dull red-brown.*
Habitat: *under pines or spruces.*

Hollow-stemmed Boletinus

Suillus cavipes

Size: *1–4 in. wide; stem 1½–3½ in. tall.*
What to look for: *cap dry, hairy, and brown, red-brown, or orange-brown; underside yellow (dingy yellow with age), with tubes running down stem; stem hollow at bottom, with thin collar (soon flattening to slight ring), yellow above collar, brown below; spores brown.* **Habitat:** *under larches.*

Painted Bolete

Suillus pictus

Size: *1–4 in. wide; stem 1½–4 in. tall.*
What to look for: *cap with dull red scales and hairs (yellow flesh often showing between scales); underside yellow (bruises brown), with tube openings; stem with collar or ring, yellow above collar, white or red below; spores brown.*
Habitat: *under Eastern White Pine.*

Greville's Bolete

Suillus grevillei

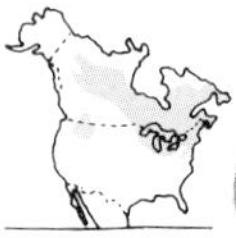

Size: *2–6 in. wide; stem 1½–4 in. tall.*
What to look for: *cap slimy, brown-red or yellow; underside yellow (bruises brown; turns olive-yellow with age), with tube openings; stem with collar, yellow above collar, streaked red-brown below; spores brown.* **Habitat:** *under larches.*

Pore Fungi

Polyporaceae and Ganodermataceae

Sometimes called bracket fungi, the two species shown at the right and those at the top of pages 552 and 553 form shelflike protuberances on trees, stumps, and logs. On the underside of the cap are pores similar in appearance and function (they produce spores) to the tubes of tube mushrooms. The pores vary greatly in size, some being visible only through a magnifying glass. In contrast to tube mushrooms, pore fungi are usually tough and woody, especially the older ones. When an Artist's Fungus is young, for example, its underside is soft enough to draw on with a sharp instrument, but it slowly dries and hardens, preserving the picture in the process. As pore fungi age, they grow, sometimes to a very large size. One specimen of the rare Noble Polypore (*Oxyporus nobilissimus*) growing on a spruce in the Pacific Northwest weighed an impressive 300 pounds.

Hemlock Polypore

Ganoderma tsugae

Size: *2–8 in. wide; stem (if present) 1–6 in. long.*
What to look for: *cap mahogany-red, fan-shaped, shiny or dusty brown; underside white or brown; stem mahogany-red, shiny, centered or attached at back.* **Habitat:** *on or near conifer stumps and lo*

Old Man of the Woods
Strobilomyces floccopus

Size: 1½–6 in. wide; stem 2–6 in. tall.
What to look for: cap scaly or shaggy (young with fringed edge), gray to black; underside white (bruises red, then black; turns gray with age), with tube openings; stem shaggy; spores black.
Habitat: under broad-leaved trees.

Bitter Bolete
Tylopilus felleus

Size: 2–12 in. wide; stem 1½–6 in. tall.
What to look for: cap tan to brown; underside white (bruises brown; turns pink, then rose, with age), with tube openings; stem white near top, brown below, with netlike ridges; spores dull pink or rose.
Habitat: near logs and stumps of conifers.

Two-colored Bolete
Boletus bicolor

Size: 2–6 in. wide; stem 2–4 in. tall.
What to look for: cap purple-red (paler with age, often cracking to show yellow); underside bright yellow (bruises blue), with tube openings; stem yellow near top, purple-red below; spores olive-green.
Habitat: under broad-leaved trees.

King Bolete
Boletus edulis

Size: 3–10 in. wide; stem 4–7 in. tall.
What to look for: cap pale brown to brown; underside white (green-yellow with age), with tube openings; stem bulbous, white near top, yellow to brown below, with netlike ridges; spores brown.
Habitat: under conifers.

Admirable Bolete
Boletus mirabilis

Size: 2–8 in. wide; stem 3–8 in. tall.
What to look for: cap dark red-brown, woolly or hairy when young; underside bright yellow, with tube openings; stem red-brown, with netlike ridges near top; spores brown.
Habitat: on or near conifer logs and stumps.

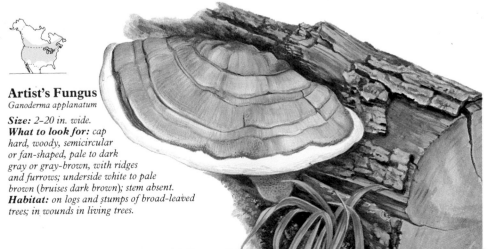

Artist's Fungus
Ganoderma applanatum

Size: 2–20 in. wide.
What to look for: cap hard, woody, semicircular or fan-shaped, pale to dark gray or gray-brown, with ridges and furrows; underside white to pale brown (bruises dark brown); stem absent.
Habitat: on logs and stumps of broad-leaved trees; in wounds in living trees.

Many-colored Polypore
Coriolus versicolor

Size: *single cap ¾–3 in. wide.*
What to look for: *clusters of thin overlapping caps, with gray, blue, and black bands or white, yellow, and brown bands; velvety or hairy zones alternating with smooth zones; underside white or yellow; stem absent.*
Habitat: *on dead wood or in wounds in broad-leaved trees; occasionally on conifers.*

Hen of the Woods
Grifola frondosa

Size: *8–25 in. wide.*
What to look for: *large cluster of overlapping caps, gray on top, white or yellow below; stem short, thick, with many branches.* **Habitat:** *near stumps or trunks, usually of broad-leaved trees.*

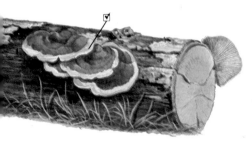

Chocolate Lenzites
Gloeophyllum sepiarium

Size: *¾–4 in. wide.*
What to look for: *cap thin, flexible, bright rusty brown (edge often white, yellow, or orange), hairy or smooth; underside with gills or pores; stem absent.* **Habitat:** *on conifer logs, stumps, and lumber.*

Sulphur Polypore
Polyporus sulphureus

Size: *2–20 in. wide.*
What to look for: *cap fleshy or firm, with ruffled edge; orange, salmon, or yellow (paler with age) above; underside sulphur yellow (paler with age); stem short or absent.* **Habitat:** *in large clusters on trunks, logs, and stumps of conifers and broad-leaved trees.*

Teeth Fungi
Hydnaceae

The fungi in this family can be soft, tough, or brittle. They also vary in appearance. Some have a cap with the teeth hanging from the underside; in others, the teeth make up most of the fungus. Spores are borne on the outside of each tooth. The Indian Paint Fungus, said to have been used by the Indians of the Pacific Northwest as a source of orange dye, causes heart rot in trees.

close-up

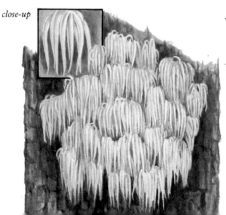

Coral Hydnum
Hericium coralloides

Size: *5–12 in. wide.*
What to look for: *numerous white branches (cream-colored with age), with iciclelike hanging spines on tips.* **Habitat:** *on logs and dead trunks of broad-leaved trees; in wounds in living trees.*

Red Belt Fungus
Fomitopsis pinicola

Size: *2-16 in. wide.*
What to look for: *cap hard or woody, thick, dark red to brown or gray to black, sticky, with red band near rounded edge; underside white to yellow (brown with age).*
Habitat: *on dead trees, stumps, or logs; occasionally on living trees.*

Bracket Fomes
Fomes fomentarius

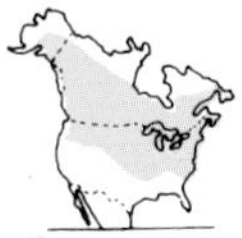

Size: *2-8 in. wide.*
What to look for: *cap hoof-shaped, tough, with hard crust, pale tan to gray-brown (gray to black with age); underside gray to brown; stem absent.* **Habitat:** *on dead trunks or logs of broad-leaved trees; in wounds in living trees.*

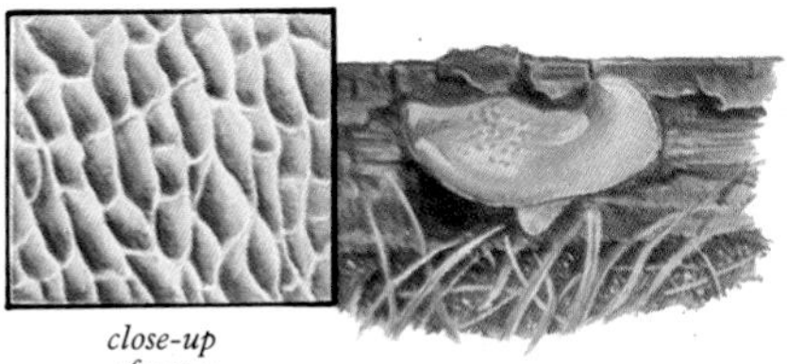

close-up of pores

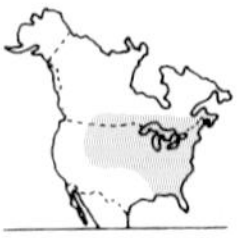

Honeycomb Bracket Fungus
Favolus alveolaris

Size: *½-4 in. wide; stem (if present) to ½ in. long.*
What to look for: *cap tough to brittle, red-yellow to brick-red (paler with age), often with small flattened scales; underside white, with texture like honeycomb; stem white.* **Habitat:** *singly or in clusters on dead wood of broad-leaved trees.*

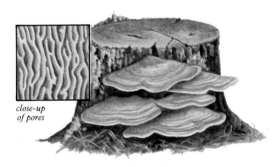

close-up of pores

Willow Polypore
Daedalea confragosa

Size: *1-6 in. wide.*
What to look for: *cap gray to brown, often banded, leathery to rigid; underside white to brown, with gills or with round or irregular long pores; stem absent.* **Habitat:** *on dead wood of broad-leaved trees; in wounds in living trees.*

Indian Paint Fungus
Echinodontium tinctorium

Size: *1½-8 in. wide.*
What to look for: *cap hoof-shaped, woody, green-black or dark brown, often cracked and moss-covered; inside orange; teeth tough, sometimes flattened, buff or brown-gray.*
Habitat: *on living conifers.*

Spreading Hedgehog Mushroom
Dentinum repandum

Size: *2-6 in. wide; stem 1-3 in. tall.*
What to look for: *cap dull to brownish orange, tan, or white; teeth white to cream or pale salmon; stem white or colored like cap.* **Habitat:** *under conifers or broad-leaved trees.*

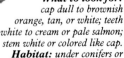

Dog Stinkhorn
Mutinus caninus

Size: 2–4 in. tall.
What to look for: pink to red, foamy-looking stalk; tip tapered, with olive-green slime; remnants of oval "egg" at base. **Habitat:** singly or in clusters on soil, humus, wood-chip mulch, or woody debris.

Eastern Stinkhorn
Phallus ravenelii

Size: 4–6 in. tall.
What to look for: cylindrical, slimy or dry fungus with gray- or olive-green head and ringed hole at tip; stem white, foamy-looking, usually with 1 or 2 thin brown rings; remnants of oval or round "egg" at base. **Habitat:** on sawdust or wood debris.

Stinkhorns   Phallaceae

An egg-shaped case resembling a puffball encloses the young stinkhorn. As the "egg" matures, the stinkhorn swells with water and lengthens rapidly—within the span of a few hours. The top of the mature stinkhorn is covered with a foul-smelling, spore-containing slime. Flies and beetles attracted to this transport stinkhorn spores to new areas.

Puffballs and False Puffballs
Lycoperdaceae and Relatives

Almost every kind of terrestrial habitat in North America, even the desert, has some kind of puffball. Children soon learn that the little round varieties are fun to step on—they explode with a pop, then squirt out the powdery spore "dust." Considering the number of spores produced by a puffball's spongelike mass, it is surprising that these fungi are not everywhere underfoot. The highly prized Giant Puffball, for example, is believed to produce about 70 trillion spores, yet it is not a common species. Some, but not all, puffballs are choice eating. Even though they seem easily recognizable, there are poisonous look-alikes, such as the button (immature stage) of an amanita—another indication of the foolhardiness of dining on wild mushrooms without expert guidance.

False Puffball
Scleroderma aurantium

Size: 1–4 in. wide.
What to look for: outside yellow-brown, cracked into small areas, each with dark wart; inside white (turning purple or black), firm (powdery with age); wall visible in cut section white, thick; spore "dust" black or brown. **Habitat:** woods or parklike areas; near trees, logs, or stumps.

Giant Puffball
Calvatia gigantea

Size: 6–20 in. wide.
What to look for: white globular fungus (turning yellow- or olive-brown with age, from center outward); attached to ground by short "cord." **Habitat:** open grassy areas, woodland edges.

Striate Bird's Nest Fungus
Cyathus striatus

Size: 1/4–1/2 in. wide; 1/4–5/8 in. tall.
What to look for: bowl-shaped fungus; outside dark brown, hairy, inside whitish or black, striped; "eggs" inside bowl disklike, dark.
Habitat: in clusters on sticks and woody debris.

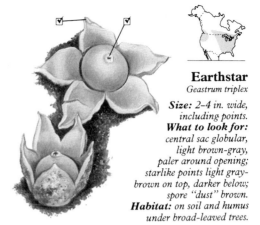

Earthstar
Geastrum triplex

Size: 2–4 in. wide, including points.
What to look for: central sac globular, light brown-gray, paler around opening; starlike points light gray-brown on top, darker below; spore "dust" brown.
Habitat: on soil and humus under broad-leaved trees.

Bird's Nest Fungi   Nidulariaceae

Each "egg" in these minuscule "nests" contains a multitude of spores. Rainwater splashes the eggs out of the nest, and their outer walls decay, spreading the spores and allowing them to germinate. Usually several nests appear together—sometimes even hundreds. In gardens fertilized with manure, the Bird's Nest Fungus (*Cyathus stercoreus*) is often found.

Earthstars   Geastraceae

On an immature earthstar, the points of the star are firmly closed, and the structure resembles a puffball. With age, an outer layer, not found in true puffballs, splits open, revealing a sac that contains the spores. If pressed by a finger, the sac squirts the spores out in a cloud. Raindrops most likely cause the release of spores in more natural situations.

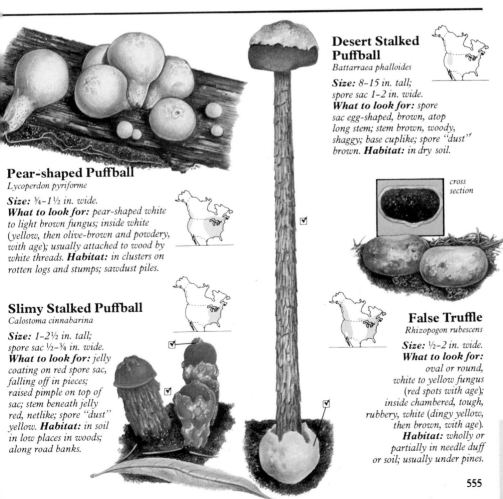

Desert Stalked Puffball
Battarraea phalloides

Size: 8–15 in. tall; spore sac 1–2 in. wide.
What to look for: spore sac egg-shaped, brown, atop long stem; stem brown, woody, shaggy; base cuplike; spore "dust" brown. *Habitat:* in dry soil.

cross section

Pear-shaped Puffball
Lycoperdon pyriforme

Size: 3/4–1 1/2 in. wide.
What to look for: pear-shaped white to light brown fungus; inside white (yellow, then olive-brown and powdery, with age); usually attached to wood by white threads. *Habitat:* in clusters on rotten logs and stumps; sawdust piles.

Slimy Stalked Puffball
Calostoma cinnabarina

Size: 1–2 1/2 in. tall; spore sac 1/2–3/4 in. wide.
What to look for: jelly coating on red spore sac, falling off in pieces; raised pimple on top of sac; stem beneath jelly red, netlike; spore "dust" yellow. *Habitat:* in soil in low places in woods; along road banks.

False Truffle
Rhizopogon rubescens

Size: 1/2–2 in. wide.
What to look for: oval or round, white to yellow fungus (red spots with age); inside chambered, tough, rubbery, white (dingy yellow, then brown, with age). *Habitat:* wholly or partially in needle duff or soil; usually under pines.

Jelly Fungi Tremellales

The jellylike look of these fungi is deceptive, for they are actually so firm they can be cut only with a sharp object. Jelly fungi dry out for long periods, only to revive and resume growth when soaked with water. The Fairy Butter and Witches' Butter, for instance, are often prominent in winter woods when melting snow moistens the logs. Each time a jelly fungus revives, it produces new masses of spores over its wrinkled surface.

Black Witches' Butter
Exidia glandulosa

Size: *1–8 in. long.*
What to look for: *irregular jellylike masses, brown to black-brown with brown warts (drying like black paint).*
Habitat: *on wood from broad-leaved trees.*

Witches' Butter
Tremella mesenterica

Size: *¾–4 in. wide; to 1½ in. tall.*
What to look for: *firm, jellylike, orange to orange-yellow fungus with brainlike shape or broad folds.*
Habitat: *on logs, stumps, and dead branches of broad-leaved trees.*

Fairy Butter
Dacrymyces palmatus

Size: *½–2½ in. wide.*
What to look for: *jellylike, tough fungus (soft and watery with age), yellow-orange, orange, or orange-red; looks like folded petals.*
Habitat: *on conifer logs and stumps.*

Yellow Jelly Fungus
Guepiniopsis alpinus

Size: *¼–½ in. wide.*
What to look for: *yellow or orange jellylike cup; narrow stem.*
Habitat: *in small clusters on conifer wood.*

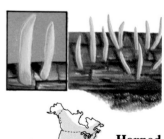

White Jelly Fungus
Pseudohydnum gelatinosum

Size: *1–2 in. wide; ¾–3 in. tall.*
What to look for: *cap translucent, whitish, jellylike, thick but pliable; underside with white spines; stem (if present) short, off-center.* **Habitat:** *on wood.*

Horned Calocera
Calocera cornea

Size: *¼–¾ in. tall.*
What to look for: *firm, jellylike needles or horns (brittle when dry), sometimes with branches; yellow or orange-yellow.*
Habitat: *on dead trees.*

Flask Fungi
Sphaeriales and Relatives

Although they are probably the largest group of fungi, the flask fungi are generally inconspicuous, many being merely black specks on plant debris. Their unassuming appearance belies their importance; some species are notorious tree-killing parasites (those that cause Dutch elm disease and chestnut blight are examples). The powdery mildews, which give a moldy appearance to the leaves of lilacs, phlox, plums, cherries, and many weeds and grasses, are also flask fungi. The plants they live on look unsightly but are not permanently harmed by their presence.

Black Knot Fungus
Apiosporina morbosa

Size: ½–1½ in. wide; 1–12 in. long.
What to look for: dull olive-green (black with age), hard, generally cylindrical fungus; tapered, clublike, or irregularly lumpy. **Habitat:** on twigs and branches of living or dead plum and cherry trees.

Dead Man's Fingers
Xylaria polymorpha

Size: ¾–4 in. tall.
What to look for: club-shaped or fingerlike fungus; outside black, rough; inside white, tough, woody. **Habitat:** on decaying wood above ground or on buried wood.

Orange-colored Cordyceps
Cordyceps militaris

Size: ¹⁄₁₆–¼ in. wide; ¾–3 in. tall.
What to look for: clublike cylindrical fungus; orange-buff or red-orange, with minute pimples on head.
Habitat: on moth or butterfly pupae buried in ground or decayed wood.

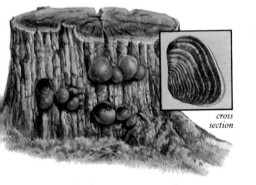

cross section

Zoned Black Fungus
Daldinia concentrica

Size: ¾–2 in. wide.
What to look for: hard, round or half-round fungus; surface dull pink-brown (blackened by spore "dust" with age); concentric zones of gray and black visible when cut. **Habitat:** on stumps and logs of broad-leaved trees.

Orange Hypomyces
Hypomyces lactifluorum

What to look for: orange or orange-red coating, with deep orange or red dots; covers entire mushroom or only gills and stem; makes gills visible only as faint ridges.
Habitat: on certain mushrooms (russulas and lactarii).

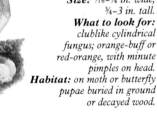

Red Pimple Fungus
Nectria cinnabarina

Size: about ¹⁄₁₆ in. wide.
What to look for: small pink to orange-red cushion (dark red with age).
Habitat: in groups on sticks or dead branches of living trees.

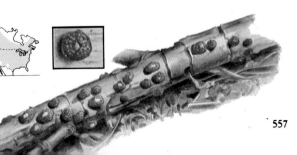

Cup Fungi
Pezizales and Relatives

The fungi in this group vary widely in appearance. The morels and false morels on the opposite page, for example, bear little resemblance to the small, colorful cups shown below. What they have in common is their microscopic spore sacs, borne on the upper or inside surface of the cups or, in the morels, on the entire outer surface. Some spring-fruiting morels are prized delicacies, but mushroom hunters should beware: false morels and other poisonous relatives appear during the same season.

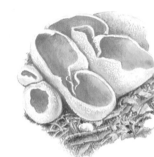

Orange Peel
Caloscypha fulgens

Size: *½–2 in. wide.*
What to look for: *cup-shaped fungus, often split or lopsided; inside yellow to orange, outside with blue-green tints or stains.*
Habitat: *in clusters in wet places under conifers.*

Scarlet Cup
Sarcoscypha coccinea

Size: *½–2 in. wide.*
What to look for: *bright scarlet cup (whitish on outside); stem very short or absent.* ***Habitat:*** *on hardwood sticks.*

Orange Fairy Cup
Aleuria aurantia

Size: *¾–4 in. wide.*
What to look for: *shallow cup or saucer; inside bright or red-orange, outside white, translucent.* ***Habitat:*** *in clusters on packed soil in dirt roads and paths.*

Confusing Peziza
Peziza badioconfusa

Size: *1–4 in. wide.*
What to look for: *shallow cup; inside brown or red-brown, outside dull yellow-brown (black all over with age).* ***Habitat:*** *on soil or humus or beside logs and stumps.*

Gray Urn
Urnula craterium

Size: *1–3 in. wide; 2–5 in. tall.*
What to look for: *urn or deep cup; inside dark brown to black, outside dark gray to brown (black with age).* ***Habitat:*** *in clusters on or near sticks and logs of broad-leaved trees.*

Pink Crown
Sarcosphaera crassa

Size: *1–4½ in. wide.*
What to look for: *deep cup with crownlike edge; inside gray-lilac to pink, outside white; stem (if present) short, thick.* ***Habitat:*** *woods; wholly or partly buried in soil.*

Yellow Cup Fungus
Bisporella citrina

Size: *⅛–¼ in. wide.*
What to look for: *shallow, bright yellow disk or cup, often fused with others into large mass.* ***Habitat:*** *in clusters on dead wood of broad-leaved trees.*

Blue-green Cup Fungus
Chlorociboria aeruginascens

Size: *¼–1½ in. wide.*
What to look for: *shallow, dull blue-green cup; very short stem.* ***Habitat:*** *in clusters on logs or dead branches of conifers.*

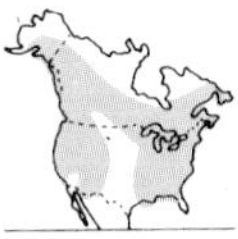

Yellow Leotia
Leotia lubrica

Size: *½–1½ in. wide;
stem ½–2½ in. tall.*
What to look for:
*oval or cushion-shaped
cap on club-shaped stem;
cap and stem slimy,
dingy yellow, buff, or brown
(sometimes with olive tint).*
Habitat: *in clusters on soil or moss in woods.*

False Morel
Gyromitra esculenta

Size: *1½–4 in. wide;
stem 1–3 in. tall.*
What to look for:
*cap wrinkled, folded
(like a brain),
irregularly shaped,
brown or red-brown,
lacking pits; stem whitish.*
Habitat: *under conifers.*

Common Morel
Morchella esculenta

Size: *1–2 in. wide;
1½–4 in. tall.*
What to look for: *cap
continuous with stem,
gray or light yellow to
brown with rounded
ridges and rounded or
irregular pits; stem
white.* **Habitat:** *old
orchards; broad-leaved
forests; grassy areas;
low wet areas; near
recently dead elms;
occasionally in gardens.*

cross section

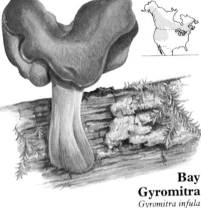

Bay Gyromitra
Gyromitra infula

Size: *1–5 in. wide; stem 1–4½ in. tall.*
What to look for: *cap generally saddle-shaped,
sometimes slightly wrinkled, buff or dark brown
or red-brown; stem whitish or tinted brown.*
Habitat: *on rotting conifer wood;
occasionally in rich woodland soils.*

cross section

Early Morel
Verpa bohemica

Size: *½–1 in. wide; 3–4 in. tall.*
What to look for: *cap bell-shaped, yellow-brown,
attached at top of stem (bottom edge free), wrinkled
or folded, with deep elongated pits; stem hollow,
whitish, yellow, or tan.* **Habitat:** *wet areas.*

Elfin Saddle
Helvella lacunosa

Size: *½–2 in. wide;
stem 1½–5 in. tall.*
What to look for:
*cap saddle-shaped,
slightly wrinkled
or folded, gray;
stem pale gray,
with deep channels.*
Habitat: *on ground
in woods; sometimes
on decaying wood.*

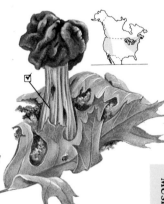

Index to Scientific Names
Page numbers in this index refer to illustrations, text, or both.

Index to Common Names

Page numbers in this index refer to illustrations, text, or both.